T0140209

Communications
in Computer and Information Science   1293

More information about this series at http://www.springer.com/series/7899

Constantine Stephanidis ·
Margherita Antona · Stavroula Ntoa (Eds.)

HCI International 2020 – Late Breaking Posters

22nd International Conference, HCII 2020
Copenhagen, Denmark, July 19–24, 2020
Proceedings, Part I

Springer

Editors
Constantine Stephanidis
University of Crete and Foundation
for Research and Technology – Hellas
(FORTH)
Heraklion, Crete, Greece

Margherita Antona
Foundation for Research and Technology –
Hellas (FORTH)
Heraklion, Crete, Greece

Stavroula Ntoa
Foundation for Research and Technology –
Hellas (FORTH)
Heraklion, Crete, Greece

ISSN 1865-0929   ISSN 1865-0937   (electronic)
Communications in Computer and Information Science
ISBN 978-3-030-60699-2   ISBN 978-3-030-60700-5   (eBook)
https://doi.org/10.1007/978-3-030-60700-5

This Springer imprint is published by the registered company Springer Nature Switzerland AG
The registered company address is: Gewerbestrasse 11, 6330 Cham, Switzerland

Foreword

The 22nd International Conference on Human-Computer Interaction, HCI International 2020 (HCII 2020), was planned to be held at the AC Bella Sky Hotel and Bella Center, Copenhagen, Denmark, during July 19–24, 2020. Due to the COVID-19 pandemic and the resolution of the Danish government not to allow events larger than 500 people to be hosted until September 1, 2020, HCII 2020 had to be held virtually. It incorporated the 21 thematic areas and affiliated conferences listed on the following page.

A total of 6,326 individuals from academia, research institutes, industry, and governmental agencies from 97 countries submitted contributions, and 1,439 papers and 238 posters were included in the volumes of the proceedings published before the conference. Additionally, 333 papers and 144 posters are included in the volumes of the proceedings published after the conference, as "Late Breaking Work" (papers and posters). These contributions address the latest research and development efforts in the field and highlight the human aspects of design and use of computing systems.

The volumes comprising the full set of the HCII 2020 conference proceedings are listed in the following pages and together they broadly cover the entire field of human-computer interaction, addressing major advances in knowledge and effective use of computers in a variety of application areas.

I would like to thank the Program Board Chairs and the members of the Program Boards of all Thematic Areas and Affiliated Conferences for their valuable contributions towards the highest scientific quality and the overall success of the HCI International 2020 conference.

This conference would not have been possible without the continuous and unwavering support and advice of the founder, conference general chair emeritus and conference scientific advisor, Prof. Gavriel Salvendy. For his outstanding efforts, I would like to express my appreciation to the communications chair and editor of HCI International News, Dr. Abbas Moallem.

July 2020   Constantine Stephanidis

HCI International 2020 Thematic Areas and Affiliated Conferences

Thematic Areas:

- HCI 2020: Human-Computer Interaction
- HIMI 2020: Human Interface and the Management of Information

Affiliated Conferences:

- EPCE: 17th International Conference on Engineering Psychology and Cognitive Ergonomics
- UAHCI: 14th International Conference on Universal Access in Human-Computer Interaction
- VAMR: 12th International Conference on Virtual, Augmented and Mixed Reality
- CCD: 12th International Conference on Cross-Cultural Design
- SCSM: 12th International Conference on Social Computing and Social Media
- AC: 14th International Conference on Augmented Cognition
- DHM: 11th International Conference on Digital Human Modeling & Applications in Health, Safety, Ergonomics & Risk Management
- DUXU: 9th International Conference on Design, User Experience and Usability
- DAPI: 8th International Conference on Distributed, Ambient and Pervasive Interactions
- HCIBGO: 7th International Conference on HCI in Business, Government and Organizations
- LCT: 7th International Conference on Learning and Collaboration Technologies
- ITAP: 6th International Conference on Human Aspects of IT for the Aged Population
- HCI-CPT: Second International Conference on HCI for Cybersecurity, Privacy and Trust
- HCI-Games: Second International Conference on HCI in Games
- MobiTAS: Second International Conference on HCI in Mobility, Transport and Automotive Systems
- AIS: Second International Conference on Adaptive Instructional Systems
- C&C: 8th International Conference on Culture and Computing
- MOBILE: First International Conference on Design, Operation and Evaluation of Mobile Communications
- AI-HCI: First International Conference on Artificial Intelligence in HCI

Conference Proceedings – Full List of Volumes

1. LNCS 12181, Human-Computer Interaction: Design and User Experience (Part I), edited by Masaaki Kurosu
2. LNCS 12182, Human-Computer Interaction: Multimodal and Natural Interaction (Part II), edited by Masaaki Kurosu
3. LNCS 12183, Human-Computer Interaction: Human Values and Quality of Life (Part III), edited by Masaaki Kurosu
4. LNCS 12184, Human Interface and the Management of Information: Designing Information (Part I), edited by Sakae Yamamoto and Hirohiko Mori
5. LNCS 12185, Human Interface and the Management of Information: Interacting with Information (Part II), edited by Sakae Yamamoto and Hirohiko Mori
6. LNAI 12186, Engineering Psychology and Cognitive Ergonomics: Mental Workload, Human Physiology, and Human Energy (Part I), edited by Don Harris and Wen-Chin Li
7. LNAI 12187, Engineering Psychology and Cognitive Ergonomics: Cognition and Design (Part II), edited by Don Harris and Wen-Chin Li
8. LNCS 12188, Universal Access in Human-Computer Interaction: Design Approaches and Supporting Technologies (Part I), edited by Margherita Antona and Constantine Stephanidis
9. LNCS 12189, Universal Access in Human-Computer Interaction: Applications and Practice (Part II), edited by Margherita Antona and Constantine Stephanidis
10. LNCS 12190, Virtual, Augmented and Mixed Reality: Design and Interaction (Part I), edited by Jessie Y.C. Chen and Gino Fragomeni
11. LNCS 12191, Virtual, Augmented and Mixed Reality: Industrial and Everyday Life Applications (Part II), edited by Jessie Y.C. Chen and Gino Fragomeni
12. LNCS 12192, Cross-Cultural Design: User Experience of Products, Services, and Intelligent Environments (Part I), edited by P.L. Patrick Rau
13. LNCS 12193, Cross-Cultural Design: Applications in Health, Learning, Communication, and Creativity (Part II), edited by P.L. Patrick Rau
14. LNCS 12194, Social Computing and Social Media: Design, Ethics, User Behavior, and Social Network Analysis (Part I), edited by Gabriele Meiselwitz
15. LNCS 12195, Social Computing and Social Media: Participation, User Experience, Consumer Experience, and Applications of Social Computing (Part II), edited by Gabriele Meiselwitz
16. LNAI 12196, Augmented Cognition: Theoretical and Technological Approaches (Part I), edited by Dylan D. Schmorrow and Cali M. Fidopiastis
17. LNAI 12197, Augmented Cognition: Human Cognition and Behaviour (Part II), edited by Dylan D. Schmorrow and Cali M. Fidopiastis

40. CCIS 1226, HCI International 2020 Posters (Part III), edited by Constantine Stephanidis and Margherita Antona
41. LNCS 12423, HCI International 2020 – Late Breaking Papers: User Experience Design and Case Studies, edited by Constantine Stephanidis, Aaron Marcus, Elizabeth Rosenzweig, P.L. Patrick Rau, Abbas Moallem, and Matthias Rauterberg
42. LNCS 12424, HCI International 2020 – Late Breaking Papers: Multimodality and Intelligence, edited by Constantine Stephanidis, Masaaki Kurosu, Helmut Degen, and Lauren Reinerman-Jones
43. LNCS 12425, HCI International 2020 – Late Breaking Papers: Cognition, Learning and Games, edited by Constantine Stephanidis, Don Harris, Wen-Chin Li, Dylan D. Schmorrow, Cali M. Fidopiastis, Panayiotis Zaphiris, Andri Ioannou, Xiaowen Fang, Robert Sottilare, and Jessica Schwarz
44. LNCS 12426, HCI International 2020 – Late Breaking Papers: Universal Access and Inclusive Design, edited by Constantine Stephanidis, Margherita Antona, Qin Gao, and Jia Zhou
45. LNCS 12427, HCI International 2020 – Late Breaking Papers: Interaction, Knowledge and Social Media, edited by Constantine Stephanidis, Gavriel Salvendy, June Way, Sakae Yamamoto, Hirohiko Mori, Gabriele Meiselwitz, Fiona Fui-Hoon Nah, and Keng Siau
46. LNCS 12428, HCI International 2020 – Late Breaking Papers: Virtual and Augmented Reality, edited by Constantine Stephanidis, Jessie Y.C. Chen, and Gino Fragomeni
47. LNCS 12429, HCI International 2020 – Late Breaking Papers: Digital Human Modeling and Ergonomics, Mobility and Intelligent Environments, edited by Constantine Stephanidis, Vincent G. Duffy, Norbert Streitz, Shin'ichi Konomi, and Heidi Krömker
48. CCIS 1293, HCI International 2020 – Late Breaking Posters (Part I), edited by Constantine Stephanidis, Margherita Antona, and Stavroula Ntoa
49. CCIS 1294, HCI International 2020 – Late Breaking Posters (Part II), edited by Constantine Stephanidis, Margherita Antona, and Stavroula Ntoa

http://2020.hci.international/proceedings

HCI International 2020 (HCII 2020)

The full list with the Program Board Chairs and the members of the Program Boards of all thematic areas and affiliated conferences is available online at:

http://www.hci.international/board-members-2020.php

HCI International 2021

The 23rd International Conference on Human-Computer Interaction, HCI International 2021 (HCII 2021), will be held jointly with the affiliated conferences in Washington DC, USA, at the Washington Hilton Hotel, July 24–29, 2021. It will cover a broad spectrum of themes related to human-computer interaction (HCI), including theoretical issues, methods, tools, processes, and case studies in HCI design, as well as novel interaction techniques, interfaces, and applications. The proceedings will be published by Springer. More information will be available on the conference website: http://2021.hci.international/

General Chair
Prof. Constantine Stephanidis
University of Crete and ICS-FORTH
Heraklion, Crete, Greece
Email: general_chair@hcii2021.org

http://2021.hci.international/

Contents – Part I

Mobile and Multimodal Interaction

Interacting with Data, Information and Knowledge

Interaction and Intelligence

User Experience, Emotions and Psychophisiological Computing

Contents – Part II

Virtual, Augmented and Mixed Reality

Learning

HCI, Culture and Art

Health and Wellbeing Applications

HCI in Mobility, Automotive and Aviation

HCI Theory, Methods and Tools

How to Think About Third Wave HCI that Questions the Normative Culture in Computer Science?

Pricila Castelini[1](✉) and Marília Abrahão Amaral[2]

[1] Federal University of Technology, Paraná, Brazil
pricilacas@hotmail.com
[2] Department of Informatics and Program in Technology and Society,
Federal University of Technology, Paraná, Brazil
mariliaa@utfpr.edu.br

Abstract. Think about normative culture in computer science and question it based on third wave Human-Computer Interaction also involves problematizing our culture, our society and us as part of livelihood. The Science, Technology and Society studies that are basing our work by feminists' optics reveal that there is no way to think about technoscience without thinking about people who are the reason for its existence. Our objective is highlight plural approaches in the computer science graduate courses documents in Brazilian Computer Science and in Bachelor in Information Systems and Computer Engineering from a public institution in Brazil based on feminist theories of Science, Technology and Society. The work results are: a) structural barriers in low women participation; b) gender disparities are not even mentioned in Computer Engineering documents; c) intersection of race, class and gender are present only in Bachelor in Information Systems documents; d) power relations in macro axes reveal intentions of those who create computer science documents in Brazil.

Keywords: Normative culture · Computer science · Brazilian Computer Science · Feminist STS · Third-wave HCI

1 Introduction

The process of interaction between people and technologies reflects values, senses, beliefs, culture and gender of those who design and use it [1]. The study on interactions between people and technologies also involve different moments and appropriations. These moments in Human-Computer Interaction (HCI) are located in three waves based on Bødker [2]. The three waves in HCI for [2] are not chronologically localized because the approaches change according to the community interests and study context.

The first wave in HCI studies cognitive science and human factors. "From human factors to human actors" [2] points second wave HCI studies. When HCI researchers start to study human factors in computer science interactions the concerns about feminism, gender, sustainability and intersectionality is part of the third wave in HCI. The third

© Springer Nature Switzerland AG 2020
C. Stephanidis et al. (Eds.): HCII 2020, CCIS 1293, pp. 3–10, 2020.
https://doi.org/10.1007/978-3-030-60700-5_1

wave focuses on use and appropriations that can occur in the public and private spheres involving daily life, cultural, social, aesthetic and situated experiences [2]. Considering the context and values of technologies in society there are also HCI strands using feminist HCI [3], gender HCI [4], intersectionality HCI [5–7]. In these researches we see the concern with diverse people participation as a way to promote moments for discussion.

In the context to answer the question about normative culture in computer science we based our research in third wave HCI, our research objective is highlight plural approaches in the documents of computer science graduate courses in a public institution in Brazil based on feminist theories of Science, Technology and Society (STS). This work is divided into: a) theoretical background discussion in intersectional HCI and feminist STS studies; b) methodological research paths to analysis the Bachelor in Information Systems and Computer Engineering documents; c) data analysis based on three categories and d) results discussion.

2 From the Perspective of Technoscience Feminists

Computer science area is based on a normative culture [8] and considering this we emphasize the importance of the intersections of race and ethnicity, gender, social class and people with disabilities. This research appropriates the concepts of feminist STS studies to discuss normative culture in computer science and also in our society to question scientific objectivity, technological determinism and science linerity that and dialogue with HCI [8–10].

Normative culture, for feminist STS studies is due to structural barriers in education, family, technologies, society, culture that permeate male values. The structural barriers can be observed by the low number of women enrolled in Science, Technology, Engineering, Mathematics (STEM) areas. According to Wajcman [8] the absence is due to the men monopoly that comes from the first computing activities with the end of World War II as an important source of power and, thus, lack of women's technical skills to appropriate computing and other activities related.

Haraway [8] and Wajcman [8] identified that research in STEM areas has been referred to male and has obscured the meaning of inventions and productions of 'women's sphere' (WAJCMAN, 2004, p. 12) and reinforce the male stereotype and normative culture of these areas. When we discuss normative culture in STEM we realize that the term technology is usually reduced to artifacts. Wajcman (2004) says that the history of technology still represents the masculine. However, for her, the concept of technology changes considering the historical and cultural process of society.

Thinking about this process of understanding values, gender and culture in design and use of technologies [3] research suggest in the book "humanistic HCI" that any HCI research or practice deploys humanistic epistemologies. In these studies the authors indicate the importance of research that embody social, cultural and feminist epistemologies as part of a whole in design and use of technological artifacts. Although the humanistic HCI points out theories and methodologies for developers and users appropriation, it is with specific studies on third wave HCI in feminist HCI, gender HCI and intersectionality HCI that agendas and methodologies are proposed.

2.1 Computer Science Normative Culture to Third-Wave HCI Studies

According to third wave HCI studies [3] discuss about feminisms and gender methods for people who design and use technologies. In gender HCI, [4] pointed out that people who develop technologies transpose their values, their culture, their gender when they design. This researches contributes to our work to question normative culture in computer science and indicate diverse people participation, for example, women or disabled person and other subordinates in the history.

Intersectional HCI theory authors highlights the multiple avenues through which racial, ethnical and gender that are experienced. The intersectional movement began with black feminists in the late 1980s that had the banner of recognizing multiple identities in women's studies. Kimberlé Crenshaw primarily used it during a lecture. After that, authors such as [5, 6] and others comment that instead of limiting intersectionality research to a specialization of content with marginal populations, this can be an analytical paradigm to study social groups, relations and contexts.

Dahmoon [7] points to go beyond the conventional scope of non-white women. From [7] discussion we based our analysis to bring difference in individual or a group of identities, such as race, gender, racialization, racism, colonialism, sexism, patriarchy, class etc. Yuval-Davis [6] present her intersectional perspective that involve social divisions in different levels for example in macro axes and social power, there are expressed in institutions, organizations, documents such as state laws, state agencies, unions and family. The authors' position contributes to our research to thinking about the documents that regulate computer science undergraduate courses in Brazil and permeate power relations and discourses of prejudice, discrimination, lack of recognition and evasion [8].

Based on intersectional studies [6, 7] and feminist STS studies [8–10] we recognize theoretical categories that base our analysis to highlight plural approaches: (a) **multiculturalism**: move towards inclusion from respect and honor of groups and communities experience. Culture as an a account of agencies, hegemonies, counter-hegemonies and unexpected possibilities of body building [6–10]; (b) **intersectionality**: bringing together people who are considered subaltern in the use and development of technologies with the multiplicity of identities and forms of oppression involving (gender, race, ethnicity and class) [5–7]; (c) **reflexivity**: involves thinking about identities to problematize scientific objectivity, technological determinism and science linearity and to consider people in different places and times pointing to more engagement and participation of different groups [8–10].

3 Research Methodology

We began our methodological research by looking at Computer Brazilian Society documents that regulate computer science undergraduate courses in Brazil. As a research clipping we chose to analyze the documents and approaches of Federal University of Technology - Paraná, Brazil undergraduate courses to continuity a first contact with students and graduate of Bachelor in Information Systems and Computer Engineering with participatory workshops too understand problems and perceptions of them in research of master's degree [11].

The first research stage was to collect the undergraduate courses documents (Bachelor in Information Systems and Computer Engineering). The second research stage was to collect and to analyze the Computer Brazilian Society documents. The third research stage was to define the categories (a), (b) and (c) based on our theoretical background. The forth research stage was to analyze the Bachelor in Information Systems and Computer Engineering documents.

About the first research stage, the Federal University of Technology - Paraná, Brazil there are thirteen campuses all over the state. We made the clipping by headquarter localized at Curitiba, Paraná capital state. The Bachelor in Information Systems and Computer Engineering have the same guidelines based on Brazilian Computer Society documents. Bachelor in Information Systems documents available in the university website[1] are: graduation general norms; complementary activities; curriculum; pedagogical course project and teaching plans. Computer Engineering documents are available on their own website[2] not in the institutional: pedagogical course project; curriculum and teaching plans. In addition to having similar documents (Pedagogical Course Project) update in 2016 in terms of standards, it is not equal in content.

In the second research stage we found the documents and guidelines of Brazilian Computer Society available on the website[3]. The main documents that base the construction of all the computer science undergraduate and postgraduate programs in Brazil are devided into: *regiment, action plan, ordinance, statute, statitcal, challenges, basic education courses references* and *postgraduate courses references*.

The *regiment* are the Rules of the Special Commitee on Information from 2018; *action plan* for them are guidelines for undergraduate and postgraduate courses and its update is from (2009–2011); *ordinance* show the classification and standards about undergraduate computer science courses; *statute* the most recent of all is from 2019 and consolidate bylaws of undergraduate computer science courses; *statitical* show the annual report but in the website the last report is from 2017; *challenges* from 2006 to 2016 present research challenge computer science in Brazil; *basic education courses references* and *postgraduate courses references* indicate the theoretical background to plan the computer science graduate and undergraduate courses in Brazil. We highlight that the concepts was analyzed in Portuguese, considering that all documents are written and organized in this language.

4 Data Analysis

As the third research stage of our work we analyzed those documents that regulate all computer courses are based on Brazilian Computer Society guidelines, so we present (a), (b) and (c) categories analyzed in this section.

---

[1] Available in: http://portal.utfpr.edu.br/cursos/coordenacoes/graduacao/curitiba/ct-sistemas-de-informacao Accessed in 13 dec 2019.

[2] Available in: http://engcomp.dainf.ct.utfpr.edu.br/estrutura.php Acessed in 13 dec 2019.

[3] Available in: https://www.sbc.org.br/ Accessed in 10 dec 2019.

4.1 Brazilian Computer Society Documents

In Brazilian Computer Society we analyzed 8 documents, considering (a) not only as closed categories, but what involves thinking about multiculturalism in terms of society, groups, identities, differences and cultures. The (b) category for us involve subaltern people and the intersections of multiplicity of identities and oppression forms (gender, race, ethnicity and class).

Table 1. Recurrences in Brazilian Computer society documents

Categories/Documents	Multiculturalism	Intersectionality
Basic education courses references	Culture, digital culture (28)	
Ordinance	Culture (2)	
Statistical		(2015) - gender (8) (2016) - gender - (12) (2017) - gender (12)
Challenges	Culture (2)	Gender (3)

The last category (c) **reflexivity** did not appear any time in the Table 1 because it cannot be quantified for us, we use category (c) to analyse how multiculturalism and intersectionality are presented in the documents. (c) for Haraway [9] is more a stance of those who write the documents that reflects on representativeness (or not) about intersections. When we question the scientific objectivity, science linearity and technological determinism we think about identities and intersections and how the documents explore it?

In the document *basic education courses references* the concept culture appear (28) times in *challenges* and *ordinance* (2) times. In a quantitative analysis "culture" is the most recurrent term in the documents, but its emphasis is shifted from the theory. We identify that the term is allied to technological culture and not as a group or identity and difference. It reinforce scientific objectivity Wajcman [12] that represent culture as a dimension of ethics sphere. In *statitical* "gender" is the most recurrent term, but they consider data of male and female participation in general. There is no mention of intersection that are not recognized in the binary - man and woman [12].

4.2 Bachelor in Information Systems and Computer Engineering Documents

When looking at two computer science undergraduate courses we observed that they follow the same guidelines, are in the same institution and in the same academic department, have similar and complementary disciplines in paths but have a different (Pedagogical Course Project) in view of discourses they prioritize (Table 2).

About the category (c) the Bachelor in Information Systems (Pedagogical Course Project) discuss normative culture in the document, question scientific objectivity, technological determinism and science linearity [9] and bring intersections as part of Pedagogical Course Project. We identify that reflexivity is a reflection of people who thought

Table 2. Recurrences in Bachelor in Information Systems and Computer Engineering documents

Categories/Pedagogical course project	Multiculturalism	Intersectionality
Bachelor in Information Systems	(2016) - culture (28)	(2016) - race (2); class (11); gender (2); ethnicity (2)
Computer Engineering	(2016) - culture (33)	

the document with intentions that led them to propose a curriculum flexibility based on students criticism.

The Computer Engineering (Pedagogical Course Project) follows the Brazilian Computer Society guidelines and documents, as well as the other graduate course, but without intending to problematize normative culture (c) in the area [7–9]. They follow the minimum of social issues such as bringing up the theme 'culture'. In addition, the Computer Engineering is longer, because has 10 periods and Bachelor in Information Systems has 6 periods. In this sense, thinking about a curriculum flexibility from students' reality is a way to minize dropout, psychological problems from excesses of subjects, tests in certain periods of the undergraduate course. The normative culture highlight in the theoretical background by Wajcman [8] and Castelini [11] show that structural barriers are in education (in documents, guidelines, laws) also in family, technologies, society and culture. The next section present some questions, results and discussions that involve the categories analysed in the documents.

5 Results

The structural barriers can be observed by the low number of women in the documents that even mention gender disparities and other oppression in computer science undergraduate and graduate courses in Brazil. The main results of this work identified that in the documents of Brazilian Computer Society and Computer Engineering intersectionality and multiculturalism is little and in some documents not even mentioned it represents the gaps in the current documents.

By contrast in the Bachelor in Information Systems documents we identified a problematization about intersections, people with disabilities and also about linearity, objectivity and determinism in science and technology. We note that this undergraduate Pedagogical Course Project brings the criticism to the area itself regardless of not having guidelines that indicate this importance. It reflects intentions and values of people participation and discussions on the margins of the area [8–10]. Therefore, identifying this gap is also important to note that changes in the area can occur within it and we need to value the people who point out these gaps, through documents at first, but also with actions in communities.

If intersectionality (race, class and gender) [6] ethnicity, age, nationality, multiculturalism, disabilities and other discussions are not in the documents and guidelines how is it in the classroom? How is it at academic events? How is it in the community through extension actions? To Yuval-Davis [6] intersectional perspective involves social divisions that are reinforced in this gap in the documents but also on a daily basis at the university, in research groups, in institutional projects, in the guidelines that regulate public institutions in the country.

For her it is in macro axes and social power that contributes to thinking about the future paths of this work that should involve criticism of documents and guidelines, but also with proposals for new approaches through intersectional bias [6]; actions with people who are and are not in computer science undergraduate courses [8–10]; with schools; with kids and with families to think with them [3, 4] about intersectional public policies.

Point out these gaps in the documents and also in community is to propose spaces, groups and actions to problematize by the lens of STS studies, intersectionality considering that our country is multicultural, and all the documents, laws and materials are made by people with intentions [1]. Haraway [9] indicates in her work that we need to question scientific objectivity, science linearity to understand that society is multiple, diverse, variable but it is not trivial to recognize (reflexivity) because the actions must be with people participation [3].

Acknowledgment. This study was financed in part by the Coordenação de Aperfeiçoamento de Pessoal de Nível Superior - Brasil (CAPES) - Finance Code 001.

References

1. Winner, L.: Artefatos têm política? Trad. Debora Pazetto Ferreira; Luiz Henrique de Lacerda Abrahão. Analytica, Rio de Janeiro, vol. 21, no. 2, pp. 195–218 (2017). https://revistas.ufrj. br/index.php/analytica/article/viewFile/22470/12527. Accessed 30 Sept 2019
2. Bødker, S.: Third-wave HCI, 10 years later—participation and sharing. Mag. Interact. **22**(5), 24–31 (2015). https://dl.acm.org/citation.cfm?id=2804405. Accessed 01 Oct 2019
3. Bardzell, J., Bardzell, S.: Humanistic HCI, 163 p. Morgan and Claypool Publisher (2015)
4. Breslin, S., Wadhwa, B.: Engendering interaction design. In: 3rd International Conference on User Science and Engineering (i-USEr) (2014). https://ieeexplore.ieee.org/document/700 2719. Accessed 01 Oct 2019
5. Schlesinger, A., Edwards, K., Grinter, R.E.: Intersectional HCI: engaging identity through gender, race and class. CHI (2017). https://www.semanticscholar.org/paper/Intersectional-HCI%3A-Engaging-Identity-through-Race%2C-Schlesinger-Edwards/27b49a706d907c5 d6858068ba97bbe873fcf687f. Accessed 01 Oct 2019
6. Yuval-davis, N.: Intersectionality and feminist politics. Eur. J. Women's Stud. **13**(3), 193–209 (2006). https://hal.archives-ouvertes.fr/hal-00571274. Accessed 14 Oct 2019
7. Dahmoon, R.K.: Considerations on mainstreaming intersectionality. SAGE (2011). https:// journals.sagepub.com/doi/abs/10.1177/1065912910379227. Accessed 18 Oct 2019
8. Wajcman, J.: TechnoFeminism. Polity Press, Cambridge (2004)
9. Haraway, D.J.: Saberes localizados: a questão da ciência para o feminismo e o privilégio da perspectiva parcial. Cadernos Pagu (5), 7–41 (1995). https://periodicos.sbu.unicamp.br/ojs/ index.php/cadpagu/article/view/1773. Accessed 01 Oct 2019
10. Lauretis, T.: A tecnologia do gênero, pp. 1–30. Indiana University Press (1987). http://mar coaureliosc.com.br/cineantropo/lauretis.pdf. Accessed 30 Sept 2019

11. Castelini, P.: Mulheres na computação: percepções, memórias e participação de estudantes e egressas. Dissertação de Mestrado em Tecnologia e Sociedade, Curitiba, Paraná, 125 p. (2018). http://repositorio.utfpr.edu.br:8080/jspui/handle/1/2944. Accessed 8 Aug 2019
12. Wajcman, J.: Feminism Confronts Technology. The Pennsylvania State University Press, University Park (1991)

Direct User Behavior Data Leads to Better User Centric Thinking than Role Playing: An Experimental Study on HCI Design Thinking

Abhishek Dahiya[✉] and Jyoti Kumar

Indian Institute of Technology Delhi, New Delhi 110016, India
abhiphd3@gmail.com, jyoti@design.iitd.ac.in

Abstract. This paper explores the difference in the effects of role-playing and usability testing on the design thinking process of novice designers. While usability testing helps in understanding user mental models by observing user behavior as the user interacts with a system, role-playing relies on a designer's own perception about the user where the designer him/herself acts as a user. The difference in user research methods that leads to a different understanding of the user might reflect in the design thinking process of a designer while ideating for solutions of an HCI design problem. This paper presents findings from an experimental study done with novice designers to understand the differences in design thinking processes when designers themselves conducted usability tests versus when they designed using role-playing on persona data given to them. The findings suggest that direct observation of user behavior leads to more consideration for users and therefore better user-centered thinking process than the imaginative role-playing.

Keywords: Design thinking · Usability testing · Role playing · Linkography · User centered design

1 Introduction

User-Centered Design (UCD) methodology aims to bridge the gaps between users' mental model and designers' mental model [1]. Among the various methods used in UCD for Human Computer Interaction (HCI) products, usability testing is one of the most prevalent one. Formative and summative usability tests are used throughout the HCI design cycles where UCD is employed. The usability tests collect behavioral reactions of users on a given design prototype. While usability tests provide actual behavioral responses on a given design, there are other non-behavioral methods often employed by HCI designers to aid in their understanding of users. For example, another tool often employed by design teams is called 'role-playing'. In role-playing, the design teams assume themselves to be users and try to behave like users. Though they do not know the actual user behavior, based on their prior experience and imagination, they try to play the role of users. This role-playing method helps the design team in the visualization of the scenario and tasks of the users.

© Springer Nature Switzerland AG 2020
C. Stephanidis et al. (Eds.): HCII 2020, CCIS 1293, pp. 11–18, 2020.
https://doi.org/10.1007/978-3-030-60700-5_2

Using this premise, this paper explores the difference in the effects of imaginative role-playing and factual usability testing on the design thinking process of novice designers. An experimental setup was created where five novice designers were given a persona for role-playing. Thereafter, they sketched design solutions for the given HCI design problem. Then the same novice designers conducted usability tests with actual users whose persona was earlier presented. Following the usability tests, the designers again sketched design solution concepts. The concept generation phase was recorded in both cases. The participants were asked to think aloud while generating design concepts. Later design moves were analyzed by using linkography and text entropy of verbal protocol. The findings from this study might have useful implications for the choice of user research methods to get more user-focused design thinking.

2   Background

2.1   User-Centered Design

User-Centered Design (UCD) has been defined as "a philosophy based on the needs and interests of the user, with an emphasis on making products usable and understandable" [2, 3]. UCD methodology was propounded to focus on users and their needs before advancing in the design process [1]. It has been argued that designers and users might have different perspectives on the problem [1, 4]. Therefore, a design solution produced without taking the user's perspective into account might not solve the actual problem. With the advent of UCD in design research and practice, various user research methods like user interviewing, shadowing, focus groups, usability testing, and role-playing, etc. were used to understand and empathize with the users. The experiment described in this paper uses usability testing and roleplaying as methods to understand and empathize with the users. The two methods were selected because these methods are very different in terms of user inputs/insights gained by the designer. While role-playing relies on a designer's own understanding of the user, usability testing produces hard factual data about user behavior while interacting with the system.

2.2   Usability Testing and Role Playing

Usability has been defined as the extent to which the target users can use the product to achieve their intended goals with effectiveness, efficiency and satisfaction in a specified context of use [5]. With the advent of web based products, usability assessment is becoming increasingly relevant especially because a user friendly website is capable of capturing and retaining a potential customer [6]. For this, various methods to evaluate usability are employed like heuristic evaluation, think aloud, questionnaire, interview, prototype evaluation and usability testing. However, literature reports usability testing to be the most used method for evaluation of software applications [7]. Usability testing has been used as a method to understand users as they perform tasks given to them. It has three main components - representative users who are asked to perform representative tasks and are then observed how they do it, where they succeed and the difficulties they face [8]. The relevance of these methods lies in extracting the direct information about how people use a particular system. This makes it possible to identify specific problems with the interface which can then be resolved in subsequent design iterations [9].

In role playing one deliberately assume a character role in a constructed scene with, or without, props. This method of user research is used to help designers empathize with the users. While doing a user role play, designers gets insights about the issues that the user might be facing during the task in the task environment. This is one of the easy and less time consuming method of user research. It is often argued that the designer is merely acting like the actual users, and the issues reported by the designer are the ones that the designer himself/herself faced while using the product. However, the method is useful to help designers reflect back on their design actions while designing.

2.3 User Information Affecting Design Thinking

Understanding design thinking processes have been an interesting topic in design research since the 1930's. Investigation in the design thinking process has been helpful in getting insights into human problem solving and was used in developing design methods, processes, and design techniques. There were several attempts to investigate the effect of various stimuli on design thinking [10]. A few attempts on how user information affects design thinking process have also been reported in literature. These studies indicated that there are differences in design thinking patterns of designers while working with user information given in various formats [11]. Other studies reported the effect of additional training exercises like empathy exercises [12] while working with user data. However, the effect of working with user data obtained through various user research methods on design thinking is still not much reported in literature.

2.4 Tools to Observe Design Thinking: Linkography

Linkography is a technique used in protocol analysis to study a designer's cognitive activities. This technique is widely used to assess the design productivity of a design thinker. Verbal protocols recorded through think aloud or interview method are first parsed into design moves which is 'a step, an act, an operation, which transforms the design situation relative to the state in which it was prior to that move' [13]. Design moves are then linked according to their relationship to form a linkograph. Linkograph produced is thus a graphical representation of cognitive activities involved in solving the design problem. In a linkograph, Link node is a point of intersection of two design moves; Backlinks are links of moves that connect to previous moves; Forelinks are links of moves that connect to subsequent moves; Critical move is design moves that are rich in links, they can be either forelinks, backlinks, or both; Link index is the ratio between the number of links and the number of moves (Fig. 1).

2.5 Entropy Measurement

Linkograph entropy has been reported as a measure of quality of creative thinking process of a designer [14]. Based on Shannon's information theory, Kan and Gero argue that a fully linked linkograph indicates no diversification of ideas, hence less opportunity for

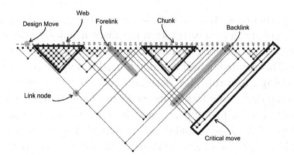

Fig. 1. Example of a Linkograph with its constituents

quality outcomes. Similarly, an unlinked linkograph indicates unrelated ideas, indicating no converging ideas, hence very low opportunity for idea development. A partially linked linkograph in which moves are interrelated but not totally connected indicates that there are lots of opportunities for good ideas with development. High entropy is indicative of a productive process, or richer idea generation process. Entropy of idea links was calculated using Shannon's formulae for entropy measurement:

$$H = -\sum_{i=1}^{n} p_i log(p_i)$$

Separate entropy for forelinks, backlinks and horizontal links was calculated and it is argued in literature that if an idea is weak, it will not have many fore-links, which is represented by low entropy [14]. Similarly, for backlink entropy, if an idea is novel, it will not have backlinks. The resulting entropy is low. Conversely if an idea is back linked to all previous ideas, it is not novel. Hence it is represented by low entropy [14]. Horizon link entropy measures opportunities relating to cohesiveness and incubation. Low horizon link entropy indicates complete cohesiveness [14].

3   A Study to Understand the Difference in Design Thinking

3.1   Experiment Methodology

Design thinking was observed through the solution generation approach to the design problem by designers. A total of five designers participated in the study. In the first case, designers were given a website redesigning task. The participants were first verbally briefed about the users. The brief about the users included their age, education, profession, digital proficiency, work culture and motivations to do use the website. The participants were given five distinct tasks that can be done using the website. They were asked to empathize and role-play their users as they perform these tasks. The participants were free to ask questions and to take notes of the usability issues that they observed during the session. After this session, the participants were asked to produce conceptual solutions for redesigning the website for the five tasks that they performed. In the second case, the participants were first briefed about the persona. Then, they were asked to conduct a usability testing session with actual users in a professional usability setup. The participant in the usability testing session was asked to perform the same tasks on the website while designers marked behavioral observations of the user performing the tasks. A usability testing report was generated by the designer on the basis of which they were asked to generate conceptual solutions for the same. The concept generation process by designers was recorded using a tabletop camera. The designers were asked to think aloud while they were generating solutions for the design problem given to them. The time given for concept generation sessions was 30 min in both cases. Verbal protocols of designers from the think-aloud session were used to analyze the difference in design thinking pattern in both cases.

Design Task. The website given to the designers to redesign was a national government service website called Digital Seva "digitalseva.csc.gov.in". The website is used by more than a million users per day. The website is able to provide more than 200 government services including insurance services, citizen ID registration, various bill payments, Income tax return filing, etc. The designers were given only five tasks that they need to redesign. These were: 1. Change Language of the website 2. Postpaid recharge 3. Electricity bill payment 4. IGL Gas bill payment 5. Logout and Login. These tasks were given to all the participants in the same sequence. Designers were asked to generate conceptual UI design solutions for the tasks described above.

Participants. Participants who volunteered to participate in this experiment were post-graduate students of Industrial Design at the Indian Institute of Technology, Delhi. A total of five students participated in this study. Participants constituted two males and three females with age range between 23–27 yrs. (average age: 25.3 yrs., Std. dev.: 1.23 yrs.).

Data Analysis. The data collected from the experiment was verbal protocols by the participants collected using think aloud method while ideating for solutions. Linkographs for conceptual design sessions were constructed to analyse design thinking process of the participants. Linkographs were constructed by using a software called Linkoder [15]. 10 linkographs were constructed for 5 participants (2 linkograph per participant). Linkographs were quantitatively and qualitatively analysed to study the design thinking process.

3.2 Observations and Results

Figure 2 shows linkographs for conceptual ideation session of five participants while generating design solutions after Role Playing and after Usability Testing with a user. By looking at the physical characteristics of the linkographs it can be said that idea links for the participants ideating after role playing session are more staggered than the idea links for the participants working after usability testing (except P2). Further, it was observed that a high density of idea links was developed in the initial part of the linkographs for the participants working after usability testing (except P2). This was the part where participants were contemplating on what they observed dusting the

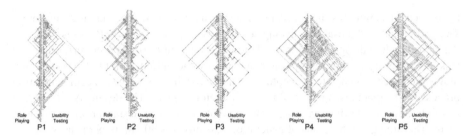

Fig. 2. Linkographs generated for participants P1 to P5 while designing.

usability testing session. The initial design moves were therefore more important to the participants which were linked more with the successive design moves.

Critical moves in linkographs are important turning points in the thinking process [13]. A higher value of link index and critical moves indicates a more productive design process [13]. Table 1 below shows number of critical moves along with link index for linkographs for role playing and for usability testing.

Table 1. Quantitative data from linkographs for Role Playing (RP) and Usability Testing (UT)

Participant	Number of critical moves		Link index		Fore link entropy		Back link entropy		Horizontal link entropy	
	RP	UT	RP	UT	RP	UT	RP	UT	RP	UT
P1	4	6	1.52	2.27	0.213	0.343	0.226	0.318	0.148	0.165
P2	6	3	1.83	1.2	0.378	0.187	0.204	0.342	0.122	0.105
P3	3	5	1.31	1.53	0.265	0.328	0.288	0.327	0.153	0.168
P4	4	9	1.25	1.78	0.201	0.269	0.197	0.225	0.125	0.188
P5	5	7	1.46	1.84	0.342	0.385	0.326	0.358	0.084	0.124
Mean	4.4	6	1.474	1.724	0.280	0.302	0.248	0.314	0.126	0.150
Std. Dev	1.14	2.24	0.23	0.40	0.08	0.08	0.06	0.05	0.03	0.03

The table above indicates that number of critical moves in usability testing case is more than role playing case except for participants P2. Similarly, the link index for participants working after usability testing session were found higher (except P2) than for the participants working with role playing. This indicates that participants working after usability session underwent a more productive design thinking process than in role playing. Gero [14] argues that by entropy of idea links, is helpful in indicating the creative thinking behaviour of the individual. Table 1 shown above indicates rise in fore link entropy, backline entropy and horizontal link entropy for most of the designers working on design problem after usability testing as compared to Role playing. Hence, it can be said that participants working with user data underwent a more creative thinking process than the participants working on a design problem without any user data. Low fore link entropy value of designers working without user data could be a result of weak ideas or more idea fixation [14]. This trend is an indicator that designers were not very sure of their initial ideas in Role playing as compared to Usability testing where designers were constantly referring to their initial design moves. The backlink entropy of designers working after usability testing is found to be more than that of Role playing. The low backlink entropy value is indicative of either a new idea generation process [14]. Designers working after Role playing session were able to produce more number of new ideas than working after usability testing. As seen in qualitative analysis of linkographs, participants working after Role playing were not able to hold on to their initial ideas. Therefore, low backlink entropy value in this case is due to sudden thoughts that came to the participants as the participants progressed in design process. High value of horizontal link entropy is indicative of cohesiveness in design thinking process. As seen in qualitative analysis of linkographs, the designers working after Role playing were not able to hold up their initial ideas and jumping randomly to add new features to design solutions. This is also reflected in the horizontal link entropy values in the table above. Whereas designers working after Usability testing session tend to reflect back more on their initial thoughts about users which resulted in more cohesive design thinking process and high horizontal link entropic value.

4 Conclusion and Discussions

With increase in User Centered Design methodology in design practice, there has been a rise in the number of methods to understand users. Along with the complexity of choosing appropriate method for user research, there has been very limited literature available on how different design methods affect the development of user understanding and hence affect the design thinking process of a designer. This paper was an attempt to investigate how user understanding from two different user research methods affect the design thinking process of a designer. Analysis of linkographs shows that most of the designers working on design concepts after usability testing underwent a richer design thinking process as compared to role playing. It was observed that designers working with user data obtained after usability testing were able to have a more structured and cohesive design thinking approach. Qualitative analysis of the verbal protocols indicated that designers working with usability data were deriving their concepts on what they observed in the usability session. Whereas designers working on design concepts after role playing session were mostly speaking and developing ideas on what they think should be the solution. Hence a more "user-centered design thinking" was seen when participants were working after conducting a usability testing session with actual users. This finding provides opportunity to discuss how more user centricity in design thinking can be obtained. This opens up the opportunity to rethink on how user research outcomes should be applied or used in design thinking process.

References

1. Vredenburg, K., Isensee, S., Righi, C.: User-centered Design: An Integrated Approach. Prentice Hall, Prentice Hall (2002)

2. Dorst, K., Cross, N.: Creativity in the design process: co-evolution of problem–solution. Des. Stud. **22**, 425–437 (2001)
3. Norman, D.: The Design of Everyday Things: Revised and Expanded Edition. Hachette UK, London (2013)
4. Nielsen, J.: Usability Engineering. Morgan Kaufmann, Burlington (1994)
5. ISO 9241-11: 1998: Ergonomic requirements for office work with visual display terminals (vdts) — Part 11: Guidance on usability. ISO (1998)
6. Murillo, B., Vargas, S., Moquillaza, A., Fernández, L., Paz, F.: Usability testing as a complement of heuristic evaluation: a case study. In: Marcus, A., Wang, W. (eds.) DUXU 2017. LNCS, vol. 10288, pp. 434–444. Springer, Cham (2017). https://doi.org/10.1007/978-3-319-58634-2_32
7. Paz, F., Pow-Sang, J.A.: Current trends in usability evaluation methods: a systematic review. In: 2014 7th International Conference on Advanced Software Engineering and Its Applications, Haikou, pp. 11–15 (2014)
8. Nielsen, J.: Usability 101: introduction to usability. Usability 101: Introduction to Usability (2012)
9. Holzinger, A.: Usability engineering methods for software developers. Commun. ACM **48**(1), 71–74 (2005)
10. Cardoso, C., Badke-Schaub, P.E.T.R.A.: Fixation or inspiration: creative problem solving in design. J. Creative Behav. **45**(2), 77–82 (2011)
11. Dahiya, A., Kumar, J.: Do design outcomes get influenced by type of user data? An experimental study with primary and secondary user research data. In: Ahram, T., Karwowski, W., Taiar, R. (eds.) IHSED 2018. AISC, vol. 876, pp. 191–197. Springer, Cham (2019). https://doi.org/10.1007/978-3-030-02053-8_30
12. Dahiya, A., Kumar, J.: Observations on design thinking in novice designers while empathizing with persona. In: Handbook of Research on Human-Computer Interfaces and New Modes of Interactivity, pp. 21–39. IGI Global (2019)
13. Goldschmidt, G.: Linkography (2014)
14. Kan, J.W.T., Bilda, Z., Gero, J.S.: Comparing entropy measures of idea links in design protocols: Linkography entropy measurement and analysis of differently conditioned design sessions. Artif. Intell. Eng. Des. Anal. Manuf. **21**, 367–377 (2007)
15. Pourmohamadi, M., Gero, J.S.: LINKOgrapher: an analysis tool to study design protocols based on FBS coding scheme. In: DS 68-2: Proceedings of the 18th International Conference on Engineering Design (ICED 2011), Impacting Society through Engineering Design, vol. 2: Design Theory and Research Methodology, Lyngby/Copenhagen, Denmark (2011)

Moving Beyond Stuck: A Design-Based Approach to Enhancing Minority Tech Startup Launches

Wanda Eugene[✉], Yerika Jimenez, Ekaterina Muravevskaia, Carmen Lopez-Ramirez, and Juan Gilbert

Computer and Information Science and Engineering Department, University of Florida,
P.O. Box 116120, Gainesville, FL 32611, USA
{weugene,jimenyer,emur,clopezramirez,juan}@ufl.edu

Abstract. Given that all of the US-based business owners ranking in the top 10 of the Forbes billionaires list helped found technology-based companies, tech entrepreneurship presents an almost unmatched potential for social mobility for company founders. Unfortunately, Black entrepreneurs in technology-based businesses receive less than 1% of the venture capital in the US. "Stuck from the start," is the characterization of the situation that Black entrepreneurs find themselves in while navigating the road to entrepreneurship (Myers and Chan 2017). The challenges faced by Black entrepreneurs stem from institutionalized racism (e.g., discriminatory lending), implicit biases, a lack of mentorship or connection to a larger network of business owners/investors (Fairlee and Robb 2008; Robb et al. 2014), a dearth of culturally-relevant curriculum, a lack of technical support, and other characteristics of the current entrepreneurial ecosystem. For the past three years, the Entrepreneurial Diversity in Information Technology (EDIT) has been iteratively refined to address some of the hurdles faced by Black tech startup founders; technical development, culturally-relevant curriculum, and targeted mentorship. With the ultimate goal of developing a scalable and sustainable model that can bring target communities into the tech-based entrepreneurial ecosystem across Florida, to date, EDIT has supported 43 Black founders in starting their entrepreneurship journey and assisted in the development of 25 technology-based startups. In this paper, we discuss the relevant background, the design-based research methodology utilized to refine the program, and the future directions for the program.

Keywords: Business startup · Pre-incubators · Black entrepreneurs · Culturally-relevant curriculum · Cross culture training

1 Introduction

During times of economic downturn, entrepreneurs, new venture creation, and small business sectors significantly contribute to the US economy creating new jobs, hiring more workers, etc. Often seen as the backbone of the U.S. economy, and employing 47.5% of the private workforce, small businesses have remained critical to societal

© Springer Nature Switzerland AG 2020
C. Stephanidis et al. (Eds.): HCII 2020, CCIS 1293, pp. 19–26, 2020.
https://doi.org/10.1007/978-3-030-60700-5_3

growth and vitality. The creation and growth of new ventures in high growth sectors such as technology account for one-quarter of high growth firms. Startups armed with seed financing stave off economic stagnation and are transformational for the broader society but also for the entrepreneurs' lives (Stangler 2010). Notoriously difficult, a little more than 50% of startups fail in the first four years. Amongst businesses that do manage to survive these first years, according to a recent Kauffman Foundation report, BIPOC (Black, Indigenous and People of Color) entrepreneurs, especially Black business owners, are extremely underrepresented among U.S. small business owners (Kauffman 2018). These findings are exacerbated when examining the tech entrepreneurship space where Black entrepreneurs receive less than 1% of venture capital funding.

What, then, is preventing the success of Black entrepreneurs generally and within tech-based businesses? Myers and Chan (2017) illustrate the financial challenges confronting Black entrepreneurs while starting and running their own businesses that foster unequal outcomes for entrepreneurs in the United States. Recent studies show that Black people have substantially lower levels of assets than their White counterparts (Bento and Brown 2020), lower startup capital (Fairlie and Robb 2008), and are unable to establish lines of credit that could support expansion plans. Further complicating the ability for Black entrepreneurs' trajectory is a lack of a robust network and supportive institutions that could provide managerial training, technical assistance, and strategic advice. In the U.S., social networks are highly racially and ethnically segregated, depriving Black entrepreneurs of novel resources that other groups, like White entrepreneurs, would benefit from (Javadian et al. 2018).

In order to address challenges faced by small business owners broadly, business incubators have served a vital role over the last three decades in propelling startups to sustainable growth and structure, after having been identified as a differentiating factor to success in for many startups (Wiggins and Gibson 2003). Incubators are organizations geared toward speeding up the growth and success of startup and early-stage companies, while accelerators are organizations that "support early-stage, growth-driven companies through education, mentorship and financing" (Hathaway 2016). Business incubators and accelerators have become a popular strategy to support the growth of entrepreneurial ventures (Anderson and Hanadi 2012; Molnar et al. 2011).

The programs are designed to address some of the networking, educational, and capital challenges that entrepreneurs face. Researchers have noted the significant role these programs have played as a source for sparking innovation development, converting the ideas into marketable products and services, and entrepreneurial success (Cohen and Hochberg 2014). Women and BIPOC, however, are not participating in high-tech incubators and accelerators at the same rate as White males. A report by JP Morgan Chase & Company found four barriers that have prevented women and BIPOC entrepreneurs from participating in high-tech incubators and accelerators: recruitment, selection biases, program design, and culture (JPMorgan Chase & Co 2018). The Entrepreneurial Diversity in Information Technology (EDIT) program addresses some of the gaps in existing programs in order to ensure Black entrepreneurs in under-resourced communities are fully supported as they move towards launching technology startups.

2 Overview EDIT Program Design

2.1 Pedagogical Approach

In its current form, EDIT provides ten-weeks training on entrepreneurship focusing on design thinking and lean startup as pillars for small business development. Our pedagogical approach combined aspects of constructivism, cultural-relevance, and situated learning. First, constructivism states that people construct their understanding and knowledge of the world through experiencing things and reflecting on those experiences. When a person encounters something new, she has to reconcile it with our previous ideas and experience, maybe changing what she believes, or possibly discarding the new information as irrelevant (Wadsworth 1996). In the EDIT program, entrepreneurs learned the entrepreneurial process by learning elements of design thinking and lean-startup and applying those elements into their own business. By doing this, we ensure that entrepreneurs are actively working, modifying, and building their business idea and entrepreneurial skills.

Next, culturally relevant pedagogy (CRP) recognizes that learning is a complex process, and students' identities, lived experiences, and culture are factors when learning. CRP is a pedagogy that addresses student achievement and helps students accept and affirm their cultural identity while developing critical perspectives that challenge inequities in society (Ladson-Billings 1995). The EDIT program used CRP throughout the curriculum in different ways. The first step taken was to ensure that instructors looked like our served population. For this reason, all cohorts were taught by people of color (one female Haitian-American and one Black male).

Finally, Lave argues that learning as it usually occurs is a function of the activity, context, and culture in which it occurs (i.e., it is situated). Social interaction is a critical component of situated learning learners become involved in a "community of practice," which embodies certain beliefs and behaviors to be acquired. As the beginner or newcomer moves from the periphery of this community to its center, they become more active and engaged within the culture and hence assume the role of expert or old-timer (Lave and Wenger 1991). The EDIT program used situated learning by taking a more participant-centered approach instead of a one-side model approach. This was done by taking into consideration who the participants were overall in order to shape the interactions within the program. The program took into account participants' needs outside the program by identifying previous experiences, challenges, or obstacles that may affect learning.

2.2 Content

The content of the program led the founders through a blend of design thinking and the lean startup methodology. Design thinking was chosen because the process allowed participants to define their business idea, understand it in-depth, create a possible solution, test it, and reflect on the results. The results of user research inform the development team to expand its ideas by improvements to physical prototypes. New prototypes are later tested by users and the results are used as inputs for the next round of development (Johansson-Sköldberg et al. 2013). According to Brown (2008), it is through the process of creating, testing, and consequently learning that entrepreneurs can improve on their initial ideas. Similarly, the lean startup methodology provides a framework for systematically validating the (solution) hypotheses in fast loops.

The blending of these two processes helps entrepreneurs to "fail many times" by establishing a fast feedback loop with participants. The methodology is founded on close and constant interaction with real customers and collection of feedback. In the first step, entrepreneurs map their business ideas into testable business model assumptions. Then through a tool termed as minimum viable products (MVPs), these assumptions will be tested. An MVP is a version of the product with the smallest set of features that are built to provide relevant information to validate or invalidate assumptions (Ries 2011). Through the objective analysis of the completed tests, the assumptions are validated or invalidated. This process is aimed at reducing the extreme uncertainty in venture creation processes through the accumulation of fine-grained and detailed information about the sources of uncertainty.

3 Program Refinement

3.1 Methodology

Using the Design-Based Research (DBR) methodology (Wang and Hannafin 2005), the EDIT program underwent five iterative cycles of design, implementation, analysis, and revisions. After each instantiation of the program, we worked to incorporate solutions to implementing the program considering participants' needs and barriers to program participation with a new set of entrepreneurs.

3.2 Program and Cycle of Design Process

1. Focus Groups and Brainstorm: Review and discuss existing incubator models, and literature on small business support, and disconnects for Black tech founders.
2. Material Gathering: Collect culturally appropriate material to be used.
3. Curriculum Design: To create a course design model
4. Pilot and Evaluation: To pilot and redevelop course modules and gather students' feedback.

Throughout the process of program development, we conducted progressive and iterative reviews. We first assessed existing programs in the local area and nationwide to support our target audience in launching innovations. We then conducted a focus group with existing, aspiring entrepreneurs and supporting entities to complete a needs analysis. We went on to design activities which we piloted with a Black female entrepreneur with previous experience in participating with entrepreneurial-like programs (Iteration 1). After we officially produced and organized the course modules, we offered Cohort 1 in the fall of 2017 (Iteration 2). We conducted external expert reviews to evaluate creatively and critically the quality of the program and the design process. Leveraging the evaluation and feedback received, Cohort 2 in the spring of 2018 (Iteration 3) used the revised program and curriculum design. We then varied the location to better asset the program design and development for Cohort 3 in the fall of 2018 (Iteration 4). The idea of a curriculum that accounts for the fluidity of culture guided every action. Finally, in the summer of 2019 (Iteration 5), Cohort 4 introduced a third-party facilitator to assess the curriculum's durability and sustainability. Table 1 shows key information related to iterations.

4 Iterations

Table 1. EDIT cohort iterations

Iteration	# of students	Scope of iteration
Iteration 1: Summer 2017	GNV, FL: 1	1. Test curriculum modules 2. Test course organization, timing, and flow 3. Try out assignments and deliverables 4. Gather student feedback
Iteration 2: Fall 2017	GNV, FL: 9	1. Field-test the completed beta course with real EDIT participants 2. Invite learners to troubleshoot course contents and modes of delivery 3. Design in-class activities 4. Invite external reviewers for expert feedback
Iteration 3: Spring 2018	GNV, FL: 8	1. Deliver the revised course 2. Recruit a different group of EDIT participants 3. Compare participants experience across cohorts 4. Modify program design to include additional support 5. Embed research in program design manual
Iteration 4: Fall 2018	MIA, FL: 14	1. Create community engagement protocol 2. Create community partnerships and alliances 3. Deliver the revised course 4. Modify Recruitment protocol 5. Recruit a different group of EDIT participants 6. Compare participants experience across cohorts 7. Embed research in program design manual
Iteration 5: Summer 2019	GNV, FL: 18	1. Deliver the course modules 2. Recruit third-party facilitator 3. Embed research in an evaluation plan

5 Analysis Within the Iterations

1st Iteration: Pilot. The pilot took place during the summer of 2017 with one participant. We held two-hour sessions twice a week for four weeks at a university in the southeast. Her insight helped the EDIT program understand what elements we should include and excluded from the curriculum based on her previous experience and knowledge gaps.

The pilot participant explained that the curriculum was too complicated and suggested to focus more on their ways of knowing and cut down more common business rhetoric to improve the curriculum.

2nd iteration - Cohort 1 – Gainesville. Cohort 1 took place during Fall 2017 in Gainesville, Florida, with a total of eight Black and one Latino entrepreneurs with ages ranging from 40 to 70 years old. Participants met twice a week for a two-hour session over twelve weeks. Cohort 1 had four main challenges: 1) length of the cohort, 2) difficulties engaging with the material and putting into practice, and 3) additional support for entrepreneurs after the program ended. The first challenge was the length (12 weeks), which led to entrepreneurs' disengagement, burnout, and apathy towards the end of the program. We solved this challenge by reducing the cohort length from 12 weeks to 10 weeks.

The second challenge arose when the cohort found it challenging to engage with the material and put the lessons they learned into practice. As a result, after each lecture ended, most founders seemed at a bit of a loss on how to enact their immediate next steps regarding building their business. It was during one-on-one sessions held to finalize the design concepts before development that they revealed this challenge.

They continued to submit requests to meet as they tried to navigate their entrepreneur journey. Many of the participants still felt hesitant to immerse themselves in their broader entrepreneurial community. This challenge was solved by providing entrepreneurs with "office hours" - 3 months of additional support to help entrepreneurs complete their business.

3rd iteration - Cohort 2 - Gainesville. Cohort 2 took place during Spring 2018 in Gainesville, Florida, with a total of eight Black entrepreneurs. This cohort took place over ten weeks, and just like the previous cohort, entrepreneurs had little technology background and needed a business idea before joining the program.

Even after correcting for changes made based on Cohort 1 feedback, some of the entrepreneurs still struggled to grasp some aspects of the curriculum. They were reluctant to speak on their misunderstandings. This challenge often occurs when adult learners return to the classroom after a long period of absence (National Research Council 1999). To address this challenge, we provide entrepreneurs with one-on-one time throughout the program to ask questions outside the classroom.

Also, many of them struggle to juggle time and resources to maintain their current responsibilities and work on their business idea. We solved this challenge by adding resource management modules to the curriculum. They helped entrepreneurs to think about how they spent their time and allow them to identify time blocks within their day where they can work on their ideas.

4th iteration - Cohort 3 – Miami. Cohort 3 took place during the Fall of 2018 in Miami, Florida, over ten weeks with 14 Black entrepreneurs. To leverage a local presence in Miami, we established partnerships with crucial Miami grassroots organizations active in the target community. These partnerships were beneficial for recruitment and making the program accessible. We also modified the information and recruitment sessions, from an in-person to a virtual platform. The virtual approach allowed us to be accessible and flexible to program applicants. We needed curriculum modifications because Cohort 4 was more exposed to disruptive innovation's impact on societal shifts. As such, they were more effective in leveraging their social capital to fill gaps and pool resources.

This cohort's biggest challenge was the need for more feedback loops for entrepreneurs, so the EDIT program hired additional support personnel to provide more hands-on feedback and faster feedback loops.

5th iteration - Cohort 4 – Gainesville. Cohort 4 took place during Spring 2019 over ten weeks with 18 Black entrepreneurs. We used the same refined course modules and program structure, and we introduced a third-party facilitator (a male Black). This change brought out opportunities to revise and improve the curriculum. The first opportunity was the need for detailed facilitator training and enhanced training materials to train future facilitators. After receiving multiple inquiries asking for more information about the curriculum and future host location, we saw this as an opportunity to expand and streamline the curriculum for prospective cohorts.

6 Summary and Future Directions

The EDIT program completed five iterations, one pilot and three full cohorts. In total, we have supported over fifty African American founders starting their entrepreneurship journey and assisted in the development of twenty-five technology-based startups. To have a successful cohort, you must build trust with the community you are serving and fully understand what the participants' cultural barriers are and how it can affect their participation in the program. As for the cohort, we learned that the length of the cohort, time management, engaging material, additional support, fast feedback loops, and detailed manuals for instructors are important elements to provide and iterate upon based on the cohort population served.

References

Anderson, B.B., Hanadi, A.M.: The gateway innovation center: exploring key elements of developing a business incubator. World J. Entrepreneurship Manag. Sustain. Dev. (2012)

Bento, A., Brown, T.N.: Belief in systemic racism and self-employment among working blacks. Ethnic Racial Stud. 1–18 (2020)

Brown, T.: Design thinking. Harvard Bus. Rev. **86**(6), 84 (2008)

Cohen, S., Hochberg, Y.V.: Accelerating startups: the seed accelerator phenomenon (2014)

Colwell, A.: The top 40 startup accelerators and incubators in North America in 2020. Sales Flare (2020). https://blog.salesflare.com/top-startup-accelerators-incubators-us-canada?fbclid=IwA R0OO5uZKDU0Eh8cjXEAkgBQk_l8RnTf3AlTjGAwlomRgR-BBHAwqG3kd8c. Accessed 18 June 2020

Davidsson, P.: The types and contextual fit of entrepreneurial processes. Int. J. Entrepreneurship Educ. **2**, 4–407 (2005)

Fairlie, R., Desai, S., Herrmann, A.: Early-Stage Entrepreneurship in the United States. Kauffman Indicators of Entrepreneurship (2019). https://indicators.kauffman.org/wp-content/upl oads/sites/2/2019/09/National_Report_Sept_2019.pdf. Accessed 18 June 2020

Fairlie, R.W., Robb, A.M.: Race and Entrepreneurial Success. MIT Press, Cambridge (2008)

Hathaway, I.: What startup accelerators really do. Harvard Bus. Rev. (2016). https://hbr.org/2016/ 03/what-startup-accelerators-really-do. Accessed 18 June 2020

Javadian, G., Opie, T.R., Parise, S.: The influence of emotional carrying capacity and network ethnic diversity on entrepreneurial self-efficacy. N. Engl. J. Entrepreneurship (2018)

Johansson-Sköldberg, U., Woodilla, J., Çetinkaya, M.: Design thinking: past, present and possible futures. Creativity Innov. Manag. **22**(2), 121–146 (2013)

JPMorgan Chase & Co.: Is Tech Still An Unwelcome Place for Black Female Founders? I JPMorgan Chase & Co. (2018). https://www.jpmorganchase.com/corporate/news/stories/is-tech-still-an-unwelcome-place-for-black-female-founders.htm. Accessed 18 June 2020

Ladson-Billings, G.: Toward a theory of culturally relevant pedagogy. Am. Educ. Res. J. **32**(3), 465–491 (1995)

Lave, J., Wenger, E.: Situated Learning: Legitimate Peripheral Participation. Cambridge University Press, Cambridge (1991)

Molnar, L., Lewis, D., Harper-Anderson, E.: Incubating Success: Incubation Best Practices That Lead to Successful New Ventures. U.S. Department of Commerce Economic Development Administration (2011)

Myers, S., Chan, P.: Stuck from the Start: The Financial Challenges of Low-and Moderate-Income African-American Entrepreneurs in the South. Prosperity Now (2017)

Ries, E.: The lean startup: how today's entrepreneurs use continuous innovation to create radically successful businesses. Currency (2011)

Robb, A., Coleman, S., Stangler, D.: Sources of economic hope: women's entrepreneurship. SSRN 2529094 (2014)

Stangler, D.: High-growth firms and the future of the American economy. SSRN 1568246 (2010)

Wadsworth, B.J.: Piaget's Theory of Cognitive and Affective Development: Foundations of Constructivism. Longman Publishing (1996)

Wang, F., Hannafin, M.J.: Design-based research and technology-enhanced learning environments. Educ. Technol. Res. Dev. **53**(4), 5–23 (2005)

Wiggins, J., Gibson, D.V.: Overview of US incubators and the case of the Austin Technology Incubator (2003)

National Research Council: How people learn: Bridging research and practice. National Academies Press (1999)

Limiting Experience and Cognition by Flexibility, Interaction Design and Cybernetics

Tore Gulden[1](✉) and Frederick Steier[2](✉)

[1] Oslo Metropolitan University, Oslo, Norway
tore.gulden@oslomet.no
[2] University of South Florida, Tampa, USA
fsteier@gmail.com

Abstract. In this paper, we discuss how flexibility in interaction design processes may lead to hinder flexibility in user praxis and thus cognition, experience, and behaviour, and for design praxis circuits and functioning, and the meta cognition about the design praxis in relation to meaning, aim, change, and inquiring dimensions of functioning, such as the purpose interaction design serve up against the cause by which they arise. A theoretical discussion of the widespread agile and lean interaction design processes in relation to cybernetic theory and the term flexibility introduced by Bateson is the basis for the discussion.

Keywords: Flexibility · Cybernetics · Interaction design

1 Flexibility of Flexibility

Interaction design is typically created with the intention of guiding users through a web page or application architecture by semantic explanations or nudging. Interaction design has left the waterfall processes and implemented agile communication techniques among others, to become more flexible and perhaps holistic while developing design solutions. This flexibility within an organization theory understanding, has led to a "more openness to change and a willingness to do things differently as opposed to the rigid" [1] formal linear-based design approaches. The flexibility thus has led to design and coding teams that can complete designs with less loops of major recoding and redesigning. This flexibility however has possibly shunned away three other layers of flexibility that has a great potential of development, namely the missing flexibility of rethinking and restructuring own development processes within the existing design paradigm, rethinking the paradigm that the design process functions, and the missing flexibility of experiencing while using or exploring interaction designs for users.

This paper has as a starting point, then, the recognition that all forms of design process, including interaction design, need seek to create a balance between structure and flexibility. Yet, rather than seeing this what this balance might look like as one that can be generalized across situations, we recognize the need for the structure/flexibility

C. Stephanidis et al. (Eds.): HCII 2020, CCIS 1293, pp. 27–31, 2020.
https://doi.org/10.1007/978-3-030-60700-5_4

balance to fit with the context, or situation. As such, we propose that interaction design must concern itself with a flexibility of flexibility. To develop this idea, we turn to cybernetics, where concepts of flexibility, in conjunction with adaptation and variety, are central.

1.1 Cybernetics

Cybernetics is about the understanding systems and "flexibility must be understood as a property of a system" [2]. A cybernetic understanding of flexibility explains how it serves as a potential of adaptive behaviour and change. Bateson defined flexibility as "uncommitted potential for change" [3]. Flexibility however, has another end to its functioning, by that it is tied to limited flexibility [1]. "To be flexible, a system must retain (or even increase) its variety of potential responses. Yet at the same time, as Bateson noted, increasing variety in one domain can lead to decreasing variety, as a compensation, in another related domain. In short, there is an economics of flexibility" Within this economics of flexibility, we need consider fully what are the consequences of related increased and decreased flexibilities [See 3 In: Steier, 2005].

2 The Making and Use of Interaction Design Can Be Understood as Circularity

The praxis of behaviour by the designer is similar as for the users. The design process describes the circuits, and the behaviour the emotions [4]. Thus one could feel being in a very flexible situation and yet be bound. Such binding is not so easy to recognize when named the opposite. For the designer and the design agency, the process is often flexible within a limited defined system functioning and goal. If a design member initiates a different way of designing in a design team, the existing design system would hinder it because the flexibility of the existing system is based on a clear goal, often related to cooperation, time, and functioning. The flexibility of the system thus, does not allow changes outside the defined area of flexibility.

2.1 Flexibility of Flexibility for the Users

When an interaction design is flexible in use it may facilitate for users to explore intended functions through multiple media, suggested similar functions and so forth. A cybernetic analysis of this flexibility involves the study of what it does not offer, or hinder users to explore or do. In order to exemplify we can look to a general online newspaper that offers a flexibility by offering of popular or connected articles, but does not suggest unpopular or less read articles, nor critical articles in other news channels for example. In extension, this flexibility function of informing about similar articles, articles that involves the same person, or other articles that readers like, disturbs the concentration of reading the initial article and narrows the area explored by the reader. Hence, analysing such a flexibility layout through a cybernetic perspective, one can say that the news service in this example, serves to hinder concentration and limit news exploration by flexibility [2] for the reader.

When an internal flexibility within the mentioned example of the newspaper article leads the user to orient the readers attention to all articles connected to an article within the same news channel, the design serves to hinder other behaviours, alternative news channels and other emotions. The flexibility instigates the continuance of use within the same sphere, possibly due to will to influence and marketing functions. Every new turn taken by the user, in an interaction design may not lead to different horizons of experience or understanding, rather they often loop (circulate) back to nodes within the internal network, and leads to a minimal learning referred to as zero learning in cybernetics [3]. A cybernetic understanding of such circularity may contribute to how we can understand and perform interaction design as a changing experience offering other types of flexibility. Circularity in interaction design thus may be understood as explanations of actions within and because of the architecture design, typically referred to as navigation. What is left out of such an understanding of experiencing design then is that the user also acts within a circular relationship [5]. This cybernetic understanding of circularity which includes the understandings of "our explanations of our actions" … "integrated together with our acting in a circular relationship" [5] involves the second order (or level) of interpretation, researching, controlling, or understanding a first order systems functioning. Furthermore, such "circularity between understanding and action" may be" exemplified in the eponymous cybernetic example of steering a ship, where the steersman's understanding of the effects of his or her action informs how he or she continues to act. This contrasts with where we try to apply theory linearly to practice or, vice versa, where we fail to situate theory in such a way that it can lead to new ways of acting" [5] for both designers and users. If the context for the steersman in this example is changed to the steering or orienting within, or experiencing interaction design, the example suggest that for every choice made by a user, effects the next action and the direction of continuing act. This space of potential emergent unforeseen acting is seldom looked upon as a design potential other than the already mentioned function of directing to similar experiences or other places in the channel/platform architecture. Effects of actions or acting as a steersman at sea (taking a turn for example) represents an abundant variety of consequences (fun, explorative, dangerous and so forth) and experiences, and the choice for further change in praxis is up to the steersman, not the service. Hence, the service is limiting the experience in a circular fashion that can lead to reading to justify opinions and worldviews rather than exploring. Flexibility of flexibility for the users then is to be freed from the flexibility presented.

2.2   Flexibility of Flexibility when Designing

That is, when designers taught in a tradition that recognizes lean and agile processes as flexible, they believe it and thereby they miss out of an autonomous work process and a mind-set to seek other flexibilities that may occur in every new horizon that the turn of the ship in new routs may present. Accordingly, limited flexibility facilitates work circuits that produce a context that enables zero learning by the binding to one understanding, rather than to seek alternative processes, situations, and functioning. The goal then within such a paradigm is to redesign design processes rather than challenging and altering the goals that led to the creation of them. Hence, the flexibility of the interaction design processes often lies within defined process, programs, goals, and content. This limited and teleological understanding of flexibility thus, which prevents thinking outside the box since the repeated behaviour circuits creates rigid habits.

2.3 Play as a Dimension of Understanding Flexibility

In research on game mechanics, play functioning is often divided into progression and emergence structure for games [6]. Progression structures allows a space to behave, like in Super Mario, where you can do a whole lot but nothing that the creator of the game did not think of. In emergence structure games like football it is the rules that initiate behaviour and emotions, and new ways of doing emerge continuously. In that sense football represents flexibility of flexibility in that it affords behaviour that is created by the player [See for example: 7]. This emergent play context thus that stimulate new behaviour, such as a new offside strategy, represents higher level of learning, namely first order learning. That is, the history of doing is challenged and therefor also the experience. One often also see second order learning by the players, where the platform or paradigm of understanding the game is changed like for example rules change by cultural adjustment etc.

3   Flexibility of Flexibility

For the interaction designer, the work environment can compare to a game structure. That is, they play according to rules often called agile communication, lean processes, and so forth and these rules compare to a progression structure platform. When recognizing the progression structure platform as flexibility, they rule out the possible first and second order learning potentials and in extension change and creation by emergence and thus they become inflexible. Accordingly, the possible worlds of variable understandings and experiences, flexibility of flexibility, offered by interaction design are often neglected or not recognized. Moreover, the experiences and cognition elicited while using the designs are limited to the history of the previous experiences in the design rather than the emergence of the future experiences and processes. We think education plays its role for this missed design potential identified. The emphasis on flexibility by agile processes has limited the space of flexibility for the users and cognition by the designers, possibly because interaction design education largely rely on flexibility as an autonomous work context.

Flexibility of flexibility thus needs to be implemented on different levels. In current praxis's the flexibility often lies within low impact system change like stock and flow of things, money, and resources, and structural change [8]. To achieve flexible flexibility however the system of work should also have opening for change of culture, systems, rules, and so forth [8]. This in for example processes of need-finding and context analysis that may lead to the acceptance of that a lot of things, behaviour, and processes are invisible to the interaction designers. Empathy processes for example will give different insights when opened up in order to discuss what to measure in order to what is quality of what function. It is for example reasonable to expect that interaction design has interactive functions and opens for the interacting in different ways for the user, other than simply cause and effect. Such interactivity however is seldom explored since the exploration of unknown unknowns represents an uncertainty beyond a common understanding of a flexible design process. That is, one miss out of the possibilities for the designer to explore real interactive systems in an interactive way- rather they are often limited by flexibility to merely testing of hypothesis. The user environments are controlling rather than open for processes of emergence or self-producing systems and flexible flexibility. Flexibility in education and in praxis thus is modelled on a progression structure rather than emergence structure.

An exploration of what types of learning and in extension design processes, experiences, an emergence structured design process can initiate or self-produce, would be an interesting continuation of this discussion.

References

1. Eriksen, T.: Mind the gap: flexibility, epistemology and the rhetoric of new work. Cybern. Hum. Knowing 12(1–2), 50–60 (2005)
2. Steier, F.: Exercising frame flexibility. Cybern. Hum. Knowing 12(f0020001), 36–49 (2005)
3. Bateson, G.: Steps to An Ecology of Mind. University of Chicago Press, Chicago (2000/1972)
4. Bunnell, P.: ASC: dancing with ambiguity. Cybern. Hum. Knowing 22(4), 101–112 (2015)
5. Sweeting, B.: Cybernetics of practice. Kybernetes 44(8/9), 1397–1405 (2015)
6. Juul, J.: Half-Real: Video Games Between Real Rules and Fictional Worlds. MIT Press, Cambridge (2011)
7. Gulden, T.: Engagement by lamination of autopoietic concentric interaction systems in games: a study of football and Pokémon GO. Hum. Technol. 14(1), 96–134 (2018)
8. Meadows, D.H., Wright, D.: Thinking in Systems: A Primer. Earthscan, London (2009)

Exploring the Social Innovation Ecosystem: Case Report and a Brief Literature Review

Wang Jing(⊠)

TONGJI University College of Design and Innovation, 281 Fuxin Road, Shanghai, China
Wangjing7733@tongji.edu.cn

Abstract. Traditional institutional logic restricted knowledge spread across organizational boundaries and affects the performance of innovation. This paper, using the beneficial aspects of institutional complexity, Proposes an ecosystem hypothesis to explore how design better promote innovation. At first part, through the cases study and synthesis of more than 100 projects, Proposes an "ecosystem" hypothesis as the theme connecting its common characteristics. The second part, through the literature research, examined its alternative structure of ecosystem, such as business model, platform, value network, knowledge alliance, etc., and proposed ecosystem analytical framework. The third part, Makes a comparative analysis of two cases, summarizes two different types of ecosystem, and deeply explores the mechanism of transformation.

The design values based on "ecology" focus on activating more actors to participate in collaborative actions to achieve more sustainable social system transformation.

Keywords: Innovation ecosystem · Design-driven innovation · "Duality" · Case study

1 Introduction

The concept of innovation came from Joseph Alois Schumpeter. In his view, innovation is an activity that brings excess profits due to the introduction of "new combinations" of production factors and conditions into the production system [1]. As a confrontational process of the new arrangement against the control belief, innovation is a product in the process of the opposite "Negation" element which is unintentionally produced by the "affirmation" element. The new arrangement is not something foreseen by the controller itself, but something contains its interests [2]. Whether to resist or to accept innovation, it may depend on whether other groups regard the innovation-related groups as negative or positive reference groups [3].

Innovation enables effective prevention of institutional rigidity. The purpose of the establishment of system is to create order and reduce uncertainty in communication. As the predictable process and rules in the process of management and control, institution is a rules system designed by the players of the game to obtain the game equilibrium to benefit their respective interests. With the advent of the era of knowledge economy, the scope

© Springer Nature Switzerland AG 2020
C. Stephanidis et al. (Eds.): HCII 2020, CCIS 1293, pp. 32–46, 2020.
https://doi.org/10.1007/978-3-030-60700-5_5

of innovation has expanded beyond the boundaries of the organization, where the traditional hierarchical organizational framework has limited the extensive cooperation. The problem of "institutional complexity" is reflected in the process of inter-domain social cooperation, which often faces different, even incompatible rules and requirements.

A large number of literatures focus on the response of institutional complexity, but with little being known about how the institutions coexist. In fact, different degrees of "conflict" and "complementarity" exist in the behavior which combines different logics, but not in the logic itself. When the conflicting logics of the opposites are cleverly bridged, there will be complementarity created between the logics [4], which is mainly reflected in the dynamic integration process, leading to the production of the positive and reciprocal inevitable results brought by the interdependence between the actors. The logic of coexistence exists by interdependence and contradiction, defining the division of specific structures, and segregating the work behaviors which belong to conflict logic, so that individual work behaviors can display the logic of coexistence in appropriate place and time [5].

Lou Yongqi believes that "any contradiction exists in a both positive and harmonious way, opposing and connecting with each other, checking and balancing one other". "Contradiction" awakens the cognitive reconstruction of actors and transforms it into innovative behavior. A lens that can be employed to look at contradictions in a correct manner is beneficial to innovation itself [6] (see Fig. 1). When the actors realize the fact that they can actively make use of the tension of the contradictions by embedding the tension [7, 8], the duality of stability and change [9], competition and cooperation [10, 11], structure and Agency [12–14], actively in the institutional matrix, they start to critically test the deep-rooted cognitive hypothesis, and set up a more generalized "cognitive ecological map" to guide and reflect on the practice behavior of their own.

"Ecosystem", based on system theory and holism, is a process of analysis and creative integration, which has great potential to respond to the challenges of institutional complexity and openness in the process of innovation. In this paper, observation is made from the perspective of ecosystem on the "duality" in the process of innovation to explore how to bridge the contradictory logics and to establish the ecological relationship of mutual benefit and symbiosis.

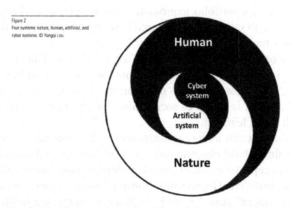

Fig. 1. The duality (Image source: Lou Yongqi, interaction of four systems)

2 Enabling Ecosystems for Social Innovation

The research of this paper is Inspired by the book *How to thrive in the Next Economy: Designing Tomorrow's World Today* by John Thackara. In this book he introduced the local innovation practices from all over the world, such as ecological restoration camps, food cooperatives, neighborhood garden, local currency, etc. The practice projects of these emerging economies present a new mode of action and value ethics, with attention paid to social justice, the importance of ecological construction to advocate a new ecological concept. This paper summarized the 8 typical projects and present the eco-innovation prototype (see Fig. 1), introducing the

As a new value ethics, "ecosystem" has experienced a lengthy process of development. In 1997, Robert Costanza emphasized the value of natural ecosystem, believing that nature provides resources to support human survival and economic development, and therefore proposed to consider the stock of natural capital in the political decision-making process. T Jackson analyzed the correlation between human development and economic growth in his *Prosperity without growth: transition to a sustainable economy* and believed that we should get rid of the obsession with economic growth and pay attention to other options of the biosphere. William Nordhaus is one of the top analysts who study the economics of climate change in the world, who proposed an economic model of climate change, DICE, to calculate the social cost of carbon (SCC) through carbon tax to take into account the social development quality of ecological benefits. At this stage, "ecosystem", as an environmental ethics, aims to make the public realize the boundary of natural ecosystem.

With the deepening of the comprehension of "ecosystem" in academic circles, the understanding of ecosystem has been extended from the global environmental problems to the basic operation mode of taking social actions to change human society. Robert W.kates believed that attention should be paid to the integration of globalization process and local ecology and the inclusion of the locality to the globality, to explain the complex behavior of self-organized system and the response of natural social system, and take ecological process as the balanced development process both globally and locally.

Ezio Manzini, viewed from the perspective of social technology system, believed that a product service system should be developed to optimize the system resources to provide integrated service portfolio, to promote the convergence of economic interests of new stakeholders, and to satisfy the social needs. He regards ecology as the construction of a green infrastructure.

Carlo Vezzoli believed that the change of ecological civilization is a continuous learning process. In view of the nature and dimensions of change involving complex politics, economy and culture, it is thus necessary to innovate at the system level. Vezzoli's ecological concept is a kind of social value concept that changes in the scale of "system" through social learning.

Ecosystem exists not only as the germination of civilization, but also as an innovation form. This paper, through the observation of more than 100 social innovation practices, observes that the concept of ecosystem extends multiple connotations in different practice contexts, and exists in different forms (the following figure provides a simple illustration). The term "design pattern" comes from Ezio Manzini mentioned in his book *Design, When Everybody Designs*, introductice a new way of doing things in cross organizational collaboration, which corresponds to the "conventional pattern". He believed that design experts should first identify the "design pattern" innovation practices, and then help them develop and grow (Fig. 2).

Prototyping Eco-innovation	Design Patterns	Construction
CASE No.1 Wild Machine Biological machines, as an art and science project, explore the connection between human technology and the biological environment.	**Meaning Construction** Plants as organizational model linking the human, technology and biodiversity, expressing the value of collaboration	Complex Networks
CASE No.2 Beehive Food Co-op Beehive co-op is a fair food platform, embedded social goal in its own development vision, focusing on fair pay for local producers.	**Problem Solving** Consider the interest of local farmers, land, river and biodiversity and make them form a collaborative community	Business Model
CASE No.3 Citizen Oasis Lending Committed to creating an ecological participation platform for citizens and provide the oasis seeds location.	**Meaning Construction** Oasis is a new lifestyle and the new perception of well-being	Value Network
CASE No.4 Citizen Lab The citizen lab, as the policy experiment scenario, provides an information platform for citizens to actively participate in urban political decisions.	**Problem Solving** Facilitate the more active interaction between citizens and policy makers. Exploring the citizen centered future government model	Platform
CASE No.5 Global Organic Farm Alliance An online community open to the global world, thinking globally, acting locally, and focusing on the deep value of local wisdom and traditional knowledge.	**Meaning Construction** The global network alliance delivering the new stories of reciprocity and connection in new life relationships	Value Network
CASE No.6 India Water Resources Participatory Management Groundwater is quantified and managed through the water unit collector, Recording the daily rainfall, water level, wellbore volume, and monitoring the daily stream flow.	**Problem Solving** Communities and stakeholders are able to monitor and manage groundwater as a public resource	Knowledge Alliance
CASE No.7 Flax Project Presenting the different scenes of flax producers, processors and users, each processing process can be traced back through the Supply chain technology.	**Meaning Construction** Showing a new to express the local products with reasonable price, and environment friendly production process	Value Network
CASE No.8 Permaculture Movement The design principle centers on the whole system, simulate and utilize the patterns and elastic features from the natural ecosystems	**Meaning Construction** Showing the philosophy of cooperation with the nature through the social movement of renewable agriculture and ecological restoration	Knowledge Alliance

Fig. 2. Prototyping the Eco-innovation (Image source: Drawing by the author researching the cases mentioned in the book of *How to thrive in the Next Economy: Designing Tomorrow's World Today by John Thackara*)

3 Literature Review

3.1 Origin of Concept

The concept of "ecosystem" originated from the business ecosystem proposed by Moore, who emphasized the importance of developing innovation capability across multiple industries for the development of enterprises and economic growth. In the report of *Maintaining the National Innovation Ecosystem* published in 2004 by the American President's Council of Advisors on Science and Technology (PCAST), the term "innovation ecosystem" was first proposed to affirm the role of ecosystem in the development of sustainable economy, and to regard the national innovation ecosystem as a dynamic system of interaction between institutions and personnel necessary for the advancement of technology and economic development. The research of national innovation system, represented by Freeman and Nielsen, focuses on the comparative study of the differences among countries in the innovation system to improve the institutional arrangement from the perspective of the macro system that affects innovation performance [15]. In a general word, the ecosystem can be divided into three categories. The first category is rooted in the national innovation system of evolutionary economics theory, and discusses how to create a macro environment to support innovation and Entrepreneurship from the national level; the second category is the business ecosystem, which takes the dynamic ability and survival capital of enterprises as the core issues, and takes the innovation ability of enterprises as the basic unit of national innovation; the third category concerns the democratic nature of knowledge, the diversity of values and lifestyles of the innovation ecosystem, to serve as a responsible innovation to promote social cohesion and local inclusive development.

3.2 Value Co-creation Ecology

Along with the transformation of national economic activities from industrial manufacturing to knowledge creation and service provision, the concept of Co-creation has been advocated more and more frequently in recent years. It reflects that the management mode in the industrial era has come to the end of the S-shaped curve. In the past, the concept of product centered value creation is transforming into a collective knowledge construction process of multi participants' collaborative creation. As an interactive economic community, ecosystem will open up an interactive "two-way lane" among the multi participants through "Networking", and tap the huge potential of collective creation [16].

From the perspective of natural system, "ecosystem" is defined as the value that collective participants pursue multiple interests, though different yet same, but all recognize the system as an important resource to continue [17]. Teece puts forward the importance of "dynamic capability" for maintaining competitive advantage in the innovation process, which is an intangible asset to deploy and protect excellent long-term business performance. Each innovation subject seeks external extension to expand various partnerships, such as industrial clusters [18], strategic alliances [19], cooperation networks [20], and these external links are designed to collect external resources and reduce transaction costs [21].

From the perspective of management structure, ecosystem as a co creation organic structure [22] is opposite to hierarchy system. Meadow applies the concepts of "organic" and "mechanical" organizational structures to working groups. An organic group tends to complete tasks in a comprehensive way, with mutual support among subjects, rather than splitting and distributing the tasks. Organically, it emphasizes the consistency structure of the multilateral partnership, and starting from the value proposition, it defines a series of interactive actors to make the proposition of value creation come into being to realize the key value based on the organic structure of mutual support.

From the point of view of natural technology science, nonlinear chaos behavior, "basin of attraction" provides a perspective to observe the dynamic interaction between ecosystem elements, with the amplification of the positive feedback of system changes, and taking the ecosystem as an exciting heterogeneous set of observations. Although some scholars claim that it can be applied to economic, ecological and social systems, its causal mechanism is too abstract, therefore further operation methods need to be found in order to encourage the application in a wider range.

From the perspective of transformation theory, ecosystem is regarded as a constantly developing knowledge system, where the actors in the system constantly check their own value system and reflect on the way of "cognition" and "existence" of the world through the process of "learning by doing", "learning by using" and "learning by interaction".

To sum up, "ecosystem" provides an attractive metaphor to describe the relationship between a series of value creation and the interrelated innovation subjects, though its concept still remains vague without any consensus on this has so far formed in the academic circle. Therefore, so far as it is concerned, it is only a flawed analogy. However, it is generally accepted in academic circles that this loose metaphor provides a new way to explore the process of interdependence, co-evolution and co-creation interaction between the innovation subjects [23, 24].

3.3 Ecosystem Construction

The word "construction" is often used to represent the architecture in urban areas, but more and more "construction" concepts are being employed in other fields, such as products [25], industry [26], and organizations. As a synthesis of forms, construction responds to functions, and when extend it to complex systems, construction can be defined as: the basic organization of a system is reflected in the relationship between its components as well as their relationship with the environment, along with the principles that guide the designing and evolution [27].

In this paper, study has been conducted on the different construction forms of innovation ecosystem. By examining the relationship between the alternative structures of ecosystem (i.e., business model, platform, value network, knowledge alliance, complex network), it aims to define the internal structure of ecosystem and to build the theoretical basis with an analysis framework for the ecosystems.

1. As a business model. Business model is "the business mode reflected in the core value proposition provided by the enterprise for customers". The business model itself describes the basic principles or other forms of value that organizational ecology creates, delivers and captures.
2. As a platform. Platform is regarded as the interface of interaction in the business field. It can promote the interaction between partners by shaping the interaction mode, so as to transfer the value from the enterprise to the network. Traditional non-platform-offering companies create value in the form of goods or services, and then sell them to the downstream of the supply chain. Unlike the linear business which creates and controls inventory through supply chain, the platform creates connections and creates value by facilitating communication between two or more interdependent groups. The joint management of many participants provides a more comprehensive business prospect for the platform, enabling participants to increase the value of the platform and to realize path control through knowledge and resource sharing.

3. As a value network. Being a set of relationships, ecosystem is a community of actors defined by network and platform relationships. Peter viewed it from the perspective of value realization and believed that the value chain is the transportation line of integrating material value. Value network is the strategic deployment of turning from individual competition to group competition. Through resource complementation, each enterprise can realize their effective reorganization of both internal and external resources through dynamic collaboration.

4. As a knowledge alliance. In the era of knowledge economy, knowledge processing, knowledge innovation and knowledge dissemination are the main activities. As the most basic economic factor, the human ability of creativeness is continuously allocated in a scientific manner with the innovation of production mode and the improvement of production efficiency. As knowledge flows as a kind of shared resource, leaders need to increase organizational learning opportunities, providing or acquiring valuable knowledge and information to or from each other through mutual learning, so as to form a strategic alliance between enterprises.

5. As a complex network. Complex networks compare "digital innovation ecosystem" to heterogeneous elements, which evolve together over time. Heterogeneous elements include technology, method, concept, business application, organization and complex configuration of institutional background [28]. In the process of co-evolution of complex networks and other networks, new elements will be introduced from the neighboring systems. Such continuous update is a significant feature of complex networks. In this process, two evolutionary mechanisms, i.e., variation and selective reservation, are also involved. Variation increases the diversity of complex networks, while selective reservation changes the centrality of dominant elements in the complex network.

4   Design-Driven: Dynamic Transformation of Duality

4.1   Design Values

Design values is a concept put forward by Terry Irwin of Carnegie Mellon University in the transformation design Seminar. He believes that "values" are beliefs, expectations and ideologies embodied in behind the socio-economic and political paradigms. Transformation designers need to re-compose the whole pattern of the society to influence the change of people's "attitude".

Alan Scheinson compared the technocratic paradigm with the planetary ecological paradigm in his *Paradigm Shift: from Technologist to Planetary Man* to study these two different values. The technocratic paradigm holds the belief of instrumental value to the non-human world, understanding nature as an object in a machine, and denies the endogenous value of the subject's life. Planetary ecology puts emphasis on symbiosis, decentralization, and community freedom.

We observe the process of social interaction, where more and more innovative projects across multiple organizations, stakeholders, producers and users are taking place, creating a new organizational form and collaborative design process. Mancini called it the "design pattern" way of doing things, which is the display of dynamic performance of human beings to actively carry out social cooperation to find solutions in the face of new difficulties. The idea of "everyone is a designer" advocated by him is a process of appreciating the "endogenous value" of others. He regards everyone as an active subject who can contribute his own knowledge, ability and resources to forms a close cooperative community around the common value and vision. Thus, it abandons the bureaucratic paradigm of technical experts and endows ordinary people with great significance in social participation.

4.2 From "Duality" to "Ecology"

Symbiotic and co-evolution relationship reorganization: activation of different participants. Due to the complexity of social problems, any isolated individual way is difficult to produce effectiveness. Only with the participation of different stakeholders, it is possible to promote the solution of the problem [29]. Design participation has the potential to promote cooperation and co creation among different partners and to promote the reproduction of social and spatial relations through the production of frameworks and stages [30]. Social innovation design regards bottom-up social action as an important resource to solve social problems, and pays attention to the creativity of ordinary people and communities. It employs the belief of trust and reciprocity as the logical framework of action, and builds a multi role cooperation framework through the community logic of emotion, loyalty, common values and personal care. Taking Gongyuanpo Food Cooperative as an example, Different from the profit oriented commercial food business, it emphasizes the joint ownership and operation of community members. Each cooperative member must work in the cooperative for 2 h and 45 min every four weeks, which means each member works 13 times a year according to this frequency. This provision creates a sense of belonging and personal relationship quality for members, emphasizing that the stakeholders form a closely connected and reliable relationship with non-instrumental mobilization and linkage.

Significance assigning and transmitting: Based on a common vision. Wilson believes that significance is accompanied by the further development of society and exposed social problems, which is the source power of social evolution [31]. "Vision" is to recognize the value of time, transcending the paradigm objective or subjective, and regard time as a kind of social coordination. Design observes human beings and the ideal world they interact with in a specific environment, and finds different views of stakeholders through normative forms of participation. Krippendorff believed that design is a human centered constructivist [32]. Through the process of human-centered communication such as storytelling and game playing, the vision is more visualized. For example, the Chart of Digital Life (CDL) project funded by the British Research Council studies how British citizens managed their digital identities during the three important transitions of human life through fictional scenarios and role settings. Conscious design of the future means creative thinking, shaping people's opportunities, goals, and beliefs through vision. By constructing the ideal future, and then reverse work it is determined the future and the current action strategy. By describing the ideal scenario in the future, it encourages more stakeholders to participate and invest, which is crucial for the decision-making or operation of the public sector.

Identity change: from labor, creation to citizen action. According to identity Cybernetics Theory (ICT), identity influences the way of role playing. The transformation of collective identity is an important foundation of social transformation. Transformation design considers that civil society plays a very important role in urban transformation and is regarded as the gear of sustainable development [33]. Nowadays, the developed network communication technology offers the material basis for citizen science. Many amateurs who are interested in science are recruited into problem-driven experimental research to contribute their own value. For example, the bee lab project applies citizen science and open design to apiculture, monitoring equipment for participant data, and data collection. These projects, known as citizen science, cover a wide scope of topics arranging from microbes to bees, to water quality and to galaxies. As a mining tool of social capital, citizen science by its essence is a mechanism for extending social ties and increasing positive contacts between members of different groups.

5   Dual Cases Comparative Study of "NICE2035" & "VP2040"

5.1   Cases Introduction

1. System Transformation: Low carbon City Project in Australia

There are few cases available of innovation and transformation of design system. The VP2040 project, jointly sponsored by the Victorian ecological innovation laboratory co-founded by the government of Australia, University of Melbourne and the University of New South Wales, adopted a vision driven design approach to develop the vision of Australia to achieve rapid de-carbonization in 2040. The design in the process of project employed mainly the physical way of "system visualization" to show the understanding of different stakeholders for the future. The core research team came from different disciplines such as the environmental policy, the design research, the strategic management, the consumer research and the energy policy. In order to deepen the understanding of the future, it employed the form of workshop to contact with project partners. During this period, 16 professional designers were commissioned to carry out visualization work, with finally 83 visualization schemes being generated. In this paper, 2 of them were selected as the exhibition. Figure 3, The "Road to Life" project on the left describes the road technology system of hybrid biology in the future. The surface of the road absorbs sunlight and converts energy to power the surrounding houses; Fig. 4, while the figure on the right describes the operation status of Melbourne CBD as an integrated network in 2040. In order to reduce the "urban heat island effect" of the central business district with a large number of green, and river pollution being treated; the bridge connecting the two rivers is specially arranged for walking and cycling.

2. Innovation and entrepreneurship community: N-ICE2035 future life prototype Street

"N-ICE2035" is a social innovation experiment initiated by Lou Yongqi, Dean of the School of Design and Creativity of Tongji University based on years of social innovation

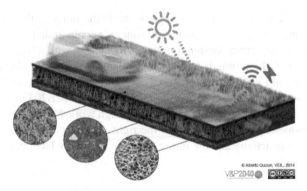

Fig. 3. "The road of life" hybrid biological technology road system

Fig. 4. Melbourne CBD operates as a green and integrated network of interconnected systems (Source of image: http://www.ecoacupuncture.com/)

design research. The project is located in Lane 1028 between Siping Road and Fuxin Road. Since 2012, the OYS project team of the social innovation college has entered Siping District, where the designers and artists have made 66 "micro update" designs around the garbage room, manhole cover, power transformation box, newspaper post and street corners. Among these cases, the most famous case includes the changing of a garbage room on Fuxin Road into "Tongji MIT Design Science Laboratory". In 2018, with the integration of universities and communities, the intermediary space between colleges and communities was created, forming a prototype laboratory community. The University Basic Research Laboratory provides outputs of knowledge and human resources, and the "Prototype Laboratory" provides the outputs of future life style prototype for product, service, system visualization and entity operation. So far as it is concerned, more than ten prototype laboratories have stationed in residence, which include Food Lab, Sound Lab, Tongji Aston Martin Lab, Design Harvest Lab, Neuni New Material Lab, and Fab-O Maker Education Lab, etc. It is a complex ecological space integrating product research and development, innovation education, entity prototype experiment, crowdfunding center and incubator functions.

Professor Lou Yongqi, the sponsor, regards the community as the source of innovation, with attention paid to the wisdom of ordinary people in daily life, and changes the design value concept from "design for whom" to "design with whom". For example, to connect Finnish fashion brands with local residents, to organize MarimeKKo joint design workshop with cloth as raw material, to jointly imagine the understanding of future lifestyle and fashion. (Figure 5 is the project site of NICE2035 Prototype Street in 1028; Fig. 6, the one in the middle is the joint design workshop held by MarimeKKo and the local residents; Fig. 7, the one on the right is the workshop of Aston Martin Laboratory open day activity and the future life style shared by laboratory students and community residents.)

Fig. 5. The project of NICE2035 future life prototype street site on lane 1028, fuxin road

Fig. 6. Finland fashion brand MarimeKKo held a co-design workshop with local residents

5.2 Case Analysis and Discussion

Projects VP2040 and NICE2035 have something in common. That is, both are vision-driven social transformation actions over a long period of time. It advocates the agenda of transformation towards the goal practice by doing experiments while learning. In the political background of foreign countries, low-carbon city transformation involves election cycle, business strategy prospect, population life cycle and other issues. Policy

Fig. 7. The open day workshop of Tongji - Aston Martin laboratory (Images sourced from NICE2035 project document)

making plays an important role in the transformation. In these two project cases, the design oriented vision of the future places the design in a special position. In addition to the narrow specialized design, the designer guides the stakeholders to create and participate based on the common vision. From the long-term social development thinking, it poses an impact on the norms, values, social identity and political and economic models of the whole society.

In these two project cases, the objects of design are different. In view of the historical effect of the city in striving for social democracy and environmental rights, VP2040 regards urban system as the key field of social transformation. 96 experts participated in the vision seminar held in Sydney. After many dialogues, they discussed the planning of urban climate change, advocated embedded experiments in real life and urban ecological acupuncture. From the output of 100 visual schemes, the way of implementation can be defined as the macro planning of national innovation system. Design participates in the two different types of outputs. The first type is the direct participation of designers, which visualized the output of the envisaged system; the second is that the field participants summarized the important role which design played in promoting vision discussion and new knowledge synthesis by reflecting on the project process records. That is to say, by bringing sticky additional information to connect different types of knowledge, it presents appropriate relationships for the whole system components.

NICE2035 put its emphasis on the social action from the bottom up, and created an "enabling ecosystem" in the community environment surrounded by university resources to arouse the enthusiasm of ordinary people and created the innovation and entrepreneurship ecology of the main living community. By such the stakeholders were connected through a series of thematic events, which included, for example, visit, lecture, project investigation, closed door publicity meeting, co-creation workshop, forum, etc. It not only attracted start-ups and small business projects to settle in, but also connected the local opinions and ideas of the community into a common dialogue platform, so that everyone could express their feelings, needs and views on the "future life". The project taking the mechanism similar to that of acupuncture and moxibustion had formed a distributed innovation network, which further attracted the participation of external partners, and developed a series of platform interfaces around the mutual correlation of D&I Tongji Design and Creative College, such as Tongji Shenzhen Needs Lab, Design

Harvest, Neili Department Store, Shanghai International Design Innovation Research Institute, etc., to form a knowledge flow ecology. Design presents a more comprehensive value output in the project of Nice2035. It respects, not only at the level of design values, but also at the same time, everyone's endogenous value with active seeking of new technologies, products, services, even value norms and economic models to meet social functions through the prototype laboratory (Fig. 8).

	NICE2035 Future Life Prototype Street	VP2040 Low-Carbon City Project
Participants	Scientific research institutions, enterprises, governments and citizens	Scientific research institutions, government
Ecosystem type	"Bottom up" innovation ecosystem	"Top down"innovation ecosystem of urban transformation
Design method	Future life prototype lab,urban micro update action of design modification	Description of the long-term vision that influences the change of social culture and social technology structure
Project Vision	Community with innovation, entrepreneurship and creativity	Low carbon city
Design values	Endogenous value of community freedom and existence	—
Key event	11 prototype labs stationed in the residence area of the local community	96 experts participated in the vision workshop held in Sydney
Role of design	Community activation, and output of future life style prototype	Output of future urban prototype, information processing and knowledge synthesis

Fig. 8. Comparison between the two ecosystems (Source: Self-developed by the author)

6 Conclusion

In this paper review is mainly conducted on the practice of social innovation from the perspective of "ecology", and finds that it has completely different implications in different contexts. When it is seen as a feature of new economy, it appears as a kind of value idea. When it is constructed as a tangible thing, it can be expressed as business model, platform, value network, knowledge alliance, etc. In Ezo Mancini's design concept, this "ecology" is a kind of design value, emphasizing the dialogue process of open design. Meanwhile, the role of design has shifted from focusing on the output of tangible things to human-oriented value co-creation process, and it also serves as a new way to integrate different types of knowledge.

The combination of future research and design is an important trend in the development of design science. According to German futurist Rolf Kreibich, future research on possible, ideal and hopeful future science provides knowledge about prediction, deconstruction, analysis and imagination of the future [34]. Futurist scholars combine the strategic foresight, the scientific orientation of system analysis with the knowledge creation orientation in design organically, which shows that current scientific research is not only to explore existing content, but also to inspire the social movement training to find new solutions. The 2012 Arizona Symposium "Artists and Scientists Redesign the Future" combines future research, design and innovative approaches. In the process of human centered communication in the design discipline, creative methods are employed to allow thinking visually outside the framework. A group of people gather together to explore and question the future, taking action to experiment, so as to promote the development of learning and knowledge. Design has an important potential to be explored in the process of future transformation.

The role of designers is on its continuous development along with the change of the social environment. Especially when people are no longer satisfied with the demand of material richness, the demand for spiritual level shall become the object of design need to think about. The design understood by the public is usually related to its physical output. However, the role of design in the process of capturing future needs and generating knowledge is not seeable. The field and boundary of design are expanding all the time. The former design methods collide with the new research fields and produce chemical reactions. Accordingly, some new design knowledge and new design methods become inevitable. This process must be exploratory and open. As Mancini pointed out, design experts should be keen to identify promising trends and help them develop.

References

1. Schumpeter, J.A.: History of Economic Analysis. Routledge, Abingdon (2006)
2. Hargrave, T.J., Van de Ven, A.H.: Integrating dialectical and paradox perspectives on managing contradictions in organizations. Organ. Stud. **38**(3–4), 319–339 (2016)
3. King, N., Anderson, N.: Innovation and Change in Organizations. Routledge, Abingdon (1995)
4. Pache, A.-C., Santos, F.: Inside the hybrid organization: selective coupling as a response to competing institutional logics. Acad. Manag. J. **56**(4), 972–1001 (2013)
5. Greenwood, R., Raynard, M., Kodeih, F., et al.: Institutional complexity and organizational responses. Acad. Manag. Ann. **5**(1), 317–371 (2011)
6. Lou, Y.: The idea of environmental design revisited. Des. Issues **35**(1), 23–35 (2019)
7. Bledow, R., Frese, M., Anderson, N., et al.: A dialectic perspective on innovation: conflicting demands, multiple pathways, and ambidexterity. Ind. Organ. Psychol. **2**(3), 305–337 (2009)
8. March, J.G.: Exploration and exploitation in organizational learning. Organ. Sci. **2**(1), 71–87 (1991)
9. Farjoun, M.: Beyond dualism: Stability and change as a duality. Acad. Manag. Rev. **35**(2), 202–225 (2010)
10. Lado, A.A., Boyd, N.G., Hanlon, S.C.: Competition, cooperation, and the search for economic rents: a syncretic model. Acad. Manag. Rev. **22**(1), 110–141 (1997)
11. Ring, P.S., Van de Ven, A.H.: Structuring cooperative relationships between organizations. Strateg. Manag. J. **13**(7), 483–498 (1992)
12. Battilana, J., D'aunno, T.: Institutional work and the paradox of embedded agency. Inst. Work: Actors Agency Inst. Stud. Organ. **31**, 58 (2009)

13. Garud, R., Hardy, C., Maguire, S.: Institutional Entrepreneurship as Embedded Agency: An Introduction to the Special Issue. Sage Publications, London (2007)
14. Walker, K., Schlosser, F., Deephouse, D.L.: Organizational ingenuity and the paradox of embedded agency: the case of the embryonic Ontario solar energy industry. Organ. Stud. 35(4), 613–634 (2014)
15. Edquist, C.: Systems of Innovation: Technologies. Institutions and Organizations. Routledge, Abingdon (2013)
16. Sanders, E.B.-N., Stappers, P.J.: Co-creation and the new landscapes of design. Co-design 4(1), 5–18 (2008)
17. Scott, W.R.: Organizations and Organizing: Rational. Natural and Open Systems Perspectives. Routledge, Abingdon (2015)
18. Marshall, A.: Industry and Trade. Macmillan, London (1920)
19. Devlin, G., Bleackley, M.: Strategic alliances—Guidelines for success. Long Range Plan. 21(5), 18–23 (1988)
20. Grandori, A., Soda, G.: Inter-firm networks: antecedents, mechanisms and forms. Organ. Stud. 16(2), 183–214 (1995)
21. Reinhardt, R., Gurtner, S., Griffin, A.: Towards an adaptive framework of low-end innovation capability – a systematic review and multiple case study analysis. Long Range Plan. 51(5), 770–796 (2018)
22. Ketonen-Oksi, S., Valkokari, K.: Innovation ecosystems as structures for value co-creation. Technol. Innov. Manag. Rev. 9(2) (2019)
23. Adner, R., Kapoor, R.: Value creation in innovation ecosystems: how the structure of technological interdependence affects firm performance in new technology generations. Strateg. Manag. J. 31(3), 306–333 (2010)
24. Frels, J.K., Shervani, T., Srivastava, R.K.: The integrated networks model: explaining resource allocations in network markets. J. Mark. 67(1), 29–45 (2003)
25. Sanchez, R., Mahoney, J.T.: Modularity, flexibility, and knowledge management in product and organization design. Strateg. Manag. J. 17(S2), 63–76 (1996)
26. Jacobides, M.G., Winter, S.G.: The co-evolution of capabilities and transaction costs: explaining the institutional structure of production. Strateg. Manag. J. 26(5), 395–413 (2005)
27. Maier, M.W., Emery, D., Hilliard, R.: Software architecture: introducing IEEE standard 1471. Computer 4, 107–109 (2001)
28. Chae, B.K.: A General framework for studying the evolution of the digital innovation ecosystem: the case of big data. Int. J. Inf. Manag. 45, 83–94 (2019)
29. Ollenburg, S.A.: A futures-design-process model for participatory futures. J. Futures Stud. 23, 51–62 (2019)
30. Akama, Y.: Politics makes strange bedfellows : addressing the 'messy' power dynamics in design practice. Politics Makes Strange Bedfellows 2009, pp. 16–19 (2008)
31. Hayduk, L.: The meaning of human existence. Can. Stud. Popul. 43, 148 (2016)
32. Krippendorff, K.: The Semantic Turn: A New Foundation for Design. CRC Press, Boca Raton (2005)
33. Frantzeskaki, N., Kabisch, N.: Environmental Science & Policy Designing a knowledge co-production operating space for urban environmental governance — Lessons from Rotterdam, Netherlands and Berlin, Germany. Environ. Sci. Policy 62, 90–98 (2016)
34. Kreibich, R., Oertel, B., Wolk, M.: Futures Studies and Future-oriented Technology Analysis Principles, Methodology and Research Questions (2012)

iVIS: Interpretable Interactive Visualization for User Behavior Clusters

Yieun Kim⬥, Yohan Bae⬥, Junghyun Kim⬥, and Yeonghun Nam(✉)⬥

Samsung Research, Samsung Electronics, Seoul, Republic of Korea
{yieun12.kim,yhan.bae,jh24.kim,yeonghun.nam}@samsung.com

Abstract. To improve Quality of Experience (QoE) and develop new features, understanding users and making a decision to target specific user groups are important to service providers. Based on the internal interviews, we find that service operators have trouble in identifying user behavior characteristics for numerous services in a short time. To address this challenge, we present iVIS, an interactive visualization system that clusters the user behaviors and visualizes the representative behavior patterns. With iVIS, service providers can interpret the user clusters (e.g., heavy/light users), and drill down to a particular cluster to get details interactively. To evaluate our system, we conduct a case study on the log data from the internal data catalog service which enables researchers to browse and use datasets. We found service operators could rapidly interpret representative user behaviors, and discover new behavior types such as *frustrated users* (i.e., users who only explored datasets for a while but not use them) or *testers* (i.e., users who used the service for testing) by refining the clustering results.

Keywords: Behavior analysis · User clustering · Interactive visualization

1 Introduction

The success of an online service is increasingly dependent on how quickly service providers (e.g., data analysts, retailers, marketers, and service managers) identify target customer characteristics and how accurately they determine their needs. Service providers can establish a market strategy, provide customized services, and develop new features aligning with consumer needs and priorities based on the behavioral analysis. However, as service functions are complicated and user characteristics are diversified, it is becoming difficult to understand user behaviors to make a decision on developing the service.

Typically, user behavioral analysis is based on collected user activity records. Request/response records, button clicks, page access paths, finger swipes and input records can all be included [1]. It takes a very long time for service providers to make data-driven decisions based on various user records. Therefore, a visual interface must be provided to help them to present the key features explaining user behaviors.

© Springer Nature Switzerland AG 2020
C. Stephanidis et al. (Eds.): HCII 2020, CCIS 1293, pp. 47–52, 2020.
https://doi.org/10.1007/978-3-030-60700-5_6

In addition, several visualization interfaces for user behavior clusters in online service cluster users with similar behavior patterns and provide indicators to identify the cluster characteristics. However, the existing cluster visualization interface has the following limitations. *First*, they mainly focus on identifying and drilling down the characteristics of each cluster. However, through preliminary interviews, we have found a need for service providers to compare the differences between clusters. *Second*, it is not allowed to transform the cluster results by additionally dividing or integrating clusters based on their domain knowledge.

To meet these challenges, in this paper, we present iVIS, an interactive visualization system that clusters users and visualizes their behavior patterns. iVIS provides information about cluster similarity and differences, and user distribution per cluster as a compressed view. Moreover, the usability for each service function is presented for each cluster, so that the cluster can be interpreted intuitively (e.g., heavy/light users). Furthermore, iVIS supports interaction to combine or divide user clusters inferred by the clustering model. In other words, iVIS helps service providers to answer key questions regarding their services, e.g., what is the difference between major and minor behavioral groups? What are the main user groups interested in? At what time or which regions are the groups distributed? What is the difference between the group that mainly uses the newly launched service function and the group that does not use it?

In summary, the main contributions of our work are as follows:

- We present iVIS, an interactive visualization system that clusters the user behaviors and visualizes the representative behavior patterns.
- We support not only the exploration of each group in detail, but also the comparison of several groups.
- We allow analysts to refine the clustering results by interactively merging the clusters or partitioning a cluster by user-defined rules.

2   Related Works

Several visualization interfaces based on user behavior clusters have been proposed in recent articles. In [1], a cluster visualization tool is proposed to explore hierarchically clustered online service users. The cluster hierarchy is presented as packed circles where more general patterns are presented as higher-level, and further identifying patterns as lower-level. In [2], a user clustering algorithm is proposed based on text analysis and topic modeling for online services, and an interactive visual analytics interface is designed to identify each group. It enables users recursively explore hierarchical behavior patterns in service function sequences. In [3], an interactive cluster exploration tool is designed to enable user-guided clustering. Users can cluster major clickstream patterns using their domain knowledge, and a semi-supervised automatic clustering algorithm is applied to assign complex patterns to the existing clusters.

3   iVIS Interface

3.1   Design Rationale

We interviewed service providers about how they analyze user behavior and what pain points they are facing while conducting the analysis. The result is summarized in the following three tasks they need help with:

Identify interesting cluster straightforwardly [DR-1]: The service providers confirm that it is important to view a cluster overview at the beginning of the analysis. Moreover, in order to reduce analysis time, they want to simply and clearly figure out interesting user groups (e.g., a group that has unexpected usage patterns or leaves the service) that will be considered as the starting point for analysis.

Drill down into individual groups and compare them interactively [DR-2]: For behavior analysis, they typically select multiple groups as the starting point, and understand the groups by interactively investigating as well as comparing characteristics. Therefore, they need a tool that supports interaction for both drilldown and comparison in a compressed view.

Customize the results based on domain knowledge [DR-3]: After analyzing the characteristics of all clusters, they want to use their domain-knowledge to customize the results. One said: "Other automated analytic tools have limitations to conduct domain-specific analysis. I want to apply my domain knowledge to the result, which is useful for understanding user segments and making decisions".

After the user interviews, we devise an interactive visualization for user behavior clusters that satisfying the requirements.

3.2   iVIS Interface

Cluster Overview (Fig. 1a). The widget represents each cluster as a circle. The radius of each circle is proportional to the number of users in the group, and the distance between circles represents the similarity between clusters. When a cluster is selected, other widgets reflect the selection and display the cluster detail. Moreover, service providers can customize the original result (Fig. 2a) using their domain knowledge by merging similar clusters (Fig. 2b) or splitting one cluster into multiple clusters with appropriate criteria (Fig. 2c).

Usage Segmentation (Fig. 1b). To provide explainable cluster characteristics, we categorize the user behavior into four usage patterns: *inactive, active only for a certain period, steady but less active,* and *steady and active.* We then visualize the proportion of each pattern in the widget.

Event Composition (Fig. 1c). The widget indicates distribution of event occurrences for each cluster. A cluster characteristic can be identified by comparing the event composition rate with the other clusters. We provide three switchable metrics to present event compositions: ratio, count, and average (which is the number of occurrences per user), so that service providers can perform various interpretations according to the selected metric.

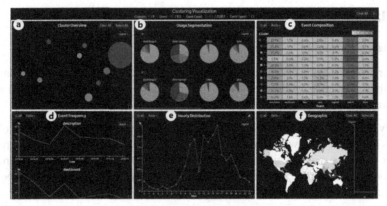

Fig. 1. Interface of iVIS. a) The number of users in each cluster and the similarities between clusters are indicated by the circle size and distances between them, respectively. b) Usage characteristics are represented by pie charts where each chart displays the usage pattern proportions for each event type. The other coordinated views show c) the event compositions, d) event frequencies over time, e) hourly event distributions, and f) geographic event distributions

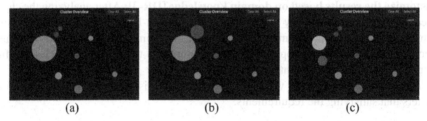

Fig. 2. Cluster overview. a) Before customizing, b) after integrating two clusters (in the upper left), and c) after dividing the cluster (in the center of the left)

Event Frequency (Fig. 1d). The widget displays the number of event occurrences over a given time range. By selecting clusters and sub-time range, they can understand the relationship among events, clusters, and the specific period. The frequency metric can be changed from the number of events to the occurrence ratio.

Hourly Distribution (Fig. 1e). The widget shows the aggregated hourly event counts. It provides information about when users in each cluster actively use the service. The unit of time can be customized by the other units such as day, day of week, and month.

Geographic (Fig. 1f). Geographic information of each cluster is visualized in the widget. The number of users in each country is represented by the color opacity. When a cluster is selected, the regions where the cluster is mainly distributed are colored.

Cross-Filtering. All widgets in the iVIS interface can be cross-filtered, thus service providers can select any interesting cluster, event type, period, hour and region as filter conditions.

4   Case Study

4.1   Study Design

To evaluate the iVIS interface, we conducted a case study with two service administrators and a developer (referred to as P1-P3 later) using the service logs collected from the internal data catalog service which allows researchers to browse and use datasets. We asked domain experts to try our interface to freely explore the given clustering results for 30 min.

4.2   Study Results

We observed how domain experts analyze user behaviors of service using iVIS and conducted interviews to understand their analysis process. At first, P1 focused on the cluster overview to understand the user groups. Subsequently, he selected interesting clusters and events in the event composition view. On the contrary, other domain experts first looked at the usage segmentation view, selected two or three clusters of interest from the cluster overview, and explored other coordinated views. P2 stated "The usage segmentation view helped me explore the distribution of usage patterns for each user group. As a result, I was able to find the user groups of interest."

They also discovered new behavior types and rapidly interpreted representative user behaviors. Two participants found previously unknown behavior types such as *frustrated users* (i.e., users who only explored datasets for a while but not use them for a certain reason) or *testers* (i.e., users who used the service for testing). According to interviews, they discovered those types by utilizing the interaction such as switching the metrics in the event composition and event frequency widgets. In addition, they showed a great passion for discovering new behavior types using our interface.

In the early user interview stage, analysts wanted to customize the clustering results by interactively merging the clusters or partitioning a cluster by user-defined rules. In the case study, they actively used those interactions and refined the results. However, P2 mentioned "I think the partitioning function is useful, but it was difficult to determine user-defined rules. The appropriate guidance may be required when we first make them."

5   Conclusion

In this work, we present iVIS, an interactive visualization system that clusters the user behaviors and visualizes the various behavior patterns. With our interface, service providers can interpret the user clusters and drill down to a particular cluster to get details interactively. The case study conducted with two service providers and a developer showed that iVIS helps them explore each user group and identify unusual behaviors. Moreover, we gained data analysts' feedback to improve our visual representations and interactions. Though data analysts are able to customize the clustering results with iVIS, they can still be dissatisfied with the results. In the future, we plan to support the use of diverse clustering algorithms. Furthermore, we will design novel visualizations that are suitable for comparing the results based on various clustering models.

References

1. Wang, G., Zhang, X., Tang, S., Zheng, H., Zhao, B.Y.: Unsupervised clickstream clustering for user behavior analysis. In: CHI '16: Proceedings of the 2016 CHI Conference on Human Factors in Computing Systems, USA, pp. 225–236. ACM (2016)
2. Nguyen, P.H., et al.: VASABI: hierarchical user profiles for interactive visual user behaviour analytics. IEEE Trans. Vis. Comput. Graph. $26(1)$, 77–86 (2020)
3. Wei, J., Shen, Z., Sundaresan, N., Ma, K.-L.: Visual cluster exploration of web clickstream data. In: 2012 IEEE Conference on Visual Analytics Science and Technology (VAST), USA, pp. 3–12, IEEE (2012)

Deciphering the Code: Evidence for a Sociometric DNA in Design Thinking Meetings

Steffi Kohl[(✉)], Mark P. Graus, and Jos G.A.M. Lemmink

School of Business and Economics, Maastricht University,
Maastricht, The Netherlands
stefanie.kohl@maastrichtuniversity.nl

Abstract. Despite the increased popularity of virtual teams, in-person teamwork remains the dominant way of working. This paper investigates to what extent social signals can be used to infer the work domain of team meetings. It reveals insights into the complex nature of team dynamics, that are not often quantified in literature, during the design thinking process. This was done by using sociometric badges to measure the social interactions of four teams over a three week development cycle. From these interactions we were able to discriminate different modes in the design thinking process used by the teams, indicating that different design thinking modes have different dynamics. Through supervised learning we could predict the modes of Need Finding, Ideation, and Prototyping with F1 scores of 0.76, 0.71, and 0.60 respectively. These performance scores significantly outperformed random baseline models, corresponding to a doubling of F1 score of predicting the positive class, indicating that the models did indeed succeed in predicting design thinking mode. This indicates that wearable social sensors provide useful information in understanding and identifying design thinking modes. These initial findings will serve as a first step towards the development of automated coaches for design thinking teams.

Keywords: HCI · Social signals · Human behaviour analysis · Predictive modeling · Field study

1 Introduction

DNA is a sequence in every cell that defines the characteristics of the organism made up of these cells. In a similar way, social signals such as voice, body motion, and relative location define the characteristics of a social interaction; Every interaction is composed of these basic elements. Like the sequence of nucleotides in DNA, we posit that sequences of social signals determine the properties of the interaction. These signals can be read using sensor technology, but the scientific community is only beginning to explore their structure. Interactions may show

© Springer Nature Switzerland AG 2020
C. Stephanidis et al. (Eds.): HCII 2020, CCIS 1293, pp. 53–61, 2020.
https://doi.org/10.1007/978-3-030-60700-5_7

different patterns of signals for different tasks, and thus have a different Sociometric DNA. As such, researchers could start relying on these patterns when studying work in team interactions.

Prior research suggests that distinct phases exist in group problem solving. Phases are identified with distinct primary needs and while relational and structural elements (such as the number of interruptions or frequency of taking turns talking) are beneficial for one phase, they are detrimental to another [20]. In a similar fashion Stempfle and Badke-Schaub [23] identify four cognitive operations which design thinking teams utilize at different stages and for different tasks. Throughout this paper, the term 'mode' will be used to differentiate interactions for different tasks within teams. These different modes require different relational and structural elements.

Although extensive research has been carried out on sociometric signals in teams, the difference between modes is not often taken into consideration. A study that did use social signals and take into account different modes has failed to draw any conclusions on how patterns of social signals differ over modes [12]. The majority of studies relying on social signals have not included differentiation of modes [16] or assume that all modes will benefit from the same signals. One example of this is the study by Woolley et al. [24] on understanding collective intelligence in teams. The study makes no attempt to differentiate between different modes in teams when determining collective intelligence, even though participants are asked to solve a wide range of tasks. The study does not attempt to identify how the relationship between different signals and collective intelligence changes for different types of tasks. This shortcoming might explain why turn taking is the only social signal found to correlate with collective intelligence. The same lack of differentiation between modes can be observed in approaches to understand collaborative problem solving within the cognitive science literature [6, 7]. While the study by Eloy et al. [7] differentiates between goal type it makes no distinction between tasks.

Given the literature on relation and structural elements within modes, can we reasonably overlook the differences in nonverbal dynamics between all modes? Is it helpful to identify social signals that predict performance for all modes if we have reason to assume that interaction dynamics are not the same for all modes?

For this paper, we rely on robust cues that have been studied in nonverbal communication. Human proxemic and paralinguistic behavior have been studied extensively since the 1920s, in a diverse set of domains such as sociology, psychology [9] and, most recently, human-robot interaction [15]. Proxemic behavior relates to how people use space when communicating, while paralinguistic behavior relates to all aspects of spoken communication (such as when someone is speaking, their tone of voice, etc.), except for the semantic content. Research on organizational science has identified areas in which measuring proxemics and paralinguistics provides important insights. Among others, research shows that face-to-face social interactions play a significant role in the workplace, ranging from job perception [11] to organizational commitment [10]. Furthermore, postural markers have been used in human activity recognition to differentiate team members group-functions [5].

This paper demonstrates that social signals can be used to identify modes in design thinking teams. The specific research questions addressed in this paper are: 1) Can the design thinking mode of an individual in a team be predicted by features extracted from social signals? 2) How do the features extracted from social signals help in predicting individual mode?

2   Meeting Dataset

To investigate the research questions, we collected social signals from a group of young professionals engaging in a new product development (NPD) sprint exercise at a large consultancy. The dataset was collected during the entire four week sprint from start to prototype development. In total 4 groups with either 5 or 4 members were observed on 13 days in an open space office floor. All teams worked without supervision, so each team structured their work days and scheduled team meetings or requested support from consultants as necessary. Participants wore sociometric badges during working hours whenever engaged in potentially work-related activities but not during lunch breaks. A sociometric badge is a wearable electronic device capable of automatically measuring social signals, derived from vocal features, body motion, and relative location.

In order to distinguish different modes, a variety of definitions of formal methods that underlie a design thinking approach have been suggested. However, three modes are commonly identified within a design thinking approach: Need Finding, Ideation and Prototyping. Need Finding are the activities related to problem definition. Ideation is the process of generating ideas and solutions. Prototyping encompasses building models to facilitate the development and selection of concepts [14,21]. In addition to the data resulting from the sociometric badges, each day, after finishing all work-related activities, participants completed a questionnaire that assessed how much time in percentages participants spent in these three different design modes. In total, for the 16 days, each team member completed this survey, resulting in a total of 222 responses.

2.1   Outcome Variable

The outcome variables, ground truth, or labels to be predicted are defined by the reported percentages for the three design thinking modes by participants. Each observation corresponds to a participant's answer on a given day. For each observation three variables were created, each describing if the participant indicated that the day was spent more than 50% on the corresponding design thinking mode. This cut off point was chosen to ensure single labelling. For example, the variable corresponding to Need Finding is positive when participants reported working on Need Finding at least 50% on a given day. Whereas the negative class is those participants who reported less than 50% Need Finding. The threshold of 50% was used for all modes.

2.2 Feature Extraction

Many different features are used to assess nonverbal signals, such as turn taking, activity levels, or proximity within the network [19]. Previous studies have shown that even with a small sample size, patterns measured by sociometric badges were significant and revealing. These patterns can successfully be used to predict a variety of outcomes such as creativity and team performance [17].

The features included in this paper have been selected to capture the rotation of nonverbal behavior in teams, specifically rotating leadership (RL), rotating contributions (RC), turn taking (TTK) and successful and unsuccessful interruptions(SI & UI). The descriptions of these are covered in the following sections. All features are derived from the speech and proximity measurements provided by the Sociometric Solutions software [22].

Rotating Leadership. Rotating Leadership [4,8,13] measures how frequently people change their centrality in the team when represented as a graph. Betweenness centrality is a measure of how central a node in a graph is, and it is calculated by dividing the times the node is located on a shortest path by the total number of paths. In our case, the nodes in the graph are participants and edges are formed when people are within close proximity as measured by both infrared and Bluetooth sensors. Rotating Leadership counts the number of local maxima and minima in the betweenness curve over time of an person. These peaks and valleys indicate how often people change from a central position to a peripheral one.

The proxemics domain has explored the theme of Rotating Leadership (or RL). RL, revealed by changing network structures where people oscillate between peripheral and more central network positions, has a relevant impact on knowledge-sharing dynamic, affects individual and group creativity [8,13], and is a predictor of innovative performance. The power of RL in predicting innovation performance has not only been observed between individuals but between organizations as well [4].

Rotating Contribution. Rotating Contribution (or RC) measures the oscillation of the Contribution Index (CI) and thus represents how frequently people change the amount of time they spend listening vs speaking [17]. We calculate the CI of each person (speaking - listening/speaking + listening) over time and count the number of local maxima and minima in the CI curve of a person.

Just like RL, RC has been shown to be a consistent indicator of creativity. For both signals, more rotation is positively related with performance during creative tasks, while less rotation is preferable for non-creative tasks [8].

Turn Taking. Turns [3,24] are speaking segments that occur after and within 10 s of another speaking segment. By default a speaking segment must be made within 10 s after the previous one has ended in order to be considered a turn. Note that the two speaking segments need not be from two different people to count as a turn, a person can pause and then start speaking again. This would count as two speaking segments, and one "self-turn".

Turn taking in groups has been associated with collective intelligence [24]. Chuy et al. [3] argue that taking turns while engaging all team members is crucial for team success. Longer mean speaking segment length, and hence lower number of turns taken, has been shown to be correlated with diminished perceptions of individual and group creativity, imagination, as well as lower levels of involvement and enjoyment [17].

Interruptions. An interruption is considered [un]successful [17] if the following scenario takes place. Person A is talking, Person B starts talking over A. If Person A talks for [more]less than 5 out of the next 10 s, then Person B [un]successfully interrupted Person A.

Similar to turn taking, interruptions have been related to creativity and work enjoyment. Successful interruptions show that different members take over and guide the discussion [17]. By the same token, teams show lower creativity if a few people dominate the discussion [24].

3 Predictive Modeling

3.1 Data Preparation

The final dataset contained a class imbalance for each of the 3 design thinking modes. Need Finding, Ideation, and Prototyping have positive labels for 49 (22%), 57 (26%), and 74 (33%) samples to classify respectively. There are a total of 222 examples to classify. In order to avoid bias, and to compensate for class imbalance and the number of examples, the training sample is over-sampled using SMOTE [2]. SMOTE creates new synthetic training examples by creating new examples in between two existing examples in the minority class. This results in a training data set that is more balanced and larger by creating synthetic observations based on the existing observations.

After features were extracted from the raw signals collected by the sociometric badges, they were further transformed by oversampling and feature scaling. The features have different ranges of values. All features were normalized between 0 and 1 using min-max scaling where the smallest value for the feature becomes 0 and the largest 1, and all other values are mapped linearly in between. This prevents features with much larger numeric values from dominating the predictions of the model.

3.2 Models and Model Evaluation

Eight different models were trained on the 222 examples, with the aim of comparing linear and nonlinear models as well as instance based and model based models. The scikit learn package [18] was used to train and test all models. Results are only reported for the three best models.

All models are evaluated using leave-one-out cross-validation which is known to be an almost unbiased estimator of model generalization performance on unseen examples [1]. The results of the three best classifiers can be seen in Table 1. Nonlinear models had higher performance suggesting that there is a more complex relationship between the features and the design thinking mode.

As this is the first approach to tackling design thinking prediction, there are no established baselines. Therefore, a stratified random baseline was created where the probability of a label occurring is proportional to the occurrence in the data set. Unpaired sample t-tests were performed between the baseline and trained model. All t-tests were significant ($p < 0.0001$) indicating that the trained models statistically significantly outperform the random baseline models according to the F1 score. This indicates that the proposed approach has predictive power for design thinking modes.

Table 1. Performance of the features on predicting design thinking mode

Model	Mode	$F1$	$F1_{pos}$	$F1_{neg}$	Precision	Recall
SVM Linear	NF	0.75	0.41	0.84	0.75	0.75
Random Forest	NF	0.73	0.39	0.82	0.73	0.72
SVM RBF	NF	**0.76**	**0.42**	**0.86**	0.76	0.77
Random Baseline	NF	0.65	0.23	0.78	0.66	0.66
SVM Linear	ID	0.69	0.29	0.83	0.68	0.72
Random Forest	ID	**0.71**	**0.44**	**0.81**	0.71	0.71
SVM RBF	ID	0.67	0.42	0.76	0.69	0.66
Random Baseline	ID	0.61	0.24	0.74	0.61	0.61
SVM Linear	PR	0.66	0.62	0.68	0.74	0.65
Random Forest	PR	**0.68**	**0.54**	**0.76**	0.69	0.68
SVM RBF	PR	0.65	0.60	0.68	0.73	0.64
Random Baseline	PR	0.55	0.34	0.67	0.56	0.56

3.3   Results

The results can be seen in Table 1. The model performance is reported as $F1$ score, Precision and Recall. In addition, $F1_{pos}$ and $F1_{neg}$ for the positive and negative classes are reported. A random baseline model is reported. The trained models always outperform the random baseline. The best performing classifiers are Random Forest and SVM RBF Kernel with F1 of 0.76 for Need Finding, 0.71 for Ideation and 0.68 for Prototyping.

The F1 for the positive class is typically 0.2 higher than that of the random baseline, indicating the positive class is predicted correctly at a rate often approaching double that of the random baseline. This indicates that the models are clearly performing better than expected by random chance and have indeed learned something from the data. These models also show high F1 for predicting the negative class with 0.86, 0.81, and 0.76 respectively, indicating low false positive predictions.

The Random Forest and SVM RBF Kernel are nonlinear models which indicates that there exists predictive performance gains in nonlinear combination of the features. The results indicate that the features have power of discrimination for predicting design thinking modes.

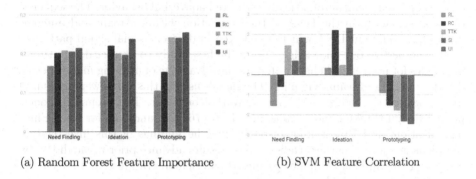

(a) Random Forest Feature Importance   (b) SVM Feature Correlation

Fig. 1. Model features

The feature importance scores indicate which signals are important for predicting each of the different design thinking modes. Figure 1a shows the feature importance for Random Forests, where UI, TTK, and SI were the top performing features for Need Finding contributing 21.4%, 20.9% and 20.5% respectively. For Prototyping, similar trends are observed with these features scoring 25.6%, 24.2% and 24.1%. In contrast, top performing cues for Ideation are UI, RC and TTK with 23.9%, 22.0% and 20.1%. In all three classification models, UI is the top performing feature. However, it should be noted that the contribution is fairly equal for all features except RL.

While Random Forests show feature importance for design thinking mode, they do not show positive or negative association. On the other hand, the coefficients of the separating hyperplane from the linear SVM in Fig. 1b show which features help predict the positive and negative classes. Where the Random Forest feature importance scores are quite similar across modes, the SVM feature scores show different correlations between features and modes. In contrast, the most important feature for all modes in Random Forests is UI, where as for SVMs this is only the case for Need Finding and Prototyping. For Ideation it is the third most important feature. It only has a positive association for Need Finding but has negative association for Ideation and Prototyping. UI is negatively associated with Ideation and Prototyping. It is very clear that features are differently positively and negatively associated for different design thinking modes. This answers our research question that different modes have different dynamics in rotation behavior.

In conclusion, rotation features can be used to infer design thinking modes. Each design thinking mode has different importance of rotation features. The direction of certain features changes for different modes.

4   Discussion and Conclusion

This paper presents evidence for a Sociometric DNA in design thinking meetings. This study indicates that differences exist between design thinking modes and can be captured using automatically extracted nonverbal behavior. The sequence of social signals form the DNA of the interaction within a team and different modes have different DNA which is reflected in different social signal patterns.

To the best of our knowledge, this is the first study to predict design thinking modes for nonverbal behavior despite the advantage of utilising mode-specific data to understand team dynamics. The signals used in this study were measured using sociometric badges capturing nonverbal behavior. The proposed models predict design thinking modes with an F1 of 0.76, 0.71 and 0.68 for Need Finding, Ideation, and Prototyping respectively. The findings of this investigation complement those of earlier studies. These results advance prior research [12] by increasing the number of modes predicted and demonstrating that they can be predicted outside of a laboratory setting.

A potential application of these findings can be found in building an automated coach. Relevant interventions can be presented to meeting participants based on their automatically classified design thinking mode. While coaching teams was previously only possible using in person coaches, this new technology can provide a coach on a much larger scale.

References

1. Cawley, G.C., Talbot, N.L.: On over-fitting in model selection and subsequent selection bias in performance evaluation. J. Mach. Learn. Res. **11**(Jul), 2079–2107 (2010)
2. Chawla, N.V., Bowyer, K.W., Hall, L.O., Kegelmeyer, W.P.: Smote: synthetic minority over-sampling technique. J. Artif. Intell. Res. **16**, 321–357 (2002)
3. Chuy, M., Zhang, J., Resendes, M., Scardamalia, M., Bereiter, C.: Does contributing to a knowledge building dialogue lead to individual advancement of knowledge. In: Connecting Computer-Supported Collaborative Learning to Policy and Practice: CSCL2011 Conference Proceedings, vol. 1, pp. 57–63. ISLS (2011)
4. Davis, J.P., Eisenhardt, K.M.: Rotating leadership and collaborative innovation: recombination processes in symbiotic relationships. Adm. Sci. Q. **56**(2), 159–201 (2011)
5. Dietzel, J., Francu, R.E., Lucas, B., Zaki, M.: Contextually defined postural markers reveal who's in charge: evidence from small teams collected with wearable sensors (2018)
6. D'Mello, S., Stewart, A.E., Amon, M.J., Sun, C., Duran, N., Shute, V.: Towards dynamic intelligent support for collaborative problem solving. In: Proceedings of the Approaches and Challenges in Team Tutoring Workshop (2019)

7. Eloy, L., et al.: Modeling team-level multimodal dynamics during multiparty collaboration. In: 2019 International Conference on Multimodal Interaction, pp. 244–258 (2019)
8. Gloor, P.A., Almozlino, A., Inbar, O., Lo, W., Provost, S.: Measuring team creativity through longitudinal social signals. arXiv preprint arXiv:1407.0440 (2014)
9. Harrigan, J.A.: Proxemics, kinesics, and gaze. In: The New Handbook of Methods in Nonverbal Behavior Research, pp. 137–198 (2005)
10. Hartman, R.L., Johnson, J.D.: Social contagion and multiplexity communication networks as predictors of commitment and role ambiguity. Hum. Commun. Res. **15**(4), 523–548 (1989)
11. Ibarra, H., Andrews, S.B.: Power, social influenced, and sense making: effects of network centrality and proximity on employee perceptions. Adm. Sci. Q. **38**, 277–303 (1993)
12. Jayagopi, D.B., Kim, T., Pentland, A.S., Gatica-Perez, D.: Recognizing conversational context in group interaction using privacy-sensitive mobile sensors. In: Proceedings of the 9th International Conference on Mobile and Ubiquitous Multimedia, p. 8. ACM (2010)
13. Kidane, Y.H., Gloor, P.A.: Correlating temporal communication patterns of the eclipse open source community with performance and creativity. Comput. Math. Organ.Theory **13**(1), 17–27 (2007)
14. Liedtka, J.: Perspective: linking design thinking with innovation outcomes through cognitive bias reduction. J. Prod. Innov. Manag. **32**(6), 925–938 (2015)
15. Mumm, J., Mutlu, B.: Human-robot proxemics: physical and psychological distancing in human-robot interaction. In: Proceedings of the 6th International Conference on Human-Robot Interaction, pp. 331–338. ACM (2011)
16. Olguin, D.O., Gloor, P.A., Pentland, A.S.: Capturing individual and group behavior with wearable sensors. In: Proceedings of the 2009 AAAI Spring Symposium on Human Behavior Modeling, SSS, vol. 9 (2009)
17. Parker, J.N., Cardenas, E., Dorr, A.N., Hackett, E.J.: Using sociometers to advance small group research. Sociol. Methods Res. 0049124118769091 (2018)
18. Pedregosa, F., et al.: Scikit-learn: machine learning in python. J. Mach. Learn. Res. **12**(Oct), 2825–2830 (2011)
19. Pentland, A.: Honest Signals: How They Shape Our World. MIT Press, Cambridge (2010)
20. Perry-Smith, J.E., Mannucci, P.V.: From creativity to innovation: the social network drivers of the four phases of the idea journey. Acad. Manag. Rev. **42**(1), 53–79 (2017)
21. Seidel, V.P., Fixson, S.K.: Adopting design thinking in novice multidisciplinary teams: the application and limits of design methods and reflexive practices. J. Prod. Innov. Manag. **30**, 19–33 (2013)
22. Solutions, S.: Sociometric Badge 03-02: Preliminary User Guide. Author, Boston (2014)
23. Stempfle, J., Badke-Schaub, P.: Thinking in design teams-an analysis of team communication. Des. Stud. **23**(5), 473–496 (2002)
24. Woolley, A.W., Chabris, C.F., Pentland, A., Hashmi, N., Malone, T.W.: Evidence for a collective intelligence factor in the performance of human groups. Science **330**(6004), 686–688 (2010)

Information Analysis with FlexIA - Reconciling Design Challenges Through User Participation

Christian Kruse[✉], Daniela Becks, and Sebastian Venhuis

Westfälische Hochschule, Münsterstraße 265, 46397 Bocholt, Germany
{christian.kruse,daniela.becks,sebastian.venhuis}@w-hs.de
https://www.w-hs.de

Abstract. Information analysis is a keystone for successful digitization projects. However, due to the inherent complexity and sheer amount of information, very often fairly aggregated top-down approaches are utilized. In addition, most of the methods treat information objects as appendages of processes and do not reflect the users' perspectives sufficiently. In this paper, the FlexIA approach for conducting a user-centered information analysis is presented. Methodologically, it is based on the concept of participatory design and the action research approach. After briefly providing information on motivation and research context, the FlexIA method and the FlexIA tool are described. Three major design challenges emanating from heterogeneous user groups, volatile work settings and agile domain contexts are addressed. It is shown, that the participatory design approach is well suited to ensure that the user's requirements are appropriately taken into account in the method and the tool.

Keywords: Participatory approach · User-centered design · Information analysis

1 Introduction

In times of industry 4.0 small and medium-sized companies (SMCs) have to cope with multiple aspects of digitization. While some of them already use modern ERP information systems and other digital tools comprehensively a significant number of SMCs still struggles with the transformation from analogue to digital work. This is due to the fact, that each step towards full digitization increases the complexity of work processes and additional technological knowledge is needed

This research and development project is funded by the European Social Fund (ESF) and the German Federal Ministry of Education and Research (BMBF) within the program "Future of work" (02L18B000) and implemented by the Project Management Agency Karlsruhe (PTKA). The authors are responsible for the content of this publication.

C. Stephanidis et al. (Eds.): HCII 2020, CCIS 1293, pp. 62–69, 2020.
https://doi.org/10.1007/978-3-030-60700-5_8

to manage the modified daily work routines. How to deal with this challenge is a central research question within the 3-year project FlexDeMo. One of its major goals is to develop a toolkit consisting of different digital assistants that support companies in participatory assembly planning and simulation. Thereby, heterogeneous users, volatile application domains as well as increasingly complex work environments are critical challenges for designing software tools that are intuitively usable. In this context a user-centered and participatory approach proves advantageous. It strictly focuses on the characteristics of the users by actively involving them in each design step. This paper describes how to reconcile the varying requirements during the design, development and evaluation process. One tool based on this approach is FlexIA which is presented within this article.

2 Information Analysis with FlexIA - Motivation and Context

The competitive environment for companies is changing more rapidly and profoundly than ever. Small and medium-sized companies are confronted with the challenge to adapt dynamically to changing market conditions parallel to coping with the need to digitize their work processes. In contrast to large companies they typically operate in specialized niche markets, are often dependent on few key customers and suffer from scarce resources.

The FlexDeMo project aims at providing SMCs with methods, tools and best practice recommendations such that they become more self-reliant in leveraging their internal capabilities to adapt to changing market conditions. The project focuses on mechanical engineering companies that manufacture to order. In this domain production and assembly processes are highly customer-specific, vary considerably in scope and need to be highly flexible to incorporate late modifications of customer requirements. Given this background, the FlexDeMo project addresses two fundamental research questions that are presented in more detail in the following two sections.

2.1 Simulating the Assembly Process

The main focus of the FlexDeMo project is to provide a digital toolkit for small and medium-sized companies which may be used to simulate and evaluate alternative assembly line forms. To achieve this goal a solid information base is required that caters for valid simulations of current as well as future assembly line variations. Quite often it can be observed that the information landscape of SMCs is not well described resulting in missing, poor or unstructured data. To facilitate an initial analysis the FlexDeMo toolkit will provide suitable tools and methods to gain these information insights.

2.2 Bridging Information Islands

In the early stages of the project it could already be seen that personalized and often tacit knowledge of the employees as well as informal communication flows are of paramount importance for efficient operations. Especially the way the information is shared between departments strongly influences the process of assembly planning. In many cases, the companie's current information landscape is characterized by numerous encapsulated information islands rather than one central shared information pool. It is highly recommendable to bridge these islands because otherwise valuable domain-specific knowledge may get lost. Introducing suitable methods and tools of knowledge management to avoid information loss and to optimize the underlying information strategy of SMCs is another central project goal of FlexDeMO.

In this application context, the need for a participatory, user-centered approach for information analysis became apparent in an early project phase. While reviewing approaches and methods for information analysis the idea was created to develop an individual toolkit called FlexIA (flexible information analysis).

3   The Philosophy of FlexIA

The conceptual research framework upon which both the FlexIA method and the FlexIA tool are based is strongly influenced by the methodology of participatory design [3,11]. In particular, the following principles are applied:

- design partnerships with participants
- co-creation and co-interpretation of design artifacts
- action research approach
- focus on system user productivity rather than system developer productivity

As emphasized by Bittner and Leimeister [2] it is of paramount importance to create a shared understanding of key concepts, mental models and relevant information and design artifacts. In addition, due to the iterative nature of the research approach, both the FlexIA method and the FlexIA tool are undergoing frequent adaptations resulting in different versions and prototypes.

3.1   The FlexIA Method

In this section the underlying method is briefly introduced as this will help to understand the functionality and use of the FlexIA tool. Therefore, Fig. 1 illustrates the steps of a typical information analysis based upon FlexIA. A comprehensive description of the FlexIA method may be found in the recent publication of Kruse et al. [7].

Information analysis starts with a fairly generic data acquisition step comprising of a value stream mapping to identify suitable processes for further investigation and a so-called self assessment survey. The goal of this initial survey is to get a first impression of the current information technological situation and the company's state of digitization.

The second step focuses on the detailed examination of the selected processes. For each, a moderated workshop is held during which information objects and resources are documented within the information supply matrix. Additionally,

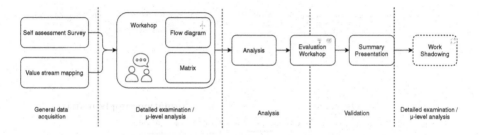

Fig. 1. Typical FlexIA analysis process

the information flow is documented within an information flow diagram. According to Hansen and Järvelin the flow of information comprises different activities like assimilation and creation and may be remarkably complex [6]. As a consequence, several actions that may be performed on the information object (e.g. transformation or move) were integrated into this diagram. After having finished this step, the collected data is analyzed both quantitatively and qualitatively.

Finally, the results are presented in participatory workshops, in which the findings are validated and possible solutions are discussed with the employees.

To perform the described information analysis specific auxiliary forms were designed including the self assessment survey, a worksheet to sketch the information flow (information flow diagram), a matrix to document the information and knowledge sources (information supply matrix) and a summarizing protocol. During the various workshops, the use of these documents proved to be not very suitable. As a consequence, it was decided to integrate these auxiliary tools into one digital assistant to make the complete process more flexible and intuitive. The prototypical realization of this tool is presented in the next section.

3.2 The FlexIA Tool

The FlexIA tool is one of serveral digital assistants that make up the comprehensive FlexDeMo toolkit. It integrates user-centered knowledge with IT-based support functionalities in a collaborative manner. This approach is well established in the realm of agile software development as exemplified by tools such as Signavio[1], Stack Overflow[2] or Confluence[3].

The screenshots presented in Fig. 2 provide a first impression of the current FlexIA prototype. As can be seen the tool comprises multiple components to support the complete analysis process introduced in Fig. 1.

When the user starts the tool, a list of all processes is displayed that have been selected for analyzing (see Fig. 2a). For each single process the user can determine the functional scope of the information analysis. This means, that they may perform either a complete information analysis starting with the interview

---

[1] https://www.signavio.com.

[2] https://stackoverflow.com.

[3] https://www.atlassian.com/software/confluence.

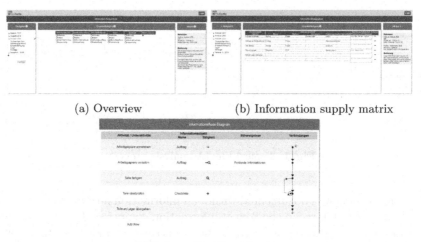

(a) Overview   (b) Information supply matrix

(c) Information flow diagram

Fig. 2. FlexIA prototype

and finishing with the evaluation. But, there is also the option to skip some information analysis steps and restrict it to only one analysis. This overview page may be seen as the homepage of the FlexIA tool.

Figure 2b illustrates the information supply matrix. It is used to describe information sources respectively objects as well as its main attributes. In addition, possible disruptive events may be recorded. They represent events that require immediate reactions by the employees. The information supply matrix is designed in table form where each row represents a single activity within the process and each column corresponds to an attribute of the information source respectively object.

The information flow diagram can be seen in Fig. 2c. Each activity correlates to a row in the diagram. On the right side a graph is displayed which represents the information flow. Typically, the information flow diagram as well as the information supply matrix are co-designed within moderated workshops as described in the section on the FlexIA method.

Currently, the prototypical components only support the detailed examination step (see Fig. 1), though the implementation has not yet been finished. During this design process the authors encountered several challenges which will be discussed in the next section.

4   Prototypical Realization of FlexIA - Design Challenges and Consequences

It is widely agreed by several authors that the context of the users and their knowledge strongly influence their information behavior and the way software is used [1,5,10]. To ensure that the FlexIA tool can be used intuitively, the system-user context needs to be comprehensively studied and modeled during the design process which is often challenging. Keeping this in mind, the context of the FlexIA tool was extensively analyzed by using e.g. guided interviews, work shadowing and the above described information analysis. Thereby several aspects aroused which are discussed in detail within the next sections.

4.1 User Context

The analysis of the FlexDeMO context revealed that there are numerous, heterogeneous users with respect to age, job position and experience as well as affinity to modern software systems. It was essential to define and systematize these user groups.

According to Grudin and Pruitt [4] personas are a very powerful tool to describe the users' personal background, their social standing and their work context which are important factors determining their preferences. Following the argumentation of Cherry and Macredie [3] it is strongly recommended to take into account these preferences to make sure that the designed system will be really used, i.e. focus on the system-user productivity.

Additionally, personas are particularly advantageous for participatory research settings [4]. As such, this approach aligns well with the underlying philosophy of FlexIA.

Keeping this in mind theses, the following five generalized personas for FlexIA and the complete FlexDeMo project were defined within a workshop.

- A worker of an company
- A manager of a medium-sized company
- A manager of a small company
- A researcher with academic background[4]
- A student

As can be easily seen, the FlexIA tool is meant to address very heterogeneous user groups. While the practically oriented users would like to quickly and easily use the tool during their daily work routines, an academic user might want to understand the underlying details of the methodology. For this reasons, multiple views were necessary to make sure that the tool can be intuitively used one the hand, but to increase user experience on the other hand. Furthermore, there exist significant differences with respect to the affinity to modern software systems which needed to be considered during the design of FlexIA. This was addressed by providing suitable support functionalities in the tool in form of tool tips, guides and explanations, in particular for novice users.

4.2 Work Context

While the challenges arising from the personal user context can be easily addressed by incorporating standard design principles as stated by Nielsen [8], the work environment necessitated a more specialized solution.

---

[4] This user group may also include consultants.

As discussed in the previous section, workers are a focal user group. Therefore, they should be able to use the FlexIA tool without interrupting their daily assembly work routines significantly. Information analysis activities are not conducted on a regular basis and do not have a high priority in their work routine. Hence, they will be interrupted regularly and continued later. As such, it was paramount for the tool to allow breaks as well as to offer an easy continuation of the analysis. Thus each tool saves continually and the work on each step can be continued.

Because SMCs typically do not have the resources to execute a complete information analysis, the FlexIA tool is designed modular meaning that each component may be used separately and selected steps can be skipped. With the help of the overview page (see Fig. 2a) the user may quickly differentiate between finished, skipped and open tasks. As a result, it is envisioned that the FlexIA tool is a daily companion that facilitates an efficient usage and sharing of information.

4.3   Domain Context

Domain and work context are closely related and both considerably influence the information behavior and the use of software systems. As already discussed at the beginning of this paper, the project focuses on small and medium-sized companies in the domain of mechanical engineering characterized by inherent dynamics resulting from changing markets and customer requirements. These unsteady settings are typical for the investigated domain and need to be taken into consideration during the whole design process. This also includes the evaluation of the tool because in order to guarantee that the developed system is really usable there is a strong need to not just investigate usability but also contextual aspects like the domain and the work setting [9]. Therefore, intensive domain-specific knowledge is necessary which can only be incorporated by means of expert evaluation. Based on this assumption, not only the method needs to be evaluated in a realistic work setting, but also the FlexIA tool needs to be investigated by experts (i.e. the employees).

5   Summary and Outlook

In this paper the current prototype as well as the underlying methodological approach of FlexIA, a tool for participatory analyzing information flows, were presented. While developing this tool specialties arising from the investigated domain of mechanical engineering (users, work context, the domain itself) strongly influenced the development of the digital assistant. Some of them were exemplary discussed in this article. To guarantee that the tool will be intuitively used by the employees of the focused small and medium-sized companies these design challenges need to be addressed within the user interface as well as the underlying method. The authors encountered these problems by incorporating standard design patterns like multiple views and tool specific solutions like the above mentioned overview page. Furthermore, comprehensive personas were defined to model the user's background and a suitable mixed evaluation design was set up.

First tests of the FlexIA method were done investigating the information landscape of one medium-sized company in the target domain and revealed promising results. In contrast, the current prototype has not yet been evaluated. For this reason, a heuristic evaluation [8] and multiple usability tests consulting domain experts will take place to analyze the user interface as well as the suitability regarding the real work environment in the near future. The feedback will be incorporated into future versions of the hitherto prototypical tool and other digital assistants developed within the FlexDeMo context.

References

1. Becks, D., Görtz, M., Womser-Hacker, C.: Understanding information seeking in the patent domain and its impact on the interface design of IR systems. In: Proceedings of the HCIR (2010)
2. Bittner, E.A.C., Leimeister, J.M.: Creating shared understanding in heterogeneous work groups: why it matters and how to achieve it. J. Manag. Inf. Syst. 31(1), 111–144 (2014). https://doi.org/10.2753/mis0742-1222310106
3. Cherry, C., Macredie, R.D.: The importance of context in information system design: an assessment of participatory design. Requirements Eng. 4(2), 103–114 (1999). https://doi.org/10.1007/s007660050017
4. Grudin, J., Pruitt, J.: Personas, participatory design and product development: an infrastructure for engagement. In: Proceedings of PDC, vol. 2 (2002)
5. Hansen, P., Järvelin, K.: The information seeking and retrieval process at the swedish patent and registration office. In: Proceedings of ACM SIGIR Workshop on Patent Retrieval (2000)
6. Hansen, P., Järvelin, K.: Collaborative information retrieval in an information-intensive domain. Inf. Process. Manag. 41(5), 1101–1119 (2005). https://doi.org/10.1016/j.ipm.2004.04.016
7. Kruse, C., Becks, D., Venhuis, S.: Flexia - a toolkit for the participatory information analysis in small and medium-sized companies. https://doi.org/10.18420/ecscw2020_p07
8. Nielsen, J., Molich, R.: Heuristic evaluation of user interfaces. In: Proceedings of the SIGCHI Conference on Human Factors in Computing Systems, pp. 249–256 (1990)
9. Sarodnick, F., Brau, H.: Methoden der Usability Evaluation. Verlag Hans Huber, s.l., 2. aufl. edn. (2011). http://sub-hh.ciando.com/book/?bok_id=240821
10. Schwab, M., Wack, K.J.: Digitalisierung der kontsruktion im sondermaschinenbau - ein erfahrungsbericht zur nutzerzentrierten gestaltung & usability-evaluation einer individuallösung. https://doi.org/10.18420/muc2019-up-0359
11. Spinuzzi, C.: The methodology of participatory design. Tech. Commun. 52(2), 163–174 (2005)

Emblem Recognition: Cultural Coaching Software via Hand Gestures

Cris Kubli$^{(\boxtimes)}$ (iD)

ArtSciLab, School of Arts, Technology and Emerging Communication, The University of Texas at Dallas, Richardson, TX, USA
criskubli@me.com

Abstract. Negotiations and casual exchanges that involve different cultures may often lead to misunderstandings and eventually adverse outcomes. These conflicts can be easily avoided if both parties are familiarized with each other's culture. This paper proposes a novel way of tackling this problem by using computer vision and identifying hand gestures that are particular to a culture. Such gestures, also known as emblems, are used frequently during interaction. There is a certain complexity to emblems, and their identification could provide vital information during communication if recognized accurately. An example for this case is the "thumbs up" gesture, where the thumb is extended while the other fingers are curled up. This gesture, while positive in the West, can be insulting in other countries. The implemented computer vision software was able to detect five distinct hand gestures that had one specific meaning in the United States, as well as other connotations in other countries. This helped inform participants with residency in the United States about additional meanings of familiar hand gestures that are commonly used in North America. The main purpose of culturally-sensitive technology is to help a user get acquainted with socio-cultural particularities of another group. Possible applications are discussed further, such as serving as a cultural interpreter during a diplomatic or business exchange or aiding in cultural sensibility training for tourists traveling to a new country.

Keywords: Human-Centered technology · Computer vision · Cultural technology · Applied anthropology

1 Introduction

In negotiations or day-to-day communication, the receiver of information must comprehend various cues of the sender in order to interpret a given situation correctly. When both parties are of different cultural backgrounds, this task has a higher risk of failure for a correct interpretation [1]. Said exchanges might also involve visual cues, such as hand gestures, which might also depend on the culture of the receiver.

Gestures are an integral part of nonverbal human communication. These unique movements are said to be a human universal and are well used around the world [2]. Knapp [3] considers that nonverbal communication comprises all types of communication except for those contexts where something is written or spoken. In popular culture,

© Springer Nature Switzerland AG 2020
C. Stephanidis et al. (Eds.): HCII 2020, CCIS 1293, pp. 70–76, 2020.
https://doi.org/10.1007/978-3-030-60700-5_9

this concept is also referred as body language. Even though the usage of arbitrary gestures in musical creation or robot remote control are useful, the detection of pre-existing gestures is equally important; especially when analyzed from a social angle, considering that various types of movements are usually dependent on the psychological and sociocultural background of a user.

Scholars that specialize in nonverbal communication divide gestures into two categories: movements that complement an exchange or conversation, and gestures that have their own meaning and do not rely on speech. Gestures that are categorized within the latter and are particular of a cultural group are labeled as either symbolic gestures or emblems [4]. In this case, emblems are the main focus of this project.

There is a certain complexity to emblems, and their identification could provide vital information during communication if recognized accurately. For Matsumoto and Huang [4], emblems can be divided into 3 discrete categories: 1) emblems that are represented differently but have the same meaning; 2) gestures that are presented the same but diverge in meaning across societies, and; 3) a particular emblem that is unique to a culture with no known equivalent. The present exercise utilizes the second category.

2   Related Work

The cultural component is no stranger to the Human-Computer Interaction (HCI) community, however there are considerably more resources on the connection between culture and user interface design; with concepts such as cross-cultural HCI, Culture-oriented HCI and Intercultural HCI to name a few [5]. On the other hand, research on the cultural implication of body language in HCI is not as plentiful. Research and improvement on gesture recognition has been fairly popular since the nineties [6], and to date there have been few groups that have explicitly specialized on emblem detection or recognition in computer vision (e.g. [7]).

Regarding Human-Robot Interaction, there are groups that have worked on the human interpretation of emblematic gestures performed by artificial means [8], and others have been involved in robots replicating gestures [9]. Peña and colleagues [10] recently unveiled a virtual animation with an auxiliary robot as a physical interface that interacts with emblematic greetings, as a way to "personalize" an interaction. Regardless, no group has tackled the issue of gestures and technology from a wide-ranging cultural perspective, with the exception of few articles that have addressed certain challenges like the importance of the "enculturation of technology" while validating the cultural background of the user [11], or the proposal of an emblem translation system [12].

3   Methods

3.1   Constructing an Emblem Recognition Software

Given the current limitations of research on cultural nonverbal communication and its recognition through computer interfaces, a modest emblem recognition model was sought as a preliminary proof of concept. Sadaival's [13] gesture recognition system was tested and chosen due to its minimalism involving hand gesture recognition. It was then modified to detect five different hand emblems which simultaneously displayed the meanings from the United States as well as corresponding meanings from abroad.

3.2   Image Processing and Software Specifics

The emblem recognition program developed in python was dependent on the Open Source Computer Vision Library, also known as OpenCV. It consisted of two windows. The main display included the visualization of a live image captured from a web camera, a region of interest designed to fit the user's hand and recognize the emblem (visualized as a green box), as well as the description of the emblem at the top of the display with meanings of the United States and abroad. The recognition of the gestures is done by standard methods in image processing, such as dilation, gaussian blur, binary image segmentation and the application of a convex hull, all of which were done in the region of interest. The program recognized the emblems by analyzing a specific ratio of the area of the participant's gesture while comparing the area determined by the convex hull. This image processing block is essential for feature extraction as it allows the identification of discrete characteristics for each hand gesture. Subsequently, the secondary window is the same size as the region of interest and is used as an aid in the detection of a gesture as it guides the user with the segmented image in case the lighting or background are not optimal.

Through a computer's web camera (Macbook Pro: 720p camera), five common static (non-dynamic) US emblems were tested, all of which had a different connotation in another culture (Fig. 1).

Fig. 1. Demonstration of the emblem recognition software.

3.3   Data Collection

The collection of data consisted of a printed questionnaire with 10 questions, as well as the testing of the program. The questionnaire had a qualitative emphasis and 7 questions were structured similarly to the Likert scale. The methodology used was the following:

First Part of Questionnaire. Before any testing occurred, the participant would answer a "before" section that concentrated on gathering data such as country of origin, number of years living in the United States, and other cultural literacy questions. This section consisted of five questions.

Testing and Debriefing. Once the initial questions were answered, individuals were asked to pose five different hand gestures with the following names: 1) Okay; 2) Thumbs Up; 3) V; 4) Hunger Games; and 5) Open Hand. Each gesture is known to have at least two meanings, one in the United States and one abroad (see Table 1). The individuals were required to use their right hand for all of the gestures. Once the exercise was finished, participants were debriefed.

Second Part of Questionnaire. Subsequently, participants responded an "after" section which evaluated the comprehension of the intent of the exercise and the educational acquisition of the new concepts. This section also consisted of five questions.

Table 1. Breakdown of emblems and their meanings in the United States and abroad.

Types of Emblems				
Okay	Thumbs Up	V	Hunger Games	Open Hand
U.S. Meaning				
Agreeing	Validating	Number 2 / Peace	Number 3	Number 5
Meaning Abroad				
Brazil: Obscene France: Number 0	Iraq: Obscene. "Up yours!"	Japan: Happiness/Smile UK: "V for victory!"	Thailand: Anti-Coup Opposition Symbol	Greece: Obscene

4 Results

A total of 17 (N = 17) individuals volunteered and engaged in the initial testing of the emblem recognition software. Participants were female and male adults familiarized with North American culture and had been living in the United States for at least 5 years. Interestingly, 14 participants (82.4%) reported to be familiar with at least one culture from abroad, either because of origin, ascendance, or personal interest. Considering the vicinity of the United States with Mexico, it is no surprise that over a third (35.3%) of the responders showed some familiarity with Mexican culture. Before the testing of the software, most participants agreed (58.8% for strongly agree; 29.4% partially agree) that hand gestures are a powerful method for communicating.

For the "after" section of the questionnaire, an overwhelming number of participants (94.1%) reported having strongly understood the nature of the exercise and visualized its potential for future applications (58.8% for strongly agree; 29.4% partially agree).

The majority (70.6%) of the people that engaged with the software knew less than three meanings of the foreign emblems, or none at all. In addition, 76.5% of the individuals strongly acknowledged having learned something new, whereas this sentiment was partial for 17.6% and neutral for 5.9% (see Fig. 2).

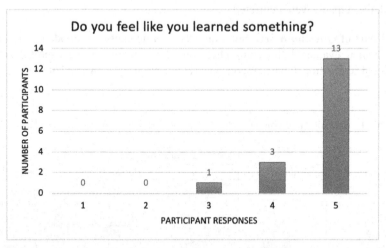

Fig. 2. Do you feel like you learned something? Most participants strongly felt that they did. Responses were assigned as Strongly Disagree (1), Disagree (2), Neutral (3), Agree (4), and Strongly Agree (5).

5   Conclusion and Future Work

The main goal of the exercise was to improve communication skills as well as cultural awareness among the volunteers, thus the concept of "cultural coaching" emerged. A simple, yet effective proof of concept was put to the test by using software to teach cultural concepts in body language; to which, most participants admitted to having learned novel information. Naturally, there are other ways of being more rigorous when selecting participants, such as in other disciplines like cultural psychology where individuals have to pass several criteria before corroborating their cultural upbringing and participate in a study. In such case, the pragmatism of the current software could be further tested for those that monocultural versus those that are multicultural.

Cultural coaching, or cultural sensitivity training, is heavily used in the medical sector, the diplomatic corps and the military. Nevertheless, if fine-tuned, this program could also be utilized by tourists and curious people alike. In addition, it shows a unique method of engagement by utilizing emblems, but other aspects could also be considered in the future, such as the volume of speech – a factor that also tends to differ from culture to culture. For upcoming work, perhaps it would be ideal that the program concentrated on targeting one culture at a time, instead of addressing various cultures.

Much like in Hasler and colleagues' [12] approach of an emblem translation system, it could potentially expand to a real-time emblem interpretation system, being utilized in any kind of human-to-human interaction such as a business exchange, where it could support already existing verbal communication translation software. Naturally, this would work more efficiently with the addition other tools such as deep learning, especially when dynamic emblems are taken into account.

The present exercise was a first step in developing culturally-sensitive technology that is able to enhance not only HCI, but also human to human interaction. As human-centered technology keeps flourishing with socio-affective inclinations in areas like social computing or emotion recognition, it is primordial to consider other factors that influence the human condition. With the development of technology that acknowledges a diverse set of cultural nuances, there is a myriad of possibilities in both research and industry, all while improving accessibility for those individuals that come from societies that are underrepresented in the current digital panorama.

Acknowledgements. I would like to thank Roger F. Malina for his invaluable support in the development of the project, as well as the members of the ArtSciLab. Additionally, I am grateful to all the volunteers that were excited to try the software with me and gave me instrumental feedback.

References

1. Littlewood, W.: Cultural awareness and the negotiation of meaning in intercultural communication. Lang. Awareness **2–3**, 189–199 (2011)
2. Archer, D.: Unspoken diversity: cultural differences in gestures. Qual. Sociol. **20**(1), 79–105 (1997)
3. Knapp, M.: Nonverbal Communication in Human Interaction. Holt, Rinehart, and Winston, New York (1972)
4. Matsumoto, D., Hwang, H.: Cultural similarities and differences in emblematic gestures. J. Nonverbal Behav. **37**, 1–27 (2013)
5. Heimgärtner, R.: Intercultural user interface design – culture-centered hci design – cross-cultural user interface design: different terminology or different approaches? In: Marcus, A. (ed.) DUXU 2013. LNCS, vol. 8013, pp. 62–71. Springer, Heidelberg (2013). https://doi.org/10.1007/978-3-642-39241-2_8
6. Quek, F., Zhao, M.: Inductive learning in hand pose recognition. In: Proceedings of the Second International Conference on Automatic Face and Gesture Recognition, Killington, VT, pp. 78–83. IEEE (1996)
7. Kanaujia, A., Huang, Y., Metaxas, D.: Emblem detections by tracking facial features. In: 2006 Conference on Computer Vision and Pattern Recognition Workshop (CVPRW'2006), New York, NY, p. 108. IEEE (2006)
8. Zheng, M., Liu, P.X., Meng, M.Q.-H.: Interpretation of human and robot emblematic gestures: how do they differ? Int. J. Robot. Autom. **34**(1), 55–70 (2018)
9. Cabibihan, J.-J., So, W., Pramanik, S.: Human-recognizable robotic gestures. IEEE Trans. Auton. Ment. Dev. **4**(4), 305–314 (2012)
10. Peña, P., Polceanu, M., Lisetti, C., Visser, U.: eEVA as a real-time multimodal agent human-robot interface. In: Holz, D., Genter, K., Saad, M., von Stryk, O. (eds.) RoboCup 2018. LNCS (LNAI), vol. 11374, pp. 262–274. Springer, Cham (2019). https://doi.org/10.1007/978-3-030-27544-0_22

11. Rehm, M., Bee, N., André, E.: Wave like an Egyptian — accelerometer based gesture recognition for culture specific interactions. People and Computers XXII Culture. Creativity, Interaction, vol. 1, pp. 13–22. Liverpool, UK (2008)
12. Hasler, B.S., Salomon, O., Tuchman, P., Lev-Tov, A., Friedman, D.: Real-time gesture translation in intercultural communication. AI Soc. **32**(1), 25–35 (2014). https://doi.org/10.1007/s00146-014-0573-4
13. Sadaival.: Hand-Gestures [Software] (2018). https://github.com/Sadaival/Hand-Gestures, Accessed 10 Mar 2020

Using the Ethical OS Toolkit to Mitigate the Risk of Unintended Consequences

Mariana Lilley[1($\boxtimes$)], Anne Currie[2], Andrew Pyper[1], and Sue Attwood[1]

[1] School of Engineering and Computer Science, University of Hertfordshire, Hatfield AL10 9AB, UK
m.lilley@herts.ac.uk
[2] Container Solutions, London EC4R 1EB, UK

Abstract. Ethical considerations relating to the use of participants' data are well-established within User Experience (UX) practices. Similarly, there is evidence of a wide understanding of what dark UX patterns are and why these violate ethical principles set out by computing codes such as the ACM Code of Ethics and Professional Conduct. However, frameworks for practitioners to reflect on the possible unintended consequences of their work are less well represented.

This paper reports on a pilot case study in which the Ethical Operating System (Ethical OS) framework was employed to bring these considerations systematically into UX work. Findings from this pilot study indicate that the use of the Ethical OS Toolkit can reveal potential unintended consequences of UX work that may not have surfaced otherwise, or that would have been recognised much later in the product's lifecycle. The work is presented as both a means of embedding the toolkit into future practitioners' education and its potential for supporting practitioners in their practice.

Keywords: UX practice · Ethics · Ethical OS framework

1 Introduction

Our experience has been that ethical considerations relating to the use of participants' data are well-established within User Experience (UX) research practices; an example of this is IDEO's 'The Little Book of Design Research Ethics' [1]. Similarly, there is evidence of a wide understanding of what dark UX patterns are (see, for example, [2]) and why these violate ethical principles set out by computing codes such as the ACM Code of Ethics and Professional Conduct [3]. A brief introduction to ethics in UX research and dark UX patterns follows.

1.1 Ethics in UX Research

Ethics is rightly a core topic in UX research teaching [5]. Indeed, at the institution of three of the authors the regulations and process for applying for ethics approval

© Springer Nature Switzerland AG 2020
C. Stephanidis et al. (Eds.): HCII 2020, CCIS 1293, pp. 77–82, 2020.
https://doi.org/10.1007/978-3-030-60700-5_10

are embedded in the curriculum. Key principles include safeguarding participants from harm, confidentiality, informed consent, and freedom to withdraw.

These are common themes across commercial entities and professional bodies' alike. For example, the principles held by IDEO of respect, responsibility and honesty [1]. The ACM ethical guidelines pertain to the conduct of computing professionals more generally, but include the fundamental principles of 'avoid harm', and 'respect privacy'.

Fundamental ethical principles therefore inform practice across technology sectors and provide a mature, strong ethical structure within which practitioners can operate. It is possible to confirm that UX research work is being conducted in accordance with these principles: either informally through professional reflection or formally by meeting stated ethical requirements. It is also possible to identify those cases when ethical standards are not being met; see, for example, [6].

1.2 Dark UX Patterns

Dark UX patterns are the intentional use of UX techniques to replace the needs of the user with the needs of the stakeholder or sponsor of users' interaction with a given system [2]. Users are effectively deceived into carrying out an action desired by the stakeholder [7] rather than an action they are seeking to perform.

Taxonomies of dark UX patterns are an active area of research; see, for example, the work of [2, 7 and 8]. Gray et al. [8] identify five categories of dark patterns: nagging, obstruction, sneaking, interface interference, forced action. For example, a nagging dark pattern may persist in requesting that the user allows an app to produce notifications but offer no way to suppress the message permanently. As another example, a sneaking dark pattern could involve an online shopping basket including an item or items that the user has not consciously added themselves.

Users may be unable to identify when they encounter a dark UX pattern and as such are vulnerable to their effects without having noticed any difficulty with their interaction. Dark UX patterns may be ubiquitous to an extent that they are part of the users' normal experience and so not remarkable enough to report [7].

Much work has gone into identifying dark patterns that are used in web applications and mobile applications; but dark patterns clearly may apply in a wide range of contexts and this is an issue that may become worse with the continuing diversity of ubiquitous computing. The effects of dark patterns that lead to users inadvertently giving up location information when they use a mobile app are already concerning. Nonetheless, these effects may be exacerbated when considered in the context of ubiquitous computing and deliberate exploitation of proxemic interactions [9, 10].

Importantly for this paper, such dark UX patterns are implemented intentionally: a user deceived into giving up their personal data is not the result of a bad design or an anti-pattern [2]; it is an effective use of the skills and knowledge of user experience design to create an interaction that is favourable for the stakeholder or sponsor. It should be noted that a number of dark UX patterns practices would be in breach of the General Data Protection Regulation (GDPR) [11], and are also under consideration as part of the DETOUR Act [12].

Ethical guidelines may allude to unintended harm and the wider impact of decisions being made. However, identifying potential unintended consequences is non-trivial and requires a systematic, structured approach. It seems that this is an area that lacks the range of mature approaches and techniques that are available to other areas of UX research and design work.

Nevertheless, it is an active area of research and development; see, for example value-sensitive design (VSD) [13], the consequence scanning kit [14] and the Ethical OS Toolkit [4]. A brief introduction to the Ethical OS Toolkit is presented next.

2   The Ethical OS Toolkit

The Ethical OS Toolkit [4] consists of eight risk zones, as listed in Table 1. Within each zone, the toolkit also provides a checklist of questions to ask. These questions form the basis for detailed discussions with stakeholders and can be used to inform discussions about unintended consequences.

As an example, if the 'Addiction and the Dopamine Economy' (Risk Zone 2) has been identified as a risk zone for a product, one of the questions would seek to identify what looks like healthy and unhealthy use of the product. Unhealthy use may manifest itself in extreme, uncontrolled use as against healthy use that may manifest itself as moderate use that may provide positive interactions for users.

The details of a pilot study where the Ethical OS Toolkit was employed by a group of undergraduate students enrolled on a UX course as a framework to identify potential unintended consequences of their UX work are presented next. The Ethical OS Toolkit was selected for this work, as it provides a detailed and pragmatic overarching framework for the consideration of risks that may apply to a product being developed. Its potential applications to industry [15, 16] were also a factor.

3   Pilot

A group of 47 undergraduate students on a UX course applied design thinking methodologies [17] to the creation of a "tech for good" high-fidelity prototype. As part of this work, they were able to explore the potential of technology to create innovative solutions to a problem affecting specific communities as identified and selected by them. Examples of their UX work included high-fidelity prototypes of a mobile app to support Sickle cell sufferers, a voice user interface to encourage users to engage more effectively with recycling, a community-led app to support single parents on low incomes. In general terms, student projects were based within one of the following four "tech for good" themes: eco-friendly transportation; education, social and inclusion; health and well-being; waste prevention and recycling.

Once their high-fidelity prototypes were produced, students were asked to reflect on the potential unintended consequences of their UX work using the Ethical OS Toolkit and select one risk zone for discussion. Table 1 presents a summary of their responses. It can be seen from the students' different selections of risk zones that in many cases more than one risk zone would apply but, for the purposes of this pilot, students were asked to expand on only one risk zone.

Findings from this pilot study indicate that students understood the importance of ethics in UX, and that the Ethical OS Toolkit was useful in supporting them to frame

Table 1. Risk zones selected for discussion by participant students (N = 47).

Ethical OS toolkit [4] Risk Zones	Eco-friendly transportation	Education, social and inclusion	Health and well-being	Waste prevention and recycling	Total
Risk Zone 1: Truth, Disinformation, and Propaganda	–	2	6	2	10
Risk Zone 2: Addiction & the Dopamine economy	–	1	3	–	4
Risk Zone 3: Economic & Asset inequalities	1	–	2	1	4
Risk Zone 4: Machine ethics & Algorithmic biases	–	–	–	–	–
Risk Zone 5: Surveillance state	–	1	1	1	3
Risk Zone 6: Data control & Monetization	–	2	8	6	16
Risk Zone 7: Implicit trust & User understanding	–	–	4	–	4
Risk Zone 8: Hateful & Criminal actors	2	2	–	2	6
Total	3	8	24	12	47

their reflections. As an example from Table 1, it can be seen that risks relating to misinformation (Risk Zone 1), access to data and how users would be supported in easily and transparently understanding what is known about them (Risk Zone 6) were particularly prominent in UX work relating to prototypes within the "health and well-being" theme. This is an important finding; students reflected on the fact that even though UX designers may not be ultimately responsible for the creation of content within a health app, the app itself can be used to propagate misinformation. It is argued that without the use of a framework such as the Ethical OS Toolkit these vital issues would not have surfaced in a systematic way.

It is also argued that the use of the Ethical OS Toolkit enabled students to consider the unintended consequences of their UX work beyond intended Primary Personas (as defined in [18]). As an example, one student who worked on a UX prototype aimed at promoting the use of public transport by providing reliable real-time data on buses in rural/less urban areas. This student selected Risk Zone 3 as their area for discussion as it was possible that some users may not necessarily have the technical resources or digital literacy to benefit from such a software artefact, should it be made live. The student also observed potential unintended consequences for bus drivers as they may constantly feel under surveillance (Risk Zone 5). It is contended that these reflections have surfaced in their UX work as a result of the application of the Ethical OS Toolkit. Similarly, concerns about algorithmic bias were raised in wider discussions within the "health and well-being" and "waste prevention and recycling" (e.g. food banks) themes.

4 Conclusion and Future Work

Ethical considerations are a critical part of building positive user experiences [19], and a foundation for UX research and design approaches. The existence of dark patterns emphasises the importance of ethics being embedded in UX design curricula and in practice. Less well represented, but also critical to ethical UX design is the need to mitigate the risks of unintended consequences.

This paper reports on a pilot study where UX students applied the Ethical OS Toolkit [4] to reflect on the implications of their UX work so that potential unintended consequences could be identified and mitigated.

The study indicates that the approach is efficacious. Using the approach, students were able to systematically identify and analyse possible unintended consequences of their UX work. The study also provides support for the idea that practitioners would benefit from the use of such a framework to identify and mitigate such risks.

Additionally, the approach demonstrates the value of embedding the approach in UX curricula: in this pilot, it was used to support students' critical reflection after they had developed their prototypes. It is anticipated that embedding the approach throughout their UX work would inculcate in students an understanding of how they can identify and mitigate unintended consequences as part of their broader UX and ethical development. Future work will study this more comprehensive embedding of the approach in UX curricula.

Another area for future work is to investigate the ways in which experienced UX practitioners are mitigating unintended consequences and the extent to which they are using formal frameworks to do this in their practice.

References

1. IDEO: The Little Book of Design Research Ethics (2016). https://www.ideo.com/post/the-lit tle-book-of-design-research-ethics, Accessed 13 Jun 2020
2. Gray, C.M., Kou, Y., Battles, B., Hoggatt, J., Toombs, A.L.: The dark (patterns) side of UX design. In: Proceedings of the 2018 CHI Conference on Human Factors in Computing Systems, pp. 1–14, April 2018

3. ACM: ACM Code of Ethics and Professional Conduct (2018). https://www.acm.org/code-of-ethics, Accessed 13 Jun 2020
4. Institute for the Future and Omidyar Network. Ethical OS Toolkit (2018). https://ethicalos.org/, Accessed 13 Jun 2020
5. Lazar, J., Feng, J.H., Hochheiser, H.: Research Methods in Human-Computer Interaction. Morgan Kaufmann, Burlington (2017)
6. Bowman, N.: The Ethics of UX Research. UX Booth, 26 August 2014. https://www.uxbooth.com/articles/ethics-ux-research/, Accessed 13 Jun 2020
7. Di Geronimo, L., Braz, L., Fregnan, E., Palomba, F., Bacchelli, A.: UI dark patterns and where to find them: a study on mobile applications and user perception. In: Proceedings of the 2020 CHI Conference on Human Factors in Computing Systems, pp. 1–14, April 2020
8. Brignull, H.: Dark patterns. Dark Patterns (2019). https://www.darkpatterns.org/, Accessed 13 Jun 2020
9. Greenberg, S., Boring, S., Vermeulen, J., Dostal, J.: Dark patterns in proxemic interactions: a critical perspective. In: Proceedings of the 2014 Conference on Designing Interactive Systems, pp. 523–532, June 2014
10. Marquardt, N., Greenberg, S.: Informing the design of proxemic interactions. IEEE Pervasive Comput. 11(2), 14–23 (2012)
11. Caruso, F.: Dark patterns: born to mislead. The European Data Journalism Network, 13 November 2019. https://www.europeandatajournalism.eu/eng/News/Data-news/Dark-patterns-born-to-mislead, Accessed 13 Jun 2020
12. GovTrack.us.: S. 1084 — 116th Congress: Deceptive Experiences to Online Users Reduction Act (2020). https://www.govtrack.us/congress/bills/116/s1084, Accessed 13 Jun 2020
13. Friedman, B.: Value-sensitive design. Interactions 3(6), 16–23 (1996)
14. doteveryone (n.d.).: Consequence Scanning – an agile practice for responsible innovators. https://www.doteveryone.org.uk/project/consequence-scanning/, Accessed 13 Jun 2020
15. Aziz, A.: How Omidyar network is building a digital code of ethics. Forbes, 8 August 2018. https://www.forbes.com/sites/afdhelaziz/2018/08/08/how-omidyar-network-is-building-a-digital-code-of-ethics/#4b0e41ef49c2, Accessed 13 Jun 2020
16. Pardes, A.: Silicon valley writes a playbook to help avert ethical disasters. WIRED, 7 August 2018. https://www.wired.com/story/ethical-os/, Accessed 13 Jun 2020
17. Dam, R.F., Siang, T.F. (n.d.) : Interaction Design Foundation: 5 Stages in the Design Thinking Process. https://www.interaction-design.org/literature/article/5-stages-in-the-design-thinking-process, Accessed 13 Jun 2020
18. Cooper, A., Reimann, R., Cronin, D., Noessel, C.: About Face: The Essentials of Interaction Design, 4th edn. Wiley, US (2014)
19. Stephanidis, C., Salvendy, G., Antona, M., Chen, J.Y., Dong, J., Duffy, V.G., et al.: Seven HCI grand challenges. Int. J. Hum.-Comput. Inter. 35(14), 1229–1269 (2019)

Perception in Human-Computer Symbiosis

Mohamed Quafafou[(✉)]

Aix-marseille University, Marseille, France
mohamed.quafafou@univ-amu.fr

Abstract. Today computers and more generally smart technology do not take into account the diversity of perception leading to the exclusion of the plurality of representation and decision even if such diversity may play a crucial role in human-computer interaction especially in our small world. We introduce in this paper a conceptual framework developing a bridge between set and perception theories to support computing with perceptions. In this context, human-machine interaction is not only guided by computation but it is also based on human-human interaction through machines and social networks.

Keywords: Perception · Interaction · Set · Accessibility

1 Introduction

Until now, a machine is said to be intelligent if its intelligence is similar to natural intelligence displayed by human especially when understanding language, learning, reasoning, and problem solving [11]. Alternatively, Human-Computer Symbiosis envisions a coupling of a human brain with intelligent machines allowing new type of thinking and data processing [10]. Nowadays, computers are connected to humans and play a human-like role, just think of Chatbots that conduct an on-line textual conversation with a human, humanoid robots that accompany old people, intelligent avatars used in e-commerce, etc. But, can computers have abilities of humans to live in the real world? Humans achieve their daily life's goals using their ability to think. From R. Descrates [1] until J. McCarthy [2], the recurring conclusion is that computers may outperform humans in calculus, but they would lack general reasoning abilities and have a limited relation to the world in general.

More generally, the emergence of intelligent interactive technologies will certainly have a great impact on the lifestyle in our society and this context emphasises significant challenges that lie ahead [9]. A crucial philosophical challenge is related to the significant role of the perception of physical environments in thinking. In fact, humans perceive the world through their five sense and act according to their perception which is in turn affected by their individual factors like

C. Stephanidis et al. (Eds.): HCII 2020, CCIS 1293, pp. 83–89, 2020.
https://doi.org/10.1007/978-3-030-60700-5_11

education, culture, psychological peculiarities, past individual experience, etc. On the contrary, computers run programs developed by human programmers encoding problem solving algorithms and methods. Consider, for example, that the following short message is broadcasted through a social network: "The meat I eat became very expensive!". Computers use efficient linguistic tools to define its semantic by applying natural linguistic methods to induce that "meat" is a noun, "eat" and "became" are verbs, the overall sentiment of the message is negative, etc. However, what is the semantic of "the meat I eat"? The answer does not depend only on linguistic considerations, but it is also related to the sender/reader of the message. In fact, Asian people eat dogs and cats, which are domestic animals for European people that eat horse meat except English persons. Furthermore, Muslims and Jewish eat cow but not pork, whereas the cow is venerated, throughout India, as a holy animal. Finally, vegetarians do not eat meat at all. In conclusion, we are facing classes, which are not only characterized by their members but they depend on their observers.

For humans, there are a number of reasons behind such diversity, which may be the consequence of sensors used to see objects, the application of community rules and the person believes, preferences, education, values, socioeconomic status, life experiences and more generally the different egocentric particulars. However, today computers do not take into account the diversity of perception and excluding consequently the plurality of representation and decision even if such diversity may play a crucial role in human-computer interaction especially in our small world. In the context of Human-Computer Confluence [5], we introduce in this paper a conceptual framework developing a bridge between set and perception theories to support computing with perceptions [6–8].

2   Perceptions, Concepts and Sets

Epistemologists have proposed various theories of what perception is and how we perceive reality, i.e., the outside world. The three main perception schools [4] are Naïve realism, Representative realism and Idealism. The Naïve realism is an Arestotelian theory, where we directly perceive the world as it is; i.e. things are what they seem, whereas Representative realism is an indirect realist theory of perception considering that real objects are only perceived indirectly, through intermediate representations, called ideas or sense data, in our consciousness. The third school is defended by George Berkeley who is persuaded by the thought that we have direct access only to our experiences of the world, and not to the world itself: to be is to be perceived.

Humans perceive objects and concepts like Car, Children, Animals, Flower, Brid, etc., where a concept C can be defined a set of individually necessary contraints for being a C. Concepts are the basic elements of thoughts generally identified with mental representations, with abilities, or with abstract objects [12–14]. Different approaches and methods that have been developed to conceptualise and represent "concepts" [15]. Formally, a concept or a classe of physical or mental objects can be represented by a set. The characteristic (membership) function of a set X, denoted 1_X, can take on only two values 0 and 1, and consequently, $1_X(x) = 1$ or 0 according as x does or does not belong to X. However, several classes of objects encountred in the real world reveal the fallacy of this assumption because such objects have not precise criteria. Hence the need to replace the boolean membership with a continuum of grades of membership [16]. Using fuzzy sets, L. A. Zadeh has introduced, in his paper [17], a computational theory of perception considering that perceptions are intrinsically imprecise and stressed the need of "a methodology in which the objects of computation are perceptions - perceptions of time, distance, form, direction, color, shape, truth, likelihood, intent, and other attributes of physical and mental objects". More recently, Z. Pawlak introduces Rough sets to express vagueness based on sets boundary regions [18,19].

3   Accessible Sets and Computing with Perceptions

At the present time, we are living in a small world allowing persons to share information and experiences even if they have different perceptions of the world. Consequently, in addition to data and knowledge, the perception will play an increasingly important role in our modern life. In fact, machines have to processes data broadcasted from different regions of the world and have to behave in a personalized way [20]. during the interaction with persons that perceive the world differently.

Let U be the universe of objects, I the set of observers, and (U, I) is the perception space. Each observer $i \in I$ has his own perception function $f_i : \mathcal{P}(U) \rightarrow \mathcal{P}(U)$, where $\mathcal{P}(U)$ is the power set of U and $f_i(X)$ is the perception of $X \in \mathcal{P}(U)$ by the observer i.

Definition 1 (Ternary relation $\in_i$). *Given a perception space (U, I), an element $x \in U$ is perceived, by the observer i, to be a member of the set $X \in \mathcal{P}(U)$, denoted $x \in_i X$, where*

$$x \in_i X \Leftrightarrow x \in f_i(X). \tag{1}$$

Definition 2 (Accessible set). *Given a perception space (U, I), a set $X \in \mathcal{P}(U)$ is said accessible, in the perception space (U, I), if and only if,*

$$f_i(X) = X \tag{2}$$

holds for each observer $i \in I$.

Perception functions are defined according to the three main perception schools developed in epistemology [4], which are Naïve realism, Representative realism and Idealism.

Following an algebraic approach, we have defined three main classes of perception functions denoted NR, RR and I, which correspond respectively to the main perception schools, i.e., Naïve Realism (NR), Representative Realism (RR) and Idealism (I). These classes cover the pessimestic, optimistic, doubtful and ignorant perceptions.

Unlike elementary perceptions, shared perceptions are alternative representations of a set X taking into account its perception by different observers.

Definition 3 (Minimal shared perception). *binarytreeNode Let U be the universe of objects, $X \subset U$, I the index set of observers, f_i the elementary perception of the observer i and $\mathbb{Q}_I(X) = (f_i(X))_{i \in I}$ is the perception of X. The set of minimal shared perception of X, denoted $\widehat{\mathbb{Q}}_I(X)$, is defined as follows :*

$$\widehat{X} \in \widehat{\mathbb{Q}}_I(X) \Leftrightarrow (\forall i \in I, \widehat{X} \cap f_i(X) \neq \emptyset) \wedge (\forall Y \subset \widehat{X}, \exists i \in I, Y \cap f_i(X) = \emptyset) \,. \quad (3)$$

Definition 4 (Space of consistent shared perceptions). *the space of consistent shared perceptions considering the set of observers I, is the sub-lattice defined by the interval $[\cap\{Y \in \widehat{\mathbb{Q}}_I(X)\}, \cup\{Y \in \widehat{\mathbb{Q}}_I(X)\}]$*

Algorithm 1. CSPS Algorithm

1: Input: The perception of X, i.e., $\mathbb{Q}_I(X) = (f_i(X))_{i \in I}$
2: Onput: The consistent shared perception space, i.e, $(CSPS, \preceq)$
3: Initialized parameters: $CSPS = \{f_i(X) : i \in I\}$
4: **repeat**
5:     $CSPSold = CSPS$
6:     $A = \{X \cup Y : X, Y \in CSPS\}$
7:     $B = \{X \cap Y : X, Y \in CSPS\}$
8:     $CSPS = CSPS \cup A \cup B$
9: **until** Convergence: $CSPS = CSPSold$
Ensure: the Consistent Shared Perception Space $(CSPS, \preceq)$.

How to compute these shared perceptions space? To answer this question we represent the perception of a set X by the hypergraph $\mathcal{H}_I(X) = (\mathcal{V}_I(X), \mathcal{E}_I(X))$, where the set of its nodes is $\mathcal{V}_I(X) = \cup_{i \in I}\{f_i(X)\}$ and $\mathcal{E}_I(X) = \{f_i(X) : i \in I\}$ is the set of its hyperedges.

Proposition 1 (Minimal shared perception). *Let $X \subset U$ a set of objects, I a finite subset of $\mathbb{N}$ and $F = \{f_i : i \in I\}$ a set of observers. The perception function of X, i.e. $\mathbb{Q}_I(X)$ is represented by the hypergraph $\mathcal{H}_I(X) = (\mathcal{V}_I(X), \mathcal{E}_I(X))$, than the set of its minimal transverses, denoted $MinTr(\mathcal{H}_I(X)$, corresponds to the set of minimal shared perception: $\widehat{\mathbb{Q}}_I(X) = MinTr(\mathcal{H}_I(X))$.*

4 The Wedding Dress Problem

Consider a girl who is getting married, how she can choose her wedding dress? Instead of using e-commerce search engines, we propose an application based on perceptions of her friends in social media like Facebook or Instagram. Here are the main steps of the process: (1) The girl chooses dresses for which she is hesitant, (2) She share these selected dresses on the wall of her social media, (3) Her friends select the ones they prefer and return their feedback (perceptions), (4) the shared perceptions is than computed, (5) the girl browses and filters dresses in the space $CSPS$ and (6) return back to (2) except if the girl considers it remains only few dresses. After that, she has to decide considering different criteria like the price, delivery of the dress, etc. In this problem, the human-machine interaction is not guided by an optimization algorithm, but humans exchange their perceptions in an iterative process, whereas computers compute the space of shared perceptions. In the following section we illustrate this processing using an example:

- (1) At the begining, the girl who is getting married selects a list of wedding dresses she is interested, and she is hesitant. Let us assume for example that this list is represented by the set

$$X = \{1, 5, 6, 7, 10, 11, 12, 13, 17, 21, 24, 26, 28, 31, 101, 102, 103\}$$

- (2) Next, she share these selected dresses on the wall of her social media like Facebook considering
- (3) Her friends select the ones they prefer and return their feedback (perceptions). For example, consider that her five friends A, B, C, D and E return the following answers:
  - $A = \{12, 21, 24\}$
  - $B = \{1, 10, 13, 21, 31\}$
  - $C = \{6, 10, 17\}$
  - $D = \{1, 7, 21, 26, 31, 101, 102\}$
  - $E = \{10, 6, 7, 11, 1, 5, 28, 103\}$
- (4) Next, we the shared perceptions are computing leading a set containing 70 minimal shared perceptions $Bd_*(X)$ that includes for example the flowing sets $\{1021\}, \{621\}, \{1012101\}, \{11217\}, \{1112131726\}, \{512131726\}, ...\}$.
- (5) The algorithm CSPS is than applied using is applied $Bd_*(X)$ to define the consistent shared perception space $(CSPS, \preceq)$.
- (6) the girl who is getting married browse the $CSPS$ space, filters the differents results and than the process returnback to the step (2) except if the girl considers that they remain only few dresses.

This example shows that the perception of the concept "Best Weeding Dress" is plural and diverse. The search task can not be resolved only using the classical human-machine interaction supported by search engine and e-business systems, but this interaction is guided by the perception of friends, the computation of the space CSPS and the intraction Human-Human, which are of prime importance.

Please note that the accessibility notion is related to the perception and can best be summarized as follows: *to be accessible is to be perceived*, which is weaker than the Berkeley's idealism, i.e *to be is to be perceived*, see [3] for more details on the work of George Berkeley.

5   Conclusion

In this paper we propose a conceptual set framework based on a perception theory where the main question about the role of perception of the world in human-machine interaction. Humans may have different perceptions of the world, whereas computers have only descriptions which are more syntactic than semantic. We introduce a new line of research that make a bridge between perception and set theories is introduced, i.e accessible sets, where the accessibility is related to the perception and can be summarized as follows "to be accessible is to be perceived". This perception is more weak than Berkeley's idealism, where objects are nothing more than our experiences of them, i.e. "to be is to be perceived". Finally, our proposal can also be seen as an attempt to define a computational theory of perceptions which can be used as a basis for integrating the diversity of perceptions in human-machine interactions.

References

1. Descartes, R.: Discourse on Method and Meditations on First Philosophy, 4th edn., p. 128. Hackett Publishing Company, Indianapolis (1999)
2. McCarthy, J.: The philosophy of AI and the AI of philosophy. Philos. Inf. **12**, 711–740 (2008)
3. Berkeley, G.: The works of George Berkeley, Bishop of Cloyne. In: Luce, A.A., Jessop, T.E. (eds.) vol. 9, Thomas Nelson and Sons, London, pp. 1948–1957 (1954)
4. Beck, L.W.: Secondary quality. J. Philos. **43**(22), 599–610 (1946)
5. Ferscha, A.: A research agenda for human computer confluence. In: Gaggioli, A., Ferscha, A., Riva, G., Dunne, S., Viaud-Delmon, I. (eds.) Human Computer Confluence Transforming Human Experience Through Symbiotic Technologies, pp. 7–17. DeGruyter Open, Berlin (2016)
6. Kirakowski, J., O'Donnell, P., Yiu, A.: The perception of artificial intelligence as "Human" by computer users. In: Jacko, J.A. (ed.) HCI 2007. LNCS, vol. 4552, pp. 376–384. Springer, Heidelberg (2007). https://doi.org/10.1007/978-3-540-73110-8_40
7. Tung, F.-W., Sato, K., Deng, Y.-S., Lin, T.-Y.: A cross-cultural study on the perception of sociability within human-computer interaction. In: Aykin, N. (ed.) IDGD 2009. LNCS, vol. 5623, pp. 135–144. Springer, Heidelberg (2009). https://doi.org/10.1007/978-3-642-02767-3_15
8. Haazebroek, P., Hommel, B.: Towards a computational model of perception and action in human computer interaction. In: Duffy, V.G. (ed.) ICDHM 2009. LNCS, vol. 5620, pp. 247–256. Springer, Heidelberg (2009). https://doi.org/10.1007/978-3-642-02809-0_27
9. Stephanidis, C., Salvendy, G.: Seven HCI grand challenges. Int. J. Hum. Comput. Interact. **35**(14), 1229–1269 (2019)
10. Licklider, J.C.R.: Man-computer symbiosis. IRE Trans. Hum. Factors Electron. **HFE-1**(1), 4–11 (1960). https://doi.org/10.1109/THFE2.1960.4503259
11. Cohen, P.R., Feigenbaum, E.A. (eds.): The Handbook of Artificial Intelligence, vol. 3. William Kaufmann, Los Alto (2014)
12. Fodor, J.: Psychosemantics: The Problem of Meaning in the Philosophy of Mind. MIT Press, Cambridge (1987)

13. Kenny, A.: Concepts, brains, and behaviour. Grazer Philosophische Studien **81**(1), 105–113 (2010)
14. Peacocke, C.: A Study of Concepts. MIT Press, Cambridge (1992)
15. Mechelen, I.V., Hampton, J., Michalski, R.S., Theuns, P. (eds.): Categories and Concepts: Theoretical Views and Inductive Data Analysis. Academic Press, New York (1993)
16. Zadeh, L.A.: Fuzzy sets. Inf. Control **8**, 338–353 (1965)
17. Zadeh, L.A.: A new direction in AI - toward a computational theory of perceptions. AI Mag. **22**(1), 73–84 (2001)
18. Pawlak, Z.: Rough sets. Int. J. Comput. Inform. Sci. **11**, 341–356 (1982)
19. Pawlak, Z.: Rough Sets, Theoretical Aspect of Reasoning about Data. Kluwer Academic Pubilishers, Dordrecht (1991)
20. Bibri, S.E.: The human face of ambient intelligence: cognitive, emotional, affective, behavioral and conversational aspects. In: Khalil, I. (ed.) Atlantis Ambient and Pervasive Intelligence, vol. 9. Atlantis Press, Paris (2015). https://doi.org/10.2991/978-94-6239-130-7

HCI Design Education at Hunan University:
A Practical Case in Chinese Design Schools

Hao Tan$^{(\boxtimes)}$ and Jialing Li$^{(\boxtimes)}$

School of Design, Hunan University, Yuelu Mountain, Changsha 410082, China
{htan,jialingli}@hnu.edu.cn

Abstract. HCI design education is rapidly developing in China, and HCI design and interaction design are in the process of becoming the main areas of specialty in Chinese design schools. This paper presents an overview of the HCI design education available at the School of Design in Hunan University as a practice case in China. We focus on the HCI design education frameworks, curricula, aspects and features at Hunan University, which lead to challenges and opportunities for our school. We discuss these and outline some of the methodological approaches we employ to deal with them, along with some examples of our education practices.

Keywords: HCI design education · Hunan university

1 Introduction

As one of the leading design schools in China, the School of Design in Hunan University can trace its history of HCI design education back to 2001, when the first master's program – usability and interface design in CAD systems - began to recruit postgraduate students [1]. In 2006, "HCI design" became one of the four education areas, called "education modules," in the new undergraduate program [2]. After eight years of development and teaching practices, we had built a relatively mature curricula structure and four aspects of HCI design education within Hunan University that became our design education features. Currently, HCI design education is the largest education module of the School of Design in Hunan University. In 2014, 72 undergraduate students graduated in HCI design, which accounted for 55% of all graduated students.

In the paper, we will introduce our curricula and discuss the four aspects and features of HCI education available at Hunan University.

2 HCI Design in Undergraduate Design Education Program

HCI design is one module of the Undergraduate Design Education Program (UDEP) in Hunan University (Fig. 1). UDEPU is a flexible and multi-disciplinary undergraduate program in design that enables students to customize their specialty and degree. There are four education modules: Transport design (T), Product Design (P), HCI Design (I) and Communication Design (C). Students can choose to specialize in one of the four modules

C. Stephanidis et al. (Eds.): HCII 2020, CCIS 1293, pp. 90–97, 2020.
https://doi.org/10.1007/978-3-030-60700-5_12

or combine any two in an interdisciplinary focus. Figure 2 shows the flexible combination between HCI design and communication design, in which students can follow the two education modules throughout the entire process of design module education.

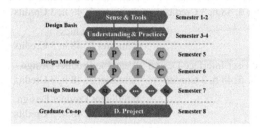

Fig. 1. Undergraduate design education program (UDEP) in hunan university.

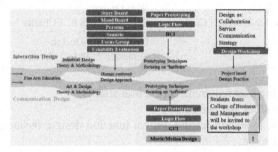

Fig. 2. Converge and combination between HCI design module and communication design module.

3 HCI Design Curricula

In HCI design curricula at Hunan University, there are eleven courses, including four key courses and seven elective courses. Table 1 shows the curricula structure of HCI design. The four key courses consist of Interaction Design Basis, Graphic User Interface Design, HCI Design and User Study. After finishing the key courses, students can select three elective HCI design courses from the seven available. The seven elective courses are HCI design practices in different fields or domains, which consist of Automotive User Interface Design, Motion Graphics, Wearable Product Design, Intelligent Product Design, Smart Home and Product Design, Web Design, and CAD System Design. In this section, we will introduce the four key courses and one elective course – Automotive User Interface Design.

3.1 Interaction Design Basis

"Interaction Design Basis" is the first course in the HCI design education module. The course introduces the process and methodology structure of HCI design and user experience design, which helps students understand the basic notion and sense of HCI design. Presented as an introduction to design practices, the contents of the course consist of:

Table 1. HCI design curricula structure.

Key courses	Elective courses
Interaction Design Basis Semester 6, 48 h, 3 Credits	Automotive User Interface Design Semester 7, 48 h, 3 Credits
	Motion Graphics Semester 7, 48 h, 3 Credits
Graphic User Interface Design Semester 6, 48 h, 3 Credits	Wearable Product Design Semester 7, 48 h, 3 Credits
	Intelligent Product Design Semester 7, 48 h, 3 Credits
HCI Design Semester 6, 48 h, 3 Credits	Smart Home and Product Design Semester 7, 48 h, 3 Credits
User Study Semester 6, 48 h, 3 Credits	Web Design Semester 7, 48 h, 3 Credits
	CAD System Design Semester 7, 48 h, 3 Credits

- Exploring/probing user requirements via user studies;
- Defining user profiles and personas;
- Concept Design, including feature design, function design, business model design, flow design and so on;
- Evaluating the business value, usability and feasibility of concepts (Fig. 3);
- Paper prototype design.

The course structure is shown in Fig. 4.

Fig. 3. Evaluate the business value of a concept in "Interaction Design Basis" course.

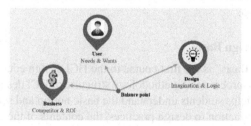

Fig. 4. Course structure of "Interaction Design Basis".

3.2   Graphic User Interface Design

"Graphic User Interface Design" focuses on designing mouse/touch-screen input and screen displays to teach students various types of GUI interactive design patterns and visualization methods (Fig. 5). In the course, students are taught to use design and development tools to build interactive prototypes based on different screens. In addition, the course emphasizes pattern transformation and innovation in different scenarios. Figure 6 shows an example of the course assignments: designing a new homepage of a mobile phone using the Chinese traditional culture element: partly hidden and partly visible, which was widely used in Chinese traditional drawing.

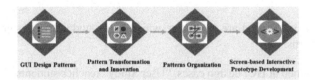

Fig. 5. Course structure of "Graphic User Interface Design".

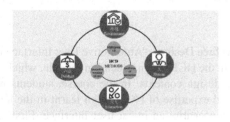

Fig. 6. An example of the course assignments of "Graphic User Interface Design" course.

HCI Design. "HCI Design" applies Human-Centered Design methodology and multimodal user interface technology to explore innovative HCI patterns (Fig. 7). The course introduces new human-computer interaction patterns, such as sound, lighting, gesture, touching, eye-movement and other interactions, and helps students to integrate them into a product design solution. At the same time, the course focuses on solving HCI problems in complex usage contexts and building interactive working demos or prototypes with development tools such as Arduino, Processing, Max/MSP, Kinect, LeapMotion and so on. Figure 8 shows a student assignment on sound analysis and design. In addition,

Fig. 7. Course structure of "HCI Design".

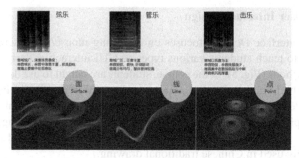

Fig. 8. Sound/music design and visualization in "HCI Design" course.

the aesthetics of interaction are our focus, which helps students to design "beautiful" interaction patterns.

User Study. Aimed at HCI design cases, "User Study" teaches students to choose suitable user study methods, conduct studies, analyze the research data and draw conclusions from studies to help the iteration design (Fig. 9). Figure 10 shows a usability study example from the course.

Fig. 9. Course structure of "User Study".

Fig. 10. Usability test in "User Study" course.

Automotive User Interface Design. "Automotive User Interface Design" is one of the seven elective courses in the HCI design education module, which are taught via design projects with practical design contexts. In the course, students need to integrate the knowledge, methods and expertise of HCI design learnt in the key courses and apply them to the new design scenario: an in-car user interface. First, a field study on cars is conducted to help students understand the drivers and passengers and find business opportunities. Then, interactive prototypes, including products and UIs, are built and tested in a driving simulation system. Finally, working demos with form, interaction and UI are "produced" by students and applied to a car. Figure 11 shows one of the working demos designed and developed by students and equipped in a car.

Fig. 11. Gesture-based HCI working demo equipped in car in "Automotive User Interface Design" course.

4 Discussion: Features of HCI Design Education at Hunan University

HCI design education at Hunan University has achieved initial success and positive impacts in Chinese internet and communication industries. For example, according to incomplete statistics from the National Education Steering Committee for Industrial Design in China, in 2013 and 2014, two top Chinese internet and communication companies – Alibaba.com and Huawei - recruited 31 HCI design students from Hunan University, which accounted for approximately 41% of all recruited graduating HCI design students in China. There are three aspects and features of our HCI design education culture and practices: (1) Localization and Internationalization; (2) Design-centered multidisciplinary education; and (3) Focusing on the aesthetics of interaction.

4.1 Localization and Internationalization

China is the largest and most complicated market in the world. The rapid development in internet and communication industries has created a huge demand for HCI designers. According to the user experience and interaction design industry's survey from IXDC China in 2014, approximately 57% of local internet and communication companies will recruit more HCI designers to match the increasing requirements of R&D [3]. The current HCI design education at Hunan University is thus mainly focused on fulfilling these requirements, which has resulted in our HCI design education becoming significantly focused on the user experience design field and the establishment of our HCI education features.

At the same time, we have built up an international design education platform, starting in 2001, in which HCI design education plays a key role. There are approximately 30 famous international companies, such as Microsoft, Google, Intel, Nokia, Samsung, Sony, Siemens, LG, GE, GM, Totota, Giugiaro Design, etc., and approximately 50 famous local global companies, such as Alibaba.com, Huawei, Haier, Tecent, etc., that provide HCI design projects, materials and teachers to our HCI design education. In addition, we have created good education cooperation and relationships with roughly 30 international design schools, such as Royal College of Art, Yale University, Politecnico Milano, Aalto University, RIT, University of Cincinnati, Ciba University, and so on.

4.2 Design-Centered Multidisciplinary Education

HCI design is multidisciplinary and the design expertise and knowledge from the fields of computer science, design, psychology and business have been increasingly integrated. We have created a design-centered interdisciplinary education system, in which designers play a key or leading role in the design and education process with students from other specialties. Firstly, the teachers of HCI design courses are from the fields of design, psychology, computer science, engineering, business and other arts, such as music, film and crafts. Additionally, all of the HCI design courses are open to all students from different specialties at Hunan University to foster a multidisciplinary design and study environment. We encourage these students, including design students and other majors, to customize their courses and degrees. There are two chances for them to change their degrees, in semesters 5 and 7. Furthermore, in semester 7, the HCI design education is conducted in a design studio, in which there are teachers, designers and researchers from different knowledge backgrounds based on the project needs. In addition, we also conduct design studies in the education process to identify defects and improve the quality of HCI design teaching.

4.3 Focusing on Aesthetics of Interaction

Aesthetics is an important attribute in the design domain and offers HCI design and research a new perspective that goes beyond the traditional use-oriented principles of HCI and usability [4]. We believe that aesthetics is one of the key areas of competitiveness in HCI design, in contrast to other specialties. In our HCI design education, the Aesthetic Attributes of Interactive System (AAIS) [5, 6] are adopted as a key education tool to help students understand, analyze, design and evaluate design objectives in an aesthetic manner. For example, "response speed" is one of the aesthetic attributes. Students in HCI courses need to learn how fast response speed is good for users' typical emotions. Often, a delayed response represents complicated and ambiguous interaction, while an instant response represents simple and clear interaction. In addition, we borrow knowledge and patterns from other art domains, such as dance, film and music, to help students create aesthetics in HCI design. Figure 12 contains photos showing how we teach students to design gesture interactions from dance and music. "Aesthetics of interaction" in HCI design education provides a strong tool for design students to use for creating breakthrough interactions, which are combined with the aesthetics of form/styling language as the design education DNA at Hunan University.

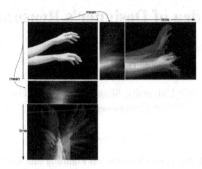

Fig. 12. Photos that students studied hand movements from dance and music in gesture interaction design.

5 Conclusion

In the paper, we introduce the HCI design education of the School of Design in Hunan University. Hunan University is one of the leading design schools in China, and is HCI design education practices are representative cases and valuable references to help HCI design educators worldwide understand the existing circumstances of HCI education in China.

Acknowledgements. The paper is supported by University-Industry Collaborative Education Program of China(201902005032) and National University Education Reform Research Program of China.

References

1. He, R.K., Ji, T., Yuan, X.: Global-competition-based design education patterns and Practices. In: Proceedings NIDEC, pp. 1–5. BIT Press (2013). (in Chinese)
2. He, R.K., Xiao, D.H., Yuan, X.: Experimental and practical teaching of art and design major in global perspectives. Exp. Technol. Manage. **27**(5), 1–4 (2010). (in Chinese)
3. IXDC. Reports on user experience and interaction design industry survey in 2014. http://wenku.baidu.com/view/57a3fb44a300a6c30d229f21.html
4. National education steering committee for industrial design of China. China design education yearbook (2014)
5. Udsen, L.E., Jørgensen, A.H.: The aesthetic turn: unravelling recent aesthetic approaches to human-computer interaction. Digital Creativity **16**(4), 205–216 (2005)
6. Wu, Y.M., Tan, H., Zhao, J.H.: An aesthetic perspective to explore aesthetic components of interactive system: a case study on music player. In: CHI 2014, pp. 2587–2592 (2014)

An Idea of Designer's Reasoning

Ye Wang[(⊠)]

Tongji University, Shanghai 200234, China
1710628@tongji.edu.cn

Abstract. In the International Congress on Planning and Design Theory, Horst Rittel supported a widespread dissatisfaction with the ability to design the worlds we live in and the vast scope of entities designed. Through facts and presenting clues, Rittel has an idea of designer's reasoning that Design is Subjective, a process as formation of judgement. The method of logic is occasional inferences during this process as Rittel believe, a 'philosophy' guiding a mode of conduct. Also, the conceivable that emerge during the process had no limits and influenced the understanding and direction of the final design. The human mind is fallible. Designer don't have choice as Rittel said. A manner problem of reasoning, perhaps. An idea of design reasoning in Rittel's work seems contrasts sharply with the ideas developed by Moholy-Nagy, Herbert Simon, and Raymond Williams. This article will trace the theme of reasoning across, indicating the points of difference that come with their different perspectives, thereby gaining more knowledge of the idea.

Keywords: Reasoning · Emotion · Argumentation · Historical analysis

1 Introduction

In the Congress on Planning and Design Theory, *Horst Rittel* supported a widespread dissatisfaction with the ability to design the *worlds* we live in and the vast scope of *entities* designed [1]. Through facts and presenting clues, Rittel has an idea of designer's reasoning that is *subjective*, a process as formation of *judgement*. The method of *logic* is *occasional inferences* during this process, a 'philosophy' guiding mode of conduct as he suggested. Also, the *conceivable* that emerge had *no limits* and influenced the *understanding* and direction of the final design. The human mind is *fallible*. Designer don't have choice as he said.

Although, for *Moholy*, it is the *knowledge and practices* that limited, the ability to *reason* and grasp which make the final design *fall very far,* due to the truth of *Nature principle* that has been misunderstood, a function problem [2]. With the method of *logic* analysis and synthesis the functional elements through the development, He believes that the designer do have a choice. However, the answer comes from the *emotion channel* of the designer, not as Rittel believe there are always *worry* in this *Mental Operations*, but *a possible* alternative may appear only before the execution takes place.

Although, the possibility for *Simon is generating* [3]. Most design resources go into discovering or generating those alternatives. The inquiry of the theme turned to

© Springer Nature Switzerland AG 2020
C. Stephanidis et al. (Eds.): HCII 2020, CCIS 1293, pp. 98–105, 2020.
https://doi.org/10.1007/978-3-030-60700-5_13

the *design process itself* to finding an *acceptable solution*. The design process appears as three subprocesses but *thoroughly intermingled*. There is no place in choice for the designer as Simon believe, because the *bounded* of *human rationality*.

The dialogue has created contradictions and respective positions. Although with underdetermination of theory, the theme was all pushed to the Social, a historical context. *Williams* believes the theme must identify as the dynamic interrelations as a *System* [4]. We must add historically varied and variable elements to see such a relationship, *a unified idea* as he believes. The analysis of such complexity must not be static as select supporting and exclude 'secondary' evidence (Fig. 1).

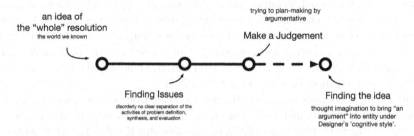

Fig. 1. The Reasoning of Designers by Horst Rittel

An idea in Rittel's work seems contrasts sharply with the ideas developed by *Moholy*, *Simon*, and *Williams*. This article will trace the theme of reasoning across, indicating the points of difference that come with their perspectives, thereby gaining more knowledge of the reasoning.

2 Games of Primitives

Rittel noted the future of design as *Science of Design* [5, p. 7]. We will accurately determine that science has a unique opinion in design activities. However, *Herbert Simon* believes this *"Pretentious"* idea of design at least shows that there are truths that can be *formulated and communicated* [3, p. 245]. The 'general truths' similar but not seems to be equivalent to 'Commonalities'. The latter pays more attention to the intersection of the mind search between the design actions of multivariate objects that may not be easily described. The former attempts to sort out the form of the process that can be conceptualized or scientifically depicted based on its existence, form or criteria known to the design. To verify the rationality of this hypothesis, considering that the reasoning of the designer could be a process of communication, probably the best choice. We can start with a process (or model) of information technology.

After Information source is reforming into messages in the initial phase of Communication, the signal generated by the Transmitter projected to another receiver via a logical channel. The transformation process is all about encoding and decoding. Imagine the brain as the machine of information Transmitter, as processing memories by encoding [6]. For the biological brain, there are short-term and long-term memories.

Following Simon's inquiry, we can see an exhaustive analysis of this brain condition. The scope of entities designed to be processed is much broader than 7–11 Plus or Minus Two, which the maximum limit in most cases [7]. However, the continuous and large amount of information, due to the low computational power of the brain, the conclusions that have been formed, and the memories that are currently being formed through cognition, and the necessary attention, will highly unstable due to the influence of "Noise Source" [6]. Similar judgments can be found in *Gestalt* and *Information Entropy*.

Under the influence of evolution, to continue to store, the brain has embraced a new strategy. Non-essential will removed, only the index to the information being held in memory [3, p. 4] and stored as commonality, characteristics, or *chunking* in long-term and stored as commonality, characteristics, or chunking in long-term. Those limited Memory, Information and Computing Power, The *Primitives*, is a designer's reasoning that begins within a process of gathering and combining. Simon believes that the designer starts with some *primitives*. Design is a game of combinatorics that played on these, which is the very heart of creation, hence of design [3, p. 247].

Although it is not intended to turn the inquiry to the Cognitive Science, a peek will reveal colossal instability and loss seem inevitable. The signs we find may not be the truth, but the fragments influence of *epistemic freedom* that Rittel suggested that knows, believes, fears, desires affected [5, p. 6]. 'Cognitive Style' is fragmentary and subjective.

Simon's inquiry formed the underline elements that help to identify and reforming that idea Rittel persuasive. We should now be able to assume the reason that the problem in the scope of Entity Designed and the knowledge diverse has become an essential issue. The creatures of bounded rationality [3, p. 3], us, the Critical Phenomena is revealed in the process of cognition of the world we living in. Simon also makes an argument about the process should see as a temporal flow and identify the underline element of one as Flexibility, novelty, and Emerge. Yet, the inquiry of general truth is restraint by only using *footnotes*. Simon suggested that we have seen that the design process is itself a temporal flow, a continuous sequence of decisions with a past, a present, and a future. Flexibility in the design process allows new knowledge to be used whenever it emerges, early or late [3, p. 254].

Also, some primitives that designer can begin with similarity to an idea of the "whole" resolution, but the difference is the primitive as a residual argument combined with those limited, as the process of converting information into messages. The word "information" is used must not be confused at all with meaning [6]. From the combinatorial process to the idea, the designer needs more than process and materials.

3 Scientific Intuition

Moholy Nagy cites 'Form follows Function' the statement of Louis Sullivan in 1947, which was easily misunderstood and distorted as a commercial slogan. In the article *Design Potentialities*, the inquiry began with a description of the French Scientist *Raoul France*: 'Every process has its necessary form, which always results in functional forms [2, p. 82].' As nature principle, when applies to human technology, however, *falls very far short of the optimum* [2, p. 2]. The same circumstance can be found through Darwin's *natural combinatorial game* [3, p. 247]. The process of combining the meaning seemly can not only by gathering information without analysis-one natural with the researcher, like Mathematics, Sociology, Phenomenology and Design Research. Also, the cognitive process begins with Combinatorial into *index, signs* or *symbols*, the *chunking* I mean. As a process of reasoning, analysis answer the questions about what the object is. The *digestion* process breaks down the object into Material, Manner, Form, and Function (or Purpose), Elements or Components. These are Fragments of *the Original Four Causes*[1].

Multi-methods in reasoning achieves the result. For instance, the *Deduction* proves the facts based on two or more premises, which mainly used in mathematics and logic, also the process of understanding what and how to result-the *Induction*, indicating operability, inferring general conclusions through a series of observations. Mainly used in the natural sciences and social sciences. Understand what and result to get a possible how. The reasoning methods used in the analysis process are not singular but multiplicative and dynamic. The goal of designer's reasoning is to see the essence. In order to form the problem from analyzed, synthesis plays a critical role in a "new whole" and defines meaning.

Comparisons appear from both the synthesis and the combinatorial in the critical positions of the cognitive "assembly" process. The two actions are consistent, or the combinatorial can be identified as the collective name for analysis and synthesis. The conclusion is uncertain.

The issue of such primitives will also be inseparable from analysis and synthesis. It will be an essential component in any action that produces meaning, among the primitives and the *"games"* that combine them. Unfortunately, in the process of synthesis, the designer always finds that not everything that we know or feel can be verbalized by a language which uses logic and reason as its main characteristics and no logical or epistemological constraints or rules which would prescribe which of the various meaningful steps to take next [5, p. 5].

The unrealistic answer to this new possibility of scientific synthesis in designer's reasoning comes from *the intuition of the designer* [2, p. 87]. Still, we must not be confused with *inspiration*, the artist's vocabulary. The word *intuition* we used means insight and sensitivity, guides for structure, proportion and form. The choices are not based upon interchangeable considerations of the single elements per se but the relationships which are created by the single as parts of an entity that produces the new meaning, the 'right' solution [2, p. 88]. It is the function or purpose of synthesis and combinatorial to see 'the whole' of new possibility in the design action, to leading the form. Only if it works well, the designer's reasoning may no longer be the primitives.

There is no place in choice for the designer's surprise at the unexpected novelties he or she creates by combining and recombining the primitives. With this in mind, the *intuition* that appears in the *Combinatorial* action seems unstable and irritable, the result of the finding action occurring in the designer's reasoning will be another alternative, a Judgement, or others new possibilities that *can be realized* [3, p. 246]. Combinatorial

---

[1] From Wikipedia: The "four causes" are elements of an influential principle in Aristotelian thought whereby explanations of change or movement are classified into four fundamental types of answer to the question "why?". https://en.wikipedia.org/wiki/Four_causes.

as Nature Principle also seems not working in artifacts, or more directional, the idea of Designer's Reasoning.

Synthesis symbols of limitation and causes of cognitive processes and the ability to reason and grasp that make Design issues seem are powerless. Though, Simon does say that the *novelty* can emerge under this circumstance [3, p. 247].

Still, the impact of the alternatives produced and the choice active in the process of design inquiry, as well as the perceived flexibility of such seemingly inevitable crises, is determined to be the inquiry focus and does not explore the meaning of these novelties. We may see the mistakenly that Nagy's inquiry believes that the scientific method will make the social sciences and the humanities intelligible and solvable, thus ignoring the functional elements of society and humanity, especially those that are illogic. Also, the problems with the designer's reasoning not only occur in the analysis of practice and process by Simon and Nagy.

4 Persuasive Imagination and Staged Process

In the article, *The Reasoning of Designers*, Horst Rittel effects two more facts. Shipping imagination that Designed into the physical world will not be a matter of design itself only but subjected to technical possibilities, commercial viability, product availability, and easy to receive interference from "noise". That is a "Solving" problem that *can be realized*. In another, the problem of transferring the 'Cognitive Style', an idea or concept, to another will be the problem of 'Persuasion' as a process of communication. We must see that the purpose of all communication is to influence the conduct of the receiver [6]. It is bidirectional, not linear. The new reasoning may be seen, from the cognitive process of the audience (or user), tries to see the imagination or idea passed by the speaker (or designer) and feedback the experience. The idea of designer's Reasoning is attempting to find the channel for the conversation.

The specific commonality or the general truth may not merely the process and methods or solve the technical problem but the social impact especially. Nagy argue that the function is not only the work to be accomplished as mechanical task, but must also fulfill *biological*, *psychophysical* and *sociological requirements* as well [2, p. 2].

Though, Rittel's idea of designer's reasoning was isolating structures of facts to become more numerous, somehow, which avoids the multiple influence factors and ignores the more comprehensive whole and details.

To see the specific commonality in actions, we must complete the shape of the form. However, the design problem will be able to realize continually reformulated during the process of design that thoroughly intermingled [3, p. 252]. At the end of the process, not only the alternatives and the idea we may find but some new goals- the criteria and constraints to be satisfied- emerge also [3, p. 251]. Those defined are also unstable due to "noise" waiting to be reforming. They converted a possible source of an idea of the "whole" resolution of the problem at the beginning of the design. We may wisely recognize that the process is not a single direction as initially assumed. In refactoring and novel, the form of the disorder contains a myriad of circuits. Even then, it will not be a *hover*; there is also inception and fulfillment. The specific commonality must not the process form itself only, but the purpose (or *spirit*) behind it.

Not just the Biological and Psychophysical, the design also needs to *satisfy* Social impact, and the core of society is culture. In the article *Dominant, Residual and Emergent, Raymond Williams* devoted to the discussion of culture and systems and pointed out the common problem of disconnection from reality. He suggested that culture discussion should not be reckless into an *epochal analysis*, but *staged in historical* [7, Ch. 8] p. 121.

Culture on the path of the times must have the current *Dominant* power, effectively seized the ruling definition of the social, leading and producing certain forms, meanings, and values; *Residual*, an element of the past may alternative or oppositional form Dominant, as effectively formed in the past, but it is still active in the cultural process and an active element of the present. A future continues to be created: *Emergent*, new meanings and values, new practices, new relationships and kinds of relationships are continually being created [4, p. 123] (Fig. 2).

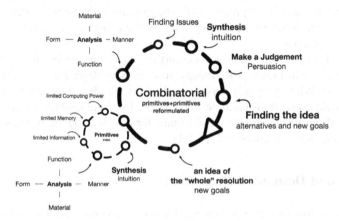

Fig. 2. Cycle of designer's reasoning as combinatorial

In itself process, Emergent and in its repeated confusion with the facsimiles and novelties of the incorporated phase. Unstable but retrospective. Willem's inquiry is not fragmented but dynamic, alternative or oppositional, Mutual influence and creation in the historical state. 'New' Emergent is not a product of the future but also the present and the past. Into the historical dynamics, we may see the designer's reasoning will also have a historical extension, past, present, and future.

What should not be forgotten is novelty can emerge, probably probabilistic and continuous. Still, no place in choice for the designer. Novelties seem to be the key to reasoning, then Willem unveiled the ambiguous: emergent in the strict sense, rather than merely novel. The former does not fully understand the manner and form to know what it is, but a novel is closely related to the combinatorial process of primitive. The conservative name should be an alternative or new gold. In confidence, it can be a new possibility. However, there is a vast gap that has a connection exists between them, hidden in the relationship between *novel* and *emergent*.

With the help of cognition, analysis, and synthesis, a Combinatorial in the present forming the Dominant, about what could be known in particular professional domain, effectively seized the ruling definition of the primitive and trying to give the specific experiences, meanings, and values. This action may also arise in the past "novel". An idea of the "whole" resolution we have at the beginning of reasoning could also form the Residual. As effectively formed in the past, but still active, alternative or oppositional, or we say "new" gold. The alternatives may open any further iterative search, and gold from the past will influence the present inquiry about possibilities and problems we have not realized it yet. It also could be Emergent in the future. It may arise from the search for the new gold, or from the pursuit of others.

What must be cautious is the interrelationship, symbiosis and exclusion, between Dominant, Residual, and Emergent. If the purpose of designer's reasoning is to find the new meanings and values, new practices, new relationships and kinds of relationships are continually being created, the "truth" Emergent. Then we need to see the threat behind the situation, must know, People without clear orientation are often confused by either sentiment or "novelty" propaganda [2, p. 10], we need to prevent the blind nostalgia and the overconfidence of the present. Only the past and the present that determines the future, and for the future of the inquiry, even an "imagination", is to verify or correct the present and the past.

Additionally, in Willem's inquiry, focus on the macroscopic perspective of the impact of cultural facts on historical. The strategy may easily be degraded into an ideological and schismatic. When we put it into the analysis of the idea of designer's reasoning, its voice should come from multiple dimensions, from the contacts of cultures, and peoples, and discipline to provide the discipline for investigating the systems of things, of experiences, and of discourses [1, p. 281].

5 An Idea of Designer's Reasoning

When we value this idea as a persuasive, Designer Reasoning such a vast world, the inquiry will no longer be static, occurs between the past and the present, between alternatives and between new goals and designers' reasoning to see Unifying ideas infinitely close to "the truth." Even if the dialogue obstructs the primitive and curtness of the one and knowledge.

We must not ignore the impact of science and give up research on methods and processes; even the reasoning is fragile, or we realize the limitations of evolution. However, the creation of technology and the study of science will make up for it. Also, the combined process from cognition will continue to advance in disorder. The functional elements come from the designer's intuition. However, we cannot readily assume that the only answer will become the truth of the idea of Designer's Reasoning. When we perceive this as a product, it will have some underline elements that must be satisfied, a form of internal impulses and external factors, and the manner will self-derivative due to the constant changes of the inquiry object. What affects these facts changes is the purpose of the inquiry as a unified idea. We should be aware that the goals that design needs to meet are not only from biology, physics but also society (Fig. 3).

When we think of this idea as a whole, we must not assume that the whole discussion object is only the ontology. The idea is to try to find the truth both in knowledge, in culture and the community. It may change the function or purpose of the designer's reasoning as original intention. Then, the more comprehensive under-standing of the idea of the

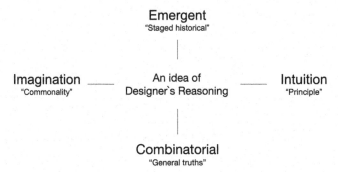

Fig. 3. An idea of designer's reasoning

"whole" resolution that Emergent at the new beginning of Designer's reasoning, may become the key to designing a closer to the "right" solution and far more significance than finding novels.

References

1. McKeon, R.: Future of the liberal arts. In: McKeon, R.P. (eds.) Freedom and History and Other Essays: An Introduction to the Thought of Richard MacKeon. University of Chicago Press, Chicago (1990)
2. Miller, George A.: The magical number seven, plus or minus two: some limits on our capacity for processing information. Psychol. Rev. **63**(2), 81–97 (1956). https://doi.org/10.1037/h0043158
3. Nagy, M..: Design Potentialities. In: Zucker, P. (eds.) New Architecture and City Planning, pp. 675–87. Philosophical Library, New York (1944)
4. Rittel, H.: The reasoning of designers. In: Protzen, J.P., Harris, D.J. (eds.) The Universe of Design: Horst Rittel's Theories of Design and Planning, pp. 171–179. Routledge, London (2010). https://doi.org/10.4324/9780203851586
5. Simon, H.A.: Problem forming, problem finding, and problem solving in design. In: Collen, A., Gasparski, W.W. (eds.) Design and Systems: General Applications of Methodology, pp. 245–257. Transaction Publishers, Piscataway (1995)
6. Weaver, W.: The mathematics of communication. Sci. Am. **181**(1), 11–15 (1949)
7. Williams, R.: Dominant, residual, and emergent. In: Williams, R., Williams, R.H. (eds.) Marxism and Literature, 2nd edn., pp. 121–127. Oxford University Press, New York (1977)

Mobile and Multimodal Interaction

Littlebits Versus Makey Makey with Scratch: An User Perception for Tangible User Interfaces

Lucas Barreiro Agostini$^{(\boxtimes)}$ ⓘ and Tatiana Aires Tavares ⓘ

Universidade Federal de Pelotas, Pelotas, RS, Brazil
{lbagostini,tatiana}@inf.ufpel.edu.br

Abstract. The main goal of this paper is to compare how different commercial systems with tangible user interfaces (TUIs) [11,12] impact the user's experience when targeting the same application. Two commercial systems were compared. The first one uses the littlebits Synth Kit [3] and the second one uses Scratch [18] and Makey Makey [5,14] together, connected to a computer. The tested application was a MIDI keyboard that was implemented using both systems. The applications were designed with the same functions even with different interfaces provided by both systems. Usability was tested with the intent of assuring that both systems had similar functionalities and, with this aspect in mind, focus primarily on the UX itself. To test the Usability, we used the System Usability Score [2], while the UX was tested using Attrakdiff [8]. As a result of the case study, it was possible to realize that, considering the user's point of view, the Littlebits Synth Kit is better than the combination of Makey Makey with Scratch. To prove so, the usability was analyzed and, since they were similar, it was possible to compare the UX, which lead to better results by the littlebits than its counterpart, the system with Makey Makey.

Keywords: Tangible User Interface · Hardware design · User evaluation

1 Introduction

Human-Computer Interaction (HCI) is a multidisciplinary area that is concerned with providing design guidelines to developers who create applications to users' needs and expectations. In this process, the HCI includes the **project**, the **implementation**, and **evaluation** of the interaction between users and the computer systems [15].

The difference for the applications based on **Tangible User Interfaces (TUI)** is the presence of physical objects as elements of interaction. In a scenario of tangible interactions, there is the object and a set of movements or actions that the user can perform with this physical element that recognizes this interaction and reacts visually or about the object itself or the environment [11,12].

ⓒ Springer Nature Switzerland AG 2020
C. Stephanidis et al. (Eds.): HCII 2020, CCIS 1293, pp. 109–115, 2020.
https://doi.org/10.1007/978-3-030-60700-5_14

Hence, if in a TUI the physical element is the input and output device of the interface, it can be assumed that the interaction process is more intuitive and natural for the user with a real-world analogy [10].

Interacting in a TUI application is different from a GUI, it is suggested that the evaluation methods currently used regularly for common graphical interfaces may not fit fully into the evaluation of a tangible application.

The objective of this paper is to compare two commercial systems using both usability [4,16] and user experience (UX) [6].

The next section presents a theoretical background about Tangible Interaction and system evaluation; Section 3 presents and discusses the results of the comparison between those systems; Section 4 discusses the results and main contribution of this paper which is to show the potential of developing specific hardware to TUIs [1].

2   Background

2.1   Tangible Interaction

Tangible Interaction is a term suggested by Hornecker and Buur to present a comprehensive field than TUI, considering social interaction through tangible applications, thus including the issue of interaction with the environment and body gesticulation [9].

Jacob et al. (2008) brought the term Reality-Based Interaction to conceptualize new user interaction styles for user skills. This context suggests that interaction with digital information is closer to interaction with the real world [13].

Reality-Based Interaction has four concepts:

- **Intuitive Physics**: the user's perception of the real world;
- **Body consciousness**: the user's notion of his body, and the ability to coordinate his gestures;
- **Environmental awareness**: the user's perception of the environment around him and his ability to interact with it;
- **Social understanding**: the perception that the user has with other users in the same environment, the communication between them and the ability to perform tasks together to achieve the same goal.

2.2   System Evaluation

The development of TUI applications is a new process and recent research is emerging that discusses a way to evaluate this type of interface. Usually, the methods that are being applied for the development of TUIs are the same methods for UI already used in daily life. Therefore, it is probable that there are specific evaluation criteria for tangible interfaces, since this is an unconventional approach to human-computer communication.

Although some research was done about this topic, many different approaches are still in use, like [6,7] which discuss different criteria for selection of instruments and evaluation methods.

The most used methods amongst the scientific community are both usability and UX. While usability focuses on the functionalities of the system per se, UX has an approach that takes into account the user perception of both the system and the interaction itself. In this paper both methods were used, usability had the purpose of granting that both systems had similar functionalities while UX was used to analyze which system was better, according to the user perceptions.

After deciding the methods used, the instruments were decided, taking into consideration the target audience of the tests and the availability of the instrument. To test both methods questionnaires were used, the System Usability Scale (SUS) [2] and Attrakdiff [8].

SUS [2] is an instrument which is widely used throughout the HCI community due to its simplicity and yet precision to determine usability issues, it is built around 10 questions that have a score from 1 to 5 ranging from "Strongly Disagree" to "Strongly Agree" and having 3 as a neutral point. The final score consists of a grade varying from 0 to 100, and higher numbers are better than lower ones.

Attrakdiff [8] is another instrument widely used, though it is built using 28 different adjective pairs, always antonyms. This instrument groups up to seven pairs of adjectives and each group represent a different set of characteristics. The four groups are Hedonic Qualities - Stimulation (HQ-S), Hedonic Qualities - Identification (HQ-I), Pragmatic Qualities (PQ), and Attractiveness (ATT).

3   Results

The tests were performed with ten different users, both men and women participated, within ages from 23 to 74 and some of them were specialists in computer science, music and some were also non-specialists in both of these areas. Even though five users usually are enough [17], it was decided to increase this number to have more precise results and uncover more issues that could have appeared through the testing.

The tests were performed in a way that let each user access both systems for five minutes, and later on answer four questionnaires, two per system, one concerning the usability (SUS) and the other was about UX (Attrakdiff). Both of these instruments were translated and adapted to Portuguese since the testers had more familiarity with the language.

After the first test, the user gave feedback that one of the systems, in this case, Littlebits, had more functionalities than its counterpart, the system with Makey Makey, specifically Littlebits had a handle to control volume and a few other buttons, so starting from the second test the users were advised to not use anything besides the piano keys on each system.

Also after a few users replied the questionnaires, it was noted that due to either a poor interpretation from the users or a poor translation of the questionaire, some adjective pairs did not present the intended results on either system, but to preserve the results they were not changed in the middle of the experiment.

As it is shown in Fig. 1, both systems presented a similar SUS score endorsing the idea of similar usability, with no statistic advantage to any of the systems.

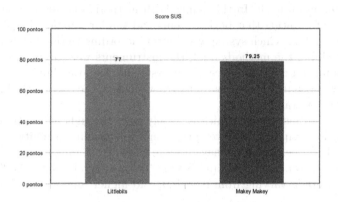

Fig. 1. System usability scale comparison

Since the comparison between usabilities shows that both systems have similar functionalities, now the UX can be considered to compare both TUIs and understand which one performs better and gives the user a better overall experience.

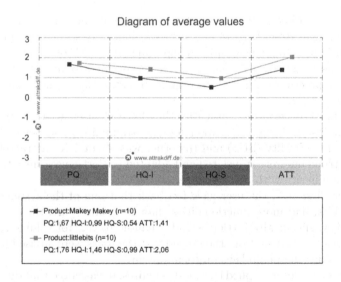

Fig. 2. Attrakdiff's average value diagram

As seen in Fig. 2, Littlebits performed better in every single group, having on average 0,41 points per adjective group. As explained previously, three adjective pairs presented an interpretation error by the users, this led to the Hedonic Qualities presenting a lower grade, on average, than PQ and ATT. Another important information about this graph is the shape that is formed between the groups, as it is seen, Littlebits and Makey Makey both had the same graph's pattern, proving again that both share similar results and functionalities.

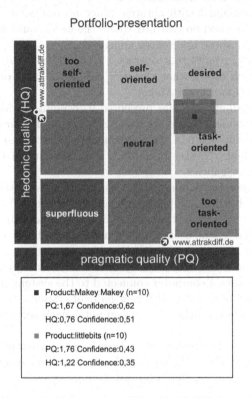

Fig. 3. Portfolio presented by Attrakdiff answers.

It is also possible to analyze through the Attrakdiff answers how a determined system can be improved, to help with this visualization the graph is shown in Fig. 3 is given. Both systems are either on the "Desired" Spectrum or close to it, this means that both commercial systems are not too self-oriented or even too task-oriented, making the user experience overall pleasant. Littlebits performed better since this graph crosses HQ and PQ to show how a determined system can be improved.

This graph also gives the confidence for each of the qualities, this is the larger box that each system has around its center. Littlebits is inside the Makey Makey confidence interval, which is bigger because users had very different answers to the same adjective pairs. Meanwhile, Littlebits has better accuracy, due to users feeling mostly the same about this system and giving similar answers to the adjective pairs.

4   Conclusion

As a result of this experiment, where two tangible user interfaces built by two different companies were tested, one can understand that users preferred Littlebits to Makey Makey combined with Scratch. Since no interviews were conducted, and the questionnaires had no text box where the users could give feedback, one can only assume why those differences appeared.

Littlebits had PQ results that averaged 1.76, while Makey Makey had PQ results of 1.67, which means that the user enjoyed a bit more the pragmatic aspect of Littlebits than Makey Makey.

Similarly, the Hedonic qualities presented 0.76 points to Makey Makey and 1.22 to Littlebits, the main reason for lower grades than PQ was because of poor interpretation and adaptation of the instruments to Portuguese and TUIs. Even though, Littlebits had a better performance in comparison to Makey Makey considering Hedonic Qualities

Both systems presented similar SUS score, within the statistical error margin, with Makey Makey having 2.25 points more than Littlebits.

The main contribution of this paper is to investigate how different commercial systems are perceived by the users, considering both usability and UX and using questionnaires with 10 users.

The main difference between those systems is that one uses dedicated hardware, and the other uses a computer connected to the system. This could potentially be explored further, testing different pairs of systems, one using dedicated hardware design while the other uses a computer with software controlling its actions.

The fact that the instruments were translated and adapted also could be explored further, since there are no available instruments specifically for evaluating tangible systems in English, even less in Portuguese.

References

1. Agostini, L.B., Tavares, T.A.: Designing and developing architectures to tangible user interfaces: a "Softwareless" approach. In: Stephanidis, C. (ed.) HCII 2019. CCIS, vol. 1033, pp. 469–475. Springer, Cham (2019). https://doi.org/10.1007/978-3-030-23528-4_64
2. Brooke, J., et al.: Sus-a quick and dirty usability scale. In: Jordan, P.W., Thomas, B., McClelland, I.L., Weerdmeester, B. (eds.) Usability Evaluation in Industry, vol. 189, no. 194, pp. 4–7. CRC Press, Boca Raton (1996)
3. Brown, S.: Big impact with littlebits. Library Technol. Rep. **54**(4), 28–31 (2018)
4. Bruun, A., Jensen, K., Kristensen, D.: Usability of single- and multi-factor authentication methods on tabletops: a comparative study. In: Sauer, S., Bogdan, C., Forbrig, P., Bernhaupt, R., Winckler, M. (eds.) HCSE 2014. LNCS, vol. 8742, pp. 299–306. Springer, Heidelberg (2014). https://doi.org/10.1007/978-3-662-44811-3_22

5. Collective, B.M., Shaw, D.: Makey makey: improvising tangible and nature-based user interfaces. In: Proceedings of the Sixth International Conference on Tangible, Embedded and Embodied Interaction, pp. 367–370 (2012)

6. da Costa, V.K., et al.: The potential of user experience (UX) as an approach of evaluation in tangible user interfaces (TUI). In: Marcus, A., Wang, W. (eds.) HCII 2019. LNCS, vol. 11586, pp. 30–48. Springer, Cham (2019). https://doi.org/10.1007/978-3-030-23535-2_3

7. Darin, T., Coelho, B., Borges, B.: Which instrument should i use? Supporting decision-making about the evaluation of user experience. In: Marcus, A., Wang, W. (eds.) HCII 2019. LNCS, vol. 11586, pp. 49–67. Springer, Cham (2019). https://doi.org/10.1007/978-3-030-23535-2_4

8. Hassenzahl M., Burmester M., Koller F.: AttrakDiff: Ein Fragebogen zur Messung wahrgenommener hedonischer und pragmatischer Qualität. In: Szwillus, G., Ziegler, J. (eds.) Mensch & Computer 2003. Berichte des German Chapter of the ACM, vol. 57. Springer Vieweg, Berlin (2003). https://doi.org/10.1007/978-3-322-80058-9_19

9. Hornecker, E., Buur, J.: Getting a grip on tangible interaction: a framework on physical space and social interaction. In: Proceedings of the SIGCHI conference on Human Factors in computing systems, pp. 437–446 (2006). https://doi.org/10.1145/1124772.1124838

10. Ishii, H.: Tangible bits: beyond pixels. In: Proceedings of the 2nd International Conference on Tangible and Embedded Interaction, pp. xv–xxv (2008)

11. Ishii, H., Lakatos, D., Bonanni, L., Labrune, J.B.: Radical atoms: beyond tangible bits, toward transformable materials. Interactions **19**(1), 38–51 (2012)

12. Ishii, H., Ullmer, B.: Tangible bits: towards seamless interfaces between people, bits and atoms. In: Proceedings of the ACM SIGCHI Conference on Human Factors in Computing Systems, pp. 234–241 (1997)

13. Jacob, R.J., et al.: Reality-based interaction: a framework for post-wimp interfaces. In: Proceedings of the SIGCHI Conference on Human Factors in Computing Systems, pp. 201–210 (2008)

14. Lee, E., Kafai, Y.B., Vasudevan, V., Davis, R.L.: Playing in the arcade: designing tangible interfaces with MaKey MaKey for scratch games. In: Nijholt, A. (ed.) Playful User Interfaces. GMSE, pp. 277–292. Springer, Singapore (2014). https://doi.org/10.1007/978-981-4560-96-2_13

15. Marsh, S.: Human computer interaction: an operational definition. SIGCHI Bull. **22**(1), 16–22 (1990). https://doi.org/10.1145/101288.101291. https://doi.org/10.1145/101288.101291

16. Nielsen, J.: Usability Engineering. Elsevier, Amsterdam (1994)

17. Nielsen, J.: Why you only need to test with 5 users (2000)

18. Resnick, M., et al.: Scratch: programming for all. Commun. ACM **52**(11), 60–67 (2009)

Sequence Based Two-Factor Authentication (2FA) Method

Devansh Amin and Yusuf Albayram[✉]

Department of Computer Science, Central Connecticut State University,
New Britain, USA
devansh.amin@my.ccsu.edu, yusuf.albayram@ccsu.edu

Abstract. Two-factor authentication (2FA) provides an extra layer of security by combining two different authentication factors that are unrelated (e.g., password and an authentication code sent to user's phone). Despite its prevalence is growing across many online services to improve individual account security, its adoption rate remains low due to various reasons (e.g., usability, privacy concerns). Though there are many 2FA methods such as SMS, One-time password (OTP) and Time-based one-time password (TOTP), U2F (Universal 2nd Factor), Push notification, all of these 2FA methods require to have a phone or a device. However, users may not be willing to provide their phone numbers due to privacy concerns about sharing their phone numbers with companies, or they may not have a device for 2FA to work. We present a new type of 2FA method where users derive OTP from a pre-generated sequence of characters. This 2FA method eliminates the need to have a physical device to use 2FA both online and offline (e.g., no cell phone service is available). Also, it can be well integrated into existing password-based authentication systems.

Keywords: Two-factor authentication (2FA) · Sequence-based authentication · Password manager · Security

1 Introduction

It is becoming increasingly difficult for users to manage and remember passwords for different online accounts. In turn, users often choose weak passwords and/or recycle their passwords across many online accounts. A secure solution is to use two-factor authentication (2FA) which combines two different authentication factors that are unrelated (e.g., password and an authentication code sent to user's phone). 2FA provides an extra layer of security as users need to provide not only password but also additional information such as one-time password (OTP) received via an SMS message or generated in app on a smartphone. Even if an attacker steals the victim's password (e.g., through phishing or password leak in the server's database), the attacker needs to have access to the other component (e.g., cell phone) to receive an OTP.

© Springer Nature Switzerland AG 2020
C. Stephanidis et al. (Eds.): HCII 2020, CCIS 1293, pp. 116–122, 2020.
https://doi.org/10.1007/978-3-030-60700-5_15

Although 2FA raises the bar for attackers and increases individual account security, it is offered as an optional feature on many online services and its adoption rate remains low due to various reasons. For example, a recent study estimated that the adoption rate of Google's two-step verification is between 2% and 6.5% [1]. Prior work identified that users' willingness to use a 2FA method can depend on the perceived value of a particular account and the available 2FA options provided by online services [2].

SMS, One-time password (OTP) and Time-based one-time password (TOTP) are the most commonly used 2FA methods in addition to commercial 2FA solutions such as YubiKey [3], Duo [4], Lastpass Grid's system which is the closest in spirit to our work. As each 2FA method has its own usability, privacy and security properties, low adoption rates may stem from users' concerns about these factors. Balancing tension between these factors is often considered as a challenge for developers, security practitioners, and researchers [5]. Therefore, there is a need for different 2FA methods that can be used as an alternative in the existing systems. Towards that, we present a new type of 2FA method where users derive OTP from a pre-generated sequence of characters, eliminating the need to have a physical device in order to use 2FA both online and offline. We discuss the details and implication of this method as follows.

2 Background and Related Work

Due to the increase in the scale and frequency of data breaches, many major service providers (e.g., Google, Microsoft, Amazon, Facebook, Twitter) are trying to improve individual account security by employing 2FA. Researchers have investigated various 2FA methods utilizing physical tokens [6], camera [7], Bluetooth [8], acoustic signals [9], ultrasound [10], ambient sounds [11] and biometrics [12]. Also, there are several commercial 2FA solutions such as YubiKey [3], Duo [4], Lastpass Grid's system which is the closest in spirit to our work. While some online services (e.g., Google) allow users to choose a variety of 2FA methods (e.g., SMS, TOTP where random code generated via an app, YubiKeys), some services are limited to SMS-based 2FA only.

These different 2FA technologies have very different security, usability and privacy properties. For instance, there are numerous articles pointing out that SMS-based 2FA should be discouraged due to the fact that text messages are not encrypted or protected making it susceptible to man-in-the-middle attacks or SIM-swapping attack [2,13–15]. In terms of usability, prior work identified that effort takes to login with 2FA and difficulty of setting up a 2FA method are perceived as the biggest obstacles for users [16,17]. While TOTP method addresses some of the drawbacks of SMS method such as not relaying on a cellular provider to deliver the one-time codes, eliminating both a potential attack surface and a problem with usability, TOTP, similar to SMS, requires users to share their phone number with vendor. Additionally, TOTP requires users to install an application on their smartphone and setup usually through QR codes, which can be deemed as a difficult task for some users. In terms of privacy, users may not be willing to provide their phone number due to concerns about sharing their phone number with companies for 2FA to work [18].

Therefore, there is a need for different 2FA methods that can improve these aspects. Also, providing different 2FA options can increase the adoption of 2FA as users may prefer to use different 2FA methods depending on the perceived value of a particular account [2,19]. Towards that, we present a new type of 2FA that can be used as an alternative in the existing systems. In this 2FA method, users derive OTP from a pre-generated sequence of characters without needing to possess a physical device in order to use 2FA both online and offline.

3   High-Level Overview of the System

To demonstrate proof of concept, we designed a password manager, called *Vault Plus* where the proposed 2FA method is used. As *Vault Plus* allows users to keep all their passwords stored in a local vault in an encrypted form, this implementation allowed us to show how an offline 2FA method for a local password manager can be used. Figure 1 shows how the user interface of *Vault Plus* looks like. In this system, there are two main processes: the setup process and login process.

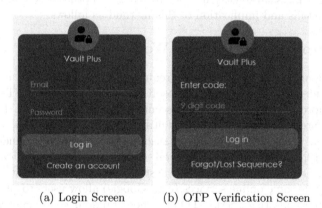

(a) Login Screen   (b) OTP Verification Screen

Fig. 1. Screenshots showing login process in *Vault Plus*.

3.1   Setup Process

To start using *Vault Plus* password manager, a new user is asked to create an account. To do so, the user is asked to enter a valid email address and master password which is hashed using SHA-256. After this, the user is assigned a randomly generated *sequence* of letter and number pairs where each letter is mapped to a number. A sequence is stored in a PDF file that is encrypted using the user's master password. The file can be printed out on paper and carried in the user's wallet. An example sequence is shown in Fig. 3. The system can also generate unique backup codes which can be used in case a user loses his/her sequence.

3.2 Login Process

Each time a user logins to the password manager that requires the 2FA method, the system asks for username and master password. If they are entered correctly, the system generates a random code (an example code is shown in Fig. 2) and shows it to the user. Subsequently, the user needs to: 1) convert the numeric code to letters using the sequence (e.g., using a sequence in Fig. 3), and 2) enter the derived letters (i.e., OTP) in the field when prompted.

For instance, for the code 879–407–304 shown in Fig. 2, the user needs to enter LMK – FJC – WZV by finding corresponding letter in the given sequence (i.e., Fig. 3) for each digit of the code. Figure 4 shows the process, where an OTP (LMK FJC WZV) is derived from a pre-generated sequence of characters for a random code (879–407–304).[1] As shown in these figures, both the sequence and random code are separated into 3 parts to make it easier for user to process. Also, the random code generation frequency is set to 60 s to allow users a sufficient time to enter the converted OTP[2]. A new random code is generated after the previous one has expired.

Your code is **879-407-304**

Fig. 2. An example random code generated by the system.

Sequence

Part 1

9:'K' | 8:'L' | 7:'M' | 6:'N' | 5:'O' | 4:'P' | 3:'Q' | 2:'R' | 1:'S' | 0:'T'

Part 2

9:'A' | 8:'B' | 7:'C' | 6:'D' | 5:'E' | 4:'F' | 3:'G' | 2:'H' | 1:'I' | 0:'J'

Part 3

5:'U' | 4:'V' | 3:'W' | 2:'X' | 1:'Y' | 0:'Z'

Fig. 3. An example sequence consisting of three parts.

---

[1] The letters corresponding to each number in each part has a color.

[2] The system can also set a maximum attempt (e.g., 5) to limit and prevent excessive trial attempts within the allowed time window.

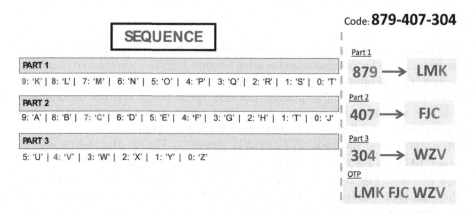

Fig. 4. Steps showing how an OTP (LMK–FJC–WZV) is derived from a pre-generated sequence of characters for a random code (879–407–304). The letters corresponding to each number are shown in the same color in each of the three phases.

4   Discussion

We proposed and described an alternative 2FA method in which users derive OTP from a pre-generated sequence of characters without a physical device.

While the proposed system generates random codes within the application to improve usability, random codes can be sent to email address of the user to further increase security. Thus, in this case, the attacker needs to access not only the sequence but also the user's email account to bypass 2FA. Also, the system can generate a new sequence after a certain period of time (e.g., every 100 days) to further enhance security, which can be done in context where security is critical such as password managers.

Comparing to the other 2FA methods, this method can work even if no cell phone service is available (e.g., being in another country or losing phone) as this method does not require a cell phone. Thus, this method can be especially appealing for those users who have concerns with sharing phone number with vendors to be able to enable 2FA.

In terms of scalability of this approach, the system can generate a total of $10! \times 10! \times 6! \times 3$ sequences, which is enough for many use cases. In terms of deployability, this 2FA method can be easily implemented in many applications ranging from password managers to banking. For instance, built-in password manager in web browsers can utilize this scheme to add an extra layer of security.

In conclusion, we propose a novel sequence based 2FA method with several important aspects in mind. We believe this 2FA method is promising and has a lot of potential for practical usage as an alternative 2FA method in addition to the existing 2FA methods.

References

1. Petsas, T., Tsirantonakis, G., Athanasopoulos, E., Ioannidis, S.: Two-factor authentication: is the world ready? Quantifying 2FA adoption. In: Proceedings of the Eighth European Workshop on System Security. EuroSec 2015, New York, NY, USA. Association for Computing Machinery (2015)
2. Reese, K., Smith, T., Dutson, J., Armknecht, J., Cameron, J., Seamons, K.: A usability study of five two-factor authentication methods. In: Fifteenth Symposium on Usable Privacy and Security (SOUPS 2019), Santa Clara, CA. USENIX Association (2019)
3. Yubico: Yubikey. https://www.yubico.com/. Accessed 6 Jun 2020
4. Duo: Secure authentication with the duo mobile app. https://duo.com/product/multi-factor-authentication-mfa/duo-mobile-app. Accessed 6 Jun 2020
5. Das, S., Wang, B., Tingle, Z., Camp, L.J.: Evaluating user perception of multi-factor authentication: a systematic review. In: Proceedings of the Thirteenth International Symposium on Human Aspects of Information Security & Assurance, HAISA 2019 (2019)
6. Das, S., Dingman, A., Camp, L.J.: Why Johnny doesn't use two factor a two-phase usability study of the FIDO U2F security key. In: Meiklejohn, S., Sako, K. (eds.) FC 2018. LNCS, vol. 10957, pp. 160–179. Springer, Heidelberg (2018). https://doi.org/10.1007/978-3-662-58387-6_9
7. Azimpourkivi, M., Topkara, U., Carbunar, B.: Camera based two factor authentication through mobile and wearable devices. In: Proceedings of the ACM on Interactive, Mobile, Wearable and Ubiquitous Technologies, vol. 1, no. 3, p. 35 (2017)
8. Czeskis, A., Dietz, M., Kohno, T., Wallach, D., Balfanz, D.: Strengthening user authentication through opportunistic cryptographic identity assertions. In: Proceedings of the 2012 ACM uonference on Computer and Communications Security, pp. 404–41. ACM (2012)
9. Han, D., Chen, Y., Li, T., Zhang, R., Zhang, Y., Hedgpeth, T.: Proximity-proof: Secure and usable mobile two-factor authentication. In: Proceedings of the 24th Annual International Conference on Mobile Computing and Networking, pp. 401–415. ACM (2018)
10. Zarafeta, D., Katsini, C., Raptis, G.E., Avouris, N.M.: Ultrasonic watch: Seamless two-factor authentication through ultrasound. In: Extended Abstracts of the 2019 CHI Conference on Human Factors in Computing Systems, LBW2614. ACM (2019)
11. Karapanos, N., Marforio, C., Soriente, C., Capkun, S.: Sound-proof: usable two-factor authentication based on ambient sound. In: 24th USENIX Security Symposium (USENIX Security 2015), Washington, D.C., pp. 483–498. USENIX Association, August 2015
12. Bhargav-Spantzel, A., Squicciarini, A.C., Modi, S., Young, M., Bertino, E., Elliott, S.J.: Privacy preserving multi-factor authentication with biometrics. J. Comput. Secur. 15(5), 529–560 (2007)
13. Mulliner, C., Borgaonkar, R., Stewin, P., Seifert, J.-P.: SMS-based one-time passwords: attacks and defense. In: Rieck, K., Stewin, P., Seifert, J.-P. (eds.) DIMVA 2013. LNCS, vol. 7967, pp. 150–159. Springer, Heidelberg (2013). https://doi.org/10.1007/978-3-642-39235-1_9
14. Hoffman, C.: Why you shouldn't use SMS for two-factor authentication. https://www.howtogeek.com/310418/why-you-shouldnt-use-sms-for-two-factor-authentication/. Accessed 30 Dec 2019

15. Whittaker, Z.: Millions SMS text messages leaked two-factor codes. https://techcrunch.com/2018/11/15/millions-sms-text-messages-leaked-two-factor-codes/. Accessed 6 Jun 2020
16. Colnago, J., et al.: "It's not actually that horrible" exploring adoption of two-factor authentication at a university. In: Proceedings of the 2018 CHI Conference on Human Factors in Computing Systems, pp. 1–11 (2018)
17. Acemyan, C.Z., Kortum, P., Xiong, J., Wallach, D.S.: 2FA might be secure, but it's not usable: a summative usability assessment of Google's two-factor authentication (2FA) methods. In: Proceedings of the Human Factors and Ergonomics Society Annual Meeting. Volume 62, SAGE Publications, Los Angeles, CA (2018) 1141–1145
18. Albayram, Y., Khan, M.M.H., Fagan, M.: A study on designing video tutorials for promoting security features: a case study in the context of two-factor authentication (2FA). Int. J. Hum. Comput. Interact. **33**(11), 927–942 (2017)
19. Redmiles, E.M., Mazurek, M.L., Dickerson, J.P.: Dancing pigs or externalities? Measuring the rationality of security decisions. In: Proceedings of the 2018 ACM Conference on Economics and Computation, pp. 215–232 (2018)

Pilot Study on the Development of a New Wearable Tactile Feedback Device for Welding Skills Training

Manabu Chikai[1]([✉]) [iD], Junji Ohyama[1] [iD], Seiichi Takamatsu[2] [iD], and Shuichi Ino[1] [iD]

[1] National Institute of Advanced Industrial Science and Technology, Central6 1-1-1, Higashi, Ibaraki, Tsukuba, Japan
m-chikai@aist.go.jp
[2] The University of Tokyo, 5-1-5 Kashiwanoha, Kashiwa, Chiba, Japan

Abstract. This study aimed to develop a new wearable tactile feedback device for application in a welder training system. This system consists of a head-mount display with its controller, a data measurement system, an open-source microcontroller board, a motion sensing input device, and the proposed wearable tactile feedback device, which is realized using a reel-to-reel microchip mounting system on thick-knitted textiles. The device consisted of a vibration motor with a flexible circuit, and its effect on the welding work of trainees was evaluated. The device provided two types of vibration stimuli to the user's forearm, based on supervised data derived from the hand motions of an expert welder during a welding task. We performed welding training trials to determine the efficacy of the tactile feedback device and evaluated its effects on the welding speed performance. Three beginners, who were randomly allocated into training and control groups, evaluated the welding speed generated using the tactile feedback device. The training group was required to provide the perceived subjective data (ease of motion), while the welder performed welding using the tactile feedback device. The results suggested that the tactile feedback device enabled the easy understanding of the operating welding velocity. In conclusion, the tactile feedback device influenced the learning process of the beginners by exploiting general information from manuals on welding operation.

Keywords: Tactile feedback device · Reel-to-reel microchip mounting system · Training system · Welder training · Motion assist

1 Introduction

This study aimed to develop a new wearable tactile feedback device for welding skill training. In Japan, there is a decline in the number of workers in the field of engineering, owing to old age. Notably, the task of welding requires a person to have a specialized skillset. Furthermore, weld quality assurance is challenging to achieve. Therefore, it is necessary to train and educate professionals over an extended period of time as opposed to classroom learning, because perfection can only be achieved after a considerable

© Springer Nature Switzerland AG 2020
C. Stephanidis et al. (Eds.): HCII 2020, CCIS 1293, pp. 123–128, 2020.
https://doi.org/10.1007/978-3-030-60700-5_16

amount of training. To this end, researchers and manufacturers have developed various types of training tools and systems to equip workers with welding skills. For example, the VRTEX® (manufactured by Lincoln Electric Company, UK) [1, 2] system provides a convenient way to conduct welding training using virtual reality (VR). This system shows the users the travel speed and the angle of the welding torch as well as the contact tip to work distance through visual information and subsequently provides the score for the performed welding task. The instructor can then teach the user, who is a beginner, through this system. Some studies have reported the use of the welding training system [3, 4]. Whether the method of teaching the welding torch control is difficult is an open question. Notably, the travel speed of the welding torch is an important factor that needs to be considered by the welder, although the systems mentioned above present the speed using the visual information [5]. We focused on the presentation method of the travel speed of the welding torch by applying vibration stimuli to the user's forearm. The vibration stimuli can induce phantom sensations [6] and rabbit sensations [7]. A previous study reported the use of the navigation system for applying the vibration stimuli to the user's forearm [8]. In this study, we focused on wearable tactile feedback device, which can be worn by the trainer on his/her forearm to present the travel speed of the welding torch via VR. In our pilot study, we designed a welding work training trial to determine the efficacy of proposed the tactile feedback device and subsequently evaluated its effects on the welding speed performance.

2 System Development

2.1 Overview

The proposed system consists of a head-mount display with its controller (VIVE, HTC Corporation, Taiwan), a data measurement system (cDAQ-9178, National Instruments, USA), an open-source microcontroller board (Arduino Uno, Arduino, Italy), a motion sensing input device (Kinect, Microsoft, USA), and the proposed wearable tactile feedback device. Figure 1 depicts the schematic diagram of the tactile feedback device. The mock-up welding torch consists of the head-mount display with its controller (VIVE, HTC Corporation, Taiwan), and the travel speed of the mock-up torch was measured by the HMD device (sampling rate: 2 Hz). The wearable tactile feedback device provided two types of vibration stimuli to the user's forearm, based on the supervised data derived from the hand motions of an expert. The users attached two tactile devices on their inner and outer forearms to perform the welding task. When the travel speed of the welding torch was slow, the users perceived high- and low-acceleration level vibration stimuli from the tactile device attached to their outer forearms. Whereas, when the travel speed was high, the users perceived the two stimuli on their inner forearms (see Fig. 1).

2.2 New Wearable Tactile Feedback Device

This tactile feedback device consists of a vibration motor (Type 310–113, Precision microdrives, UK), and a reel-to-reel microchip mounting system on thick knitted textiles [9]. The vibration stimuli provide by this device has the following acceleration

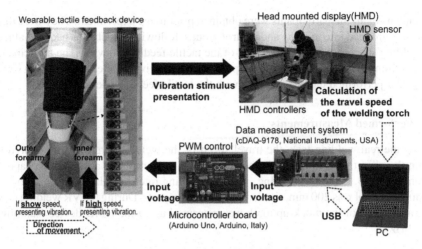

Fig. 1. Schematic of the tactile feedback device.

levels: high; 26.4 mm/s^2, and low level; 3.9 mm/s^2. These acceleration levels were measured by the acceleration sensor (Type4384, Brüel & Kjær, Denmark) and the data acquisition system (NR-600, NR-HA08, NR-CA04, Keyence Corporation, Japan) prior to the experiment.

2.3 Construction of the Supervised Data of Experts

Our training method was based on supervised data derived from the hand motions of a welding expert during a welding task. He is a welding instructor and has been working in welding for decades. First, the travel speed of the welding torch in semi-automatic arc welding was used for constructing the supervised data. The welding expert was monitored to obtain objective data (three-dimensional torch motion) using a 3D motion capture system (Flex 13, Natural Point, Inc., USA). The motion capture system collected data at the rate of 120 samples/s (a 120 Hz sampling frequency) for each task, and the length of the welding material was 200 mm. The locus of the hand motion was used to calculate the average of the welding torch travel speed; this was obtained by dividing the moving distance by the travel time. For this reason, we focused on the effect of the haptic feedback method for beginners, and as such, this system did not present the travel speed at the point of each moment. From these results, the average of torch operation velocity of the expert was estimated to be 24.2 cm/min. In the system, the travel speed of the torch in the supervised data was 24.0 cm/min.

3 Materials and Methods

3.1 Participants

Three young male participants were recruited in this study. Each of them was provided with an e-manual that provided guidelines regarding the welding process. Verbal agreements of all the participants were obtained prior to the experiment. They were then randomly grouped into training and control groups, following which they had to evaluate the welding speed generated by the use of the tactile feedback device. The participants of the training group had to provide the perceived subjective data (ease of motion) while the welder performed the welding task with the tactile feedback device.

3.2 Performed Measurements

During the real welding task, the travel speed of the welding torch was monitored to obtain the objective data (three-dimensional torch motion) using a 3D motion capture system (Flex 13, Natural Point, Inc., USA) (sampling rate: 120 Hz). The length of the welding material was 200 mm, similar to that of the experts. During the VR welding task, the travel speed of the mock-up torch was measured using the HMD device (sampling rate: 2 Hz).

3.3 Protocols

First, all the participants performed welding using semi-automatic arc welding machines. Next, each participant of the training group performed welding skill training using the VR system in five trials. However, participants of the control group did not train without using the VR system. After training, the travel speed of the welding torch for all participants was estimated.

3.4 Data Analysis

During the real welding task, the locus of hand motion was used to calculate the average of the welding torch travel speed by simply dividing the moving distance by the travel time. Whereas, in the VR welding task, we measured the welding torch travel speed and compared the difference in the distance between the supervised data and the participants' measured data on the expert's welding task for each trial. The difference in the distance was estimated by comparing the travel speeds of the participant and expert (24.0 cm/min) during the trials.

4   Results and Discussions

During the first trial of the real welding task, the travel speed of the welding torch for all the participants was lesser compared to that of the expert. In the subsequent trials of the real welding task, the participants of the control group did not show any improvement in the capability of operating the welding torch. However, their performance were improved by the VR system. Experimental results demonstrated that the distance difference in the supervised data of the expert's welding task decreased as the training progressed (see Fig. 2); the difference distance of the first VR trial was 15.2 cm, whereas in the fifth trial, it was 9.3 cm. From these results, it was assumed that the participant was able to perform welding by focusing on the travel speed of the welding torch with the aid of the tactile feedback methods. This showed that the system can accommodate the participant to the expert's welding work. Furthermore, the subjective data regarding the welding training method that involves the application of vibration stimuli to the user's forearm based on the supervised data was assessed by all the participants. All the participants reported that "*the operation of the welding torch could not be understood just by the electric manual.*" However, the participant of the training group reported that "*the tactile feedback stimuli were easy to understand for adjusting the operation of torch speed, so, it was easy to get welding training.*" That is, the tactile feedback device was effective in training by exploiting the general information from the manuals on welding operation.

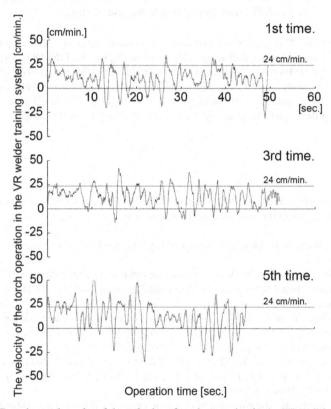

Fig. 2. Experimental results of the velocity of torch operation in the VR training system.

5   Conclusions

This study was aimed at the quantitative evaluation of the effect of a wearable tactile feedback device for welding skills training, prior to the development of a welding training system using VR technology. The main conclusions of this study can be summarized as follows:

- A welding training method was proposed that involved the application of a vibration stimulus to the user's forearm based on the supervised data derived from the hand motions of an expert during welding, and a new wearable tactile feedback device was developed using the reel-to-reel microchip mounting system on thick knitted textiles.
- The tactile feedback device was found to influence the learning process by exploiting general information from manuals on welding operation.

In future works, we plan to increase size of the data and comprehensively discuss the effect of the tactile feedback on the training process, while considering the various aspects involved in its application, in addition to the use of stimuli.

Acknowledgement. This paper was based on results obtained from a project commissioned by the New Energy and Industrial Technology Development Organization (NEDO). This work was partly supported by JSPS KAKENHI Grant Number JP17K12733. We would like to thank all the participants of this study, as well as the Japan Welding Engineering Society (JWES), Prof. Shinji Mizuno of the Aichi Institute of Technology, and FORUM 8 Co., Ltd, and Mitsubishi Electric Corporation, for their outstanding technical assistance and many productive discussions.

References

1. The lincoln electric company: VRTEX 360 virtual welding trainer. https://www.lincolnelectric.com/en-gb/equipment/training-equipment/vrtex360/pages/vrtex-360.aspx. Accessed 30 Mar 2020
2. Stone, R.T., Watts, K.P., Zhong, P.: Virtual reality integrated welder training. Weld. J. **90**(7), 136s (2011)
3. Fast, K., Gifford T., Yancey, R.: Virtual training for welding. In: Proceedings of the Third IEEE and ACM International Symposium on Mixed and Augmented Reality (2004). https://doi.org/10.1109/ismar.2004.65
4. Wang, Y., Chen, Y., et al: Study on welder training by means of haptic guidance and virtual reality for arc welding. In: Proceedings of the 2006 IEEE International Conference on Robotics and Biomimetics (2006). https://doi.org/10.1109/robio.2006.340349
5. Chen, S.J., Huang, N., Liu, Y.K., Zhang, Y.M.: Machine-assisted travel speed control in manual welding torch operation. Int. J. Adv. Manuf. Technol. **76**(5), 1371–1381 (2014). https://doi.org/10.1007/s00170-014-6310-9
6. Alles, D.S.: Information transmission by phantom sensations. IEEE Trans. on Man Mach. Syst. **11**(1), 85–91 (1970)
7. Geldard, F.A., Sherrick, C.E.: The cutaneous "rabbit": a perceptual illusion. Science **178**(4057), 178 (1972)
8. Aggravi, M., Salvietti, G., Prattichizzo, D.: Haptic wrist guidance using vibrations for human-robot teams. In: Proceedings of the 25th IEEE International Symposium on Robot and Human Interactive Communication, pp. 113–118 (2016)
9. Takamatsu, S., Yamashita, T., Itoh, T.: Development of reel-to-reel microchip mounting system for fabrication of meter-long LED lighting tapes. Microsyst. Technol. **20**(12), 2247–2253 (2013). https://doi.org/10.1007/s00542-013-1925-6

User-Specific Interfaces of Teaching Devices for Manipulation of Collaborative Robot

Jeyoun Dong[1(✉)], Seong Hyeon Jo[2], Wookyong Kwon[1], Dongyeop Kang[1], and Yunsu Chung[1]

[1] Electronics and Telecommunications Research Institute (ETRI), Daegu, South Korea
jydong@etri.re.kr
[2] Kyungbuk National University, Daegu, South Korea

Abstract. As the use of robotics in manufacturing and industrial settings continues to advance, expand, and evolve at a speedy pace, efficient collaboration between robots and workers becomes increasingly important. Known as cobots, collaborative robots are highly designed so they can perform tasks continuously and accurately alongside human workers in a safe mode. However, it is not easy to control cobots proficiently and directly in case of scaling of industrial robots for the beginners and skilled engineers. Thus, research for human-robot interaction (HRI) still remains to be challenged. Particularly, users who work with collaborative robot currently need robust and facile methodologies for human-robot collaboration to enhance user experience (UX) and to use direct teaching affordably. Up to date, teaching devices considering more intuitive graphical user interface (GUI) have been intensively exploited, thereby eliminating the need for safety barriers. However, it is still inevitable to consider safety issues that may arise when users work with cobots. Therefore, it is important to properly assign well-adapted functions to each user. There is still a big challenge to develop a more efficient way to authorization of suitable functions to different users.

This paper deals with the user-specific interface considering the user's role for improving the usability and convenience. It provides multiple functions of teaching devices simply used by not only the robot engineers but also developers and operators. We applied the method of user experience such as user journey map and persona to develop the interfaces of teaching device that can operate appropriate tasks with ease by users. In the present study, we introduce the user-specific interfaces for developers, operators, and robot engineers including beginner and experts.

Keywords: User-Specific interface · Teaching device · Human-Robot Interaction (HRI) · Collaborative robot

1 Introduction

Robots have already come out of the laboratory and are turning in to a more complex manufacturing environments for humans. In particular, industrial robots are well established in the production environments for more than 30 years and are used for tasks such as stacking, casting, painting, sorting, welding, soldering parts, and etc.

© Springer Nature Switzerland AG 2020
C. Stephanidis et al. (Eds.): HCII 2020, CCIS 1293, pp. 129–133, 2020.
https://doi.org/10.1007/978-3-030-60700-5_17

The newly designed role of collaborative robot is to deploy flexible human-robot mixing processes and to drive collaboration with small and medium-sized factories, thereby reflecting the diverse knowledge structures of successful installation, control, management, modification, and process adaptation [1, 2].

Generally, site workers, as known as robot engineers, use teaching pendant-like devices for direct teaching. Experienced specialists take advantages of the available input devices connected to the robots, thus guiding them to a specific location in the available work cells and selecting the orders of instructions from the sequence plans with the best effort and knowledge [3–5].

Currently, the studies of teaching devices have been focusing on easy UX for the beginners and experts. However, in the teaching devices, functions for only one user are still provided without distinguishing users who need other functions. It is necessary to provide functions of teaching devices for depending on the user's proficiency, work type and safety issues. It is affected by the increase in the number of sides associated with the human engineer, for example, the level of skill required to use the device, the knowledge of operating the functions of the system, and the level of education necessary to analyze and find the ideal sequence of work. Thus, it strongly demands to provide suitable interfaces that can provide a connection between the robot and the production process by providing a customized UX to other users with different understanding [5, 6].

Therefore, this study aims at introduction of the user interfaces to operate the teaching device suitable for each user. We develop user modeling to understand the needs and factors of users with different levels of proficiency.

This paper is organized as follows; we start a paper by providing UX conception for user interface in Sect. 2 and Sect. 3 describes user modeling. Finally, our conclusions and future works are summarized in Sect. 4.

2 UX Conception for User Interface

Since human users with teaching pendants and robots are in different coordinate systems, this programming method requires the acquisition of certain skills in robot kinematics. Implementation of direct teaching can make the curriculum more convenient [5, 7]. It cannot stress enough the direct teaching in both robot and teaching device. Unique features for different users are described as below;

2.1 Direct Teaching Classification by Users

The existing programming and direct teaching using robot are very difficult. It is only for experts. Thus, we replace these environments with categorizing 4 types of users. For the robot engineers, especially not trained beginner, we provide easy teaching using buttons of robot's arm, robot programming using graphical programming icons and tools for easy teaching. In case of expert site workers, we provide tree-based programming. They are very good at using all functions of teaching device. For a developer, we give all access authorization of all functions. For an operator, we just provide functions for robot operation and management. They do not need a direct teaching function.

End User Programming (Experts). The teaching device provides a programming mainly to accomplish the result of a program for specific and immediate tasks for end-user in the user interface. The graphical interface presents the programs as hierarchical tasks with tree-based representations.

Intuitive Teaching -Programming based on block-module (Beginner). This study shows how to use the benefits of block-based programming to perform complex robotic programming, a complex task that is easier for beginners to access to beginners or beginners. Thus, as an effective programming interface for situations caused by non-experts, it provides an empirical basis for block-based programming. Dragging and dropping instructions are provided to write a block-based program on screen.

Accurate Direct Teaching. In the case of direct teaching using the robot's arm, the teaching device provides the exact coordinates about the movement of the robot arm. Also, when using the teaching pendant, it provides accurate robot arm coordinates. An operator cannot use this function.

Safe Direct Teaching. The teaching device provides functions and authority for each user such as robot engineers including beginners, experts, and developers for safe use of the teaching device. Especially, as one of our remarkable UX concepts, this authority has not yet been applied to other teaching devices.

3   User Modeling

We design the user modeling for each user mentioned in Sect. 2. User modeling identifies the users of the teaching devices and the user's goals for interacting with the teaching devices and collaborative robot. We define the personas by site-workers including non-experts, engineers, developers and add each unique function to teaching devices.

3.1 Persona

The development of persona supports the design process by prioritizing and identifying the roles and characteristics of key users for the teaching device, then making composite individuals to represent the main character [8].

Three types of persona such as site-workers including non-expert, engineers and developers are created. For example, the persona of site worker type is shown in Fig. 1.

3.2 User Journey Map

User journey map is a visualization of a user's relationships with a teaching device over time and across different channels [9]. In addition, there are three types of user journey maps, and is one type of user journey map is shown in Fig. 2.

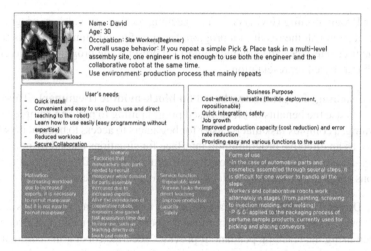

Fig. 1. The persona for site workers (Beginner)

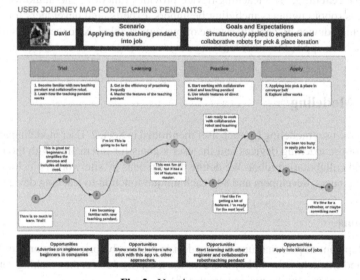

Fig. 2. User journey map

4   Conclusion

This study describes user-specific interfaces based on human-centered UX modelling applied to teaching devices for multiple users. It can be suitably used by all users including beginners, experts, developers as well as operators.

In this study, we introduced UX modelling depending on users for collaborative robots. It is also important to place intuitive and versatile interface elements that are appropriate for all users to use in the teaching pendant and to derive a GUI that reflects user-centered information.

In future work, the teaching devices with designed UX will be completed and reflected in the working environment. In addition, usability assessments will be performed for users of four types.

Acknowledgements. This work was supported by Electronics and Telecommunications Research Institute (ETRI) grant funded by the Korean government. [20ZD1130, Development of ICT Convergence Technology for Daegu-GyeongBuk Regional Industry].

References

1. Holmes, A., et al.: Intuitive interfaces in human-robot interaction. In: Giulian, M., Assaf, T., Giannaccini, M.E. (eds.) Towards, Autonomous Robotic Systems. 19th Towards Autonomous Robotic Systems (TAROS) Conference. LNCS. Springer, Cham (2018)
2. Khan, S., Germak, C.: Reframing HRI design opportunities for social robots: lessons learnt from a service robotics case study approach using UX for HRI. Future Internet **10**, 101 (2018)
3. Tonkin, M., Vitale, J., Herse, S., Williams, M., Judge, W., Wang, X.: Design methodology for the UX of HRI: a field study of a commercial social robot at an airport. In: HRI 2018 Proceedings of the 2018 ACM/IEEE International Conference on Human-Robot Interaction, pp. 407–415 (2018)
4. Yoo, S.: Development and validation of block coding based human-robot teaching pendant UX. J. Integr. Des. Res. **17**(4), 9–18 (2018)
5. Kraft, M., Rickert, M.: How to teach your robot in 5 minutes: applying UX paradigms to human-robot-interaction. In: 26th IEEE International Symposium on Robot and Human Interactive Communication, pp. 942–949 (2017)
6. Balázs, D., Korondi, P., Sziebig, G., Thomessen, T.: Evaluation of flexible graphical user interface for intuitive human robot interactions. Acta Polytechnica Hungarica **11**(1), 135–151 (2014)
7. Hartson, R., Pyla, P.S.: The UX Book: Process and Guidelines for Ensuring a Quality User Experience. Elsevier, Amsterdam (2012)
8. Examples of UX personas. https://qubstudio.com/blog/4-examples-of-ux-personas/
9. A beginner's guide to user journey mapping. https://uxplanet.org/a-beginners-guide-to-user-journey-mapping-bd914f4c517c

Bridging the Gap Between Desktop and Mobile Devices

Tyler Kass[✉], John Coffey, and Steven Kass

University of West Florida, Pensacola, FL 32514, USA
tyjkass@gmail.com

Abstract. As cell phones have adapted to becoming personalized computers, the functionality of these two different devices has converged. Conversely, the way people interact with these two platforms is vastly different. With much less space, different controls, and lower specifications, mobile interface design looks and feels significantly different than that of desktop devices. This paper aims to analyze what makes UI design for desktop applications different from mobile devices and how developers can ease this transition when porting from one device to another. The results of a survey found that computing power was a large factor in which device users chose for a particular task, while screen size was not quite as important. Through identifying differences in these applications and suggesting solutions, the awkward transition from bulky, powerful devices to the small screens of everyday mobile devices can be alleviated.

Keywords: Smart phone · Mobile device · Interface · User preferences · Desktop · Cross-platform

1 Background

1.1 Overview

Mobile devices have evolved over the last 15 years. What started as simply a way to call someone from anywhere has evolved into miniature computers in peoples' hands. Yet, despite their similarity to modern desktop computers, the means of conveying information are still vastly different. These differences may lead to confusion for new users going from one to the other, as what may end up being intuitive on one device may not carry over to another. For example, minimizing or closing a web browser window is relatively the same across all desktop devices (i.e., click "x" in the upper-righthand corner to close). However, mobile devices do not necessarily follow this same convention. Minimizing a window in Android involves hitting a circle, but what happens to the window isn't clear. This button may not be present on many newer devices, so there's no way for one to know just by looking at the screen what to do. In addition, unifying one application to run on multiple platforms can save companies a lot of time and money if they only must develop an application once. Both mobile devices and desktops can be used for similar tasks, browsing social media, using simple applications, and making

C. Stephanidis et al. (Eds.): HCII 2020, CCIS 1293, pp. 134–141, 2020.
https://doi.org/10.1007/978-3-030-60700-5_18

calculations. However, given the differences between the devices, the same application may have to be used in a completely different way. A Venn diagram of the two devices' functionality and similarity of usage would show little overlap. While the overlap has increased, it can still go further. The purpose of this study is to see how big that overlap can get, what the limitations are, and potential solutions to widening that overlap.

1.2 Solutions in the Field

The act of unifying interface design on multiple platforms has been attempted in the past. Apple's app system allows for a similar display of applications from its desktop computers to its phones. Windows has the Universal Windows Development Platform which allows for an application to be developed and distributed across any modern Windows device. Facebook's React-Native and Google's Flutter also attempt to allow cross-platform development using one codebase. These technologies can cut down on development time, but they don't solve the issue of varied interfaces across a device. A phone app will still behave like a phone app and a desktop application will still feel like a desktop application. To unite these interfaces, the device's operating system itself would have to be modified.

The main interface factor that seems to vary the most between handheld and desktop operating systems is the window system, or how applications are displayed. Phones make the best use of screen space by displaying the window across the length and width of the screen and only allowing one screen to be shown at a time. Windows, however, is a lot messier. Windows can allow these screens to be stacked, set side-by-side on one display, minimized, full-screened, and more. The "why" of this is quite simple: using smaller screens requires the most use out of the screen in order to even be visible. If multiple windows could be shown on one screen at once, it would clutter the screen and little information may be seen from each window.

1.3 The Key Differences

Weiss [1] discussed several key differences between desktop and handheld computers. He categorized the differences into reasons for use, form factor, mobility, connectivity, input, display size, memory, and storage. While these differences can help distinguish what a mobile device can and should be used for, this list can be expanded upon in modern devices with the addition of categories "orientation" and "feedback." The differences in these factors are what makes a user choose a handheld device over a desktop computer, or vice-versa. By studying these key differences, it can give an idea as to not only what device a person is most likely to use for a task, but it also gives insight as to what is just not possible to incorporate into a handheld device or desktop computer with today's technology.

For this study, the primary differences are defined by their reasons for use, form factor, mobility, display size/orientation, connectivity, input and feedback, and memory/storage. Some of these groups, such as memory/storage and connectivity are grouped together in the survey because the reasons people would prefer one device over another are similar, the speed of the device. Reasons for use is defined as what someone uses the device for. For example, smart phones are often used for voice calls and desktop computers can be used for complex computations. Form factor is the actual overall size and shape of the device. This key difference is related to the screen size/orientation as well, as the size of the display often closely matches the form factor. Mobility also ties into these two key differences, as a small form factor tends to make for a more mobile device, though other factors can come into play, such as needing cables to keep a charge. Connectivity is the ability to connect to a range of other devices. For example, a desktop computer may be able to connect quickly to the web using ethernet cables, but phones often have other means of communications such as cell towers and Bluetooth connectivity. Input and feedback have to do with the controls of the device, such as a touchscreen or a full-sized keyboard. Finally, memory and storage apply to the capacity of short term and long-term storage. More memory, RAM, leads to more powerful computers and more storage means more files and programs that can be stored on the device.

1.4 Importance of This Study

With a better understanding of the differences between these two types of devices, future technology may make development easier for programmers. By uniting some newer technologies, the future may blur the line between handheld phones and desktop computers. By identifying what is most important to users regarding desktop versus smartphone usage, priority for what to improve can be established. This study aims to identify how close to a desktop computer the mobile device can approach and vice versa.

Some of the benefits of making smartphones and desktops more similar include cost reduction on application development, as well as introducing portable technologies that close the disjoint between desktop and mobile productivity. With both technologies being able to perform similar tasks in similar ways, users will have an easier time transitioning work, school, and leisure from one device to another.

2 Methods

For this study, a survey was used to gather information on what people found the most important when deciding what device to use, as well as how many hours a day a participant used a device.

Volunteers were obtained through the Psychology Research Pool at a mid-sized university in a Southeastern state in the US. All participants were at least 18 years of age and had access to a smartphone and a desktop computer. No personal identifying information was stored, and all data were password protected.

The items on the survey were intended to identify participants' preferences regarding mobile versus desktop devices and what aspects of the device were most critical to them. For items asking how critical an aspect was, a Likert-type rating scale of 1-5 was used and each response option explained that level on the scale. Data on what the devices were primarily used for (i.e., leisure, work, and school) were also gathered.

Participants were asked to rank how critical four of the previously mentioned key differences were to their device usage. Those key differences were screen size, speed (memory, storage, and connectivity), mobility (and form factor), and controls.

3 Results

Overall, 46 participants completed the survey. The average age of participants was 24.28 years (18–52). Nearly all participants were from fields of health, social science and/or psychology with only 1 coming from a technology field. A majority (69.6%) of participants took this survey on a laptop computer as opposed to a desktop computer (19.6%) or a phone (10.9%). Most participants (65.9%) used Windows 8/10 as their primary operating system, 27.3% of participants used macOS, and 6.8% used Windows 7. Two participants answered with something that was not an operating system, so those values were removed. A large majority (71.7%) of participants used iOS as their phone operating system, with Android being the second most common (23.9%), followed by Windows (4.3%).Participants were evenly split on which device they used for most tasks with 50% responding smartphone, and 50% responding desktop.

Out of the 23 who preferred to use their smartphone for most tasks, four used Android, 18 used iOS, and one used Windows. For the 23 who preferred to use their desktop for most things, one used Windows 7, 16 used Windows 8/10, and five used a mac.

When asked how critical the size of their screen was in choosing which device to use, a majority were in the middle of the road. Most people (32%) said that it was only somewhat critical, a rating of 3. The average rating for participants with a preference for using a smartphone was 2.96, while the average rating for participants with a preference towards desktop computers was 3. Participants with a preference for using a smartphone answered 3 the most, while participants with a preference for a desktop computer answered 2 the most.

When asked how important speed was, a majority of participants (39%) reported that it was very critical and if a device did not have sufficient speed, they would not use it, a rating of 5, with 32% rating it as a 4. Of the 15 participants who answered that speed was critical, nine participants responded that they preferred to use their smartphones for most things, while six participants answered they preferred to use their desktop for most things. The average rating for people who used primarily a smartphone was 4.04, while the average rating for people who used primarily a desktop computer was 3.74. Participants with a preference for using a smartphone answered 5 the most, while participants with a preference for a desktop computer answered 4 the most.

When asked how important mobility was, 32% said it was pretty critical and they would only use a non-mobile device if they really needed it (a rating of 4). Similarly, 28.26% of participants reported that mobility was somewhat critical (a rating of 3), 26% of participants reported that mobility was a little critical (a rating of 2). Participants who reported that they used primarily smartphones rated the importance of mobility with an average score of 3.65, while participants who primarily used a desktop computer rated the importance of mobility as an average score of 2.65. Participants with a preference for using a smartphone answered 4 the most, while participants with a preference for a desktop computer answered 2 the most.

When asked how important controls were, 35.6% said it was pretty critical and they would only use a device without their preferred controls if they absolutely needed it (a rating of 4). Thirteen participants (28.9%) reported controls were somewhat critical (a rating of 3), and 15.6% of participants reported that controls were only a little critical (a rating of 2). Participants who used smartphones for most tasks rated the importance of controls to an average of 2.77, while the participants who used their desktop computers for most tasks rated the importance of controls to an average of 3.52. Participants with a preference for using a smartphone answered 3 the most, while participants with a preference for a desktop computer answered 4 the most.

Participants were asked to rank their favorite peripheral controls in order from most favorite to least favorite, with 1 being their most favorite, and 7 being the least favorite. A majority placed keyboard as their number one choice (53.5%), 9.3% ranked mouse/rollerball as their number one choice, 27.9% ranked touchscreen as their number one choice, 7% ranked voice controls as their number one choice, and one person (2.3%) ranked gamepad/controller as the number one peripheral control.

For second choice, 30.23% of participants chose mouse/rollerball as their number two choice, 27.9% chose keyboard, 27.9% chose touchscreen, 7% chose digital pen/stylus, 2.3% chose motion controls, and 4.65% chose voice controls as their number two peripheral controls.

Participants were also asked what devices they preferred to use for the following apps: YouTube, MyUWF (a university portal the participants use), Discord, OneNote, Google Docs, Slack, Skype, and email. For YouTube, 79% of participants preferred using a mobile device. For email, 69.6% of participants preferred using a mobile device. For the school portal, 91.3% of participants preferred using the desktop computer. For Discord, 67.4% did not use the app, and 23.9% of participants preferred to use it on a desktop computer. For OneNote, 57.8% of participants did not use the app, and 33.33% preferred using the app on a desktop computer. For Google Docs, 93% of participants preferred to use the app on a desktop computer. Most participants (84%) did not use Slack. For Skype, 39.1% of participants did not use it, 23.9% preferred to use Skype on a mobile device, and 36.9% preferred to use it on a desktop computer.

On average, participants reported that they used their smartphones for an average of 5.72 h a day (SD = 2.27), and their desktop computer for an average of 4.43 h per day (SD = 2.94). The participants were also asked how they used this time on each device, divided out into leisure, work, and school. For smartphones, participants reported using their devices for leisure an average of 4.24 h, for work 1.36 h, and for school 2.12 h. For desktops, users reported using their device for leisure an average of 2.31 h, for work, 2.53 h, and for school 4.13 h.

4   Discussion

4.1   Findings

This survey identified what people preferred to use, desktop or mobile device, and why they had a preference. By identifying the most prevalent causes of the divide between smartphones and desktop computers, better discussions can be made regarding improvements to minimize the gap between them. Surprisingly, there was a clearly evident split between people who used desktop computers for most tasks and people who used smartphones for most tasks. This even divide between users seems to imply that one device is not inherently better than the other. This question was added to the survey, in part, to identify if there was a device that needed to be more like the other, such as making desktop computers more mobile or making smartphones more powerful. Instead, these two devices may converge more towards the middle ground from both ends.

When analyzing what was important to participants regarding which device they used, it was noteworthy that screen size made very little difference. Most users were okay with waiting until they gained access to a larger screen and having a bigger screen wasn't urgent. With modern phones having such high resolution, it may be fair to assume a bigger and higher-resolution screen is not critical to most tasks. When identifying what devices people preferred when using certain apps, a similar trend occurred. The video streaming app, YouTube, was shown to be preferred on mobile devices by a large majority. It could be possible that modern pixel density on phone screens have become so good that this is no longer an issue. Instead, instant gratification of viewing videos may be a larger determinant of what device is used to watch videos. If a phone is close enough to one's face, then maybe even many video games can be played on such a small screen with little drawbacks. In fact, with virtual reality headsets, this idea seems to hold up very well, as the headsets contain screens often with no more pixel density than a smartphone [5, 6].

The aspect that people seemed to find the most critical was speed. With how fast information moves between people, it has become more and more critical that devices can keep up with the demand. As mentioned previously, communication speeds have been increasing substantially, and one day, many computations may not even need to be done on mobile devices themselves. Since speed seems to be the greatest barrier between using a phone versus using a desktop computer, this aspect may be the wall between uniting the two different devices.

Participants who used phones more often also valued mobility more on average. While expected, this finding also raises questions about how to get desktop devices to be more portable. Powerful, portable laptops exist, but it is hard to use the laptop while moving. They may be mobile, but laptops are still meant to be used while stationary. As mentioned before, VR backpacks include some technologies that make high computations on the go more feasible. The remaining issue, however, is the controls.

On a scale from 1 to 5, participants who used desktops more rated controls as more critical than participants who used smartphones more. Controls and peripherals would be more important to a desktop user, especially keyboard and mouse controls which were rated as users' favorite peripheral controls in the survey. But these peripherals are much harder to use on the go. Typing on a keyboard is faster and the lack of a mouse also may lead to poor screen accuracy and many controls are taken away such as hovering, right-clicking, and middle-clicking. Bringing these controls to a mobile platform would be another challenge or barrier which would require a lot of user interface experimentation. Perhaps a new form of control could develop in the future that could replace the phone keyboard. The phone keyboard has been replaced before, from number pad controls to touchscreen controls with realistic haptic feedback. Thinking that digital keyboards would be the last phone input controls could be short-sighted.

In general, this research has given insight into uniting mobile and desktop platforms. Device needs are converging, and the technologies to help are in development. By converging these technologies, development processes can also be united. An application wouldn't need to be made for desktop, then for web, and then again for mobile, each with its own technologies they need to utilize. Instead, development time could be shortened greatly and would be much easier to manage post-release.

4.2 Error and Limitations Analysis

One thing to note about the study was that a good portion of the time the survey was open, the country was advised to social distance due to the Coronavirus pandemic of 2020, and several respondents were confined to their homes. At this time, smartphone usage may have been less frequent as people were not away from their computers for as often and computer usage may have been higher.

Another limitation of the current study was the rather small convenience sample. Only 46 respondents, most of whom were psychology students, completed the survey. Future studies should employ a larger sample to include other academic majors and larger age range.

4.3 Implications

There are many places where technology could go from here, and with how fast new ideas are developing, it is hard to accurately predict what will happen. However, using what was gathered from this survey and some technologies available now, new ideas can be proposed. One potential future for devices is portable desktops. If VR backpacks become as commonplace as laptops, then it's possible that information could be streamed from a more powerful device on one's back to a handheld device, allowing for activities such as 3D computer-aided design to be performed on a large smartphone. Many powerful laptops exist, but require a work surface to use, and it is not as convenient to go hands-free. With a setup like this, users could save progress in an application, place the device in a pocket, and start a conversation with the person next to them.

Another possibility could be cloud computing. Using the cloud for computations, mobile devices could potentially utilize less on-board hardware and implement hardware from other places. The main assumption for cloud computing to be as useful as onboard hardware would be that internet speeds continue to increase.

Peripherals for these two options may be challenging. With the current application already fighting for screen space, it may be hard to also include a keyboard on more advanced devices. Getting past this limitation would require a major reimagining of input controls. Perhaps something external, such as a grip with keys built in to make use of all 10 fingers, or alternate input methods with predictive typing, may be the future of input control. Google has also developed the Soli [7], a sonar chip that allows for advanced gesture control. Gesturing may be the next leap in user interaction. However, whatever may come next, it will probably take time to catch on, which, unfortunately, would be a major hurdle for developers trying to push a new input peripheral.

One final idea is to make phones and desktops modular with each other. In other words, keep mobile devices weaker, yet portable, while giving it a docking station that boosts its power. For example, a user could be taking pictures on a mobile device, and when more computing power and keyboard shortcuts are needed to do advanced editing, the device is simply plugged into a stronger, more powerful device. This connection wouldn't necessarily unite phones and desktops in the same way as proposed earlier, and it would require a new way to think about how to design apps. But, instead of relying on every application to utilize a cloud service for storage and transfer between two devices, the device would just be able to pick up where it last left off, but now with the power to do more.

These ideas, of course, could very well be obsolete when something completely new is developed. It will still be interesting to see what develops and speculating on ideas for the future may lead to inspiring others who will shape the future of technology.

5 Conclusion

Mobile devices are becoming more and more powerful but are unable to keep up with desktop stationary devices. Many applications have versions both on desktop and mobile devices, but the difference requires two sets of code and controls. This need for different device-dependent controls increases the need and cost to maintain software and can slow development times. Mobile devices have steadily gained an overlap in functionality and usability to desktop computers, but their differences keep them from being seamlessly usable with one another. This study found that some of the most important differences to people may be alleviated through modern and future technologies to help bring mobile and desktop application development together.

References

1. Weiss, S.: Handheld Usability. Wiley, Chinchester (2002)
2. Griggs, K., Bridges, L.M., Rempel, H.G.: Tips on designing and developing mobile web sites. Code4Lib J. **8**, 1940–5758 (2009). https://journal.code4lib.org/articles/2055
3. "Speedtest Global Index." Speed Test. https://www.speedtest.net/global-index#fixed. Accessed 1 May 2020
4. Hlatshwayo, C.M., Zuva, T.: Mobile public cloud computing, merits and open issues. In: 2016 International Conference on Advances in Computing and Communication Engineering (ICACCE), Durban, pp. 128–132 (2016)
5. Gajsek, D.: HTC vive vs oculus: an in-depth guide on which headset is better for business and personal use. Circuit Stream. https://circuitstream.com/blog/htc-vs-oculus/. Accessed 3 May 2020
6. Spoonauer, M.: Samsung Galaxy S20 Review." Tom's guide. https://www.tomsguide.com/reviews/galaxy-s20. Accessed 3 May 2020
7. "Soli" Google. https://atap.google.com/soli/. Accessed 3 May 2020
8. "HP VR Backpack." HP. https://www8.hp.com/us/en/vr/vr-backpack.html. Accessed 3 May 2020

Palm-Controlled Pointing Interface Using a Dynamic Photometric Stereo Camera

Yoshio Matsuda[1], Takashi Komuro[1(✉)], Takuya Yoda[2], Hajime Nagahara[2], Shoji Kawahito[3], and Keiichiro Kagawa[3]

[1] Saitama University, Saitama, Japan
komuro@mail.saitama-u.ac.jp
[2] Osaka University, Suita, Japan
[3] Shizuoka University, Hamamatsu, Japan

Abstract. In this paper, we propose a user interface that allows pointing operation with a user's palm orientation by measuring the normal directions in the palm region using a dynamic photometric stereo camera based on a multi-tap CMOS image sensor. Our system allows users to control a pointer smoothly with small hand movement. We implemented two types of user interface designs and an interactive game to show the applicability of hand gesture operation using the proposed system.

Keywords: Hand gesture input · Normal map · Multi-tap CMOS image sensor

1 Introduction

User interfaces using hand gestures from a distance have been developed. Though hand gestures enable intuitive and flexible operation, there is a problem that users have to move their hand largely, which often makes them tired.

To solve this problem, there is a study that enabled pointing operation on a large display from a distance only with small movement of a finger [1]. However, it requires users to put markers on their hand, which may lead to physical and mental fatigue of the users.

On the other hand, there is a study that realized pointing operation from a distance without attaching any markers or devices [2]. The posture of a pointing finger is recognized with high accuracy using multiple cameras. However, it is necessary to place multiple cameras in the environment and to calibrate each camera.

In this study, we use the dynamic photometric stereo camera proposed by Yoda et al. [3], which can obtain the normal map of a dynamic scene. By using this camera, it is possible to acquire the normal directions on the surface of a human hand, and the user interface that allows pointing operation with a user's palm orientation is realized. In this paper, we show an implementation of our proposed interface and some application examples.

© Springer Nature Switzerland AG 2020
C. Stephanidis et al. (Eds.): HCII 2020, CCIS 1293, pp. 142–147, 2020.
https://doi.org/10.1007/978-3-030-60700-5_19

2 Dynamic Photometric Stereo Camera

Techniques for sensing three-dimensional information include the stereo method, structured light method, time-of-flight method, and photometric stereo method. These methods are roughly divided into methods that obtain depth maps and methods that obtain normal maps. The stereo method, the structured light method, and the time-of-flight method obtain depth maps, while the photometric stereo method obtains normal maps. It is possible to obtain a normal map by applying spatial differentiation to a depth map, but if the depth map contains some noise, a smooth normal map cannot be obtained unless the noise is reduced under some assumption. Since the photometric stereo method directly obtains the normal map, detailed normal directions on the surface of an object can be estimated without such correction.

The original photometric stereo method requires at least three images illuminated from different directions to obtain the normal map. Since these images correspond pixel to pixel, there is a condition that the camera or the object should not move while the image is captured. As photometric stereo methods that is applicable to dynamic scenes, a method using multispectral illumination [4, 5] and a method using a high-speed camera [6] have been proposed. However, the former assumes that the object has uniform color and reflectance, and the latter has a problem that the accuracy of the obtained normal map is low because the SN ratio of the captured images becomes low due to short exposure time.

On the other hand, the dynamic photometric stereo camera used in this study can obtain normal maps even in a dynamic scene using a multi-tap CMOS (Complementary Metal-Oxide-Semiconductor) image sensor [7]. A multi-tap CMOS image sensor is an image sensor that can divide and store the electric charge generated in a photodiode in different floating diffusion (FD) in each pixel, and that can simultaneously capture multiple images with different exposure patterns.

Figure 1 shows the appearance of the dynamic photometric stereo camera. The exposure control for the image sensor is synchronized with three controllable light sources. Each light source is repeatedly turned on and off in synchronization with the exposure pattern. By switching the light sources sufficiently fast, it is possible to ignore the time difference between the three images and to obtain the images of dynamic scenes illuminated from different light sources.

Figure 2 shows the pixel structure of the multi-tap CMOS image sensor and the exposure patterns of the multi-tap CMOS image sensor. Figure 3 shows the normal map of an object obtained using the dynamic photometric stereo camera. A smooth surface of the object, which cannot be obtained using a TOF (time-of-flight) camera, can be obtained.

3 Palm Detection and Tracking

The system determines the palm area by detecting and tracking a user's palm and estimates the palm orientation from the normal directions in the palm area, which is used to control the position of the pointer.

Palm detection and tracking are performed using the detector and tracking algorithm implemented in Dlib [8]. The detector is constructed based on a machine learning

Fig. 1. Appearance of the dynamic photometric stereo camera.

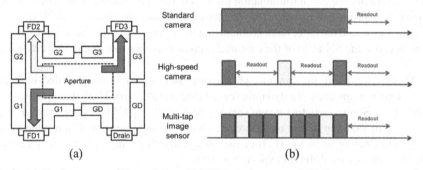

(a)   (b)

Fig. 2. (a) Pixel structure of the multi-tap CMOS image sensor, and (b) Exposure patterns of the multi-tap CMOS image sensor.

Fig. 3. Normal map of an object obtained using the dynamic photometric stereo camera.

method using HOG (Histogram of Oriented Gradients) features and SVM (Support Vector Machine). It is used to detect the user's right hand with the entire palm visible in a grayscale image obtained from the camera. Then, tracking of the palm is carried out using a correlation filter-based tracking algorithm with making the position of the detected palm to be the initial position and a rectangular region around the detected palm to be the palm region.

Figure 4 shows tracking examples of the palm region. The region in the blue box is the tracked palm region. The palm region is detected and tracked stably even when it is tilted.

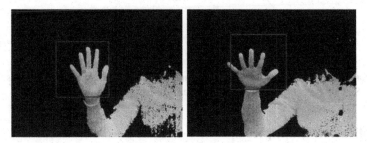

Fig. 4. Hand tracking examples.

4   Pointing Interface Controlled with Palm Orientation

In the proposed user interface, the user can control a pointer by tilting his/her palm. Figure 5 shows how the pointer is controlled using this interface.

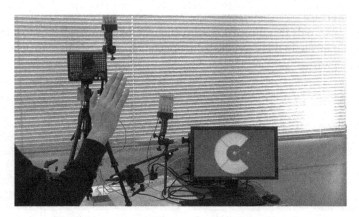

Fig. 5. A user controlling a pointer by tilting his palm.

The orientation of the average of the normal vectors in the rectangular palm region is used as the palm orientation. However, considering that the normal directions around the palm center and wrist are more important than those around fingers, only the normal vectors around the center and bottom of the rectangular region are averaged.

Figure 6 shows the change in x and y coordinate values of the controlled pointer when a hand is moved sideways or up and down. From this result, it is confirmed that the pointer smoothly moves both in the x- and y-axis directions.

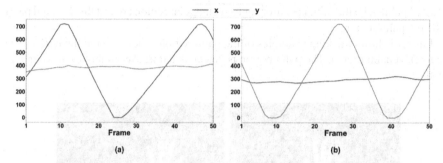

Fig. 6. Examples of pointer trajectories. (a) a hand was tilted sideways, (b) a hand was tilted up and down. Smooth trajectories were obtained even without using a smoothing filter.

5 Application Examples

We implemented two types of user interface designs (Fig. 7) and an interactive game (Fig. 8) as application examples of the proposed user interface.

Tile Layout Interface
This interface allows a user to make rough selection of items by controlling a pointer and selecting tiles. Like joystick control, the displacement that is determined depending on the palm orientation is added to the current position of the pointer.

Pie Menu Interface
This interface uses only two-dimensional directions of the palm orientation to select items from a circular menu. In this case, the palm orientation is directly used to determine the direction of an arrow.

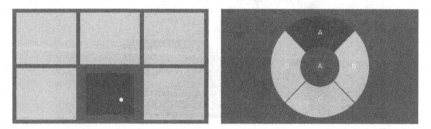

Fig. 7. Tile layout interface (left) and pie menu interface (right).

Interactive Game
In this game, red balls fall one after another from the top of the screen, and the user moves the bar at the bottom of the screen left and right to receive them. The bar becomes smaller every time it receives a ball. When the bar becomes a certain size, the fall speed of the ball increases, which makes the game more difficult.

Fig. 8. Example of an interactive game.

6 Conclusion

In this study, we proposed a user interface that is operated with a user's palm orientation using a dynamic photometric stereo camera. We also showed application examples of the proposed user interface and confirmed that the interface was able to be operated with small hand movement.

References

1. Vogel, D., Balakrishnan, R.: Distant freehand pointing and clicking on very large, high resolution displays. In: 18th Annual ACM Symposium on User Interface Software and Technology, pp. 33–42 (2005)
2. Hu, K., Canavan, S., Yin, L.: Hand pointing estimation for human computer interaction based on two orthogonal-views. In: 20th International Conference on Pattern Recognition, pp. 3760–3763 (2010)
3. Yoda, T., Nagahara, H., Taniguchi, R., Kagawa, K., Yasutomi, K., Kawahito, S.: The dynamic photometric stereo method using a multi-tap CMOS image sensor. Sensors **18**(3), 786 (2018)
4. Christensen, C., Shapiro, L.: Three-dimensional shape from color photometric stereo. Int. J. Comput. Vision **13**(2), 213–227 (1994). https://doi.org/10.1007/BF01427152
5. Hernandez, C., Vogiatzis, G., Brostow, G., Stenger, B., Cipolla, R.: Non-rigid photometric stereo with colored lights. In: 11th International Conference on Computer Vision (2007)
6. Vlasic, D., et al.: Dynamic shape capture using multi-view photometric stereo. ACM Trans. Graphics **28**(5), 1–11 (2009)
7. Han, S., Takasawa, T., Yasutomi, K., Aoyama, S., Kagawa, K., Kawahito, S.: A time-of-flight range image sensor with background canceling lock-in pixels based on lateral electric field charge modulation. IEEE J. Electron Devices Soc. **3**(3), 267–275 (2015)
8. King, D.: Dlib-ml: a machine learning toolkit. J. Mach. Learn. Res. **10**, 1755–1758 (2009)

Analysis of Multimodal Information for Multi-robot System

Artem Ryndin[ID], Ekaterina Pakulova[✉][ID], and Gennady Veselov[ID]

Southern Federal University, Rostov-on-Don, Russia
epakulova@sfedu.ru
http://ictis.sfedu.ru

Abstract. In this paper, we consider the possible set of modalities for UAVs systems for finding people in case of emergency. Modalities allow to identify and monitor the physiological state of a found person. We consider modalities from acoustic and visual communication channels such as speech, facial structure and skin temperature. We also outline the possible signals of input modalities and describe the interchange format for them.

Keywords: Multimodal data · UAVs · Interchange formats

1 Introduction

Today human-computer interaction is relevant. We communicate not only through words but also by intonation, gaze, hand and body gestures and facial expressions. These verbal and nonverbal signals have a role in the communicative process. They add, modify, substitute information in discourse and are highly linked with each other. The ease and robustness of human-human communication are due to extremely high recognition accuracy, using multiple input channels, and the redundant and complimentary use of several modalities. Human-computer interaction can benefit from modelling several modalities in analogous ways. Multimodal systems represent and manipulate information from different human communication channels at multiple levels of abstraction.

At the same time, multimodal systems allow us to design various adaptive [7] or monitoring multimodal systems. These systems interact with a user or monitor human's condition (smart home, smart vehicle, eHealth systems, etc.). Monitoring systems allows keeping the system informed about the physiological and psycho-emotional state of a user both in ordinary life and in emergencies.

In emergencies scenarios (rescue operations, rallies, etc.), unmanned aerial vehicles (UAVs) have several advantages over humans. Firstly, UAVs can be sent to any location without the operator knowing the exact conditions in the target area. Moreover, using the latest tracking and communication techniques,

Granted by the Russian Foundation For Basic Research (grant 19-37-90129) and Council on grants of the President of the Russian Federation.

C. Stephanidis et al. (Eds.): HCII 2020, CCIS 1293, pp. 148–155, 2020.
https://doi.org/10.1007/978-3-030-60700-5_20

UAVs can scan a large area in a short period. Here RGB, infrared, and thermal cameras combined with state-of-the-art machine learning (ML) can be used for identifying and tracking humans.

Due to the computational overhead required by such a use case and given the limited power supply of UAVs, the processing of collected data by a UAV is a challenging issue. Nowadays, depending on the UAV type, batteries available in the market do not allow UAV a lot [21]. So, doing any processing with video and audio onboard UAVs is not rational. The obtaining and transmission only modalities to a control centre may be regarded as a solution.

Assume that we have a system of finding people in emergencies which uses the UAVs, reads off user modalities and transmit necessary information to control point, which decides on further actions. Modalities allow to identify and monitor the physiological state of a user. Multimodal interfaces allow for a join input of information from a variety of different sensors, passive and active form of user input. These interfaces may adapt to a user, task, current dialogue and environment condition.

However, the parameters of different user modalities have different statistical characteristics. Moreover, different modalities have different requirements to a network. The contribution of the current research is the analysis of the parameters of possible modalities for a system of finding people in emergencies and interchange format in a heterogeneous network.

2 Related Works

The idea to use UAVs in monitoring the subject area is not new. The authors of [20] described possible scenarios of UAVs using in rescue operations. In [8], the framework that supports multimodal communication along with an effective and natural mixed-initiative interaction between the human and the robots is proposed. The multimodal interaction in this project should allow the operator to communicate with the robots in a natural, incomplete, but robust manner exploiting gestures, vocal, or tablet-based commands. In [13], the authors investigated the use of natural user interfaces (NUIs) in the control of small UAVs. In their experiment, they captured whole-body gestures and had visual markers (for localization and commands). They demonstrated that natural user interfaces are effective enough for higher level UAV communication. Project described in [3,4,9] are also consider the usage on multimodal interfaces for UAVs control and management.

3 Modalities Classification

In [5], the authors proposed a taxonomy of interaction modalities which is based on humans' capabilities to provide input to and perceive output from computer systems. In this paper, the authors also considered existed useful taxonomies and classification schemes to categorize and describe Human-Computer Interaction (HCI) methods from 1974 [14] until 2014 [28]. In [29] the taxonomy of input/output modalities in the three media of graphics, acoustics and haptics is presented. In [6], the authors considered the taxonomy for acoustic, visual, text, haptic and olfactory communication channels. There is also various task-based communication channels classification. For example, in [22], we consider a user communication channels classification for multimodal authentication procedure. Inspired by these researches we outline the task-based categorization for the UAVs for finding people in emergencies (Fig. 1).

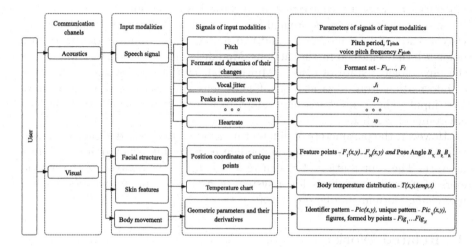

Fig. 1. User communication channels for UAVs in finding people scenario

The acoustic communication channel combines vocal (paralinguistic) and extralinguistic channels. In the vocal channel, messages are transmitted via the verbal (speech) channel, and in the extralinguistic channel, elements unrelated to speech are transmitted (cough, laughter, sigh, etc.) [11]. Moreover, it is possible to extract the heart rate from the speech signal [24]. The visual communication channel conveys the external biometric differences of the user and the manifestation of his behavioural characteristics (facial expressions, body movement, etc.) through photo and video recording by various technical devices. It allows to analyze both unique static (the user uses a specific pose) and dynamic (performed actions over some time) identifiers, as well as considering their combinations.

3.1 Speech Signal

For our proposed scenario the speech signal may be used for speech recognition and identification purposes. In speaker recognition, there are differences between low-level and high-level information. High level-information is valued like a dialect, an accent, the talking style and subject manner for context. These features are currently only recognized and analyzed by humans. The low-level information is denoted like pitch period, rhythm, tone, spectral magnitude, frequencies, and bandwidths of an individual's voice. These features are used by speaker recognition systems [31] and reflect the variety of input voice parameters to multimodal system. We outline only some of them in a following way.

The Pitch frequency is defined as follows $F_{pitch} = \frac{1}{T_{pitch}}$, where T_{pitch} is a pitch period calculated by [19]. The harmonics of pitch frequency may be calculated as $F_k = k \cdot F_0, k \in N$, where k is a number of formant frequency [10], [12]. The peaks in acoustic wave are defined by $P_i = \frac{\mu \tau}{v^2} exp(-\frac{\tau}{v})$, where τ is width, v is parameter determined by the ratio of the maximum analyzed level and quasi-maximum level, μ is a parameter depending on the maximum level analysis [10]. The Jitter J_j is calculated as it was proposed in [23].

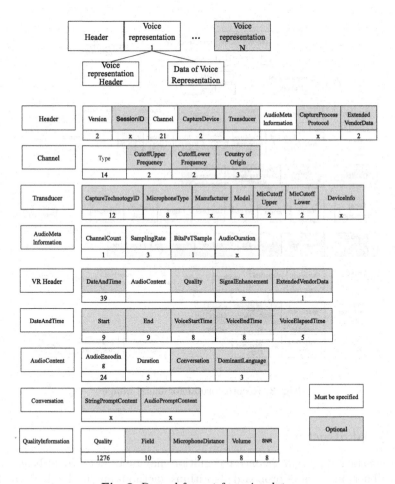

Fig. 2. Record format for voice data

Speech is an unsteady signal, but within a short period of time (10–40 ms) the characteristics of the speech signal do not change (due to the inertness of the speech path) and can be considered stable [25]. Therefore, a scan of the input speech signal by a short-term sliding window is usually used, within which one feature vector is generated.

For equal data interchange format of biometric data of various types, the series of ISO standards (19794) was proposed. The [2] specifies a data interchange format that can be used for storing, recording, and transmitting digitized acoustic human voice data (speech) assumed to be from a single speaker recorded in a single session. According to this standard the data interchange format for voice data is provided by XML format. The structure of the XML elements is shown in Fig. 2.

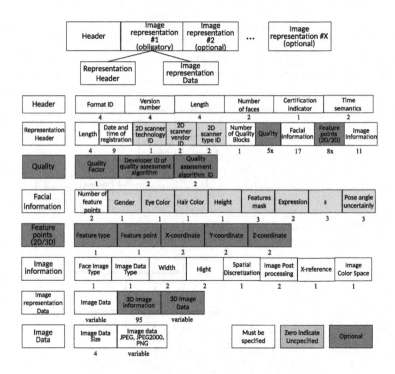

Fig. 3. Record format for facial image

3.2 Facial Structure

In our considered system the face recognition may be used for identification of a person. There are a lot of proposed algorithms, methods and tools which are dedicated to the problem of face recognition (for example, [17, 18, 21]). Video-based face recognition methods use a face image, or a series of face images captured by a video camera. Typically, a face image is captured, and then the face feature points are affixed. For example, the arrangement of the eyes, mouth, and nostrils may be used for the creation of a unique pattern. Three-dimensional face models can be created in a variety of ways, such as projecting an infrared grid ("structured light"), merging multiple images, or using halftone information in a separate image. The thermal imaging of the face displays the amount of heat caused by the flow of blood to the face. The thermal imager captures an invisible pattern of blood vessels under the skin caused by heat. Since illumination is not necessary when capturing face images with IR cameras, systems can capture images in the dark. However, IR cameras are more expensive than other types of camcorders.

The [1] defines the format for recording facial images in face recognition applications that require data exchange. The standard provides the normative requirements for all the four types of face images: basic, frontal, full frontal and token frontal. These image-type specific requirements include expected specification of a facial image like its encoding format, degree of rotation, camera position, lighting condition, resolution of the image. The detail implementation of this format is as shown in Fig. 3.

This organization of the record format includes fixed-length (17 bytes) Header containing information about the overall record, including the number of facial images represented and the overall length in bytes and an Image representation block for each facial image. This data consists of Facial Information block, the length size of which is from 47 bytes up to $(47 + 5x + 8y)$ byte (where x is the number of Quality blocks, y is a number of Feature Points blocks). The Facial Information block describes the features of the subject such as gender, multiple (including none) fixed length (8 bytes) feature points block describing feature points in a facial image. A fixed-length (11 bytes) Image Information block describing digital features of the image such as face image type and dimensions such as width and height.

3.3 Skin Features

For receiving thermal images of a victim, the thermal cameras are used. Thermal cameras are passive sensors that detect infrared radiation emitted by all objects that has a temperature above absolute zero [15]. In [30], the author considered the thermal camera's options. In [15], the sophisticated analysis of applications and features of thermal cameras is done. In [26] the authors presented a technique which allows detecting humans at a high frame rate on standard hardware onboard an autonomous UAV in a real-world outdoor environment using thermal and colour imagery. They used two video cameras. One of them delivers thermal video, and the second one is a standard colour camera. The image is first thresholded to find regions of human body temperature. Shapes of the regions are analyzed, and those which do not resemble a human body (i.e. the wrong ratio of minor and major axes of the fitted ellipse and incorrect area) are rejected. Additionally, regions which lie on the image border are rejected as they may belong to a bigger warm object. Once human body candidates are found in the thermal image, corresponding regions in the colour image are calculated. From the other hand, thermal images may be used for extracting physiological state of a person [16] such as heart rate or body temperature. It may be useful for measuring the body temperature of people on the street, for example.

We analyzed proposed solutions we may claim that typically, the work of the UAV sends the real-time aerial videos/images from the targeted area to the Ground Control System. These videos and images are analyzed by the rescue team to direct the search and rescue operations optimally [27].

4   Conclusion

Today multimodal approach for various communication systems is very relevant. Monitoring systems allows keeping the system informed about the physiological and psycho-emotional state of a user both in ordinary life and in emergencies. In this case, the UAVs may help to get acoustic or visual modalities for person recognition. In this paper, we consider the set of possible modalities and defined the interchange format for them. At the next step, we are going to collect statistic information about each modality and make a multimodal format.

References

1. Information technology-biometric data interchange formats-19794-part 5: Face image data (2014)
2. Information technology-biometric data interchange formats-19794-13: Voice data (2018)
3. Abioye, A.O., Prior, S.D., Thomas, G.T., Saddington, P., Ramchurn, S.D.: The multimodal speech and visual gesture (mSVG) control model for a practical patrol, search, and rescue aerobot. In: Giuliani, M., Assaf, T., Giannaccini, M.E. (eds.) TAROS 2018. LNCS (LNAI), vol. 10965, pp. 423–437. Springer, Cham (2018). https://doi.org/10.1007/978-3-319-96728-8_36
4. Abioye, A.O., Prior, S.D., Thomas, G.T., Saddington, P., Ramchurn, S.D.: Quantifying the effects of varying light-visibility and noise-sound levels in practical multimodal speech and visual gesture (msvg) interaction with aerobots. In: 2018 IEEE International Conference on Applied System Invention (ICASI), pp. 842–845. IEEE (2018)
5. Augstein, M., Neumayr, T.: A human-centered taxonomy of interaction modalities and devices. Interact. Comput. **31**(1), 27–58 (2019)
6. Basov, O., Saitov, I.: The main interpersonal communication channel and their projection on infocommunication systems. SPIIRAS Proc. **7**(30), 122–140 (2013). in Russian
7. Bezold, M., Minker, W.: Adaptive Multimodal Interactive Systems. Springer, New York (2011). https://doi.org/10.1007/978-1-4419-9710-4
8. Cacace, J., Finzi, A., Lippiello, V.: Multimodal interaction with multiple co-located drones in search and rescue missions. arXiv preprint arXiv:1605.07316 (2016)
9. Cacace, J., Finzi, A., Lippiello, V.: Robust multimodal command interpretation for human-multirobot interaction. In: AIRO@ AI* IA, pp. 27–33 (2017)
10. Campbell, W.M., Assaleh, K.T., Broun, C.C.: Speaker recognition with polynomial classifiers. IEEE Trans. Speech Audio Process. **10**(4), 205–212 (2002)

11. Campoy-Cubillo, M.C., Querol-Julián, M.: Assessing multimodal listening. In: Crawford, B., Fortanet-Gómez, I. (eds.) Multimodal Analysis in Academic Setting: From Research to Teaching, pp. 193–212. Routledge, London (2015)
12. Engemann, K.J., Yager, R.R.: A general approach to decision making with interval probabilities. Int. J. Gen Syst **30**(6), 623–647 (2001)
13. Fernandez, R.A.S., Sanchez-Lopez, J.L., Sampedro, C., Bavle, H., Molina, M., Campoy, P.: Natural user interfaces for human-drone multi-modal interaction. In: 2016 International Conference on Unmanned Aircraft Systems (ICUAS), pp. 1013–1022. IEEE (2016)
14. Foley, J.D., Wallace, V.L.: The art of natural graphic man-machine conversation. Proc. IEEE **62**(4), 462–471 (1974)
15. Gade, R., Moeslund, T.B.: Thermal cameras and applications: a survey. Mach. Vis. Appl. **25**(1), 245–262 (2013). https://doi.org/10.1007/s00138-013-0570-5
16. Hessler, C., Abouelenien, M., Burzo, M.: A survey on extracting physiological measurements from thermal images. In: Proceedings of the 11th PErvasive Technologies Related to Assistive Environments Conference, pp. 229–236 (2018)
17. Hsu, H.J., Chen, K.T.: Face recognition on drones: issues and limitations. In: Proceedings of the First Workshop on Micro Aerial Vehicle Networks, Systems, and Applications for Civilian Use, pp. 39–44 (2015)
18. Jain, A.K., Li, S.Z.: Handbook of Face Recognition, vol. 1. Springer, London (2011). https://doi.org/10.1007/978-0-85729-932-1
19. Markel, J.D., Gray, A.J.: Linear Prediction of Speech, vol. 12. Springer, Berlin (2013). https://doi.org/10.1007/978-3-642-66286-7
20. Mayer, S., Lischke, L., Woźniak, P.W.: Drones for search and rescue (2019)
21. Motlagh, N.H., Bagaa, M., Taleb, T.: UAV-based IoT platform: a crowd surveillance use case. IEEE Commun. Mag. **55**(2), 128–134 (2017)
22. Pakulova, E., Ryndin, A., Basov, O.: Multi-path multimodal authentication system for remote information system. In: Proceedings of the 12th International Conference on Security of Information and Networks, pp. 1–4 (2019)
23. Pakulova, E., Vatamaniuk, I., Budkov, V., Iakovlev, R., Nosov, M.: Using the random components of the jitter of speech pitch period to assess the state of the user of social-cyber-physical system. Telfor J. **11**(2), 102–107 (2019)
24. Poleshenkov, D., Pakulova, E., Basov, O.: Research on dependences of speech pitch parameters on pulse and heartbeat signals. In: Young Scientist's Third International Workshop on Trends in Information Processing, vol. 2500 (2019)
25. Rabiner, L.: Fundamentals of speech recognition (1993)
26. Rudol, P., Doherty, P.: Human body detection and geolocalization for UAV search and rescue missions using color and thermal imagery. In: 2008 IEEE Aerospace Conference, pp. 1–8. IEEE (2008)
27. Shakhatreh, H., et al.: Unmanned aerial vehicles (UAVs): a survey on civil applications and key research challenges. IEEE Access **7**, 48572–48634 (2019)
28. Turk, M.: Multimodal interaction: a review. Pattern Recogn. Lett. **36**, 189–195 (2014)
29. Tzovaras, D.: Multimodal User Interfaces: From Signals to Interaction. Springer, Berlin (2008). https://doi.org/10.1007/978-3-540-78345-9
30. Verhoeve, B.: Modifiable drone thermal imaging analysis framework for. Master's thesis (2018)
31. Yee, K.M., Khaing, M.M., Aung, T.Z.: Classification of language speech recognition system. Int. J. Trend Sci. Res. Dev. **3**, 946–951 (2019)

FAmINE4Android: Empowering Mobile Devices in Distributed Service-Oriented Environments

Ioanna Zidianaki[1]([⊠]), Emmanouil Zidianakis[1], Eirini Kontaki[1], and Constantine Stephanidis[1,2]

[1] Foundation for Research and Technology – Hellas (FORTH), Institute of Computer Science, 70013 Heraklion, Crete, Greece
{izidian,cs}@ics.forth.gr

[2] Department of Computer Science Heraklion, University of Crete, 70013 Crete, Greece

Abstract. The domain of distributed services is constantly growing, enabling interoperability between applications that run on different operating systems. The increasing availability and use of wireless mobile devices gave rise to opportunities for new types of mobility-distributed applications. This poster presents the FAmINE4Android middleware, which facilitates the development of service-oriented mobile applications by providing all the necessary mechanism and tools, through a seamless and intuitive Application Programming Interface (API). In addition, it caters for the creation of distributed services by enabling the exposure of software and hardware resources to the service-oriented environment. In order to demonstrate the features of the middleware and its suitability for the inclusion of mobile devices in distributed computing platforms, a mobile museum guide application has been developed as a case study, communicating with a Windows-based person tracking service. The preliminary evaluation of the mobile guide application verified the effectiveness and efficiency of the proposed middleware.

Keywords: Service oriented architecture · Distributed Service-Oriented environments · Middleware · Wireless mobile devices · Android · Ambient intelligence environments

1 Introduction

Over the past few years, a large number of advances in computing and communication technologies have made it possible for computing to occur anywhere. The increasing availability and use of wireless mobile devices entails opportunities for new types of distributed applications. In a distributed environment, the communication technology should abstract over the intricacies, machine architectures and operating systems, hiding the distribution of different parts that comprise the system, and enable programs written in different programming languages to communicate seamlessly. In this respect, a middleware contributes to the development of distributed applications, supporting libraries and services in any programming language. In communication middleware platforms, applications of different programming languages interact with third-party applications

© Springer Nature Switzerland AG 2020
C. Stephanidis et al. (Eds.): HCII 2020, CCIS 1293, pp. 156–164, 2020.
https://doi.org/10.1007/978-3-030-60700-5_21

or services, reflecting the synchronous and asynchronous request/response communication protocol. In particular, in the context of a distributed communication middleware, the following set of requirements should be met [1]:

- failure isolation
- elimination of single points of failure within the core middleware infrastructure
- restarting of failed services, before the clients that use those services are affected
- provision of mechanisms for notifying higher level entities about the irreparable failure of a specific service
- security throughout all the layers of a service-oriented environment.

Although many middlewares facilitate the interoperability of heterogeneous distributed services hosted in diverse platforms, their majority does not provide support for mobile devices.

This work presents the FAmINE4Android middleware, which aims to facilitate the development process of distributed Android mobile applications in service-oriented environments. The proposed approach caters for the creation of distributed services, enabling the exposure of software and hardware resources, and providing the required mechanisms and tools in order to support remote communication with distributed objects running on PCs and Android mobile devices. The proposed middleware provides mechanisms for service discovery, event driven communication and remote procedure calls through a seamless and intuitive Java API, allowing Android software engineers to develop applications enabled with distributed computing capabilities in an effortless manner. The remaining of this poster is structured as follows: Sect. 2 provides an overview of related middleware approaches; Sect. 3 presents the FAmINE4Android middleware; Sect. 4 describes a use case, in which the proposed middleware has been used, exemplifying its contributions for the development of distributed and pervasive services; finally, Sect. 5 concludes this work and highlights directions for future work.

2 Middleware Approaches

During the last decade, many middleware technologies have been established, aiming to facilitate the development process of interconnected objects in distributed service-oriented environments. A major property of these technologies is heterogeneity, meaning the support of multiple programming languages and computing platforms. Another crucial characteristic is the support for synchronous and asynchronous request/response communication and the ability of using encrypted communication channels, providing essential security to all entities in a distributed environment. This section presents well-defined existing communication technologies for service-oriented environments.

CORBA, which stands for Common Object Request Broker Architecture [2] and makes use of the Interface Definition Language (IDL) [3], is a popular middleware that defines a mapping between IDL definitions and constructs of the target programming language. It supports synchronous and asynchronous communication between services, encompassing fault tolerance mechanisms in order to allow the infrastructure to function properly, even if a fault has occurred. Moreover, this middleware uses encrypted communication channels as part of the security infrastructure that prevents hackers from accessing code inside the network. Although there are many open source implementations for each target programming language, *CORBA* is generally considered difficult to use [17].

Motivated by the need to improve unnecessary complexity of *CORBA*, the *ICE* middleware has been proposed. *ICE* stands for Internet Communication Engine [4] and relies on the *CORBA* architecture, purveying protocols to reduce network bandwidth and creating robust security systems. A considerable restriction of this middleware is that *ICE* applications and services have to be implemented under the *ICE* General Public License (GPL) and each extra feature has a corresponding fee.

Another communication middleware that builds upon CORBA libraries is *FAmINE,* which stands for FORTH Ambient Intelligence Network Environment, enabling the implementation and deployment of software abstractions [16], supporting many different programming languages such as Java, C++, Python and .NET in order to constitute a viable platform for developing distributed services. Although this middleware facilitates the interoperability of heterogeneous distributed services hosted in diverse platforms, it does not provide support for mobile devices.

A lightweight software communication middleware, which supports many different programming languages and enables Android applications to communicate with each other, is *ORBexpress* for Android [12]. This middleware provides an easy-to-use communication protocol, as well as features beyond *CORBA*, along with a development environment for building reliable distributed systems. Nevertheless, the main drawback is the lack of open-source availability due to the license fee required.

A communication platform that imports distributed services in many different programming languages is *Thrift* [6]. *Thrift*, like *CORBA*, uses IDL, which enables the invocation of attributes and operations between distributed services. Even if this approach is very well structured and efficient, *Thrift* does not import Naming and Notification Service, something that makes asynchronous communication impossible. A middleware that supports efficiently synchronous and asynchronous communication is *Etch*. *Etch* is a cross-platform, language- and transport-independent middleware for building network services [7], using a Network Service Description Language (NSDL). This approach provides the functionality for a service-oriented environment; however, it is incomplete because it is not provide the required mechanism for invocation of attributes and operations between distributed services. A flexible communication middleware platform, which supports synchronous and asynchronous communication between the interacting services, is *ROS* that stands for Robot Operating System [8]. Although *ROS* supports asynchronous messaging, it does not support synchronous request/response interaction between processes. In general, it provides many of the recommended functionalities of a distributed middleware, but it is very restrictive given that it runs only on Debian and Ubuntu and targets only a limited number of programming languages, such as C++, Python, LISP and JavaScript. Another dynamic communication middleware supporting the deployment and management of distributed systems is *RIO* [9]. It purveys a policy approach based on fault detection and recovery, scalability and dynamic deployment. Although it turns a network of computing resources into a dynamic service, providing a policy-based approach for fault detection and recovery, scalability and dynamic deployment, it is restrictive due to the limited number of running platforms that it supports.

A new perspective on modern distributed systems is *Web Services*. Using an XML-based protocol, *Web Services* allow applications to publish data across the Web [5]. While universal firewall traversal is very important for geographically distributed services, it is not essential in the context of a service-oriented environment, where the majority of the deployed services are restricted within a Local Area Network (LAN). Whereas this middleware supports synchronous and asynchronous communication between services, the programming of *Web Service* abstractions requires libraries and tools that are not available for many programming languages. As a result, this approach is insufficient as a middleware due to the absence of high level programming idioms and communication guarantees.

An interesting open source application-networking platform, which implements the open Web Application Messaging Protocol (WAMP) is *Crossbar.io* [12]. There are several WAMP clients that have already been implemented for almost twelve different programming languages, thus constituting *Crossbar.io* a communication middleware platform, encompassing a wide variety of technologies. In addition, *Crossbar.io* can be used from any Web application that is able to serve HTTP/POST requests, providing many of the requested functionalities for distributed environments. However, the implementation of WAMP does not provide full remote object passing between distributed services like CORBA.

Overall, among the aforementioned communication technologies, *CORBA* and *ICE* approaches are more effective in providing implementation for service-oriented environments. They both satisfy the requirements for a distributed communication middleware, such as heterogeneity, synchronous and asynchronous request/response communication, encrypted communication channels and ease of use via the intuitive usage of each target language. These factors make *CORBA* and *ICE* technologies independent of target domain, with the exception that *ICE* services have to be implemented under the ICE's General Public License (GPL).

Building upon good practices that are exhibited in existing middleware platforms, the proposed *FAMINE4Android* aims to bridge the existing lack for supporting mobile devices in pervasive environments, in a flexible and open-source approach, as explained in the next section.

3   FAmINE4Android Middleware

The FAmINE4Android middleware employs a freely available, open-source, and standards-compliant real-time C++ CORBA implementation, which is called The ACE ORB (TAO) and aims to facilitate the development process of distributed Android applications. FAmINE4Android builds upon the FAmINE middleware [16] and caters for the creation of distributed services, enabling the exposure of software and hardware resources in service-oriented environments. The proposed middleware consists of three core components, each responsible for a specific functionality, such as service registration, call functions and sending events, by provisioning a connection bridge between the native implementation (JNI) and the Java API. In addition, it provides the required mechanisms and tools in order to support service discovery, facilitating service registration or resolve, event driven communication and remote procedure calls, through a seamless and intuitive API.

The main components that contribute the overall architecture's synthesis and functionality are illustrated in Fig. 1 and are the following:

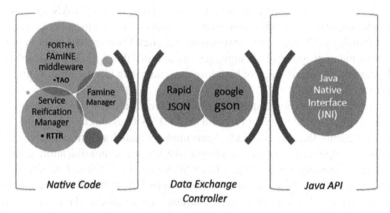

Fig. 1. High-level architecture of FAmINE4Android middleware

- *Native Code,* which consists of: 1) FAmINE middleware that builds upon TAO [2], 2) *Service Reification Manager* that implements a service type agnostic approach based on the Run Time Type Reflection (RTTR) library [14] and 3) *FAmINE Manager* that facilitates the service registration and resolve process, keeping all the required information (e.g. about the available service types) in internal data structures.
- *Data Exchange Controller* that implements a lightweight data exchange format approach, based on the JSON framework [19] in order to facilitate the object passing between Java API side and Native Code side.
- *Java API,* which is responsible for service discovery and remote procedure calls and is provided to software engineers as a unified AAR library.

Aiming at empowering the interconnection between Java and C++ native code, *FAmINE4Android* embeds advanced communication mechanisms, hiding the heterogeneity issues between Java and C++ code. The following sections present the developed mechanisms facilitating the data exchange process between Java and internal native functionality.

3.1   Run Time Type Reflection Library

Given that the implementation approach of *FAmINE4Android* middleware is based on the C++ CORBA implementation, the contribution of the reflection mechanism was crucial in order to support the collaboration of unknown type variables and objects with generic type code. Even if many programming languages provide built-in reflection mechanisms,

C++ does not support it. In this respect, *FAmINE4Android* employs the Run Time Type Reflection (RTTR) library [1413] that facilitates reflection in a semi-automated manner, where pre-defined information (e.g. regarding method signatures, types, etc.) is required by the developer.

3.2 Light-Weight Data Exchange Format Library

A mechanism responsible for facilitating the differences of data types was necessary in order to support interconnection between Java and C++ native code. Specifically, JNI native functions were used to smoothly accomplish the conversion of primitive or complex types, such as integer and data structures, between the two languages. The conversion approach of Java primitive types (e.g. Integer) to native equivalents was facilitated by underlying functionality of JNI, since the data and types' names remain identical in both Java and C++. The exchange process of complex data from Java to native code was facilitated by the Gson Java library [15], which converts Java objects to their JSON representation and vice versa. Accordingly, a mechanism able to facilitate the data transportation from C++ to Java code was implemented. Primitive type variables were converted into the JNI's generic data type (i.e., jobject), which were subsequently passed to the Java-side. Specific JNI functions that enclose their type for further type retrospection from Java were used in the conversion process. Similar functionality to the JSON approach was followed in order to transport complex type values from native code to Java-side.

4 Use Case Study: Museum Guide Android Application

The *FAmINE4Android* middleware has been employed in the implementation of a *Museum Guide* application, aiming to facilitate museum visitors by delivering real-time guidance support in an automatic manner based on their location.

For this purpose, a C++ tracking service approach, able to provide human body recognition and localization information [13] was used, in order to deliver implicit location-based guidance to any third party registered service. The underlying tracking service's infrastructure consists of an RGBD camera network and builds upon advanced computer vision algorithms that run on Windows OS. Specifically, the Museum Guide application, engaged *FAmINE4Android* as the middleware communication tool, in order to interconnect with a Windows tracking service. In order to facilitate data exchange between the C++ tracking service and the Museum Guide application, the implementation of the corresponding C++ tracking service's Interface Definition Language (IDL) [3] was necessary. IDL includes the signatures of tracking methods and variables, allowing the remote communication with the distributed service objects, call of the related methods and handle of the resolved events that keep updated Android side for recognition and localization information of humans.

The application supports four core functionalities, availed through its home screen, as presented in Fig. 2, namely: a) navigation, b) points of interest, c) map, and d) info.

In navigation mode, when a visitor is located adjacent to an artefact, information related to the artifact is automatically presented as depicted in Fig. 3. In addition,

Fig. 2. Main menu of Museum Guide application

Fig. 3. Using the mobile application to browse the digital exhibits, based on tracking technology

the user has access to a representative image of the selected exhibit as well as to relevant multimedia content. By selecting the points of interest menu option, visitors can see the full list of available exhibits within the museum and view further information about them. Finally, visitors can navigate in the museum through the map option, which depicts the floor plan illustrating all the artifacts according to their physical location in the museum.

In the context of assessing the reliability of the mobile Museum Guide application, a multiuser informal testing took place in the simulation space located in the Ambient Intelligence Facility of FORTH-ICS [18]. The simulation space was customized to accommodate some replicas of Macedonian artifacts. In detail, two golden artefacts and a fresco of ancient Greece were placed around the observed area, acting as real exhibits within a museum exhibition area. Four users, aged between 25 and 30, were invited to participate in the preliminary user-based evaluation. First, they were asked by the evaluator to download and install the application to their mobile phones. Afterwards, they were asked to launch the Museum Guide application and experiment with the four provided options. Thereafter, the evaluator asked them to walk freely within the exhibition area and show their interest to any of the three installed exhibits, by standing in front of it. All four users were able to access information related to the nearby exhibit and iterate through the artifact description and multimedia content that was automatically presented on their mobile screens. Additionally, they all were able to familiarize themselves with the map presentation and navigate easily within the exhibition area.

This case study showed that *FAmINE4Android* could stand as a real-time remote communication middleware, contributing to the development process of Android mobile applications, since it efficiently responded to the communications requirements of such heterogeneous networking environment, C++ Windows's services and Android mobile devices. During the preliminary trials, information was delivered in a timely manner to users' mobile devices, demonstrating the efficiency of the proposed communication framework.

5 Conclusions and Future Work

This work presented the *FAmINE4Android* middleware, which aims at empowering Android mobile devices in distributed service-oriented environments. *FAmINE4Android* builds upon CORBA implementation in C++ and caters for the creation of distributed services enabling the exposure of software and hardware resources in service-oriented environments. The presented approach provides the required mechanisms and tools in order to support service discovery, event driven communication and remote procedure calls, through a seamless and intuitive API. Efforts have been focused on the provision of a service type agnostic solution so that any distributed service, can be integrated in a seamless and effortless manner. Interoperability issues stemming from hosting native code in an Android Java application have been successfully addressed. In addition, a mechanism responsible for data exchange between Java and native code has been implemented. This mechanism is able to exchange the format of primitive or complex data types in order to address the data type variations between Java and native code.

The features of the *FAmINE4Android* framework were demonstrated by implementing the Android Museum Guide mobile application. *FAmINE4Android* was used as the middleware communication tool with a tracking C++ service that runs on Windows OS, providing information automatically, based on users' physical location.

Regarding future work, an evaluation strategy with the active contribution of Android developers in order to measure the applicability and usability of *FAmINE4Android* from a programmer perspective is considered essential. Moreover, the framework will be extended to support more platforms, such as iPhone devices, in order to holistically address the mobile computing market.

References

1. Georgalis, Y., Grammenos, D., Stephanidis, C.: Middleware for ambient intelligence environments: reviewing requirements and communication technologies. In: Stephanidis, C. (ed.) UAHCI 2009. LNCS, vol. 5615, pp. 168–177. Springer, Heidelberg (2009). https://doi.org/10.1007/978-3-642-02710-9_20
2. The ACE ORB (TAO). http://www.cs.wustl.edu/~schmidt/TAO.html
3. IDL. https://en.wikipedia.org/wiki/IDL_(programming_language)
4. ZeroC. http://www.zeroc.com
5. Web Services. https://en.wikipedia.org/wiki/Web_service
6. Slee, M., Agarwal, A., Kwiatkowski, M.: Thrift: scalable cross-language services implementation. Facebook White Paper. April 1, 5(8) (2007)
7. Etch. https://cwiki.apache.org/confluence/display/ETCH
8. ROS. http://www.ros.org/core-components/
9. Rio Dynami9c Distributed Services. http://www.rio-project.org/docs/index.html
10. Crossbar.io. http://crossbar.io
11. WAMP. http://www.wampserver.com/en/
12. ORBexpress for Android. http://www.ois.com/Products/communications-middleware.html
13. Galanakis, G., Zabulis, X., Koutlemanis, P., Paparoulis, S., Kouroumalis, V.: Tracking persons using a network of RGBD cameras. In: Proceedings of the 7th International Conference on Pervasive Technologies Related to Assistive Environments, pp. 1–4, 27 May 2014
14. Run Time Type Reflection. http://www.rttr.org/f

15. Gson Library. https://github.com/google/gson
16. Georgalis, I.: Architectures, methods and tools for creating ambient intelligence environments. Dissertation, Computer Science Department, University of Crete (2013). https://www.didakt orika.gr/eadd/handle/10442/29423
17. The Rise and fall of CORBA. https://dl.acm.org/doi/pdf/10.1145/1378704.1378718
18. Stephanidis, C., Antona, M., Grammenos, D.: Universal Access Issues in an Ambient Intelligence Research Facility. In: Stephanidis, C. (ed.) UAHCI 2007. LNCS, vol. 4555, pp. 208–217. Springer, Heidelberg (2007). https://doi.org/10.1007/978-3-540-73281-5_22
19. Json framework. https://www.json.org/json-en.html

Interacting with Data, Information and Knowledge

Design and Construction of a Device
for Obtaining Three-Dimensional Coordinates
in Different Topographic Surfaces Through
the Use of Wireless Networks, Gps and Altimeter

Marlene Ballestas[1]([⊠]), Vladimir Pinzón[1], Ruben Guerra[1], Alonso Barrera[2],
and Jesús Vergara[1]

[1] ITSA University, Soledad, 18 Street, #39-100 Atlántico, Colombia
mballestas@itsa.edu.co
[2] Universidad de La Costa, 58 Street, Barranquilla #55-66, Colombia

Abstract. The present investigation is done through processes that permit to find the value of the unknown term "R". The procedure for data collection disposed the transmitter and the receptor two meters apart, measuring the value of the parameter RSSI a total of twenty times; repeating this process every two meters, until the forty meters. The procedure for data collection disposed the transmitter and the receptor two meters apart, measuring the value of the parameter RSSI a total of twenty times; repeating this process every two meters, until the forty meters. In relation to the statistical treatment of the data, there were applied dispersion measurements or variability of the sample, such as the sample's variation, the standard deviation of the sample and the error. The results established the existence of the relation between the two principal variables involved in the study. Potency (dBm) as independent variable and the distance as dependent variable, in conclusion, this is prove that the bigger the distance between the transmitter and the receptor is, the less power it expresses.

Keywords: Three-dimensional · Topography · Planimetry

1 Introduction

Obtaining the three-dimensional coordinates allows comprehending in a clearer way the different topographic characteristics from a surface [1]. Various studies have addressed the need to use new methods for innovation in the use of altimetry and planimetric aspects [2, 3]. Based on those arguments, the present investigation is done through processes that permit to find the value of the unknown term "R".

© Springer Nature Switzerland AG 2020
C. Stephanidis et al. (Eds.): HCII 2020, CCIS 1293, pp. 167–175, 2020.
https://doi.org/10.1007/978-3-030-60700-5_22

2 Method

2.1 Variables and Formulas

In this case, the quantitative variable can be measured with a more precise grade and depends on measuring instruments [4]. The value of the variable relies on a value range of infinites numbers, for instance, the Time of Reaction of 22.54 g is 22.547 s, object's temperature (36.22 °C), thereby, the limitations to stablish that number, is based on the measuring instrument that was applied.

For the determination of the RSSI value, where d is the distance between the sender and receiver, the value of A is the RSSI magnitude measured from the sender to the receiver 1 m away, therefore, we have the next equation:

$$n = -(RSSI - A) * log(10)\ 10 * log(d)$$

The distance would be expressed as follows:

$$d = 10^{-\frac{(RSSI - A)}{10*n}}$$

2.2 Experimental Method

Problem Statement on this study is to Determine the distance in R3 from a Point A to a Point B, with the determination of the potency of sent and received signals between two Xbee s2c pro, through the RSSI parameter. The Hypothesis Statement is directed to that if the potency of sent and received signals between two radio frequency devices, according to the equation is: The received potency is inversely proportional to the squared distance that exists between the sender and the receiver and this distance influences over the RSSI parameter, which indicates, that while the received potency is lower, the value of RSSI will be lower as well.

The variable Definition proposes that the independent variable is the RSSI parameter, obtained by the application of the experimental method applied in this investigation, and the dependent variable is the distance between the sender and the receiver which relies on the RSSI parameter. Other variables that could interfere with the experiment design would be: Attenuation, The Free Space Loss, Atmospheric Absorption, Multipathing, refraction and thermal noise.

For this investigation the design is a correlational-causal cross-sectional study, and its goal is to describe the relationships that exist between two or more categories, concepts or variables, in a specific moment [5]. This design, measures (quantitative approach) o evaluates (qualitative approach) the relationship between the variables in a determined amount of time.

Data Collection: the sender and the receiver will be separated by 2 m and the values of the RSSI parameter will be measured twenty times. This will go on every 2 m, until completing 40 m.

Statistical Treatment: it will be applied the statistical dispersion over the samples through the variation of the sample, the standard deviation and the mistake. They will be made by the accomplished along the empirical and theoretical measures, exposed by graphics and tables. With the application of the mentioned procedures it's wanted to obtain the distance from any Point A to a Point B in R3, with the appliement of the RSSI parameter, through non-temporary measures following the experiment design.

3 Results

The results of each of the three scenarios developed in this study are shown below

3.1 First Scenario

They are shown below in table one and two the Parameter (A) Measurement (see Table 1) and Linear Data Gathering (see Table 2):

Table 1. Parameter (A) Measurement

Parameter (A) Measurement	Local	Remote	Average	Rounding
1	−28	−28	−28	−28
2	−27	−27	−27	−27
3	−28	−28	−28	−28
4	−28	−28	−28	−28
5	−28	−27	−27,5	−28
6	−28	−27	−27,5	−28
7	−28	−27	−27,5	−28
8	−28	−27	−27,5	−28
9	−28	−27	−27,5	−28
10	−28	−27	−27,5	−28
11	−28	−27	−27,5	−28
12	−28	−27	−27,5	−28
13	−28	−27	−27,5	−28
14	−27	−27	−27	−27
15	−28	−27	−27,5	−28
16	−27	−27	−27	−27
17	−28	−28	−28	−28
18	−27	−28	−27,5	−28
19	−28	−27	−27,5	−28
20	−28	−28	−28	−28

Table 2. Linear Data Gathering

Data from Urban Location Carrera 68 # 74-161 Barranquilla-Colombia

Distance (m) ➡	5	10	15	20	25	30	35	40	45	50
Number of the sample ⬇	dBm	dBm	dBm	dBm	dBm	dBm	dBm	dBm	dBm	dBm
1	50	63	60	68	74	76	76	78	79	81
2	51	57	65	69	71	73	75	80	80	82
3	51	61	65	69	68	74	75	79	80	80
4	51	59	63	69	73	78	77	77	81	80
5	51	56	66	70	73	73	76	79	82	80
6	51	60	66	66	69	72	76	78	80	82
7	50	54	68	69	71	75	78	77	81	82
8	51	57	64	68	74	75	79	80	78	84
9	52	62	64	73	71	76	78	79	81	83
10	50	60	67	70	75	76	78	80	80	83
Σ	508	589	648	691	719	748	768	787	802	817
Average	50,8	58,9	64,8	69,1	71,9	74,8	76,8	78,7	80,2	81,7

Using equation to determine the constant (n) (Table 3):

Table 3. Constant (n) for each measure

3.26	3.09	3.13	3.16	3.14	3.17	3.16	3.16	3.16	3.16

Calculating the average of the (n) values the result for the constant is:

$$n = 3.16$$

Now calculating the distance from the transmitter to the receptor with equation, this is then compared to the real distance, where Ed = Experimental distance and Rd = Real distanc (Table 4):

Table 4. Ed and Rd comparison

Ed (m)	5,27	9,51	14,62	20,00	24,52	30,30	35,05	40,26	44,91	50,10
Rd (m)	5,00	10,00	15,00	20,00	25,00	30,00	35,00	40,00	45,00	50,00
Difference (m)	−0,27	0,49	0,38	0,00	0,48	−0,30	−0,05	−0,26	0,09	−0,10

3.2 Scenario 2

They are shown below tables the Parameter (A) Measurement (see Table 5) and Linear Data Gathering (see Table 6):

Table 5. Parameter (A) Measurement

Parameter (A) Measurement	Local	Remote	Average	Rounding
1	−32	−32	−32	−32
2	−32	−32	−32	−32
3	−31	−31	−31	−31
4	−32	−32	−32	−32
5	−32	−31	−32	−32
6	−32	−30	−31	−31
7	−32	−32	−32	−32
8	−32	−32	−32	−32
9	−32	−32	−32	−32
10	−32	−32	−32	−32
11	−32	−32	−32	−32
12	−32	−32	−32	−32
13	−32	−32	−32	−32
14	−32	−32	−32	−32
15	−32	−32	−32	−32
16	−32	−32	−32	−32
17	−32	−32	−32	−32
18	−30	−30	−30	−30
19	−31	−31	−31	−31
20	−32	−30	−31	−31

Table 6. Linear Data Gathering 2

Data from Wooded Location Tubara-Colombia

Distance (m) ➡	5	10	15	20	25	30	35	40	45	50
Number of the sample ⬇	dBm	dBm	dBm	dBm	dBm	dBm	dBm	dBm	dBm	dBm
1	48	55	59	61	64	69	70	73	76	76
2	47	56	57	60	65	67	74	75	73	78
3	48	55	57	64	67	67	71	73	78	77
4	49	55	61	64	66	69	68	73	76	76
5	49	56	55	64	64	71	73	76	75	78
6	49	54	57	61	55	72	71	75	76	79
Σ	290	331	346	374	381	415	427	445	454	464
Average	48.33	55.17	57.67	62.33	63.50	69.17	71.17	74.17	75.67	77.33

Using equation to determine the constant (n) (Table 7):

Table 7. Constant (n) for each measure

2.34	2.32	2.18	2.33	2.25	2.52	2.54	2.63	2.64	2.67

Calculating the average of the (n) values the result for the constant is:

$$n = 2.44$$

Now calculating the distance from the transmitter to the receptor with equation, this is then compared to the real distance, where Ed = Experimental distance and Rd = Real distance (Table 8):

Table 8. Ed and Rd comparison

Ed (m)	4,67	8,89	11,26	17,47	19,51	33,29	40,20	53,34	61,45	71,91
Rd (m)	5,00	10,00	15,00	20,00	25,00	30,00	35,00	40,00	45,00	50,00
Difference (m)	0,35	0,63	2,32	3,06	6,38	6,60	8,15	6,80	9,37	8,27

3.3 Scenario 3

They are shown below tables the Parameter (A) Measurement (see Table 9) and Line-ar Data Gathering (see Table 10):

Table 9. Parameter (A) Measurement

Parameter (A) Measurement	Local	Remote	Average	Rounding
1	−32	−31	−32	−32
2	−32	−31	−32	−32
3	−33	−32	−33	−33
4	−34	−33	−34	−34
5	−34	−33	−34	−34
6	−32	−33	−33	−33
7	−34	−34	−34	−34
8	−33	−34	−34	−34
9	−34	−33	−34	−34
10	−34	−34	−34	−34

Table 10. Elevated Data Gathering

Data from Itsa University HQ Soledad-Colombia					
Distance (m) ➡	2	3	4	5	6
Number of the sample ⬇	dBm	dBm	dBm	dBm	dBm
1	48	49	59	59	62
2	47	48	59	56	62
3	47	49	58	55	59
4	48	49	60	61	64
5	46	50	61	61	62
6	43	50	60	63	60
7	45	45	59	63	61
8	44	45	60	59	64
9	44	49	58	61	64
10	45	48	59	63	64
Σ	457	482	593	601	622
Average	45.70	48.20	59.30	60.10	62.20

Using equation to determine the constant (n) (Table 11):

Table 11. Constant (n) for each measure

3.89	3.40	4.53	4.02	3.88

Calculating the average of the (n) values the result for the constant is:

$$n = 3.94$$

Now calculating the distance from the transmitter to the receptor with equation, this is then compared to the real distance, where Ed = Experimental distance and Rd = Real distance (Table 12):

Table 12. Ed and Rd comparison

Ed (m)	2.23	2.58	4.92	5.16	5.83
Rd (m)	2.00	3.00	4.00	5.00	6.00
Difference (m)	−0.23	0.42	−0.92	−0.16	0.17

4   Conclusions

The current techniques for obtaining the topographical survey were documented; meanwhile other different methods for device location through wireless net were identified. This information led to conclude that any topographical survey process involves wireless systems for obtaining tridimensional coordinates.

The applied methodology for the three contemplated scenarios resulted in the obtaining of distances very similar to the real ones, some of them with less than 20 cm of discrepancy; Within this methodology, other measurements were apart enough to dismiss using this technology in certain spaces with Xbee pro S2C devices. It is important to highlight that nowadays there are RF signal transmitters and receptors capable of trespassing objects which communication field it extends for many kilometers, so the results provide a great view for the application of this technology in the topographical area.

The calculation of the distance between point A and point B for the three contemplated scenarios developed the following conclusions:

- Scenario 1: The devices were located in an urban zone (Xbee) creating an uninterrupted vision line and measuring the parameters RSSI (dBm) obtaining a minimum difference of 0 (m) and a maximum one of 0.49 (m) between Rd and Ed.

- Scenario 2: The devices were located in a wooded zone (Xbee) creating an uninter-rupted vision line and measuring the parameters RSSI (dBm) obtaining a minimum difference of 0.33 (m) and a maximum one of 22 (m) between Rd and Ed.
- Scenario 3: The devices were located in an open zone (Xbee) creating an uninterrupted vision line and measuring the parameters RSSI (dBm), creating a right-angled triangle which one of its sides' length increased to obtain a minimum difference of 0.16 (m) and a maximum de 0.92 (m) for the hypotenuse between Rd and Ed.

Establishing the relation between the two principal variables involved in the study (potency (dBm) as independent variable and distance as dependent variable), led to confirm that the longer the distances between the transmitter and the receptor, the less the value of potency.

References

1. Rugeles, J., León, D.: Técnicas de localización de nodos inalámbricos mediante redes de sensores. grupo de GISSIC. Universidad militar Nueva Granada, Colombia (2010)
2. Segura, J.: Sistema de auto localización a partir de una red WIFI. Universitat de Lleida, Spain (2010)
3. Gualdrón, O., Pinzón, S., De Luque, L., Díaz, I., Vásquez, S.: Una herramienta para la predicción de la de intensidad de la señal recibida, (RSSI) para wireless Lan 802.11b. Revista Colombiana de Tecnologías de Avanzada 7 (1) (2007)
4. Ramirez, E.: El método experimental. Univerrsidad de Jaén, Spain (2010)
5. Hernández Sampieri, R., Fernández Collado, C., Baptista Lucio, P.: Metodología de la investigación. Mcgraw-hill, Mexico (2010)

Data Curation: Towards a Tool for All

José Dias[1], Jácome Cunha[1,2(✉)], and Rui Pereira[2]

[1] University of Minho, Braga, Portugal
a78494@alunos.uminho.pt, jacome@di.uminho.pt
[2] HASLab/INESC Tec, Braga, Portugal
ruipereira@di.uminho.pt

Abstract. Data science has started to become one of the most important skills one can have in the modern world, due to data taking an increasingly meaningful role in our lives. The accessibility of data science is however limited, requiring complicated software or programming knowledge. Both can be challenging and hard to master, even for the simple tasks.

With this in mind, we have approached this issue by providing a new data science platform, termed *DS4All.Curation*, that attempts to reduce the necessary knowledge to perform data science tasks, in particular for data cleaning and curation. By combining HCI concepts, this platform is: *simple* to use through direct manipulation and showing transformation previews; allows users to *save time* by eliminate repetitive tasks and automatically calculating many of the common analyses data scientists must perform; and suggests data transformations based on the contents of the data, allowing for a *smarter* environment.

Keywords: Human-centered data science · Data cleaning · Data curation

1 Introduction

The use of data cannot be dissociated from our daily lives - data supports, e.g., social media, is fundamental to guide us in traffic and is being used in precision medicine by promising health-care avenues. In order to support all these data-based services, the amount of data which are produced these days are tremendous, and are still expected to increase significantly within the near future. For example, Facebook experiences about 2.5 billion likes and 300 million photo uploads on a regular day [22]. Of course data by itself, even if in massive amounts, has very little value. Indeed, it is the information extracted from data which has the potential to change and improve our lives. However, the information extraction process is complex, requiring cleaning, transforming, understanding, analyzing and interpreting data [21]. This is what is currently called Data Science (DS) [3], and one incorrect or inaccurate decision in any

This work is financed by National Funds through the Portuguese funding agency, FCT - Fundação para a Ciência e a Tecnologia within project UIDB/50014/2020.

C. Stephanidis et al. (Eds.): HCII 2020, CCIS 1293, pp. 176–183, 2020.
https://doi.org/10.1007/978-3-030-60700-5_23

step of the process is sufficient enough to compromise the extracted information [7]. However, the challenge for any data scientist is that performing these steps requires a variety of skills including mathematics, statistics, machine learning (ML), data structures, algorithms, and correlation or causation [9]. Nevertheless, there is a worldwide movement towards pushing everyone to have DS skills. For instance, a study by IBM advocates that academia must ensure data literacy for any student in any field of education [5]. Similarly, the Portuguese Government has also defined that until the end of 2023 all students with higher education must have the opportunity to learn DS [15]. In fact, many other countries have defined national strategies for DS [3]. However, to teach advanced techniques and tools to an entire academic community is challenging, tedious, and difficult to entirely fulfil. Indeed, a study by Kaggle, with more than 16.000 answers from DS practitioners, shows that textual programming languages (PLs) such as Python or R are the most used tools (76.3% and 59.2%, respectively) [6]. Unfortunately, programming is a very challenging task, taking years to train and master. While there are other tools targeting inexperienced users, such as Tableau or Excel, these are much less used (20.4% and 13.7%, respectively [6]). Moreover, there is no empirical evidence of their efficiency and efficacy amongst non-expert users.

Human-computer interaction (HCI) related communities have been proposing several methodologies to aid users in developing their own software. These users are usually termed end users, i.e. computer users with no (or little) software development background, yet still need to develop software, i.e. end-user programming [10]. The proposed methodologies include visual programming [2], programming by example [4] or direct manipulation [19].

In this work we build on such works to further design methodologies and a tool (termed DS4All.Curation) that can be productively used by any end user for performing DS, particularly focusing on data cleaning and curation. The curation and transformation of data is generally a very complex and time consuming process for an experienced data scientist [7,14]. Oftentimes, several tools or programming languages (a PL can also be seen as a tool) are used for this. But to do so, data scientists must properly learn to use these. This is a larger issue for end user data scientists, with their limited (or inexistent) computer science background.

Thus, we believe that a visual development environment for data science (DS) direct manipulation will help diminish such difficulties and limitations. Naturally, data should be represented in a way that (end) users can actually see and manipulate it using some tabular format, e.g., resembling Excel. Whenever a user wishes to apply a certain transformation, they should also be able to see a preview of how their data will be altered. Such a side-by-side look at the dataset, prior and post changes, aims to help remove a level of abstraction of how data will be changed. Additionally, a user should be able to, at any point, directly manipulate the data within such a dataset previewer, such as updating cell values, or through a drop down menu to allow changes or filtering data on a specific column. For many operations related to data curation [13] this should be sufficient. In essence, this environment must be *simple*.

Such a visual environment must also help guide the user to more efficiently perform their work. Indeed, prior studies suggest DS environments should guide their users [21]. For example, it is very common to calculate the statistical information (average, min, max, etc.) or grouping/clustering of data prior to manipulating the data [18]. Such statistics help data scientists summarize the contents of their data, understanding if there are any outliers present, or if something appears to be incorrect. For such operations, data scientists have to repeatedly turn to using programming or complex tools to perform such common tasks each time and every time they tackle a new dataset. We propose that such common tasks should be automatically performed within our visual environment, in order to facilitate the end user data scientists' work, and in turn *save time*.

We propose to go one step further and use such information to automatically present suggestions of common (or uncommon) transformations to the user, which can be automatically applied by the system. An example would be, in a column representing gender, when detecting similar values such as FEMALE and female, to suggest replacing one entry by the other or by a new value. Another example would be for columns inferred as numerical, where a suggestion to remove data entries based on minimum and maximum bounds may be presented. The system should also learn with the user, by understanding what operations they repeatedly need and/or use, and intelligently offer suggestions. Offering both statistical information on the data and suggested operations to be performed will lower the amount of time taken to perform such tasks, reduce errors, and also reduce the possibility of incorrectly programming the tasks. As such, the final requirement of a data science environment for any use is that it must be *smart*.

In summary, we propose that a visual data science development environment must be *simple*, *saves time*, and is *smart*. Section 2 presents our initial steps in providing data science end users with an environment adhering to these three principals. In Sect. 3 we discuss related work and in Sect. 4 we summarize out contribution and discuss future work.

2   DS4All.Curation: A Data Curation Tool for All

In accordance to what we have previously discussed, we believe there are several paths one may take when developing a visual environment for the direct manipulation of data. We have developed a prototype of a humanized data cleaning tool, termed DS4All.Curation[1], shown in Fig. 1, that we now describe. The dataset represents Android smartphone usage information [12].

Since we are proposing methodologies and tools for data science, it seems natural that data should be represented in a way users can actually see and manipulate it using some tabular format, e.g., resembling Excel. Indeed, shown

---

[1] DS4All.Curation can be found at https://github.com/Zamreg/HDC.

in Fig. 1 - V (*Original dataset*), we have the original and unaltered dataset shown at all times, allowing the end user to better accompany their transformations. All such transformations would be shown and previewed in Fig. 1 - III (*Preview dataset*). This side-by-side look at the dataset before and after applying changes aims to help remove a level of abstraction of how data will be changed, and directly present such actions. At any point, the user may directly manipulate the data within the *Preview dataset*, such as updating cell values, or through a drop down menu (as shown in Fig. 1 - IV) to allow changes or filtering data on a specific column. For many operations related to data cleaning/curation [13] this should be sufficient.

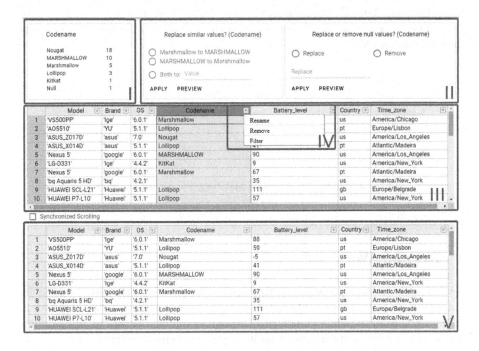

Fig. 1. Humanized Data Cleaning Example Interface

When the user selects one specific column, a *statistics card* is displayed in order to help summarize the contents of the chosen column. An example is shown in Fig. 1 - I, where the `Codename` column is selected and a *statistics card* detailing the different data entries (and their quantification) is shown. In addition to displaying a *statistics card*, a collection of *suggestion cards* are automatically displayed (shown in Fig. 1 - II), where each presents a data transformation action, based on the statistics and data inference. Following our example, the system detects two very similar values: `Marshmallow` and `MARSHMALLOW`, and thus suggests replacing one data value by the other or by a new value. In the same example, it also detected the presence of `null` or empty values, and suggests either replacing them with a new value or removing such data entries. Shown in Fig. 2, is another example of such cards if one would choose the `Battery_level` column. In this case, as the column is inferred to be numerical, a set of common numerical metrics are shown, followed by a suggestion to remove data entries based on minimum and maximum bounds. Knowing that a smartphone's battery level could not be higher than 100% nor lower than 1%, such data entries might present themselves as dirty data and could accordingly be removed through the *suggestion card*.

Such *statistic cards* and *suggestion cards* aim to remove another layer of complexity in data cleaning by automatically presenting common statistical information which users otherwise have to calculate, and by suggesting transformations based on their data. In both cases, the user would have to resort to either programming or using complex tools to gather the statistical information and apply their transformation.

Fig. 2. Numerical statistics and suggestion card example

3   Related Work

Several authors have proposed related approaches to make DS more accessible. Potter's Wheel provides an interactive data transformation and cleaning system that allows users to define transforms through graphical operations or examples and see the effects instantly, making it easy to experiment with different transformations [16]. Unfortunately, the project ended about 20 years ago and does not seem to have been evaluated with users.

Milo [17] and BlockPy [1] are tools that offer a block-based language for users, but focus on different aspects. While Milo aims to help users with no computer science background to only perform machine learning techniques, we propose a tool for data cleaning. BlockPy is a visual interface for the Python programming language to motivate students to start learning how to program. In our case, our visual environment is designed for data cleaning, and not a programming language interface.

Wallace et al. propose a tool to allow users with less statistical skills to make use of advanced models written using the R language [20]. Their motivation is similar to ours although their goal is to provide a graphical user interface for a given R model whilst we provide a tool specific for data cleaning tasks.

DataScience4NP is a web platform aiming to provide an intuitive user interface for users to build sequential DS workflows [11]. This system intends to perform all the steps of extracting knowledge from data, which includes data insertion, pre-processing, transformation, mining and interpretation/evaluation of results, without requiring users to program. However, similarly to Milo, this platform is focused on data mining techniques whilst ours focus on data cleaning.

Industry and open-source communities have also proposed several tools for DS. Popular tools include Microsoft PowerBi[2], Tableau (Prep)[3], Jupyter (notebooks)[4], and RapidMiner[5]. These tools allow their users to make data exploration, data mining, visualization and reporting tasks through visual interactive dashboards. However, there does not seem to exist any scientific evidence of their effectiveness amongst end user data scientists. In fact, Jupyter notebooks have been found to be messy by some users [8].

4 Conclusions

In this work we propose a platform for data cleaning/curation intended for end user data scientists. We achieve this by relying on suggestions and direct data manipulation. Currently as we're still improving upon what we have we plan to explore suggestions further and explore programming by example as a way to transform data where the user can specify input and output examples. This has the potential to easily allow users to normalize data, map it to other representations, and further remove a layer of abstraction of data and mental work for our end user data scientists. We also intend to empirically evaluate our tool comparing its usability (effectiveness, efficiency and satisfaction) against other popular tools.

References

1. Bart, A.C., Tibau, J., Tilevich, E., Shaffer, C.A., Kafura, D.: BlockPy: an open access data-science environment for introductory programmers. Computer **50**(5), 18–26 (2017). https://doi.org/10.1109/MC.2017.132
2. Burnett, M.M.: Visual programming. In: Wiley Encyclopedia of Electrical and Electronics Engineering. Wiley, Hoboken, December 1999. https://doi.org/10.1002/047134608x.w1707
3. Cao, L.: Data science: a comprehensive overview. ACM Comput. Surv. **50**(43) (2017). https://doi.org/10.1145/3076253

---

[2] https://powerbi.microsoft.com.
[3] http://tableau.com.
[4] https://jupyter.org.
[5] https://rapidminer.com.

4. Gulwani, S.: Programming by examples (and its applications in data wrangling). In: Dependable Software Systems Engineering, vol. 45, pp. 137–158. IOS Press, April 2016. https://doi.org/10.3233/978-1-61499-627-9-137
5. IBM and Business-Higher Education Forum and Burning Glass: The Quant Crunch: How the Demand for Data Science Skills Is Disrupting the Job Market (2017). https://www.ibm.com/downloads/cas/3RL3VXGA
6. Kaggle Inc.: The State of Data Science & Machine Learning (2017). https://www.kaggle.com/surveys/2017
7. Kandel, S., Paepcke, A., Hellerstein, J.M., Heer, J.: Enterprise data analysis and visualization: an interview study. IEEE Trans. Visual. Comput. Graph. **18**(12), 2917–2926 (2012). https://doi.org/10.1109/TVCG.2012.219
8. Kery, M.B., Radensky, M., Arya, M., John, B.E., Myers, B.A.: The story in the notebook. In: Proceedings of the 2018 CHI Conference on Human Factors in Computing Systems - CHI 2018, vol. 2018-April, pp. 1–11. ACM Press, New York, New York, USA, April 2018. https://doi.org/10.1145/3173574.3173748
9. Kim, M., Zimmermann, T., DeLine, R., Begel, A.: The emerging role of data scientists on software development teams. In: Proceedings - International Conference on Software Engineering, pp. 96–107 (2016). https://doi.org/10.1145/2884781.2884783
10. Ko, A.J., et al.: The state of the art in end-user software engineering. ACM Comput. Surv. **43**(3), (2011). https://doi.org/10.1145/1922649.1922658
11. Lopes, B., Pedroso, A., Correia, J., Araujo, F., Cardoso, J., Paiva, R.P.: DataScience4NP -A Data Science Service for Non-Programmers. In: 10° Simpósio de Informática - INForum 2018 (2018)
12. Matalonga, H., et al.: Greenhub farmer: real-world data for android energy mining. In: 2019 IEEE/ACM 16th International Conference on Mining Software Repositories (MSR), pp. 171–175. IEEE (2019)
13. Muller, M., et al.: How data science workers work with data: discovery, capture, curation, design, creation. In: Proceedings of the 2019 CHI Conference on Human Factors in Computing Systems. CHI 2019, Association for Computing Machinery, New York, NY, USA (2019). https://doi.org/10.1145/3290605.3300356
14. Pereira, P., Cunha, J., Fernandes, J.P.: On understanding data scientists. In: IEEE Symposium on Visual Languages and Human-Centric Computing (VL/HCC) (2020, to appear)
15. Portuguese Government: Contrato para a Legislatura com o Ensino Superior para 2020–2023 (2019). https://www.portugal.gov.pt/download-ficheiros/ficheiro.aspx?v=d2607a18-51c9-489c-a61c-1ff420dab2f0
16. Raman, V., Hellerstein, J.M.: Potter's wheel: an interactive data cleaning system. In: VLDB 2001 - Proceedings of 27th International Conference on Very Large Data Bases, pp. 381–390 (2001)
17. Rao, A., Bihani, A., Nair, M.: Milo: a visual programming environment for Data Science Education. In: 2018 IEEE Symposium on Visual Languages and Human-Centric Computing (VL/HCC), vol. 2018-October, pp. 211–215. IEEE, October 2018. https://doi.org/10.1109/VLHCC.2018.8506504
18. Refaat, M.: Data preparation for data mining using SAS. Elsevier (2007). https://doi.org/10.1016/B978-0-12-373577-5.X5000-5
19. Shneiderman, B.: Direct manipulation: A step beyond programming languages. Computer **16**(8), 57–69 (1983). https://doi.org/10.1109/MC.1983.1654471
20. Wallace, B.C., et al.: Closing the gap between methodologists and end-users: R as a computational back-end. J. Statist. Softw. **49**(5), 1–15 (2012). https://doi.org/10.18637/jss.v049.i05

21. Wongsuphasawat, K., Liu, Y., Heer, J.: Goals, process, and challenges of exploratory data analysis: an interview study. arXiv preprint arXiv:1911.00568, November 2019
22. Zikopoulos, P.C., DeRoos, D., Parasuraman, K., Deutsch, T., Corrigan, D., Giles, J.: Harness the power of Big Data : the IBM Big Data platform. McGraw-Hill, New York (2013)

BIMIL: Automatic Generation of BIM-Based Indoor Localization User Interface for Emergency Response

Yanxiao Feng[1], Julian Wang[1(✉)], Howard Fan[2], and Ce Gao[3]

[1] Department of Architectural Engineering, Pennsylvania State University, Pennsylvania, US
julian.wang@psu.edu
[2] Department of Electrical Engineering and Computer Science, University of Cincinnati, Cincinnati, US
[3] Aoyuan Commercial Property Group, Guangdong, China

Abstract. Effective communications among team members enable them to stay resilient and make rapid decisions when they are facing uncertainty and complexity during an incident with time and resource constraints. With the rapidly-expanding indoor positioning technologies that support public safety operations, a more efficient and effective building information platform is needed to support indoor location data visualization and coordination efforts. On the other hand, building information modeling (BIM) has been widely accepted in the Architecture, Engineering, and Construction (AEC) industry as a central repository of building information. BIM does not only include accurate geometric building data and sufficient semantic information but also could be integrated with real-time smart building data. The ultimate goal of this research effort is to bridge the technology gap between various emerging indoor positioning technologies and abundant building information and thus to overcome the main shortcoming of the existing indoor building model. A BIM-based Indoor Location (BIMIL) portal is designed in this work for automatic data extraction, visualization, and transformation of BIM emergency-related data for public safety purposes. Subsequently, the new generalized building 3D model can be overlaid with indoor positioning data to support emergency responses.

Keywords: BIM · Emergency Response and Management · Indoor location · Automatic Data Extraction and Generation · User Graphic Interface

1 Introduction

Building Information Modeling (BIM) is a digital representation of all physical and functional characteristics of a building throughout its entire life cycle [1–3]. While most other building information sources such as drawings, images, and databases may be more accessible to public safety organization (PSO) officers, these traditional repositories only contain either geometric or semantic information. Comparatively, BIM is a database for both and can be expanded with more functions as well. Precise definitions for building

© Springer Nature Switzerland AG 2020
C. Stephanidis et al. (Eds.): HCII 2020, CCIS 1293, pp. 184–192, 2020.
https://doi.org/10.1007/978-3-030-60700-5_24

elements such as stores, doors, windows, and spaces in the BIM model will provide pivotal information for emergency response-related needs. For instance, annotations (i.e., semantic information) in BIMs (e.g., room numbers, room functions, etc.) will facilitate communication between the incident commander and deployed first responders, so that the latter can quickly follow commands such as finding a specific location to deploy a node or rescue an occupant. We should also consider the integrated spatial relationships among building elements that are made clear in BIM (e.g., stairways linking two floors together, walls containing several door openings and their dimensions, etc.) and will enable navigation functions and evacuation routing analyses.

Although the current accessibility of first responders to BIM may be low, deployment by AEC as a central repository of building information is increasing [4]. It has been reported that 38% of AEC users and managers use BIM, and the percentage is expected to increase by nearly 20% in the next three to five years [5]. One can easily envision BIM-compliant resources dominating building lifecycles from design to construction and throughout the operation. Meanwhile, recent BIM-related studies and practices have captured existing buildings without the original BIM format documentation through various means (e.g., 3D laser scanners, photogrammetry), in order to obtain as-built building information [6]. Furthermore, building owners are moving BIM to the forefront of project delivery methods. A growing number of owners are developing guidelines for BIM deliverables to extract design and construction benefits today [7]; there is also an eye toward the future use of these data for building facilities operation and maintenance (O&M) that are tightly linked to smart building sensors and devices. A few emerging projects have used BIM as the platform to implement intelligent building systems [8, 9].

To survive in this new and rapidly-expanding era of digital technologies that support public safety operations, the ultimate goal of this research effort is to bridge the technology gap between emerging indoor technologies and abundant building information, and overcome the main shortcoming of existing indoor building model development (i.e., that resource-intensive generation must be done in isolation without informative user-based feedback, and when completed, the pervasive lack of up-to-date connections). Note that what is presented in this paper is not to develop new indoor location or navigation systems but rather to establish the linkage between BIM datasets and various indoor location services for public safety purposes. Particularly, in this paper, we mainly introduce the first stage of this platform development; that is, a methodology of automatically extracting the key emergency-related BIM data and generating a user interface for indoor location coordination. A user interface for BIM file uploading and converting is also yielded at this stage.

2 Prior Work

The necessity of enhancing the 3D spatial representation of the indoor layout and outdoor buildings to understand and plan their actions has been addressed in some studies, and the applications of such information in analyzing natural disasters and their corresponding navigation were investigated [10–12]. Various solutions and algorithms have been proposed and developed to integrate the detailed building information in indoor navigation systems, but there are still limitations of these solutions to be widely and efficiently used. Researchers in [13, 14] utilized the BIM model to check the emergency evacuation during the design of the construction projects to evaluate the pre-designed plan. Studies in [15] further designed the shortest paths for emergency evacuation tasks using the input geometric information and graphs constructed for network modeling without supporting real-time information updates nor considering the realistic and ever-changing indoor environment. BIM-oriented modeling was developed in the study [2] to transform the BIMs to a new geoinformation domain while the spatial relationships and semantics information in the new compact object model were preserved. However, the new spatial file was converted using a translator software and the results were unstable due to the data types applied for representing object geometries. Many studies have shown and emphasized the importance of an appropriate level of detail for the building geometry data as well as semantics information. Also, the limitations of real-time collaboration between the dynamic indoor building information and the positioning system were also identified.

In general, an indoor positioning system (IPS) using various technologies such as infrared systems, Wi-Fi-based systems, and acoustic systems [16], would be integrated as the main component of the indoor navigation tool. One nonnegligible problem with the application is the limited application scenarios for each system, which makes the collaboration between the indoor positioning technologies and building information more inconvenient. Researchers in [17] used a combined navigation platform for real-time location sensing with the collaboration of exported CAD building information in the format of Industry Foundation Classes (IFC) to provide the location information of the rescuers and support the route network generation. Nonetheless, the building information exported from CAD format was simplified spatial maps and could not reflect the critical information which may be dynamic in an emergency such as the fire resistance hours for building structure materials. Some researchers in [18] developed an indoor network model by extracting both semantic and geometric information from BIM and combined such information with GIS analysis to enable both indoor and outdoor routing analysis, but without addressing the real-time indoor positioning. There are also studies that integrate a wireless sensor network into emergency monitoring and disaster prevention as well as a response system. Researchers in [19] developed an infrastructure network using wireless sensors to capture and share the sensing data to improve emergency response efficiency. Studies in [20] proposed a BIM-based intelligent system for fire detection and disaster response system that integrated the building sensors, indoor positioning design and rescue route planning. However, automatic building information data extraction, processing, and regeneration for public safety purposes have not been addressed yet.

3   BIMIL Portal Design

In this work, we proposed and designed a BIM-based Indoor Location (BIMIL) portal based on a system architecture in which a modified building information model (mBIM) serves as the front end to disparate information including indoor location data and an abundance of smart building data; this would serve as a "one-stop shop" for public safety purposes. The PSO officers can utilize this portal, without a need of specific software installations and skills in BIM and data process, to import BIM files from local files or Web Services and then export processed indoor spatial information in the formats of IndoorGML, DXF, OBJ, or SKP, which is also integrated with indoor positioning data and smart building data. Figure 1 illustrates the overall schematic diagram of the designed portal. This BIM-IL portal provides end-users with a simple and graphical interface through which they can process BIM files for the building models and related datasets required for various indoor location technologies. The portal may hide technical details and provide a single, unified interface to provision applications on connected smart building systems. This will be constructed based on Web technology such as HTML5 and JavaScript in the future and will require no additional software on the user's (i.e., the PSO's) side. The system architecture of the BIM-IL portal is illustrated in Fig. 2 below. The interface accesses the core functionalities necessary to support user requests. It consists of three main screens in which users are able to create new projects, upload BIM files, and link O&M data. The function of linking O&M data is possible through either offline or online sources based on existing O&M data formats, such as COBie [7, 21], CMMS [22], CAFM [23], and IWMS [24].

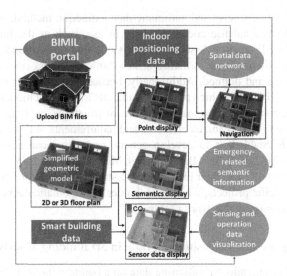

Fig. 1. Schematic diagram of the workflow of the BIMIL portal.

After uploading the BIM files and connecting the O&M dataset, the portal communicates with the server that delegates the call to the BIM Manager, which is the central algorithm package for automatically generating various models/dataset from BIMs. This layer has four modules: geometric data, the data network, emergency-related semantics, and smart building data. The modules will be linked as a collaborative workflow to support streamlined user operations, but users determine the module selection, based on their needs. In the end, in the data access layer, users can access all generated data and files, including 2D/3D layouts for simple indoor positioning presentations, various network models for further navigation purposes, and sensing and operating datasets. All generated data are associated with the identified spatial objects IDs/names and coordinates so that they can be integrated into one platform.

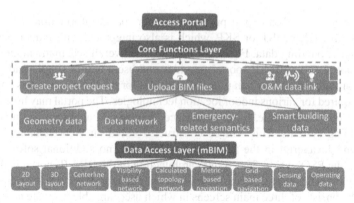

Fig. 2. BIMIL portal architecture.

3.1 Automatic BIM Data Extraction for Public Safety Purposes

In order to establish a generic and automatic data extraction method, we reviewed the national and international fire codes currently in use, such as the International Fire Code, National Fire Protection Association Fire Code, and International Building Code, and distilled from them a clear structure of how building egress-related elements and information are set and defined. Additionally, because the most commonly accepted BIM file format is IFC [25], which provides standards for product modeling schema, we also conducted a comprehensive search in terms of structures and types within the IFC schema according to the organized elements and requirements of the available building information. This enabled us to develop generic codes that can retrieve the needed parameters for all IFC-compliant BIM datasets. Meanwhile, it is also worth mentioning that modelers may still have their preferences to structure and define the egress-related information in specific projects, which may hinder the automatic data extraction based on the developed codes in this work (Table 1).

3.2 Overlaying the Indoor Positioning Data in 3D Building Models

In order to overlay the indoor positioning data on a building model (either a 2D layout or 3D map), the first requirement is to understand the indoor positioning data generated from different technologies and systems. In general, indoor positioning data can be classified into two broad categories: symbolic and point. Symbolic positioning data represent a position as a symbol, such as the room, predefined grid, and zone numbers [26, 27] mainly generated by proximity-based positioning systems (e.g., ultrasonic sensor-based [28] and Bluetooth systems [29]) when a user is in the proximity of a positioning signal modules. A number of positioning systems also output position data as grids of predefined variable sizes, which can also be further classified into the regular or irregular-shaped room/zone data [30]. Point positioning data are typically described as coordinate points that can be further classified into absolute (which has a global reference/origin) and relative (which has a local reference/origin [31]). Examples of absolute point positioning data include Wi-Fi-based positioning systems [27] that output data in the global coordinate system of a building, while examples of relative point positioning

Table 1. Key emergency-related elements and their structures in IFC.

Element	Building Codes		Defined in IFC schema
Smoke barrier	NFPA 105	Yes	P_SINGLEVALUE/IfcLabel
Fire walls, barriers, partitions	NFPA 80	Yes	P_SINGLEVALUE/IfcLable
Fire doors	SDI	Yes	P_SINGLEVALUE/IfcBoolean
Fire alarms	NFPA 72	Yes	P_SINGLEVALUE/IfcIdentifier
Automatic sprinkler system	NFPA 13	Yes	P_ENUMERATEDVALUE/IfcLable/PEnum_SprinklerActivation
Portable fire extinguisher	NFPA 10	No	N/A
Smoke and heat vents	NFPA 204	Yes	P_SINGLEVALUE/IfcLabel
Carbon dioxide fire extinguishing system	NFPA 12	Yes	P_BOUNDEDVALUE/IfcPositiveRatioMeasure
Halon 1301 fire extinguishing system	NFPA 12A	Yes	P_BOUNDEDVALUE/IfcPositiveRatioMeasure
Standard pipe system	NFPA 14	Yes	P_SINGLEVALUE/IfcIdentifier
Deflagration venting	IBC	No	N/A
Egress doors	IFC section 1010	Yes	P_SINGLEVALUE/IfcBoolean
Egress windows	IBC sec 1030	Yes	P_SINGLEVALUE/IfcBoolean
Egress ramps	IFC section 1012	Yes	P_SINGLEVALUE/IfcBoolean
Stairways	IBC	Yes	P_SINGLEVALUE/IfcBoolean
Exit signs illuminated	NFPA 101	Yes	P_SINGLEVALUE/IfcBoolean
Egress path markings	IFC sec 1025	No	N/A
Types of doors	IBC	Yes	P_SINGLEVALUE/IfcLable
Types of windows	IBC	Yes	P_SINGLEVALUE/IfcLable
Room tags and dimensions	IBC	Yes	P_SINGLEVALUE/IfcAreaMeasure

data are generated via inertial sensors [32] that report only displacements relative to the previously reported location. In our work, an indoor location system via LTE direct-mode radio signal operations can generate point coordinates that are within a relative coordinating system defined by a couple of the LTE signal modules [33]. Subsequently, we developed a calculation procedure linking the defined origins in the LTE direct-mode operations and the 3D building model, which converted the relative coordinates generated from the LTE direct-mode indoor location system to the global coordinating system of the building model.

Figure 3 provides a case study we carried out to test the BIM data extraction and positioning data integration. In this case study, a campus building's BIM file (i.e., Revit) was uploaded into the developed BIMIL portal and then automatically generated a 3D building model in which the fire rating hours of building walls were automatically extracted and visualized. The color scheme represents the levels of fire rating hours. The points' indoor positioning data in Fig. 3 (inverted cones) were generated by the LTE signal modules, representing first responders' real-time locations in the building.

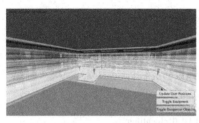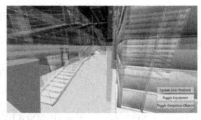

Fig. 3. A case study of the BIMIL portal use and indoor location data visualization

4   Conclusions

The importance of obtaining critical building information to improve emergency response time and reduce safety risks has been emphasized in some studies. Still, the building information platform development is both labor-intensive and knowledge-demanding as the egress-related information is not only geometric but also spatial, ambient, and semantic related. In this paper, we introduced a new BIM-based indoor location support platform that includes the key egress-related building information and can be expanded to integrate the smart building data. The basic architecture and data flow were also illustrated, and the procedure of how to integrate the indoor location data was discussed.

Acknowledgements. We acknowledge the financial support by the US NIST, Public Safety Innovation Acceleration Program Award 2017: First Responder Indoor Location Using LTE Direct Mode Operations via BIM.

References

1. Isikdag, U., Zlatanova, S., Underwood, J.: A BIM-oriented model for supporting indoor navigation requirements. Comput. Environ. Urban Syst. **41**, 112–123 (2013)
2. Van Nederveen, G.A., Wolfert, R., Van de Ruitenbeek, M.: From BIM to life cycle information management in infrastructure. eWork Ebus. Archit. Eng. Constr. ECPPM 2014, 115 (2014)
3. Wang, J., Li, J., Chen, X.: Parametric design based on building information modeling for sustainable buildings. In: Proceedings of 2010 International Conference on Challenges in Environmental Science and Computer Engineering, vol. 2, pp. 236—239. IEEE (2010)
4. Azhar, S., Khalfan, M., Maqsood, T.: Building information modelling (BIM): now and beyond. Constr. Econ. Build. **12**, 15–28 (2015)
5. Business Advantage. BIM Trends (Building Information Modelling). (2016). http://www.business-advantage.com/blog/bim-trends/. Accessed 19 Oct 2018
6. Volk, R., Stengel, J., Schultmann, F.: Building information modeling (BIM) for existing buildings — literature review and future needs. Autom. Constr. **38**, 109–127 (2014)
7. Pishdad-Bozorgi, P., Gao, X., Eastman, C., Self, A.P.: Planning and developing facility management-enabled building information model (FM-enabled BIM). Autom. Constr. **87**, 22–38 (2018)
8. Chen, K., Lu, W.S., Xue, F., Zheng, L.Z., Liu, D.D.: Smart gateway for bridging BIM and building. In: Chau, K.W., Chan, I.Y.S., Lu, W., Webster, C. (eds.) Proceedings of the 21st International Symposium on Advancement of Construction Management and Real Estate, pp. 1307–1316. Springer, Singapore (2018). https://doi.org/10.1007/978-981-10-6190-5_115
9. Balaji, B., et al.: Brick: Metadata schema for portable smart building applications. Appl. Energ. **226**(15), 1273–1292 (2018)
10. Li, J., Zlatanova, S.: A 3D data model and topological analyses for emergency response in urban areas. Geospatial Inf. Technol. Emerg. Response (ISPRS Book Ser.) **143**, 168 (2008)
11. Zlatanova, S.: SII for emergency response: The 3D challenges. in Chen, J., Jiang, J., Nayak, S. (Eds.), In: Proceedings of the XXI ISPRS Congress, Part B4-TYC IV, pp. 1631–1637. Beijing (2008)
12. Isikdag, U., Underwood, J., Aouad, G.: An investigation into the applicability of building information models in geospatial environment in support of site selection and fire response management processes. Adv. Eng. Inform. **22**(4), 504–519 (2008)
13. Wang, C.H., Moh, R., Kang, S.M., Lee, W.L., Pei, T.J., Hsieh, S.H.: BIM-based application development of underground MRT stations emergency evacuation-time evaluation for Taipei MRT design checking. In: International Conference on Construction Applications of Virtual Reality (ConVR), pp. 113–121. Taipei, Taiwan (2012)
14. Choi, J., Choi, J., Kim, I.: Development of BIM-based evacuation regulation checking system for high-rise and complex buildings. Autom. Constr. **46**, 38–49 (2014)
15. Chen, A.Y., Chu, J.C.: TDVRP and BIM integrated approach for in-building emergency rescue routing. J. Comput. Civ. Eng. **30**(5), C4015003 (2016)
16. Brena, R.F., García-Vázquez, J., Galván-Tejada, C.E., Rodríguez, D.M., Rosales, C.V., Fangmeyer, J.: Evolution of indoor positioning technologies: a Survey. J. Sens. (2017)
17. Rueppel, U., Stuebbe, K.M.: BIM-based indoor-emergency-navigation-system for complex buildings. Tsinghua Sci. Technol. **13**, 362–367 (2008)
18. Teo, T.A., Cho, K.H.: BIM-oriented indoor network model for indoor and outdoor combined route planning. Adv. Eng. Inform. **30**(3), 268–282 (2016)
19. Ochoa, S.F., Santos, R.: Human-centric wireless sensor networks to improve information availability during urban search and rescue activities. Inform. Fusion **22**, 71–84 (2015)
20. Cheng, M.Y., Chiu, K.C., Hsieh, Y.M., Yang, I.T., Chou, J.S., Wu, Y.W.: BIM integrated smart monitoring technique for building fire prevention and disaster relief. Autom. Constr. **84**, 14–30 (2017)

21. Lavy, S., Jawadekar, S.: A case study of using BIM and COBie for facility management. Int. J. Facil. Manag. **5**, (2014)

22. Rastegari, A., Mobin, M.: Maintenance decision making, supported by computerized maintenance management system. In: 2016 Annual Reliability and Maintainability Symposium (RAMS), pp. 1–8. Tucson, AZ (2016)

23. Moshrefzadeh, M., Donaubauer, A., Kolbe, T.H.: A CityGML-based Façade Information Model for Computer Aided Facility Management. In: Bridging Scales-Skalenübergreifende Nah-und Fernerkundungsmethoden, 35. Wissenschaftlich-Technische Jahrestagung der DGPF (2015)

24. Hanley, B.P., Brake, D.J.: Putting asset data at the heart of organisational decision-making using an Integrated Workplace Management System. In: Asset Management Conference (AM 2016), London (2016)

25. Borrmann, A., Beetz, J., Koch, C., Liebich, T., Muhic, S.: Industry foundation classes: a standardized data model for the vendor-neutral exchange of digital building models. In: Borrmann, A., König, M., Koch, C., Beetz, J. (eds.) Building Information Modeling, pp. 81–126. Springer, Cham (2018). https://doi.org/10.1007/978-3-319-92862-3_5

26. Lu, H., Yang, B., Jensen, C.S.: Spatio-temporal joins on symbolic indoor tracking data. In: 2011 IEEE 27th International Conference on Data Engineering, pp. 816–827. Hannover (2011)

27. Li, H., Lu, H., Shou, L., Chen, G., Chen, K.: In search of indoor dense regions: an approach using indoor positioning data. IEEE Trans. Knowl. Data Eng. **30**, 1481–1495 (2018)

28. Khyam, M.O., Noor-A-Rahim, M., Li, X., Ritz, C., Guan, Y.L., Ge, S.S.: Design of chirp waveforms for multiple-access ultrasonic indoor positioning. IEEE Sens. J. **18**, 6375–6390 (2018)

29. Faragher, R., Harler, R.: An Analysis of the accuracy of bluetooth low energy for indoor positioning applications. In: Proceedings of the 27th International Technical Meeting of the Satellite Division of The Institute of Navigation (ION GNSS+2014), pp. 201–210. Florida (2014)

30. Tamas, J., Toth, Z.: Classification-based symbolic indoor positioning over the Miskolc IIS Data-set. J. Locat. Based Serv. **12**, 2–18 (2018)

31. Hightower, J., Borriello, G.: Location systems for ubiquitous computing. Computer **34**, 57–66 (2001)

32. Kok, M., Hol, J.D., Schon, T.B.: Indoor positioning using ultrawideband and inertial measurements. IEEE Trans. Veh. Technol. **64**, 1293–1303 (2015)

33. Fan, H., Kilari, A., Vemuri, K., Daffron, I., Wang, J., Ramamurthy, V.: Indoor location for emergency responders using LTE D2D communications waveform. In: CEUR Workshop Proceedings, vol. 2498, pp. 347–354. CEUR-WS (2019)

Towards Supporting Tools for Editors of Digital Scholarly Editions for Correspondences

Tobias Holstein[1,2]([⊠]) [iD] and Uta Störl[2] [iD]

[1] Mälardalen University, Västerås, Sweden
[2] Darmstadt University of Applied Sciences, Darmstadt, Germany

Abstract. Digital (scholarly) editions are considered to be imperfect tools that are unable to meet the expectations of their users. Based on a previous study with expert users and literature research, tasks and challenges in the process of creating a digital (scholarly) edition were identified. Referring to the term computer-aided digital humanities, we looked into the different tasks and how tools could provide the required "computer-aided" support. In the context of text-based tasks, we identified several support levels from simple syntax checks in XML-Editors, to WYSIWYA-Editors, and finally to context-sensitive support, which utilises data from the same context, e.g., documents of the same author, or from the same writing date. Furthermore, we present concepts and prototypes as work in progress, which focus on support of editors of digital (scholarly) editions.

Keywords: Digital scholarly edition · Tasks · Computer-aided support · Digital humanities · Interdisciplinary

1 Introduction

Digital editions, or digital scholarly editions, are one way of preserving documents of great literary value for future generations. "Scholarly" refers to critical components of an edition, which are for example annotations or other content that provides context to a document. In comparison, a pure facsimile (digitised picture of a document), or a set of those, does not qualify as a digital edition, nor as digital scholarly edition [7]. Sahle defines editions to be scholarly "when it is based on scholarly knowledge and critical engagement" [14].

There exist already hundreds of digital editions [7], preserving letters, books, notes, diaries and other artefacts. This trend slowly replaces the previously established standard of printed editions, which came in a specific print format (e.g. books). With the rise of the digital age, print editions lack the flexibility and agility of digital equivalents, or as Sahle positively states "offer the opportunity to overcome the limitations of print technology" [14]. Thereby a new digital paradigm is introduced that opens a manifold of new possibilities, but also challenges, as for example:

© Springer Nature Switzerland AG 2020
C. Stephanidis et al. (Eds.): HCII 2020, CCIS 1293, pp. 193–200, 2020.
https://doi.org/10.1007/978-3-030-60700-5_25

- accessibility (e.g., in digital libraries [15] or digital editions [6]),
- searchability (e.g., in digital editions [13])
- overall usability and utility, i.e. usefulness (e.g., focusing on users [8])
- computability (e.g., Data in Digital Humanities [2])
- user experience (e.g., in digital editions [6])

As an example, we describe accessibility in the following, which does not mean that the other possibilities, and challenges, are in any way less important. Accessibility aims to increase access to content for people with disabilities. Following accessibility guidelines, such as WCAG [4], editors and developers make sure that content of a digital (scholarly) edition is available to screen readers, or that the design is responsive and thus allows the users to increase or decrease font sizes, contrast, etc. Digital editions core contribution is text, i.e. digital text (e.g., transcriptions of handwritten documents, comments, annotations, etc.). Thus, how the text is presented to the user, should depend on the user's preferences and not be restricted by the system. A state-of-the-art digital (scholarly) edition can provide necessary interfaces and be designed to allow all types of users to access its content. It requires careful attention by both, editors and developers, regarding how content is prepared, which in consequence requires the right tools to create and digital edition platform to deliver the content.

According to Sahle, a digital (scholarly) edition can be seen as a "data driven fluid publication", and thus it is "always open to change and amendments". Furthermore, he states "in theory, it never closes down and never reaches a final state. There is always something left to do" [14]. This is an important aspect of digital (scholarly) editions because changes and amendments can become cumbersome and can require a high effort if tools do not provide specific support. Imaging a digital edition containing thousands of transcribed documents is subject of being migrated from TEI (an XML Standard) to a different data format, such as JSON, without having the right tools.

In a previous study, we looked into the process of how digital scholarly editions are created and identified a manifold of tasks and challenges that editors have to handle [10]. In this context, we conducted a literature study and competitive analysis to find the state of the art in creating digital scholarly editions. A previous study by Franzini et al. [8] found that "digital editions are imperfect tools unable to meet the expectations of every single user". We can confirm this statement, as it aligns with our observations. There is a high potential for improvements for creating, but also for using digital (scholarly) editions. Thus, we are looking into supporting tools, that support and aid editors of digital (scholarly) editions in their tasks.

This paper is structured as follows. In Sect. 2 typical tasks of creating a digital scholarly edition are described. Section 3 describes the different levels of support based on examples. The last sections provide a discussion, conclusion and future work.

2   Tasks While Creating a Digital Scholarly Edition

The following list of tasks serves as a framework, which allows a comparison and to coordinate improvements based on an exemplary workflow. Keep in mind that editors may vary their process by adding, changing or removing tasks for a specific edition. They might vary the order, skip or repeat certain tasks, as they see fit in their editorial process. Another important aspect is parallel work on different tasks, especially when there is not a single editor, but a team of editors distributing tasks among each other. The whole process is mostly sequential, certainly iterative. E.g., transcriptions can be reviewed and improved iteratively, and comments and annotations can also be added in later iterations. However, a document has to be acquired, digitally or analogue, before it can be transcribed, therefore there are also strictly sequential parts of the process.

Acquisition
   How artefacts (i.e., documents) are acquired, requested, found, etc.
Editorial Guidelines
   The editorial that editors/creators have set, which serves as a guideline on how data is entered into the system, e.g., what to annotate, the categorisations used, or when to add additional meta-comments.
Digitisation/Facsimiles
   The process of digitising analogue artefacts, and related tasks, such as the image processing (e.g., colour-correction) or image cropping.
Document Management
   E.g., sorting, ordering, grouping, or tracking of changes of documents.
Metadata
   Adding metadata to a document, such as the date of writing, information about materiality of the original artefact (paper size, writing style, etc.), or other properties of the document that could be of use in future research.
Transcription
   Transcribing text from the facsimile or original artefact.
Annotation
   Annotating the transcribed text with entities (person, place, etc.), or annotating text corrections (e.g., characters being replaced by an author with another text).
Comments/Meta Comments
   Comments by the editor which give context to a certain part of the text, or meta comments to give context to the whole document. Both provide a critical representation of the document (in case of scholarly editions).

When software features are added to the editing platform, editors might also improve the content, if useful or necessary. For example, adding a software feature that allows cross-referencing text and selected parts of facsimiles (e.g., the stamp of a postcard), might cause another iteration in which parts of a facsimile are linked/referenced in comments.
   The workflow or process of the editing team is often parallel to a software engineering and design process. This interdisciplinary combination allows user

(i.e., editor) needs and problems to be analysed, and solutions to be developed. Thus actual usable features will resolve impediments to provide the best and most efficient set of tools (or one tool to rule them all), which aids the editors in their task of creating a "data driven fluid publication".

3   Support for Editing (Text-Based) Tasks

Tasks can be supported on different levels and by different tools. However, the context of use is important. Researchers who look into text processing might rather work with an XML-Editor, whereas editors of a scholarly edition, who focus on a critical representation of historic documents, might prefer a What You See Is What You Annotated (WYSIWYA) Editor. This section shows examples of the different levels of aid and support for text-based tasks. Additionally, we report preliminary results of user tests with prototypes built and tested in different levels in a current state of work in progress.

3.1   XML-Editors

XML-Editors provide support with syntax, conformity and validation. Advanced versions provide auto-complete features that help users while entering XML. E.g., the first characters of an XML node or attribute will cause the XML-Editor to suggest a list of possible options to complete the already written text, hence auto-complete. This feature becomes more powerful if the XML-Editor knows the XML standard, such as TEI [1] or TEI-correspDesc. In this case, the auto-complete might only suggest options, which fit in the current context. It is however still necessary for the user to understand the meaning of nodes, their attributes, how nodes can be nested, i.e. how the structure of the XML document is supposed to be according to the chosen standard. The next level of support is reached when auto-complete features also suggest options for values of attributes, e.g., a value for setting a text left-aligned, the name of a person, or even an id to an external data set.

3.2   WYSIWYA-Editors

Another way of support are "What You See Is What You Annotated" (WYSIWYA) editors, which show a visualisation of a data structure, instead of the actual data format and structure, such as XML. This allows users to focus on annotations, commenting, etc. How the WYSIWYA-Editor stores the information is now decoupled and not part of the user's tasks, even though there are hybrid-editors that allow editing the underlying structure as well as the representation of it. However, the main advantage of a WYSIWYA-Editor is the loss of complexity for editing documents and new opportunities to visualise the text and its annotations, as shown by CATMA [12,16], or INCEpTION [11].

XML-Editors as well as WYSIWYA-Editors focus on one document, and not necessarily can access a back-end or database. There are of course plug-ins

Fig. 1. Screenshot of remote test task one: an example facsimile to be described is depicted on the left, the WYSIWYA-Editor prototype with an example text and comments on the right (cmp. [9]).

providing features that allow referencing data from external sources, e.g., other XML documents, a database or similar, but the support does usually not go beyond search and insert. Creating a WYSIWYA-Editor for digital scholarly editions has many challenges. One of them is, the requirement to allow integration into the overall editing platform, instead of being a stand-alone solution. Thus, APIs have to be provided, so that data source can be connected. Also the WYSIWYA-Editor has to cope with a variety of requirements from different editions since not all editions use the same editorial guidelines. In summary, a WYSIWYA-Editor must be flexible and generic in its configuration, but also provide specific support for a specific edition.

We have developed a high-fidelity WYSIWYA-Editor prototype that encompasses all of those requirements (see Fig. 1). E.g. text can be annotated with all types of entities over a single auto-complete field. The WYSIWYA-Editor knows the internal type of the entity (person, place, etc.), and sets the right XML node for a chosen entity. Furthermore, it allows to set comments and meta-comments, which can also contain annotations. This allows to search or filter comments, or documents with comments, that contain certain annotation, or that have a reference to a certain entity. The editor can reference external APIs, and provide a flexible configuration to add or remove annotation options. E.g., if editors require another type of annotation, they can just add it to the configuration.

The WYSIWYA-Editor was tested in an unmoderated remote test. The test included a questionnaire to collect data about participants profession, experience with XML, WYSIWYA, and other types of editors, as well as expectations towards editors for digital editions. Two specific tasks were included, and a post-task feedback questionnaire. The first task required to transcribe and annotate a short letter. The second task required to correct and change an already annotated letter. 27 participants (out of 52 participants) completed both tasks and the survey. The feedback in this stage of development was constructive and helpful to improve the editor. E.g., one user stated that it would be nice to be able to see the XML code, another suggested to add a feature to change start and end of an annotation by visually dragging the start or end after an annotation has been set. Many other participants reported several errors while using the editor, which caused difficulties to complete the given tasks. Therefore, the results were inconclusive regarding efficiency and task-completion time. The complete evaluation can be found in [9]. We aim to conduct a moderated usability test to get a better insight for the improvement of future releases.

3.3   Context-Sensitive Support

A higher level of support can be achieved by providing context-sensitive information to the user. Assuming a digital scholarly edition focuses on correspondences (i.e. letters, post-cards, etc.). All correspondence items can be grouped into conversations between at least two persons, i.e. tuples of author(s) and addressee(s). Multiple correspondence items may exist for each tuple. Whenever a new correspondence item is added to an existing conversation, just by declaring the metadata of author and addressee, information from other correspondence items might be of use. Persons, events, or other entities likely reappear in a conversation. Thus, entities that have appeared in other correspondence items of the same conversation, can be shown with a higher priority/ranking in auto-complete, or similar controls.

However, showing contextual information based on the entered text could offer even more support. Using natural-language processing, it would be possible to detect and mark date and time expressions in the text. The editor-system could show a calendar upon request, presenting events, person dates of birth or death, or documents with a writing date in a certain time frame that already exist in the database (or via external services) in parallel to the transcribed text. This might allow to see and find co-relations to other entities, e.g. events, documents, etc.

This led to another concept, that we call "rule based check". Whenever entities are annotated in the text, the metadata of those entities can be used for comparisons in context of the document. An example as follows: If a text has an annotated entity of type person, the person likely has a date of birth and date of death. It is now possible to check, whether the person was alive or dead at the time of the supposed writing date of the document. Thus, the check can provide hints to the editor stating that a person cannot have written the document, because s/he was not alive at the time.

In preliminary interviews, several editors of digital scholarly editions have stated that contextual information while working with correspondence items can be useful [10]. In multiple interviews, we saw, that external resources are used to confirm transcribed text. E.g., one editor used a phone book to confirm an address. Another editor used a integrated authority file (GND) system to search and confirm a date of birth. Based on this feedback, we created mock-ups and a first working mid-fidelity prototype that was used to demonstrate how it might work, look and feel like. We received positive feedback from expert users.

However, the actual benefit in practice remains to be seen and further studies have to be conducted to confirm that this type of feature improves the work positively, e.g., in terms of efficiency or task-completion time.

4   Discussion and Conclusion

In this paper, we have presented how editors of digital (scholarly) editions can benefit from different levels of support. We explained the different levels from the simple syntax checks of XML-Editors to complex features providing context-sensitive support, to improve the computer-aided work (cmp. [3]) of editors of digital (scholarly) editions.

According to Sahle, "a digital edition is more like a workplace or a laboratory" [14]. The insight into how tools may support editors in their tasks can help to improve and create future "virtual research environments", that provide additional computer-aided support. Ease-of-use, usability, utility and their attributes should be the focus so that impediments can be resolved. Additionally, tools should take the diversity in editorial guidelines, and different aims of edition projects, into consideration. Many tools tend to be research tools for specific purposes, not fit for standard tasks of an editor. Other tools are very generic, but in consequence, not specific enough for a digital (scholarly) edition. There might just be not a single solution that fits all digital (scholarly) editions.

However, a component-based approach, like the herein introduced WYSIWYA-Editor, allows to assemble components for a digital (scholarly) edition platform. Making components configurable, allows them to be easily adapted to different needs, which can potentially lower the effort of creating and starting new edition projects.

5   Future Work

The remaining future work is manifold. We aim to provide the WYSIWYA-Editor with interfaces for XML standards like TEI [1], or variants of TEI like TEI-correspDesc, as an open-source project. We use a user-centred design process to improve the work of editors [10] and explore opportunities accordingly. E.g., we are looking into how context-sensitive support can be improved by facilitating research from the information retrieval domain. Is natural-language-processing (NLP) able to provide additional insight for editors while creating a digital (scholarly) edition? What and how can an editor benefit from technologies like that? The increasing amount of information stored in a digital (scholarly) editions poses the question of how users (not just editors) may access the information at hand in different ways. There is a need to investigate how different user groups use digital (scholarly) editions, what their tasks or aims are, and how to support those users to make them achieve their goals.

Acknowledgements. This work has been funded by the German Research Foundation (DFG), grant #389236467. The implementation of the WYSIWYA-Editor prototype, as well as the implementation of the survey, has been conducted by Johannes Goebel in context of his master thesis [9].

References

1. TEI P5: Guidelines for electronic text encoding and interchange. Text Encoding Initiative Consortium (2020). http://www.tei-c.org/
2. B. Lee Eden Book Review Editor, Brooklyn College (CUNY), B.N.: The shape of data in digital humanities: Modeling texts and text-based resources. J. Electron. Res. Librarianship, **31**(3), 214–214 (2019). https://doi.org/10.1080/1941126X.2019.1635787
3. Bruderer, H.: There Are No Digital Humanities (2018). https://cacm.acm.org/blogs/blog-cacm/232969-there-are-no-digital-humanities/fulltext
4. Campbell, A., Cooper, M., Kirkpatrick, A.: Web content accessibility guidelines (WCAG) 2.2. W3C working draft, W3C February 2020. https://www.w3.org/TR/2020/WD-WCAG22-20200227/
5. Driscoll, M.J., Pierazzo, E. (eds.): Digital Scholarly Editing: Theories and Practices, vol. 4, 1st edn. Open Book Publishers, Cambridge (2016)
6. Farindon, P.: Foundations for digital editing, with focus on the documentary tradition. In: Richard, J., Lane, R.S. (eds.) In: Constance Crompton,Doing Digital Humanities : Practice, Training, Research, Chap. 13, vol. 1, pp. 201–213. Routledge, London (2016)
7. Franzini, G., Terras, M., Mahony, S.:A Catalogue of Digital Editions. Digit. Scholar. Edit. Theor. Pract. **4**(5), 161–182 (2016)
8. Franzini, G., Terras, M., Mahony, S.: Digital editions of text: surveying user requirements in the digital humanities. J. Comput. Cult. Herit. **12**(1), 1:1–1:23 Feburary 2019. https://doi.org/10.1145/3230671, http://doi.acm.org/10.1145/3230671
9. Goebel, J.: Konzipierung und Entwicklung eines TEI-WYSIWYA-Editors für historisch-kritische Editionen. Master's thesis, University of Applied Sciences Darmstadt, Darmstadt (2020)
10. Kurosu, Masaaki (ed.): HCII 2020. LNCS, vol. 12181. Springer, Cham (2020). https://doi.org/10.1007/978-3-030-49059-1
11. Klie, J.C., Bugert, M., Boullosa, B., de Castilho, R.E., Gurevych, I.: The inception platform: machine-assisted and knowledge-oriented interactive annotation. In: Proceedings of the 27th International Conference on Computational Linguistics: System Demonstrations, pp. 5–9. Association for Computational Linguistics June 2018. http://tubiblio.ulb.tu-darmstadt.de/106270/
12. Meister, J.C., Petris, M., Gius, E., Jacke, J., Horstmann, J., Bruck, C.: Catma June 2018. https://doi.org/10.5281/zenodo.1470119
13. Morcos, H.J.: Digital Edition and Linguistic Database: A Fully Lemmatized and Searchable Model (2019). https://doi.org/10.34894/G59HGN
14. Sahle, P.: What is a scholarly digital edition?. Digit. Schol. Edit. Theor. Pract. **4**(5), 19–39 (2016)
15. Spina, C.: Wcag 2.1 and the current state of web accessibility in libraries. Weave: J. Libr. User Exp. **2**(2) (2019)
16. Sullivan, D.: Tech services on the web: Catma: computer aided textual markup & analysis. Tech. Serv. Q. **30**(3), 337–338 (2013). https://doi.org/10.1080/07317131.2013.788370; http://www.catma.de/

Body Map Pathway: Visual Guidance of Human Body to Diagnosis Efficiently

HyunJin Jo[(⊠)] ⓘD

Royal College of Art, London SW7 2EU, UK
guswls1994@gmail.com

Abstract. It is important that clinicians continuously use clinical reasoning skills to verify the diagnosis [1]. The current app strives to provide a train and practice service to improve this necessary skill. It is a skill of combining individual symptoms and signs to arrive at a diagnosis. The app provides texts and simple icons that users can start from the medical specialties. Since the users are mostly novices who have little experience in real diagnosis, they had a hard time selecting options from the first page. To overcome this existing problem, a Body Map Pathway designed to ease the choice from the first page. The new service offers visualized guidance that supports users spontaneously choose the part of the body that links with symptoms. A visual test and moderate remote usability test carried out to check the usability of the new service. The participants in this case study are 1 GP and 1 medical doctor. The case study showed participants valued the remembrance of differentials in the process of diagnosis. And appreciated intuitiveness of the Body Map Pathway that eases the choice of the first page. Further development will be planned to improve the Body Map Pathway to meet the expectation of the medical information hierarchy.

Keywords: Mobile health · mHealth · Application interface design

1 Introduction

To maintain and improve a certain level of diagnosis, it is important that medical students and professionals continuously use clinical reasoning skills and practice diagnosis [1]. The existing app aims for medical students, nurses, and junior doctors to improve their clinical diagnostic-reasoning skills. However clinical reasoning is challenging to teach and learn because it is complex, implied experience, and effectively invisible for students [2]. With this in mind, this case study proposes a visualized diagnosis service to support young medical professionals to train efficiently. This case study only focuses on redesigning the previous diagnosis app by providing a new visualized experience. However, it does not include redesigning the system of diagnosing.

2 Existing Service Problem

The previous service has a feature that helps users to experience the diagnosis. It provides texts and simple icons that users can start from the medical specialties. Specialty is a

© Springer Nature Switzerland AG 2020
C. Stephanidis et al. (Eds.): HCII 2020, CCIS 1293, pp. 201–208, 2020.
https://doi.org/10.1007/978-3-030-60700-5_26

branch of medical practice that focused on a defined group of patients, diseases, skills, or philosophy. The first page is designed to select from medical specialties such as respiratory, cardiology, or gastroenterology. Then users can narrow down to specific categories of symptoms. Users select an appropriate symptom that matches their patient's presentation. Once users click the symptom of patients, the next screen will present the most important clarifying question (e.g., the duration of a symptom or other associated features). The app will continue to ask clarifying questions to help get users to a final diagnosis (see Fig. 1). A chief executive officer and a medical director who have the medical background in the team found inconvenience in this previous service. Since the users are mostly students who have little experience in real diagnosis, they had a hard time selecting specialties and symptoms from the first page. Also, some doctors who are familiar with their specific field had a hard time looking up the other specialized area. This makes doctors hard to choose the options from the first step. This is because the existing service only provides text-oriented information which includes the plain text of the systems and icons. This can be tricky for the users who are unfamiliar with each different type of field and get confuse what kind of different symptoms belongs to each area.

Fig. 1. Specialty pathways service

3   Solution

To overcome this existing problem, a Body Map Pathway is designed to ease the selection from the first page. Users can select a Body Map Pathway or Specialty Pathways which is the previous service that provides the categories of medical specialties to start training their diagnosis. The Body Map Pathway is a visual guide that shows the body figure from head to toe. It provides different patient types of body figures including woman, man, and child. It helps users spontaneously choose the part of the body from the first screen. The first screen also provides general symptoms and skin options. By clicking these option buttons, users can diagnosis general symptoms such as fever or dermatopathy. Other symptoms are recategorized to fit into each body part. Users can click the upper levels of the body (e.g., head) and narrow down to particular body parts (e.g., scalp, face, eyes, nose, ears, and mouse). When users chose the specific body parts (e.g., eyes), it will then provide the symptoms (e.g., red eye, visual disturbance, double vision or abnormal eye movement problems, etc.) related to the body part (see Fig. 2).

Fig. 2. New Body Map Pathway service

4   Case Study

Due to the COVID-19 pandemic, all user tests were conducted by remote using Google Forms and Lookback.io. Lookback.io is a mobile UX user recording tool that captures screen interaction, voice and video of the user directly from the user's device. Participant 1 is a GP and participant 2 is a medical doctor. Both of them worked more than 5 years in the UK and participated in the case study to test the usability and feasibility.

4.1   Testing User's Perceptions of Visual Design

Visual details are a notable factor to determine the service's brand image. To measure this critical factor, structured visual testing is needed. Nielsen Norman Group's test methods are used to test visual design details in this case study. These test methods guide two main approaches to measure visual design. One is exposing participants to visual stimuli. It shows participants the visual design, which could be a static image, a prototype, or a live interactive website or application. Second is an assessment of user reactions to the stimulus. This measures users' reactions to the design using either open-ended or strictly controlled questions [3]. For the current study, Google Forms is used for the remote user test which allows testing users who are hard to meet in person.

Visual Design Test Stimulus. The test stimulus is the visual representation of the design. In this case study, it means all visual assets including the human body pictures (PNG files), clickable human body parts (SVG lines), and function buttons (UI). To test the first impressions of the service, the test presents the visual stimulus to the participant from the first question. It shows static images of man's human body pictures. One with a full front body and the other zoomed in picture of man's head part. Both pictures are positioned in the iPhone mockup images (see the first and second mock-up images of Fig. 2).

Assessing User Reactions. Once participants have been exposed to the design, the next step is to measure their responses. People's aesthetic impressions can be very idiosyncratic and will need to be systematically analyzed to identify meaningful trends [3]. First, the questionnaire used 'Open Word Choice'. Participants are asked to list 3 words to describe the given pictures which are one with a full front body and the other zoomed in picture of man's head (see Fig. 2). This format ensures you get at least some specific feedback, while still keeping the question open-ended to discover factors you may not have considered, but which are significant to your audience [3].

4.2   Moderated Remote Usability Test

User Goals and Task Scenarios. The purpose of the moderated remote usability test is to better understand how real users interact with the service and to improve the service based on the results. The test includes checking the functionality of features (UI) and end to end Body Map Pathway service experience. This study asked users to find the Body Map Pathway from the menu list and to find a tasked symptom by using the Body Map Pathway. To conduct user test, I used Lookback.io which is a remote user testing tool can be done by users themselves or with a facilitator. A live test with a facilitator performs remote user research, in real-time which enables a facilitator and participant to communicate directly with users and see what they see and get their reactions. The main goals that users have to accomplish are understanding the whole journey and able to use given interfaces to navigate the Body Map Pathway. Also, to approve the Body Map Pathway is useful for choosing the first step of practicing diagnosis. The task scenarios are reliable to use since given by medical specialists. Based on the main goals, the given task scenarios and their user goals are

Scenario 1: "24-year-old woman comes with mild fever without any serious problem. Most likely diagnosis?"
Goal: Use General Symptom Button (UI) to diagnose and change the man into woman,
Scenario 2: "A 55-year-old man presented with acute onset of redness in his left eye, which he noted upon awakening in the morning. He had no pain, ocular discharge, photophobia, blurry vision, or a history of blunt trauma. On examination, He was normotensive. His pupils were equal and reactive, and his corrected vision was 20/20. Most likely diagnosis? [4] "
Goal: Click the head of the man, then tick the eye of the head, and narrow down the symptom to diagnose,

Scenario 3: "43-year-old man comes to the hospital with upper back spine pain. He shows focal tenderness. He says it doesn't get worse during the morning but uncommon. It gets a bit worse when he lifts something heavy. Most likely diagnosis?"
Goal: Use Back Button of man (UI) to change position, click the thoracic spine from the man's back, and narrow down the symptom to diagnose,
Scenario 4: "Parents bring in their 2-year-old son in concerned about a flat dark red-purplish lesion on the infant's neck. They note the lesion has deepened in color from a pink stain present at birth, although it doesn't seem to trouble the child. Most likely diagnosis?"
Goal: Change the body into a child and use Skin Button (UI) to diagnose.

The Procedure of Moderated Remote Usability Test. Participants were tested individually in sessions lasting approximately 30 to 40 min. After participating in visual design testing provided by Google Forms, participants were guided to take a moderated remote usability test by clicking a link to Lookback.io. The facilitator helps the testing in 3 ways. Setting the test before and after, introducing the test, and help participants to complete the tasks. The facilitator guides through setting the test environment including downloading the application and connecting the screen sharing as well as voice and face recording. After finishing arranging the environment, the facilitator introduced the basic information of the existing service and the new service. Then the facilitator instructs participants to keep say out loud anything that comes out from their mind while they are performing task scenarios [5]. This is known as the 'think-aloud' method and the facilitator nudges them to keep the talking. The facilitator helps the test flowing, provides simple directions, and keeps the participant focused. When participants do not speak their thinking, the facilitator asks to keep a running narration. After finishing each task scenario, the facilitator asked the participants about the difficulties or feedbacks to validate the smoothness of the test.

4.3 User Test and Visual Elements Validation

After finishing the moderated remote usability test, participants were asked to go back to Google Forms and finish the questionnaire. Post user test questionnaire asks the smoothness of the user test process. And then asks the appropriateness of the usage of the visual elements (see Fig. 3). The question checks body pictures including man, woman, and child are clear enough to identify. Also, it asks about the separation of the body (green line) is precise enough to apply (see the last right picture of Fig. 3).

5   Result

Qualitative data from the case study with the medical professionals support findings.

5.1   User's Perceptions of Visual Design Evaluation

The goal of the 'Open Word Choice' is to get feedback about the design of the new service. One is to ensure that the image of the new service fits the previous brand image.

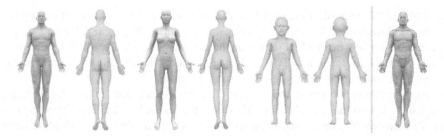

Fig. 3. Static images for visual testing (Color figure online)

The second is to see the factors that are significant to the users at first glance. A good approach for this analysis is to categorize terms as generally positive, negative, or neutral, then group terms with similar meanings, and evaluate whether they match your target brand attributes [3]. This is why 'Open Word Choice' is organized as the first test. The participants described the new service as 'Clean, Confusing, Simple, Cold, Blue, Male'. These descriptions then categorized as positive, neutral, negative. 'Clean, Simple' belongs to positive, 'Confusing' belongs to negative, and 'Cold, Blue, Male' belongs to neutral feedback. The positive feedback matches the previous brand image as well as the goal of new service which is making an easy guideline to navigate the diagnose. In contrast, 'Confusing' word appeared in negative feedback. To clarify, 'Clean' and 'Simple' refer to graphics and the layout style used for the new service. But, the word 'Confusing' means, 'Looking at the pictures for the first time, it is confusing.' It means without the introduction from the facilitator, it is hard to assume the purpose of the new service. The user interface and the general concept of the Body Map Pathway design needs a description for first-time users to guide the service.

5.2 Moderated Remote Usability Test Evaluation

The goal of scenario 1 was to see the participant can use Dropdown Button to change the gender of the human body and click General Symptom Button to help them diagnose. Both participants 1 and 2 showed no problem with finding the General Symptom Button. But both participants did not aware of Dropdown Button and could not change the gender of the human body. The goal of scenario 2 was clicking body parts to narrow down the symptom. From the task, the participants had to click the head of the man's body and then click the eyes to solve the given task. Both participants had no difficulty clicking the body parts. However, the interaction of showing the symptom list might not be intuitive. Since the list of symptoms is positioned below the Body Map Pathway and hidden from the screen, participants have to scroll down to check the symptoms. It means scrolling down to see the list is less practical for the users. The goal of scenario 3 was using the Back Button of the human body to rotate the position. Participants had to click the thoracic spine from the man's back and narrow down the symptom to diagnose. Both participants easily selected the body parts to perform the task and showed no impediment in this stage. The goal of the last scenario was to change the body into a child and use Skin Button to diagnose. Both of the participants showed no problem changing the body and applied Skin Button to finish the task.

Participant 2 expressed a few uncertainties about organizing the interfaces of the Body Map Pathway. One is the Button interfaces used in the service. Providing text as well as image buttons at the same time makes the participant confusing because these buttons do not feel like a coherent interface. Also, from the medical professional's point of view, general symptoms, demagogical condition (skin), and the Body Map Pathway should be the same level of choice. The Body Map Pathway looks intuitive, but it does not seem like the same option as General Symptom or Skin Button. The given tasks enabled the researcher to discover insights to develop the design further. Unclear steps to start the Body Map Pathway and inaccurate medical information hierarchy should be improved to match the user's expectation. This means the onboarding process might be needed to use the Body Map Pathway for first-time users. And the options of the Body Map Pathway, general symptoms, and demagogical condition (skin) should be reorganized to match the information hierarchy.

5.3   User Test and Visual Elements Validation Feedbacks

After finishing the user test, participants were requested to go back to Google Forms and finish the questionnaire. The questionnaire includes the validation of the overall user test experience and interface design correctness. In the feedbacks, participants agreed that the user test was smooth enough as a whole to perform the tasks. Participants acknowledged that the body pictures [Fig. 3] were clearly showing the different types of gender and age. Also, they conceded that the separation of the body by green lines seen [the last picture of Fig. 2] is accurate enough to understand and fits in the human structure.

6   Conclusion

This case study intended to test the effectiveness of a new service which is a guidance of symptom diagnose by using intuitive visualization of the human body. The results of the case study showed that the Body Map Pathway service supported the users to practice diagnosis by recalling the memory that they have learned before. They experienced the Body Map Pathway itself was intuitive enough to choose symptoms quickly that match body parts. Based on these findings, the use of the Body Map Pathway has potential benefits in practicing the symptom diagnosis and eases the choice of specialties and symptoms by showing visual guidelines. The result also indicates that the visual images used in the Body Map Pathway are accurate and the visual design matches the current brand image. Subsequent studies will be conducted to offer more advanced services to reduce the inconvenience of the text information-oriented diagnosis practice at the first stage. And will further improve the hierarchy of information to match the expectation of the medical professionals' point of view.

Acknowledgments. I like to thank the Dem Dx team for working hard on a new project of the Body Map Pathway. And appreciate the participants who are fighting in the frontline for the patients.

Novel Cluster Analytics for Analyzing COVID-19 Patient Medical Data

Joseph E. Johnson[1]([✉]) [iD] and Dezhi Wu[2] [iD]

[1] Department of Physics and Astronomy, University of South Carolina, Columbia, SC 29208, USA
jjohnson@sc.edu
[2] Department of Integrated Information Technology, University of South Carolina, Columbia, SC 29208, USA
dezhiwu@cec.sc.edu

Abstract. The ongoing global COVID-19 pandemic has caused more than 440,000 deaths among more than 8 million cases globally by Mid-June, 2020. This pandemic has caused a staggering worldwide socioeconomic impact and loss of lives. This research proposes an innovative technological approach to analyze COVID-19 patient data for new analytical insights via developing a transformative pattern identification algorithm for cluster analysis in tabular numerical data tables, e.g., patient medical data files and in disease networks. The underlying mathematics is based upon Lie algebras and continuous Markov transformations that are foundational in quantum theory, relativity, and theoretical physics. Our novel algorithm does not use an arbitrary concept of proximity or nearness but instead is based upon an information flow model where clusters are identified, and rank ordered by the matrix eigenvalues. The component clusters identify the degree of patient cluster participation by the nodal weight given by each associated eigenvector. Medical metadata tags in the tables are automatically linked to the cluster eigenvalue and eigenvectors to facilitate interpretation of the analytics. The core algorithm has been coded and will be ported to a cloud environment allowing other investigators to submit data files for cluster analytics. We plan to analyze COVID-19 patterns and expect to work with other medical research teams on pattern identification in deidentified medical patient data sets. We expect this ongoing research to lead to significant practical and theoretical insights and a greater understanding of our transformative network clustering algorithm at the individual COVID-19 patient level, hospital level and beyond.

Keywords: COVID-19 · Cluster algorithm · Network clusters · Analytics · Medical metadata · HIT · Health informatics

1 Introduction and Study Motivation

Based on a recent World Health Organization (WHO) report [1], the ongoing COVID-19 global pandemic has caused over 8 million cases and more than 440,000 deaths as of June 18, 2020, so the COVID-19 pandemic turns out to be the most severe global

© Springer Nature Switzerland AG 2020
C. Stephanidis et al. (Eds.): HCII 2020, CCIS 1293, pp. 209–216, 2020.
https://doi.org/10.1007/978-3-030-60700-5_27

crisis in the last century. Although many efforts are ongoing with medicine and other science areas, the causes of such a deadly disease are still mysterious. Even with global lockdown in Spring 2020, there are many uncertainties still ahead of us to effectively handle the current COVID-19 virus crisis. As such, it is urgent to have a novel way to discover the root causes of this disease to be able to identify appropriate solutions. Traditional medicine and clinical methods have their rigorous means of uncovering this myth but being constrained with its efficiency to connect to all available patient data to provide a more holistic view of this disease, however, with today's modern computing sciences, artificial intelligence, machine learning, big data analytics, and other emerging technologies on large cyberinfrastructures (e.g., smart devices, Internet of Things (IoTs)), we may have an opportunity to better understand this disease and trace back its root causes in a more efficient and accurate way due to many electronic medical health records (MHR) available in the current health IT systems. As such, this research proposes a novel cluster analytics algorithm based on Lie algebra, Lie group and continuous Markov transformation theory rooted in theoretical physics to dynamically identify unique patterns of COVID-19 patients through network clusters that can be powerfully integrated with individual social networks.

This paper is proceeded as follows. Following the introduction section, we describe the foundations of the proposed novel cluster analytic methodology, and then we present the current applications and new COVID-19 initiatives in healthcare domain. After discussing our ongoing research efforts on this project, we conclude this paper with study implications and future research directions.

2 Foundations of Novel Cluster Analytic Methodology

2.1 Two Fundamental Types of Numerical Data

There are two fundamental types of numerical data that are captured by humans: The first type is a table of the properties (in columns) of entities or things (in rows) T_{ij}. This began for commerce with accounting systems dating back more than 7,000 years in Mesopotamia. Tables now represent massive scientific data on the properties of living things, galaxies, alloys, and medical files of people as well as accounting reports and performance reports of corporate entities. Numerical tables capture our most exacting knowledge. The second type is a network matrix that represents the strength of connection between pairs of things (nodes) C_{ij}. The capture of extensive network data only emerged in the last century (with the computer and internet). Networks capture the foundation of the structure of our civilization as the vast interconnectivities of the strength of connections between pairs of things (nodes) C_{ij}. Networks capture (a) all communication among people (and soon, the Internet of Things) such as internet traffic, phone calls, mail, etc. (b) all financial transactions from entity i to entity j, (c) all utility system structures such as the flow of electricity, water, gas lines, etc., (d) all transportation systems (land, sea, air) of things moved from node i to node j, (e) all communicable disease networks, and not the least of these is (f) the network representing the evolution of all living things including the genetic passing of human DNA and its mutations (as well as virus and bacteria) to descendants. Essentially all of these and other related networks collectively represent the fabric and essence of living things. Thus, T and C capture the essence of our knowledge of the universe and of our civilization. A third type of information is the free and unstructured information in the form of text along with inflection and gestures. Such information constitutes relatively 'fuzzy' information including 'language.' The fuzzy aspect of language is not a bad but a good thing because it can be generated rapidly and is extremely useful in describing general values. For example, it is very important to be able to say "Bob is tall" rather than having to take the time to get Bob and measure his height as 2.11382 meters. It is only necessary to indicate that Bob is taller than most men and more accuracy is not needed in this circumstance. This brings up the topics of (a) the cost of a measurement at a given level of accuracy, and (b) the value of the different levels of that information. Finally, a fourth type of information is captured in photography, video, drawings, paintings, music, and the other art forms. This is perhaps the oldest form. We will address information that is numerical and embodied in (a) tables, even if it is just a single numerical value, or a list, or two (or higher) dimensional tables, and (b) networks as are described above.

2.2   The Mathematical Structure of Networks and Data Tables

Consider a social network of people where C_{ij} is defined as the strength of connection between person i and person j as defined perhaps by the number of emails, bits of information, number of phone calls, or time spent in contact in personal conversations. People group into clusters where C represents a tighter connectivity among some members perhaps based upon interest in music, athletic events, work projects, gardening, or intellectual interests. A person can belong to many different such groups or clusters often with names for the groups such as impressionistic art collecting, or fitness routine advocates. There are over 100 computer algorithms in use for analyzing networks to identify such clusters. In fact, networks represent one of the most difficult domains of mathematics as they are defined as a non-negative square matrix C_{ij} that specifies the strength of linkage between node i and node j. Each value of C must be zero or positive as there is normally no meaning to a connection less than zero. Furthermore, there is no meaning to the connection of a thing with itself, so it follows that the diagonal of this matrix is undefined, not zero, but undefined. Networks can be of any size and normally are functions of time C_{ij} (t). The mathematics of such objects is challenging especially due to the fact that the matrix diagonal is undefined, and all off-diagonal elements are non-negative. Such network clusters are normally defined by groups of nodes that are "strongly connected" and given some name but this is ambiguous because proximity is "in the eye of the beholder." Next consider tabular data such as the table of the properties of the chemical elements (with properties of density, thermal and electrical conductivity, ...) or the state of a person (as physical profile exam + blood + urine + athletic performance + mental performance + knowledge + emotional profile...) at a given time (as specified by their 'properties'). Things (minerals, foods, or even people) which have very similar properties can also be grouped to form "clusters" such as plants, trees, foods, minerals, and medical patients. Words in our language: nouns, verbs, adjectives, and adverbs give names to identified clusters of things with similar properties and so our language is based upon the fundamental concept of a "cluster." Finally, consider unstructured language and documents: Our very language, with nouns, verbs, and qualifying adjectives, and adverbs, are names for these clusters which we then join to form more complex structures. Words are symbols (names) for clusters. Thus, the unstructured information in the form of language represents, in grammatical form (similar to expressions in logic), an extremely complex network of linkages among clusters from networks and tabular data, via sentences, paragraphs, and documents. Thus, the mathematics of clusters in both networks and tables is foundational to information.

2.3 Foundation for Numerical Clusters in Network and in Tabular Forms

Johnson [2]'s previous work in decomposing the general linear group in n dimensions, GL(n,R), provided a new methodology for understanding all linear transformations (Lie groups) that are continuously connected to the identity and the (Lie) algebras that generate them. Specifically, he proved that the general linear group can be decomposed into two different Lie algebras: (a) the first was the Abelian algebra, "A(n)", of exponential growth or decay of each separate element of the vector that is acted upon. This gives a scaling group. The other component (b) was the Markov Type (MT) Lie algebra that continuously took a fraction of any one component of a vector and added it to another component thus preserving the sum of the two values. Such transformations "Rob Peter to pay Paul." All in all then it becomes the Lie group of transformations on a vector that preserves its sum, and thus moves the vector over a plane perpendicular to the unit vector $(1, 1,...1)$. This contrasts with the continuous rotation group, which rotates a system in two or three dimensions and preserves the sum of the squares rather than the sum of the components. When later working on the mathematics of networks, he discovered that every network, C, is exactly represented by one member of the Lie algebra that generates the transformations for the MT group. But only positive linear combinations are allowed of the basis elements in order to keep the off diagonal elements of the network positive. This correspondence between the MT algebra and any network then automatically defines the diagonal of the Lie algebra to be the negative of the sum of the elements in that respective column. This means that a study of the MT Lie algebra and more explicitly the Markov group that it generates is precisely a study of all networks. Actually, the restriction to off-diagonal non-negative values removes the inverse of the MT group and generates a Markov Monoid (MM) instead of a full group. It is critical that the MM generates continuous flows of a conserved entity (e.g., the sum of the elements of a vector such as money), and its eigenvalues represent the "normal nodes" of exponentially moving the vector to an equilibrium point over time. This is because Markov transformations represent diffusion. They model the increase of entropy and the second law of thermodynamics. The eigenvector defined by this eigenvalue is that linear combination of the vector components that exponentially decreases collectively with a unique rate of exponential decrease. Thus, to summarize: Every network defines a specific MM matrix transformation, and conversely, every MM transformation defines a specific network. They are said to be isomorphic [2]. Thus we can now use all the mathematical power of Markov theory and Lie algebras to analyze networks.

2.4 The Renyi Entropy Spectral Curve of a Network

The MM transformation matrix generated by any network contains only non-negative elements, and the sum of the values in each column is exactly "1." Thus each column can be considered as a probability distribution. This allows a Shannon, or better yet a Renyi entropy, to be defined for that column. The collection of these n Renyi entropies (one value for each column) can be sorted, giving a Renyi Information (or entropy) spectral curve that characterizes the network very well. Any network could be expanded as a finite lossless series of such spectral curves [3]. Series expansions are critically important throughout mathematics, science, and engineering, with their ability to address succeeding levels of approximation. Often a non-linear set of equations can be well approximated by a linear set which then can be studied in view of the next most important effect (approximation). For two networks to be identical, that the (very computationally fast) comparison of their Renyi spectra must be identical. A "distance metric" between two networks was then further defined by taking the distance between (square root of the sum of squares) of two Renyi spectral curves. This process could be done on a single network between two adjacent time intervals, thus giving a foundation for a theory of network dynamics as the time derivatives of the changes of the distance between spectral curves. As a result, every single network matrix C exactly determines one Markov algebra element which generates a Markov type (MT) transformation that conserves the sum of elements of any vector. The meaning of the spectral entropy curve is of the information flow rate in or out of a given node. This entropy spectral curve has been used [3–5] to monitor internet traffic (or the dynamics of any time-dependent network) to study attacks, intrusions, and anomalies of network performance.

2.5 Network Clusters as MM Eigenvectors

The clusters of a network can be defined as the eigenvectors (weighted linear combinations of nodes) corresponding to each eigenvalue of the MM for that network. The eigenvalues give the collective rate of approach to equilibrium for that eigenvector and thus measure the "strength" of that cluster. In this definition, each cluster is defined by the eigenvector and thus is a linear combination of nodes. Higher values represent nodes near the center of the cluster, and one can choose any cutoff desired to "define" the most important nodes in a cluster. There is no arbitrary definition of "distance between nodes" in this system. The clusters can be sorted by the associated eigenvalue, which gives the "cluster strength," a well-defined critical concept for cluster analysis and again, which is not arbitrary. Note that if the network is not symmetric, then one can do the same analytics on the transpose matrix, which means that one then replaces the diagonal values effectivity with the sum of the values in the rows to define the Lie algebra and thus another MM matrix.

2.6 Cluster Analytics for Tabular Data

Realizing the power of the Renyi entropy and cluster analytics of networks using the Lie algebra and MM model of networks, Johnson [2, 3] began to study the application of this research to tabular data as expressed in a rectangular numerical n × m matrix where column 0 has unique strings that label the rows (entities or things) and row 0 has unique strings that label the columns (properties of those entities). Allowance is made for metadata tags, which are identified by row and column labels preceded by a "%" but which are not used in the Renyi and cluster analytics but are used to describe the clusters and nodes later more fully.

As an example, considering the chemical elements, one knows that gold is more like iron than calcium, and far more like iron than like hydrogen as measured by its properties. So, we sought to define a network among the rows of a table based upon the difference or "distance" between their properties. But each column has highly diverse values as the columns (density, electrical conductivity, …) are in different units of measurement. To obtain comparable row vectors, the values must all be fully dimensionless. There is a method for such standardization of a table T_{ik} as follows. Compute the mean and standard deviation of each column. Note that members of that column must first be converted to the same units if not already done. Then create a new table, T_{ij}, where each value is the number of standard deviations (of that column) from the mean (of that column). Then define distance in the normal manner as between two row vectors as $C_{ij}^r = \exp\left(-\text{Sqrt}\left(\sum_k \left(T_{ik} - T_{jk}\right)^2\right)\right)$. Note that the elements of C_{ij}^r will be "1" if i and j are essentially the same since one gets exp(0) which is "1," and the elements of C_{ij}^r will be "0" if the rows are extremely different since one gets exp(-large number) which is "0." This is exactly what we desire to define a network among the rows. Likewise, one can define another network, C^c_{ij}, among the properties (columns) as $C_{ij}^r = \exp(-\text{Sqrt}(\sum_k \left(T_{ik} - T_{jk}\right)^2))$ which gives the same range. This will show that electrical conductivity and thermal conductivity are very tightly clustered (since conduction of heat and electricity are highly correlated), and both also somewhat clustered with the property of "density."

2.7 The Potential of Clustering All Networks and Tables

With the emergence of the internet, one increasingly can find tables of numeric data and also be able to define networks of connectivities of all types, such as with social networks or banking transactions. Then one can envision the creation of an automatic search and processing system to find and create all associated networks (within the domain of allowable access) and then execute the clustering and Renyi spectral algorithms continuously on the public (under appropriate security), private networks such as banking, communication, utility, transportation, and health and even ancestry. Each identified resulting cluster can be automatically named by the IP address of the source and will contain the clusters sorted by eigenvalue strength and named by the dominant eigenvalue nodes which may have attached metadata making the name more readable.

3   Past Applications and New COVID-19 Initiatives

3.1   Initial Study of Internet Traffic as an Example of Network Data

Our initial work [3] was to address the general domain of network security and to identify potential attacks and network anomalies. To identify complex, even nonlinear patterns in numerical data, we used a powerful new mathematical approach based upon the Lie algebra, Lie group, and continuous Markov transformation theory that is foundational in theoretical physics. The Markov Monoid generated by a given network, and the Renyi entropy spectral curve that is computed from its columns, were described above. Our discovery in this period was that (a) the Renyi information spectral curves and (b) the Markov Monod eigenvalue/eigenvector analysis, both identified complex patterns in the network of internet traffic [3–5].

3.2 Healthcare IoTs Applications

Now consider just the collection of all health-related data of humans with rows named by a patient ID (PID) + Date of periodic physician visits. The columns (i.e., attributes) would consist of physical + blood + urine + diagnosis numerical values along with pharmaceutical and diagnosis metadata. Next, consider the IoT data collection from one's smartphone or watch with steps taken each hour, blood pressure, pulse, temperature, movement acceleration, blood sugar, etc. on a frequent basis. Then add the IoT interfacing of exercise equipment with phone Bluetooth and periodic laptop tests of a person's vision, hearing, memory, reasoning, and other mental and emotional parameters. Then the agent described above can process the dynamical movement of the clusters that represent the person and their proximity to cluster profiles for stroke and other clusters [6, 7].

3.3 Ongoing Development of the Core Cluster and Information Pattern Identification Software for Cloud Use

Up to this point, we are in the process of designing, building, deploying and testing this software based on the novel and transformative cluster and spectral pattern identification analytic approach in a secure cloud environment. This new application will offer double authentications for user registration along with substantial general operating information to understand the processing at multiple levels of mathematical sophistication. The core of this initial website prototype is expected to be completed in the summer of 2020 and opened up to users for pilot testing and usability evaluations in the fall of 2020. We will invite multiple research scientists in medical and data science domains to test this new cluster algorithm and Renyi entropy spectral curves on extensive networks and their transposes as well as the same analysis for tabular data for both entities (rows such as medical patient ids) and their attributes (columns of fields & properties). Then our next goal would be to perform the requisite underlying mathematical and computational research to extend, validate, and better understand the related tools and the comparison of these analytics to other systems.

4   Study Implications and Future Research Directions

To test the viability and utility of the cluster analysis component of this system, we plan to use tabular numerical medical patient data (e.g., patient ID in rows). The increasingly extensive numerical properties can represent the entire spectrum from the human health profile to the clustering of patients as clustered with associated metadata tags and also equally the clustering of medical attributes, fields, and properties to understand their interdependence with particular emphasis on COVID-19. To extend the application of this analytic methodology as described in this document to all numerical scientific fields, including material science, physics, chemistry, pharmacology, all domains of engineering, the social sciences including social networks, and finally, mathematical economics.

Acknowledgement. The authors would like to acknowledge the funding support from the University of South Carolina's VP For research and Prisma Health Seed Funds for this research. The views and conclusions contained in this document are those of the authors and should not be interpreted as representing official policies and opinions, either expressed or implied, of the funding agencies.

References

1. WHO website. https://www.who.int/dg/speeches/detail/who-director-general-s-opening-rem arks-at-high-level-video-conference-on-belt-and-road-international-cooperation—18-june-2020. Accessed 18 June 2020
2. Johnson, J.E.: Markov-type lie groups in GL(n, R). J. Math. Phys. **26**(2), 252–257 (1985)
3. Johnson, J.E.: Networks, Markov lie monoids, and generalized entropy. In: Gorodetsky, V., Kotenko, I., Skormin, V. (eds.) MMM-ACNS 2005. LNCS, vol. 3685, pp. 129–135. Springer, Heidelberg (2005). https://doi.org/10.1007/11560326_10
4. Johnson, J.E., Campbell, W.J.: Mathematical foundations of networks supporting cluster identification. In: KDIR 2014 International Conference on Knowledge and Information Retrieval (2014)
5. Campbell, W.J.: Network Analysis and Cluster Identification Using Markov Theory, M.S. Thesis, University of South Carolina, USA (2014)
6. Bennett, K.J., Yuen, M., Blanco-Silva, F.: Geographic differences in recovery after the great recession. J. Rural Stud. **59**, 111–117 (2018)
7. Bennett, K.J., Probst, J.C., Vyavaharkar, M., Glover, S.: Missing the handoff: post-hospitalization follow-up care among rural medicare beneficiaries with diabetes. Remote Rural Health **12**(3) (2012)

A Study on Infographic Design of Door Dehumidifier

Junyoung Kim[1], Eunchae Do[2], and Dokshin Lim[3(✉)] (iD)

[1] Graduate School of Creative Design Engineering, UNIST, Ulsan, Korea
[2] Department of Visual Communication Design, Hongik University, Seoul, Korea
[3] Department of Mechanical and System Design Engineering, Hongik University, Seoul, Korea
doslim@hongik.ac.kr

Abstract. Millennials in Korea tend to live in a small studio alone. We focused on a common problem that this kind of one-person households have, which is that most of them suffer from laundry process due to the lack of drying feature in the built-in washing machines in their studios. "Door Dehumidifier" is a conceptual product that we propose to solve this problem. Installing our "Door Dehumidifier" in place of the existing door of their built-in washing machines will enable to manage the humidity automatically both inside and outside area of washing machines. The present paper describes how the infographic LED display of the new concept "Door Dehumidifier" communicate with the users. We designed the infographic with effectiveness and efficiency of the human-machine interaction in mind. Applying calm tech philosophy, we propose five infographics of "Door Dehumidifier" which we test and go through iterations to improve the final infographic design.

Keywords: One-person household · Dehumidifier · LED display · Infographic · Calm tech

1 Introduction

1.1 Background

Often in an environment where the Millennial Generation's one-person households live, they have no choice but to use washing machines, a basic built-in home. Many of these users suffer from a double whammy of the lack of drying on the devices provided, and their lifestyle is difficult to take out immediately after the washing is finished. There is also a prior study [1] in which ideas are proposed and recognized on these issues. The "Door Dehumidifier" referred to in this study provides the ability to install in a built-in washing machine and manage the internal humidity after the washing is automatically finished. This could be one of the new concepts that will improve the inconvenience experienced by the aforementioned users during the drying process. However, if this concept is introduced, there is a new weakness that the transparent washer door is changed

© Springer Nature Switzerland AG 2020
C. Stephanidis et al. (Eds.): HCII 2020, CCIS 1293, pp. 217–224, 2020.
https://doi.org/10.1007/978-3-030-60700-5_28

to opaque, blocking the user's visual information through the transparent door. Through this study, LED infographic designs were developed to complement this weakness in developing a new category of products called "Door Dehumidifier" but to be a good enough design choice.

1.2 Purpose

The market competition structure of products such as refrigerators, washing machines and air conditioners, commonly referred to as the "big three", has become no longer differentiated by functional benefits according to the law of diminishing marginal utility. Manufacturers are struggling to gain an upper hand in the competition through the positive emotional benefits of the joy, pleasure, and surprise they experience in using the product or the services associated with it [2].

This empirical benefit requires a different design approach than simply providing benefits by adding functionality, of which "Calm Tech" is the one that is drawing attention from Internet of Things (IOT) smart products where Door Dehumidifier are attributed. With the addition of smart functions, users surrounded by the increasing number of functions and the amount of information are feeling tired from the overflowing information and cognitive burden on complex decisions. "Calm Tech" is a combination of "calm" and "technology", meaning quiet, and Dr. Mark Weiser, a computer science professor who foretold the "Calm Tech" era, called it "a high-tech technology that gives information but does not require attention" [3]. How will the user interaction mechanism design and user interface design of sensor-intensive smart appliances permeate the daily lives of natural users in line with the "Calm Tech" philosophy?

This will be possible only if the utility of smart appliances is interpreted as the benefit felt by users in their daily lives by utilizing data and communicated easily and at the right time. Sensors should also play an active role in understanding the user's status to realize Calm Tech, as well as enhance the product's basic functionality. In this study, the design guidelines were drawn by presenting Door Dehumidifier infographic alternatives and conducting verification of target users through various case studies of infographic designs that affected products used in the home, the representation of air quality management information, and the method of communicating utility in real time, especially in Door Dehumidifier in millennial household washing machines.

2 Infographic Design

2.1 Research for Design Trends

Based on the research objective, design trends were investigated focusing on the user interface of the latest home appliance devices. We could see that the main design of the user interface fits the Calm Tech philosophy was the "glanceable" user interface design. Glanceable user interface refers to an interface that provides users with quick and easy access to information, and this has been considered particularly important for peripheral displays [4]. The examples in Table 1 shows that a glanceable user interface with just a dot of LEDs is sufficiently designable, and that this information is not over-represented in everyday life, with light of the weak century and simple color composition, an aesthetic design can also be reached.

Table 1. Examples of interface design on the latest home appliance devices.

Sample image	Product	Explanation for Interface
	AWAIR	Numerical values such as temperature, humidity, etc. are expressed in the number of LED.
	Google Nest Protect	Carbon monoxide is expressed in light color
	BRUNT AIRJET	Colorful representation of indoor fine dust and outdoor air
	Google Home	Presenting the state of the device as 12 lights

2.2 Infographic Design

Door Dehumidifier, which are designed for this study, will also say that it is desirable to pursue glanceable user interface design. Therefore, by utilizing small LEDs for dehumidifiers, users did not perceive it as loud noise in their daily lives and designed it intuitively with simple light intensity and color (Fig. 1).

First of all, LEDs are composed of 12 dots to represent dehumidification times of up to 12 h. These information-transmitting media can be given roles depending on the wavelength, intensity and continuity of light [5]. Therefore, the color is composed of blue, which is an intuitive reminder of water from washing and dehumidification, and orange, which can be reminiscent of a negative warning image when referring to Fig. 2 below, while also calling for user action, such as a positive and meaningful sign of progress, and an indication of dehumidification, and an error.

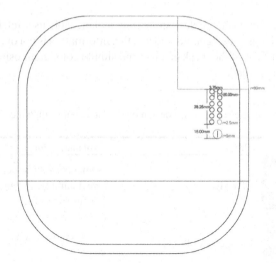

Fig. 1. Overall layout for the interface design on Door Dehumidifier.

In addition, the layout of the LEDs and power buttons in this user interface design is closely configured with the handle of the washing machine door so that users can recognize the operation/state of the washing machine door with no significant movement as they open and close the washing machine door (Table 2).

Table 2. Exact interface designs of each state.

Each State	Explanation of movement	Example image
1. Water level rising	Two dots of LEDs in the same line light up with water level rising.	
2. Washing mode	A dot of 12 LEDs goes out with rotating.	
3. Device filled with water	Dots of LEDs with color of orange rotate quickly.	
4. Dehumidifying	A dot of LEDs with color of blue turn to white per hour.	
5. Error detected	All dots of LEDs with color of Orange.	

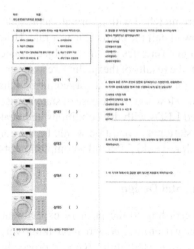

Fig. 2. Questionnaire.

3 Experimental Design and Results

3.1 Primary Experimental Design

Previously, a total of five films were prepared by combining the design for each state with the digital model of the product. Questionnaires were also prepared for use later in the experiment.

Prior to the experiment, this study and the Door Dehumidifier were presented verbally. The subjects checked the status of the prepared films on TV screens and conducted a qualitative assessment of the reasons and conditions for each of the processes. After all status checks were completed, a questionnaire was used to provide a quantitative assessment of how each state was perceived by the user.

3.2 Primary Experimental Result

The quantitative evaluation results of the preceding experiment are shown in Fig. 3.

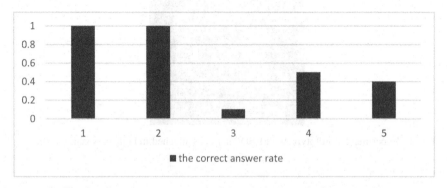

Fig. 3. The correct answer rate of the primary quantitative evaluation

State 1 and State 2 were matched with information presented by all 10 subjects naturally and State 4 also showed half the correct answer rate. However, states 3 and 5 have significantly lower correct answer rates and most subjects match incorrect information.

During the experiment, the results of the qualitative assessment for each state through interviews are as follows. For states 1, 2, 4, it was confirmed that each state could easily come up with what it meant. However, in the case of state 3, we could identify a tendency to associate orange-colored LEDs with dry conditions and heat, and in the case of state 5, we could predict that a stationary condition would be the completion of a process or, in relation to an orange color, would predict the completion of drying.

3.3 Secondary Experimental Design

Improvement Design. According to the primary experimental results, improvement designs for states 3 and 5 have been devised with more intuitively conveying the meaning. It consists of a motion that stops and blinks without proceeding or rotating to prompt the user to act with audible information. For more specific information transmission, the alphabet "F" was shaped from "Full" to state 3 and "d" was shaped from "door error" to state 5.

Secondary Experimental Design. The second experiment was also conducted in the same order as the first, but instead of the film, the experiment was carried out as a prototype of the real thing. The prototype uses a general built-in washing machine and has a programmed LEDs attached to the 3D printed Door Dehumidifier, which is similar to the actual use environment. In addition, after the questionnaire progresses, we provided a description of the state of Door Dehumidifier to see if the subjects could easily understand the interface design (Fig. 4).

Fig. 4. Experimental prototype with LED interfaces attached in built-in washing machine.

3.4   Secondary Experimental Design

The quantitative evaluation results of the preceding experiment are shown in Fig. 5.

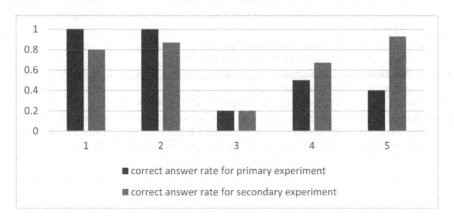

Fig. 5. The correct answer rate of the primary and secondary quantitative evaluations

According to the test conducted on 20 people, states 1, 2, 4 also showed a high correct answer rate. In particular, it can be seen that the correct rate has increased significantly in the state 5 where the improvement design has been applied. However, state 3 still has a significantly lower answer rate.

The results of the qualitative assessment of the states in which the improvement plan was applied through interviews during the experiment are as follows. In case of state 5, as intended by the design, subjects could easily associate "door" with the alphabet "d", and the tendency to predict a problem with the door could be seen through hearing information such as red-colored LEDs and repeated flickering and warning tones. However, in case of state 3, we could check the tendency of connection with the situation of completion by referring to "Finish" rather than "Full" by the alphabet "F".

4   Conclusions and Limits

The qualitative and quantitative assessment of the first and second experiment indicated that the overall evaluator experienced positive emotions in the design of this interface. In addition, although somewhat less intuitive, we were able to see that the purpose of this interface design was to match the intent of implementing Calm Tech and glanceable designs.

The design of the primary and improved versions of state 5 also confirmed that a clear intuitive design beyond quiet is needed to prompt users to take action. However, both the primary and improved versions of state 3 showed a low correct answer rate. This refers to the lack of intuitiveness to alarming device filled with water. In particular because condition of device filled with water exists only in function of dehumidifiers, research on the state will be needed in the future through a case study on the interface of various type of dehumidifiers.

References

1. Nameui, L., Sung Yeon, K., Frank, B.: Design guidelines for user-friendly washing machines for young single people based on the goal-directed design process. In: Contemporary Engineering Sciences, vol. 7, no. 21, pp. 1079–1086. HIKARI Ltd. (2014). http://dx.doi.org/10.12988/ces.2014.49135
2. Minho, K.: Back to the Basic. TurnAround Inc., Korea (2018)
3. Calm Tech. https://calmtech.com. Accessed 21 Dec 2016
4. Tara, M.: Designing and evaluating glanceable peripheral displays. In: Proceedings of the 6th conference on Designing Interactive systems, pp. 343–345. Association for Computing Machinery, New York (2006). https://doi.org/10.1145/1142405.1142457
5. Bit-Na, B., Hyeon-Jeong, S., Myong-Suk, K.: Context information representation applying light attributes-representation of abstracted context information using LED. In: Archives of Design Research, vol. 25, no. 1, pp. 207–218. Korean Society of Design Science (2011)

DNA as Digital Data Storage: Opportunities and Challenges for HCI

Raphael Kim[✉] [iD]

Queen Mary University, London, UK
r.s.kim@qmul.ac.uk

Abstract. DNA molecules can retain information in high densities, with high durability and low overall energy cost. This would make DNA-based data storage system a compelling solution in placating the increasing gap between global data production and our current means to store data. While key technical developments in recent decades have allowed DNA-based data storage systems to slowly progress closer to mainstream usage, there has been an overall lack of discourse surrounding potential implications of the system in the context of human computer interaction (HCI). This article introduces the DNA-based technology, followed by highlights of some of the potential opportunities and challenges it brings to the HCI community. In summary, DNA-based data storage systems offer a new research topic for user experience studies and data physicalization, and these are driven by inherent biological qualities of the DNA. As a tool, given the longevity of DNA, the system could also function as a multi-lifespan information management product, designed to help in addressing long-term wicked problems. In terms of challenges, ethical implications surrounding the technology ownership, and communication hurdles for HCI researchers working with the new technology, should also be considered and addressed.

Keywords: DNA · Data · Storage · Biodigital · Archive · BioHCI

1 Introduction

Over the last few decades, there has been a number of technological breakthroughs [1] that indicate gradual removal of barriers for mainstream adoption of DNA-based data storage systems. Contrary to this progress, and to the extensive discourses within life science and biotechnology fields, there has been relatively little discussion within the HCI community on the implications of the new data storage system.

Some of the preliminary and long-term questions remain unexplored: How would these data storage systems function, how would we interact with them, and what are their possible social and cultural ramifications for HCI research and design?

This article intends to serve as an opening for prospective dialogues that explore the aforementioned questions through the HCI lens. The article is roughly divided into three components: A brief introduction of the DNA data storage system, followed by a set of opportunities it presents, and then an outline of challenges that may arise in light of its application.

© Springer Nature Switzerland AG 2020
C. Stephanidis et al. (Eds.): HCII 2020, CCIS 1293, pp. 225–232, 2020.
https://doi.org/10.1007/978-3-030-60700-5_29

2 System Overview

2.1 DNA

Short for deoxyribonucleic acid, DNA is a molecule that carry genetic information in living organisms. They are found in nature, but they can also be synthesized artificially. There are four types, known as bases: Adenine (A), Thymine (T), Cytosine (C), and Guanine (G). Each DNA base can potentially hold up to two bits (binary digits) of electronic data. For example, a sequence of 00, 01, 10, and 11 can be coded as A, T, C, and G, respectively, as DNA.

Several attributes make DNA an ideal candidate for data storage. Firstly, the recovery and reading of DNA that is hundreds of thousands of years old [2] suggest DNA's high stability, and the potential to offer high retention capability as a data storage medium. Moreover, DNA offer low energy of operation [1], making it an economically attractive alternative to existing forms of data storage.

DNA's strongest attribute, however, is its impressive storage capacity. Capable of retaining up to 10^{18} bytes of information per cubic millimeter, DNA provides density that is roughly six orders of magnitude higher than the currently available, densest storage media [3]. To give a better sense of perspective, such density would allow all information produced around the world over a one-year period, to be stored in just 4 g of DNA [3].

Overall, these attributes would help in making DNA-based data storage systems to address the issue of exponentially growing digital data production [4] in outpacing the growth of traditional digital data storage systems (e.g., tape or hard disk drives, Blu-ray, and flash).

2.2 The Process

In terms of explaining how DNA fits into the overall process of data storage system, Fig. 1 provides the generic framework, illustrating the basic steps that are involved. Digital data is firstly encoded into DNA sequences, which are subsequently artificially synthesized into real DNA strands. These are then stored/archived away in either of the two formats. The first format, which is more commonly researched, is in vitro (either as frozen liquid or dried-down "powder" format). The second format involves insertion of the DNA into a host cell (in vivo), such as *E.coli* bacteria, effectively creating a type of microbial "memory unit" [5] (p. 3).

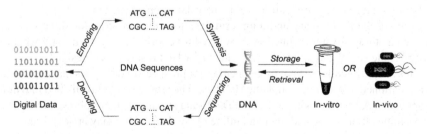

Fig. 1. Simplified process flow for a DNA-based digital data storage system

In order to request and retrieve back the data, an appropriate method for random access is carried out on the stored DNA batch (e.g., through polymerase chain reaction (PCR), not shown in Fig. 1), followed by a use of a sequencing machine to read the DNA, and then the final step of decoding the sequences back into an electronically compatible form.

3   Opportunities

DNA-based data storage systems, with their distinct attributes, open up a new space for HCI research, in the context of how they could shape the way we perceive, interact, and use data in the future. This article highlights just a handful of the many opportunities that the new technology brings to the HCI community.

3.1   User Experience Studies

In some ways, DNA is a somewhat ambiguous matter that does not fit neatly into either a virtual or a physical category. In the strictest sense, DNA is a physical molecule, but given its miniscule size and its invisibility to the naked human eye, it would be difficult to regard it as a tangible artefact in the context of people's expectations and experiences of it.

Likewise, the three thematic qualities identified by Odom et al. [6] as characteristic of virtual artefacts – placelessness, spacelessness, and formlessness – do not all apply when it comes to DNA. While the molecules may be spaceless and formless, in a sense that they "*largely do not intrude into people's physical space*" ([6], p. 985) and "*can be easily reproduced*" ([6], p. 985), they are not placeless, meaning that the molecules will have a designated place (e.g., a lab) and thus cannot simply be accessed from anywhere.

In addition, the ability of DNA to transition from its present state to either a macro-molecular or a digital form add further ambiguity. DNA is a step away from being translated by enzymes into larger, and more tangible macromolecules as proteins, which are responsible for organisms' phenotypes. On the other hand, it is also a step away from being translated into binary digits, which can be used to create a type of virtual artefact.

As such, should DNA become a new, encoded form of personal artefacts, that carry digital information (e.g., family photo albums, favorite songs, emails, etc.), it would be difficult to predict how people would perceive and experience the artefact, given its ambiguous status. It is also not known, whether the users' preconceptions about DNA, such as its traditional roles (e.g., "*DNA is a molecule that only carries genetic information (and no other types of information)*"), and of its previous applications (e.g., "*DNA is responsible for enabling genetically-modified organisms and food*") – may shape their experiences of it as an artefact.

Therefore, the creation of DNA-based artefacts would bring new research opportunities to find people's perceptions and experiences of them, and to subsequently better design the information system in response to the findings.

3.2 Data Physicalization

The advantages of data physicalization in helping users to explore, understand and communicate data [7] may also be applicable to physicalization of DNA-based data too. One of the ways to "physicalize" DNA, would involve incorporation of the DNA into a living cell (e.g., a bacterium). The host cell would then translate the DNA into proteins that could, with careful molecular programming, result in physical and visual changes. These changes include (but not exclusive to) pigment production, growth, antibiotic resistance, and death.

With such set up, several questions arise. For designers, what are the distinct advantages of using a dynamic, (and 'living') form of physicalization – such as those derived from DNA and bacteria – over more conventional static forms, to communicate data? And for prospective audiences, how would their experiences relate in comparison to 1) static data physicalizations, and 2) findings from previous studies on interactive systems that integrate living materials? For example, would the realization by the audience that the artefact contains living component significantly contribute towards certain aspects of their experiences, such as increased empathy [8], and enhanced sensory and imaginative immersion [9]?

3.3 Multi-lifespan Information for Wicked Problems

Once fully developed, the new data storage system could contribute towards some of the ongoing research initiatives in the HCI community, in addressing challenges that are unlikely to be solved within single human lifespans [10].

Given the longevity of DNA and its encoded data, it would lend itself well as a 'multi-lifespan' information system, that can outlast modern digital data storage systems, and more significantly, human lifespans. Not just generations, but possibly thousands (and perhaps even hundreds of thousands) of years' worth of archived data would be at a user's disposal as DNA, which could be accessed and used to tackle wicked problems [11] that demand long timeframes.

Long-term meteorological data would help towards prediction of climate change, whilst the archived genomic data of certain species would assist in effective visualization and analysis of their evolution (and also their possible extinction) [12].

In terms of social and cultural applications, DNA-based systems could assist in archival and curation of historical events that has occurred or will occur over multi-generations, thereby facilitating long-term endeavors such as international peace-building, finding genocidal justice [13], retention of family memory [14], and managing post-death legacy [15].

4 Challenges

4.1 Ethical Implications

So far, much of the discussions in academic research on the challenges faced by DNA-based data storage systems, have been mostly technical in nature. Reducing system latency, making it scalable, reducing cost of operation, and striving for full automation, are some of the technical discussions that have been published so far (e.g., [1]).

On the other hand, discussions on social implications of the technology has been lacking overall: What are the potential ethical issues surrounding our prospective interactions with the new technology, and what are the possible ways to be address them?

Technology Ownership. In the early years of market adoption, DNA-based data storage systems will most likely be available to the public as an online data storage service, rather than as hardware that users can own and operate the physical steps involved. The machine(s) and reagents that enable different steps, such as data encoding and decoding, would simply be too expensive, with some of the protocols involved also possibly patent protected.

As such, the technology's most likely initial owners, which would include co-operations (e.g., Microsoft [16]), government bodies (e.g., Defense Advanced Research Projects Agency (DARPA) [17]), and academia in partnership with either of these organizations, would have most of the control in gathering, storing, and using data.

Historically, handing personal data to such organizations have led to issues associated with data privacy breaches and data misuses in the past [18–21]. And crucially, there is currently no convincing guarantee that such issues cannot rise again with the usage of the new technology through third parties.

A possible long-term solution to these potential issues could involve designing better or alternative systems that are affordable and accessible for public use, thereby handing the agency of data management to the user in how and why certain data are to be archived and retrieved.

A possible shorter-term solution, on the other hand, would involve gaining better awareness and insight into 1) how DNA-based storage systems work, 2) their potential pitfalls, 3) the overall business model of the storage services offered, and 4) their associated customer rights.

4.2 Communication

One of the main ingredients that is needed to create meaningful and productive dialogue in a research community is effective and clear communication of ideas and arguments. This may be achieved through verbal or written channels, or through artefact designs that project or embody the ideas and arguments.

As the concepts of alternative, biological data storage and retrieval systems permeate the HCI community, effective ways to communicate the technology between those who may be designing and/or studying such systems would be one of the challenges that should need to be overcome.

As an example, on a basic level, the process of encoding digital data into DNA, and decoding it back to binary bits, allow languages of molecular biology and computer programming to intertwine, which may pose technical difficulties for those that may be unfamiliar with either of the two disciplines.

These type of issues will add to the constantly widening HCI curriculum for biology based HCI training [22], which could be delivered as 1) cross-disciplinary participatory workshops [23], 2) design and testing of educational gadgets [22], 3) seminars, and 4) formation of special interest groups within HCI.

5 Conclusion

DNA molecules, with its special qualities, make for compelling media for alternative data storage systems. Key technological developments over the recent years have allowed the prospect of DNA-based digital data storage systems (and services) to edge closer to mainstream usage. Despite these progressions, there has been little discussions within the HCI research community on the implications of this technology. This paper highlights just a few prospective opportunities and challenges presented by DNA-based data storage systems.

Overall, DNA-based data storage systems remain a largely open research topic for HCI, and the questions that have been raised here are by no means exhaustive. They are intended to serve as an opening for further in-depth discourse and explorations.

The opportunities can be broadly divided into two types. First type of opportunity is the fact that the technology brings a new research topic for user experience studies. This paper identified four of DNA's associated qualities, which hints at delivering new types of user experiences that may not be observed with conventional forms of data storage and/or artefacts. These qualities are 1) Spacelessness and formlessness of DNA; 2) User preconceptions of DNA; and 3) Transitionary capability of the DNA to undergo physicalization.

The second type of opportunity presented by DNA-based data storage was as a tool – which could harness the longevity of the DNA, in helping to address the multi-lifespan demands of several genres of wicked problems.

In terms of challenges, some of the ethical implications were highlighted, on the potential issues that may arise from corporate and governmental ownership of the data storage technology, and the possible ways to mitigate them. And finally, the need for creating a better "school" of communication of the technology amongst HCI designers and researchers were also mentioned, with some suggestions on ways to fulfill such types of needs.

DNA-based information storage will bring back drastic changes in how we store and use data. However, without consideration of its HCI-specific opportunities, as well as its social and ethical implications, we risk falling short of 1) fully capitalizing the new technology, and 2) better preparations for potentially negative ramifications.

Acknowledgements. I would like to thank friends, and colleagues at Media and Arts Technology (MAT) program at Queen Mary University, for helpful comments.

References

1. Ceze, L., Nivala, J., Strauss, K.: Molecular digital data storage using DNA. Nat. Rev. Genet. **20**(8), 456–466 (2019). https://doi.org/10.1038/s41576-019-0125-3
2. Ball, J.: Ancient horse bone yields oldest DNA sequence. BBC News. https://www.bbc.co.uk/news/science-environment-23060993. Accessed 15 June 2020

3. Rutten, M.G.T.A., Vaandrager, F.W., Elemans, J.A.A.W., Nolte, R.J.M.: Encoding information into polymers. Nat. Rev. Chem. **2**, 365–381 (2018). https://doi.org/10.1038/s41570-018-0051-5

4. Baraniuk, R.: More is less: signal processing and the data deluge. Science **331**(6018), 717–719 (2011). https://doi.org/10.1126/science.1197448

5. Kim, R., Poslad, S.: The thing with E. coli: Highlighting opportunities and challenges of integrating bacteria in IoT and HCI. arXiv preprint (2019). arXiv:1910.01974

6. Odom, W., Zimmerman, J., Forlizzi, J.: Placelessness, spacelessness, and formlessness: experiential qualities of virtual possessions. In: Proceedings of the 2014 Conference on Designing Interactive Systems (DIS 2014), pp. 985–994. Association for Computing Machinery, New York (2014). https://doi.org/10.1145/2598510.2598577

7. Jansen, Y., et al.: Opportunities and challenges for data physicalization. In: Proceedings of the 33rd Annual ACM Conference on Human Factors in Computing Systems (CHI 2015), pp. 3227–3236. Association for Computing Machinery, New York (2015). https://doi.org/10.1145/2702123.2702180

8. Cheok, A.D., Kok, R.T., Tan, C., Fernando, O.N.N., Merritt, T., Sen, J.Y.P.: Empathetic living media. In: Proceedings of the 7th ACM Conference on Designing Interactive Systems (DIS 2008), pp. 465–473. Association for Computing Machinery, New York (2018). https://doi.org/10.1145/1394445.1394495

9. Kim, R., Thomas, S., van Dierendonck, R., Kaniadakis, A., Poslad, S.: Microbial integration on player experience of hybrid bio-digital games. In: Cortez, P., Magalhães, L., Branco, P., Portela, C.F., Adão, T. (eds.) INTETAIN 2018. LNICST, vol. 273, pp. 148–159. Springer, Cham (2019). https://doi.org/10.1007/978-3-030-16447-8_15

10. Friedman, B., Nathan, L.P.: Multi-lifespan information system design: a research initiative for the HCI community. In: Proceedings of the SIGCHI Conference on Human Factors in Computing Systems (CHI 2010), pp. 2243–2246. Association for Computing Machinery, New York (2010). https://doi.org/10.1145/1753326.1753665

11. Rittel, H.W.J., Webber, M.M.: Dilemmas in general theory of planning. Pol. Sci. **4**(2), 155–169 (1973)

12. Cox, J.P.: Long-term data storage in DNA. Trends Biotechnol. **19**(7), 247–250 (2001). https://doi.org/10.1016/s0167-7799(01)01671-7

13. Yoo, D., et al.: Envisioning across generations: a multi-lifespan information system for international justice in rwanda. In: Proceedings of the SIGCHI Conference on Human Factors in Computing Systems (CHI 2013), pp. 2527-2536. Association for Computing Machinery, New York (2013). https://doi.org/10.1145/2470654.2481349

14. Jones, J., Ackerman, M.S.: Co-constructing family memory: understanding the intergenerational practices of passing on family stories. In: Proceedings of the 2018 CHI Conference on Human Factors in Computing Systems (CHI 2018), pp. 1–13. Association for Computing Machinery, New York (2018). https://doi.org/10.1145/3173574.3173998

15. Gulotta, R., Odom, W., Faste, H., Forlizzi, J.: Legacy in the age of the internet: reflections on how interactive systems shape how we are remembered. In: Proceedings of the 2014 Conference on Designing Interactive Systems (DIS 2014), pp. 975–984. Association for Computing Machinery, New York (2014). https://doi.org/10.1145/2598510.2598579

16. Microsoft. DNA Storage. https://www.microsoft.com/en-us/research/project/dna-storage/. Accessed 15 June 2020

17. DARPA. Turning to Chemistry for New "Computing" Concepts. https://www.darpa.mil/news-events/2017-03-23. Accessed 15 June 2020

18. Culnan, M.J., Bies, R.J.: Consumer privacy: balancing economic and justice considerations. J. Soc. Issues **59**(2), 323–342 (2003)

19. Oh, Y., Obi, T., Lee, J.S., Suzuki, H., Ohyama, N.: Empirical analysis of internet identity misuse: case study of south Korean real name system. In: Proceedings of the 6th ACM Workshop on Digital Identity Management (DIM 2010), pp. 27–34. Association for Computing Machinery, New York (2010). https://doi.org/10.1145/1866855.1866863

20. Korolova, A.: Privacy violations using micro targeted ads: a case study. J. Privacy Confidential. **3**(1), 27–49 (2011)

21. Lyon, D.: Surveillance, snowden, and big data: capacities, consequences, critique. Big Data Soc. 1–13 (2014). https://doi.org/10.1177/2053951714541861

22. Kim, R., Poslad, S.: Growable, invisible, connected toys: twitching towards ubiquitous bacterial computing. In: Proceedings of the Halfway to the Future Symposium 2019 (HTTF 2019), pp. 1–9. Association for Computing Machinery, New York (2019). https://doi.org/10.1145/3363384.3363387

23. Kim, R., Thomas, S., van Dierendonck, R., Wood, C., Poslad, S.: Toward growable computer games: insights from biotic game ideation workshops. Interactions **27**(2), 82–85 (2020). https://doi.org/10.1145/3378563

Decision Making Process Based on Descriptive Similarity in Case of Insufficient Data

Ahto Kuuseok[✉]

Estonian Business School, Estonian Police and Border Guard Board, Tallinn, Estonia
akuuseok@gmail.com

Abstract. This paper examines the possibilities and tools for quantifying the similarity of situations and developments, especially in relation to the outbreak of armed conflict. In previous works, the author has discussed structural similarity and descriptive similarity, plausibility. In the case of descriptive similarity, descriptions of events in situations and sets of statements have been used. Their numerical assessments of similarity are based on an assessment of the similarity of the respective situations and developments. This numerical estimate is based on the concept of the so-called descriptive similarity coefficient and the calculation prescript. In the investigation of descriptive similarity of situations and developments, they are viewed as algebraic systems in which the goal is to relate similarity to plausibility. It turned out that in the case of the security developments examined, there were very few allegations from descriptions found in public sources that reflected the real causes of the armed conflicts that had erupted. Probably partly because historical approaches have different views and the real reasons are contained in non-public databases. This explains why the searched common part was not found. As we did not find intersection among the allegations selected and observed and from the descriptions of the military attacks, we had to look for something else to replace it. For this purpose, the associators and, through them, the associations of descriptions (as relevant sets of claims) have been used below. Figuratively speaking, associators are statements from different descriptions that could be equated with each other - associations are a set of descriptions that are linked to each other by statements from different associatiors. We are trying to find a threshold above which it would be sensible to "hear warning signs". The author's relevant experience since working in the respective services has also been helpful.

Keywords: Descriptive similarity · Situations and developments · Similarity assessment procedures · Similarity and plausibility · Associations and associators · Stages of crisis development · Thresholds as a basis for decision making

1 Introduction

In many situations that often require decision-making and often quick decision-making, there is a lack of reliable statistics (time series, etc. are not available). At the same time,

© Springer Nature Switzerland AG 2020
C. Stephanidis et al. (Eds.): HCII 2020, CCIS 1293, pp. 233–240, 2020.
https://doi.org/10.1007/978-3-030-60700-5_30

you have to rely on something to manage situations. This is often done on the basis of similarity. This may be based on the experience of decision-makers in similar situations.

In the best case scenario, there are materials that have already been studied for the situation(s) to be played out or for the development(s) similar to the development. This approach helps to make credible decisions. It also helps to plausible analyze the past, the present and the plausibly expected future.

Similarity is a suitable instrument for recognition. Recognition is expressed, for example, by the following sentences (and not only in situations related to the job): "these situations are similar", "these developments are similar", "the future is likely to be similar" etc. Recognition is an area that is developing exponentially and in which the use of computers and sensors is expanding. Examples include other areas: the use of biometric evidence, fingerprints, eye irises, face detection etc. The difference simply depends on the detection technology and sensors, but the reasoning is philosophically the same: It all depends on how to teach computers to use the data from the sensors to get hold of them and evaluate the same or similar data.

There is no doubt that in the future, it will be essential to use computers to analyze crises, situations and developments. However, this requires a lot of preliminary work to understand how people would do this when teaching computers. In his previous work on situations and developments, the author has studied how to obtain numerical estimates of similarity. To this end, strategic texts, failed IT projects, business-critical value systems, as well as security situations were compared [1]. One of the results was the Crisis anatomy table [1], on the basis of which we analyze the matches of the statements in the descriptions of the development of military conflicts discussed in it and previously examined. We also compare the results with those obtained through associators and associations and examine how they correlate with developments in situations. We treat descriptions as a set of statements that characterize an area that describes an area (e.g., a situation immediately prior to an armed conflict), that is, as a set of relevant statements. The primary interest is to determine whether these descriptions have some intersection: some statements that could be noticed in all the descriptions analyzed. At the same time, of course, the material to be analyzed must be limited so that, for example, resources are not spent on irrelevant comparisons (e.g. due to too many different political, historical, cultural, geographical, etc. factors) [2]. In the research related to this work, the author has formulated appropriate criteria for selecting the conflicts that have taken place so far and deserve to be addressed from the aspect of security of the Republic of Estonia [3]. Based on these criteria, 16 conflicts were screened and their descriptions were taken into account.

2 Some Explanations of the Mathematical Concepts Applied in the Work

In dealing with the similarity of situations and developments, this work has been limited to the use of appropriate descriptions. It is assumed that the descriptions consist of statements: preferably those that could be "translated" into the formulas of one or another algebraic system theory [10], if necessary. Or more generally, descriptions are assumed to consist of statements that can be translated into a predicate calculation language.

Thus, we are dealing with so-called sets of numbers. Firstly, the set of descriptions of the situations or developments under investigation. Secondly, each description, as the set of relevant statements. As noted above, the approach of the present work is largely related to numerical estimates of descriptive similarity. As an appropriate estimate, we used the Lorents coefficient [1, 2], which differs from the Jaccard coefficient [5, 6] in that the Jaccard coefficient is based on the number of two sets of identical elements and the Lorents coefficient on the number of equated elements. There is no doubt that the Lorentz coefficient is appropriate for assessing the similarity of situations and developments, based on descriptions of relevant claims, as it is not reasonable to limit the use of strictly identical claims to those that could be equated (e.g. because they carry the same content). Of course, it must be clearly stated and fixed which type of identification is involved, as different identification methods may also give rise to different values of the coefficients. There are several other aspects to the use of identical statements instead of the same ones. For example, how to deal with the lack of an intersection of descriptions (i.e., the same statements that are searchable in all descriptions). These (i.e. Intersections), if any, would be one of the strongest features that are usually sought to be relied upon when examining similarity, as this is where it is expected to answer the question: what do the things under consideration have in common? The associations and associates proposed by Lorents are helpful here [7]. In short, among the given descriptions, those associations are those which:

(I)   are so-called directly associated because they have equated statements
(II) are so-called indirectly associated, as they have descriptions that form a "chain" from one description to another, in which "neighbors" are directly associated with each other

An association associate is made up of all such statements, e.g. **S1** and **S2**, which come from different descriptions belonging to the association, e.g. **D1** and **D2**, but these statements are equitable with each other.

3   Methods

The theoretical basis of the approach is to rely on the coefficient of descriptive similarity introduced by P. Lorents [1]. In order to implement it, the descriptions of the "eve" of conflicts must be formed into sets of relevant statements by two conflicts, e.g. **C1** and **C2 - D1** and **D2**. Then, pairs of equateble statements (e.g. pair **S1** and **S2**) must be identified by pairing the statements from one and the other set F in a fixed manner. It is important to emphasize here that these are equated things, not necessarily the same things. As described above, this is a significant difference in the nature of the Jaccard coefficient [5, 6] and the Lorentz coefficient: to calculate the Jaccard coefficient of two sets, the common part of the two sets, i.e. the same part, must be found; however, to calculate the Lorents coefficient, an equated part must be found. Thus, for two given sets, it is conceivable that the application of different identification methods may result in several different coefficient values. One can be the value of the corresponding Jaccard coefficient: namely, if the equation relation " $=$ " is selected as the identification method.

There are undoubtedly several possibilities for equalization in the case of two sets of claims, e.g. **D1** and **D2**. For example, relying on the logical equivalence of the appropriate predicate calculation formulas for the two statements. Or relying on the same meaning of the two statement. But whatever it would not be relied on in this case - in any case, the method of equalization used must be exhibited in order to apply the Lorents coefficient.

Denoting the method of equalization used by the symbol F, the part of the two sets of statements D1 and D2 identified by it with the notation **equF(D1, D2)** and the number of elements of a finite set H by the notation E(H) - we can use the Lorentz formula to calculate: $\mathbf{Des_F(D1,D2) = E(equ_F(D1,D2))/(E(D1) + E(D2) - E(equ_F(D1,D2)))}$ [1].

Examination of the descriptions **D1, D2... Dn** of the "eve" of the armed conflicts selected using the above-mentioned "filtering criteria" [3] revealed a somewhat startling result: for the sets of descriptive statements, the intersection turned out to be empty - that is, that $\mathbf{D1 \cap D2 \cap ... \cap Dn = \emptyset}$ [2]. And what is even stranger - the identified part also turned out to be empty [2]. This result raised the question of what could be "something" that would, in essence, "resemble" the common part as much as possible and help to highlight those statements that are not found in all descriptions D1, D2... but are encountered in so many enough. The mathematical aspect of this question (for relevant definitions, calculation rules, statements and proofs) was dealt with by P. Lorents [7], the content and applications of which remained the concern of the author of this paper.

4 Results

First, some numerical values: In the selected 16 descriptions, 138 statements were highlighted to describe the situations. In 1 of the 16 descriptions, no statement was found that could have been identified with the statements in another description. These 16 situations were selected by a selection method developed by the author [3]. The result was the associators of the sets of (statements), the application of which to the sets D1, D2... Dn revealed 7 statements that could be found in several descriptions [4]. Many of these statements appeared in only a few descriptions at a time, some in only 3, for example (see Table 1). Of course, a new question immediately arose: what could be the "reasonable level" for the statements that emerged in a given associate, i.e. the proportion of such numbers in which the given statement can be found. Obviously, such a level is not, for example, "pair set", "down", etc. Interviews with practitioners who are actually involved in hazard analysis and forecasting revealed that there is usually an interest in a few or three "higher frequencies". We have also outlined them below with brief explanations. The difference in the number of allegations was multiple. The highest number of occurrences was in the observed descriptions, according to A1 we had in the descriptions of the selected and observed situations of the parties (see Table 2).

Compared to the results of the author's previous works, the use of the association is much more meaningful. Recall that the similarity coefficients for pairwise equalization and comparison was "completely scattered" and surprisingly remained very low (average 0.299), and in addition, no intersection was found [2]. In previous works, the author also studied word comparison using "emerged search words" analysis [2] with keywords taken from the crisis anatomy table [1]. In this case, the results were higher, but also scattered and did not point out direct triggers that would need close attention when the possibility of an emergency situation is in question.

Using the same selected examples that appeared in more than one description, and looking at the associators (i.e., sets of statements whose elements were identified in more than one description), we obtained the following tables:

Table 1. Statements, associators, occurrence in association

	Statements from associators	Occurrence of maches								Descriptions in which there were claims identical to the claim	The descriptions shall include a total of the claims identified as such
A1	international condemnation but no consequences	1	3	4	5	6	7	10	16	8	9
A2	influence of great powers in conflict (both sides)	1	2	5	6	13	15			6	20
A3	prior annexation	3	4	5	7	9	10			6	15
A4	aspirations of national groups for freedom	3	4	6	10	15				5	3
A5	ethnic armed conflict (established)	5	6	9	13	15				5	6
A6	the predominant influence of economic interests as a major reason	2	8	11	12					4	15
A7	UN peacekeeping presence	1	13	15						3	15

Table 2. Coefficient of presentation in association

Total of cases	16	
Association	Total of presence in of descriptions	Coefficient
A1	5	0,3125
A2	8	0,5
A3	5	0,3125
A4	3	0,1875
A5	4	0,25
A6	6	0,375
A7	6	0,375

Important note: this example is a so-called maximum association, i.e. an association that "can no longer fit anything".

Statement A1: "There is international condemnation but no real results". This is an important danger sign for people working in security. This stems from the general recognition that "international cooperation based on recognition and diplomacy is one of the cornerstones of security" [9]. In other words, if the alarm clock and condemnation no longer receive attention, there is certainly cause for more serious concern. Statement A2: "strong influence of big players (on both sides)", also statement A3: "prior annexation" (by an aggressor who seems to be able to justify an ideological attack using some argument to establish historical justice), are also noteworthy danger signs.

The method described and based on previous work is intended as a so-called quick decision assistant for the expert, to give an initial assessment: To plan and decide on further steps in the future. It can also be simply forcing the risk assessment forward and raising awareness of the danger. In order to form a risk assessment not only within the framework of this work, it should also provide for the fulfillment of other preconditions describing a similar risk. Here are just 3 important questions that a risk assessment designer should ask themselves in order to assess a military threat even without having classified information [8].

1. Technical ability: is the aggressor able to carry out the desired attack quickly? To answer this question, it would be necessary to analyze a number of military-technical calculations, which is not appropriate to do here, as it would not fit into the scope of this work. This will be done by the relevant experts each time as necessary.
2. 2. Rhetoric: Has the aggressor expressed a political will to carry out a similar attack, has such rhetoric been covered in the domestic or foreign media? This issue deserves attention if such a message is conveyed by the direct official head of state, government officials or leaders of leading parties. The assessment of the answer to this question would also be based on the opinion of experts.
3. Are there any other signs that the aggressor was preparing his country and people for a crisis with a direct use of specific military force or a real possibility of using it? This assessment would also be based on expert opinion.

If these conditions are met and the main associates who have emerged in the descriptive association speak the same language, there is reason to make an in-depth analysis of the situation after a rapid and preliminary assessment. Once again, the above is not a universal model of prediction, but provides an opportunity and quick assessment for emergencies in the event of sudden emergencies.

5 Summary

Monitoring security situations and making appropriate decisions often takes place in situations where the necessary information is lacking and decisions need to be taken quickly (as an example: should travel restrictions be imposed? should their citizens be recalled? should something be and can be done to save assets and money? should force be used to protect their interests? etc.). In such a case, there is often no other way to reach a decision than to rely on the similarity of existing descriptions (on the one hand, a description of a "threatening" conflict, on the other hand, descriptions of some things that have already happened). Here, however, there is a danger of underestimating the workload.

On the one hand, it seems that due to the paucity of available data, experts will be able to "shred through" it. On the other hand, these are "hidden" large numbers: for example, an examination of the descriptions of the sixteen cases examined in this paper revealed that there is only one "more serious" association (containing 15 descriptions) and one "singular" association (containing only one description). However, we note that associations are (not-empty) parts of a set of descriptions. However, there are $2^{16} - 1 = 65535$ for 16 descriptions. And only for 16 descriptions!

Obviously, computer assistance is needed to cope with this (exponentially growing) volume. However, it cannot (at least initially) be limited to computers. The reason is that the equalization of claims is carried out by human experts based on their experience and intuition.

Consequently, it is necessary, at least initially, to try to rely on the establishment and implementation of appropriate dialogue systems, in order to "translate" the statements presented in the so-called natural language into the predicate calculation formulas [11–13]. At the same time, it is worth thinking immediately about the connection of this type of dialogue system with IT tools capable of "self-learning" (e.g. suitable neural networks, etc.). Thus, it can be said that the topic of this work is organically related to the field, which is characterized by the words: Human-Computer-Interaction. The current selection and calculation of examples has been done so-called manually, their aim was to create a system and methodology through calculations and comparisons - how to quickly manage decision-making in the presence of limited data, if a decision is needed in any case. Numerical values of similarity were used for this purpose, which in turn helps to assess the plausibility of the occurrence of one or another further situation. The field of security is only one of its kind, but obviously there are other areas where similarity assessments can be effectively applied: the technology sector, business (takeovers, etc.), as well as medicine, etc. The method of associations and associators created by Lorents [7] used in this work provides an opportunity to find a numerical assessment of situations even if there is no direct intersection in the descriptions of similar situations. It would certainly be necessary to create tools for the implementation of computers for the described method, combining learning machines and best artificial intelligence practices. In the world of security, there are typically too few relevant data and examples that do not allow the use of statistical methods (no statistical significance). Therefore, it can be assumed that based on the scarce descriptions of the initials and the implementation of self-learning IT systems, we could perform data mining, and reach results that we cannot expect today. Human-computer interaction could also lead to significantly better results in this area in the future. Unfortunately, proposing this solution does not fit into the scope of this work, but it is waiting to be done. In the present work, the methods are limited to mathematical and substantive analysis. The problem to be solved in the future is how to teach computers to calculate in the same way as people in order to obtain numerical estimates based on the desired and sought similarity.

References

1. Lorents, P., Matsak, E., Kuuseok, A., Harik, D.: Assessing the similarity of situations and developments by using metrics. In: Czarnowski, I., Howlett, R.J., Jain, L.C. (eds.) IDT 2017. SIST, vol. 72, pp. 184–196. Springer, Cham (2018). https://doi.org/10.1007/978-3-319-59421-7_17
2. Lorents, P., Kuuseok, A., Lorents, E.: Applying systems' similarities to assess the plausibility of armed conflicts. In: El Moussati, A., Kpalma, K., Ghaouth Belkasmi, M., Saber, M., Guégan, S. (eds.) SmartICT 2019. LNEE, vol. 684, pp. 83–93. Springer, Cham (2020). https://doi.org/10.1007/978-3-030-53187-4_10
3. Kuuseok, A.: Procedure of mining relevant examples of armed conflicts to define plausibility based on numerical assessment of similarity of situations and developments. In: Ahram, T., Karwowski, W., Vergnano, A., Leali, F., Taiar, R. (eds.) IHSI 2020. AISC, vol. 1131, pp. 619–626. Springer, Cham (2020). https://doi.org/10.1007/978-3-030-39512-4_96
4. Kuuseok, A.: Application of associations to assess similarity in situations prior to armed conflict. In: ICAI 2020. Springer (2020)
5. Jaccard, P.: Étude comparative de la distribution florale dans une portion des Alpes et des Jura. Bulletin de la Société Vaudoise des Sciences Naturelles **37**, 547–579 (1901)
6. Jaccard, P.: Distribution de la flore alpine dans le bassin des Dranses et dans quelques ré-gions voisines. Bulletin de la Société Vaudoise des Sciences Naturelles **37**, 241–272 (1901)
7. Lorents, P.: Comparison of similarity of situations in associations. In: ICAI 2020. Springer (2020)
8. Raag, I.: How to assess the threat of war without classified information (2015). https://edasi.org/29178/ilmar-raag-kuidas-hinnata-sojaohtu-ilma-salajase-teabeta/Edasi.org
9. Vienna Convention on Diplomatic Relations 1961. https://legal.un.org/ilc/texts/instruments/english/conventions/9_1_1961.pdf
10. Maltsev, A.I., Малъцев, А.И.: *Алгебраические системы.* "Наука". Москва (1970)
11. Matsak, E.: Dialogue system for extracting logic constructions in natural language texts. In: Proceedings of the International Conference on Artificial Intelligence. IC – AI 2005. Volume II, Las Vegas, Nevada, USA, pp. 791–797. CSREA Press (1970)
12. Matsak, E.: System DST for transforming natural language texts, representing estimates and higher order. Predicates and functionals. In: Proceedings of the 3-rd International Conference on Cyberneticsand Information Technologies, Systems and Applications: CITSA 2006 (2006)
13. Matsak, E., Lorents, P.: Decision-support systems for situation management and communication through the language of algebraic systems. In: 2012 IEEE International Multi-Disciplinary Conference on Cognitive Methods in Situation Awareness and Decision Support (CogSIMA 2012), CogSima 2012, pp. 301–307. IEEE Press (2012)

Fortune at the Bottom of the Information Pyramid: Leveraging Data Logs to Derive Experience Insights, a Reflective Case Study

Rutuja More[✉]

Barclays Global Service Centre Pvt. Ltd.,
Gera Commerce Zone SEZ, DP Farms Road, Kharadi, Pune 411014, India
`rutuja.more@barclays.com`

Abstract. In this case study, we aim to discuss and reflect on the methodology adopted by the UX team to come up with user and usage analytics insights in the absence of the same by using data generated from system logs and creating custom queries to derive reports to measure user experience. Thus data led to information. This then helped UX designers to derive behaviour and usage insights which translated to design recommendation hypothesis which were then validated against business objectives through stakeholder interactions. Thus information created knowledge and helped create a business value as well as evangelise UX within a technology driven organisation. Through this exercise designers learnt how data could be leveraged as a medium to create qualitative insights. The business witnessed the RoI of design as the findings were backed by data. This study also paved a path for engagements that are in progress between designers and data scientists to collaborate using Splunk and other analytics tools to mine richer user insights and drive strategy through data driven design approach.

Keywords: B2B · O2O · UX evangelisation · Data designer · UX in enterprise · UX in banking · Qualitative & quantitative research

1 Introduction

Banks have moved away from products to providing financial services. In a global organisation like Barclays the business and the actual end users (primarily investment bankers) were located in the US and the design and technology teams were in Pune, India. Hence a complex domain, lack of access to actual end users made it difficult for UX teams to understand the user technology landscape and their behavioural pain points. Yet all these applications have very thorough and rich system logs which help the development teams to trace bugs in case of any failures.

The DIKW pyramid is a hierarchical format that explains the four components of data, information, knowledge and wisdom. An analytical process starts at gathering context, assimilating information and reflect on the learnings to ultimately create business value. In the process that we gathered data from system logs and technology usage analytics dashboards, analysed the export reports and tried finding user usage patterns that could be leveraged to form experience insights. Thus backing the business asks with user needs and ultimately creating UX value within the organisation.

© Springer Nature Switzerland AG 2020
C. Stephanidis et al. (Eds.): HCII 2020, CCIS 1293, pp. 241–245, 2020.
https://doi.org/10.1007/978-3-030-60700-5_31

2 Background

Due to a geographic disparity, finding access to actual end users in investment banking domain is a challenge its hard to get time and attention within business hours. There was also a large time difference as the UX team and the end users were located in different geographies. So we had to come up with a sustainable approach to conduct user research remotely. Designing for expert users was another challenge as expert users know what they want and aren't afraid to ask for it. The users also have a strong mental model of existing legacy systems, learnt behaviours and other technological biases for performing tasks once they also resist changes. Studying behaviour through analytics gave us an understanding into the user's psychic but also backed our findings trough data.

3 Methodology

3.1 Data Gathering

The CRM Application which was a primary multi-functional applications based on a centralised client information warehouse that we were working had no means to capture user behaviours or feature utilisation through analytics but the system was capturing logs to keep a track of all events incase of any failure or downtown. These logs were intended to help the support team incase of any incidents were raised by users. The UX team would sit with the database developers and ask them to create a query that would give a list of events that were tracked in the application and then export that to excel file. UX designers would later massage the data reports generated and trace patterns for UX pain points and find opportunities for enhancements.

Some of the analytics dashboards that were used by senior management had some level of usage analytic information captured. But this application was primarily designed to understand the system capabilities like

- Number of users using the application and their usage frequency
- License and access management
- Monitor server health and RAM utilisation
- Overall action log that was needed for regulatory audits and development support

So the data captured was technology centric and not the way in which analytics captures usage data to find patterns and understand user behaviours right away.

Impersonation was another way for gathering data. It is a method in which one person can login as another and get a view of the UI through the other user profile. Impersonation helps when there are multiple user profiles accessing the same system, but the application tweaks itself based on the roles. By impersonating a user the designers could understand what is the interface that the actual user was seeing and how do they organise their data. It helped us understand how user roles personalised their dashboards and we could find parallels in roles and feature preferences through this exercise. Thus impersonation became a powerful tool to understand the user mental model and information hierarchy for various user profiles.

3.2 Analysis and Insights

Through the excel reports, we could track certain parameters like session start and end times, or most clicked page urls, the system was programmed to count events based on user clicks. This could generate quantitative answers to design questions. Hence the KPIs were centred around these quantitative parameters. Through the data logs we could get answers to when users access the system in their day, how long does a session last, what are the most and least accessed features/pages for various profiles easily. We also deep dived in their action logs to get secondary behaviours like whose profiles do users goto, what data are they interested in, this analysis led us to reach insights like peer comparison was essential for users but the UI didn't provide these feature.

Through the exercise we could derive the following information:

- Most and least frequent user profiles
- Frequency of accessing application
- Feature priority list
- Information categorisation and mental models.

3.3 Impact on UX Maturity

Insights gathered trough secondary research helped in creating micro-personas and user journey/experience maps. Access to users that had posed as a challenge was not so anymore as information needs and experience goals were derived from the data trails allowing us to create a design business case for stakeholders. The findings when presented to business proved of value and were included in the next development phases.

4 Summary

Lack of UX centric analytics allowed us to look at the data trails generated by systems in their data logs and mould it as per our needs to find patterns and gather insights. The methodology used allowed us to create a design business case for the stakeholders and helped in kick starting user research. The design findings also validated business asks as the findings were backed up by data. The process proved to be an effective means of secondary user research when there was a lack of it and also increased the credibility for user research within a technology centric organisation and moved the UX maturity index in a positive direction (Fig. 1).

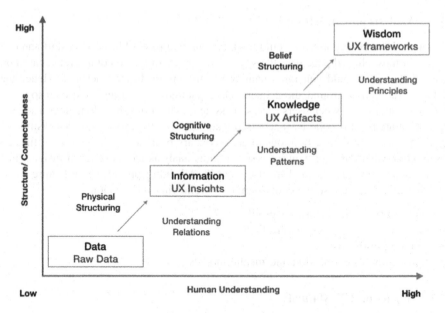

Fig. 1. DIKW hierarchy model flow applied to UX maturity

5   Moving Forward

As the methodology provided some groundwork of a sustainable remote user research framework, the team is now working with analytics team to create a richer data gathering tool for UX KPIs. The aim is to leverage data science technologies to gather more number of user interactions and help in finding answers to qualitative as well as quantitative experience questions. Designers are learning how can they frame the right problem statements to get the right data from systems for richer insights.

Thus though we started at the ground level of no formal analytics in the system, through this design methodology we could take the raw data analyse it in information insights, which helped in creating knowledge in the form of the design artefacts like personas and user journeys. Through the value creation we are now working on creating frameworks for generating user insights through data science which would help in increasing the UX maturity, thus making the organisation wiser than before.

Acknowledgements. I would like to thank Mr. Shrikant Ekbote, my manager who encouraged me to question and reflect of the work that we do and promoting data driven research frameworks to drive usability and experience. BI and tech teams at Barclays who have helped us in providing all required help and support in understanding technology frameworks.

References

1. Why I design for the enterprise and why you should, too. https://medium.com/swlh/why-i-design-for-the-enterprise-and-why-you-should-too-4547e01d7df3. Accessed 12 Mar 2020
2. Designing for expert users. http://usablemachine.com/designing-for-expert-users-2/. Accessed 10 Mar 2020
3. DIKW   chain.   https://slidemodel.com/templates/dikw-model-powerpoint-template/powerpoint-model-dikw-chain/. Accessed 26 Jan 2020
4. What are micro personas and do you need them? https://smallbusiness.yahoo.com/advisor/resource-center/if-youve-read-this-blog-or-heck-any-blog-about/. Accessed 25 Jan 2020

Real-Time Video Stream Reduction on Mobile Devices for Generation of Ground Truth Data for Indoor Localization

Benny Platte[✉][ID], Christian Roschke, Rico Thomanek, Tony Rolletschke,
Ruben Wittrin, Claudia Hösel, Frank Zimmer, and Marc Ritter

Hochschule Mittweida, Technikumplatz 17, 09648 Mittweida, Germany
platte@hs-mittweida.de

Abstract. We would like to offer users an easy way to generate smart pre-selected high quality Ground Truth Data for location detection.

We use the hardware-accelerated computation in image buffers available in modern smartphones and investigate the automatized "picking" of the most suitable images out of the running video stream. Furthermore we investigate the real-time capability of the selection algorithms and ask the question: How do the reduced reference data perform after the training of image classifiers compared to the "stupid all-saver"?

In summary, a factor 10 reduction of the image quantity is achieved in real time by intelligent selection directly at the source on the smartphone without losing recognition quality.

Keywords: Indoor localization · Ground truth generation · Annotated data · Smartphone application

1 Introduction

The investigation is part of a project in which we examine infrastructure independent indoor positioning. The high computing power of modern smartphones enables the internal camera to examine a video stream in real time and to store annotated single images to train neural networks.

Let's consider the user who has been tasked with indoor localization annotation as the center: he wants to generate reference data quickly and straightforwardly. For this purpose he wants to walk through the rooms with his smartphone and tag locations. The reference data should be comprehensive and of high quality (e.g. image sharpness), but at the same time not take up too many resources. These competing demands require intelligent pre-selection. With this selection, we do not want to annoy the user, but instead perform it automatically.

What are the requirements? The individual frames of a video stream, recorded in motion, are often blurred. This leads to our hypothesis: The blurred images only inflate the required resources of the image classification algorithm, but do not result in an advantage in recognition quality. From this hypothesis

© Springer Nature Switzerland AG 2020
C. Stephanidis et al. (Eds.): HCII 2020, CCIS 1293, pp. 246–254, 2020.
https://doi.org/10.1007/978-3-030-60700-5_32

the following question arises: Can the mobile device select the images *in real time* and immediately sort out the majority of them, i.e. not save them at all?

In this study, we investigate an automated realtime selection of meaningful single images from the image stream *directly during generation in the mobile device* (Fig. 1). Our goals are:

1. Complete real-time capability.
2. Maintaining recognition quality: no compromises in the quality of the final classifier. The model performance after the training of the classifiers should at least be equivalent to that of the model that was trained with all images.
3. Reference Image count reducing to 20%.

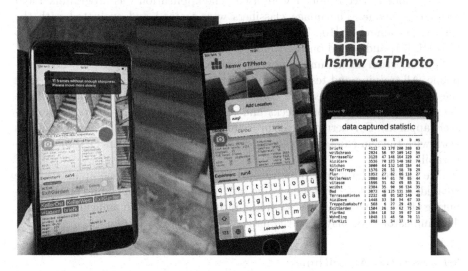

Fig. 1. iOS application for indoor location ground truth creation

2 Related Work

The calculation of the sharpness of images plays an important role especially in the development of cameras and their autofocus systems [1,2]. Usually it concerns the evaluation of certain edge categories. The most common area of application is the resharpening of noisy images such as in fingerprint recognition [3]. Less frequently, the selection of images from a larger contingent is examined [4]. If so, then mostly in the medical sector. The use case is similar to ours: there are substantially more images than needed, and an automated selection has to be made, e.g. the brightest sharp images [5]. Other approaches to dataset reduction like MRMR [6] are based on the identification of characteristics. However, these require the existence of the entire dataset to use scoring and clustering methods. The present study does not intend to generate a ground truth dataset and then cluster it, *we don't want to create it in the first place.* We do have data available for selection, but only in small batches. Based on these small groups, the decision must be made in real time: "Delete or keep".

3   Methods

A smartphone application for iOS devices [7] created by us provides the basis for the study. With this application we capture the reference data and extract different categories of filtered reference image sets from the video stream in real-time using hardware accelerated DSP-matrix calculations of the *Accelerate* framework [8, 9].

As mobile device iPhone 7 were used. The application was programmed and created in Xcode. The image classifiers were trained and evaluated with the turicreate-framework [10]. The models with the best metrics were converted to CoreML [11] and tested on the smartphone.

The selection algorithms were implemented and tested directly on the smartphone. All training and test data was recorded directly and simultaneously with the smartphone under real-life conditions. This allows a fast iteration of the development. Possible bottlenecks and performance problems become immediately apparent. Furthermore, this procedure ensures that all selection algorithms work with the same data in the concrete mobile device and thus guarantee comparability.

We reduced the video frame rate to 10 fps. The smartphone application we created (Fig. 1) uses a dynamic frame rate based on this: depending on the computing effort of the filters, the sampling rate is lowered or dynamically increased. This indicator is displayed to the user.

3.1   Selected Algorithms

We selected 3 filters for the implementation of the sharpness rating: "Scharr", "Sobel" and "Laplace". These 3 are supplemented by a manual image selection in 2 variants for comparison purposes. Together with the basic method there are 6 methods of image selection for comparison, listed in Table 1.

Each of the 3 automatic methods calculates the respective output by a discrete convolution based on its own convolution matrix ("kernel"). After the calculation of the convoluted luminance layer, it is normalized and the standard distribution of the edge values over the whole image area is calculated. We use this measures as scores for image sharpness.

3.2   Implementation

The smartphone analyzes every single frame of the video stream. Each frame gets an identifier. The stream of frames is passed to the selection algorithms ("frame picker"). The framepickers are each independent classes and were implemented in the form of the GoF-strategy pattern [12] as concrete algorithms of

Table 1. Frame selection algorithms ('Framepicker')

`allSaver`	Basis of all comparisons will be this "stupid All-Saver". This algorithm will store *every image*. Therefore, we refer to it as the "stupid"
`manual Immediately`	Without any automation, pure user-based selection: The user presses a button. The next frame is then immediately saved
`manual Sharpest`	`manualImmediately` with assistance: By pressing the above button the sharpest of all frames of the previous two seconds will be searched and saved
`scharr`	First order edge detection method: calculation of the sharpness score by "Scharr"-Filter
`sobel`	First order edge detection method: calculation of the sharpness score by "Sobel"-Filter with vertical kernel
`laplacian`	Second order edge detection method: calculation of the sharpness score using a laplace kernel

an abstract framepicker algorithm. They create independent frame objects with a reference to the real frame. Each frame is thus used to create several frame objects enriched with still empty metadata (type of processing, score value), one in each frame picker. Each frame picker now checks the frame for its parameters from Table 1. This modularization allows easy exchangeability and extensibility of the algorithms to be used. They can be dynamically changed at runtime. For the examined edge detection filters, the frame with the highest sharpness score is saved after 2 s without user interaction. If none of the images reaches the minimum value, no image is saved and the user is notified ("move Smartphone slower please").

If the respective frame picker decides that the image meets the criteria, it assigns appropriate metadata to it and forwards the frame object together with metadata to the archiving class. This class saves the image to the file system of the smartphone and the metadata to a database. If several frame objects are passed to the storage class that refer to the same physical frame, the file is only saved once. The metadata database then contains several entries with different metadata that all refer to the same frame.

Optimization. Performance plays a major role in full-screen image calculations. Since we want to reduce the generated ground truth data immediately on the mobile device, all calculations must be performed by the mobile device. It is worth to examine the whole pipeline from the image sensor to the file for optimization potential. The selected image classifiers "resnet-50" and "squeezenet v1.1" work with image resolutions of 224×224 and 227×227 pixels, respectively. The image sensor has therefore been parameterized to give a low resolution as close as possible to that at which even the preview image is still meaningful for the user. VGA with 640 × 480 has proven to be practical here. At the same time, the user can see the preview image well enough at this resolution during data acquisition.

Only a grayscale image is needed for the calculation of the edge detection filters. To avoid generating a grayscale image from the color layers, the image data was read from the image sensor in YpCbCr pixel format ("420YpCbCr8BiPlanarFullRange"). This format represents the luminance of the image on one layer and the color information on separate layers. The 3 edge detection filters were implemented in image buffers by hardware accelerated computation. For this we used the Accelerate Framework [9].

Aquisition. The iPhone application shown in Fig. 1 was used to record ground truth data for a building. In order to test the user experience, 3 different user images were recorded on different days. Each user received a short briefing.

Training. To create the image classifier models the 3 variables listed in Table 2 plus the 6 selection algorithms from Sect. 3.1 are available. With each of the possible 48 combinations a separate classification model was trained and evaluated.

Table 2. Methods for splitting train and test data.

network	network used for training
main_split	first stage of splitting training and evaluation data: "random" means random selection from whole dataset, separate_days get evaluation data from completely different recording days with partly different furniture and different sunlight. Here we expect worse results in recognition, as the situations, lighting conditions and positions vary greatly. The similarities between training and test images are greatest here.
per_label_ split_ method	In order to determine statistical skewness due to the possible types of train-test splitting, the splits were made label-specific in different variants:
	fractional random — get the same relative amount from each class; completely random distribution. Disadvantage: possibly undetected clustering due to unequal image distributions in the individual classes.
	same quantity — same nominal part of training data from each class regardless of the number of data available in that class
	as it is — with main_split = separate_days no further splitting is applied.

4   Results

A total of 52810 images were recorded in 20 classes. In addition to the training data, each selection algorithm ("Framepicker") adds about 2% test data. The test data has already been separated during the main_split which refers to the entire dataset. Users pressed the shutter button almost 1500 times during recording. The framepicker manualSharpest from Table 1 which supports manual triggering selected 639 images (+2%).

Table 3. Comparison of key statistics and performance of all 48 trained image classifiers.

comparison basis best picking algorithm		model average AUC						dataset image count						
		Values in ‰						test	train					
main_split	per label split method	"stupid" allSaver	manual Immed.	manual sharpest	laplacian	scharr	sobel	all methods	"stupid" allSaver	manual Immed.	manual sharpest	laplacian	scharr	sobel
resnet 50 random	fractional	994	976	973	993	937	976	982	51828	1456	1156	3501	3306	3756
	random	994	971	968	994	974	978	982	51828	1436	1163	3517	3354	3812
	same quantity	996	971	971	994	921	979	980	51830	1446	1157	3500	3407	3754
separate Days	as it is	879	843	853	875	851	854 ②	4703	48107	923	639	2340	2289	3402 ⑤
		proportional part of AllSaver in ‰:												
squeeze-net v1.1 random	fractional	952	922	916	942	877	940		1000	28	22	68	64	72
	random	955	926	926	950	897	960		1000	28	22	68	65	74
	same quantity	952	923	913	939	877	950		1000	28	22	68	66	72
separate Days	as it is	834	811	784	827	754	816		1000	19	13	49	48	71
mean over all models		945	918	913	939	886	932		1000	26	20	63	60	72
Difference to mean of "allSaver"		①	26	31	③ 5	58	12					④		

In the evaluation variation `separate_days`, described in Table 2, 4703 images were recorded. These 4703 images form a completed test set. With this set, all selector models were evaluated in another separate run. The user interaction-free selection algorithms selected about 2300 (2289+2%) to 3900 (3812+2%) images (⑤ in Table 3). This corresponds to about 68–74‰ of all recorded images. The ratio of the selected image numbers shows Fig. 2 in column 3.

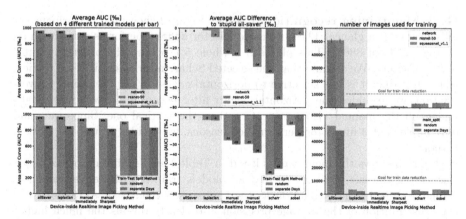

Fig. 2. Comparison of the averaged model metrics: `allSaver` is highlighted in yellow, the best automated selection model in green.

All values based on the `allSaver` represent the reference metric. This is marked yellow in all tables and figures. The mean value of all area under curve reference metrics is 945‰, see ① in Table 3. As expected, the values for the `main_split = separate_days` are below the randomly split datasets (mean 857‰ vs. 974‰ and thus 117‰ below).

With an AUC of 916% the two manual selection procedures range between the fully automated models. The automatic selectors scharr, laplacian and sobel are within a range of 53% respectively 5.3 %. The selection algorithm `laplacian` has the highest recognition quality with an average AUC value of 939% (③ in Table 3). This value is 5% below the average AUC of `allSavers`.

The used iPhone 7 reaches almost 7 fps in the developer mode of the application. The biggest performance drop was caused by the re-conversion of the filtered images to store the calculated filter images for the present investigation. No DSP function could be used here. The conversion required half the computing time.

5   Discussion

Goal: Training Data Reduction to 20%: The manual selection method `manualImmediately` performs better in the average AUC 5% than the supported manual method `manualSharpest`. We assume that this is due to the fact that the users pressed the shutter button several times per second when they noticed an important object and kept moving the smartphone. This resulted in several manual images, while the supporting algorithm in this case only selected one or none of them. One of the given goals was to reduce the amount of comparison images to 20% ($\equiv$200%). With 68–74% all automatic selectors are within the target corridor or far below. All automatic selectors therefore reach this target.

Goal: Maintaining recognition quality: Figure 2 shows the performance of all selectors at a glance. The automatic selector **scharr** performs worst with an average AUC of 886%. This places it a whole 5% behind the other two automatic selectors. We assume that the selected Scharr filter is sensitive to vertical edges, but that it is less sensitive to horizontal edges. In the preliminary investigation, we excluded the horizontal Scharr filter because it selected less sharp images in the manual visual inspection than the vertical one. Since we could only implement 3 filters for performance reasons, we decided to use the vertical variant.

Figure 3 shows the mean values listed in Table 3 as distribution of the single classes. On the left you can see that all models trained with `laplacian` show similar results in the evaluation as the comparison models of `allSaver`. The class distribution of the average precision also clearly reveals the much higher performance of the resnet network in Fig. 3 on the right.

The best automatic selector is `laplacian` with an AUC of 939% (③ in Table 3), closely followed by `sobel` with 932 ‰. `laplacian` is only 6% behind the reference metric `allSaver` in the mean AUC. With slightly better performance he also selected 8% fewer images than `sobel`. Thus `laplacian` is also the most effective automatic selector.

Let's look at the use case in later practice: A trained classifier model runs on a smartphone and analyzes images of places the user has in front of him. These images do not come from a random splitting of the set of ground truth data, but represent a new day, different light conditions or other inventory. The performed `main_split=separate days` simulates just this practical use case: here the `laplacian` selector is at 875% and thus a whole 21% before the `sobel` selector (②) in Table 3). The distance to the allSaver is now only 2‰. In this case, the AUC of the `laplacian` selector is equal to the comparison metric. The slightly lower precision of this more realistic use case `separate days` is also clearly visible in the distribution of the single classes in the middle of Fig. 3.

The performance of the `laplacian` selector in the middle AUC over all trained models is only 6% below the `allSaver`. Thus it is on par in performance, but only needs 6–8% of the image set (Fig. 2 and Table 3).

Goal: Realtime Capability: The consulted users considered the achieved sampling rate of 7 fps with full automatic sharpness selection to be sufficient in practical use. It should be noted that the application for the present study ran in developer mode. In this mode it additionally stores all calculated filter images. The greatest performance loss occurred due to the necessary reconversion of the filter images. No hardware-accelerated DSP functions could be used here. The conversion took half the computing time. This is not necessary in later normal operation. This would significantly increase the frame rate.

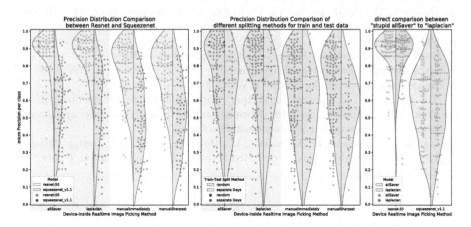

Fig. 3. Precision distribution of the individual classes. Shown are the benchmark metric `allSaver`, the best automatic selector `laplacian` and the two manual selectors for comparison.

6   Conclusion

The investigation is part of a larger project for indoor localization without external infrastructure components. In the present work it could be shown that it is possible to reduce the necessary ground truth data for a comprehensive image-based acquisition of a building already within the mobile device to less than one tenth by using suitable methods. The quality of the image classifiers generated with this method is equal to that of the classifiers based on all data.

This solution offers various advantages: users can collect data in the building up to ten times longer until they reach the memory limits of the smartphone. Furthermore, the time required to train the classifiers is significantly less.

References

1. Ba-Tis, F., Ben-Mrad, R.: Autofocus and optical image stabilizer system. U.S. pat. 20190373174A1. Faez Ba-Tis, Ridha Ben-Mrad 5 December 2019
2. Pertuz, S., Puig, D., García, M.Á.: Analysis of focus measure operators for shape-from-focus. Pattern Recognit. **46**, 1415–1432 (2013). https://doi.org/10.1016/j.patcog.2012.11.011
3. Abdul-Kader, S.A.: Comparative study for edge detection of noisy image using sobel and laplace operators. J. Coll. Educ. Women **23**, 11 (2012)
4. (PDF) Efficient Method of Detecting Blurry Images. https://www.researchgate.net/publication/265198032_Efficient_Method_of_Detecting_Blurry_Images
5. Moreno-Díaz, R., Pichler, F., Quesada-Arencibia, A.: Computer Aided Systems Theory - EUROCAST 2015: 15th International Conference, Las Palmas de Gran Canaria, Spain, February 8–13, 2015, Revised Selected Papers. Springer, Heidelberg (2015). Google Books: RjQ3CwAAQBAJ
6. Gulgezen, G., Cataltepe, Z., Yu, L.: Stable feature selection using MRMR algorithm. In: 2009 IEEE 17th Signal Processing and Applications Conference, pp. 596–599 (2009)
7. Swift - Apple Developer. https://developer.apple.com/swift/
8. Metal. https://developer.apple.com/metal/
9. Introducing Accelerate for Swift - WWDC 2019
10. Turi Create API Documentation. https://apple.github.io/turicreate/docs/api/
11. Core ML | Apple Developer Documentation. https://developer.apple.com/, https://developer.apple.com/documentation/coreml
12. Gamma, E., Johnson, R., Vlissides, J.M., Helm, R., Fowler, M.: Design Patterns: Elements of Reusable Object Orientated Software. Pearson Education, Upper Saddle River (2020)

Challenges of Simulating Uncertainty of Information

Adrienne Raglin[1]([⊠]) [iD], Somiya Metu[1] [iD], and Dawn Lott[2] [iD]

[1] Army Research Laboratory, Adelphi, MD 20783, USA
{adrienne.raglin2.civ,somiya.metu.civ}@mail.mil
[2] Delaware State University, Delaware, USA
dlott@desu.edu

Abstract. Human information interaction including human computer interaction is complex given the variability of the human and now the ever-increasing amount of information available. While more information seems to be ideal, most would agree that having the needed information at the time required maybe the ideal. This is particularly true for decision-making. At each step along the decision-making process, different information may be needed so that the goal of generating the best decision is reached. However, information is not perfect and comes with uncertainties. Our approach has been to explore what we have termed uncertainty of information (UoI) and its impact on decision-making. We have selected Gershon's taxonomy of imperfect information as variable descriptors to represent potential sources of uncertainty. Using terms from the taxonomy we have created an algorithm that can capture the uncertainty from this point of view. In addition, we have developed simulations to begin to explore the how UoI from various sources can influence decision-making. Consequently, we have been faced with the difficulties of building a general comprehensive model for simulating UoI. These difficulties range from how to express the behavior of the human to how to express the behavior of the computer and devices that may be providing the information. The difficulties also include how to incorporate the different factors and underlying dependencies that contribute to the UoI value.

Keywords: Human information interaction · Uncertainty of information · Simulations

1 Introduction

1.1 Objective

The overarching objective is to research generating, presenting, and visualizing uncertainty so that the decision maker can make risk informed decisions. Understanding the uncertainty of information (UoI) and how it influences the decision is key particularly for decisions that the military faces. Therefore, the goal of the model is twofold: allow the examination of decision-making theories and aid the analysis and assessment of relevant underlying sources of uncertainty in this context. This paper discusses some of the

© Springer Nature Switzerland AG 2020
C. Stephanidis et al. (Eds.): HCII 2020, CCIS 1293, pp. 255–261, 2020.
https://doi.org/10.1007/978-3-030-60700-5_33

challenges in simulating the concept and the approach to those challenges. This paper also beings to expand on UoI concept and algorithm allowing for different taxonomies and variables to be used for various decision-making tasks.

1.2 The Motivation

Although not strictly a new concept, the military's answer to the joint operations question has become the multi domain operation (MDO). Leveraging and combining capabilities across air, land, sea and space, "offers the freedom of action necessary to attain mission success" [1]. Due to rapid advances in technology, one of the main factors that fuels this transition is the growth of information. From the perspective of military decision-making, information particularly in MDO is a vital component. These future MDOs will be much more fluid and dynamic, all decision makers including commanders will need to 'cope with unprecedented complexity, uncertainty, and op-tempo" [2]. All decision-making, even high-level ones, happen even when there are unknowns, unfortunately not all information is know when needed. The choices in this environment come with a degree of risk. This uncertainty creates the fog of war. Whether the uncertainty is connected to the adversaries' capability and intent or not it remains a crucial challenge. In earlier phases of this work [3] representing uncertainty and [4] the investigation of expressing uncertainty were initially explored. In this phase of the work, a numerical expression is selected and although there exists several features that can represent uncertainty, Gershon's taxonomy of imperfect information is selected. Thus, the uncertainty of information is used to form a single value. However, the algorithm allows this single value to be expanded so that the various sources and types of uncertainty can be reviewed for use in the decision-making process.

2 Review of Uncertainty of Information

2.1 The Algorithm

Initially, the uncertainty of information (UoI) was a weighted sum

$$UoI = \sum_{i,j=1}^{n,m} T_i * S_j \tag{1}$$

where T are the weights per taxonomy for each individual entry for the sources, S. In [5], the algorithm was expanded using operations research approach referred to as LRM version of UoI is discussed in detail. As new applications are being considered the algorithm will be modified to utilize categories of sources that are composed of multiple source types; for example, devices may be further differentiated into sub-categories of sources (ex. devices: cameras to include IoT and traditional cameras such as pan and tilt, multispectral, polarimetric, etc....). In addition, the weights may include those generated in various ways (ex. entered interactively by the decision maker, composite of expert recommendations, calculated from AI/ML, or based on other and additional uncertainty taxonomies and expressions). Initially the taxonomies were based on Gerhson's concept of imperfect information [6] as the following:

- Corrupt data and information with any type of error
- Incomplete data and information whether missing or inaccessible
- Inconsistency in data and information with previous known data
- Difficulty in understanding complexities of the data
- Imperfect presentation of data that is delayed or perceived incorrectly
- Uncertainty in the data perceived by the user

This revised version of the UoI is:

$$UoI = \sum_{a,b=1}^{k,l} T_{a,b} * S_{a,b} + \sum_{c,d=1}^{m,n} W_{c,d} * D_{c,d} \tag{2}$$

where D are variables that express components of decision-making that may be key factors for the task and W are the weights associated with the importance of those component. In addition, T will be the categories of taxonomy weights and S will be the categories of sources. In the expanded version of UoI the taxonomies can come from other concepts. Additional ones from Gershon [6] can include:

- Inappropriate device used to present the data and information
- Imperfect representation in the appearance or proximity of the data
- Information overload that prevents taking in and understanding the data
- Inappropriate presentation that causes misunderstanding of the data

As mentioned in [7] taxonomies can be come from other work on uncertainty and how it can be presented and visualized as the first two listed below or inspired by other work such as the third listed below is inspired by Gershon:

- Uncertainty in acquisition
- Uncertainty in transformation
- Inappropriate sensor or system

Given the potential complexities of decision-making for a wider set of applications, the UoI may be modular where various sub-UoI values are integrated into an overall UoI value. This may include creating various versions of UoIs for different phases in the decision-making process. This approach could support different decision-making theories whether it is the military decision-making process, the OODA loop or Herb Simon's model. A UoI could be generated at each step and concatenated together or combined at the final decision-making point. Ideally this approach would be sufficiently flexible so that decision navigation can be supported. In this version, UoIs could be calculated along the progression of the mission allowing the commander and other decision makers to adapt to new challenges, new conditions, new data, and changing strategies of the adversary.

2.2 The Current Application Simulation

Currently the application of the existing UoI algorithm is internet of things (IoT) focused. This application uses four broad general sources: IoT device, Information from the device, the Network that is the platform for the device, and the Visualization system used with the device [8]. The simulations of the UoI were done using SAGE. SAGE is a multi-agent-based framework for system automation from the Naval Research Laboratory. Once the operations research inspired algorithm was generated, simulations were done where source and taxonomy ranking were randomly generated using MATLAB.

3 Challenges of Simulation

3.1 SAGE Simulation

As with any research, the challenge of complexity is usually present. With the extensive features of SAGE, a simple approach was initially adopted. We developed a scenario in SAGE with single agents that represented the decision-maker, sources and control. The different types of agents within the developed SAGE Scenario are described below:

Decision Maker Agent: The decision makers are responsible for performing decision tasks. The decision-making agent performance is governed by its defined behavior, current options are Risky, Random or Conventional. Simple rules were created for each behavior type. Each type of decision maker has an inherent numerical decision attribute. The predefined rules determine the increase or decrease of the attribute for different choices given the UoI value at the time a decision needs to be made.

Source Agent: Currently there are four types Device, Information from Device, State of Network and Visualization. Unconsciously single source types were set (ex. information was from one device on one network with one visualization system). An UoI value is generated for each of these sources.

Controller Agent: The controller monitors the state of the sources and provides an overall UoI value from the individual source UoI values. The individual source UoI values are referred to as the VIND (Visualization, Information, Network, Device) numbers. The controller agent gives the value to the decision-making agent and acts as a repository for the UoI values over time.

For the simulation, we chose a simple task to actuate an IoT device or not. In order to make this decision, the decision maker agent communicates with the controller agent to request the UoI values and the VIND numbers. Upon receipt of this request, the controller agent prepares and sends back the UoI values from each of the sources individually and collectively. Once the decision maker receives the UoI values from the controller, the final decision task is performed. Once the decision is decided the decision attribute is calculated based on the rules.

Different types of simulations in SAGE were performed in which the UoI value was classified as "High", "Medium" or "Low". Each simulation consisted of a decision maker performing fifteen decisions. These simulations were run hundred times and the decision attribute value of the decision makers were aggregated over the course of the simulation. The graphs below depicts two different simulations with different UoI classification range and summarizes the performance of different decision makers.

As depicted in the graph above (see Fig. 1), different UoI value ranges and threshold levels yielded different results in terms of performance of the decision makers. In Fig. 1(a) the threshold levels were preset prior to simulation runs. In Fig. 1(b) the threshold levels

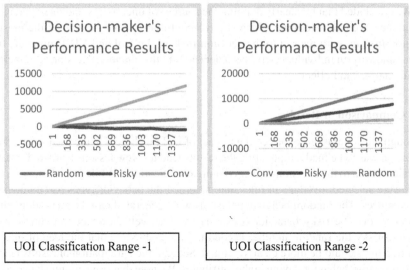

Fig. 1. (a) On the left the results with preset threshold levels. (b) On the right the results with threshold levels determined after the range of UoI values are calculated.

were set after the range of UoI values were known. In near real-time applications the range of values cannot be calculated prior to setting the thresholds they will change as the ranking and decision factors change. The differences that clearly impact the performance attribute results indicate the need for further investigation for an optimal UoI value ranges and corresponding threshold levels.

3.2 MATLAB Simulation

The LRM version of the UoI algorithm [5, 9] was utilized to simulate a compound, yet simple experiment to investigate how the UoI can influence decisions, particularly at the point of the final decision step. This version of the algorithm utilizes mathematical tools of operations research to maximize the level of uncertainty from the sources. In the simulation, random numbers or preset numbers were used to rank the importance of the taxonomies and sources that would support decision-making in a simple military relevant inspired task. In the future, a user study based experimentation will collect data from participants for the ranking with more detailed military relevant scenarios to provide the context in which decisions will be made.

The present simulation task consisted of making a yes or no decision at fifteen decision points, in succession. At each decision point, the Decision-maker was provided the UoI and the VIND numbers which are computed using the LRM method and are based on the data supplied by each source regarding each Source_Taxonomy pair. From this work, we were able to gauge the performance of various types of decision-makers in terms of the value of their decision attribute after performing a certain number of decision tasks. The results of simulations conducted provide corroborating evidence that uncertainty and its causal effects have an influence on decision-making.

We concluded that by clearly defining the sources of uncertainty and there perceived importance, we can determine which sources contribute to and are valued the most in decision-making with respect to the decision-maker. The UoI and VIND numbers link to how and why an individual arrives at a decision. In this manner, decisions can include causal analysis and effects.

3.3 Comparison of Results

Although the simulations explored the impact of UoI on choices at the final stage where a decision was to be made, replicating the results lead to a few lessons learned. First, the behaviors given to the decision-makers require modifications. While only three behavior types were selected, overlaps in rules that governed the behavior-types had unintended consequences. The random behavior decisions were generated based on a random number generator. The risky behavior decisions were as well, however to express some notion of risky the random number needed to be weighted so that the idea of making risky decisions could be more clearly defined. Second, the anticipation of results lead to the conservative behavior having higher attributes. We note that in no circumstance could the conservative behavior have any poor choices, which is not always realistic. Lastly, it was unclear if the risky or random behavior should produce the higher attributes between the two. Giving well-defined and distinct behavior to each decision-maker might yield definitive answers to this question.

Additional challenges were encountered during the MATLAB simulations that impacted the SAGE simulations. A method for choosing the thresholds for low, medium, and high UoI values needed to be defined based on a combination of simulation outcomes to determine the appropriate range. A relative ratio for the weights of the sources had to be maintained. If the weights did not add up to the same number for each simulation, then the ranges of UoI would be significantly different for each simulation. Currently, the number of sources defines how much data we have available to create the optimization. If more sources are added, then the number of additional equations needed in the optimization grows multiplicatively. The introduction of additional sources requires the formulation of new constraints for the UoI algorithm and these constraints must also be consistent with the military task being simulated.

4 Conclusion

The simulations of the LRM version of the UoI uncovered several things that are needed that had not been considered prior. By selecting a relative simple task and rules for the simulation we were able to begin addressing the issues that emerged. This is definitely the benefit to simulating the expression for the UoI with two systems. The MATLAB simulation allowed us to implement the operations research inspired LRM version of the UoI. The SAGE simulation allow us to implement this version in an environment we hope will allow more complex behaviors for the agents. Ideally, we would like to explore how close to near real time the simulations allow us and validate the ranking of importance of the taxonomies and sources with participants in an experimental user study. Although faced with challenges in simulating UoI it has set the stage for expanding the UoI concept further. In future research, expanding UoI that is potentially flexible and robust to apply to a wider range of applications will be the objective.

References

1. Reilly, J.M.: Multidomain operations: a subtle but significant transition in military thought. Air Force Research Institute Maxwell AFB, USA (2016)
2. Gyllensporre, D.T.: Decision navigation: coping with 21st-century challenges in tactical decisionmaking. Milit. Rev. **83**(5), 20 (2003)
3. Raglin, A.: Presentation of information uncertainty from IoBT for military decision making. In: Streitz, N., Konomi, S. (eds.) HCII 2019. LNCS, vol. 11587, pp. 39–47. Springer, Cham (2019). https://doi.org/10.1007/978-3-030-21935-2_4
4. Raglin, A., Dennison, M., Metu, S., Trout, T., James, D.: Decision making with uncertainty in immersive systems. In: Virtual, Augmented, and Mixed Reality (XR) Technology for Multi-Domain Operations, vol. 11426, p. 114260L. International Society for Optics and Photonics, April 2020
5. Lott, D.A., Raglin, A., Metu, S.: On the use of operations research for decision making with uncertainty for IoT devices in battlefield situations. In: 2019 IEEE 5th International Conference on Collaboration and Internet Computing (CIC), pp. 266–297. IEEE, December 2019
6. Gershon, N.: Visualization of an imperfect world. IEEE Comput. Graphics Appl. **18**(4), 43–45 (1998)
7. Pang, A.T., Wittenbrink, C.M., Lodha, S.K.: Approaches to uncertainty visualization. The Vis. Comput. **13**(8), 370–390 (1997)
8. Metu, S., Raglin, A., Lott, D.: Automation of IoT based decision making with uncertainty, No. 2824. EasyChair (2020)
9. Lott, D.A., Raglin, A., Metu, S.: On the use of operations research for decision making with uncertainty for IoT devices in battlefield situations: simulations and outcomes. In: Proceedings of Virtual, Augmented, and Mixed Reality (XR) Technology for Multi-Domain Operations, vol. 11426, p. 1142609 (2020). https://doi.org/10.1117/12.2557870. Event: SPIE Defense+Commercial Sensing, 2020, Online Only, California, USA

Discontinued Public Spheres? Reproducibility of User Structure in Twitter Discussions on Inter-ethnic Conflicts

Anna S. Smoliarova⑩, Svetlana S. Bodrunova$^{(\boxtimes)}$ ⑩, Ivan S. Blekanov⑩,
and Alexey Maksimov ⑩

St. Petersburg State University, Saint Petersburg, Russia
{a.smolyarova,s.bodrunova}@spbu.ru

Abstract. Recently, communication scholars have paid attention to the growing dissonant and dissipative character of the public spheres, especially in their
connection to networked discursive spaces. While substantial dissonance of the
discussions is well addressed, structural discontinuity of public discussion remains
under-explored. Reproducibility of the discussions on similar issues or events in
time, we argue, needs to be seen as a marker of stability of public spheres. In this
paper, we compare the user and influencer structure of two similar discussions on
German Twitter of 2016 (the Cologne mass harassment) and 2019 (the Chemnitz
killing). We show that the overall reproducibility of the discussions is extremely
low, and the only structural element that reproduces are influential media, mostly
of national reach. But even the stability of media presence must be questioned, as
both intensity of their presence within the discussion and user engagement with
their tweets varies much from one discussion to the other. Thus, one may conclude
that the structural stability of public discussion of similar events on Twitter is not
reached.

Keywords: Computer-mediated communication · Germany · Twitter · Cologne ·
Chemnitz · Conflictual discussion · Inter-ethnic conflict · Influencer · Discussion
structure · Public sphere · Media on Twitter

1 Introduction

Recently, communication scholars have stated that today's public spheres [1] have
become increasingly dissonant [2] and disintegrated. They rarely have consensus as
a goal and, to a large extent, consist of *ad hoc* discussions [3] that have no continuity
and quickly dissipate. Disconnection also emerges through 'ever-more-fiercely negative
campaigns, increasing political polarization, and public debates filled with prejudices
and false assumptions' [2: 59]. One dimension of this disintegration has remained virtually unexplored, which is time. In traditionally mediated public spheres [4], the main
structure of information flows organized by media and institutions remained stable in
years or even decades; but we hardly know whether the user and influencer structure of
networked discussions remains stable or changes with time, and to what extent. How

© Springer Nature Switzerland AG 2020
C. Stephanidis et al. (Eds.): HCII 2020, CCIS 1293, pp. 262–269, 2020.
https://doi.org/10.1007/978-3-030-60700-5_34

can we expect public discussions to come to definitive conclusions stably accepted or at least discussed, if the very participant structure is unstable?

We argue that reproducibility of the discussion structure may be viewed as a sign of the long-term continuity of the public spheres and, thus, work as their quality metric. Long-term studies of networked discussions (*e.g.* their polarization) remain rare despite the measurement's tools accessible at the platform such as networking, tweeting and content-producing behavior of users [5]. 'Most longitudinal network studies have confounded the processes of new tie formation and old tie maintenance, resulting in an incomplete understanding of the processes of network change' [6]. Studying Twitter data in timelines and investigating timeline narratives longitudinally are, till today, atypical approaches to data gathering and analysis [7]; comparisons between structures of similar discussions of various times are next-to-absent.

Conflictual discussions online are vivid forms of expression of the public sphere [8]. Among them, Twitter discussions are the most rapidly growing and, sometimes, most quickly dissipating. Our previous findings have shown that Twitter 'is more complicated than the imaginary cocooned talk in echo chambers, especially for issues beyond elections and direct policing' [8: 130]. Moreover, according to the studies of digital protest and 'hashtag activism', Twitter may enable longitudinal campaigning that changes structure and content of public discussions for long enough time periods [9]. Technological affordances equally contribute to the formation of social movements and the spread of false beliefs in the 'unedited public sphere' [10] that emerges on social media. They also simultaneously allow for keeping the talk alive and forgetting it as soon as it goes beyond the Twitter scroll.

Case studies of Twitter discussions on selected conflicts paid more attention to the content of debate and the character of public communication than to who and how long participates in the discussion [11]. Also, comparative approaches have mostly been applied to simultaneous cases in different countries, not to similar discussions that happened within one national context in varying times, with few exceptions when the scholars talk about a social/political movement with its evolving dynamics of activities (e.g. #blacklivesmatter).

This study aims at comparing two national-level discussions in German-language Twitter about ethnicity-related conflicts: the one on the 2016 New Year's Eve sexual assaults in Cologne and that on the 2018 protests in Chemnitz that took place after the death of a Cuban-German man. We ask to what extent the structure of influencers (ordinary users, media, and institutions) has remained similar, since the issue and public polarization behind it were the same. Comparison within the national context reduces bias present in cross-national studies, as the variety of influencers cannot be explained by varying national political cultures.

The structure of this paper is organized as follows. The next sections presents our research questions and methodology (Sect. 2) and the findings of our study (Sect. 3). We conclude with a short summary of our results (Sect. 4).

2 Research Questions and Methodology

As stated above, the study aims at comparing two national-level discussions in German-language Twitter about ethnicity-related conflicts: the one on the 2016 New Year's Eve sexual assaults in Cologne and that on the 2018 protests in Chemnitz that took place after the death of a Cuban-German man. Our general assumption is that the structure of participation, as well as the structure of influencers, should remain similar, as the issue and public polarization behind the discussions were the same.

We conducted vocabulary-based web crawling to collect the discussion content and to analyze their structure. A special web crawler has been developed to bypass the limitations of Twitter API [12]. The total number of users in the two datasets included 12,382 users for Cologne and 22,973 users for Chemnitz.

As we moved from step to step in our research, we corrected the research questions and hypotheses based on the findings of the previous steps. Here, we will describe the RQs and methods used for each step, but the hypotheses are attached to the description of our results.

RQ1. Did Twitter users who discussed the Cologne case join the Twitter discussion about the Chemnitz case?

To answer RQ1, we assessed the general reproducibility of the discussions by defining the number of all users and influencers who participated in both discussions.

RQ2. Does the structure of politically relevant (institutionalized political, grassroots political, and media) influencers repeat from Cologne to Chemnitz?

To answer RQ2, we assessed the structure of influencers. For this, we sampled 50 top users for each of eight user metrics: number of tweets; number of interactions (likes, comments, and retweets); centralities – indegree, outdegree, betweenness, and pagerank. Then we merged them in aggregate lists of top users and eliminated the duplicates. As many users were within the top lists by many metrics, the final top lists included 230 users for the Cologne case and 207 users for the Chemnitz case. We manually coded the users in the final lists for their offline status in the following way. We coded an account as 'ordinary user' if its owner mentioned neither an institutional status nor political positioning in the user self-description at the top of the Twitter blog. If any political positioning or support of political values have been mentioned in the description, the account has been coded as 'politically active blogger/activist.' As 'media' we coded the accounts that either have a clear connection to a media project outside Twitter or position themselves as Twitter-only media projects. Institutional political actors included the accounts run by state authorities of any level and their individual representatives; political parties; individual politicians. Any other possible classification based on the description in the user account was marked as 'other'.

RQ3. Does the salience of intersecting influencers differ in the two cases?

To answer RQ3, we have defined the list of relevant intersecting influencers and have calculated their activity ratio and user engagement ratio. The former is the number of tweets published by the account in the first case divided by the number of tweets published in the second case; the latter is the ratio of the according numbers of user comments.

These ratios show whether the status of these influencers, both actively pursued and user-supported, has been stable in time.

3   Findings

3.1   Reproducibility of the General User Structure in the Discussions

RQ1. Did Twitter users who discussed the Cologne case join the Twitter discussion about the Chemnitz case?

Hla. *Ad hoc* publics that emerged around the Cologne and Chemnitz cases repeat to a significant share (over 30% of the participants who discussed Cologne also discussed Chemnitz).
H1b. The list of top users changed less than the general sample of users taking part in the discussion, as influencers are the structural carcass of the issue-based debates.

To prove Hla we compared two general samples crawled for the Cologne case and for the Chemnitz case. From the whole dataset, we excluded those users who have not posted at least once and only interacted with those who tweeted by liking or sharing. (These users were crawled because they were necessary for the graph reconstruction of the discussions; we consider them irrelevant for RQ1.) The datasets for RQ1 included 12,382 users who tweeted about Cologne and 22,973 users who tweeted about Chemnitz. Only 1,735 users (circa 14% of Cologne sample and 7,5% of Chemnitz sample) participated in both discussions posting at least one tweet with at least one hashtag that defines the corpora of each discussion. 17% of them published the same amount of posts (from 1 to 7 tweets in each discussion), 57% tweeted more about Cologne and 26% were more active in posting about Chemnitz. The total number of unique users amounts to 33,620 users; thus, the share of intersecting users is 5,2%. If we exclude those who posted less than three tweets in both cases, the share of users participated in both discussions decreases even to 1,2%. Therefore, Hla has to be rejected: the *ad hoc* publics the emerged around the Cologne and Chemnitz events vary by 95%.

To check H1b, we selected the top users (influencers) for both cases by the aforementioned procedure, which resulted into 222 users for the Cologne case and 207 users for the Chemnitz case, 413 unique users in total. Only 16 top users – 7% from the Cologne top list and 7,7% from the Chemnitz top list – have participated in both discussions (3,9% of the total number of unique users; for the accounts, see Table 1). This also means that the list of top users changed slightly more than the general sample, but the difference seems not to be incredibly significant. Thus, H1ba is rejected, too.

3.2   Reproducibility of the Influencer Structure: Politicization and Political Polarization

RQ2. Is the structure of politically relevant (institutionalized political, grassroots political, and media) users among the influencers similar in both cases?

Table 1. Intersecting influencers

Institutional type	Accounts	Number of users
National media	BILD, DLFNachrichten, faznet, ndaktuell, SPIEGELONLINE, SZ, tagesschau, tazgezwitscher, welt, ZDFheute, zeitonline	11
Regional media	WDR and ZDFnrw	2
Journalists	MatthiasMeisner	1
Bloggers	Korallenherz	1
Politicians	HeikoMaas	1

H2a. The media segment of the influencer structure is the most stable (as media are the key actors in the mediated public sphere).

H2b. The political segment (both institutional and grassroots) is more salient in the Cologne case (due to the political resonance of the case) (Table 2).

Table 2. Institutional character of influencers

Institutional type	Cologne	Chemnitz
Institutional political actors	5,22%	14,98%
Media	23,48%	24,15%
Activists and politically active bloggers	11,26%	27,05%
Ordinary	50,00%	18,36%
Other/irrelevant	11,74%	14,49%
Total N	230	207

H2a is fully supported: the share of media accounts in both cases remained the same. Moreover, as shown in Table 1, 13 out 16 users that were high-ranked in both discussions are editorial mass media that operate mostly on the national level in Germany.

As for H2b, our findings demonstrate that political actors were much more visible in the discussion around events in Chemnitz that in Cologne: the share of institutionalized politicians has almost tripled. One might explain this tendency by the growth of Twitter activity of German politicians in general. SPD, die Linke, and FDP, as well as AfD, were fighting for users' attention and gaining authority in an online discussion.

The salience of the AfD representatives has doubled. Four members of the right-wing party are present among the high-ranked users driving Twitter-discussion about events in Cologne in 2016, among them Björn Höcke, one of the founders of AfD Thuringia, the speaker of the parliamentary group of the AfD and the spokesman of the Thuringia Regional Association. In the discussion about Chemnitz in 2018, 8 accounts associated with AfD are found on the list of top users. All of them are ranked high by pagerank; 4 of 8 accounts are also ranked high by indegree and 1 by retweets.

Also, the rise of the grassroots politicization is clear. In our previous research on the Cologne case, we have shown that 'many ordinary users have a clear political position that can be understood from their tweets, but they don't define themselves as activists' [13: 141]. The Chemnitz case shows a clear difference: the share of ordinary people who explicitly declare their political position or another official status in their account descriptions has increased from 11% to 27%. This is another sign of politicization and political polarization during the case, as well as the sign of structural instability. Thus, H2b has not been supported.

3.3 Reproducibility of Intersecting Users and Their Roles: Media as the Carcass of Networked Discussions

RQ3. Does salience of the intersecting accounts differ in the two cases?

H3a. The activity ratios of the intersecting users remain stable (in between 0,8 and 1,2).
H3b. The user engagement ratios of the intersecting users remain stable (in between 0,8 and 1,2).

We have shown above that media influencer accounts were, en masse, the only group of influencers that stably repeated in the two discussions. Hence, we have decided to assess the 13 media accounts that were discovered in both top user lists in terms of their activity and user engagement ratios.

Almost all media outlets tweeted more about Cologne than about Chemnitz (see Table 3). For public service TV, the difference is the most significant: @ZDFnrw posted in January 2016 almost 12 times more tweets than in August-September 2018. Nationwide news program @tagesschau is the second account that was much more active in January 2016: they posted 7 times more tweets about Cologne. Interestingly, two media outlets that paid more attention to the Chemnitz case than to the Cologne events – @welt and @tazgezwitscher – represent the two opposite sides of the political spectrum (right-wing and left-wing, respectively), which, again, is a sign of political polarization. Thus, H3a is rejected.

Contrary to the fact that media outlets tweeted significantly more about Cologne, the users' involvement seems to follow the opposite trend. The biggest difference between users' engagement rate between two cases is revealed for *@ZDFnrw*, despite this media account has tweeted 12 times less about Chemnitz than about Cologne. Users of *@tagesschau* were 5 times more involved into the discussion of about Chemnitz than by tweets about Cologne. The same gap is observed for another public broadcaster, the national radio station *@DLFNachrichten*. Thus, national/regional PSB has lost its positions in terms of user engagement, despite the growing efforts in Twitter reporting.

Unlike the PSB TV, media with clear political positioning like the conservative *@BILD* and *@welt* and the left-wing *@Tazgezwitscher*, received higher user attention in the Chemnitz case – again, which tells of user polarization. There is no media account

Table 3. Activity and user engagement ratios for media influencers in the two discussions

	Cologne	Chemnitz	Activity ratio (Cologne to Chemnitz)	User engagement ratio (Cologne to Chemnitz)
ZDFnrw	83	7	11, 86	0,07
Tagesschau	123	18	6,83	0,2
Faznet	66	19	3,47	0,77
DLFNachrichten	52	15	3,47	0,21
BILD	16	5	3,2	3,79
SZ	21	7	3	0,49
WDR	31	15	2,066	0,08
SPIEGELONLINE	43	24	1,79	0,42
Ndaktuell	54	31	1,74	0,54
Zeitonline	40	23	1,74	2
ZDFheute	32	28	1,14	0,36
Tazgezwitscher	16	29	0,55	1,07
welt	10	21	0,48	1,55

except for *@Zeitonline* that would fit into our expected ratio divergence values. Thus, both H3a and H3b need to be rejected. This, in its turn, is a sign of unstable positioning of the only segment of influencers that continued to the second Twitter discussion.

4   Conclusion

Our findings suggest that the level of general reproduction of the structure of *ad hoc* conflictual discussions is extremely low. Comparing the two general samples crawled for Cologne and Chemnitz we revealed that the lists of users who have posted at least once match by 5% only. The list of top users changed even more significantly, contrary to expectations. Among the top users, the media segment has been the most stable, which supports the idea of media remaining the key actors in the mediated public sphere [4]. But even this media cluster did not preserve its positioning, neither in terms of activity nor in terms of user engagement. While media accounts tweeted significantly more about Cologne, the users' involvement seems to follow the opposite trend. Political actors were much more visible in the Twitter discussion on Chemnitz than on Cologne: the share of institutionalized politicians has almost tripled, and the number of grassroots activists has more than doubled. This shows that politicization of the discussion became more formal, while the issue itself became relevant for non-politicized people. We can conclude that media remain the carcass of the public spheres which discontinue around them.

Acknowledgements. The research has been supported in full by the Russian Science Foundation, grant 16-18-10125-P.

References

1. Habermas, J.: Political communication in media society: does democracy still enjoy an epistemic dimension? The impact of normative theory on empirical research. Commun. Theory **16**(4), 411–426 (2006)
2. Pfetsch, B.: Dissonant and disconnected public spheres as challenge for political communication research. Javnost – Public **25**(1-2), 59–65 (2018)
3. Bruns, A., Burgess, J.E.: The use of Twitter hashtags in the formation of ad hoc publics. In: Proceedings of the 6th European Consortium for Political Research (ECPR) General Conference 2011, pp. 1–9, August 2011
4. Calhoun, C.J. (ed.): Habermas and the Public Sphere. MIT Press, Cambridge (1992)
5. Garimella, V.R.K., Weber, I.: A long-term analysis of polarization on Twitter. In: Proceedings of the 11th International AAAI Conference on Web and Social Media, pp. 528–531, May 2017
6. Fu, J.S.: Unpacking the influence of informational, organizational, and structural factors on the longitudinal change of the NPO follower-followee network on Twitter. Int. J. Commun. **13**, 3802–3825 (2019)
7. Brooker, P., Vines, J., Barnett, J., Feltwell, T., Lawson, S.: Everyday socio-political talk in twitter timelines: a longitudinal approach to social media analytics. In: Proceedings of the 7th 2016 International Conference on Social Media & Society, July 2016
8. Bodrunova, S.S., Blekanov, I., Smoliarova, A., Litvinenko, A.: Beyond left and right: real-world political polarization in Twitter discussions on inter-ethnic conflicts. Media Commun. **7**, 119–132 (2019)
9. Bonilla, Y., Rosa, J.: #Ferguson: digital protest, hashtag ethnography, and the racial politics of social media in the United States. Am. Ethnol. **42**(1), 4–17 (2015)
10. Bimber, B., de Zúñiga, H.G.: The unedited public sphere. New Media Soc. **22**(4), 700–715 (2020)
11. Groshek, J., Tandoc, E.: The affordance effect: gatekeeping and (non) reciprocal journalism on Twitter. In: Proceedings of the 7th 2016 International Conference on Social Media & Society, pp. 1–10, July 2016
12. Blekanov, I.S., Sergeev, S.L., Martynenko, I.A.: Constructing topic-oriented web crawlers with generalized core. Sci. Res. Bull. St. Petersburg State Polytech. Univ. **5**(157), 9–15 (2012)
13. Smoliarova, A.S., Bodrunova, S.S., Blekanov, I.S.: Politicians driving online discussions: are institutionalized influencers top twitter users? In: Kompatsiaris, I., Cave, J., Satsiou, A., Carle, G., Passani, A., Kontopoulos, E., Diplaris, S., McMillan, D. (eds.) INSCI 2017. LNCS, vol. 10673, pp. 132–147. Springer, Cham (2017). https://doi.org/10.1007/978-3-319-70284-1_11

A Design and Evaluation of Coefficient of Variation Control Chart

Chauchen Torng[✉] and Haoren Jhong

National Yunlin University of Science and Technology, Yunlin 64002, Taiwan, ROC
torngcc@yuntech.edu.tw

Abstract. Statistical Process Control (SPC) is widely used in practice, and the control chart is a main tool in SPC. The control chart monitors process quality and detects process variations in real time to reduce the defective products. Regulatory maps are used in clinical trials and agronomic industries, and the mean and variance are not constants, and the coefficient of variation is an indicator of the reliability of chemical tests. However, the coefficient of variation control chart (CV Chart) monitors the coefficient of variation, and the ability to detect small shift sizes is not good. This study uses a double sampling plan combined with a coefficient of variation control chart (DS CV chart) to improve the performance of CV Chart. A design model of DS CV chart is also created to optimize its parameters. The results of the study show that the good performance of DS CV chart in small shift detection.

Keywords: Coefficient of variation · Double sampling control chart · Average run length

1 Introduction

Statistical process control is widely used in today's manufacturing, and the control chart is an important tool in detecting the process variations. In recent years, the control chart has been widely used in clinical trials, chemical tests, and agronomic improvement in the manufacturing industry. Connett and Lee (1990) indicates that coefficient of variation (CV) is often used to measure in repetitive experiments, it was found that the standard deviation increases or decreases proportionally with the increase or decrease of the mean, so the use of the CV is a more useful statistic than the standard deviation of the sample.

Kang et al. (2007) proposed a coefficient of variation control chart (CV Chart) to monitor the variation of process CV, but this chart is not good in detecting the small shift sizes for quality characteristic. Therefore, to improve the monitoring variation of CV control chart with less sample size becomes a challenge.

Daudin (1992) first proposed a double-sampling (DS) Xbar control chart, which combines the concept of a double-sampling plan in an acceptable sampling plan with a traditional Shewhart's control chart to improve the effectiveness of monitoring process

© Springer Nature Switzerland AG 2020
C. Stephanidis et al. (Eds.): HCII 2020, CCIS 1293, pp. 270–278, 2020.
https://doi.org/10.1007/978-3-030-60700-5_35

variation. Some studies used the same concept of DS scheme to combine with the S control chart and to extend the multiple sampling control charts (He and Grigoryan 2002; He and Grigoryan 2003; He et al. 2002). In Lee (2013), it was found that the design using DS control charts can effectively improve the detection ability. This study will combine the CV control chart with DS method to increase the ability in the monitoring of process CV variations. A design model also proposes to obtain its optimal parameters.

2 Review of Control Charts

2.1 DS Xbar Control Charts

The DS Xbar control chart proposed by Daudin (1992), and this chart integrated two Shewhart's Xbar control charts with different widths of control limits.

Under an assumption that true process state is in control, the range of each region can be defined as $I_1 = [-W, W]$, $I_2 = [-L_1, -W) \cup (W, L_1]$, $I_3 = (-\infty, -L_1] \cup [L_1, +\infty)$, $I_4 = [-L_2, L_2]$ and $I_5 = (-\infty, -L_2] \cup [L_2, +\infty)$.

Daudin (1992) had established the procedure of DS Xbar control chart. First, take a small sample size, n_1, and calculate its sample mean $\bar{X}_1$. Then, calculate z using a standardized method, that is, $z = \sqrt{n_1}(\bar{X}_1 - \mu)/\sigma$. If z is in the regions of I_3, this chart signals an out-of-control state. If z falls in I_1, the process will be determined an in-control state. For the case that z falls in I_2, it is necessary to take a second-stage sampling with the second-stage control chart. With the second-stage sampling occurring, the sample size will be n_2 (usually $n_1 < n_2$) and its mean $\bar{X}_2$ of the second-stage sampling needs to be calculated. Then, the total sample mean $\bar{X}^*$ for both samplings can be calculated with $\bar{X}^* = (n_1\bar{X}_1 + n_2\bar{X}_2)/(n_1 + n_2)$. Afterward, standardized $\bar{X}^*$ will be represented with z^*, $z^* = \sqrt{n_1 + n_2}(\bar{X}^* - \mu)/\sigma$. When z^* is falling in I_4, the process indicates an in-control state. Otherwise, the process is an out-of-control state, the process mean may be occur shift.

The following two indicators were always used to measure the ability of the chart:

1) Average Run Length (ARL) is the time of average sampling form the process variation starting to signaling this variation.
2) The Average Sample Size (ASS) is the average size of each sampling.

Let μ_0 and σ be the initial mean and standard deviation of the process, respectively. When an assignable cause occurs, the process mean shifts to $\mu_1 = \mu_0 + \delta\sigma$, where δ is the shift size coefficient. If $P(\delta)$ represents the probability that the sample mean falls in the out-of-control region, then the average run length (represented by $ARL(\delta)$) is $1/P(\delta)$.

Irianto and Shinozaki (1998) and He et al. (2002) showed the calculation of $P(\delta)$ under normality, and that is

$$P(\delta) = 1 - \left[p(z \in I_1 | \delta\mu_1 = \mu_0 + \delta\sigma) + p(z \in I_2 | \mu_1 = \mu_0 + \delta\sigma)\right]$$
$$\times p\left(z^* \in I_4 | \delta\mu_1 = \mu_0 + \delta\sigma\right)$$
$$= 1$$
$$- \left\{ \Phi\left(W + \delta\sqrt{n_1}\right) - \Phi\left(-W + \delta\sqrt{n_1}\right) \right.$$
$$\left. + \int_{z \in I_2} \begin{bmatrix} + \Phi\left(L_2\sqrt{\dfrac{n_1 + n_2}{n_2}} + \dfrac{n_1 + n_2}{\sqrt{n_2}}\delta - z\sqrt{\dfrac{n_1}{n_2}}\right) \\ - \Phi\left(-L_2\sqrt{\dfrac{n_1 + n_2}{n_2}} + \dfrac{n_1 + n_2}{\sqrt{n_2}}\delta - z\sqrt{\dfrac{n_1}{n_2}}\right) \end{bmatrix} \phi(z)dz \right\} \quad (1)$$

where $\Phi(\bullet)$ is the cumulative distribution function of standard normal distribution, $\phi(\bullet)$ is the probability density function of standard normal distribution; I_i means region i, $p(z \in I_i | \bullet)$ or $p(z^* \in I_i | \bullet)$ means the probability that z or z^* falls in region i.

Since the widths of the warning regions determine the probability for the occurrence of the second-stage sampling, the expected sample size ASS will be

$$E_{DS-\bar{x}}(N|\delta) = n_1 + n_2 p(z \in I_2 | \mu_1 = \mu_0 + \delta\sigma) = n_1 + n_2$$
$$\times \left[\Phi\left(-W + \delta\sqrt{n_1}\right) - \Phi\left(-L_1 + \delta\sqrt{n_1}\right) + \Phi\left(L_1 + \delta\sqrt{n_1}\right) - \Phi\left(W + \delta\sqrt{n_1}\right)\right] \quad (2)$$

where $E_{DS-\bar{x}}(N|\delta = 0)$ means the sample size of in-control process, $E_{DS-\bar{x}}(N|\delta \neq 0)$ means the out-of-control sample size.

2.2   CV Control Charts

Iglewicz and Myers (1970) defined that the following conditions are appropriate to use the coefficient of variation as a statistic:

1) The mean and standard deviation are not a fixed constant. The standard deviation will increase or decrease as the mean increases or decreases.
2) The coefficient of variation (CV) is used to compare the degree of dispersion of two data, especially in the following situations:

   a. The gap between the two data values is too large.
   b. When the two data units are different.

The research hypothesis of the coefficient of variation control chart proposed by Kang et al. (2007) is:

1) The mean and standard deviation are not a fixed constant. The standard deviation will increase or decrease as the mean increases or decreases, and the mean and standard deviation must be greater than zero.
2) Data follow a normal distribution.

Suppose the quality characteristic $X = \{x_1, x_2, \ldots, x_n\}$ is an independent random variable and follows a normal distribution with mean μ and standard deviation σ. The CV γ of the quality characteristic X is defined as

$$\gamma = \sigma/\mu \tag{3}$$

where the $\mu > 0$, n is the sample size, CV > 0.

Kang et al. (2007) proposed that the CV control chart monitors the coefficient of variation and defines the sample CV $\hat{\gamma}$ is

$$\hat{\gamma} = S/\bar{X} \tag{4}$$

where

$\bar{X} = \sum_{i=1}^{n} x_i/n,$

$S^2 = \sum_{i=1}^{n} \left(x_i - \bar{X}\right)^2/(n-1)$

Kang et al. (2007) proposed the CV control chart to monitor the coefficient of variation, and defined the sample CV $\hat{\gamma}$ as $(0, +\infty)$, and the probability distribution of $\hat{\gamma}$ was

$$F_{\hat{\gamma}}(x|n, \gamma) = 1 - F_t\left(\frac{\sqrt{n}}{x}\bigg|n - 1, \frac{\sqrt{n}}{\gamma}\right) \tag{5}$$

where $F_t\left(\frac{\sqrt{n}}{x}|n - 1, \frac{\sqrt{n}}{\gamma}\right)$ is the cumulative distribution function of noncentral t distribution with degree of freedom of $n - 1$. The invers cumulative distribution function of $\hat{\gamma}$ is

$$F_{\hat{\gamma}}^{-1}(\alpha|n, \gamma) \cong \frac{\sqrt{n}}{F_t^{-1}\left(1 - \alpha|n - 1, \frac{\sqrt{n}}{\gamma}\right)} \tag{6}$$

The upper and lower control limits (UCL, LCL) of CV control chart can be obtained by

$$UCL_{cv} = F_{\hat{\gamma}}^{-1}\left(1 - \frac{\alpha}{2}|n, \gamma_0\right)$$

$$LCL_{cv} = F_{\hat{\gamma}}^{-1}\left(\frac{\alpha}{2}|n, \gamma_0\right) \tag{7}$$

where the α is the occurrence probability of false alarm that the $\hat{\gamma}$ falls the outside of control limits, but the process does not occur variation.

3 DS_CV Control Charts

This section presented the establishing of DS CV control chart. Figure 1 shows the DS CV control chart. The UCL_1 and LCL_1 are the upper and lower control limits of 1st stage sampling, respectively; the UWL and LWL indicate the upper and lower warring limits of 1st stage sampling, respectively; and the UCL_2 and LCL_2 are the upper and lower control limits of 2nd stage sampling.

The DS CV control procedure includes:

(1) To take a sample of size n1, calculate the sample mean $\bar{X}_1$ and standard deviation S_1 and then calculate the sample CV $\hat{\gamma}_1$ with Eq. (4);
(2) if the $\hat{\gamma}_1$ falls in I_1, the process will be considered as an in-control state;
(3) if $\hat{\gamma}_1$ falls in I_3, the process will be determined as an out-of-control state;
(4) if $\hat{\gamma}_1$ falls in I_2, then takes second sample of sizes n_2, calculates the sample mean $\bar{X}_2$ and standard deviation S_2;
(5) calculate the total sample CV

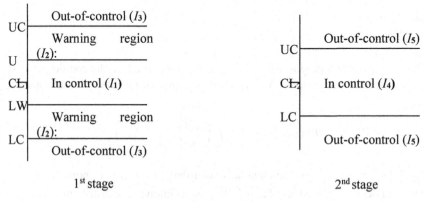

Fig. 1. DS CV control chart.

Let the in-control process CV be γ_0. If the process occurs variations, the process CV shifts to $\gamma_1 = \gamma_0 * \delta$ from γ_0, and the δ is shift size and can be obtained by $\delta = \gamma_1/\gamma_0$. Let ρ be the probability that a sample point falls in out-of-control regions. The power $\rho(\delta)$ of DS CV chart for a specific shift size δ is

$$\rho(\delta) = P\left(\hat{\gamma}_1 \in I_3 | \gamma_1 = \gamma_0 * \delta\right) + P\left(\hat{\gamma}_1 \in I_2 \cap \hat{\gamma}^* \in I_5 | \gamma_1 = \gamma_0 * \delta\right) \qquad (8)$$

The ARL for a specific shift size δ is

$$ARL(\delta) = 1/\rho(\delta) \qquad (9)$$

The ASS for a specific shift size δ can be calculated by

$$E_{DS-CV}(N|\delta) = n_1 + n_2 \times P\left(\hat{\gamma}_1 \in I_2 | \gamma_1 = \gamma_0 * \delta\right) \qquad (10)$$

These probabilities $P(*)$ can be obtained by a simulation procedure. The simulation procedure is as:

(1) Generate n_1 data from a normal distribution and calculate the sample CV $\hat{\gamma}_1$ in stage 1.
(2) Repeat step (1) 100,000 times to obtain 100,000 sample CV $\hat{\gamma}_1$.
(3) Record the number of sample CV $\hat{\gamma}_1$ that falls in I_2 and I_3 respectively and then divide them by 100,000 respectively to estimate the $P(\hat{\gamma}_1 \in I_3 | \gamma_1 = \gamma_0 * \delta)$ and $P(\hat{\gamma}_1 \in I_2 | \gamma_1 = \gamma_0 * \delta)$. Here the number of sample CV $\hat{\gamma}_1$ that falls in I_2 is represented by U.
(4) Generate n_2 data from a normal distribution to calculate the sample mean and standard deviation of second-time sampling $\bar{X}_2$ and S_2 and then calculate the total sample CV $\hat{\gamma}^*$.
(5) Repeat step (4) for U times.
(6) Record the number of total CV $\hat{\gamma}^*$ that falls in I_5 and divide it respectively with U to calculate the $P(\hat{\gamma}_1 \in I_2 \cap \hat{\gamma}^* \in I_5 | \gamma_1 = \gamma_0 * \delta)$.

4 The Design Model of DS_CV Charts

This study chose 8 design parameters of the DS CV chart using a design model to optimize its parameters. This model minimizes the out-of-control ARL values for the shift size $\delta = \tau$ to design this chart and maintains the in-control ARL values of 370.4 and the in-control ASS of 5 and 10 to perform its ability in detecting shifts. The design model of DS CV chart is

$$Min \ ARL(\delta > 1)$$

$$Subject \ to$$
$$ARL(\delta = 1) = 370.4$$
$$E_{DS-CV}(N | \delta = 1) = EN$$
$$0 < LCL_1 < LWL < UWL < UCL_1$$
$$0 < LCL_2 < UCL_2$$
$$2 \leq n_1 < E_{DS-CV}(N | \delta = 1) < n_2 \leq 30$$
$$n_1 \ and \ n_2 \in Integer$$

The Matlab optimization toolbox uses a nonlinear constrained optimization algorithm to solve nonlinear models. Ascione et al. (2019), Ali and Kairouani (2016), Razaa et al. (2019) and Lee (2013) used the Matlab optimization toolbox to solve the model.

5   The Performance Studies

This study considers the in-control CVs $\gamma_0 = 0.05, 0.1$ and 0.15, $EN = 5$ and 10, and shift sizes $\delta = 1.1, 1.2, 1.5, 2$ and 2.5 to compare the performance of DS CV chart with CV chart of Kang et al. (2007). Table 1 and 2 show the optimal design of DS CV control chart, and these charts have the same in-control ASS and ARL value.

Table 1. The optimal design of DS CV chart with EN $= 5$ and in-control ARL $= 370.4$

γ_0	δ	n_1	n_2	UCL_1	LCL_1	UWL	LWL	UCL_2	LCL_2
0.05	1.1	3	27	0.2641	0	0.0817	0.0135	0.0678	0.0332
	1.2	3	27	0.2641	0	0.0817	0.0135	0.0678	0.0332
	1.5	4	22	0.1388	0.0016	0.0712	0.0227	0.072	0.0298
	2	4	22	0.1388	0.0016	0.0712	0.0227	0.072	0.0298
	2.5	4	22	0.1388	0.0016	0.0712	0.0227	0.072	0.0298
0.1	1.1	3	29	0.4266	0	0.1489	0.0344	0.1364	0.066
	1.2	4	29	0.4087	0.0001	0.1341	0.0512	0.1386	0.0645
	1.5	4	29	0.4087	0.0001	0.1341	0.0512	0.1386	0.0645
	2	4	29	0.4087	0.0001	0.1341	0.0512	0.1386	0.0645
	2.5	4	23	0.4176	0.0001	0.1333	0.0518	0.1445	0.0597
0.15	1.1	3	25	0.4979	0.0013	0.2322	0.0478	0.2104	0.095
	1.2	3	25	0.4979	0.0013	0.2322	0.0478	0.2104	0.095
	1.5	4	23	0.4777	0.0027	0.2119	0.0704	0.2169	0.0902
	2	4	21	0.3879	0.0098	0.2052	0.0747	0.2244	0.0848
	2.5	4	19	0.3657	0.0132	0.2024	0.0765	0.2374	0.0761

Table 3 presets the out-of-control ARL values of CV charts and DS CV charts. These CV charts in Table 2 have common in-control ARL values and ASS values with DS CV charts. Since the Table 2, it can be found the DS CV charts have better detecting ability in all shift sizes than CV charts. When the shift size increases, the ARL values of DS CV charts decreases. For different in-control CVs γ_0, the out-of-control ARL values of DS CV charts in different shift sizes do not change obviously. Therefore, the detecting ability of DS CV charts is insensitivity in the change of the in-control CVs γ_0. DS CV charts is suitable for monitoring the different in-control CVs γ_0.

Table 2. The optimal design of DS CV chart with EN $= 10$ and in-control ARL $= 370.4$

γ_0	δ	n_1	n_2	UCL_1	LCL_1	UWL	LWL	UCL_2	LCL_2
0.05	1.1	7	31	0.119	0.0055	0.0718	0.0266	0.0678	0.0334
	1.2	8	30	0.1024	0.0108	0.0669	0.0308	0.0693	0.0322
	1.5	8	30	0.0962	0.0134	0.0641	0.0329	0.0706	0.0312
	2	8	30	0.0962	0.0134	0.0641	0.0329	0.0706	0.0312
	2.5	8	30	0.0962	0.0134	0.0641	0.0329	0.0706	0.0312
0.1	1.1	9	31	0.2855	0.0047	0.1405	0.0579	0.1369	0.0661
	1.2	9	31	0.2647	0.0074	0.1282	0.0671	0.1388	0.0646
	1.5	9	30	0.2655	0.0073	0.1244	0.0701	0.1401	0.0636
	2	9	30	0.2655	0.0073	0.1244	0.0701	0.1401	0.0636
	2.5	9	30	0.2655	0.0073	0.1244	0.0701	0.1401	0.0636
0.15	1.1	8	31	0.485	0.004	0.202	0.0922	0.2077	0.0978
	1.2	8	31	0.485	0.004	0.202	0.0922	0.2077	0.0978
	1.5	9	31	0.4464	0.007	0.198	0.0967	0.209	0.0969
	2	10	28	0.3497	0.0236	0.2017	0.0951	0.2129	0.0939
	2.5	10	28	0.3497	0.0236	0.2017	0.0951	0.2129	0.0939

Table 3. The out-of-control ARL values of CV charts and DS CV chart

EN	δ	$\gamma_0 = 0.05$		$\gamma_0 = 0.1$		$\gamma_0 = 0.15$	
		CV	DS CV	CV	DS CV	CV	DS CV
5	1.1	162.2	71.1	162.4	71.5	162.9	73.3
	1.2	64.6	20.9	65.8	21	66.3	21.6
	1.5	10.6	4.2	10.8	4.2	11.1	4.4
	2	2.9	1.8	2.9	1.9	3.1	1.8
	2.5	1.7	1.3	1.8	1.3	1.8	1.4
10	1.1	119.8	65.1	121.9	66.2	121.6	67.9
	1.2	37.0	15.2	37.7	15.5	38.6	16
	1.5	4.8	2.4	4.9	2.4	5.1	2.5
	2	1.5	1.2	1.6	1.2	1.6	1.2
	2.5	1.1	1.1	1.1	1.1	1.2	1.1

6 Conclusions

In real process control, the mean and standard deviation may be not a fixed constant. The standard deviation will increase or decrease as the mean increases or decreases. The DS CV control charts were created to monitor this process in this study. The DS CV control charts improved the disadvantage of CV charts in detecting shift slowly without increasing the sample size. The calculations and simulation procedures of ARL and ASS values for DS CV control charts were also presented in this study. A statistical design model was developed to optimize the DS CV control charts. Since the design of control charts, a cost model is suggested to consider in design model of DS CV control chart for reducing the control cost. The future research can focus on the economic design of DS CV control chart.

References

Ali, M.B., Kairouani, L.: Multi-objective optimization of operating parameters of a MSF-BR desalination plant using solver optimization tool of Matlab software. Desalination **381**, 71–83 (2016)

Ascione, F., Bianco, N., Mauro, G.M., Napolitano, D.F.: Building envelope design: multi-objective optimization to minimize energy consumption, global cost and thermal discomfort. Application to different Italian climatic zones. Energy **174**, 359–374 (2019)

Connett, J.E., Lee, W.W.: Estimation of the coefficient of variation from laboratory analysis of split specimens for quality control in clinical trials. Control. Clin. Trials **11**, 24–36 (1990)

Daudin, J.: Double sampling Xbar charts. J. Qual. Technol. **24**, 78–87 (1992)

He, D., Grigoryan, A.: Construction of double sampling s-control charts for agile manufacturing. Qual. Reliab. Eng. Int. **18**, 343–355 (2002)

He, D., Grigoryan, A.: An improved double sampling s chart. Int. J. Prod. Res. **41**, 2663–2679 (2003)

He, D., Grigoryan, A., Sigh, M.: Design of double-and triple-sampling X-bar control charts using genetic algorithms. Int. J. Prod. Res. **40**, 1387–1404 (2002)

Iglewicz, B., Myers, R.H.: Comparisons of approximations to the percentage points of the sample coefficient of variation. Technometrics **12**, 166–169 (1970)

Irianto, D., Shinozaki, N.: An optimal double sampling Xbar control chart. Int. J. Ind. Eng. **5**, 226–234 (1998)

Kang, C.W., Lee, M.S., Seong, Y.J., Hawkins, D.M.: A control chart for the coefficient of variation. J. Qual. Technol. **39**, 151–158 (2007)

Lee, P.H.: Joint statistical design of Xbar and s charts with combined double sampling and variable sampling interval. Eur. J. Oper. Res. **225**, 285–297 (2013)

Razaa, S.A., Abdullakutty, F.C., Rathinam, S., Govindaluri, S.M.: Multi-objective framework for process mean selection and price differentiation with leakage effects under price-dependent stochastic demand. Comput. Ind. Eng. **172**, 698–708 (2019)

A Study on Presentation Method of Video Thumbnail on SNS Using Micro-Moments

Wonseok Yang[1](✉) and Cliff Shin[2]

[1] Shibaura Institute of Technology, 3-9-14 Shibaura, Minato-ku, Tokyo 108-8548, Japan
yang@shibaura-it.ac.jp
[2] University of Illinois Urbana-Champaign, 608 Lorado Taft Dr, Champaign, IL 61820, USA

Abstract. It is necessary to conduct research find out effective format of video thumbnails that users gain information in Micro-Moments when video thumbnails are being presented to users. The methodology we used is to find elements that influence their decisions by providing content that can be recognized and that has an interesting element while the participants are using SNS in a short period. The textual information and fast-forwarding format were effective to comprehend contents regardless of intensity and amount of movement. Authors believe that it would be better for the audience that contents can be intuitively recognized as video clips because comprehension of con-tents and interests can be changed by audiences' interests when contents have many moving elements. However, fast-forwarding is an effective method to attract audiences' interests for contents that have subtle moving elements. Therefore, the contents that have subtle moving elements can in-duce fast-forwarding. This research of video clips on SNS administers micro-moments that can increase in contents understanding and thumbnail method that the audience can effectively recognize contents. In terms of understanding content, it was effective for the audience to increase under-standing by a combination of fast-forwarding and textual information.

Keywords: SNS · Information management · Human behavior

1 Introduction

Lately, social networking services (SNS) or blogs have become more popular and increased in the number of users. Among the users, young users have been utilizing social media as a communication tool to share their pictures, videos, or any type of visual material. Within the SNS environment, there are two types of users - content providers(CPs) and contents consumers(CCs) – and CPs can simultaneously become CCs and vice versa. It is common for CPs in SNS to share their everyday lives. Since CPs who share their lifestyles don't have an obligation to provide certain content, the first impression in micro-moments is critical for CPs to capture content consumers' attention from the contents. CPs have reduced the size of images, eliminated a certain amount of content when the contents exceed as the size of data while the contents are being suggested on SNS. Lately, the contents on SNS have been greatly evolved with

© Springer Nature Switzerland AG 2020
C. Stephanidis et al. (Eds.): HCII 2020, CCIS 1293, pp. 279–287, 2020.
https://doi.org/10.1007/978-3-030-60700-5_36

contents that contain video footage because the information has a variety of formats that cannot be expressed with text and expanded its size. Most content providers tend to place play icons on video thumbnails. The placement of the play icon has been used since the services created and has not been explored to increase in capturing audiences" attention. Therefore, it is necessary to research to find out the effective format of video thumbnails that users gain information in micro-moments when video thumbnails are being presented to users. The purpose of the research is to investigate elements that affect users' decision-making process when video thumbnails are presented during micro-moments on SNS (Fig. 1).

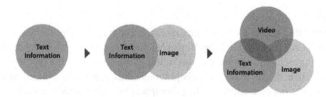

Fig. 1. Changes in information that can be shared online

2   Significance of Micro-Moment on SNS

In 2015, Google started using the terms, "Micro moment". It is referring to a moment that a user feels that leads to a certain action, "I would like to do something like that in everyday life". There are many different types of desire that occurs in daily life. If there is something unknown, users would want to find out what it is. If there is something wish to own, users would want to purchase it. The micro-moment is the desire of "I would like to do".

2.1   Utilization to Micro-Moments

As Fig. 2 indicates, there are several distinctive desires – "I would like to know", "I would like to visit", "I would like to do", and "I would like to buy" in the micro-moment. However, it is more critical to provide instantaneous references that users can assess values through micro-moments.

Many content providers implement micro-moments in their marketing mechanism. Video clips have been effective for self-evaluation when desire has occurred in daily life. Therefore, there is a close relationship in our everyday lives between micro-moments that require instant valuation and our lives.

2.2   Micro-Moments in SNS

Content providers on SNS share their contents in different formats such as text, images, and movie clips. Moreover, the content providers can both instantaneously and proactively respond to information that was created by audiences clicking on "likes" or leaving

Fig. 2. About micro-moments

comments. CCs evaluates whether the contents appear to be interested in scrolling the contents being presented. The concept of the micro-moment can play a critical role because the micro-moment can provide more precise information to CCs while CCs are making decisions. Therefore, the contents of micro-moment should be presented and include contents that draw attention to CCs. To initiate interactions from CCs and establish communication, the contents by CPs should meet or exceed CCs' expectations. If not, the contents could be ignored even though the contents were something CCs were looking for. It is very important for either individual content providers (ICPs) or commercial content providers (CCPs) to understand that micro-moment on SNS has become an initial point of interaction with CCs that would lead to continuous communication between CPs and CCs.

3 Methodology

The methodology we used is to find elements that influence their decisions by providing content that can be recognized and that has an interesting element while the participants are using SNS in a short period.

a) Investigating a method when amount contents including texts, images, and video clips are exceeded in a capacity of size of the screen within current SNS services.
b) Conduct survey usage of SNS in order to find out the reaction of watching video clips.
c) Conduct an experiment to investigate the existence of differences depending on the number of dynamic elements in the contents.
d) Conduct interviews of content providers to find out what makes content providers share the video clips on SNS.
e) conduct experiment that shows contents as fast-forwarding except for contents that consist of text and find out the level of comprehension for the contents.
f) Video thumbnail from Instagram was shown to participants and conduct experiments to find out the level of comprehension and interests.

4 Analysis

4.1 Evaluating Existing SNS Services

We have identified popular five (5) services to investigate from providing content to consuming content based on several users and level of content quality. Within 5 services, authors investigate methods to present contents when there was an excess of the number of contents (Fig. 3).

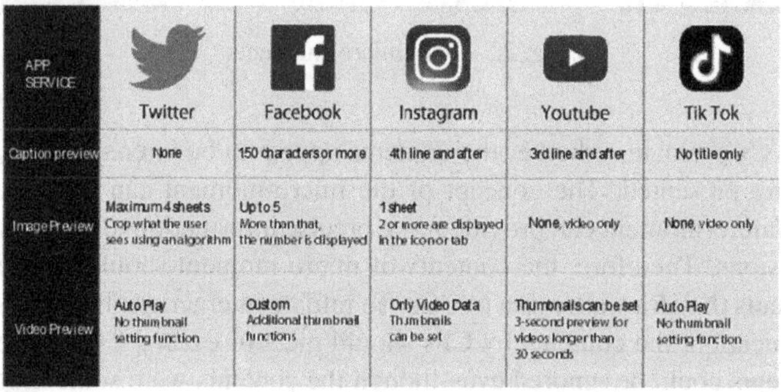

APP SERVICE	Twitter	Facebook	Instagram	Youtube	Tik Tok
Caption preview	None	150 characters or more	4th line and after	3rd line and after	No title only
Image Preview	Maximum 4 sheets Crop what the user sees using an algorithm	Up to 5 More than that, the number is displayed	1 sheet 2 or more are displayed in the icon or tab	None, video only	None, video only
Video Preview	Auto Play No thumbnail setting function	Custom Additional thumbnail functions	Only Video Data Thumbnails can be set	Thumbnails can be set 3-second preview for videos longer than 30 seconds	Auto Play No thumbnail setting function

Fig. 3. Presentation method when there is a large amount of information on the Timeline

As a result, most services used a method that leads to the use of search engines due to the high level of interest by being exposed to a preview of contents on either text or images. However, it was difficult to identify triggers to consume the contents in case of praying a video clip. It indicates that there was not an optimized method to present video clips to draw attention. Authors suspect that CPs have failed to establish an optimized method and been attempting many different ways in search of an effective method whereas texts and images have methods to draw attention.

4.2 Survey on SNS Usage

Conduct survey usage of SNS focusing on video clips. Content consumers think that the optimal duration for playing video clips is around 10 s. 91% of content consumers watch video clips with no sound. It is a phenomenon that mobile devices are being used to browse SNS by content consumers while waiting on public transportations or between quick breaks.

4.3 The Experiment of Comprehension or Drawing Attention When Contents Have Dynamic Elements While Being Presented

Authors investigated four (4) patterns of video thumbnail on SNS; using texts for contents, using images for contents, three (3) images video and fast forward. The purpose of the pilot experiment is to understand the differences between contents with dynamic moves and contents with subtle moves while video clips are being presented. The experiment shows that its contents with dynamic elements are more effective than contents with fast-forwarding. However, there was some unexpected results base on the characteristics of the contents (Fig. 4).

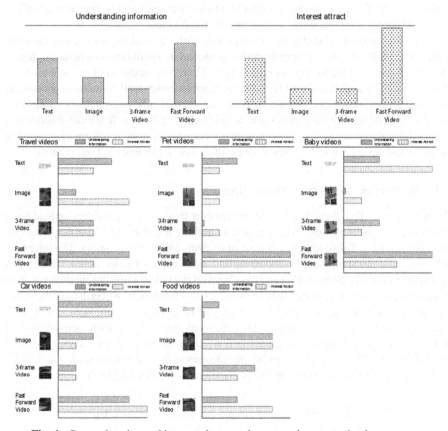

Fig. 4. Comprehension and interests between images and contents that have moves

Level of Comprehension

Effective contents for fast-forwarding: video clips such as pets, babies, and automotive share a common characteristic, in which most events occur in a short period and contents are dynamic. Therefore, the fast forward method is effective when contents that have events occur in a short period need to be presented.

Effective contents for subtle moves (including texts or images): video clips for travel and food use textual information in order to compensate lack of context information with still images and video clips. Therefore, subtle moves are effective for contents that need to be understood the context.

Content Trigger to Show Interests

Effective contents for dynamic moves: video clips for pets and automotive are not necessary to have contexts to understand the contents and, typically, events occurred in a short period of time. Dynamic moves are effective to draw attention to intermittent events.

Effective contents for subtle moves: travel, food relates.

Traveling or food-related content works well with subtle elements because contents with subtle elements provide opportunities to appreciate small details whereas dynamic elements have less time to interact with details. Therefore, authors believe that contents that consist of images work well if audiences need to understand contexts or if contents need to capture audiences' attention. However, textual information works well with contents that have a lot of moves such as video clips of babies. If textual information successfully draws audiences' attention that's because of textual information that has funny or humorous expression, not because of dynamic elements in their contents.

4.4   The Purpose for Video Clips for SNS

Authors believe that there were different reasons that content providers upload their video clips according to the experiment. The authors interviewed 13 participants who had sightseeing in Tokyo and they consist of students and foreign visitors. The interview was focused on the purpose of videotaping and the contents of videotaping. Participants uploaded their video clips on SNS and have been taking videotaping during their vacation because the authors believe that they are students and foreigners. According to the chart, the participants videotaped when they thought that the context and atmosphere were hard to describe with text or still images. Also, they videotaped for dynamic elements such as fireworks. Sightseeing during vacations is a unique opportunity for either students or foreign visitors. Therefore, the number of videotaping has been increased, which leads to more opportunities for uploading those video clips to SNS (Table 1).

Table 1. The purpose and dynamic elements of the video

View	-Scenery and atmosphere of overseas towns -The atmosphere of the train arriving at the station is different from the home country -It is rare for a tram to run with a car -Differences in cityscape and landscape	Early August	Want to share the atmosphere and situation Remember later when seeing that
Tradition	Rare things		
Fireworks	-Sound and power when listening / flow / volume of people -Atmosphere including movement -Sharing emotions felt by light	Mid-August	For sharing fun and memories
Drink	-Fun and atmosphere at that time -The atmosphere of nostalgia and friends at the same time	Late August	Sharing differences in nationality and Nuance Remember when to look back later
Food	-Fire flickering and atmosphere during barbecue -The atmosphere of freshly baked hamburger oil and steam		

The authors conducted interviews for finding out why the participants would want to videotape in various activities. As a chart suggests, the participants would want to videotape when the participants thought that it would be hard to explain context with words and to capture strong feelings that occurred during the event as still images.

4.5   Comprehension Measures Between Contents with Textual Information and Without Information

The previous experiment has shown it is effective for the content consumer to comprehend contents and express interests with the method that has dynamic elements. The authors observed the same phenomenon from the previous experiment when the contents with textual information were being presented. The authors compared content comprehension between subjective and objective except the experiment for contents with textual information (Table 2).

Table 2. Recognition of information presentation without text Information

	Subjective understanding	Actual understanding
Travel videos	41%	**1.8%**
Pet videos	86%	**27%**
Baby videos	88%	**16%**
Car videos	55%	**20%**
Food videos	79%	**17%**

Participants' subjective comprehension can be interpreted by selecting words that have been pre-arranged based on contents. On the other hand, it means that participants may not be able to comprehend the content provider's objective or intention. Therefore, it is not enough for content providers to present contents with dynamic elements. Authors believe that it is necessary for the content provider to add textual information when content is being presented.

4.6   Experiment Between Comprehension and Interest

Based on data from previous experiments, authors created 5 video clips that are differently combined with dynamic or subtle elements besides the method of Instagram and conducted another experiment for comprehension and interests on pre-arranged samples. As a result, textual information and fast-forwarding format were effective to comprehend contents regardless of intensity and amount of movement (Table 3).

Authors believe that it would be better for the audience that contents can be intuitively recognized as video clips because comprehension of contents and interests can be changed by audiences' interests when contents have many moving elements. However, fast-forwarding is an effective method to attract audiences' interests for contents that have subtle moving elements.

Table 3. Analysis of variance results

Content with a lot of Movement			N=20
	Average	Variance	Standard Deviation
Understand	3.482	0.8147	0.9026
Interest	2.695	1.8204	1.3449

	Understand	Interest
1 : Play button	0	11
2 : Fast forward video	11	12
3 : Play button + fast forward video	4	9
4 : Short text + fast forward video	29	8
5 : Play button + short text + fast forward video	2	6

Content with fewer of Movement			N=23
	Average	Variance	Standard Deviation
Understand	3.652	0.8790	0.9375
Interest	2.326	1.2197	1.1044

	Understand	Interest
1 Play button	2	9
2 Fast forward video	6	24
3 Play button + fast forward video	1	5
4 Short text + fast forward video	34	5
5 Play button + short text + fast forward video	3	3

5 Conclusion

This research of video clips on SNS administers micro-moments that can increase in contents understanding and thumbnail method that the audience can effectively recognize contents. In terms of understanding content, it was effective for the audience to increase understanding by a combination of fast-forwarding and textual information. When contents have a lot of movements, subtle elements capture audiences' interests and vice versa. Also, the authors have confirmed that the method to present video thumbnail needs to alter depending on the number of contents of the move. It has a potential risk that the essence of contents can be distorted by altering moving elements in dynamic content presenting. Also, there are alternative ways to create video content through interesting icons or digital stamps. Therefore, content providers need to carefully consider moving elements itself within contents as well as a nuance of contents.

References

1. Kawasaki, T., Ideguchi, T.: Factor analysis of video picture impression and influence of video transcribing speed on each factor. Inst. Electron. Inf. Commun. Eng. **85**(9), 1022–1025 (2002)
2. Ohmukai, I.: Current status and future perspectives of social networking services. Natl. Inst. Inf. **47**(9), 993–1000 (2006)
3. Saito, S.: Proposal of a new design for responsive web. In: Proceedings of Japan Telework Society Conference, vol. 17, pp. 37–42 (2015)
4. Toshiki, M., Wonseok, Y., Naoya, S.: The consistency of the visual information in web design. In: The 63st Annual Conference of JSSD
5. Yuki, A., Maekawa, T.: An adaptive content presentation system for web browsing using cellular phones. J. Inf. Process. Soc. Jpn. **47**(12), 3149–3164 (2006)
6. Yuki, A.: 9 button browsing system: a web browsing system for cellular phone users. Database Soc. Jpn. **5**(4), 9–12 (2007)
7. Ito, S.: Worth of social media for the consumer. Fukuoka Univ. Rev. Commer. Sci. **60**(3), 381–405 (2016)

8. Maruya, T., Tano, S., Hashiyama, T., Ichino, J.: Quantitative evaluation of effects on comprehension of learning from text, illustration, and animation. In: 31st Fuzzy System Symposium in Japan, pp. 322–327 (2015)
9. Iguchi, H., Abe, K., Misawa, T., Kimura, H., Daido, Y.: Recognition of grouping patterns in trademarks based on the gestalt psychology. IEEJ Trans. Electron. Inf. Syst. **127**(6), 844–853 (2007)

Enabling Authors to Produce Computable Phenotype Measurements: Usability Studies on the Measurement Recorder

Limin Zhang[1]([✉]) [iD], Hong Cui[1], Bruce Ford[2] [iD], Hsin-liang Cheng[3] [iD], James Macklin[4], Anton Reznicek[5], and Julian Starr[6]

[1] University of Arizona, Tucson, AZ 85705, USA
liminz@email.arizona.edu
[2] University of Manitoba, Winnipeg, MB R3T 2N2, Canada
[3] Missouri University of Science and Technology, Rolla, MO 65409, USA
[4] Agriculture Agri-Food Canada, Ottawa, Canada
[5] University of Michigan, Ann Arbor, MI 48019, USA
[6] University of Ottawa, Ottawa, ON, Canada

Abstract. We believe authors are the most authoritative in defining characters they record. Currently, it is professional curators to convert phenotype characters in publications from human language to computable language using ontology. Such a curation process is not only slow and costly, but it is also jeopardized by significant inter-curation variation issues that are well-known but not systematically addressed. In an effort to make scientific publication semantically clear at the time of publication, we are designing, developing and evaluating a series of ontology-aware software prototypes to support authors to produce phenotypic data that can be readily harvested by computers. One of this series, Measurement Recorder, has been developed to assist authors to define numerical measurements of characters. Two usability studies have conducted with 22 undergraduate students who majored in information science and 32 biology undergraduate students respectively.

Results obtained from the questionnaires and user interaction log data suggest that users can use the Measurement Recorder without training and find it easy to use. Users also appreciate semantic features that enhance data quality. A set of software design issues have also been identified and new features/modifications have been approved by three botanists on the team and implemented to address these issues. This module will be included in a larger Character Recorder platform where both categorical and numerical characters are supported. Future work includes representing the semantic data as RDF knowledge graph and characterizing the division of work between authors as domain knowledge providers and ontology engineers as knowledge formalizers.

Keywords: Phenotype characters · Author curation · Usability study · Measurement recorder · Inter-curator variation · Semantic-aware software

© Springer Nature Switzerland AG 2020
C. Stephanidis et al. (Eds.): HCII 2020, CCIS 1293, pp. 288–296, 2020.
https://doi.org/10.1007/978-3-030-60700-5_37

1 Introduction

Phenotypes are the set of observable characteristics of an individual resulting from the interaction of its genotype with the environment. Despite a tremendous amount of manuscripts have been published and are being published, only a small portion of them are "computable" [1]. By "computable", we mean that data are written without ambiguity, so that can be used by computers for analytical research. The proportion is relatively low due to the fact that there are no uniform rules for computer-readable phenotypical data. The process converting incomputable data into computable is referred as ontologization, where the semantics of a phenotype description is made explicit by translating it to some formal statements with terms and relations in some ontologies [2]. The entire conversion process relies heavily on human curators with domain knowledge [3]. Human involvement brings variations, known as "inter-curator variation" and has been widely reported in different data curation settings [4–7]. In the case of phenotypic character curation, the variation at the level of 40% among three curators who have worked on the same project and followed the same curation guideline has been reported [8, 9].

Unlike the current curation practice, we proposed a project, "Authors in the Driver's Seat", to investigate a different paradigm with authors hold the pens [10]. There are a number of critical reasons for this approach. First, authors are the most authoritative interpreter of the original meaning of the characters they recorded. Second, authors' terminology choice and character formation jointly create and develop the conceptual model of a taxonomy group. Third, the most simple reason is that there are not enough human resources to convert all published and future papers into computable languages. In the project, we plan to develop and evaluate a set of software to support authors expressing the semantics of their characters at the time of recording characters. One of the software prototype, Measurement recorder, has been designed, developed,and then evaluated through usability experiments. The findings collectively answer these following research questions: (1) Functionality: Are the users able to use this software without instruction to define characters and add terms to ontology? (2) User adoption factor: Do the users appreciate the Measurement Record for its data quality control functionality? (3) User adoption factor: Do the users appreciate the support for character illustrations and character reuse?

The paper is organized as follows: starting by the design goals and targeted users, then presenting the Measurement Recorder, following by introducing the experiment design in the Method section. Relevant results from all the experiments will then be presented around the three research questions in the Results and Analyses section. Following a discussion of the results, we conclude the paper with a few concluding remarks and future work.

2   Method

2.1   Design Goals, Target Users and High-Level Functionality of the Measurement Recorder

The Measurement Recorder is designed for numerical measurement characters. The specific design goals are: (1) to assist users in defining characters and recording measurements in semantical explicit language, and to allow measurements to be described graphically; (2) be easy to use without training; (3) support features that would incentivize user adoption of the application. Through user research, we create a user persona: "They are taxonomists or other evolutionary biologists. They are savvy users of analytical software applications including a spreadsheet. They do not have the time or patient to navigate a complex software system to complete a routine task of documenting measurements".

Employ the methodology established in [11], in designing the Measurement Recorder, a conceptual mode was first established with a user persona and an application domain as the context. The conceptual model is then mapped to functions or features that need to be implemented in the software. Several versions of user interface sketches were drafted and evaluated by the designers before one version is selected and implemented. See https://drive.google.com/open?id=1tSpBS for the screenshots of prototype.

2.2   Usability Study Experiment Design and Subjects

We conducted two usability experiments, "Individual" and "Shared", in succession. The Individual one was designed to evaluate the general usability of the software. The tasks were measuring four common objects (length of leaf, distance between pupils, width of leaf, and cellphone screen size) and the participants (24) were recruited from the undergraduate programs in the School of Information of the University of Arizona. The researchers manipulated the ontology for this experiment by including different number of useful terms or illustrations to make the tasks more or less difficult. Participants were asked to ignore characters created by others, hence the name "Individual" for this experiment. The Shared Experiment was designed to evaluate software data quality features, in addition to the general usability of the software for biologists. Thirty-four undergraduate were recruited from two different classes in the Department of Biology of the University of Manitoba. One class (15 participants) covers flowering plants in general, and the other class (19 participants) covers the genus *Carex*. We shall refer to the first group as "shared-ns" (non-expert participants) while the second group as "shared-es" (expert participants) hereafter. Shared-es and shared-ns groups completed the same set of tasks given in the same order in the same computer lab, one group after the other. User tasks in Shared Experiment involved technical measurements of plant structures, which are length of Perigynium, length of Inflorescence, width of Spike, length of Perigynium Beak. Participants were encouraged to review and reuse characters created by others, hence the name "Shared" for this experiment. The basic procedure for both Individual and Shared Experiment are watching the introduction video; completing the measurement tasks in a given order, completing a questionnaire relevant to an experiment.

There was no training on the use the software for the participants. All participants received $10 for their participation and some of them also received course credits offered by their instructor. The study was proved by relevant Human Subject Research review authorities of the University of Arizona and the University of Manitoba and the experiments was carried out from September to November 2018.

3   Results and Analyses

22 of the 24 participants in the Individual Experiment completed all four tasks. Among these, 10 completed the tasks in the "easy to hard" order and 12 in the "hard to easy" order. Data from the other two participants were excluded from the analyses because they failed to follow the experiment instruction. 32 of the 34 participants completed the entire session in the Shared Experiment. Among these, 13 were in the "shared-ns" group and 19 were in the "shared-es" group. The two participants did not complete the tasks due to system overload issues. Data collected from responses to the questionnaires and from the system's user logs are analyzed to answer the research questions.

3.1   Research Question 1: Is Measurement Recorder Intuitive Enough to Be Used Without Instructions?

Survey questions relevant to RQ1 and their mean scores with standard deviations (SD) are grouped into the "easy to use" and "hard to use" indicators in Table 1.

As shown in the Table 1, Responses from both Individual and Shared Experiments were largely consistent. The data show that, in general, participants agree that they have the skills to use the MR (Q1), it becomes ease to use after some practice (Q3), and having more built-in assistance would make the tool more effective (Q6), although they do not feel particularly apprehensive when using the tool (Q4). This set of self-reported scores indicates that the software can be used without instruction, although more built-in help is desired. To verify this finding, task completion time were extracted from the system's user logs. Statistical significant differences were found between the task completion times for the first and second tasks in each of the l experiment settings: Individual Experiment's easy-to-hard and hard-to-easy orders, Shared Experiment's es and ns groups (Welch Two Sample T-test, p-value < 0.001). No significant differences were found in task completion time among Tasks 2, 3, and 4 in all experiment settings. In other words, regardless of perceived difficulty levels of the 4 tasks, the initial task is always the most time consuming, and all the other tasks take about the same amount of time.

3.2   Research Question 2: Do Users Appreciate the Measurement Recorder for Its Data Quality Control Functionality?

Survey questions related to Research Question 2 and their mean scores with SDs are presented in Table 2. Because participants in the Shared Experiment are biology majors, a set of questions closely related to biological data quality that were not used in the Individual Experiment were included in the Shared Experiment questionnaire, and vice

Table 1. Questions and their agreement scores related to Research Questions 1

Category	Questions	Individual EXP mean score* (N = 22)	Shared EXP mean score* (N = 32)
Easy to use indicator	Q1 I have the skills necessary to use Measurement Recorder	4.18 (1.006)	4.13 (0.871)
	Q2 Figuring out how to operate Measurement Recorder is easy for me	3.77 (1.152)	3.50 (1.078)
	Q3 I find Measurement Recorder is easy to use after some practice	3.86 (0.941)	4.13 (0.871)
Hard to use indicator	Q4 I feel apprehensive about using Measurement Recorder	3.09 (0.971)	3.09 (0.780)
	Q5 I find Measurement Recorder difficult to use at the beginning	3. 91 (1.192)	3.28 (1.780)
	Q6 I could complete a task more effectively using Measurement Record if there were more help built into the system	4.00 (0.926)	4.09 (0.818)

Mean score = 5*(# of strongly agree) + 4* (# of agree) + 3*(#of neither agree or disagree) + 2* (# of disagree) + 1*(# of strongly disagree)/# in total. This is also applied to Table 2 and 3.

versa. Questions that were not included in the questionnaire for a specific experiment have a score of "N/A" in the table.

The findings from the Individual Experiment and the Shared Experiment are again consistent with this research question. The data shows a relatively strong agreement that Measurement Recorder would help improve data quality in terms of accuracy and consistency (Q 1, 2, 3, 4, 5), that it is preferable over Excel for data quality control (Q 6, 7, 8), with a stronger agreement amongst biology participants, and that it does not make data recording more boring (Q9), again with a slightly stronger agreement amongst biology participants. Comparing the mean agreement scores and their standard deviations between Shared Experiment and Individual Experiment, biology participants seem to embrace the Measurement Recorder more strongly. In addition, biology participants strongly agree that the Measurement Recorder could be a useful tool for teaching biological measurements (Q2).

Table 2. Questions and their agreement scores related to Research Questions 2

Category	Questions	Mean score (SD)*	
		Individual EXP (N = 22)	Shared EXP (N = 32)
Data quality control	Q1 I find Measurement Recorder useful for explaining how a measurement is taken	3.818 (1.140)	4.281 (0.634)
	Q2 I think Measurement Recorder could be a useful tool for teaching biological measurements	N/A	3.844 (0.448)
	Q3 Using Measurement Recorder is NOT a good idea for data quality control	2.5 (0.802)	N/A
	Q4 Measurement Recorder will help increase the accuracy of measurements in scientific publications	3.864 (0.834)	4.313 (0.535)
	Q5 Using Measurement Recorder is NOT a good idea for improving consistency amongst different researchers	N/A	1.813 (0.535)
Compare to excel	Q6 If a task requires measurement definitions, I would prefer Excel over Measurement Recorder.	3.318 (1.129)	N/A
	Q7 If a task requires measurement definitions (explaining how a measurement is taken), I would prefer Measurement Recorder over Excel	N/A	4.156 (0.808)
	Q9 Using Measurement Recorder enables me to accomplish the measurement takes more accurately than using Excel	3.545 (1.057)	4.188 (0.780)
User experience	Q9 Measurement Recorder makes data recording more interesting	3.409 (1.054)	3.625 (0.793)

3.3 Research Question 3: Do the Users Appreciate the Support for Illustrations and Character Reuse?

The set of questions related to Research Question 3 and their agreement scores are shown in Table 3. Again, "N/A" indicates a question was not included in the questionnaire for a specific experiment.

As shown in Table 3, responses to definition related questions (Q2, 3) show a relatively strong level of agreement that participants were not confident in their definitions for the characters, even though they may not perceive writing the definition as a difficult task (Q3). It is interesting to note that more biology participants find it hard to write definitions (Q3), and this is because definitions involved in their tasks require a good level of biology knowledge.

Table 3. Questions and their agreement scores related to Research Questions 3

Questions	Mean score (SD)*	
	Individual EXP (N = 22)	Shared EXP (N = 32)
(1) Measurement illustrations shown in the "Method" section make my work more efficient	3.905 (0.995)	4.500 (0.672)
(2) I was worried that my measurement definitions may not be the best	3.682 (0.995)	3.969 (0.822)
(3) Writing definitions for terms was difficult for me	3.045 (1.090)	3.219 (1.211)
(4) If allowed to view the definitions created by other users, I would feel more comfortable using the Measurement Recorder	3.818 (0.795)	N/A
(5) I used "clone and enhance this" function to create my character	N/A	20 [YES] 12 [NO]
(If 5 = YES) "Clone and enhance this" makes it quicker to create a character I needed	N/A	4.600 (0.754)

Despite that participants in the Individual Experiment were instructed not to use others' characters, the user interaction log shows that 20 out of 88 total characters were created through reusing characters created by others via methods "use this" or "clone and enhance it". 77% of the participants expressed a desire to view characters created by others (Q4). Participants in the Shared Experiment were encouraged to review and reuse existing characters if needed. In each group (shared-ns and shared-es), all participants noticed the relevant characters created by others and a vast majority did check characters created by others. And 20 out of 32 participants indeed reused some characters created by others via "clone and enhance it" and found the feature increased efficiency (Q5). From this, we can infer that the other way of reusing characters, "use this", would have a similar effect because the two mechanisms are very similar, and "use this" requires even fewer user actions.

4   Improvement Suggestions

Based on the issues identified above, along with the comments participants left in an open-ended question in the questionnaires, a set of improvements have been identified and implemented in the Measurement Recorder. All of these have been approved by the three botanists on the project.

First, when characters accumulate, it can become difficult to select relevant characters for reuse. To address this issue, tool-tips are added in the character search/dropdown selection. Mouse-over a character triggers the display of the character's verbal or visual definition. Second, to bring users attention to the unit information, a mechanism is added to send the user to the unit section automatically after they fill out the definition form. Third, as an error prevention mechanism, and to further address the unit issue, a series of confirmation dialogs are added for the user to review both the definition and the unit before saving a character when they Use This or C&E a character. A light-weight form for forming character names is now provided. Forth, to maintain consistency in character naming, the form of *"character* of/between *structure"* is adopted in the Measurement Recorder, and the form will eliminate character naming errors such as *leaf length* as the correct form is *length of leaf*. Fifth, a set of labels are changed, for example, the new label for the search/create character box is now "Search or Create Character". See https://drive.google.com/drive/folders/1rxRH_ajDNoURxXagyWtmx__W6h 5Nmq_x?usp=sharing L for updated UI.

5   Conclusion and Future Work

In this paper, we motivate the need for a software platform that help authors to semantically describe their phenotype data, in this case, numerical measurable characters. We describe a software prototype, the Measurement Recorder, and the usability studies with three different user groups possessing different levels of domain knowledge. Results obtained from the questionnaire and user interaction log data suggests that users can use the Measurement Recorder without training and find it easy to use. Users also appreciate the semantic features that enhance data quality. Participants with more biological knowledge also favor the Measurement Recorder more. A set of software design issues have also been identified and new features/modifications have been approved by three botanists on the team and implemented to address these issues.

Based on the lessons learned from this study, we have already implemented a Character Recorder prototype platform where both categorical and numerical characters are supported. The Measurement Recorder becomes an integral part of the platform. In the near future, we will conduct experiments with a number of *Carex* experts to characterize and quantify the division of work between authors as domain knowledge providers and ontology engineers as knowledge formalizers.

Funding.   This work was supported by UA National Science Foundation # 1661485.

References

1. Dahdul, W., Dececchi, T.A., Ibrahim, N., Lapp, H., Mabee, P.: Moving the mountain: analysis of the effort required to transform comparative anatomy into computable anatomy. Database (Oxford) **13**
2. Mabee, P.M., et al.: Phenotype ontologies: the bridge between genomics and evolution. Trends Ecol. Evol. **22**(7), 345–350 (2007)
3. Ware, M., Mabe, M.: The STM Report: an overview of scientific and scholarly journal publishing. 4th edn. International Association of STM Publishers (2015)

4. Camon, E.B., Barrell, D.G., Dimmer, E.C.: An evaluation of GO annotation retrieval for BioCreAtIvE and GOA. BMC Bioinf. **6**, 17 (2005)
5. Söhngen, C., Chang, A., Schomburg, D.: Development of a classification scheme for disease-related enzyme information. BMC Bioinf. **12**, 329 (2011)
6. Wiegers, T.C., Davis, A.P., Cohen, K.B., Hirschman, L., Mattingly, C.J.: Text mining and manual curation of chemical-gene-disease networks for the comparative toxicogenomics database (CTD). BMC **10**, 326 (2009)
7. Endara, L., et al.: Building the "plant glossary"—a controlled botanical vocabulary using terms extracted from the floras of North America and China. Taxon **66**(4), 953–966 (2017)
8. Dahdul, W., et al.: Annotation of phenotypes using ontologies: a gold standard for the training and evaluation of natural language processing systems. Database: J. Biol. Databases Curat. **2018** (2018)
9. Cui, H., et al.: CharaParser+ EQ: performance evaluation without gold standard. Proc. Assoc. Inf. Sci. Technol. **52**(1), 1–10 (2015)
10. Cui, H., et al.: Incentivising use of structured language in biological descriptions: author-driven phenotype data and ontology production. Biodivers. Data J. **6** (2018)
11. Johnson, J., Henderson, A.: Conceptual Models: Core to Good Design. Morgan & Claypool Publishers

Interaction and Intelligence

Experiencing AI in VR: A Qualitative Study on Designing a Human-Machine Collaboration Scenario

Alexander Arntz[✉] and Sabrina C. Eimler

Institute of Computer Science, University of Applied Sciences Ruhr West,
Bottrop, Germany
{alexander.arntz,sabrina.eimler}@hs-ruhrwest.de

Abstract. This paper describes the setup and results of a qualitative interview study, in which participants were given the opportunity to interact with an AI-based representation of a robotic-arm in a virtual reality environment. Nine participants were asked to jointly assemble a product with their robotic partner. The different aspects of their experiences, expectations and preferences towards the interaction with the AI-based industrial collaboration partner were assessed. Results of this study help to inform the design of future studies exploring working arrangements and communication between individuals and robots in collaborating together.

Keywords: Human-machine collaboration · Artificial intelligence · Virtual reality · Qualitative study

1 Introduction

Recent advancements in Artificial Intelligence (AI) and industrial robotics enabled the first step towards true Human-Machine Collaboration (HMC), which allows for new concepts of industrial production [14]. Envisioning these upcoming production scenarios in the age of digitalization is a major advantage for creating optimized and efficient workplaces [7]. Virtual Reality (VR) delivers the tool to validate concepts for production processes of the future before they become reality [4]. This allows to explore how individuals behave, when confronted with AI-enhanced industrial robots in a safe and controlled virtual environment, that can be adjusted for any scenario or robot manifestation or behavior. One of the key aspects of HMC is that a human and a robot entity work as equal parties together to accomplish a task [9]. Apart from the technical implementation of the machine, the human factor should not be neglected. One of the major problems is the outward appearance of the robot, considering that a robot in such a scenario is not antropomorphic but embodied as an industrial robot-arm. The lack of verbal communication paired with the absence of body language hampers the interpretation of the machine's intention [2]. This is critical as an autonomously

© Springer Nature Switzerland AG 2020
C. Stephanidis et al. (Eds.): HCII 2020, CCIS 1293, pp. 299–307, 2020.
https://doi.org/10.1007/978-3-030-60700-5_38

acting machine, that is unpredictable in terms of communicated behavior, might induce aversion [11]. In addition, according to a study by the European Union, the disdain against autonomous machines and AI-systems is already widespread among the industrial workforce [12]. These unfavorable opinions, currently aimed towards the fear of being replaced and loss of the job, might be fueled by poorly designed HMC workplaces, thus leading to a fail of the concept. This renders the need for investigating how AI-enhanced robots in such scenarios should behave and communicate. This paper presents results from an exploratory qualitative study, in which 9 participants from different levels of prior experiences with robotics interacted with an AI-driven robot-arm in a virtual reality workspace environment. A qualitative method was used to gain insights into users' feelings, expectations and thoughts in pursuing a joint construction task with the AI-driven robotic-arm. The following parts describe research questions, scenario description and methods used. Results and implications are discussed.

1.1   Research Questions

The projected VR-experimental approach demands to design the robot-arm with a comprehensible interface that communicates the robot's action to the participants enabling an efficient collaboration process. As outlined earlier, it is especially important to determine which expectations people have towards an AI-enhanced collaborative robot-arm, in which ways they want to communicate with the system and which characteristics evoke participants feeling of an intelligent robot. Therefore, the interview was guided by the following research questions:

- **RQ1:** What are participant's expectations towards a collaborative robot-arm?
- **RQ2:** Which communication methods are requested by the participants?
- **RQ3:** Which characteristics make the robot-arm appear as an intelligent system?

2   Study Setup and Procedure

The study involved 9 participants, with 3 assigned for each of the 3 conditions. Every condition consisted of 2 males and 1 female participant. All of them were students recruited from the University of Applied Sciences Ruhr West (Bottrop, Germany). A purposive sampling was chosen according to preselected criteria e.g. age, gender, experience with robots, technical expertise and previous knowledge in manufacturing work. Each condition contained a virtual software agent driven robot-arm, capable of autonomously reacting to the participant's input and collaborating with them. The conditions differed only in the way the virtual robot communicated its actions to the participants, based on suggestions found in prior Human-Robot interaction related studies [3,8,13]. The first condition contained generic text instructions (e.g. "component is removed", "task successful") placed right next to the user (Fig. 1(A)). The second used instructions written in first person (e.g. "I am now placing the component into the container"), adapted from the natural communication pattern established by voice assistants (Fig. 1(B)). In the third condition the robot merely relied on gestures to communicate its intentions to the user (Fig. 1(C)). Participants were given 10 minutes to collaborate with the robot in an assembling task, self-determining working speed, procedure and coordination with their robot partner. Afterwards, each participant received a debriefing and was interviewed.

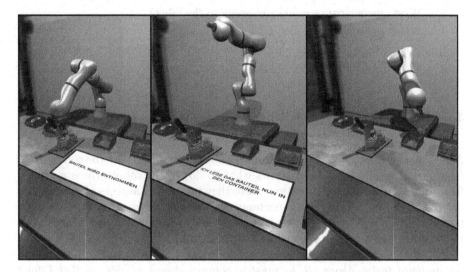

Fig. 1. The 3 conditions from left to right: (A) generic instructions condition, (B) personalized instructions condition, (C) gestures condition

The interviews were conducted with each participant individually after the interaction with the system. The interviews took place in a prepared seating area, enabling participants a more comfortable environment for the interrogation. A total of 7 predefined questions helped to structure the interview (Table 1). The questions were derived from the already stated research questions. During the interview, participants were encouraged to voice their thoughts and explain their answers in detail. For analyzing purposes, all interviews were audio recorded and transcribed. On average, the time spend with the participants was about 20 minutes. The interview language was German, thus all quotes were translated for this paper. Transcribed answers were categorized along the research questions.

3   Findings

This section presents the main themes which emerged during the conducted interviews and the subsequent data analysis.

Table 1. Questions asked in the qualitative interview.

No.	Question
1	How did you feel about the cooperation with the robot?
2	What expectations towards a robot do you have, if you have to work with it?
3	Which forms of communication of the robot did you perceive?
4	What additional forms of communication would you wish for, if you had to work with the system?
5	What characteristics would you assign to the robot?
6	Which aspects of the robot did you find unpleasant?
7	Which characteristics would the robot have to have for you to perceive it as an intelligent system?

3.1   RQ1: What Are Participant's Expectations Towards a Collaborative Robot-Arm?

Across all conditions, participants from both genders stated that the competence (the robot knows its task and knows what to do) of the robot-arm is a crucial factor for a successful collaboration. Also, they referred to aspects of uncertainty avoidance, in highlighting the importance of a) reliability (no need to control the robot, it reliably does its job) and b) trust (does not hurt people). The ability to work independently is a recurring theme stated by the participants.

"That he does the tasks he's supposed to do, that I don't have to work beyond my assigned tasks. Above all, he must be competent and reliable, so that I don't have to constantly keep an eye on if the tasks were being completed. I have to know that I only have to do my part"

(female participant no. 2, gestures condition)

"I expect that I can trust the robot to do his job competently. Also that he can work independently"

(male participant no. 2, personalized instructions condition)

"So the main criteria is that I can trust the robot to do its job. But also that it can work independently. That he doesn't hurt me and that everything is working smoothly".

(male participant no. 1, generic instructions condition)

Further quotes gathered from other participants corroborate the shared expectation of a robot-arm that is capable to conduct the instructed task, minimize or prevents failures and decreases workload for the person that is collaborating with it. The theme of competence was put forward by all participants, independent of the condition or prior exposure with robots. One aspect on the perceived competence that is associated with the robot is the communication, covered by the second research question.

3.2   RQ2: Which Communication Methods Are Requested by the Participants?

Although participants exposed to the condition with the personalized text output (condition B) stating the robot's intentions) rated the collaboration process more favourably than participants from other conditions, additional ways for the robot to express itself such as light signals were recommended.

"I only recognized the text output as a communication form there and that he also waits for me if I haven't done something yet. I would like to have a color signal, a light or something similar, directly on the robot. I always had to look back and forth between the text field and the moving robot. The robot and the text was not in my field of vision and forced me to look back and forth between them. A control lamp, like a traffic light on the robot, yellow, green, red, so that you know the next step is due. Then I would find it easier to work with the robot".

(male participant no. 3, generic instructions condition)

In addition to criticising the monitors' location that forced participants to continuously shift their view between the robot-arm and the text, participants commented that the monitor displaying the text should be placed in vicinity of the robot-arm.

"I had not associated the text instructions directly to the robot. I think it would help if the text was written as if it came from the robot itself. For example, I do this and that instead of the robot does this and that. Also the monitor should be directly in front of the robot, so you can see both at the same time. Then it also looks like the statement is coming directly from the robot"

(male participant no. 2, generic instructions condition)

The implementation of gesture based communication (condition C) turned out unfavourably as no consensus in the interpretation of the meaning emerged among participants. The only gesture that was uniformly recognized was the termination of motion, once the robot-arm detects that the participant approximates to close for safe operations.

"I wasn't paying attention directly at it. But there were certain movements where he didn't go directly to the component but hinted at something. But I can't tell you exactly what it meant.

(male participant no. 3, gestures condition)

"I could not recognize gestures. I only noticed sometimes that the robot came unnecessarily far forward, what that means I don't know. But what was clear was that I should not get too close to the robot".

(male participant no. 1, gestures condition)

"I did not really notice any gestures apart from that I just tested if it would stop when I put my hand in its way and it did. So when you put yourself in danger, that it stops and waits. If you take your hand away, it continues".

(female participant no. 2, gestures condition)

3.3 RQ3: Which Characteristics Make the Robot-Arm Appear as an Intelligent System?

Independent of the condition, most participants stated that the robot-arm adapting to actions outside of the procedure is the greatest indicator for intelligence. The variety of descriptions of intelligent behaviors ranged from a) adaptation, in the sense of compliance with predefined rules, b) a reflection-based reaction and self-determined selection of behavior and c) showing signs of spontaneous behavior outside of parameters.

"The robot must be able to cope with unforeseen events. That would be a form of intelligence for me. But just that it can tell when you get too close and it stops, shows a representation of logic. That the robot not stubbornly does something, but that it constantly evaluates its environment and acts according to it".

(male participant no. 2, personalized instructions condition)

"For me to call the robot intelligent it would have to show some form of spontaneity. Spontaneity in the sense that the robot does not work with predetermined steps but can react to new situations"

(male participant no. 1, personalized instructions condition)

Occasionally, participants were unsure whether or not the robot-arm needs some sort of intelligence. While others stated that the impression of intelligence is linked to human like characteristics such as the presence of a face. Thus, the perception of the robot-arm as an intelligent system can be evoked by adjusting the way it communicates.

"An intelligent system, mmmh difficult question. Well, I couldn't say at this point if the robot is intelligent or not. Overall, it did the tasks it was designed to do. I don't think there's any need for more intelligence".

(male participant no. 1, generic instructions condition)

"Sounds a bit cliché, but maybe the robot should have a face. Of course, in terms of an industrial scenario, I don't know. I got the instruction through this text box. Maybe it just needs to be designed differently to relate better to the robot. That probably changes the perception of intelligence as well".

(female participant no. 3, generic instructions condition).

4 Discussion

The gathered data from the qualitative interviews delivered valuable insights in the expectations people might have for a HMC scenario involving AI-enhanced industrial robots and was a first step for determining the communication design of the robot, which was at that time under development. It also shows the diverse requirements for such a system to be faced in order to be accepted by people. Minute aspects in the communication design determine the perception of the robot and can possibly repell people, fueling existing negative attitudes towards the robot. This is especially prevalent in non anthropomorphic robot representations, which are generally perceived as more cool and dismissive compared to their android counterparts [10]. A major factor for the concept of HMC is the execution of the work by both parties as equal partners. For this reason it was necessary to investigate, at what degree the participant would qualify the system a form of intelligence. A convergence can be made on spontaneous reactivity, as the majority of participants valued it, apart from the actual competence on the task, as the highest indicator of a intelligent system. Although such high expectations a difficult to meet in terms of technical implementation, the impression of such reactivity can be made by adding more and refined communication interfaces (i.e. the light signals, visual feedback along the text output). Apart from safety precautions for collision avoidance, the usage of gestures turned out not effective enough as a communication basis in such a scenario. However, there are some limitations to the results, the limitations of the study are needed to be acknowledged. As previously stated, the majority of participants that formed the sample consisted of students recruited from the University of Applied Sciences Ruhr West. Even tough, the sample does not represent the overall population, the composition of the sample was cast from diverse technical backgrounds, offering wide range from no prior exposure and knowledge of robotics and AI-systems to expert level. Also, the sample size is small and, although this could lead to inadequate depth for collecting data, the interviews indicated repeating concepts without new emerging themes. Additional HMC scenarios with a diverse range of tasks remain to be explored in further studies and should help continuously refine the communication capabilities of the robot in order to meet user expectation and supplying an effective way for collaborative work.

5   Conclusion

The ongoing digitalization of the industrial working environment is in full motion [5]. It is expected that this will have a major influence on the workforce, as it is not only introducing new production processes but also new concepts of how employees interact with machinery such as robots [6]. Through continuous advancements in artificial intelligence and machine learning algorithms, the concept of equal collaboration between human workers and robotic entities is not some far-fetched vision of the future anymore [1]. However, the implications that such a major shift in sociotechnical systems will bring, have to be investigated. Results of this exploratory interview study will be taken into account, i.e. adding light signals and shifting the communications display in vicinity of the robot, to enhance future VR-based HMC studies that will explore different working arrangements.

Acknowledgments. The authors thank Prof. Dr. H. Ulrich Hoppe, Dustin Keßler, Nele Borgert, Dr. Carolin Straßmann and Sarah Zielinski for their contributions, comments and reviews regarding the study design and execution, as well as all participants contributing to the study.

References

1. Arntz, A., Eimler, S., Handmann, U.: Artificial intelligence driven human-machine collaboration scenarios in virtual reality (poster) (2018). http://www.handmann. net/pdf/IA-Poster-ArnEimHan2018.pdf

2. Embgen, S., Luber, M., Becker-Asano, C., Ragni, M., Evers, V., Arras, K.: Robot-specific social cues in emotional body language. In: Proceedings - IEEE International Workshop on Robot and Human Interactive Communication, pp. 1019–1025, September 2012. https://doi.org/10.1109/ROMAN.2012.6343883

3. Ende, T., Haddadin, S., Parusel, S., Wüsthoff, T., Hassenzahl, M., Albu-Schäeffer, A.: A human-centered approach to robot gesture based communication within collaborative working processes, pp. 3367–3374, September 2011. https://doi.org/ 10.1109/IROS.2011.6094592

4. de Giorgio, A., Romero, M., Onori, M., Wang, L.: Human-machine collaboration in virtual reality for adaptive production engineering. Proc. Manuf. **11**, 1279–1287 (2017). https://doi.org/10.1016/j.promfg.2017.07.255

5. Hermann, M., Pentek, T., Otto, B.: Design principles for industrie 4.0 scenarios: a literature review, January 2015. https://doi.org/10.13140/RG.2.2.29269.22248

6. Kirschner, D., Velik, R., Yahyanejad, S., Brandstötter, M., Hofbaur, M.: YuMi, come and play with me! A collaborative robot for piecing together a tangram puzzle. In: Ronzhin, A., Rigoll, G., Meshcheryakov, R. (eds.) ICR 2016. LNCS (LNAI), vol. 9812, pp. 243–251. Springer, Cham (2016). https://doi.org/10.1007/ 978-3-319-43955-6_29

7. Mueller-Abdelrazeq, S.L., Stiehm, S., Haberstroh, M., Hees, F.: Perceived effects of cycle time in human-robot-interaction. In: 2018 IEEE Workshop on Advanced Robotics and its Social Impacts (ARSO), pp. 25–30. IEEE (2018). (27092018– 29092018). https://doi.org/10.1109/ARSO.2018.8625819

8. Scheunemann, M.M., Salge, C., Dautenhahn, K.: Intrinsically motivated autonomy in human-robot interaction: human perception of predictive information in robots. In: Althoefer, K., Konstantinova, J., Zhang, K. (eds.) TAROS 2019. LNCS (LNAI), vol. 11649, pp. 325–337. Springer, Cham (2019). https://doi.org/10.1007/978-3- 030-23807-0_27

9. Shah, J., Wiken, J., Williams, B., Breazeal, C.: Improved human-robot team performance using chaski, a human-inspired plan execution system. In: Billard, A., Kahn, P., Adams, J.A., Trafton, G. (eds.) Proceedings of the 6th International Conference on Human-Robot Interaction - HRI 2011, p. 29. ACM Press, New York (2011). https://doi.org/10.1145/1957656.1957668

10. Straßmann, C.: All eyes on the agent's appearance?!: Investigation of target-group-related social effects of a virtual agent's appearance in longitudinal human-agent interactions. Ph.D. thesis, June 2018

11. Straßmann, C., von der Pütten, A.R., Yaghoubzadeh, R., Kaminski, R., Krämer, N.: The effect of an intelligent virtual agent's nonverbal behavior with regard to dominance and cooperativity. In: Traum, D., Swartout, W., Khooshabeh, P., Kopp, S., Scherer, S., Leuski, A. (eds.) IVA 2016. LNCS (LNAI), vol. 10011, pp. 15–28. Springer, Cham (2016). https://doi.org/10.1007/978-3-319-47665-0_2

12. European Union: Special eurobarometer 382: public attitudes towards robots (2014). https://data.europa.eu/euodp/de/data/dataset/S1044_77_1_EBS382. Accessed 13 Mar 2020

13. Yanco, H., Drury, J.: A taxonomy for human-robot interaction, pp. 111–119, December 2002
14. Zheng, P., Sang, Z., Zhong, R., Liu, Y.: Manufacturing systems for industry 4.0: conceptual framework, scenarios and future perspectives. Front. Mech. Eng. **13**, 137–150 (2018)

Interacting with a Salesman Chatbot

Charlotte Esteban[1][(✉)] and Thomas Beauvisage[2]

[1] Orange Labs SENSE, Lisst-Cers, Chatillon, France
esteban.charlotte@orange.fr
[2] Orange Labs SENSE, Chatillon, France
thomas.beauvisage@orange.com

Abstract. In recent years, chatbots have been spreading on social networks and brand websites, and interactions between users and commercial chatbots have become an ordinary experience in the range of human-computer interactions. Yet, whereas automated conversation has been analyzed in various experimental contexts, only a few studies describe real-world interactions with voicebots [1–3] or chatbots [4–6]. How do interactions with chatbots actually take place? What is an AI-driven commercial conversation in practice? To address these questions, we conducted a sociological study of interactions with chatbots, based on the quantitative and qualitative analysis of interaction logs with a vending chatbot, deployed on a French online telecom company. The study relies on a dataset of 9 months of ComBot usage logs in 2019, representing roughly 47,000 interaction sessions. Our analysis shows that interactions with the commercial chatbot are a highly hybrid format between click-based interfaces and conversational interactions. A majority of users mobilize the conventions of commercial conversation to express their need in plain text. However, the rest of the dialogue mainly combines response-buttons, short input text, and hyperlinks. The use of politeness shows that users are keen on following the conversational interaction format offered to them, even if they don't use it entirely.

Keywords: Chatbots · Interaction logs · Automated commercial dialogue

1 Studying Chatbots Usage in the Wild

The spread of smart speakers since 2017 accelerates a trend that began a few years earlier with Apple's (Siri) and Google's voice assistants on smartphones: these objects are becoming quite ordinary. More sophisticated, more efficient and open to a wide variety of players in the form of a platform, the conversational interface is moving away from its generalist paradigm to be deployed in a wide variety of contexts [5].

However, there are still little empirical studies of how conversational interfaces are used in various contexts. An important attention has been paid recently to voice bots: studying Amazon Echo, Porcheron et al. [1] observe that the use of smart speakers is framed and embedded in the family life situations of the home. Sciuto et al. [2] underline the specificity of the early interactions with smart speakers, and how afterwards users tend to focus on a small set of commands. The use of chatbots is less described in

© Springer Nature Switzerland AG 2020
C. Stephanidis et al. (Eds.): HCII 2020, CCIS 1293, pp. 308–314, 2020.
https://doi.org/10.1007/978-3-030-60700-5_39

the academic literature. Jain et al. [4] focused on user expectations from chatbots in terms of "personnality" and self-disclosure. In the context of marketing and customer services, Følstad et al. [7] showed that users are particularly sensible to the capacity of chabots to correctly interpret their request. An array of works describes the resulting repair strategies deployed in human-computer conversations. Myers et al. [8] showed that NLP failures are a major issue in voice bots, and that users handle it mainly by repeating commands rather than reformulating them. Beneteau et al. [3] insist on the "burden" that deployment of repair strategies is for users, and their variety of strategies with Amazon Echo failures. Ashktorab et al. [9] underline that performing repair turns is hard for machines and that this issue needs to be taken into account in the design of conversational services.

This study aims to complement these works on a large empirical basis, and to describe and understand how users interact with a commercial chatbot, based on a sociological analysis of the bot's logs. How do users address the chatbot? What form of "conversation" do they establish with the robot? How do these interactions take place?

2   Objectives and Empirical Material

ComBot (the name has been changed) is a commercial chatbot implemented on the website of a French telecommunication company. Its purpose is to answer questions related to purchasing of a mobile phone, changing mobile operator or subscription plans. The bot is thus programmed to answer to a dozen of themes related to the acquisition of a mobile phone. This chatbot is developed with a natural language processing solution, which allows to process users requests in ordinary language. However, the bot may also suggest response buttons that users can click, particularly when the NLP system faces difficulties to interpret a user's input. The chatbot may also route users to other customer support means on the company's website, such as online forms, FAQ, or product pages.

The study is based on the analysis of 9 months of anonymized usage logs of ComBot, from December 2018 to August 2019, or 47,474 chatbot interaction sessions. The data contains a timestamped dump of the text of interaction between the users and the chatbot. However, compared to the original texts of the interactions, emojis are not available in the data. Also, the logs do not contain explicit information on the interaction modality performed by users (free text, button-based response, or link), but we could identify them afterwards based on a list of the 350 formulas proposed by the bot in its buttons response.

3   Results

3.1   Quantifying and Qualifying Turn-Takings

The ambition of conversational interfaces is to allow users to express themselves as they wish, in their own words. So, how do the users interact with the chatbot? What do these conversations look like?

First, the sequences of interaction with ComBot are quite short: users perform an average of 4.1 turns of speech during interaction with the bot. In half of the cases, the user counts 1 to 3 turns, which is not much.

Second, interactions with the chatbot involve a combination of free text and clickable buttons (Table 1), and constitute a hybrid format conversation and web and application interfaces. When considering the overall interaction sequences, users use response buttons in 68% of them, and click on Web links in 21%. Free text is present in 100% of interaction sequences, since the user is asked to express his need in free text at the beginning of the interaction; but in the rest of the conversation, free text is present in 58% of the interaction sequences only.

When considering the overall 200.000+ user inputs (Table 1), we see that free text is still the main modality of interaction (57%), but mainly because of the first expression of intent (24%). Free text input are quite short: 9.0 words on average, with a peak at 15% of these texts consisting of a single word. Response buttons are responsible for more than one third of users input. Interestingly, 13% of users input are free text, avoiding a response button, showing that free text can be used at any time by users.

Table 1. Input types in users turns

Input type	% of users turns
Free text	57%
- 'hello'	*3%*
- First expression of need	*24%*
- Avoiding response buttons	*13%*
- Other free text	*17%*
Response buttons	37%
Urls	6%
Overall	100%

3.2 How Users Express Their Need

Within the free writings of users, the expression of need takes on a particular character: it is the first interaction requested from the user, and it is on this basis that the chatbot will have to build its interpretation of the need and guide the rest of the interaction. With what words do users formulate their request?

First of all, despite the chatbot's explicit invitation to express his need ("What can I do for you?"); the expression of the need does not systematically occur in the first round. In fact, the convention of civility is superimposed on this injunction to say why the bot is used, usually marked by turns of presentation and civility. Thus 14% of the first turns are simple "hello" and its variants, the need being expressed in the next round.

Secondly, users express their need in a plurality of forms. Several distinctions can be made: 1) length: intents are 12 words-long on average, but the median is 6 words; 2) syntax: verb-free input account for 12%; 3) posture: 61% of intents are formulated at the first person ("I", "my"); 4) politeness: 31% of intents include words like "hello" or "please"; 5) semantic: 36% express a specific need, while 22% ask a question.

This detailed examination of the various forms led us to identify two main dimensions structuring the expression of intent:

- *Keywords (20%) vs. sentences (80%).* Short forms without conjugated verbs ("change mobile", "change plan"), as opposed to phrased forms, in the first or third person ("I'm looking for a mobile plan starting at 1go", "hello I would like to take advantage of the 50 giga offer on my 2 mobile phones").
- *Intent vs. situation.* The expression of an explicit need (change of plan, question about portability, request for advice on choosing a terminal, etc.), as opposed to formulations that describe the user's situation, and where the need is going to be implicit, or not discernible ("I received a text message announcing promotions on open plans", "Hello, at the moment I have a galaxy J3", "I'm looking at Iphone offers with a 24-month commitment").

Based on these two dimensions, we established a typology of the expression of their needs by users, detailed in Table 2.

Table 2. How users express their need: a typology

Expression type	Description	% of expressions of the need
Search query	The intention is expressed in the form of a nominal group, in a few words (avg: 3.9)	12%
Synthetic query	This group is close to keywords, but uses a verb with an infinitive, sometimes politeness	8%
Explicit need	The user expresses a clearly identified need, with the use of forms such as "I want to", or "I wish to"	32%
Question	The need is clearly identified, but expressed with the interrogation's form	30%
Narrated situation	The user primarily states his or her situation, in the form of a narrative, the need is not clearly identified	18%

3.3 To Be or not to Be Civil with a Bot

The question of the relationship with bots has been a major concern in the researches on conversations interactions, especially on the subject of emotions. The way people spontaneously express their need tend to show that users align their interactions with the existing modalities of interaction with companies: through customer services (face to face or by phone), or websites and apps. In that sense, observing the human-to-human interaction habits when conversing with chatbots is rather a question of civility than a question of emotions. In this last part, we investigate the use of civility and politeness in users' free text inputs, and try to interpret it regarding the relation with the bot. What does politeness towards the chatbot say about the relationship with the tool? To what extend do users stick to the traditional frames of conversations, as in interactions with salesmen or customer services representatives?

The first cue concerning civility is *vouvoiement*. In French, "vous"/"votre" are the plural or polite form of the pronouns "you"/"your", and "tu"/"ton" are the singular and familiar one. In our data, 4% of the users' first turn use this *vouvoiement* when addressing the chatbot in the first turn, and 7% of their other interactions in free text. *Vouvoiement* is certainly a mark of civility with the chatbot, as used in ordinary interactions with customer services. But it marks also as a relationship of agentivity with the chatbot: thus giving the chatbot the status of an "actor". This position invites the chatbot to respond to particular expectations, such as advice ("what do you think of the motorola?") or types of negotiation ("Hello, I would like to see what you can offer me?"). Through *vouvoiement*, users also engage in an interaction with the brand as an entity, thus comforting the chatbot as a point of contact between customers and brands. Placing the chatbot as an "interlocutor-person" engages a relational relationship with the brand, even an emotional and "physical" relationship ("I can reach you by phone?"). Thus, when the user resorts to *vouvoiement*, the chatbot is considered as much as a brand ambassador as an interlocutor. In this sense, like customer services or salespeople, chatbots are both a mediator between the customer and the brand's products and services, and a company representative, who speaks and negotiates on its behalf.

The second marker of civility that can inform the nature of the relationship with the chatbot is the "hello/thank you/goodbye" trio, which we can easily and unambiguously identify in the data. These three markers of politeness are also three procedural markers of the conversation: a "hello" does not, in principle, appear anywhere else than in the first or second turn, while a "goodbye" cannot appear in the first turn: in principle, these words appear punctually and unevenly in the dialogue. "Thank you", in contrast, can be met at moment of the interaction, although it can rather be expected at the end; we wanted to focus on the concluding "thank you". These three markers are decreasingly met in the sequences of interaction (Table 3): while almost half of the opening turns include a "hello", only 7% include a "thank you", and the closing "goodbye" is seldom used.

Table 3. Politeness during sequences of interaction

Markers of politeness	% in interactions
Opening the interaction with "Hello"	45% of 1st turn
"Thank you"	7% (except 1st turn)
"Goodbye"	0,5%

How should we interpret the difference between the observance of civility in the opening and the closing of the interaction? In some cases, the commercial interaction can be continued on other communication means after being redirected by the chatbot:

in that case, performing the closing sequence is not expected; but this case is not the majority. In addition, the chatbot has the particularity of never explicitly ending the interaction, and never performing a closing sequence: rather, it claims to be "always available for further need". However, we believe that the gap between the use of "hello" and "goodbye" also demonstrates a change in the reference interactional frame occurring during the interaction. At the beginning, the chatbot mobilizes the forms of commercial conversation, by introducing itself and requesting "what can I do for you", while response-buttons, redirections and the absence of closing sequences breaks this conventions. Rather, the chatbot presents itself as a disposable automated information point, making civility pointless. Hence, the conversational framing of the exchange evolves from an interactional necessity towards a corporate politeness, held by the chatbot, as in any other person-less interfaces (apps, websites, etc.).

4   Discussion

Our study, based on the analysis of 9 months of logs, shows that the interactions generated by the chatbot appear in practice as an original composition of elements from self-care interfaces (web, applications) and exchange modalities with vendors (telephone, chat). This mix is based in particular on the use of "conversation" as a reference frame for the exchange, even if it uses reply buttons as soon as possible. The user initially expresses his need in free text, and this conversational framing of the exchange is rather followed, since a majority of users write complete sentences, and use forms of civility.

The first implication for design if this study deals with the setup of NLP tools in conversational interfaces. The chatbot's logs shed light particularly well on the various forms that users formulate their needs. This diversity is both lexicometric and syntactic and current tools face difficulties when dealing with short real-world texts from ordinary users. Yet, our typology of the way users express their need can help guiding NLP tools by identifying patterns of expressions, and distinguishing the expression of needs from the description of situations.

The second implication is about how conversation acts on the interaction. As shown in [10] and [4], personnification is rare, and the users of convesrational interfaces favor tools that explicitly tell what they are capable of, and do not pretend to be as human. Our study complements these results: the chatbot we examined presents itself as a bot, and often underlines its limits, and makes large use of response buttons to guide the interaction. In this case, conversation is not a way of building a convincing pereonnality for the chatbot, but rather a convention on how to interact with the system, and make it usable.

References

1. Porcheron, M., Fischer, J.E., Reeves, S., Sharples, S.: Voice interfaces in everyday life. In: Proceedings of the 2018 CHI Conference on Human Factors in Computing Systems - CHI 2018, pp. 1–12. ACM Press, Montreal (2018)

2. Sciuto, A., Saini, A., Forlizzi, J., Hong, J.I.: "Hey Alexa, what's up?": A mixed-methods studies of in-home conversational agent usage. In: Proceedings of the 2018 on Designing Interactive Systems Conference 2018 - DIS 2018, pp. 857–868. ACM Press, Hong Kong, China (2018)

3. Beneteau, E., Richards, O.K., Zhang, M., et al.: Communication breakdowns between families and Alexa. In: Proceedings of the 2019 CHI Conference on Human Factors in Computing Systems, pp. 243:1–243:13. ACM, New York (2019)

4. Jain, M., Kumar, P., Kota, R., Patel, S.N.: Evaluating and informing the design of chatbots. In: Proceedings of the 2018 on Designing Interactive Systems Conference 2018 - DIS 2018, pp. 895–906. ACM Press, Hong Kong (2018)

5. Følstad, A., Skjuve, M., Brandtzaeg, P.B.: Different chatbots for different purposes: towards a typology of chatbots to understand interaction design. In: Bodrunova, S.S., et al. (eds.) INSCI 2018. LNCS, vol. 11551, pp. 145–156. Springer, Cham (2019). https://doi.org/10.1007/978-3-030-17705-8_13

6. Bittner, E., Shoury, O.: Designing automated facilitation for design thinking: a chatbot for supporting teams in the empathy map method (2019)

7. Følstad, A., Nordheim, C.B., Bjørkli, C.A.: What makes users trust a chatbot for customer service? An exploratory interview study. In: Bodrunova, S.S. (ed.) INSCI 2018. LNCS, vol. 11193, pp. 194–208. Springer, Cham (2018). https://doi.org/10.1007/978-3-030-01437-7_16

8. Myers, C., Furqan, A., Nebolsky, J., et al.: Patterns for how users overcome obstacles in voice user interfaces. In: Proceedings of the 2018 CHI Conference on Human Factors in Computing Systems - CHI 2018, pp. 1–7. ACM Press, Montreal (2018)

9. Ashktorab, Z., Jain, M., Liao, Q.V., Weisz, J.D.: Resilient chatbots: repair strategy preferences for conversational breakdowns. In: Proceedings of the 2019 CHI Conference on Human Factors in Computing Systems, pp. 254:1–254:12. ACM, New York (2019)

10. Purington, A., Taft, J.G., Sannon, S., et al.: "Alexa is my new BFF": social roles, user satisfaction, and personification of the Amazon echo. In: Proceedings of the 2017 CHI Conference Extended Abstracts on Human Factors in Computing Systems - CHI EA 2017, pp. 2853–2859. ACM Press, Denver (2017)

An Empirical Study on Feature Extraction in DNN-Based Speech Emotion Recognition

Panikos Heracleous[1(✉)], Kohichi Takai[1], Yanan Wang[1], Keiji Yasuda[2],
Akio Yoneyama[1], and Yasser Mohammad[3]

[1] KDDI Research, Inc., 2-1-15 Ohara, Fujimino-shi, Saitama 356-8502, Japan
{pa-heracleous,ko-takai,wa-yanan,yoneyama}@kddi-research.jp
[2] Nara Institute of Science and Technology,
8916-5 Takayama-cho, Ikoma 630-0192, Japan
ke-yasuda@dsc.naist.jp
[3] Data Science Laboratories, NEC, Japan,
2-4-7 Aomi, Koto-ku, Tokyo 135-0064, Japan
yasserm@aun.edu.eg

Abstract. The current empirical study focuses on speech emotion recognition using speech data extracted from video clips. Although many studies reported speech emotion recognition, the majority of the studies presented were based on using acted and clean speech. A more challenging and realistic task would be using spontaneous noisy speech from video clips. In the current study, the modern and state-of-the-art i-vector features are applied and experimentally evaluated. Comparisons with the widely used low-level descriptors (LLDs) and functionals are also presented. To improve the classification accuracy, a method based on late fusion is investigated. Using the proposed method, higher accuracies were achieved compared to the sole use of individual features. For classification, a fully connected deep neural network (DNN) with several hidden layers was used.

Keywords: Speech emotion recognition · Feature extraction · i-vectors · Late fusion · Deep neural networks

1 Introduction

The task of speech emotion recognition is to automatically recognize the human emotion being expressed from uttered speech. Speech emotion recognition plays an important role in human-computer interaction and its real-world applications [1].

Due to the high importance of speech emotion recognition, a large number of studies have investigated and reported methods and results in this research area [2–6]. However, the majority of studies presented focused solely on using clean acted emotional speech, while few studies reported results using real-world

© Springer Nature Switzerland AG 2020
C. Stephanidis et al. (Eds.): HCII 2020, CCIS 1293, pp. 315–319, 2020.
https://doi.org/10.1007/978-3-030-60700-5_40

noisy data [7]. The current study focused on speech emotion recognition using speech data extracted from video clips. In the current study, state-of-the-art features were applied and experimentally compared by evaluating the methods using deep neural networks (DNNs) [8]. Specifically, i-vector features [9] were applied and compared with low-level descriptors (LLDs) and functionals [10] extracted automatically from the video clips. To improve the classification accuracy using a fully connected DNN, late fusion based on weighted likelihood scoring was applied.

Table 1. Speech samples used for training and testing.

Data set	Emotional classes			
	Positive	Neutral	Negative	Total
Training	802	923	936	2661
Testing	302	280	184	766
Total	1104	1203	1120	3447

2   Methods

2.1   Data

In the current study, the Video Group AFfect (VGAF) database [11,12] was used. The video clips were collected from YouTube English videos with the commons creative licence. The database is freely available for research purposes. To select the appropriate video clips, groups of related keywords were used. The specific keywords reflect various emotions and cohesion such as interview, festival, party, etc. The video clips are of different resolutions to generalize the database. Following the selection and extraction procedure, the video clips were divided into short clips with a duration of 8 to 25 ms. The data were annotated by three human raters using three classes namely, positive, neutral, and negative. Further details regarding video collection and processing are found in [11].

In the current study, all video clips were a duration of 5 s. The data consisted of 2661 video clips for training, and 766 video clips for testing without overlapping. Using the *ffmpeg* Linux tool, the raw speech signals of 44.1 kHz sampling rate were extracted from the video clips. The speech samples were then down sampled to 16 kHz to be used for feature extraction and further processing. Table 1 shows the speech samples used in the current study.

2.2   Feature Extraction and Classification Approach

The basic acoustic features used were 12 mel-frequency cepstral coefficients (MFCCs) [13], pitch, and energy. Twelve MFCC features were extracted from the emotional speech signal every 10 ms with a window-length of 20 ms. Due to the effectiveness of the shifted delta cepstral (SDC) [14] feature vectors in language identification, SDC coefficients concatenated with the basic features were also used to form the feature vectors. The parameter configuration of SDC was optimized to 11,1,3,3.

Following MFCC extraction, i-vectors of 200 dimensions were constructed. To further improve the discrimination ability of the emotion models, supervised linear discriminant analysis (LDA) [15] was also performed on the extracted i-vectors, which resulted in a 2-dimension final emotion vectors. In addition to the i-vectors, LLDs were also used. Specifically, the AVEC2013 [16] and IS09 [17] feature settings were applied to extract feature vectors of dimensions 2268 and 384, respectively. In addition to the sole use of individual features, late fusion was also applied to integrate i-vectors and LLDs features.

DNN is an important method in machine learning that has been applied in many areas. DNN is a feed-forward neural network with many (i.e., more than one) hidden layers. The main advantage of DNNs compared with shallow networks is the better feature expression and the ability to perform complex mapping. Deep learning explains several of the most recent breakthroughs in computer vision, speech recognition, and agents that achieved human-level performance in several games, such as go and poker. The DNN architecture used in this experiment is a standard fully connected network with three hidden layers of 128, 64, 32 neurons, followed by a Softmax layer with 3 neurons for classification. All neurons employed the ReLU activation function. Stochastic Gradient Descent with Nestrov initialization and 0.9 momentum was employed for training (learningrate = 0.01). Data were presented to the network in 100 epochs without early stopping. The batch size was set to 128.

To improve the emotion classification accuracy, late fusion of two different features was also applied prior to the final decision. The approach used for late fusion was based on weighted likelihood scoring. Specifically, two parallel classifiers were applied and the obtained probabilities were combined to form the final score. The following equation shows the way the two scores λ_1 and λ_2 were combined using the weight α to produce the final λ score.

$$\lambda = \alpha * \lambda_1 + (1 - \alpha) * \lambda_2 \tag{1}$$

In the current study, the weight α for the i-vectors was set to 0.617, and for the AVEC2013 features to 0.383. When using the IS09 in late fusion, the weight α for i-vectors was set to 0.848, and for the IS09 features to 0.152. In both cases, the weights were empirically adjusted to maximize the classification accuracy.

3   Results

Table 2 shows the results obtained using individual features and late fusion of different features. As can be seen, using i-vectors higher performance was obtained compared with using LLDs. Furthermore, using i-vectors with LDA, the accuracy was improved to 55.87%. This is a very promising result and significantly higher to the result obtained in [11], where the same data but with less speech samples was used (i.e., 50.23% accuracy). When the i-vectors with LDA were fused with AVEC2013 features, the highest accuracy was achieved. In this case, the accuracy was as high as 58.49%. In the case of IS09 with i-vectors and LDA, the accuracy was 57.98%. The results show that i-vectors can be effectively used in speech emotion recognition with clean and noisy real-world speech data. The reason is because i-vectors explains the variability of speaker, channel, and emotion.

Table 2. Classification accuracy using various features and late fusion.

Features	Dimension	Accuracy [%]
i-vectors	200	53.13
i-vectors(LDA)	2	55.87
AVEC2013	2268	53.01
IS09	384	46.56
i-vectors(LDA) + AVEC2013	2270	58.49
i-vectors (LDA) + IS09	386	57.98
[G. Sharman et al. [11]]	6373	50.23

4 Conclusions

A study was presented on feature extraction in speech emotion recognition. State-of-the-art features were evaluated and compared using real noisy data extracted from video clips. Furthermore, late fusion was also proposed and applied, which improved the accuracy. The highest accuracy obtained was 58.49%, which is a very promising result and significantly higher compared with the accuracy obtained in a similar study [11]. Currently, early fusion and other late fusion methods are under investigation.

References

1. Busso, C., Bulut, M., Narayanan, S.: Toward effective automatic recognition systems of emotion in speech. In: Gratch, J., Marsella, S. (eds.) Social Emotions in Nature and Artifact: Emotions in Human and Human-Computer Interaction, pp. 110–127. Oxford University Press, New York (2013)
2. Pan, Y., Shen, P., Shen, L.: Speech emotion recognition using support vector machine. Int. J. Smart Home **6**(2), 101–108 (2012)
3. Nicholson, J., Takahashi, K., Nakatsu, R.: Emotion recognition in speech using neural networks. Neural Comput. Appl. **9**(4), 290–296 (2000)
4. Stuhlsatz, A., Meyer, C., Eyben, F., Zielke1, T., Meier, G., Schuller, B.: Deep neural networks for acoustic emotion recognition: raising the benchmarks. In: Proceedings of ICASSP, pp. 5688–5691 (2011)

5. Han, K., Yu, D., Tashev, I.: Speech emotion recognition using deep neural network and extreme learning machine. In: Proceedings of Interspeech, pp. 2023–2027 (2014)
6. Lim, W., Jang, D., Lee, T.: Speech emotion recognition using convolutional and recurrent neural networks. In: Proceedings of Signal and Information Processing Association Annual Summit and Conference (APSIPA) (2016)
7. P-Cabaleiro, E., Costantini, G., Batliner, A., Baird, A., Schuller, B.: Categorical vs dimensional perception of italian emotional speech. In: Proceedings of Interspeech, pp. 3638–3642 (2018)
8. Hinton, G., et al.: Deep neural networks for acoustic modeling in speech recognition: the shared views of four research groups. IEEE Signal Process. Mag. **29**(6), 82–97 (2012)
9. Dehak, N., Kenny, P.J., Dehak, R., Dumouchel, P., Ouellet, P.: Front-end factor analysis for speaker verification. IEEE Trans. Audio Speech Lang. Process. **19**(4), 788–798 (2011)
10. Schuller, B.W., et al.: The INTERSPEECH 2016 computational paralinguistics challenge: deception, sincerity & native language. In: Proceedings of Interspeech, pp. 2001–2005 (2016)
11. Sharma, G., Ghosh, S., Dhall, A.: Automatic group level affect and cohesion prediction in videos. In: 2019 8th International Conference on Affective Computing and Intelligent Interaction Workshops and Demos (ACIIW), pp. 161–167 (2019)
12. Dhal, A., Sharma, G., Goecke, R., Gedeon, T.: EmotiW 2020: driver gaze, group emotion, student engagement and physiological signal based challenges. In: ACM International Conference on Multimodal Interaction 2020 (2020)
13. Sahidullah, M., Saha, G.: Design, analysis and experimental evaluation of block based transformation in MFCC computation for speaker recognition. Speech Commun. **54**(4), 543–565 (2012)
14. Bielefeld, B.: Language identification using shifted delta cepstrum. In: Fourteenth Annual Speech Research Symposium (1994)
15. Fukunaga, K.: Introduction to Statistical Pattern Recognition, 2nd edn. Academic Press, New York (1990). Chap. 10
16. Valstar, M., Schuller, B., et al.: AVEC 2013 - the continuous audio/visual emotion and depression recognition challenge. In: Proceedings of AVEC 2013, pp. 3–10 (2013)
17. Schuller, B., Steidl, S., Batliner, A.: The INTERSPEECH 2009 emotion challenge. In: Proceedings of Interspeech, pp. 312–315 (2009)

Develop an Interactive Model of Impact of Basketball Players and Team Performance

Yun-Chi Huang[✉]

Kang-Chiao International School, Taipei, Taiwan
yunchihuang@hotmail.com.tw

Abstract. This study aims to develop an analytical model of basketball team performance based on substitution method (Rotational, Fatigue, Best Fit), player's usage percentage, and individual's point produce (Calculation extended with field goal percentage/attempt of 2P, 3P and FT). The model is expected to predict game results and analyze team management strategies. This study develops four strategies based on the interactive model: (Rotational versus Best fit) Substitution and (Star player versus Average) Usage Rate with scoring value X (The individual player's value of shooting percentage) and value S (The summation index of all scoring value). It is found that scoring performance of Best fit Substitution and star player Usage Rate strategy is highly predictable. Also scoring performance of Best fit Substitution is usually more precise than Rotational Substitution.

Keywords: Rotational system · Substitutional method · Player usage percentage

1 Introduction

Professional sports generate huge amounts of data with great potential to analyze and optimize athletes' performance. Performance analysis like statistical modeling in sports is important to decision-making and strategy development. NBA as one of the most professional sports leagues in the world has the best statistics organization and professional players (Sampaio et al. 2015). Performance analysis with critical variables can maximize NBA players' court efficiency. Critical variables include game's final result, scoring percentage, field goal percentage, 3PA (3-Point Field Goal Attempts) and FTA (Free Throw Attempts), and rate of scoring (Nibras 2018; BigDataBall 2020). Taking Washington Wizards' 2018 season as an example, Fig. 1 and 2 show the total number of points scored by field goals and free throws (PTS) of starters.

Aforementioned background information has pointed out the importance of big data analyses. A trend of professional sports league is to develop player's rotation strategy according to data analytics for on court efficiency/output. This study aims to develop an analytical model of basketball team performance based on substitution method (Rotational, Fatigue, Best Fit), player's usage percentage, and individual's point produce

© Springer Nature Switzerland AG 2020
C. Stephanidis et al. (Eds.): HCII 2020, CCIS 1293, pp. 320–324, 2020.
https://doi.org/10.1007/978-3-030-60700-5_41

(Calculation extended with field goal percentage/attempt of 2-Point, 3-Point and Free Throw) (Nibras 2018; BigDataBall 2020). The model is expected to predict game results and analyze team management strategies across cultures. Again taking Washington Wizards' 2018 season as an example, Fig. 3 and 4 show 2-Point Shot usage rate and 3-point Shot usage rate of starters.

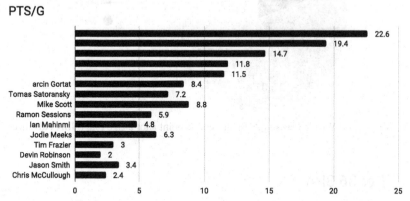

Fig. 1. 2018 Washington Wizards season 2018 starters' PTS/G (NBA Advanced Stat 2020)

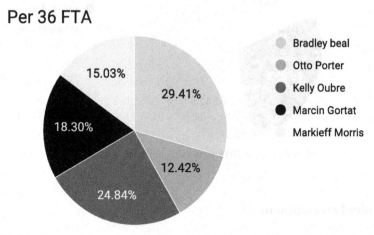

Fig. 2. Washington Wizards season 2018 starters' free throw usage rate (NBA Advanced Stat 2020)

Per 36 2PA

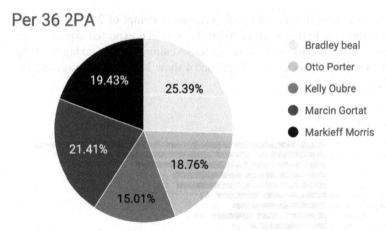

Fig. 3. Washington Wizards season 2018 starters' 2-point shot usage rate (NBA Advanced Stat 2020)

Per 36 3PA

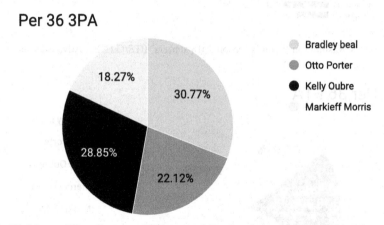

Fig. 4. Washington Wizards season 2018 starters' 3-point shot usage rate (NBA Advanced Stat 2020)

2 Model Development

The correlation between team substitutional decision and player's usage percentage shows that rotational time management (starter playing 36 min and bench players playing 12 min) is more efficient than relying on star players and several bench players. Starters' performance usually slows down, declines, and even loses points after playing 36 min on court. For example, James Harden, NBA scoring leader for the 2018–2019 season, had 78 game starts with 54 games of disappointing performance in the fourth period (NBA Advanced Stat 2020).

In competitive professional sports like NBA, athletes require lots of stamina and have enough endurance to stay on the court and injury-free. Team coaches consider players' stamina and on-court condition to make player adjustments. Coach substitution method highly based on individual player's condition.

A great team systematic rotation depends on coach decisions. Taking Golden States Warriors season 2017 as an example, coach Steve Kerr prefers 3 point contest shot and screen motion to playing high low motion, so he relies on 3 point shooter and athletic players. Thus center players may not play as much time as the point guard and shooting guard. This model also considers the best-fit substitution method to reduce the deviation of rotational system.

$$X(Player\ Usage\ Factor) = \frac{Individual\ attemptment}{Total\ attemptment}$$

$$S = \sum_{1}^{3} FGA*X$$

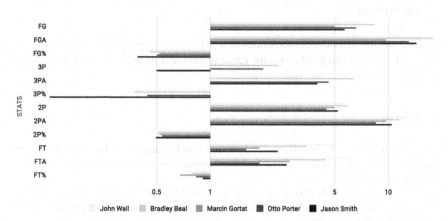

Fig. 5. Statistics of critical variables of Washington Wizards season 2018 starters

The model consists of offensive variables predicting scoring, as well as individual team player's on court efficiency and win share rate. It is usual to consider field goal (combination of two point and three point shots) attempt (FGA) and field goal percentage the most effective among all variables. The model also includes shooting ratio as the third important variable. Defensive statistics are excluded because they do not have direct effects on scoring. Again taking James Harden as an example, he scored 36.1 points in an average 37 min of playing time (NBA Advanced Stat 2020). Taking Washington Wizards' 2018 season as an example, Fig. 5 and 6 show statistics of critical variables and prediction of performance.

There are four strategies based on the interactive model: (Rotational versus Best fit) Substitution and (Star player versus Average) usage rate with scoring value X (The individual player's value of shooting percentage) and value S (The summation index of all scoring value). It is found that scoring performance of Best fit Substitution and star player usage rate strategy is highly predictable. Also scoring performance of Best fit Substitution is usually more precise than Rotational Substitution.

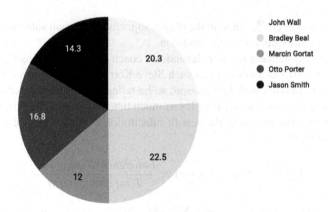

Fig. 6. Prediction of Washington Wizards season 2018 starters

3   Conclusion

The aforementioned model demonstrates how offensive rating components predict team scoring. The model can predict future game results and to analyze team management strategies.

References

Sampaio, J., McGarry, T., Calleja-Ganzalez, J., Saiz, S.J., del Alcazar, X.S., Balciunas, M.: Exploring game performance in the national basketball association using player tracking data. PLoS One **10**(7), e0132894 (2015)

Nibras, N.: Assessing NBA player similarity with Machine Learning (R) (2018). https://tow ardsdatascience.com/which-nba-players-are-most-similar-machine-learning-provides-the-ans wers-r-project-b903f9b2fe1f

NBA Advanced Stat: James Harden (2020). https://stats.nba.com/player/201935/

BigDataBall: NBA Datasets (2020). www.bigdataball.com/nba-datasets/

Human-Centered Artificial Intelligence: Antecedents of Trust for the Usage of Voice Biometrics for Driving Contactless Interactions

Rohan Kathuria[1], Ananay Wadehra[2], and Vinish Kathuria[3]([✉]) [iD]

[1] The Shriram School, Gurgaon, India
[2] Delhi Technological University, Delhi, India
[3] Indian Institute of Management, Lucknow, India
efpm07014@iiml.ac.in

Abstract. Covid-19 driven pandemic situation has brought greater visibility to contactless interactions with consumer IoT devices. As industries explore transitioning away from shared touch devices, the role of voice biometrics for authentication becomes critical. Voice biometrics is utilized for voice recognition through analysis of an individual's pitch, speech, voice, and tone and has been used in back-office operations for customer verification, fraud avoidance, and password reset. However, not much research has been done in the consumer sector and the critical role of trust in driving usage and the adoption of such services.

Using the existing research on trust in e-commerce and automation, we bring together models from psychology (Theory of Planned Behaviour) and technology (Human-Centered Artificial Intelligence), to explore the various antecedents of consumer trust for voice authentication (Ease of use, self-efficacy, perceived usefulness, reliability, the perceived reputation of the service provider, perceived security, perceived privacy, fraud, and social influence). Special attention is given to the use of vernacular voice, two-step authentication, and their impact on trust. Speaker recognition is a pattern recognition problem and incudes various technologies like frequency estimation, hidden Markov models, Gaussian mixture models, pattern matching algorithms, neural networks, decision trees, and linear predictive coding.

Through a combination of custom build prototypes, usage scenarios, and qualitative and quantitative analysis, we intend to highlight the components that drive trust for voice authentication so that it can help in the societal transition to contactless interactions. Early results show that people value Security, Privacy, and Reliability as top factors impacting trust in Voice Biometrics. Multi-level authentication, vernacular voice, and initial usage for transactional and low-value financial transactions can help drive trust in the voice biometrics ecosystem.

Keywords: Artificial intelligence · Human-machine interaction · Voice biometrics · Contactless · Covid-19

C. Stephanidis et al. (Eds.): HCII 2020, CCIS 1293, pp. 325–334, 2020.
https://doi.org/10.1007/978-3-030-60700-5_42

1 Introduction and Market Evidence

Covid-19 driven pandemic situation has brought greater visibility to contactless inter-actions with consumer IoT devices in retail, healthcare, hospitality, financial services, entertainment, and more (Choudhary 2020; Singh 2020). Coronavirus is making touch-free shopping a necessity (Rubin 2020) as contactless is considered the more hygienic and safe way of transacting. Marketers have started to explore the shift of marketing messages away from convenience toward safety and health (ABI Research 2020). Mastercard has reported a 40% jump in contactless payments as shoppers fear germs on cash and credit cards (Rooney 2020), and an additional 110 million contactless payment cards are expected to be issued in 2020 when compared to pre-COVID-19 forecast expectations (ABI Research 2020). COVID-19 has galvanized the authentication industry (Stokel-Walker 2020).

As industries explore contactless interactions, the role of voice biometrics for authentication becomes critical in shared touch devices, from simple elevator buttons & doorbells to point of sales & shared kiosks for ordering & payment, to personal voice assistants. Voice biometrics is utilized for voice recognition through analysis of an individual's pitch, speech, voice, and tone and is usually employed as a 'gatekeeper' to provide access to a secure system (Lancker and Kreiman 1984). It has been used in back-office operations for customer verification (Groenfeldt 2016), fraud avoidance, and password reset, and numerous patents have been issued on the topic. However, there is limited adoption in the consumer sector and limited research has been done in investigating the critical role of trust in driving usage and the adoption of such services. Voice authentication, like other biometric technologies, faces challenges in terms of customer acceptance (Turner et al. 2006). For example, the ability of bad actors to replicate a person's voice is an existing limitation that impacts trust (Ahaskar 2020) and hence it becomes imperative to look at the critical role trust plays in its adoption.

What is trust and why is understanding trust important for implementing voice authentication? Voice authentication shares characteristics with both speech systems and biometrics. Does that overlap impact people's trust? Do users trust voice biometrics at the same level as existing authentication mechanisms? Are there cultural, demographic, and use case differences that are worth investigating? To address the research questions presented here, we leverage existing research on trust in e-commerce and automation and bring together models from psychology (Theory of Planned Behaviour) and technology (Human-Centered Artificial Intelligence) to propose and test, an integrated model that highlights different antecedents of trust in voice authentication. Through a combination of custom build prototypes, usage scenarios, and qualitative and quantitative analysis, the researchers intend to highlight the components that drive trust for voice authentication. In this research, we present the initial findings from a qualitative study that demonstrates that while people believe in uniqueness of voice biometrics, similar to fingerprints, face or eyes, concerns with security and fraud may restrict the vast consumer adoption.

2   Literature Review

Voice Interaction and Biometrics. Voice interaction is the ability to speak to a device, have it process the request, and act upon whatever is being asked. People associate voice with communication with other people rather than with technology and hence voice interaction systems can significantly enhance the naturalness of human-machine interactions. Media Equation Theory (Nass et al. 1996) posits that computers are social actors and that social rules from traditional human-to-human interaction also apply to people's interaction with computer devices. Voice biometrics or Speaker recognition is the identification of a person from characteristics of voices like pitch, speech, voice, and tone (Poddar et al. 2018).

Technology. Voice interaction systems are dependent on speech recognition, an inter-disciplinary subfield of computational linguistics that develops methodologies and tech-nologies that enables the recognition and translation of spoken language into text by computers. Today, many aspects of speech recognition have been taken over by a deep learning method called Long short-term memory (LSTM), a recurrent neural network (Hochreiter and Schmidhuber 1997). Speaker recognition is a pattern recognition prob-lem and incudes various technologies like frequency estimation, hidden Markov models, Gaussian mixture models, pattern matching algorithms, neural networks, matrix repre-sentation, vector quantization, decision trees, and linear predictive coding (Gupta 2016). Voice recognition systems monitor the cadence and accent, as well as indicate the shape and size of the larynx, nasal passages, and vocal tract of a person, to help identify and authenticate the individual (Chinnaswamy 2018).

Trust. In general, trust is viewed as a three-dimensional construct, composed of com-petence, integrity, and benevolence (Gefen et al. 2003). Competence is the belief in the trustee's ability to perform as expected by the trustor. Integrity is the belief that the trustee will be honest and keep its promises. Benevolence is the belief that the trustee will not act opportunistically, even given the chance. In sum, a trust gives the trustor the confidence that the trustee will behave capably (ability), ethically (integrity), and fairly (benevolence) (Pavlou and Fygenson 2006). A review of trust in automated sys-tems concluded that understanding trust in automation is important because people are willing to use and rely on automation they trust and refuse to use automation they do not trust (Lee and See 2004). Just as trust mediates relationships between people, it may also mediate relationships between people and automation (Lee and See 2004).

People attribute intentionality and impute motivation to automation as it becomes increasingly sophisticated and takes on human characteristics, such as speech commu-nications (Lee and See 2004). Listeners' perceptions of speech systems are strongly influenced by qualities of the system's voice and language, or the 'persona' the system presents to users (Cohen et al. 2004) and these perceptions of voice characteristics are positively correlated with system trust.

Antecedents of Trust. Research shows that consumers exhibit variability in their per-ceptions of privacy, security, and trust, and hence variables of perceived privacy and per-ceived security are used for the study (Chellappa and Kvlou 2002). Preserving privacy using multi-factor authentication and principle of trust management has been demonstrated by Anakath et al. 2017. Researchers have investigated the role of consumer self-efficacy in customer's adoption of B2C services mediated by the trust (Dash and Saji 2008) and have also empirically derived four key dimensions of B2C transactions - information content, design, security, and privacy (Ranganathan and Ganapathy 2002). Research has shown that company reputation and willingness to customize products and services can significantly affect initial trust (Koufaris and Hampton-Sosa 2004). Researchers have identified four of our types of trust-inducing forces for mobile banking - institutional offering (structural assurances), cognition (perceived benefits), personality (personal propensity) and firm characteristics (firm reputation) (Kim et al. 2009). Lee and Turban (2001) demonstrated the role of four antecedent influences on consumer trust in Internet shopping, e-trustworthiness of the Internet merchant, the trustworthiness of the Internet as a shopping medium, infrastructural (contextual) factors (e.g., security, third-party certification), and other factors (e.g., company size, demographic variables). Research on biometrics has shown that customer acceptance is based on factors unique to biometrics. False Rejection Rate and Failure-to- Enroll rates are related to perceived system reliability. Major concerns points are around reliability, social acceptance, perceived intrusiveness, social-impact, and data privacy (Turner et al. 2006). The antecedent variables are moderated by the individual consumer's degree of trust propensity, which reflects personality traits, culture, and experience (Lee and Turban 2001).

Theory of Planned Behaviour. Human behaviour is guided by three kinds of consideration: behavioural beliefs, normative beliefs, and control beliefs (Ajzen 2002). Behavioural beliefs produce a favourable or unfavourable attitude toward the behaviour, normative beliefs result in a subjective norm, and control beliefs give rise to perceived behavioural control. In combination, these lead to the formation of a behavioural intention (Ajzen 2002). The concept of social influence has been assessed by the social norm and normative belief on whether they are expected by their friends, family, and the society to perform the recommended behaviour. While most models are conceptualized within individual cognitive space, the theory of planned behaviour considers social influence based on collectivistic culture-related variables (Ajzen 2002). Research Objectives and Conceptual Framework

Human-Centered Artificial Intelligence Well-designed technologies that offer high levels of human control and high levels of computer automation can increase human performance, leading to wider adoption. At the heart of human-centered AI is the desideratum - AI systems need to be able to understand humans; AI systems need to help humans understand them; and Computational creativity (Riedl 2017). The Human-Centered Artificial Intelligence (HCAI) framework clarifies how to (a) design for high levels of human control and high levels of computer automation to increase human performance, (b) understand the situations in which full human control or full computer control are necessary, and (c) avoid the dangers of excessive human control or excessive computer control (Shneiderman 2020). The methods of HCAI are more likely to produce designs that are Reliable, Safe & Trustworthy (RST). The fundamental shift is from traditional one-dimensional thinking that designers had to choose a point on the one-dimensional line from human control to computer automation (Sheridan and Verplank 1978), to the decoupling of these concepts leads to a two-dimensional HCAI framework, which suggests that achieving high levels of human control and high levels of computer automation is possible (Shneiderman 2020), as shown in Fig. 1. The lower left quadrant is the home of simple devices such as clocks, music boxes, or mousetraps; the lower right quadrant is home of computer autonomy requiring rapid action, for example, airbag deployment, anti-lock brakes, pacemakers, implantable defibrillators, or defensive weapons systems. The upper left quadrant, with high human control and low automation, is the home of human autonomy where human mastery is desired to enable competence building, free exploration, and creativity in activities such as bicycle riding, piano playing, baking, or playing with children. The upper right quadrant, with High Human Control and High Automation, can produce solutions that are Reliable, Safe & Trustworthy (RST). The HCAI framework is based on the belief that people are different from computers. Therefore, designs that take advantage of unique computer features including sophisticated algorithms, voluminous databases, advanced sensors, information abundant displays, and powerful effectors are more likely to increase performance.

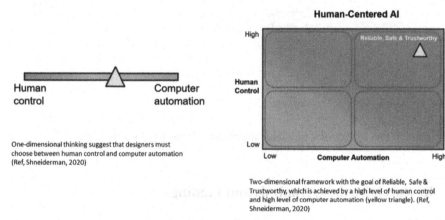

Fig. 1. Human centered artificial intelligent framework as compared to traditional human computer interaction framework (Ref. Shneiderman 2020)

3 Research Objectives and Proposed Model

The underlying objective of the research is to investigate what would it take an average user to get comfortable with the AI-driven voice biometric system and accordingly, our research objectives are RQ1: What are the key drivers for people's trust in Biometrics solutions and Voice Biometrics in particular? RQ2: Does people's evaluation of trust change based on the type of usage scenario? RQ3: Is it possible to do a segmentation of population-based on their trust level of Voice Authentication? Are there demographic and/or psychographic segments that are more inclined than others? RQ4: Does the use of a multi-level authentication process impact trust? Is there a difference (wrt trust) between a hybrid (text + voice) usage and a pure voice scenario? RQ 5: Does the role of Vernacular voice impact people's trust in Voice Biometrics?

Based on academic research, we propose a model with four main antecedent influences on consumer trust in Voice Authentication: Perceived Quality of the solution, Perceived Competency of the solution provider, Perceived Security, and Social Influence. Our model consists of nine constructs: Ease of use, self-efficacy, perceived usefulness, reliability, the perceived reputation of the service provider, perceived security, perceived privacy, fraud, and social influence, as shown in Fig. 2.

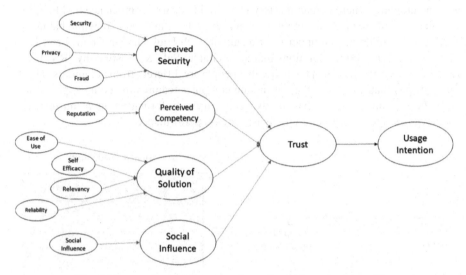

Fig. 2. Proposed model for antecedents of trust for voice biometrics

4   Research Method, Analysis and Findings

Research in the current study is qualitative and exploratory in nature. Online focus groups that included a moderator and a group of participants discussing concepts of interest (Miller 2005), were used for the survey of 15 people. A demonstration of speaker authentication was given using solution from Voice IT (a company specializing in voice biometrics) and inhouse developed voice authentication solution. Eight different scenarios were shared with the respondents corresponding to the four categories of use cases, as shown in Table 1. A discussion guide was prepared to get relevant information and the conversation was moderated for each to gather responses. The respondents were also asked to fill a small survey post focus group. The aim at this stage was to find where the user draws a subconscious line perceiving the system as a Reliable, Secure and Trusted system, as per the HCAI framework. Each use case and discussion brought more clarity to the answer being sought.

The overall analysis indicates that participants believe that just like face ID and fingerprint, voice biometrics is unique to their identity and thus can be trusted. However, the level of trust varies and is currently a fraud and security threat as others could record their voice as well. The inclusion of multi-factor authentication and vernacular voice

Table 1. Results of different use cases and respondents' comfort with RST

Category of Use Cases	Use Cases	Personal / Shared	Voice / Speaker Recognition	Critical – Expectation of Confidentiality	Reliable	Safe	Trustworthy
Transactional	Elevator	Shared	Voice	Low	Yes	No	Yes
	Online Tests	Personal	Speaker	Medium	Yes	Yes	Yes
	Phone ON / App access	Personal	Speaker	Medium	Yes	Yes	No
Financial, Low Criticality	Online Ordering (low amount, repeat purchase)	Personal	Speaker	Medium	Yes	Yes	Yes
Financial, High Criticality	Online Ordering (high amount)	Personal	Speaker	High	No	No	No
	Kiosk Usage (ATM, Banking Transaction)	Shared	Speaker	High	Yes	No	No
Vernacular Voice and 2 Factor Authentication	Online Ordering (high amount)	Personal	Speaker	High	Yes	No	Yes
	Kiosk Usage (ATM, Banking Transaction)	Shared	Speaker	High	Yes	Yes	Yes

seems to indicate an increase in trust, while concerns with reliability remain. There were various assumptions and preconceived notions that were held by the focus group and act as a guide for deeper research. Some of them included - (a) the difference in trust between solutions being used indoor and outdoor, (b) the voice authentication technology being used was perceived to be an 'expensive technology', (c) the accuracy of the system was inherently less than a fingerprint and other biometrics, (d) the system would be far less reliable when the authentication was done through a 'voice call' than by a 'professional microphone' present locally (e.g. a phone or personal assistant) in the immediate vicinity.

Using the HCAI framework as a guide, we analysed the results of the focus group to understand the gaps in reliability, safety, and trustworthiness in each of the use cases and to explore the probable modification of our assumed model. Some participants have home automation and home assistant devices, activated by voice. Their comfort for voice authentication appeared to be higher than others, who do not have a home voice-activated device. However, the reliability experience varied with current users of the voice assistant. Deeper conversations also brought out the presumed role of "home comfort" in differentiating between 'at home' and 'away from home' use cases and the decrease in fraud perception between the two locations.

For use cases associated with ordering and payments, the transaction size seems to have an impact on trust. A higher level of comfort was demonstrated for lower ticket size, repeat orders (like a subscription service) than for a pure shopping experience with a relatively expensive item. The role of trust and safety is critical for financial transactions and was evident from the conversations. Users preferred ATM over phone banking (assuming ATM was in a safe location), however for both the inclusion of multiple biometrics solutions (voice biometrics in conjunctions with another biometric) increased the level of trust in the solution. A couple of statements bring out the essence of the analysis – "Even e-banking solutions are not entirely reliable" and "2-factor authentication makes us feel safer". The vernacular voice was preferred, but there were concerns around loss of accuracy (aka decrease in reliability).

5 Discussions and Future Implications

Through a combination of custom build prototypes, usage scenarios, and qualitative and quantitative analysis, the researchers intend to highlight the components that drive trust for voice authentication so that it can help in the societal transition to contactless interactions. Early results show that people value Security, Privacy, and Reliability as top factors impacting trust in Voice Biometrics. This has significant managerial implications since it indicates a need for a cohesive category level strategy across different companies to develop and demonstrate a secure solution that people trust (maybe similar to https and encryption in online transactions). The order of preference Transactional > Low critical Financial > High critical Financial also shows that industry should make the effort to educate and get people comfortable with the voice technologies on an everyday basis before asking them to use it for critical solutions. Multi-level authentication, vernacular voice, and initial usage for transactional and low-value financial transactions combined with an industry level education and technology advancement initiatives can help drive trust in the voice biometrics ecosystem. Numerous studies have looked at technology adoption curves and the same could be a value add in this scenario as well. The use of vernacular voice and multiple-factor authentication was well received and their role in developing and enhancing consumer trust should be explored further.

The researchers plan to augment research through an empirical, quantitative analysis covering respondents across multiple geographical regions. Structural Equation Modelling techniques would be used to evaluate the validity of the model and the impact of different antecedents on research. The multi-group analysis would be used to look at the impact of different moderators (Age, Gender, Culture, Home vs Away, Financial Transaction sizes, Attitude towards Biometrics, etc.). The inhouse technical solution would also be modified to include vernacular and multi-factor authentication scenarios.

References

ABI Research: COVID-19 Will Drive Global Contactless Payment Card Issuance Above the 2 Billion Mark in 2020. ABIResearch, 13 May 2020 (2020). https://www.abiresearch.com/press/covid-19-will-drive-global-contactless-payment-card-issuance-above-2-billion-mark-2020

Ahaskar, A.: Voice biometrics are cleverer now, but still need more work. Live Mint, 6 February 2020 (2020). https://www.livemint.com/technology/tech-news/voice-biometrics-are-cleverer-now-but-still-need-more-work-11581011267941

Ajzen, I.: Perceived behavioral control, self-efficacy, locus of control, and the theory of planned behavior. J. Appl. Soc. Psychol. **32**(4), 665–683 (2002)

Anakath, A .S., Rajakumar, S., Ambika, S.: Privacy preserving multi factor authentication using trust management. Clust. Comput. **22**(5), 10817–10823 (2017). https://doi.org/10.1007/s10586-017-1181-0

Chellappa, R.K., Pavlou, P.A.: Perceived information security, financial liability and consumer trust in electronic commerce transactions. Logist. Inf. Manag. **15**(5/6), 358–368 (2002)

Chinnaswamy, S.: The Future is calling: using voice recognition for authentication. Tata Consulting Services, 17 September 2018 (2018). https://www.tcs.com/blogs/using-voice-recognition-for-authentication

Choudhary, P.K.: Using artificial intelligence to tackle epidemics: the COVID-19 model. Healthwire, 9 May 2020 (2020). https://healthwire.co/using-artificial-intelligence-to-tackle-epidem ics-the-covid-19-model/

Cohen, M.H., Giangola, J.P., Balogh, J.: Voice User Interface Design. Addison Wesley, New York (2004)

Dash, S., Saji, K.B.: The role of consumer self-efficacy and website social-presence in customers' adoption of B2C online shopping. J. Int. Consum. Mark. **20**(2), 33–48 (2008)

Gefen, D., Karahanna, E., Straub, D.: Trust and TAM in online shopping: an integrated model. MIS Q. **27**, 51–90 (2003)

Gefen, D., Straub, D.: The relative importance of perceived ease-of-use in is adoption: a study of e-commerce adoption. J. AIS **1**(8), 1–30 (2000)

Groenfeldt, T.: Citi Uses Voice Prints to Authenticate Customers Quickly and effortlessly. Forbes, June, 2016

Gupta, S.: Application of MFCC in text independent speaker recognition. Int. J. Adv. Res. Comput. Sci. Softw. Eng. **6**(5), 805–810 (2016). (806)

Hochreiter, S., Schmidhuber, J.: Long short-term memory. Neural Comput. **9**(8), 1735–1780 (1997)

Koufaris, M., Hampton-Sosa, W.: The development of initial trust in an online company by new customers. Inf. Manag. **41**(3), 377–397 (2004)

Kim, G., Shin, B., Lee, H.G.: Understanding dynamics between initial trust and usage intentions of mobile banking. Inf. Syst. J. **19**, 283–311 (2009)

Van Lancker, D., Kreiman, J.: Familiar voice recognition: patterns and parameters. Part I: recognition of backward voices. J. Phonet. **13**, 19–38 (1984)

Lee, M.K.O., Turban, E.: A trust model for consumer internet shopping. Int. J. Electron. Commer. **6**(1), 75–91 (2001)

Lee, J.D., See, K.A.: Trust in automation: designing for appropriate reliance. Hum. Factors **46**, 50–80 (2004)

Miller, L.: Case study of customer input for a successful product. In: ADC 2005 Proceedings of the Agile Development Conference, pp. 225–234 (2005)

Nass, C., Fogg, B., Moon, Y.: Can computers be teammates? Int. J. Hum Comput Stud. **45**, 669–678 (1996)

Pavlou, P., Fygenson, M.: Understanding and predicting electronic commerce adoption: an extension of the theory of planned behavior. MIS Q. **30**, 115–143 (2006)

Poddar, A., Sahidullah, M., Saha, G.: Speaker verification with short utterances: a review of challenges, trends and opportunities. IET Biometr. **7**(2), 91–101 (2018)

Ranganathan, C., Ganapathy, S.: Key dimensions of business-to-consumer web sites. Inf. Manag. **39**(6), 457–465 (2002)

Riedl, M.: Human-centered artificial intelligence. Medium.com, 21 July 2017 (2017). https://med ium.com/@mark_riedl/human-centered-artificial-intelligence-70b019f956d1

Rooney, K: Contactless payments jump 40% as shoppers fear germs on cash and credit cards, MASTERCARD says. CNBC, 29 April 2020 (2020)

Rubin, B.F.: Coronavirus is making touch-free shopping a necessity. CNet, 15 April 2020 (2020). https://www.cnet.com/personal-finance/coronavirus-is-making-touch-free-sho pping-a-necessity/

Sheridan, T.B., Verplank, W.L.: Human and computer control of undersea teleoperators. Massachusetts Institute of Technology, Cambridge, Man-Machine Systems Lab (1978)

Singh, A.: Contactless, tech-driven shopping to drive India's retail segment post COVID-19. The Week, 6 May 2020 (2020). https://www.theweek.in/news/biz-tech/2020/05/06/contactless-tech-driven-shopping-to-drive-indias-retail-segment-post-covid-19

Shneiderman, B.: Human-centered artificial intelligence: reliable, safe & trustworthy. Int. J. Hum.-Comput. Interact. **36**, 6 (2020)

Stokel-Walker: How COVID-19 galvanised the authentication industry. Raconteur, 5 May 2020 (2020). https://www.raconteur.net/technology/authentication-methods-coronavirus

Turner, C., Safar, J., Ramaswamy, K.: The Effects of use on Acceptance and Trust in Voice Authentication Technology. In: Proceedings of the human factors and ergonomics society annual meeting, vol. 50, pp. 718–722 (2006)

An HCI Approach to Extractive Text Summarization: Selecting Key Sentences Based on User Copy Operations

Ilan Kirsh[1]($\boxtimes$)(iD) and Mike Joy[2](iD)

[1] The Academic College of Tel Aviv-Yaffo, Tel Aviv, Israel
kirsh@mta.ac.il
[2] University of Warwick, Coventry, UK
M.S.Joy@warwick.ac.uk

Abstract. Automatic text summarization is a very complex problem. Despite being intensively researched, automatic summaries are still considered to be of lower quality than manual summaries. This paper introduces a novel HCI approach to web page summarization. The proposed Crowd-Copy Summarizer follows the extractive text summarization approach of summarizing by selecting sentences within the text. The selection is performed by examining how frequently users copy certain sentences to their clipboards, for their own purposes. The most frequently copied sentences are included in the summary. Results from an early experiment are promising, as key sentences, such as introductory sentences, definitions, and important highlights, are copied frequently. Consequently, the generated summaries can provide good coverage of the main topics. This novel text summarization approach combines the best of both worlds: summarization based on collective human wisdom, without the expensive burden of manual summarization work.

Keywords: Automatic extractive text summarization · Clipboard · Copy and paste · Website · Web page · Document · Text · Crowd wisdom

1 Introduction

The need for automatic text summarization becomes increasingly apparent as the amount of textual information available grows. Despite decades of extensive research, the quality of automatic summaries is still inadequate [8].

There are two main approaches to automatic text summarization: the extractive approach and the abstractive approach [2,7,8]. Extractive methods select key sentences from the text and compose a summary from these selected sentences, without changing them. Abstractive methods use Natural Language Processing (NLP) techniques to analyze the text and build a summary that may also contain synthetically generated sentences. Since abstractive summarization

© Springer Nature Switzerland AG 2020
C. Stephanidis et al. (Eds.): HCII 2020, CCIS 1293, pp. 335–341, 2020.
https://doi.org/10.1007/978-3-030-60700-5_43

is very complex, abstractive summarization methods often rely on elements of extractive summarization [1].

Extractive methods usually calculate a score for every sentence and then select the sentences with the highest scores and include them in the summary. Scores assigned to sentences are often based on scores given to individual words, as the importance of a sentence may be related to the importance of the words that it contains. Many different scoring methods have been studied [9]. The evaluation process usually combines information from the document (e.g. the frequency of a word in the document, where a higher frequency implies higher importance), with external knowledge (e.g. the frequency of a word in general, where a higher frequency implies lower importance) [7].

This paper introduces a new, "crowd wisdom" approach to text summarization of web pages. It follows the extractive approach (forming a summary by selecting important sentences within the text), only instead of selecting sentences using conventional methods, the new approach uses a novel source of information: copy operations of web users on web pages (for their own purposes). The most frequently copied sentences are included in the summary. To the best of our knowledge, this approach has never been studied before.

This paper is organized as follows. Section 2 describes the Crowd-Copy Summarizer implementation. Section 3 demonstrates the summarization of a sample web page. Section 4 analyzes the results. Section 5 concludes this paper.

2   Implementation

Figure 1 shows the architecture of the Crowd-Copy Summarizer. A reference to a *Copy Script* is embedded in all the web pages. As a result, every request for a page of the website returns a revised version of the page that triggers an additional request to load the *Copy Script* from the *Summarizer Server*. The script tracks JavaScript clipboard copy events and reports them back to the *Collector* component in the *Summarizer Server*. The *Collector* stores the data anonymized in a dedicated database, adhering to industry standards of data anonymization and user privacy preservation. The *Summarizer* uses the copy operations data and the original web page to produce the summary.

Users copy strings of various types to the clipboard [4,5], including, for example, words or sequences of words to look up or translate elsewhere [3,6] and code fragments from code examples (copied by programmers to paste in their IDEs) [5,6]. Therefore, the Summarizer ignores copy operations of the following types of content:

- content in a PRE HTML element, which usually contains code, and so is irrelevant in text summarization;
- content consisting of less than 8 words, which could be copied with the intention of searching for more information on the internet;
- content with more than 40 words, since including complete or large parts of paragraphs in summaries is likely to add noise.

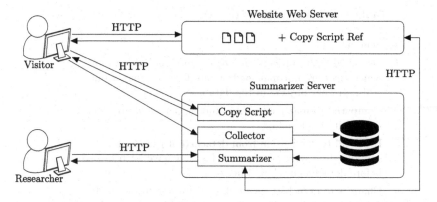

Fig. 1. High-level architecture of the crowd-copy summarizer

The 8–40 words range was found to be reasonable through experimentation, but it is not necessarily optimal. The Summarizer breaks the text in every accepted copy operation into its constituent sentences and assigns one point to each complete sentence (partial sentences are ignored). The resulting summary is simply generated by joining all the sentences that exceed a minimum score threshold, ordered by their position in the original text.

3   Sample Summary

The Crowd-Copy Summarizer was tested on technical documentation web pages of the ObjectDB website[1]. This website contains learning materials on the Java Persistence API (JPA), the standard API for accessing databases from Java in an object-oriented way. Copy operations performed by visitors have been recorded for a period of three months, ending in March 2020.

Table 1 presents the text summarization of a sample page, which was viewed 3,847 times during that period. 312 copy operations have been recorded in total. 68 copy operations (consisting of 74 sentence occurrences) remained after applying the filtering process (as described in Sect. 2). All the sentences with a score of 3 or above, ordered by their position in the page, are included in Table 1.

To provide a brief context, JPA refers to an ordinary object that represents data in the database as 'managed', and this sample web page introduces a different type of object, 'detached'.

Different summaries of various lengths can be generated from the results in Table 1 by setting different minimum score thresholds. For example, setting the threshold to any value between 9 and 16 will generate a very short summary, consisting of a single sentence. This is the most important sentence, which defines the term detached, so it is probably the best possible one-sentence summary. This is the first indication that there is a positive correlation between the frequency of a sentence being copied and its importance.

---

[1] https://www.objectdb.com.

Table 1. Summarization of the "Detached Entity Objects" Page

#	Sentence	Score
1	Detached entity objects are objects in a special state in which they are not managed by any EntityManager but still represent objects in the database	16
2	Compared to managed entity objects, detached objects are limited in functionality	7
3	Retrieval by navigation from detached objects is not supported, so only persistent fields that have been loaded before detachment should be used	3
4	Changes to detached entity objects are not stored in the database unless modified detached objects are merged back into an EntityManager to become managed again	8
5	Detached objects are useful in situations in which an EntityManager is not available and for transferring objects between different EntityManager instances	4
6	When a managed entity object is serialized and then deserialized, the deserialized entity object (but not the original serialized object) is constructed as a detached entity object since is not associated with any EntityManager	5
7	Marking a reference field with CascadeType.DETACH (or CascadeType.ALL, which includes DETACH) indicates that detach operations should be cascaded automatically to entity objects that are referenced by that field (multiple entity objects can be referenced by a collection field)	5
8	Detached objects can be attached to any EntityManager by using the merge method	6
9	Marking a reference field with CascadeType.MERGE (or CascadeType.ALL, which includes MERGE) indicates that merge operations should be cascaded automatically to entity objects that are referenced by that field (multiple entity objects can be referenced by a collection field)	3

Page: https://www.objectdb.com/java/jpa/persistence/detach
Sentences are ordered by their appearance order in the page.

4   Analysis

We can expect a good summary to cover the most important information in the text, to eliminate redundancy, and to be readable. This section uses these three criteria in analyzing the summary that is produced from Table 1 by applying a score threshold of 3 (i.e. the summary that includes all the sentences in Table 1). Most of the arguments in this discussion are applicable also to other thresholds (which produce shorter summaries).

4.1 Covering Important Information

The coverage of a summary can be assessed by examining if it answers the most important questions about the topic. In the context of a technical web page, the key questions about a new concept may be: What is it? When should we use it? How does it work? What are the differences between this new concept and other familiar concepts? We can see that most of the selected sentences in Table 1 answer these key questions:

- What are detached objects? Sentence #1 is the definition.
- How are they different from ordinary objects? Answered by #3 and #4.
- When are detached objects needed? Answered by #5.
- How do objects become detached? Answered by #6 and #7.
- How do objects stop being detached? Answered by #8 and #9.

These indeed seem to be the key questions. It seems that one important sentence is missing in Table 1: another part of the answer to the basic question of "How do objects become detached?" (by using the detach method). This sentence has not been selected as it was only copied once.

It is interesting to analyze the distribution of the copied sentences on the web page. This sample web page contains a preface and 5 sections. The 9 sentences in Table 1 are distributed as follows: 5 in the preface and one in each of sections 1, 2, 4, and 5. Section 3 (Bulk Detach) seems to be perceived as less important by the website users.

4.2 Avoiding Redundancy

The examined web page contains 6 headers, 26 sentences (9 of which are shown in Table 1), and 4 code boxes containing code fragments.

Examining sentences that were not copied by users (or rarely copied) shows that they discuss low-level details. For example, many sentences explain which exceptions are thrown when things go wrong, and these sentences are rarely copied by users. The general impression (to be verified in further work) is that sentences copied more frequently are indeed more important, and therefore, including them in the summary is justified.

One counter-example is sentence #2 in Table 1 that does not provide much value on its own. In fact, 6 out of the 7 copies that it scored were due to copy operations of both sentences #1 and #2 (which are adjacent in the text) combined. Counting only the first sentence in each copy operation may produce better summaries. In the summarization of this web page, it would only affect sentence #2: reducing its score from 7 to 1, removing it from Table 1, and eliminating it from any derived summary.

4.3 Preserving Readability

The resulting summary is quite readable (and so are other summaries produced from Table 1 using other thresholds). It seems that users tend to copy standalone sentences more frequently than sentences that depend on other sentences or code fragments (e.g.. sentences that explain code). As a result, these self-contained sentences can be combined into a summary that does not feel fragmented.

5 Conclusions

This paper presents a new approach to extractive text summarization: composing a summary from sentences that are frequently copied by users.

Users copy to the clipboard strings of various types and for different purposes. Words and phrases are often copied to the clipboard in order to look them up on the internet. It is quite unlikely that complete sentences are copied for this purpose, as long strings are not effective in search. Full sentences may be copied in order to use them in summaries or as citations in documentations, presentations, blogs, websites, answers on forums (such as StackOverflow), or even in private communications between colleagues who work on a project together. Key sentences are probably copied more frequently, and therefore, the frequency of copying a sentence can be used in extractive text summarization as an indicator of its importance.

An initial analysis of the results is promising. Key sentences, such as introductory sentences, definitions, and important highlights, are copied more frequently. Consequently, summaries produced using this approach could provide good coverage of the main topics presented in web pages. Further work should include a full evaluation of this approach, including a comparison against conventional text summarization methods.

References

1. Allahyari, M., et al.: Text summarization techniques: a brief survey. Int. J. Adv. Comput. Sci. Appl. **8**(10) (2017). https://doi.org/10.14569/IJACSA.2017.081052
2. Kiani, F., Tas, O.: A survey on automatic text summarization. Press Start **5**, 205–213 (2017). https://doi.org/10.17261/Pressacademia.2017.591. http://pressacademia.org/archives/pap/v5/29.pdf
3. Kirsh, I.: Automatic complex word identification using implicit feedback fromuser copy operations. In: Proceedings of the 21st International Conference on Web Information Systems Engineering (WISE 2020). Lecture Notes in Computer Science. Springer, Cham (2020). https://doi.org/10.1007/978-3-030-62008-0_11
4. Kirsh, I.: What web users copy to the clipboard on a website: a case study. In: Proceedings of the 16th International Conference on Web Information Systems and Technologies (WEBIST 2020). INSTICC, SciTePress, Setúbal, Portugal (2020, forthcoming)
5. Kirsh, I., Joy, M.: A different web analytics perspective through copy to clipboard heatmaps. In: Bielikova, M., Mikkonen, T., Pautasso, C. (eds.) ICWE 2020. LNCS, vol. 12128, pp. 543–546. Springer, Cham (2020). https://doi.org/10.1007/978-3-030-50578-3_41

6. Kirsh, I., Joy, M.: Splitting the web analytics atom: from page metrics and KPIs to sub-page metrics and KPIs. In: Proceedings of the 10th International Conference on Web Intelligence, Mining and Semantics (WIMS 2020), Biarritz, France, pp. 33–43. Association for Computing Machinery, New York, June 2020. https://doi.org/10.1145/3405962.3405984

7. Rajasekaran, A., Varalakshmi, R.: Review on automatic text summarization. Int. J. Eng. Technol. (UAE) **7**, 456–460 (2018). https://doi.org/10.14419/ijet.v7i2.33.14210

8. Saggion, H., Poibeau, T.: Automatic text summarization: past, present and future. In: Poibeau, T., Saggion, H., Piskorski, J., Yangarber, R. (eds.) Multi-Source, Multilingual Information Extraction and Summarization. Theory and Applications of Natural Language Processing, pp. 3–13. Springer, Heidelberg (2013). https://doi.org/10.1007/978-3-642-28569-1_1

9. Sajjan, R., Shinde, M.: A detail survey on automatic text summarization. Int. J. Comput. Sci. Eng. **7**, 991–998 (2019). https://doi.org/10.26438/ijcse/v7i6.991998

Infrequent Use of AI-Enabled Personal Assistants Through the Lens of Cognitive Dissonance Theory

Nicole O'Brien[1] and Maarif Sohail[2(✉)]

[1] Sawyer Business School, Suffolk University, Boston, MA 02108, USA
nobrien@suffolk.edu
[2] DeGroote School of Business, McMaster University, Hamilton, ON L8S4L8, Canada
sohaim9@mcmaster.ca

Abstract. The current availability of several versatile and powerful Artificial Intelligence-Enabled Personal Assistants (AIEPA) along with the unique phenomena of far less usage of these devices serve as the primary reason for motivation for the development and contribution of this research. This research explores the infrequent usage of commonly available commercial Artificial Intelligence Enabled Personal Assistants (AIEPA) like Alexa and Google Assistant with the help of Cognitive Dissonance (CD) theory. We propose a model that helps to investigate the phenomenon of infrequent usage. We also share our view that the theory of cognitive dissonance can be a way forward to study the usage behavior of the end-users, which can improve the performance of these devices as well as reduce concerns that act as barriers in adoption, acceptance, and usage.

Keywords: Infrequent usage · Artificial intelligence personal assistants · Cognitive dissonance

1 Introduction

We live in an era of change and disruptions, where vicissitudes surface intrinsically as well as extrinsically. These changes bring complexities to an individual's life and warrant assistance from smart or artificial intelligent (AI) technology. AI makes use of advanced information technology (IT) capabilities, including computer vision (CV), speech recognition (SR), and natural language processing (NLP), (Anthes 2017). We identify the commercially available smart assistants as Artificial Intelligence enabled Personal Assistants (AIEPAs) as they make good use of characteristics of advanced information technologies, namely CV, SR, and NLP. Common voice-based AIEPAs available in the consumer market include Alexa, Siri, Cortona, Bixby from Amazon, Apple, Microsoft, and Samsung, respectively; Besides, there are smart assistants like Amazon Echo, Samsung S-Voice, IBM's Watson, so on and so forth. AIEPAs are not only innovative but also representative of one of the more common forms of Human-Computer Interaction (HCI) and help businesses in a socio-cultural environment (Business Dictionary 2020).

© Springer Nature Switzerland AG 2020
C. Stephanidis et al. (Eds.): HCII 2020, CCIS 1293, pp. 342–350, 2020.
https://doi.org/10.1007/978-3-030-60700-5_44

Researchers have studied popular AIEPAs like Siri, Alexa, Cortana, and Google Assistant to compare and contrasts their speech-based natural user interactions (Lopez et al. 2017). In the future, AIEPAs will make use of Automatic Speech Recognition (ASR) and Natural Language Understanding (NLU) abilities to simulate human to human communication (Knote et al. 2019). We are cognizant of the fact that AIEPAs have many things in common with Intelligent Personal Assistants (IPAs). Research literature recognizes AIEPAs as digital assistants, personal assistants, smart assistants, universal assistants or virtual assistants, for the sake of clarity, when we use the researchers selected term, we are referring to AIEPAs. AIEPAs, also known as Intelligent Personal Assistants (IPAs), have been around for a while in different forms, including Voice-Activated Smart Phone Assistants (VASPA). VASPAs, with their hands-free operations, will be of special benefit to individuals, businesses, and society in situations like covid19 (Sohail 2020).

Ironically there is no formal definition for AIEPAs. One of the earliest definitions focuses on the function, "an application that makes use of the user's voice as an input. Furthermore, contextual information to provide assistance by answering questions in natural language, providing endorsements and executing tasks" (Baber 1993). Subsequent definitions emphasize human interaction with computer systems more human-like, using natural language to accomplish their schedules, complete an assortment of tasks and services (Van Biljon and Kotze 2007), gathering information, automating complex tasks and cooperating with other IPAs (Czibula et al. 2009). AIEPAs (IPAs) are mobile, autonomous, and software agents capable of performing tasks or services on behalf of humans (Garrido et al. 2010). AIEPAs require a powerful computing infrastructure and the internet. Thus AIEPAs are often considered with the ubiquitous computing environment, as explained by Satyanarayanan (2001) and the internet of things (IoT) perspective (Jara et al. 2013). Thus AIEPAs can, with the help of IoT, can carry out different tasks and communicate with other devices on the internet. Thus the end-users using these different devices form a virtual community. The computing devices of today, besides human input, can learn on their own (LeCun et al. 2015). At the same time, there is a tendency among the end-users to avoid these AI-enabled technology devices (Yang et al. 2017; Yu et al. 2013). AIEPAs make use of artificial intelligence (AI), machine learning (ML), natural language processing (NLP), and various actuation mechanisms to sense and influence the environment (Knote et al. 2018). AIEPAs help humans by substituting human efforts, enhance human abilities, or work as an AI plus human hybrid system (Rai et al. 2019). AIEPAs are usually voice-activated (White 2018).

All these definitions lead to our understanding of how social interaction between the end-user and the AI device takes place. The AI technologies have enabled humans to maintain a closer and personal interaction with the computing systems of today, in reality, the very essence of the HCI-AI paradigm in days to come.

HCI within the realm of AI is often explained with the help of similarity–attraction hypothesis, which undertakes that humans like to interact with other humans of similar personality (Byrne and Griffitt 1969), we can extend this to the personalization of AIEPAs. This is, however, challenged by another theory, the Uncanny Valley effect (Mori 1970), especially when the AIEPAs are given humanness or anthropomorphic characteristics (Wagner and Schramm-Klein 2019). The uncanny effects tend to influence the user behaviour towards AIEPAs, often leading to individuals preferring to use the AIEPAs infrequently or discontinue the usage (Braun and Alt 2020). Voice-activated digital assistants (Amazon Alexa, Google Assistant, Apple Siri) are rapidly rising in popularity and provide users with a novel way to interface with technology (Koon et al. 2020). Conversational user experience (UX) makes the switch to a human form of communication as if a human is having a normal conversation with another person (Bors et al. 2020).

The improvements in technology, as well as changes in age, income levels, and status, prompt a change in taste for the same individual. A change in taste can lead to a change in usage patterns along with adoption, acceptance, or rejection of various new innovative technologies. Also, since AIEPAs use the internet, the AIEPA users become a part of a virtual community comprising of AIEPA users. These changes influence the Human-Computer Interaction in profound ways. The changes in human behavior can result in the same person liking or disliking a product or a service after using it for a finite period of time. In other words, a decline in the frequency of use can be observed with users being identified as frequent users or infrequent users.

Even though AIEPA devices are available in different forms and at different prices, it is a common fact that these devices have an infrequent usage. The logical reasons for infrequent usage include demographic factors, the difference in user expectation about AIEPA performance and the actual AIEPA performance, user privacy violations and security issues related to hackers, as well as lack of trust on AI which leads to a feeling of unpleasantness and display of avoidance behaviour by some individuals for these devices. We posit that AIEPAs use the internet. Thus the AIEPA users become a part of a virtual community comprising of AIEPA users. We are interested in exploring whether being a part of a virtual community increases the use of AIEPA or not. Thus our central research question (CRQ) is

CRQ: Does Cognitive Dissonance, along with technology overload and dehumanization, prevents an AIEPA end-user in becoming a member of the virtual community?

We wish to explore the distinction between frequent and infrequent users, from the Cognitive Dissonance theory, whether the end-user carries similarity-attraction towards AIEPA leading to frequent use or the uncanny effect leading to infrequent use of AIEAP. This strategy is in line with the research perspective that "Cognitive Dissonance" is observed or present, where our beliefs, behaviors, and attitudes conflict.

The remainder of the research article is structured into different sections. The next section captures the Literature Review. Succeeding the Literature Review section is the part that presents theoretical foundations. The penultimate section provides Methodology. The final section offers conclusions.

2   Literature Review

We use the Webster and Watson (2002) guidelines for our Literature Review to tease out factors of interest that help us address our research question. The body of knowledge presents the fact that researchers within the context of AIEPA make use of Technology adoption model (Davis, 1986, 1989) and its sophisticated extensions and subsequent critiques (Davis and Venkatesh 1996) along with Theory of Reasoned Action (Ajzen and Fishbein 1975) and Theory of Planned Behaviour (Azjen 1985, 1991). There is no evidence that researchers have used CDT to study AIEPAs.

The literature on the context of the application of AIEPA usage has been studied in varied contexts like device being used for improving the social bonds of elders (Reis et al. 2017), for understanding and measuring the user experience of these AI devices (Kocaballi et al. 2019). Some researchers have studied how product characteristics can influence the behaviour of the end-user (Kepuska and Bohouta 2018) while others have tried to address the communications of devices with end-users (Peter and Kühne 2018).

Studies analyze the effect of Security/Privacy risk on the adoption of IPAs while focusing on the Para-social Relationship Perspective (Han and Yang 2018). There is a stream of literature that explores how gesture and context-aware influences user satisfaction, can be used to predict context-aware user satisfaction with AIEPA (Kiseleva and Rijke 2017). Certain studies have talked about the Effectiveness, Controllability, Reliability, Accuracy, Usefulness, Ease of Use, Satisfaction, and Loyalty for these devices (Orehovački et al. 2018). The Internet of Things have provided these AIEPA devices with capabilities of knowledge and awareness about their surroundings (Santos 2016). These capabilities are often not used judiciously.

Studies pivot on the reason that unused capabilities of these devices often lead to device abandonment (Xu et al. 2015). Significant studies have identified how the end-users ace obstacles to make use of the device (Myers et al. 2018). An essential dimension pertains to the proactive behaviour of these devices (Myers and Yorke-Smith 2007). In recent studies, the uncertainty in the time taken for these devices to respond (Rong et al. 2017) as well as the privacy issues (Datta et al. 2018), have been studied, as factors leading to avoidance behavior. We observe that there is a gap that these AIEPAs have not been studied with the lens of Cognitive Dissonance Theory (CDT).

3 Theoretical Foundations

Cognitive Dissonance Theory (CDT) elucidates the fact that when an individual holds two or more cognitions that are contradictory, she will feel an unpleasant state, recognized as "dissonance" till she can remove this state by changing her cognitions (Festinger 1957). This theory of social psychology has been used extensively in management to address employee behaviour issues. One of the earliest studies on testing this theory is attributed to Festinger and Carlsmith (1959), who found that after accomplishing unpleasant conduct, if the individuals are provided with small incentives, they can change their attitudes to favor the behavior. In another study, Aronson and Mills (1959) found that forceful socialization (e.g., hazing) leads to increased commitment.

We use CDT to study avoidance behavior associated with the use of AI-enabled devices in general and VAs in particular. The model represents the relationship amongst different constructs, namely cognitive dissonance, Techno overload, dehumanization, Virtual Community Involvement. These essential relationships are reflected in our research model displayed in Fig. 1 below.

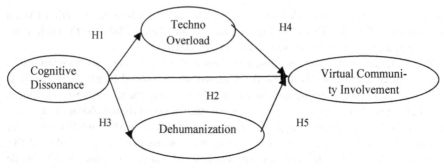

Fig. 1. Research model

The techno overload construct relates to the use of technology by an end-user as out of compulsion and not by choice. This refers to situations where individuals are expected to work more and faster, or even multitask to match the working demands when using technology at Workplaces, (Tarafdar et al. 2011; Weil and Rosen 1997; 1998). We extend this concept to apply to AIEPAs usage at home. This does not take away the fact that Techno overload forms one of the more critical components of technostress (Tarafdar et al. 2011). Dehumanization represents "the denial of qualities associated with meaning, interest, and compassion" toward others (Barnard 2001). People who engage in dehumanization do not perceive the human qualities of others (Bandura 2004). We will apply this concept to AIEPAs as individual users initially apply the humanness or anthropomorphism to these AIEPA devices, and then due to gap in user expectation and AIEPA performance, start showing condescending or dehumanization behaviour towards AIEPA. The virtual community concept (Koh et al. 2003) and its subsequent measurement (Blanchard 2007) suggests that a person using AIEPA to communicate and interact with her contacts is making use of the online interaction. Thus our premise for the model is that cognitive dissonance, techno-overload, and Dehumanization influence the virtual community involvement on the adoption, usage, and infrequent usage of AIEPAs. We propose the following hypotheses.

H1: The higher the cognitive dissonance, the higher the Techno Overload faced by the end-user.
H2: The higher the cognitive dissonance, the lower is the relationship with Virtual Community Involvement
H3: The higher the cognitive dissonance, the higher is the dehumanization feeling experienced by the end-user.
H4: The higher the Techno Overload, the lower is the relationship with Virtual Community Involvement
H5: The higher the Dehumanization, the lower is the relationship with Virtual Community Involvement

This parsimonious model may help us to understand that if factors like task complexity and device characteristics can be removed to make a meaningful prediction about the device usage by the end-user.

4 Methodology

We will use quantitative analysis to test our model. We will examine the instruments before we advance to collect data from the sample of VA end users. The survey instruments include a demographic section capturing the end-users' age, gender, income, and time of usage, followed by questions based on the constructs. Cognitive dissonance will be measured as per Tsang (2019) by asking the end-users, whether using AIEPA made them angry, disgusted, frustrated, and irritated. We will use a modified version of the Dehumanization scale used by Alnuaimi et al. (2010). Similarly, we will measure the Techno-Overload construct by using the scale of Ragu-Nathan et al. (2008), and finally, we will modify the virtual community involvement scale used by Kim et al. (2012) to suit our research.

Using smart PLS 3, we will carry out an analysis of the structural and measurement models. We will ensure that our study demonstrates acceptable measurement properties. The PLS analysis will generate path coefficients for the structural model. The structural model will show whether our five hypotheses are supported or not.

5 Discussion, Limitations, and Conclusions

The research will explore the efficacy of Cognitive Dissonance Theory to understand the infrequent use of AIEPAs. This study will help to investigate whether by removing the factors that create end user's cognitive dissonance with AIEPAs, the infrequent use can be converted to continuous or more frequent use. The research will also investigate the performance of the AIEPAs is one of the reasons that limit the public use of AIEPAs. This may be of interest to practitioners as well as manufacturers.

6 Future Research

To meet the criteria of generalizability, we propose that this research should be replicated in different settings at different locations inside and outside North America. Also, for future studies, we recommend including the effects of privacy, security, and trust as moderating variables.

References

Ajzen, I.: From intentions to actions: a theory of planned behavior. In: Kuhl, J., Beckmann, J. (eds.) Action Control. SSSSP, pp. 11–39. Springer, Heidelberg (1985). https://doi.org/10.1007/978-3-642-69746-3_2

Ajzen, I.: The theory of planned behavior. Organ. Behav. Hum. Decis. Process. **50**, 179–211 (1991)

Alnuaimi, O.A., Robert, L.P., Maruping, L.M.: Team size, dispersion, and social loafing in technology-supported teams: a perspective on the theory of moral disengagement. J. Manag. Inf. Syst. **27**(1), 203–230 (2010)

Anthes, G.: Artificial intelligence poised to ride a new wave, pp. 19–21 (2017)

Aronson, E., Mills, J.: The effect of severity of initiation on liking for a group. J. Abnormal Soc. Psychol. **59**, 177–181 (1959)

Baber, C.: Developing Interactive Speech Technology. Taylor & Francis Inc, Routledge (1993)

Bandura, A.: Selective exercise of moral agency. In: Thorkildsen, T.A., Walberg, H.J. (eds.) Nurturing Morality. Issues in Children's and Families' Lives, vol. 5, pp. 37–57. Springer, Boston (2004). https://doi.org/10.1007/978-1-4757-4163-6_3

Barnard, A.: On the relationship between technique and dehumanization. In: Advancing Technology, Caring, and Nursing, pp. 96–105 (2001)

Blanchard, A.L.: Developing a sense of virtual community measure. Cyber Psychol. Behav. **10**(6), 827–830 (2007)

Bors, L., Samajdwer, A., van Oosterhout, M.: Designing a conversational user experience. In: Oracle Digital Assistant, pp. 17–43. Apress, Berkeley (2020)

Braun, M., Alt, F.: Identifying personality dimensions for characters of digital agents. In: El Bolock, A., Abdelrahman, Y., Abdennadher, S. (eds.) Character Computing. HIS, pp. 123–137. Springer, Cham (2020). https://doi.org/10.1007/978-3-030-15954-2_8

Business Dictionary: Socio-cultural environment (2020). http://www.businessdictionary.com/definition/socio-cultural-environment.html. Accessed 15 Jan 2020

Byrne, D., Griffitt, W.: Similarity and awareness of similarity of personality characteristics as determinants of attraction. J. Exp. Res. Pers. (1969)

Czibula, G., Guran, A.-M., Czibula, I.G., Cojocar, G.S.: IPA-an intelligent personal assistant agent for task performance support. In: 2009 IEEE 5th International Conference on Intelligent Computer Communication and Processing (2009), pp. 31–34. IEEE (2009)

Datta, P., Namin, A. S., Chatterjee, M.: A survey of privacy concerns in wearable devices. In 2018 IEEE International Conference on Big Data (Big Data), pp. 4549–4553. IEEE, December 2018

Davis, F.D., Venkatesh, V.: A critical assessment of potential measurement biases in the technology acceptance model: three experiments. Int. J. Hum. Comput. Stud. **45**(1), 19–45 (1996)

Davis, F.D.: Perceived usefulness, perceived ease of use, and user acceptance of information technology. MIS Q. **13**(3), 319–340 (1989)

Davis, F.D.: Technology acceptance model for empirically testing new end-user information systems theory and results. Unpublished Doctoral Dissertation, MIT (1986)

Festinger, L., Carlsmith, J.M.: Cognitive consequences of forced compliance. J. Abnorm. Soc. Psychol. **58**, 203–210 (1959)

Festinger, L.: A Theory of Cognitive Dissonance. Stanford University Press, Stanford (1957)

Fishbein, M., Ajzen, I.: Belief. Attitude, Intention, and Behavior: An Introduction to Theory and Research, vol. 578 (1975)

Han, S., Yang, H.: Understanding adoption of intelligent personal assistants. Ind. Manag. Data Syst. **118**(3), 1411–1430 (2018)

Jara, A., Ladid, L., Gómez-Skarmeta, A.F.: The internet of everything through IPv6: an analysis of challenges, solutions and opportunities. J. Wirel. Mob. Networks Ubiquitous Comput. Dependable Appl. **4**(3), 97–118 (2013)

Jean Tsang, S.: Cognitive discrepancy, dissonance, and selective exposure. Media Psychol. **22**(3), 394–417 (2019)

Kepuska, V., Bohouta, G.: Next-generation of virtual personal assistants (Microsoft Cortana, Apple Siri, Amazon Alexa, and google home). In: 2018 IEEE 8th Annual Computing and Communication Workshop and Conference (CCWC), pp. 99–103. IEEE, January 2018

Kim, H.-W., Chan, H.C., Kankanhalli, A.: What motivates people to purchase digital items on virtual community websites? The desire for online self-presentation. Inf. Syst. Res. **23**, 1232–1245 (2012)

Kiseleva, J., de Rijke, M.: Evaluating personal assistants on mobile devices. arXiv preprint arXiv: 1706.04524 (2017)

Knote, R., Janson, A., Söllner, M., Leimeister, J.M.: Classifying smart personal assistants: an empirical cluster analysis. In: Proceedings of the 52nd Hawaii International Conference on System Sciences, January 2019

Knote, R., Janson, A., Eigenbrod, L., Söllner, M.: The what and how of smart personal assistants: Principles and application domains for IS research (2018)

Kocaballi, A.B., Laranjo, L., Coiera, E.: Understanding and measuring user experience in conversational interfaces. Interact. Comput. **31**(2), 192–207 (2019)

Koh, J., Kim, Y.G., Kim, Y.G.: Sense of virtual community: a conceptual framework and empirical validation. Int. J. Electron. Commer. **8**(2), 75–94 (2003)

Koon, L.M., McGlynn, S.A., Blocker, K.A., Rogers, W.A.: Perceptions of digital assistants from early adopters aged 55+. Ergon. Des. **28**(1), 16–23 (2020)

LeCun, Y., Bengio, Y., Hinton, G.: Deep learning. Nature **521**(7553), 436–444 (2015)

López, G., Quesada, L., Guerrero, L.A.: Alexa vs. Siri vs. Cortana vs. google assistant: a comparison of speech-based natural user interfaces. In: Nunes, I. (eds.) Advances in Human Factors and Systems Interaction, AHFE 2017. Advances in Intelligent Systems and Computing, vol. 592. Springer, Cham (2017). https://doi.org/10.1007/978-3-319-60366-7_23

Satyanarayanan, M.: Pervasive computing: vision and Challenges. IEEE Pers. Commun. **8**(4), 10–17 (2001)

Mori, M.: The uncanny valley. Energy **7**(4), 33–35 (1970)

Myers, C., Furqan, A., Nebolsky, J., Caro, K., Zhu, J.: Patterns for how users overcome obstacles in voice user interfaces. In: Proceedings of the 2018 CHI Conference on Human Factors in Computing Systems, pp. 1–7, April 2018

Myers, K., Yorke-Smith, N.: Proactive behavior of a personal assistive agent. In: Proceedings of the AAMAS Workshop on Metareasoning in Agent-Based Systems, Honolulu, HI, pp. 31–45, May 2007

Orehovački, T., Etinger, D., Babić, S.: The Antecedents of Intelligent Personal Assistants Adoption. In: Nunes, Isabel L. (ed.) AHFE 2018. AISC, vol. 781, pp. 76–87. Springer, Cham (2019). https://doi.org/10.1007/978-3-319-94334-3_10

Garrido, P., Martinez, F.J., Guetl, C.: Adding semantic web knowledge to intelligent personal assistant agents. In: Proceedings of 9th International Semantic Web Conference, Shangai, China, 7–11 November 2010, pp. 1–12 (2010)

Peter, J., Kühne, R.: The new frontier in communication research: why we should study social robots. Media Commun. **6**(3), 73–76 (2018)

Ragu-Nathan, T.S., Tarafdar, M., Ragu-Nathan, B.S., Tu, Q.: The consequences of technostress for end users in organizations: conceptual development and empirical validation. Inf. Syst. Res. **19**(4), 417–433 (2008)

Rai, A., Constantinides, P., Sarker, S.: Editor's comments: next-generation digital platforms: toward human–AI hybrids. MIS Q. **43**(1), iii–x (2019)

Reis, A., Paulino, D., Paredes, H., Barroso, J.: Using intelligent personal assistants to strengthen the elderlies' social bonds. In: Antona, M., Stephanidis, C. (eds.) UAHCI 2017. LNCS, vol. 10279, pp. 593–602. Springer, Cham (2017). https://doi.org/10.1007/978-3-319-58700-4_48

Rong, X., Fourney, A., Brewer, R.N., Morris, M.R., Bennett, P.N.: Managing uncertainty in time expressions for virtual assistants. In: Proceedings of the 2017 CHI Conference on Human Factors in Computing Systems, pp. 568–579, May 2017

Santos, J., Rodrigues, J.J.P.C., Silva, B.M.C., Casal, J., Saleem, K., Denisov, V.: An IoT-based mobile gateway for intelligent personal assistants on mobile health environments. J. Netw. Comput. Appl. (71), 194–204 (2016)

Sohail, M.: Exploring User Satisfaction with AI-enabled Voice-Activated Smart Phone Assistants. In: PACIS, p. 13 (2020)

Tarafdar, M., Tu, Q., Ragu-Nathan, T.S., Ragu-Nathan, B.S.: Crossing to the dark side: examining creators, outcomes, and inhibitors of technostress. Commun. ACM **54**(9), 113–120 (2011)

Van Biljon, J., Kotzé, P.: Modelling the factors that influence mobile phone adoption. In: Proceedings of the 2007 annual research conference of the South African Institute of Computer Scientists and Information Technologists on IT Research in Developing Countries, pp. 152–161 (2007)

Wagner, K., Schramm-Klein, H.: Alexa, Are You Human? Investigating Anthropomorphism of Digital Voice Assistants–A Qualitative Approach (2019)

Webster, J., Watson, R.T.: Analyzing the past to prepare for the future: writing a literature review. MIS Q. xiii–xxiii (2002)

Weil, M., Rosen, L.D.: Techno Stress: Coping with Technology at Work at Home at Play. Wiley, New York (1997)

White, R.W.: Skill discovery in virtual assistants. Commun. ACM **61**(11), 106–113 (2018)

Xu, C., Peak, D., Prybutok, V.: A customer value, satisfaction, and loyalty perspective of mobile application recommendations. Decis. Support Syst. **79**, 171–183, (2015)

Yang, H., Lee, H., Zo, H.: User acceptance of smart home services: an extension of the theory of planned behavior. Ind. Manag. Data Syst. **117**(1), 68–89 (2017)

Yu, J., Zo, H., Choi, M.K., Ciganek, A.P.: User acceptance of location-based social networking services. Online Inf. Rev. (2013)

Concept for Human and Computer to Determine Reason Based Scene Location

Adrienne Raglin[(⊠)] [iD] and Andre Harrison [iD]

Army Research Laboratory, Adelphi, MD 20873, USA
`adrienne.raglin2.civ@mail.mil`, `andre.v.harrison2.civ@mail.mil`

Abstract. The motivation of human computer interaction (HCI) is to improve how humans use computers. One approach can be developing technology that allows the human and computer to collaborate. In some cases creating this type of collaboration or joint approach to for example solve a problem or identify an important piece of information. While some researchers investigate ways that do not include the human, HCI focuses on keeping the technology linked to the human. At this stage in our research, the human is the collaborator utilizing the computer as a teammate to accomplish the task. The task for this work falls under the area of ongoing research in scene understanding. We present a concept that allows the location of an image to be determined based on object detection performed by the computer and the human using reasoning to generate possible candidates for the location that an image can represent. The human may use his or her own knowledge to reason about the options or again working with the computer to glean from reasoning engines that include knowledge. The paper will present this idea and the work that has started.

Keywords: Human information interaction · Artificial reasoning · Scene understanding

1 Introduction

1.1 Motivation

The motivation of human computer interaction (HCI) is to improve how humans use computers. The list of considerations within HCI research include the way systems are designed and implemented to improve efficiency and learning, as well as the way systems are developed to improve information discovery and management. One approach can be developing the technology that allows the computer to communicate information to the human in a similar manner that humans communicate information to each other. Another approach can be developing technology that allows the human and computer to collaborate. In some cases, creating this type of collaboration or joint approach is helpful for solving a problem or identifying an important piece of information. A lot current research outside of the HCI space focuses on developing new systems that do not include the human, while HCI focuses on keeping the technology linked to the human advances in AI are moving the placement of this link. The idea of human in

© Springer Nature Switzerland AG 2020
C. Stephanidis et al. (Eds.): HCII 2020, CCIS 1293, pp. 351–358, 2020.
https://doi.org/10.1007/978-3-030-60700-5_45

the loop as the controller is moving to human on the loop as the supervisor. At this stage in our research, the human collaborators with the computer systems to accomplish the task. At this stage the systems are tools that receive and provide information to a person. The work presented in this paper falls under the area of ongoing research in scene understanding. This paper considers how the task of understanding the location an image represents can be accomplished using a team consisting of humans and computer systems. We present a concept that allows the location of an image to be determined based on object recognition performed by the computer and the human using reasoning to generate possible candidates for the location that an image can represent. The human may use his or her own knowledge to reason about the options or again work with the computer to glean that knowledge using reasoning engines. The paper will present this idea and the work that has been initiated.

1.2 Interaction Systems and Humans

The question of where the human interaction takes place in systems that are being designed and created to provide capabilities that only humans traditionally perform is an ongoing one. Human in the loop takes advantage of the strengths of humans and machines to create models, the human interaction is always required along the cycles of the loop. Human on the loop is where human interaction is required only to override the intended action of the machine if needed. Human off the loop is where there is no interaction; the machine is fully autonomous. Any system that aides the human in decision-making or problem solving that includes the human in the loop approach can lead to beneficial methods as technology and capabilities expand. As we strive to develop this system enabling it to capture and utilize similar knowledge as humans is an important component. The goal is to allow the system to take advantage of reasoning approaches for finding information and connecting that information to solve possible locations for scenes represented in images. The human evaluates the outcomes of the system and determines if additional steps are needed. Moreover, the human uses the reasoning system guiding the responses that contribute to the goal of the tasks. In this way, the human adds his or her knowledge to the limited knowledge that the reasoning engine may have at this stage of development.

1.3 Reasoning

Reasoning is defined as the "mental process of deriving logical conclusion and making predictions from available knowledge facts, and beliefs ... a way of to infer facts from existing data." [1] Reasoning is used to make decisions, solve problems and to make evaluations. Reasoning can be done formally or informally, by using top down or bottom up processing, and changes or is impacted by uncertainty and partial truths [2].

Reasoning in artificial intelligence has the goal of enabling a machine to think and perform as a human would. According to information found in [1–4] reasoning under artificial intelligence falls in several categories:

1. Deductive reasoning is where new information is generated from logically related known information. In this case, the conclusion is valid when the arguments leading

to a conclusion must be true and when the premises are true, it uses propositional logic requiring rules and facts, and is a top down process.

2. Inductive reasoning is where conclusions are arrived by using a limited set of facts to reach a general conclusion; it is based on propositional logic, and is a cause-effect or bottom up process. The true premises do not guarantee the truth of the conclusion but are a probable support to the conclusion.

3. Abductive reasoning is for explaining observations like inductive reasoning but allows for a best guess, it is considered less rigorous than deductive reasoning and is used when uncertainty exists and is applied to decision making and troubleshooting.

4. Common Sense reasoning is an informal experienced based process, allowing a person to make "presumption about events" of every day occurrences; it "relies on good judgment rather than exact logic and operates on heuristic knowledge and rules" [1].

5. Monotonic reasoning is where additional information is added to the knowledge base but the conclusion stays the same, the additional knowledge does not reduce the set of prepositions derived, valid conclusions are from the facts only.

6. Non-Monotonic reasoning is where conclusions can be invalidated through added information and "deals with incomplete and uncertain models" [1].

Any of the reasoning individual processes or a combination of the process can be used to address challenges in various areas of research. Since reasoning approaches utilized by people can also be integrated into computer systems this is one way of allowing human in the loop approaches to inform decision making and problem solving. In our approach, we look at analogical reasoning which is a form of inductive reasoning. An analogy is a comparison between two objects or systems of objects in ways where they are similar. It "cites accepted similarities between the objects to support the conclusion that some further similarities exists" [3].

Reasoning processes that do not fall under deductive logic can use ampliative reasoning. Ampliative reasoning allows information to be added through a series of questions and answers with logical inference steps. The question can come from an observation or an experiment. The answer can be from a database or a person. [4] Analogical reasoning can be categorized as ampliative reasoning, where the conclusions are "supported with varying degrees of strength" [4].

2 Flow of Application Concept

2.1 A Subsection Sample

The concept for this reason based scene location application takes advantage of the human and currently developed computer systems. As discussed in previous sections the human supports and evaluates the work that the computer systems performs. This work is an extension of the ideas presented in [5]. This concept leverages work from [6] on semantic vector space and [7] question and answering as well as work on image saliency [8]. The outline of this concept is as follows:

Step 1: Input is an image

Step 2: Use a library of object detection algorithms to find and label as many objects as possible from the image and along with the probability of correct detection associated with the objects

Step 3: Create an object list for that image using only high confidence detections (See Fig. 1 that shows steps 1–3)

Fig. 1. Input image analyzed by library of algorithms to find objects. The objects are stored in list database.

Step 4: in present concept, a person would enter the objects into the reasoning system. Future versions of this concept could remove human involvement in this step and have it performed automatically or with the option of including human input for refinement.

Step 4a: Using the reasoning engine, generate a list of objects that are related to the objects previously identified. These new objects would be related by reasoning predicates (ex. part of, near to, …). This list is used to verify the entries in the object list and to determine if there are any additional objects not previously identified. Currently a human is required to specify the relevant reasoning predicates. In future, the reasoning engine could also accept this information from the database entries.

Step 4b: Using the reasoning engine generate the possible locations list based on the objects found and associated additional objects as well. This list would be related to the objects by reasoning predicates (ex. used for,…). This list of locations become the possible choices for the scene.

(See Fig. 2 that show steps 4a, 4b)

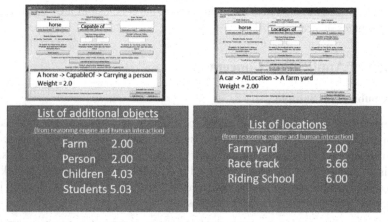

Fig. 2. Reason based engine (EZ Vector) used to find additional objects and locations linked to initial set of objects.

Step 4c: If any of the objects from step 4a are not part of the initial object list additional algorithms maybe used to attempt to detect them with a lower detection threshold due to their increased expectation or from the image searched by a person.

Step 5: An image saliency algorithm will be used to boost potential objects by either: strengthening the link of the object within the reasoning engine (thus creating an augmented knowledge base) and highlighting areas where key objects are located that the algorithm did not identify. In the latter case a person can determine if the object should be added to the object list and what strength it should be given. In both cases an augmented knowledge base is created and can be transferred

(See Fig. 3 that shows step 5)

Fig. 3. Saliency algorithm that highlights were key objects may be located. The results of the saliency algorithm can boost the strength of the objects and highlight possible areas where additional objects may be and those can be added to the object list as well.

Step 6: A knowledge database is created to store the links for the image with the objects and possible locations.

Step 7: The best location is selected based on the reasoning engines strongest candidate for the location given the objects

(See Fig. 4 that shows steps 6 and 7)

Step 8: Repeat with additional image(s)

Image ID No.	Key Objects	Location
1	Car	~~Farmyard, Race Track,~~ Riding School
	Dog	~~Farmyard, Race Track,~~ Riding School
	Horse	~~Farmyard, Race Track,~~ Riding School
	Person	~~Farmyard, Race Track,~~ Riding School
	Farm	~~Farmyard~~
	Children	~~Farmyard, Race Track,~~ Riding School
	Students	~~Farmyard, Race Track,~~ Riding School

Fig. 4. Database information that can be transferred to knowledge base aides in refining which objects and locations remain. This example shows that the riding school location would be selected as the "best" scene description for this image.

3 Application

3.1 Object Detection and Classification

The set of object recognition algorithms consists of well-known pre-trained object recognition models out of the TensorFlow object detection API[1]. Currently two object recognition algorithms are used during the first pass, the Single Shot multibox Detector (SSD) using the MobileNet backbone, for feature extraction, and the faster-RCNN model using the ResNet101 feature extractor, both of which have been trained on the MS-COCO dataset [9–12]. The SSD model with MobileNet backbone is typically used in computationally limited applications where resources are limited, but accurate and real-time implementation is still desired. Faster R-CNN is a more computationally demanding object recognition model, but can generate more accurate object recognition predictions across many domains. Together these models represent different approaches to object recognition and while still fairly accurate are likely to differ in which objects they recognize more consistently in different locations. The common objects in context (COCO) dataset is an object recognition focused dataset aimed at the detection of objects within

---

[1] https://github.com/tensorflow/models/blob/master/research/object_detection/g3doc/detection_model_zoo.md.

different contexts. This lends itself as a good starting point for object based scene recognition as the location of the scene heavily influences the context of the objects. Hence, the object recognition models are likely to work in many commonly occurring scene locations.

3.2 Lists for Future Database of Knowledge

As images are entered into the application concept discussed earlier, the lists associated with the objects and locations can be used to create a database (See Fig. 4). Ideally, this database becomes a method for correctly finding the scene location of new images as the number of images grows supporting the object list and location list information in the database. Thus, the lists form a database of knowledge for scene understanding.

3.3 Reasoning Engine

The EZ Vector Knowledge Base (KB) is the reasoning engine application utilized in this concept [13]. The interface is shown in Fig. 2. Based on the Vector KB [6] it takes advantage of the facts within ConceptNet integrated with the reasoning approach within Vector KB. A key advantage to EZ Vector KB is the ability to search for reasoning links for either the head, predicate or tail term. EZ vector KB also allows new information to be added to the knowledge base if necessary. EZ vector KB allows modification of the strengths of the links from the search. If a relational link is listed lower in the list that strength can be increased based on the importance of that relationship for the particular context. The item can be decreased if needed. These features are key to implementing steps in the concept presented earlier. In future, a method for entering a justification may be added to document and track the modification of entries.

3.4 Saliency Boost

For supporting the identification of important objects, we propose using the saliency algorithm in the Ideal Observer Model (IoM) [8] to provide a saliency boost. The results from the IoM would highlight key objects (see Fig. 3). Then a person can use these results to increase (or decrease) the strength of the object in the reasoning engine. This modification may be very context driven thus the modification maybe only applicable for a specific set of images or related tasks that requires the scene understanding. Additionally, since the objects from the IoM can be "ranked" (for example only the top 20 objects can be highlighted), objects lower than this threshold could be reviewed by a person and if considered important this maybe another criteria for adding these boosted objects to the list.

4   Conclusion

As research continues in advancing systems that aid humans in accomplishing tasks efficiently the interaction between humans and computers, as well as other systems will be essential. As the balance between whether these systems have the human in the loop or on the loop utilizing what the human does well and what the computer does well can form an effective team. In the future applications may become more autonomous, however in this concept for a reason based scene location system we consider the human and the computer working together to perform the task. The ability of image processing algorithms to analyze numerous images paired with a person using a reasoning engine to build knowledge for successfully categorizing the location of scenes is the objective. In this paper, we presented the concept and the techniques that are currently being used in the implementation. As this work continues, we will focus on interconnecting the elements of the concept and addressing the challenges in the individual components and the overall application system.

References

1. https://www.javatpoint.com/reasoning-in-artificial-intelligence
2. https://simplicable.com/new/reasoning
3. https://plato.stanford.edu/entries/reasoning-analogy/
4. Ampliative reasoning can be studied, and answer are understood broadly. https://www.britan nica.com/topic/applied-logic/Strategies-of-deductive-reasoning
5. Raglin, A., Harrison, A., Summers-Stay, D.: Fused reasoning under uncertainty for soldier centric human-agent decision making. In: 2018 IEEE Southwest Symposium on Image Analysis and Interpretation (SSIAI), pp. 1–4. IEEE, April 2018
6. Summers-Stay, D., Li, D., Raglin, A.: Reasoning with Vector-Based Knowledge Representations (2018)
7. Li, D., Sutor, P., Raglin, A.: Query Answering by Deductive and Analogical Reasoning in a Semantic Vector Space
8. Harrison, A., Etienne-Cummings, R.: An entropy based ideal observer model for visual saliency. In: 2012 46th Annual Conference on Information Sciences and Systems (CISS), pp. 1–6. IEEE, March 2012
9. Liu, Wei., et al.: SSD: single shot multibox detector. In: Leibe, Bastian, Matas, Jiri, Sebe, Nicu, Welling, Max (eds.) ECCV 2016. LNCS, vol. 9905, pp. 21–37. Springer, Cham (2016). https://doi.org/10.1007/978-3-319-46448-0_2
10. Howard, A.G., et al.: MobileNets: efficient convolutional neural networks for mobile vision applications. arXiv preprint arXiv:1704.04861(2017)
11. Ren, S., et al.: Faster R-CNN: towards real-time object detection with region proposal networks. In: Advances in Neural Information Processing Systems (2015)
12. He, K., et al.: Deep residual learning for image recognition. In: Proceedings of the IEEE Conference on Computer Vision and Pattern Recognition (2016)
13. Green, M., Raglin, A., Summers-Stay, D.: Knowledge Base Management Simplified with EZ Vector KB

A Neural Affective Approach to an Intelligent Weather Sensor System

John Richard[✉], James Braman[✉], Michael Colclough[✉],
and Sudeep Bishwakarma[✉]

Community College of Baltimore County, Baltimore, MD 21239, USA
{ric986124,col953764,bis949947}@email.ccbcmd.edu,
jbraman@ccbcmd.edu

Abstract. The ability to capture data from our surrounding environment while learning user preferences has the potential to make our everyday decisions more straightforward and informed. Based on the idea of capturing weather data, we present our current design of a weather sensor network using several Raspberry Pi's, combined with external resources, that presents recommendations based on personalized affect data. The goal of the system is to learn user preferences in combination with providing emotive output utilizing a neural network. The system has visualization capabilities that can interface with the web, along with other features based on preferences set by the user. This paper presents an overview of the system prototype.

Keywords: Weather sensors · Neural net · Affective computing

1 Introduction

The multitude of data provided by various devices connected to the internet has the potential to revolutionize the efficiency of choices we make every day. These data-driven choices can range from helping with simple tasks such as deciding what food items to purchase for the week to better home energy management configurations to reduce costs. For example, refrigerators can help keep track of food products we buy and when we run out [1]. Homes using smart energy management devices help occupants make better decisions for settings based on time, outdoor and indoor temperatures and adjust accordingly even when not home [2]. While some of these decision-making improvements may seem trivial, combined with other enhancements, or used in a broader context, these improvements can be beneficial.

Given the benefit of collecting data through sensors that can be embedded in many everyday devices around us, a major question that emerges is what to do with all this data? Can this data be combined with other data sources in some way to be made useful? Is there a context that needs to be addressed for a home or individual? Consider a home sensor network that collects data on an older adult living alone. Data collected via a wireless sensor network could be used to provide insight on daily behaviors, activities, and well-being of the older person to guide healthcare providers in decision making

© Springer Nature Switzerland AG 2020
C. Stephanidis et al. (Eds.): HCII 2020, CCIS 1293, pp. 359–365, 2020.
https://doi.org/10.1007/978-3-030-60700-5_46

better [3]. There are endless possibilities as to what data can be collected and how this data can be used to improve our lives. All these internet-connected devices are part of the Internet of Things (IoT). IoT can be considered as consisting of devices (things) that exchange data which can communicate with each other, having an Internet or other network connection. Estimates place the number of IoT devices at around 10 billion devices by the year 2020 and 22 billion by 2025 [4].

The ability to purchase and modify IoT devices such as the Raspberry Pi, Arduino and Particle, more people can experiment and create smart sensors and devices for everyday use. In this paper, we describe our project that focuses on a weather sensor system, combining elements from both IoT and affective computing while utilizing a neural network. Using the Python programming language, we have designed a weather sensor network using several Raspberry Pi's that combined with external resources, present recommendations based on personalized affect data. The system has visualization capabilities that can interface with the web, along with other features based on preferences set by the user.

2 Background

Weather is based on atmospheric conditions over a short period of time such as hours or days and is often thought about in terms of temperature, humidity, precipitation, cloudiness, brightness, visibility, wind, and pressure [5]. These factors, in combination, have some impact on not only our environment but on decisions and to some degree, potentially our mood. For some individuals, certain weather conditions could cause distress, annoyance and other unpleasant conditions affecting our daily plans. Other times when the weather is sunny with warmer temperatures, it may invoke thoughts of visiting the beach or planning outdoor activities. For some, aspects of weather, temperature, humidity and even air quality influence mood. However, there are studies that debate this association or suggest that the association is weak [6]. [7] found that no significant effect was found between weather on positive affect. This study did note that sunlight was found to have a significant main effect on tiredness [7]. Interestingly, several studies have reported a positive impact from weather, such as increases in gratuity left in restaurants on sunny days [8].

Even if there is no correlation between weather and emotion state, weather can have a significant influence on how we plan the day. In our research, we are making the assumption that weather at least influences to some degree and influences some decisions or behaviors we make. For instance, if we know that the weather will be freezing, we will dress appropriately. If the weather is forecasted to have heavy rain, we will bring an umbrella with us when we leave the house. We are also assuming that there is at least some emotional influence of the weather. Several factors would need to be considered and are unique to everyone as to why weather could potentially have an impact. As noted by [9], sunny days could lead people to go outdoors, leading to more leisurely activities which could lead to increased happiness. The increased level of happiness is not due solely with it being a sunny day, but rather the context of how it influenced the decision to go outside. Alternatively, some individuals may prefer a more cloudy or rainy day.

The premise is to provide users with helpful information that would be relevant to their daily decision making based on environmental factors (i.e. weather) while considering one's potential emotional state (i.e. mood). Using various sensors, weather data is collected and combined with other data sources to assist in this process.

3 Developing the Intelligent Weather Sensor System

The design of the system can be broken down into three components: a) System Input, b) Processing Component, and c) Interface. Figure 1 depicts the main elements of the weather system. Some parts are still being tested and improved. The system's hardware components hinged upon several key factors: availability of system components, ease of component integration, and scalability.

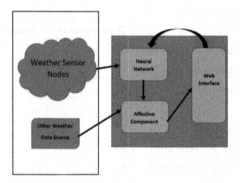

Fig. 1. System overview

3.1 Weather Sensor Nodes

The initial system build for each weather node in the network consisted of a Raspberry Pi 2 B single-board computing device running Raspbian Stretch paired with a DHT11 weather sensor (Fig. 2). This sensor was capable of measuring temperature ranges from 0 to 50 °C (±2 °C accuracy) and a humidity range between 20% and 90% relative humidity (±5% relative humidity accuracy). With these pieces in place, we used a Python script to automate sensor readings every hour and recorded data to a shared Google Sheet file for storage and ease of access. Later iterations were tested connecting to a web database.

These weather sensor nodes were designed to run independently to collect simple temperature and humidity data. In the future, other types of information can be collected and integrated into the system architecture. A selected sample dataset is provided in Table 1 below. The Python script extracts temperature and humidity data as recorded from the sensor, converts the reading to Fahrenheit, formats the information and transmits via a live wireless internet connection. Currently, nodes are being placed near a direct power source and have wireless internet connectivity. In the future, we intend to use battery-powered or solar options for a power source for more remote locations. The

Fig. 2. DHT11 sensor

Table 1. Sample dataset collected from a weather sensor node

DHT11 Sample		
Date/time	Temperature (F)	Humidity (%)
Wed Mar 20 19:00:08 2019	62	33
Wed Mar 20 20:00:08 2019	62	33
Wed Mar 20 21:00:09 2019	62	32
…	…	…
Sun Jul 7 09:00:08 2019	75	95
Sun Jul 7 10:00:07 2019	80	95
Sun Jul 7 11:00:09 2019	82	95

goal is to have numerous sensors for each site to improve monitoring and to personalize results better. As each sensor in the system can record various attributes at different time intervals, the amount of data that could be potentially collected could be quite significant if continued over a long period.

3.2 Other Weather Data Sources

To gather additional weather and environmental data from the surrounding area, an outside weather data source was selected to include with the program. Using the free version of the API from OpenWeather, we were able to extract additional information for testing purposes [10]. A more comprehensive set of data is available through paid subscription services. Using Python's urllib library and a free account and API key, we were able to request temperature and humidity data for a zipcode using a separate script. As shown in Fig. 3, there is additional information that can be quite useful which is returned such as wind speed, sunrise and sunset time, the specific time zone for the area, visibility, air pressure and more. Currently, we are mainly focused on temperature and humidity.

```
Enter zip code
21221
b'{"coord":{"lon":-76.45,"lat":39.31},"weather":[{"id":501,"main":"Rain","description":"moderate
rain","icon":"10d"}],"base":"stations","main":{"temp":302.23,"pressure":1013,"humidity":89,"temp
_min":300.15,"temp_max":304.26},"visibility":11265,"wind":{"speed":2.6,"deg":120},"clouds":{"all
":75},"dt":1563462730,"sys":{"type":1,"id":4995,"message":0.018,"country":"US","sunrise":1563443
612,"sunset":1563496205},"timezone":-14400,"id":0,"name":"Essex","cod":200}'
>>>
```

Fig. 3. Sample API response for local zip code from OpenWeather

3.3 Neural Network

The program used a neural network to take weather data, parse it, and produce meaningful output. The network consisted of a two-input perceptron model with one hidden layer and one output node (Fig. 4).

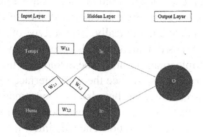

Fig. 4. Simplified visualization of the neural network

As the network parsed the input values, it repeatedly made use of the sigmoid activation function and its derivative to produce an output consisting of a floating-point number between 0.0 and 1.0. Using backpropagation (backpropagation of error) the network recognized errors and adjusted the weight values within the network accordingly. Using this method, we were able to feed the output value into our affective component. The input consisted of various weather data from the sensor network and the external sources. Whereas the output consists of an affective value which is used to alter the web-based visualization for the user.

3.4 Affective Component

This work was partially inspired by a separate project that involved the use of an agent architecture for human assistive technologies that account for emotional influence. In this other project, the output produced by the human user includes mediation methods between the human output with the output of an artificial agent to provide a "better" decision [11, 12]. Affective computing can be described as "computing that relates to, arises from or deliberately influences emotions" [13, p. 1]. To this end, a unique component of the system is its affective computing element as a factor in its interface presentation. We posit that weather influences decision making on some level for certain daily decision making. Also, emotional factors also play a role in decision making at some level. Consider someone that is looking forward to having an outside wedding, but the weather that day has become overbearingly hot and humid, or if it rains that day. This would have an impact on one's emotions. Compare this to another day when someone is heading off to work or school, and it begins to snow or rain. This may impact a person's decision on what to wear to go outside. Besides a certain level of annoyance or excitement, the emotional effect might not be as intense in this case (unless there is a great deal of snow or rain that would cause distress from icy conditions or floods). This weather system aims to combine this weather data along with learned emotional impacts from a user, and combined makes suggestions for the day.

3.5 System User Interface

A web-based interface serves as the main output of the system and as a means of displaying recommendations to the user. Taking input from the affective component module, the web interface will automatically adapt based on various input provided. Using a combination of JavaScript and Cascading Stylesheets (CSS), the entire layout of the interface can adapt the style and update automatically. A prototype of the interface will consist of using various color schemes to match "moods" provided by the affective component that reflects the user. Multiple images can also be included in the page that is appropriate for the current weather conditions. We see the web interface of the system as a means to gain insight on the current forecast, but also as a systematic set of suggestions for the day. As an example, a user who enjoys the outdoors, and lives in an area where the forecast is bright and sunny but not too hot. The web interface receiving input from the system knowing the user preferences and weather information can present this information to the user using bright colors, appropriate imagery as well as a list of outdoor activities, local events taking place (of which could potentially be weather dependent) and other suggestions. As another example, a user that does not like rainy weather and is ill-prepared for the week's upcoming storms could assist in pre-planning by suggesting appropriate attire and various indoor activities or a to-do list.

4 Conclusions and Future Work

Based on the idea of capturing weather data, we have designed a weather sensor network using several Raspberry Pi's that combined with external resources, present recommendations based on personalized affect data. The system has visualization capabilities that can interface with the web, along with other features based on preferences set by the user. This paper presents an overview of the system prototype.

At this time, we have not tested the system for accuracy on a larger set of users for affect suggestion. Testing of the system will be conducted as part of our future work which includes modifications to the actual sensor network. Improvements are needed to stabilize the web-interface and to make it simple and easy for the user to select and "agree" with the solutions presented via the neural network to learn preferences. Testing of the interface will include user satisfaction surveys, interface surveys and surveys on accuracy on the prediction. Additional data sources are planned to be integrated into the system other than weather alone.

Some hardware limitations need to be overcome, such as instances where there was noticeable interference with the temperature sensors and the Pi due to heat transference. Care was needed to consider where the sensor was placed in relation to other devices and power cords as to decrease temperature reading accuracy. As noted earlier, more sensors are required and need to be installed independent of dedicated power supply in some cases.

References

1. Osisanwo, F., Kuyoro, S., Awodele, O.: Internet refrigerator–a typical internet of things (IoT). In: 3rd International Conference on Advances in Engineering Sciences & Applied Mathematics, London (2015)
2. Anvari-Moghaddam, A., Monsef, H., Rahimi-Kian, A.: Optimal smart home energy management considering energy saving and a comfortable lifestyle. IEEE Trans. Smart Grid **6**(1), 324–332 (2015)
3. Suryadevara, N.K., Mukhopadhyay, S.C., Wang, R., Rayudu, R.K.: Forecasting the behavior of an elderly using wireless sensors data in a smart home. Eng. Appl. Artif. Intell. **26**(10), 2641–2652 (2013)
4. Lueth, K.: State of the IoT 2018: Number of IoT devices now at 7B – Market accelerating. IoT Analytics. https://iot-analytics.com/state-of-the-iot-update-q1-q2-2018-number-of-iot-devices-now-7b/. Accessed 26 July 2019
5. NASA.: What's the difference between weather and climate. National Aeronautics and Space Administration. https://www.nasa.gov/mission_pages/noaa-n/climate/climate_weather.html. Accessed 02 June 2020
6. Hardt, J., Gerbershagen, H.U.: No changes in mood with the seasons: observations in 3000 chronic pain patients. Acta Psychiatr. Scand. **100**(4), 288–294 (1999)
7. Denissen, J.J., Butalid, L., Penke, L., Van Aken, M.A.: The effects of weather on daily mood: a multilevel approach. Emotion **8**(5), 662 (2008)
8. Cunningham, M.: R: Weather, mood, and helping behavior: quasi experiments with the sunshine samaritan. J. Pers. Soc. Psychol. **37**(11), 1947 (1979)
9. Connolly, M.: Some like it mild and not too wet: the influence of weather on subjective well-being. J. Happiness Stud. **14**(2), 457–473 (2013)
10. OpenWeather.: OpenWeather Weather Forecast. https://openweathermap.org/city. Accessed 26 June 2019
11. Vincenti, G., Braman, J., Trajkovski, G.: Emotion-based framework for multi-agent coordination and individual performance in a goal-directed environment. In: 2007 Fall AAAI Symposium, Arlington, VA, USA (2007)
12. Vincenti, G., Braman, J., Trajkovski, G.: Hybrid emotionally aware mediated agent architecture for human-assistive technologies. In: AAAI 2008 Spring Symposium, Palo Alto, California, USA (2008)
13. Picard, R.W.: Affective Computing-MIT Media Laboratory Perceptual Computing Section Technical Report No. 321, Cambridge, MA, 2139 (1995)

Role-Based Design of Conversational Agents: Approach and Tools

Ilaria Scarpellini and Yihyun Lim[(✉)]

Design Lab, Massachusetts Institute of Technology, Cambridge, MA 02139, USA
yihyun@mit.edu

Abstract. The wide adoption of conversational agents in delivering services to users asks for user-centric approach to design of the experience. We propose a Role-Based design approach, introducing 9 archetypal roles/purposes of conversational agents, resulting from case study research of conversational interfaces available in the market. These roles cover a range of behaviors (reactive, proactive) and features (relational, operational) that will enable the design of human-like, bi-directional conversational experience. We exemplify this approach through workshop sessions that involved stakeholders from financial industry in using the developed toolkits to envision financial service experiences enabled by conversational-agent.

Keywords: Human-product interaction · Conversation agents · Conversational UX · User-centered design · Design research · Design toolkit

1 Introduction

Conversation is a mode of communication to exchange information and ideas through natural dialog. Explorations in applying human communication modalities to interface with machines have been an active area in both academic and industry research. However, to convey meaning beyond the exchange of words in a conversation, it is important to clarify the goal and purpose of a conversation which are usually implicit in human dialogs [8].

The development of conversational AI technologies was mostly in the domain of engineers, and hasn't yet offered opportunities for non-technical experts to be engaged in the design process. To create a human-centric service experience with conversational agents, it is important to discuss the values, roles, needs of the users and to embed these insights. In this paper, we aim to address the approach to designing a conversational agent with specific focus on identifying 'roles' of conversational agents to deliver customized services to its users.

2 Related Work

2.1 Conversational Agents

Conversational agents (CAs) are intelligent systems that are designed to be communicated in a human-like conversation way, using natural language [11]. It refers to both

© Springer Nature Switzerland AG 2020
C. Stephanidis et al. (Eds.): HCII 2020, CCIS 1293, pp. 366–375, 2020.
https://doi.org/10.1007/978-3-030-60700-5_47

text-based and speech-based systems, such as text-based chatbots on mobile and web interfaces, and speech-based virtual/digital assistants that are widely available through home devices such as Alexa and Google Home [10, 13, 19]. With the advancement in natural language processing and machine learning, capabilities of these CAs have improved greatly. We're seeing increasing adoption of conversational agents beyond 'general-purpose' CAs that can talk about any topic (e.g. Apple's Siri), to more topic-specific expert CAs as found in the financial industry (e.g. Bank of America's Erica and Bradesco's BIA). Moreover, as 'Conversational AI' is being widely integrated into smart products as Conversational UI/UX, the term Conversational Smart Products (ConvSP) is being introduced to include physical, networked products that are augmented by a digital counterpart. These include Conversational User Interfaces (CUI) in the form of Vocal User Interfaces (VUI), Embodied Conversational Agents (ECA), Virtual Personal Assistants (VPA), and chatbots [20].

2.2 Conversational Design Approaches

Conversational Design refers to interactions that mimic the human conversation, which is bidirectional and turn-based [16] where exchange of information occurs and conversation builds based on memories of past turns. There are two archetypal approaches to Conversational Design.

The first is a technology-driven approach used by tech companies that are focused on industry application. Microsoft provides a series of Conversational AI tools that is mainly focused on aiding the quick and easy building and deploying of Conversational Agents on multiple platforms rather than the actual design of the conversation with respect to UX [3]. IBM mostly proposes guidelines about technical aspects of AI and CA and principles about conversation in general, rather than an integrated approach to design the interaction and therefore communication between artificial systems and humans [11]. In the 'Guides' section of Google Cloud's online documentation for Dialogflow, it addresses technical aspects of Agent Design such as ML training and best practices from the business and brand image perspective [6].

Second approach is a human-centric design approach to conversation design, fostered by the awareness that CAs are the UI of the future since they can bridge the gap between humans and technology [2]. If designed by applying former principles of human cognition and communication theory this approach can provide the potential to overcome the need for humans to 'learn the language' of technology, which happens in cases of GUIs. This kind of approach is well conveyed and exemplified by Erika Hall's Conversational Design Book, where she notes: "Conversation is how humans interact with one another, and have for millennia. We should be able to use the same principles to make our digital systems easy and intuitive to use by finally getting the machines to play by our rules".

In terms of application domains, conversation design has been much explored in customer service, in attempts to increase service encounter quality and efficiency of customer experience that are traditionally performed by a human. Gnewuch et al. have outlined an approach to design cooperative and social CAs that can display human characteristics to increase service quality in customer service [7]. However, CAs can also become a double-edged sword, and when it becomes the main touch point of a service it needs to be carefully designed to deliver a coherent UX and a positive customer experience (CX). To have a meaningful conversation, it needs to be more than an exchange of phrases, should start with an unspoken agreement (hidden expectation) that is followed by collaborative actions between the CA and the user in reaching towards a goal [8].

3 Role-Based Design of Conversational Agents

Understanding the relation between context of use (industry), purpose (reason why users' interact with it) and characterizing traits of a CA (success factors) is key to identify its role with respect to the service delivery. This enables to frame users' expectations accordingly and to design conversational agents that are able to enhance the customer experience. In this section we will primarily discuss the role and purpose of CAs and its related success factors, while the relation to the context of use was investigated by means of participatory sessions with stakeholders, and will be further explained in chapter 4 of this paper.

3.1 Purpose of CAs

The first part of the framework concerns the definition of the role of CAs, with respect to its intended purpose. Defining the role of a CA is key in order to design the user experience since it determines the expectations of the users in terms of performance, behavior and service delivered. We gathered over 50 case studies across different types of hosting platforms (operative systems, applications, messaging apps, home assistants) and across various fields of application (mobility, finance, gaming, wellbeing, entertainment, culture, domotics, etc.). This broad area of research was needed to understand how CAs differ in purpose. Results have been mapped along two axes - behavior (passive or proactive) and features (operational vs. relational) - to reveal clusters of related groupings (Fig. 1).

Behaviors of CA: Reactive vs. Proactive. The level of initiative a system takes in interacting with the user differentiates one conversational system from another [14], and when a 'chatterbot is enhanced with proactivity it can be regarded as an intelligent conversational agent' [1]. We used the reactive-proactive dimension to seek for analogies between CA purposes and real human character's role and behavior in the delivery of a service (i.e.: the user is aware that he needs to call a plumber to fix a sink, while a financial advisor is expected to proactively notify the customer when 'good' investment opportunities are available).

Features of CAs: Operational vs. Relational. CA's overall smartness relies on its performance across different dimensions. Similar to Rijsdijk and Hultink's six dimension of product intelligence [18] our case study also identified number of distinctive features which serve as criteria to assess a CA's level of smartness. These consisted of a full spectrum of cognitive capabilities ranging from purely utilitarian (Operational) to purely social ones (Relational).

Using these two axes to cluster case study results, we identified 9 archetypal purposes/roles of CAs as shown in Table 1, which are defined from the perspective of the user and described in terms on CA capabilities.

Table 1. Archetypal Purposes of CAs

	Purpose of AI	Description of purpose from the perspective of the user	Examples of CA capabilities
Ability	Control	Performing a task ordered by the user and involving third parties such as devices or services	• Ordering a pizza • Turning on the light
	Guide	Support the user in accomplishing the steps needed to perform a task	• Fill in tax forms • Managing an insurance policy
	Assist	Helping the user organizing and performing tasks by managing to-do's and agenda	• Set up meetings • Find a dentist • Geo-locate to-do's
Trust	Inform	Provide the user with needed information, and presenting them in a relevant way	• Customized news lists • Walking time calculated based on user's actual pace
	Advise	Helping the user to evaluate a situation by comparing, predicting and gathering feedback from the net	• Recommend a product or a service • Suggest improvements
	Educate	Enabling the user to learn about a certain topic by a more or less scholastic approach	• Support students in solving math problems • Learn and practice a language
Affinity	Coach	Accompanying the user to reach her objectives by monitoring, training and providing motivation	• Stop smoking • Following a diet • Personal growth paths
	Entertain	Interacting with the user with no other aim than that of passing the time	• Exchanging jokes • Find fun facts • Have hilarious conversations
	Bond	Reaching a certain level of emotional engagement through empathy with the user	• Share intimate thoughts • Engage emotionally • Express opinions

Success Factor of CA Purposes. These purposes drive users' perception and expectations of the CA, as it entails that a CA needs to convey specific characteristics (success factors) in the interaction with the user in order to deliver a successful UX. These success factors need to be taken into account in the design of CA. Above 9 purposes of CA can be grouped into three success factors:

- **Ability:** Ability refers to those CAs whose purpose is mostly focused on the achievement of a pragmatic aim and need to be effective in performing their task in an efficient way.

- **Trust:** Trust refers to those CAs whose purpose is to aid the user in achieving their aim, such as being up to date or help decision making, and need to be reliable and explicative.
- **Affinity:** Affinity refers to those CAs whose purpose is focused on the connection that is established with the user, and need to be able to fine-tune with users' attitudes and preferences.

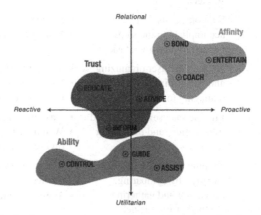

Fig. 1. Purpose and success factors of conversational agents

Design Toolkit. In order to make these findings available in the design of CA experiences, we designed a toolkit composed of three tools (Purpose Cards, Desired Purpose Worksheet, Envisioned Experience Worksheet). The key component of this toolkit is the CA Purpose Cards. Card-based tools are effective in conveying the results of the research to workshop participants because cards decks (design tools) are an 'intermediate-level' knowledge that can bridge the gap between theory and design practice [4, 5, 12]. Details of these tools will be provided in the following section.

4   Envisioning CA Experiences Workshop

We conducted a co-creation workshop with industry partners to rethink the role of CA in delivering financial services, utilizing the design tools created from applying the aforementioned framework. The workshop involved internal stakeholders from a Brazilian bank. In total, 20 people participated in the full-day workshop. All participants were corporate bank employees from various departments, selected on the basis of their roles and expertise (marketing, customer care, innovation department, insurance branch, IT).

4.1   Method

During the two-day workshop, participants were divided into small groups of 3–4 persons, and were taken through a series of hands-on activities. A set of design tools and worksheets were prepared to guide the participants through the process.

1. **Envisioning the future context.** As a first step we asked participants to envision the future context in which the CA will play a role. Inspired by Hekkert and Van Dijk's Vision in Product Design approach [9], this involved reflecting on the current societal context, on what will stay and what may change in the future in different domains.
2. **Target segments and users.** Using a variation of the empathy map, we asked participants to discuss and explore their projected user's (within their selected target segment) behaviors, expectations, influences, concerns, and preconceptions. In-lieu of performing their own user studies, we asked participants to refer back to the customers they have worked with in the past and/or current work.
3. **Define the Role of the CA.** CA purposes card set was used in order to define the role of the CA for enabling the delivery of both existing and new banking and insurance services, and also to assess the importance of each success factor with respect to the target group's expectations.
4. **Experience Vision.** The identified purposes and related success factors oriented the selection of the qualitative aspects of the UX and the definition of an 'Experience Vision', expressed through metaphors [15]. The use of metaphors as inspiration helped participants to generate concepts and detail the interaction between the CA and the user.
5. **Conversation Pattern.** As a final exercise, we asked participants to roleplay a sample conversational pattern between CA and user, that takes account of the specific role of CA and user's expectations and needs.

4.2 Toolkits

To support the workshop activities, we prepared a set of design worksheets and cards that were informed by the proposed design framework.

Tool 1: Purpose cards. These cards are designed (tailored) to inform participants [17], about the different role that CA can play and its key characteristics. The Purpose card deck (Fig. 2) presents the 9 identified purposes labeled by success factor. It provides a definition, a description of its capabilities and a pragmatic example to ease understanding.
Tool 2 - Desired Purpose worksheet: The aim of the worksheet is to funnel decision making and reporting choice of the purpose of the CA in relation to the target user and also with respect to the different components of the service offerings.
Tool 3: The Envisioned Experience worksheet. This worksheet helps to create a shared vision and to aid the ideation of the interaction between users and the CA (Fig. 3). The use of adjectives to envision the interaction with a product and using metaphors to express it is commonly used in the field of design [15]. To engage non-designers (e.g. company stakeholders) in brainstorming of CA-enabled services and related UX, we created a worksheet with pre-selected adjectives/qualities that could match well with the different CA purposes.

Fig. 2. Purpose cards

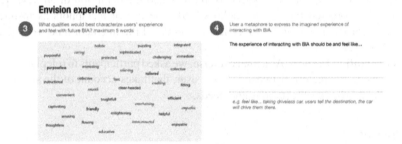

Fig. 3. Image of Tool 3 'Envisioned Experience' worksheet

4.3 Results

Results from workshop activities showed examples of attributing specific behavioral and communication characteristics (role) to CA to design new ways of delivering services targeting a specific customer segment. Characterizing CA by purpose allowed the participants (non-designers) to generate clearly distinguishable financial offer concepts and UX which enabled to convey CA's capabilities to the user, providing cues for usability and opportunities to match users' expectations. The input gathered from the stakeholders also helped to define a service offer map entirely based on the role played by the Conversational Agent. Table 2 lists select concepts that were discussed during the workshop.

The WS proved that our toolkit was useful to facilitate the co-creation with bank stakeholders, as participants were able to make a connection between their assigned target group, the most fitting purpose of the CA with respect to that target user and relate it back to bank's products offerings.

Table 2. Role-based concepts from the workshop

Concept title	Target User	Role of CA	Metaphor	Metaphor
Budget partner	Young adults looking for financial stability	Coach (Affinity)	…as the Jiminy Cricket watching over their shoulder to make sure they don't get lost along the way	• Setting financial goals • Expenses pattern recognition • Budgeting training • Tax filing reminders and aid
Risk Fella	Large and wealthy families travelling a lot	Inform (Trust)	…as the magic umbrella, an omnipresent shelter that appears at the right moment to protect users from unavoidable and unpredictable mishaps	• Analysing transactions • Forecasting purchase related risk • Snack insurance • Vocal activation
Personal Advisor	Investors and traders	Advice (Trust)	…like the genie in a bottle, always ready to satisfy users desires but also giving wise advice	• Stock-market custom predictive analysis • Concierge service for business and personal life
Bailout Buddy	Low income class	Educate (Trust)	…as an older brother, giving you tips and advice to better face life, in a friendly way	• Audio explanations about economics fundamentals • Smart governmental funds request
Account Guardian	Retail customers	Guide (Ability)	…as the tip of the scale, an incorruptible judge able to clearly distinguish good from bad	• Voice print recognition • Cards location usage map

5 Discussion

We started from the assumption that when interacting with an artificial system, users' expectations and perception of the experience is influenced by three main aspects: the intent of the user (purpose), the capabilities of the CA (operational vs. relational), and its field of application (context). Considering that the consistency of these three elements is key to deliver a positive human-product interaction and UX, the presented archetypes aim at providing a starting point to open up a discussion for the co-design of a coherent CA rather than providing a comprehensive set of guidelines to be used by experts in the field [3, 11]. We aim to further test the usefulness of the proposed approach through additional workshops with stakeholders from a diversity of services and target segments.

As conversational agents are widely adopted across industries, we'll see more demand for 'specific CAs' that are experts in knowledge with the human-like abilities to communicate. These CAs should have its own character and personality, driven by the expected roles and purposes. For example, interacting with a CA for airlines to find about flight info would be different from interacting with a financial CA that advises on investment strategies. Similarly, as general-purpose CAs widen its knowledge base, it could use the role-based approach to develop different personas/personalities to interchange depending on its assumed role. As one of the participants said after the workshop, *"Communicating a well defined role through the UX is key to ease the comprehension of the system from users…and clearly define the boundaries of the system."*

Designing of CAs should be inclusive that brings engineers, designers and non-designers on the table together, and we hope the proposed approach and toolkit makes the design process accessible and easy to envision and ideate services enabled by CAs.

Acknowledgement. We'd like to thank Banco Bradesco for providing funding to conduct the research and supporting with the workshops.

References

1. L'Abbate, M., Thiel, U., Kamps, T.: Can proactive behavior turn chatterbots into conversational agents?. In: IEEE/WIC/ACM International Conference on Intelligent Agent Technology, pp. 173–179. IEEE (2005)
2. Actions on Google, Conversation Design Process - Create a Persona. https://designguidelines.withgoogle.com/conversation/conversation-design-process/create-a-persona.html#create-a-persona-how-do-i-create-one. Accessed 15 June 2020
3. Cheng, L., Microsoft Conversational AI tools enable developers to build, connect and manage intelligent bots, 15 August 2018. https://azure.microsoft.com/it-it/blog/microsoft-conversational-ai-tools-enable-developers-to-build-connect-and-manage-intelligent-bots/. Accessed 10 June 2020
4. Chung, D.W., Liang, R.H.: Interaction tarot: a card-based design of knowledge construction for brainstorming in HCI. In: Proceedings of the 6th IASDR Conference on Design Research (IASDR 2015) (2015)
5. Deng, Y., Antle, A.N., Neustaedter, C.: Tango cards: a card-based design tool for informing the design of tangible learning games. In: Proceedings of the 10th Conference on Designing Interactive Systems, pp. 695–704. ACM Press, New York (2014)

6. Google Cloud, Agent Design. https://cloud.google.com/dialogflow/docs/agents-design. Accessed 30 May 2020

7. Gnewuch, U., Morana, S., Maedche, A.: Towards designing cooperative and social conversational agents for customer service. In: ICIS (2017)

8. Hall, E., Maeda, J.: Conversational design (2018)

9. Hekkert, P., van Dijk, M., Lloyd, P.: Vision in product design: Handbook for innovators (2011)

10. Hill, J., Ford, W.R., Farreras, I.G.: Real conversations with artificial intelligence: a comparison between human-human online conversations and human-chatbot conversations. Comput. Hum. Behav. **49**, 245–250 (2015)

11. IBM Design for AI, Chatbots and Conversational Agents. https://www.ibm.com/design/ai/conversation/#chatbots-and-conversational-agents. Accessed 28 May 2020

12. Löwgren, J.: Annotated portfolios and other forms of intermediate-level knowledge. Interactions **20**(1), 30–34 (2013)

13. McTear, M. F., Callejas, Z., Griol, D.: The conversational interface, vol. 6, no. 94, p. 102. Springer, Cham (2016). 10.1007/978-3-319-32967-3

14. Nishio, S., Nakanishi, H., Fujinami, T.: Investigating human nature and communication through robots. Front. Psychol. **7**, 1784 (2016)

15. Pasman, G., Boess, S., Desmet, P: Interaction vision: expressing and identifying the qualities of user-product interactions. In DS 69: Proceedings of E&PDE 2011, the 13th International Conference on Engineering and Product Design Education, London, UK (2011)

16. Pearl, C.: Designing Voice User Interfaces: Principles of Conversational Experiences. O'Reilly Media, Inc., Sebastapol (2016)

17. Peters, D., Loke, L., Ahmadpour, N.: Toolkits, cards and games–a review of analogue tools for collaborative ideation. CoDesign, pp. 1–25 (2020)

18. Rijsdijk, S.A., Hultink, E.J.: How today's consumers perceive tomorrow's smart products. J. Prod. Innov. Manag. **26**(1), 24–42 (2009)

19. Shah, H., Warwick, K., Vallverdú, J., Wu, D.: Can machines talk? comparison of eliza with modern dialogue systems. Comput. Hum. Behav. **58**, 278–295 (2016)

20. Vitali, I., Arquilla, V.: Conversational smart products: a research opportunity, first investigation and definition. In: Colombo, S., Lim, Y. (eds.) DESFORM 2019. Beyond Intelligence, pp. 60–68 (2019)

How Users Reciprocate to Alexa

The Effects of Interdependence

Florian Schneider[✉]

Julius-Maximilians University Wuerzburg, 97070 Würzburg, Germany
`florian.schneider@uni-wuerzburg.de`

Abstract. With the launch of *Siri*, a conversational assistant presented by *Apple* in 2011, voice-enabled personal assistants have since been accessible to the masses (Hoy 2018). As speech is the main channel for communication between humans (Flanagan 1972; Schafer 1995) and is considered to be an innate human behavior (Pinker 1994), interacting with a voice interface is intuitive (Cohen, Giangola and Balogh 2004). Studies conducted under the Computers Are Social Actors (CASA) paradigm indicate that speech-output and interactivity are two main factors to elicit social reactions in users (Nass et al. 1993). Users adopt human principles like reciprocity and team affiliation when interacting with computers (Nass and Moon 2000). As voice assistants are able to send social cues we assumed that subjects will show social reactions towards an *Amazon Echo*. Focussing on the social norm of reciprocity, we measured if people provide more help to the assistant after being told that they are interdependent of each other when compared to being independent.

A laboratory experiment with 120 participants was conducted. Participants played an interactive game using an *Amazon Echo*. Team affiliation was manipulated by telling one group their game performance would be rated individually while telling the interdependent group that they are being assessed on their joint performance with the assistant. To operationalize reciprocity, we opted for a behavioral measurement to assess participants' willingness to help the assistant: Participants were asked to name potential cities in which the game could take place. Participants were able to name any number of cities, assuming a relationship between the number of cities named and the level of cooperativeness towards the assistant.

Results show a significant main effect of interdependence on the evaluation of Alexa as well as the number of cities named meaning participants did show reciprocal behavior towards the voice assistant.

Keywords: CASA · Voice assistants · Reciprocity · Media equation

1 Introduction

Conversational interfaces have established themselves as one of the breakthrough technologies of the 21st century. With the launch of Siri, a conversational assistant presented by *Apple Inc.* in 2011, voice-enabled technology has since been accessible to the masses.

C. Stephanidis et al. (Eds.): HCII 2020, CCIS 1293, pp. 376–383, 2020.
https://doi.org/10.1007/978-3-030-60700-5_48

Initially, these services were only available on smartphones. However, since the *Amazon Echo* was released in 2014, there have been stand-alone devices, so-called smart speakers. These are equipped with intelligent personal assistants aiming to make people's everyday life easier (Hoy 2018). Siri, Alexa, Google's Assistant, Cortana and other intelligent assistants can currently perform basic functions that the user can trigger via voice command. They send messages, create shopping lists or retrieve information from the Internet - overall, they perform tasks on demand.

Spoken dialogue interfaces take advantage of human evolutionary behavior which is why interacting with them appears intuitive and easy (Cohen et al. 2004). Speech is the primary medium of human communication (Flanagan 1972; Nass and Gong 2000; Schafer 1995) and thus a means of interaction whose use one is usually unaware of. Voice assistants appear to have human characteristics like comprehending speech, generating voice and being inherently socially interactive (Purington, Taft, Sannon et al. 2017) and thus send social cues to users. Based on the findings of research conducted under the Computers Are Social Actors (CASA) paradigm (Nass et al. 1994; Nass et al. 1993), for the present study we assume that the blurring of the boundary between medium and interaction partner, in this case voice assistants, leads to the mindless application of innate social rules. During interactions with computers it was confirmed that the norm of reciprocity (Fogg and Nass 1997) and the application of politeness (Nass et al. 1999) retain their validity. It has been shown that by creating team affiliation between computers and users, findings from the domain of group research can also be applied to Human-Computer Interaction (HCI) (Nass et al. 1996). For example, the authors found that interdependent subjects had the feeling that they were aligning their responses with those of the computer, showed a greater willingness to conform to the computer's suggestions and were more open to being influenced (Nass et al. 1996). Interdependence was found to affect the willingness to help (Van der Vegt and Van de Vliert 2005; Wagemann 1995) and to increase cooperation among group members (Crawford and Haaland 1972). In line with this, cooperating with a non-helpful teammate leads to a decrease in prosocial behavior (Velez 2015).

The present study sets out an empirical examination of the effects of interdependence on the users' behavior towards a voice assistant, specifically Amazons Alexa.

2   Theoretical Framework

2.1   Speech in Human-Human Interaction

Speech is an essential aspect of human-human interaction (Flanagan 1972; Nass and Gong 2000; Schafer 1995) and, referring to socio-evolutionary research, an inevitable tool for survival (Nass and Gong 2000). In ancient times, it was a vital need of the homo sapiens to bond with other humans for hunting and for mating to make sure that the species will survive natural selection (Nass and Gong 2000). As speech was an easy to perceive and highly accurate cue of humanness, it became a central tool for interactions, such as building and maintaining social bonds, describing the environment and expressing internal processes. All of this led to the innate rule of decision to perceive everything that produces speech as a human being (Nass and Gong 2000).

Transferring it to technology results in the most humanlike interaction with technological devices, so far. Technology evolves rapidly - from unidirectional communication of a user giving commands to the device and waiting for an answer to bidirectional communication between the technological agent and the human user. One of the greatest advantages of speech technology is the intuitive operation of the devices. Since spoken language skills are an innate behavior (Pinker 1994) and do not have to be learned first, the handling of language-based systems is familiar and easy (Cohen et al. 2004). The technological progress and the resulting new conditions of technology use call for an in-depth analysis of the underlying psychological processes: If human users communicate with conversational agents will they adopt social norms originally known from human-human interaction?

2.2 Previous Research: Computers Are Social Actors

The theory of CASA maintains that social scripts are activated when interacting with a computer resulting in behavior that is well known from human-human interaction (Nass and Moon 2000). Several studies carried out in this domain were based on the same principle: a methodological approach known from interpersonal social research was taken and replicated in such a way that at one point the human being was substituted by a computer (Nass et al. 1994). Following this procedure, it was demonstrated that users classify computers into social categories such as gender and ethnicity, adopting predictions of stereotypic behavior and character traits (Nass et al. 1994; Nass et al. 1997; Nass and Moon 2000). Furthermore, people tend to attribute personality characteristics to computers (Nass et al. 1995) and adopt social norms such as politeness when interacting with computers (Nass et al. 1994) as well as smartphones (Carolus et al. 2019).

Speaking naturally with a computer is a truly ubiquitous method of user access (Cox et al. 2000). Giving the fact that a voice assistant is able to send social cues and thus appears to have human characteristics like comprehending speech, generating voice and being "inherently a socially interactive device, since it requires social interaction to function" (Purington et al. 2017), it is reasonable to assume that voice assistants are perceived as social actors and as a result treated as such.

2.3 The Effects of Interdependence

From an evolutionary perspective, the desire for social bonding among individuals is a vital advantage of human species (Baumeister and Leary 1995). As the societal system of humans depends on group membership, building and maintaining relationships is one of the core motives of an individual's actions (Leary and Cox 2008). It was found that interdependence influences the behavior of individuals within a group. By manipulating the level of interdependence, it could be examined that being dependent on each other leads to increased cooperation among group members (Crawford and Haaland 1972) as well as a higher willingness to help each other (Van der Vegt and Van de Vliert 2005; Wagemann 1995).

Since studying the effects of group membership is one of the main topics in social psychology, this field of research was also of great interest to the followers of the CASA paradigm to be investigated in the context of interaction with computers. Nass et al.

(1996) were the first to conduct fundamental research on the effects of team affiliation in HCI. Creating dependency between users and computers led to higher levels of cooperation, higher conformity of the computer's opinion and higher ratings of friendliness and intelligence (Nass et al. 1996; Nass and Moon 2000).

2.4 Hypotheses

The CASA literature indicates that users tend to perceive a computer as a social entity which leads to the application of social rules in interactions with computers. Following the Minimal Group Paradigm, team affiliation between humans and computers can simply be induced by telling subjects that they are being assessed on their joint performance with the computer (Johnson and Gardner 2007; Nass et al. 1996). There is evidence in literature that interdependence leads to increased cooperation among group members (Crawford and Haaland 1972) as well as a higher willingness to help each other (Van der Vegt and Van de Vliert 2005; Wagemann 1995). The inherent obligation to respond to helpfulness is defined under the norm of reciprocity (Gouldner 1960). Considering the findings from Fogg and Nass (1997) showing that manipulating interdependence can influence subject's reciprocal behavior towards a computer, we predict the following:

H1: Subjects in the interdependent condition provide more help to Alexa by naming cities than participants in the non-interdependent condition.

Since interdependence leads to increased prosocial behavior and revaluation among group members, we predict that manipulating interdependence would also lead to differences in a voice assistant's evaluation:

H2: Subjects in the interdependent condition evaluate the voice assistant's performance to be significantly better than participants in the non-interdependent condition.

3 Method

3.1 Participants

120 volunteers participated in our experimental study conducted at the University of Würzburg, including $n = 39$ (32.5%) male and $n = 81$ (67.5%) female subjects. Participants ranged in age from 18 to 30 years ($M = 21$ years, $SD = 2.23$ years). In terms of education, 86.7% reported to hold a higher education entrance qualification.

3.2 Procedure

In order to evaluate the research questions, we conducted a laboratory experiment with a between-subject factorial design (interdependent/non-interdependent). On arrival, subjects were randomly assigned to one of the conditions and were prompted to play a game that involved interacting with an Amazon Echo device.

The game was developed especially for the present study and consisted of a storyline written in HTML so that it could be accessed in a web browser. In addition to that, an Alexa Skill was programmed. Participants navigated through several web pages to play the game. Each page consisted of a short text that continued the story (participants took on the role of a spy decoding a secret message), a task to be given to Alexa, a question for which the correct answer was mandatory in order to continue and an input field for this answer. The only way the player could obtain the correct answer was from the speech output of the voice assistant, which forced users to interact with Alexa. A total of 21 tasks had to be fulfilled to solve the game and complete the mission. Once the participants completed the last task of the game, they received feedback on their performance in the game. The wording of the feedback differed depending on the level of interdependence, as subjects in the interdependent condition expected to be assessed on their joint performance with the assistant. All participants received the same feedback based on the condition.

In a second task, the user's willingness to help Alexa was measured. Following the feedback, Alexa pretended that the participant could help fill a database with cities where the plot of the game could alternatively take place. Participants were able to name any number of German cities before ending the interaction. To detect a valid city entry, a list of 1055 German cities was used. In this way it was possible to compare the voice input with the existing list and only increase the city counter if a valid input had been made.

Lastly, participants filled in an online questionnaire to rate the voice assistant's performance. The scale consisted of six items (e.g. 'How well did Alexa perform?') and was derived from the 'computer performance' scale used by Johnson and Gardner (2007). All answers were given on a 7-point-likert-scale.

4 Results

Table 1 shows the descriptive results of cities named for both experimental groups revealing that participants in the interdependent condition were more willing to help the voice assistant after concluding the game.

Table 1. Means and standard deviations of "cities named"

Interdependent	Non-interdependent
M 8.13, *SD* 3.64	*M* 5.77, *SD* 3.56

Our first hypothesis stated that the level of interdependence has a positive effect on the participants' reciprocal behavior towards Alexa. For calculations, reciprocity was quantified by counting the absolute value of cities mentioned when Alexa asked the subjects for help to extend a library. A one-way ANOVA between the experimental groups revealed that perception of interdependence had a significant effect on reciprocity, $F(1, 116) = 5.83$, $p = .017$, $\eta^2 = .048$. Subjects in the interdependent condition named significantly more cities to Alexa than subjects who were told they are being assessed on their performance individually (non-interdependent). Therefore, the hypothesis can be confirmed.

Hypothesis 2 focused on between-group differences of interdependence on the evaluation of the voice assistant's performance. As expected, there was a significant difference between the interdependent and the non-interdependent group, $F(1, 116) = 6.35$, $p = .013$, $\eta^2 = .051$. Subjects in the interdependent group rated Alexa's performance to be significantly better compared to subjects in the non-interdependent group.

5 Discussion

Interdependence was found to elicit numerous forms of prosocial behavior (Crawford and Haaland 1972; Van der Vegt and Van de Vliert 2005; Wagemann 1995). One of the most dominant features of social interaction is the norm of reciprocity (Cialdini 2009; Fehr and Gächter 2000). The goal of this study was to examine the effects of this norm during human-voice-assistant interaction based on previous CASA research. The results confirmed the positive effect of interdependence on reciprocal behavior. Subjects who were told that they are being evaluated on their joint performance with the spoken language system were more willing to help the system than participants in the non-interdependent condition. The significance of the results confirms that our manipulation of interdependence was effective and noticeable and that it is sufficient to tell the participants that they are dependent on the voice assistant to create a sense of team empathy. This can be seen as a verification that the social cues sent by a voice-based system causes the user to view the system as a social actor.

The obligation of the members to help their group achieve joint success is closely linked to the feeling of belonging to this group. If this social norm is violated, the group punishes the uncooperative participant (Fehr and Gächter 2000). In his study, Velez (2015) was able to demonstrate that the non-helpfulness of a teammate led to a significant decrease in the prosocial behavior of the participants. He further noted that this effect is not limited to the ingroup but is independent of the group affiliation of the recipient of the reciprocal action (Velez 2015). Our results show that when asked to evaluate the performance of a voice assistant after interacting with it, participants rated it to be higher when a sense of interdependence was induced, thus falling in line with previous research concerning group behavior in human-human interaction and confirming that a perceived sense of interdependence affects the behavior of the user.

6 Conclusion

To conclude, transferring the CASA paradigm to voice assistants has been shown to be a heuristically fruitful approach for future analyses. They seem to elicit seemingly inappropriate social reactions in their users which are the result of psychological mechanisms deeply rooted in mankind.

The assumption of subject's perceiving a smart speaker as a social actor was confirmed by significant results regarding reciprocal behavior in an interdependent team constellation. Subjects who were told that they are being evaluated on their joint performance with the spoken language system were more willing to help the system than participants in the non-interdependent condition. Thus, this thesis provides a further contribution to the extension of the CASA paradigm with focus on the medium of speech. The indication that interacting with a voice assistant can elicit social behavior opens up new questions regarding the concept of trust, influence and dependency in the highly relevant field of voice interaction.

References

Baumeister, R.F., Leary, M.R.: The need to belong: desire for interpersonal attachments as a fundamental human motivation. Psychol. Bull. **117**(3), 497–529 (1995). https://doi.org/10.1037/0033-2909.117.3.497

Brown, P., Levinson, S.C.: Politeness: Some Universals in Language Usage. Cambridge University Press, Cambridge (1987)

Carolus, A., Schmidt, C., Münch, R., Schneider, F.: Impertinent mobiles. Effects of polite and impolite feedback on the evaluation of smartphones. Comput. Hum. Behav. **93**, 290–300 (2019). https://doi.org/10.1016/j.chb.2018.12.030

Cialdini, R.B.: *Influence: The Psychology of Persuasion* [Epub Edition]. Collins, New York (2009)

Cohen, M.H., Giangola, J.P., Balogh, J.: Voice User Interface Design. Addison-Wesley, Boston (2004)

Cox, R., Kamm, C., Rabiner, L., Schroeter, J., Wilpon, J.: Speech and language processing for next-millennium communications services. Proc. IEEE **88**(8), 1314–1337 (2000). https://doi.org/10.1109/5.880086

Crawford, J.L., Haaland, G.A.: Predecisional information seeking and subsequent conformity in the social influence process. J. Person. Soc. Psychol. **23**(1), 112–119 (1972). https://doi.org/10.1037/h0032870

Fehr, E., Gächter, S.: Fairness and retaliation: the economics of reciprocity. J. Econ. Perspect. **14**(3), 159–181 (2000). https://doi.org/10.1257/jep.14.3.159

Flanagan, J.N.: Speech Analysis Synthesis and Perception, 2nd edn. Springer, Berlin (1972)

Fogg, B.J., Nass, C.: How users reciprocate to computers. In: Extended Abstracts on Human Factors in Computing Systems, CHI 1997, pp. 331–332 (1997). https://doi.org/10.1145/1120212.1120419

Gouldner, A.W.: The norm of reciprocity: a preliminary statement. Am. Soc. Rev. **25**(2), 161–178 (1960). https://doi.org/10.2307/2092623

Hoy, M.B.: Alexa, Siri, Cortana, and more: an introduction to voice assistants. Med. Ref. Serv. Q. **37**(1), 81–88 (2018). https://doi.org/10.1080/02763869.2018.1404391

Johnson, D., Gardner, J.: The media equation and team formation: further evidence for experience as a moderator. Int. J. Hum.-Comput. Stud. **65**(2), 111–124 (2007). https://doi.org/10.1016/j.ijhcs.2006.08.007

Leary, M.R., Cox, C.B.: Belongingness motivation: a mainspring of social action. In: Shah, J.Y., Gardner, W.L. (eds.) Handbook of Motivation Science, pp. 27–40. The Guilford Press, New York (2008)

Nass, C., Fogg, B., Moon, Y.: Can computers be teammates? Int. J. Hum.-Comput. Stud. **45**(6), 669–678 (1996). https://doi.org/10.1006/ijhc.1996.0073

Nass, C., Gong, L.: Speech interfaces from an evolutionary perspective. Commun. ACM **43**(9), 36–43 (2000). https://doi.org/10.1145/348941.348976

Nass, C., Moon, Y.: Machines and mindlessness: social responses to computers. J. Soc. Issues **56**(1), 81–103 (2000). https://doi.org/10.1111/0022-4537.00153

Nass, C., Moon, Y., Carney, P.: Are people polite to computers? Responses to computer-based interviewing systems1. J. Appl. Soc. Psychol. **29**(5), 1093–1109 (1999). https://doi.org/10.1111/j.1559-1816.1999.tb00142.x

Nass, C., Moon, Y., Fogg, B.J., Reeves, B., Dryer, C.: Can computer personalities be human personalities? In: Conference Companion on Human Factors in Computing Systems - CHI 1995, pp. 228–229 (1995). https://doi.org/10.1145/223355.223538

Nass, C., Steuer, J., Tauber, E.R.: Computers are social actors. In: Proceedings of the SIGCHI Conference on Human Factors in Computing Systems Celebrating Interdependence - CHI 1994, pp. 72–78 (1994). https://doi.org/10.1145/191666.191703

Nass, C., Steuer, J., Tauber, E., Reeder, H.: Anthropomorphism, agency, and ethopoeia. In: INTER-ACT 93 and CHI 93 Conference Companion on Human Factors in Computing Systems - CHI 1993, pp. 111–112 (1993). https://doi.org/10.1145/259964.260137

Pinker, S.: The Language Instinct: How the Mind Creates Language. W. Morrow and Co., New York (1994)

Purington, A., Taft, J.G., Sannon, S., Bazarova, N.N., Taylor, S.H.: Alexa is my new BFF. In: Proceedings of the 2017 CHI Conference Extended Abstracts on Human Factors in Computing Systems - CHI EA 2017, pp. 2853–2859 (2017). https://doi.org/10.1145/3027063.3053246

Schafer, R.W.: Scientific bases of human-machine communication by voice. Proc. Natl. Acad. Sci. **92**(22), 9914–9920 (1995). https://doi.org/10.1073/pnas.92.22.9914

Van Der Vegt, G.S., Van De Vliert, E.: Effects of perceived skill dissimilarity and task interdependence on helping in work teams. J. Manag. **31**(1), 73–89 (2005). https://doi.org/10.1177/0149206304271382

Velez, J.A.: Extending the theory of bounded generalized reciprocity: an explanation of the social benefits of cooperative video game play. Comput. Hum. Behav. **48**, 481–491 (2015). https://doi.org/10.1016/j.chb.2015.02.015

Wageman, R.: Interdependence and group effectiveness. Adm. Sci. Q. **40**(1), 145–180 (1995). https://doi.org/10.2307/2393703

User Experience, Emotions and Psychophisiological Computing

Affective Analysis of Visual and Vibro-Tactile Feedback During Floor Cleaning Task Using Heart Rate Variability

Kodai Ito[1]([✉]) [iD], Tsubasa Maruyama[2] [iD], Mitsunori Tada[1] [iD], and Takuro Higuchi[3]

[1] Artificial Intelligence Research Center, National Institute of Advanced Industrial Science and Technology (AIST), Tokyo, Japan
{kodai.ito,m.tada}@aist.go.jp
[2] Human Augmetation Research Center, AIST, Kashiwa, Japan
tbs-maruyama@aist.go.jp
[3] Kao Corporation, Tokyo, Japan
higuchi.takuro@kao.com

Abstract. In this study, we analyzed the electrocardiogram (ECG) against visual and vibro-tactile feedback during floor cleaning task using sheet-type mop for proposing physiological indexes to estimate the emotional changes during the task. For this purpose, we developed a real-time measurement and feedback system of the floor cleaning. In this system, the swept area by the mop and trunk posture of the cleaner were estimated from the motion sensor data attached to the body and the mop. Based on these estimation, the vibro-tactile and visual feedbacks were provided to the cleaners for improving the efficiency of the cleaning and for letting them know their current posture. During the task, we measured ECG to perform heart rate variability (HRV) analysis. After the task, the participants were asked to answer the questionnaires for collecting their subjective emotions. The results of the analysis demonstrated that male subjects tended to feel achievement from the visual feedback of the swept area which can be detected by RMSSD, one of the HRV index, of the ECG signal. It was also shown that LF/HF, the other HRV index, is suitable to detect concentration in the task. Our results demonstrated the potential of the HRV indexes for measuring daily emotions which can be used to optimize the contents of the feedback based on their emotional state for reducing the daily mental workload.

Keywords: Floor cleaning · ECG · Physiological indexes · Emotions

1 Introduction

Daily household work generally makes negative effects on our emotions, such as tired, bothersome and more. We focused on floor cleaning using a sheet-type mop. Improving the emotion with some feedbacks may be able to reduce daily mental workload.

Makabe et al. developed a prototype system of floor cleaning, where the tactile and auditory feedbacks were provided to the subject for increasing the swept area by the

© Springer Nature Switzerland AG 2020
C. Stephanidis et al. (Eds.): HCII 2020, CCIS 1293, pp. 387–393, 2020.
https://doi.org/10.1007/978-3-030-60700-5_49

sheet-type mop [1]. In this system, vibro-tactile feedback or 3D surround sound were provided to the cleaners for letting them know the unswept area or for navigating them to the unswept area. The results show the potential of the gamificated feedbacks on the emotions and efficiency of the cleaning.

However, the effects of feedbacks were not clarified due to accuracy of estimation of body motion. We developed a real-time measurement and feedback system of the floor cleaning. Based on the estimation of motion, vibro-tactile and visual feedbacks were provided to the cleaners. Maruyama et al. evaluated the effect of feedbacks from the body motion and cleaning task performance aspect [2]. Based on this system and experiment, we focused on evaluating the emotional changes.

Recently, some previous study suggest possibility to measure emotions using biosignals, such as electrocardiogram (ECG), Electroencephalogram (EEG) and more [3]. However, the physiological indexes to measure emotions for various situation were not clarified. In this study, we analyzed the ECG against visual and vibro-tactile feedback during floor cleaning task using sheet-type mop for proposing physiological indexes to estimate the emotional changes during the task.

2 Measurement and Feedback System of the Floor Cleaning

2.1 Overview

We developed a real-time measurement and feedback system of the floor cleaning. In this system, the swept area by the mop and trunk posture of the cleaner were estimated from the motion sensor data attached to the body and the mop.. The details were described in Maruyama's paper [2]. Based on these estimation, the vibro-tactile and visual feedbacks were provided to the cleaners for improving the efficiency of the cleaning and for letting them know their current posture. We used oscillator for vibro-tactile feedback and LCD display for visual feedback (Fig. 2).

2.2 Vibro-Tactile and Visual Feedbacks

Our system has following three type feedbacks using vibro-tactile and visual.

- No feedback (NFF, NFL):

Participants equipped our sensors and feedback system and performed the cleaning task. These trials were performed before (NFF: No feedback at first) and after (NFL: No feedback at last) other three feedbacks.

- Sweep count feedback (SF):

In the sweep count feedback, the vibro-tactile feedback was provided to the cleaner according to the number of swept at the current mop position. The strength of the oscillation decreases logarithmically. If participants sweep the same area more than twice, the oscillation will be stopped.

- Visual feedback (VF):

In the visual feedback, the swept area was visualized on the LCD display as shown in Fig. 1. On this display, the room model is rendered from top. According to the number of swept for each cell, the cells is colorized on the floor model. If participants sweep once, the floor cell will be green. If they sweep twice, it will be red and it don't have no more changes.

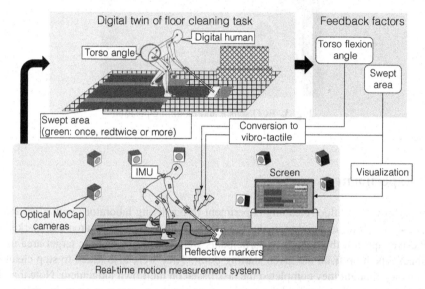

Fig. 1. Overview of the floor cleaning measurement and feedback systems [2]

Fig. 2. Sensors and oscillator attached on the sheet-type mop [2]

- Motion feedback (MF):

In the motion feedback, the vibro-tactile feedback is provided to the cleaner according to the current torso flexion angle. The degree of the oscillation increases logarithmically, continuously from 0 to 100 with the increase of the torso flexion angle.

2.3 Measurement of Biosignals

During the task, we measured ECG of participants with ZMP ECG-2 [4] (Fig. 3). We calculated their heart rate, R-R intervals (RRI) and several heart rate variability (HRV) indexes. We used following HRV indexes [5] for estimate emotional changes: SDNN, RMSSD, LF/HF and RMSSD.

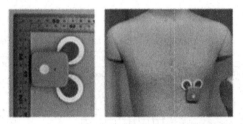

Fig. 3. ECG sensor and mounting position

3 Experiment

We performed the floor cleaning experiment in our living laboratory with eight males (age: 40.3 ± 10.6) and eight females (age: 38.4 ± 11.3). The target area was marked by adhesive tapes on the floor. The participants were asked to clean the target area using a sheet-type mop from the given starting point. They were also asked to stop cleaning when they thought they completed the task based on their own judgement. Note that the order of the cleaning area and the number of sweeping were not restricted.

Five trials were performed for each participant. In each trial, the participant performed the task with one of the three feedbacks (SF, VF, or MF) in random order. In addition, two trials without the feedback were measured first and last (NFF, NFL).

The task completion time was 108 s on average, with the shortest and longest time of 56 s and 174 s, respectively. After the task, the participants were asked to answer the questionnaires for collecting their subjective emotions about achievement and workloads for each task. The experiment was approved by the ethical review board of the authors' institute.

4 Results and Discussions

4.1 Results of the Questionnaire

Participants answered their feelings about achievement, physical workload and mental workload after each task. Figure 4 and Fig. 5 shows the results of the questionnaire. There is no significant difference. Then, we compared the results of the questionnaire by gender. As a result, we found that achievement was NF < VF ($p < 0.05$) for males. These results suggest that male subjects tended to feel achievement from the visual feedback of the swept area (Fig. 6).

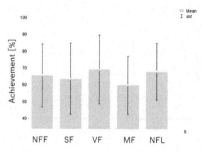

Fig. 4. Results of the questionnaire in each condition (achievement)

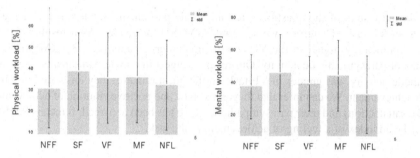

Fig. 5. Results of the questionnaire in each condition (workload)

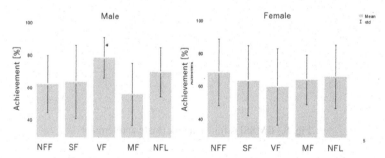

Fig. 6. Results of the questionnaire in each condition (achievement, male and female)

4.2 Results of HRV Analysis

We calculated SDNN (Fig. 7), LF/HF and RMSSD of all participants and compared between tasks. However, there is no significant difference.

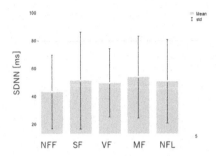

Fig. 7. SDNNs of all participants in each condition

In the results of the questionnaire, only male participants tended to feel achievement in VF task. Therefore, we separated RMSSD by gender. As a result, RMSSD was significantly higher in the VF task for male participants (Fig. 8). RMSSD is an index of parasympathetic activity. Our results suggest that male participants' parasympathetic activity was greater in VF task. In the questionnaire, they answered that they felt achievement. We can infer that they got a static and positive emotion of achievement (like satisfaction) and their parasympathetic nerve has been activated. It means RMSSD may be an index of a feeling of achievement in the task.

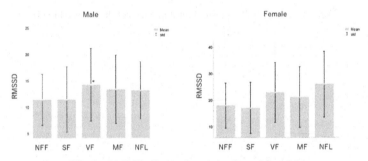

Fig. 8. RMSSDs for each task (male and female)

We performed the questionnaires with a 100-point rating. We considered that 50 point is turning point and divided participants into two group based on the NFF score, high score and low score. As a result, we found that LF/HF was significantly higher in the SF task for high achievement score group and high mental workload score group participants (Fig. 9). LF/HF is an index of sympathetic activity. In the SF task, participants needed to guess the strength of vibration to know swept area. Therefore, we can infer that participants concentrated cleaning and felt a emotion of achievement. Our results suggest that LF/HF may be an index of a concentration in the task.

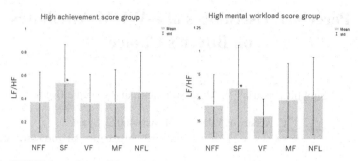

Fig. 9. LF/HFs in each condition (high achievement/high mental workload score group)

5 Conclusion

In this study, we analyzed the ECG against visual and vibro-tactile feedback during floor cleaning task using sheet-type mop for proposing physiological indexes to estimate the emotional changes during the task. For this purpose, we developed a real-time measurement and feedback system of the floor cleaning using a sheet-type mop and performed the cleaning experiment The results of the analysis demonstrated that male subjects tended to feel achievement from the visual feedback of the swept area which can be detected by RMSSD, one of the HRV index, of the ECG signal. It was also shown that LF/HF, the other HRV index, is suitable to detect concentration in the task. Our results demonstrated the potential of the HRV indexes for measuring daily emotions which can be used to optimize the contents of the feedback based on their emotional state for reducing the daily mental workload. However, there is few deference in questionnaire results among tasks. Our feedback contents did not affect not so big impact for participants' emotion. There is possibility that improving the feedbacks can indicate more clear results. Thus, our future work will be addressed to evaluate and compare several kinds of feedback to find more affective feedbacks.

References

1. Makabe, R., Ito, K., Maruyama, T., Miyata, N., Tada, M., Ohkura, M.: Development and evaluation of gamified multimodal system to improve experience value of floor wiping. In: Stephanidis, C. (ed.) HCII 2019. CCIS, vol. 1032, pp. 371–377. Springer, Cham (2019). https://doi.org/10.1007/978-3-030-23522-2_48
2. Maruyama, T., Ito, K., Tada, M., Higuchi, T.: The effect of visual and vibro-tactile feedback during floor cleaning task on motion and task performance. In: Stephanidis, C., Antona, M. (eds.) HCII 2020. CCIS, vol. 1224, pp. 261–269. Springer, Cham (2020). https://doi.org/10.1007/978-3-030-50726-8_34
3. Ohkura, M., Hamano, M., Watanabe, H., Aoto, T.: Measurement of Wakuwaku feeling of interactive systems using biological signals. In: Fukuda, S. (ed.) Emotional Engineering, pp. 327–343. Springer, London (2011). https://doi.org/10.1007/978-1-84996-423-4_18
4. ZMP ECG2. https://www.zmp.co.jp/products/sensor/vital-sensor/ecg. Accessed 20 Mar 2020, in Japanese
5. Guidelines: Heart rate variability: Standards of measurement, physiological interpretation, and clinical use. Eur. Heart. J. **17**(3), 354–381 (1996)

Perceived Usefulness of e-WOM Attributes on Buyer's Choice

Shobhit Kakaria$^{(\boxtimes)}$, Aline Simonetti, and Enrique Bigné

University of Valencia, Valencia 46022, Spain
{shobhit.kakaria,aline.simonetti,enrique.bigne}@uv.es

Abstract. Online reviews are a prevalent practice in the digital space to dissem-
inate and acquire information about products and services which has immense
effects on consumers' decision making. The study aims to measure the direct
and the interaction effects of the two review attributes of online reviews: review
content and review authenticity during the pre-purchase stage on subsequent purchase intention. We conduct a between-subject 2×2 experimental online study
with 251 participants manipulating review authenticity (verified vs unverified) and
review content (general vs specific). While consumers often use online reviews for
choosing experiential as well as material products, the present study results show a
differential impact of review content and review authenticity on the product type.
Results displayed a significant effect of review authenticity and review content on
self-reported purchase intention for material product. However, we could not find
a similar effect for experiential product. The results showed no interaction effect
between review authenticity and review content.

Keywords: Online reviews · Product type · Purchase intention

1 Introduction

With the flourishing of e-commerce platforms, the concept of consumers sharing reviews
about their purchases online, which are visible to a large audience of strangers (e.g.,
Amazon.com, Booking.com) is gaining momentum. Consumers often have access to
more than dozens of reviews across products and services from other consumers to
obtain product information and evaluate product alternatives. Each of these reviews can
potentially add value to the prospective buyer. Often online reviews help in product
evaluation and reduce uncertainty in the minds of the buyers [1].

Online reviews contain rich information about experiences with products and services. Various e-commerce websites facilitate consumers to add open-ended comments
for a product and ratings (usually presented in the form of stars). But these very reviews
also pose a challenge for the consumers. It is practically difficult for the consumer to
process all the reviews written for a particular product. To curb this overwhelming information, consumers might only selectively focus on review attributes that seem to be
helpful for their decision [2].

© Springer Nature Switzerland AG 2020
C. Stephanidis et al. (Eds.): HCII 2020, CCIS 1293, pp. 394–401, 2020.
https://doi.org/10.1007/978-3-030-60700-5_50

Perceived helpfulness of online reviews is considered as a cognitive cue and emotional response driven by heuristic processing [3]. The main drivers of perceived helpfulness can be sorted in the truthfulness of the sender's comment (e.g. verified by the platform), and the content. Previous research on verified online reviews is scarce [4] and no previous research has addressed the interaction of authenticity and the type of content.

In order to test such interaction, the current research uses two product categories, experiential and material purchases. Van Boven and Gilovich [5] define experiential purchases as *"those made with the primary intention of acquiring a life experience: an event or series of events that one lives through"* and material purchases as *"those made with the primary intention of acquiring a material good: a tangible object that is kept in one's possession."* Limited research has focussed on how consumers evaluate experiential and material products at the pre-purchase stage [6]. The current study explores the evaluation of review attributes for experiential and material products and their impact on subsequent purchase intentions.

Previous research has shown the direct effect of authentic reviews on material product sales [7], but the research is still laggard for experiential products. Further, prior research on online reviews has narrowly focused on the role of language style using hedonic and utilitarian products types [8], but scarcely in case of both experiential and material product evaluations.

The content of eWOM can be sorted in different ways [9, 10], including the scope of it as a general versus specific content. Previous research has suggested that the scope of a review content affects consumer decision dissimilarly [9]. However, previous research has scarcely focused on the interaction between review content and product type.

Therefore, our study addresses the following research questions: *(1)* Does the authenticity of focal reviews of experiential and material products impact purchase intention? *(2)* Does the style of the review content of experiential and material products influence purchase intention? (3) Does the interaction between review authenticity and review content impact purchase intentions?

This research contributes to the body of research inspecting consumer behaviour through the following findings. First, we highlight the critical role of review authenticity in subsequent purchases intentions. Second, we reveal that the linguistic style of the review content influences purchase intentions. Third, we attempt to highlight the interaction between authenticity and content on subsequent purchase intentions of different product types. Lastly, the findings identify that the material and experiential nature of a product determines the impact of authenticity and linguistic style of the review on purchase intention.

2 Background and Hypotheses

Review Authenticity. Verified or unverified reviews have been identified as two sources of generating reviews [11]. Reviews with a verification tag would be considered more trustworthy since their purchase history is traceable [11]. Authentic reviews have been defined as verified reviews based on the personal statement or checking by a platform. Platforms have adopted different ways of showing such authenticity. For instance, Amazon a 'Verified Purchase' badge in *September 2009* to indicate whether the purchase history of the reviewer could be verified by Amazon. In tourism, Booking.com only accept reviews from customers who have actually booked and stayed at a hotel through their website; but other platforms (e.g., TripAdvisor) permit all reviews to be displayed centred on the trust they place in users' affirmations concerning their visits, who need not provide proof of the booking at the hotel or service [4].

In this study, we define authentic reviews as verified reviews, meaning reviews with the presence of a 'Verified Purchase' badge; and non-authentic reviews as unverified reviews, meaning reviews with the absence of a 'Verified Purchase' badge. The reasoning behind this is that a review of a consumer with a 'Verified Purchase' badge reflects a genuine experience with the product – an experience not all reviewers have - making their reviews authentic. Previous research has shown that the reviews written by consumers with a verified purchase badge have greater explanatory power in predicting future sales and price than the mean review rating [7]. Intuitively, the higher the percentage of verified reviews, the more the consumers will perceive the reviews to be credible.

An authentic review generates trustworthiness and credibility among readers that the person who has written the review has bought the product and has experience of using the product, whereas non-authentic reviews can be written by a competitor or a paid critic and can be fake or deceivingly written by a reviewer, without even having purchased the product before, compromising the credibility of the review [7]. Hence, our first hypothesis:

H1: Purchase intention will be higher for products with verified reviews than for unverified reviews.

Review Content. The content of the review encompasses various reasons for the purchase of the product in different linguistic styles such as comments in straightforward language or complex language [8]. The credibility of a review is facilitated more by product-specific content (objective review) than by personal experience interpretations (subjective review) [12]. In a review content, consumers can share either factual information of a product *(e.g. I chose the phone because..)*, or indicate their emotions regarding the product *(e.g. I liked the phone because..)*. Moore [10] divided review content into two parts, *'explained actions'* and *'explained reactions'*. Explained actions or objective criteria refer to a review wherein the reviewers specify why they choose the product that was bought whereas explained reactions or subjective criteria is when the reviewers explain why they feel what they feel about the product they bought. The study revealed that for utilitarian products, explained actions were more helpful than explained reactions, whereas for hedonic products explained reactions were more helpful than explained actions [10]. Following Moore [10], we define a general comment as a comment that describes the individual's feeling of using or experiencing the product. In contrast, a specific comment is defined as a comment that describes an individual's objective of why they choose the product, focusing on its functions and details. Hence our second hypothesis:

H2: Purchase intention will be higher for products with specific content than for general content.

Additionally, we hypothesize an interplay between the two main factors:

H3: Purchase intention will be higher for verified reviews with specific content than unverified reviews with specific content.

H4: Purchase intention will be higher for verified reviews with general content than unverified reviews with general content.

3 Method

The selection of the two products was based on three criteria: a) the products should have a sufficiently large number of reviews available on e-commerce platforms; b) they should raise the interest in knowing the opinions of other consumers regarding the products; and c) the product should be divided easily into a materialistic product or an experiential product. Therefore, a tablet and a trip destination were chosen for materialistic and experiential products, respectively. Afterwards, we selected reviews for each product. The number of reviews and the number of words in a review were kept constant for all conditions. The selected reviews were collected, curated and adapted from the actual product online reviews to reflect the manipulation intended.

3.1 Design

A 2 × 2 mixed design was used, with review content (general/specific) and review authenticity (verified/unverified) as the between subject's independent variables, and product (a tablet and a trip destination) as the within-subjects' variable. The dependent variable used was the probability of purchase measured on a continuous scale of 0–100% as it has been usually developed in the literature. The reviews also contained a 5-stars rating sign for each review comment, that was kept constant across reviews and products. In totality, there were four conditions for four types of online reviews coded as, (I) Specific-Verified, (II) Specific-Unverified, (III) General-Verified and, (IV) General-Unverified. Each participant was exposed to the same condition for each product. For comparative purposes, each product, tablet and trip destination were analysed separately.

3.2 Participants

251 participants answered the survey (52% females; age range: 20–58 years; mean age: 36.4 years (SD = 8.43); Occupation: 67% workers, 25% unemployed, 6% students; Education: 20% High School, 59% college/university, 21% Graduates; Gross income: 43% above $40,000, 19% up to $20,000; frequency of shopping online in past 1 year: 75.7% bought often). The participants were monetarily compensated for completing the experiment. The data were collected in May 2020. The experiment was conducted online in the United States of America, using Clickworker platform.

3.3 Procedure and Task

We developed a fictitious scenario of purchase for both the tablet and the trip destination, wherein the participant looked at the product, and subsequently, read the reviews of the product. At the beginning of the experiment, the participants read the instructions and then the scenario. When facing the tablet, they were asked to imagine that they want to buy a new tablet and that they found the following comments about it on Amazon.com; for the trip destination condition, the participants were asked to imagine that they are planning their next vacation to Sri Lanka and they found the following comments related to a trip destination on an online provider.

Participants were presented with a picture of a generic tablet (for the tablet scenario) and a beach landscape (for the trip destination scenario) with no brand or price information followed by the scenario description. In doing so we removed the scope of brand and price as they can confound purchase intentions. Then they were shown four reviews for each product. The composition of the reviews was mixed. For each condition, $1/4^{th}$ of the reviews (i.e., one of the reviews) were of the opposite condition; for example, in the General-verified condition, three comments had general content with a verified purchase sign and the 5-stars rating sign, and one of the comments (placed always in the third position) had a specific content without the verified purchase sign and a 1-star rating sign. This was done to make the reviews seem genuine to the participants. Right after the last comment, participants rated the intention to purchase the product in a slider bar ranging from zero to 100%, followed by a demographic questionnaire. The order of the presentation of products was randomized across participants.

3.4 Pre-test

We conducted a within-subject online experiment using Clickworker to define and assess the linguistic content style of the review comments. The respondents scored 16 comments (eight for tablet and eight for trip destination) on the scale of 1(*mostly general content*) to 5 (*mostly specific content), with the middle point (3) indicated as "neither general not specific".* Based on the scorings, we selected twelve comments for the main experiment.

4 Results

4.1 Pre-test

A total of 44 participants (mean age = 35.3 years; $SD = 9.60$) responded to the pre-test survey. In total three comments per condition were chosen resulting in six general content comments and six specific content comments (half of them for the tablet and the other half for the trip destination). The chosen comments had individual means below three for general comment and means above three for specific comments.

A related-samples Wilcoxon signed-rank test showed that there were significant differences in general and specific comments for the tablet ($Z = 975, p < .000$) as well as for trip destination ($Z = 935, p < .000$). The means of each condition were: $M_{general\text{-}tablet} = 1.75, SD = 0.82; M_{specific\text{-}tablet} = 4.48, SD = 0.98; M_{general\text{-}trip} = 1.80, SD = 0.84; M_{specific\text{-}trip} = 3.92, SD = 0.92.$

4.2 Online Study

To test the hypotheses, we conducted a general linear model analysis with the probability of purchase as the dependent variable, and authenticity of a review (verified and unverified) and content style of a review (general and specific) as independent variables, on tablet and trip destination. The data were analysed using Statistical Package for the Social Sciences (SPSS, Version 26.0).

In the case of a tablet, this revealed a main effect of review content style $(F (1, 247) = 23.99, p < .001)$, in which the condition with specific comments led to a higher purchase intention than general comments $(M_{specific} = 69.00, SD = 23.90; M_{general} = 53.71, SD = 26.11)$, and a main effect of review authenticity $(F(1,247) = 4.23, p = 0.40)$, on purchase probability, with the condition with verified comments leading to a higher purchase intention than unverified comments $(M_{verified} = 64.38, SD = 24.92; M_{unverified} = 58.20, SD = 27.06)$. In the case of trip destination, there was neither a main effect of review content $(F (1, 247) = 3.21, p = .74; M_{specific} = 69.24, SD = 26.23; M_{general} = 63.40, SD = 25.96)$, nor of review authenticity, $(F (1, 247) = 2.09, p = .14; M_{verified} = 68.60, SD = 24.29; M_{unverified} = 63.97, SD = 27.95)$, on purchase probability was observed. There was no significant interaction of authenticity and content observed in both product categories.

5 Conclusion

This research compared the extent to which people are influenced by review authenticity and review content for experiential purchases and material purchases during the pre-purchase stage, and see their differential impact on the purchase probability for materialistic, rather than experiential purchases. The influence of review authenticity and review content on the probability of purchase was found to be significant for the tablet, but not for the trip destination. This indicates that consumers indicate a higher intention to purchase the product when encountering verified reviews compared to unverified reviews for the tablet, whereas for the Trip destination this element has no influence. The same effect was found considering the style content of the review. Consumers reported a higher probability of purchasing the tablet when they read specific comments reviews than general ones, but not for the Trip destination. Although the data revealed that there is a trend for the experiential product to follow the same patterns found for the materialistic product, we saw no changes in the probability of purchase for the trip destination for any of the conditions. This yields only partial support to our H1 and H2. We also looked for the interaction between review authenticity and review content for each product categories but found non-significant interactions, which implies no interplay between review authenticity and content on subsequent purchase probability of the product. This yields no support for H3 and H4. We conclude that there are differences in evaluation for comments for materialistic and experiential products and attributes such as review authenticity and review content are more important for materialistic than experiential products in self-reported purchase intention.

6 Implications, Limitations, and Future Directions

The study showed that the verified purchase badge (vs no verified purchase badge) impacts purchase intention strongly for materialistic purchases than experiential purchases. This could be because a tablet is tangible, lasts over time and is kept in physical possession of the consumers. However, the experience of the trip is intangible and cannot be physically possessed over time, it can only be experienced once. Thus the consumer might give weightage to authentic reviews more for materialistic goods than experiential goods at the pre-purchase stage. The study also showed that the specific review comments (vs. the general reviews), detailed the product's functions and could be considered to be more appropriate; implying that they might contain sufficient, necessary information to make the purchase decision, but only in the case of materialistic products (not experiential products). This may be because consumers find the attributes of materialistic products more quantifiable than experiential products at the pre-purchase stage. The current research offers a practical implication for review websites to develop a strategy based on diverse product types which can assist consumers with easier product evaluations.

The study has its limitations. First, we only used positively valence comments to see the effect of independent variables pronouncedly. Future studies should take valence as an independent variable with negative and neutral comments included. Secondly, not all products are strictly experiential or materialistic, they can be mixed and context-dependent. Further research should take a larger pool of products across the materialistic-experiential spectrum. In the same vein, future research can examine how the experiential-material purchase type interacts with other categories such as hedonic (vs. utilitarian). Another fascinating line of research would be to explore the differences in evaluation of product types by using neurophysiological tools such as eye-tracker to see more nuanced effects of review attributes.

Acknowledgements. The authors gratefully acknowledge the financial support of Rhumbo (European Union's Horizon 2020 research and innovation program under the Marie Skłodowska-Curie Grant Agreement No 813234).

References

1. Ismagilova, E., Slade, E.L., Rana, N.P., Dwivedi, Y.K.: The effect of electronic word of mouth communications on intention to buy: a meta-analysis. Inf. Syst. Front. (2019). https://doi.org/10.1007/s10796-019-09924-y
2. Gottschalk, S.A., Mafael, A.: Cutting through the online review jungle—investigating selective eWOM processing. J. Interact. Mark. **37**, 89–104 (2017). https://doi.org/10.1016/j.intmar.2016.06.001
3. Ruiz-Mafe, C., Bigné-Alcañiz, E., Currás-Pérez, R.: The effect of emotions, eWOM quality and online review sequence on consumer intention to follow advice obtained from digital services. J. Serv. Manag. (2020). https://doi.org/10.1108/JOSM-11-2018-0349
4. Bigné, E., William, E., Soria-Olivas, E.: Similarity and consistency in hotel online ratings across platforms. J. Travel Res. **59**, 742–758 (2020). https://doi.org/10.1177/0047287519859705
5. Van Boven, L., Gilovich, T.: To do or to have? That is the question. J. Pers. Soc. Psychol. **85**, 1193–1202 (2003). https://doi.org/10.1037/0022-3514.85.6.1193
6. Dai, H., Chan, C., Mogilner, C.: People rely less on consumer reviews for experiential than material purchases. J. Consum. Res. **46**, 1052–1075 (2020). https://doi.org/10.1093/jcr/ucz042

7. He, J., Wang, X., Vandenbosch, M.B., Nault, B.R.: Revealed preference in online reviews: purchase verification in the tablet market. Decis. Support Syst. **132**, 113281 (2020). https://doi.org/10.1016/j.dss.2020.113281
8. Chen, Z., Yuan, M.: Psychology of word of mouth marketing. Curr. Opin. Psychol. **31**, 7–10 (2020). https://doi.org/10.1016/j.copsyc.2019.06.026
9. Bigne, E., Ruiz, C., Curras-Perez, R.: Destination appeal through digitalized comments. J. Bus. Res. **101**, 447–453 (2019). https://doi.org/10.1016/j.jbusres.2019.01.020
10. Moore, S.G.: Attitude predictability and helpfulness in online reviews: the role of explained actions and reactions. J. Consum. Res. **42**, 30–44 (2015). https://doi.org/10.1093/jcr/ucv003
11. Wan, Y.: The Matthew effect in social commerce. Electron. Markets **25**(4), 313–324 (2015). https://doi.org/10.1007/s12525-015-0186-x
12. Mudambi, S.M., Schuff, D.: What makes a helpful online review? A study of customer reviews on amazon.com. MIS Q. Manag. Inf. Syst. **34**, 185–200 (2010). https://doi.org/10.2307/20721420

Feasibility of Healthcare Providers' Autonomic Activation Recognition in Real-Life Cardiac Surgery Using Noninvasive Sensors

Lauren R. Kennedy-Metz[1]([✉]), Andrea Bizzego[2], Roger D. Dias[3], Cesare Furlanello[4], Gianluca Esposito[2,5], and Marco A. Zenati[1]

[1] Medical Robotics and Computer-Assisted Surgery Lab, Harvard Medical School and VA Boston Healthcare System, Boston, MA, USA
lauren.kennedy-metz@va.gov, marco_zenati@hms.harvard.edu
[2] University of Trento, Trento, Italy
{andrea.bizzego,gianluca.esposito}@unitn.it
[3] Human Factors and Cognitive Engineering Lab and STRATUS Center for Medical Simulation, Brigham and Women's Hospital, Boston, MA, USA
rdias@bwh.harvard.edu
[4] HK3 Lab and Bruno Kessler Foundation, Trento, Italy
cesare.furlanello@hk3lab.ai
[5] Nanyang Technological University, Singapore, Singapore

Abstract. Cardiac surgery is one of the most complex specialties in medicine, akin to a complex sociotechnical system. Patient outcomes are vulnerable to surgical flow disruptions (SFDs), a source of preventable harm. Healthcare providers' (HCPs) sympathetic activation secondary to emotional states represent an underappreciated source of SFDs. This study's objective was to demonstrate the feasibility of detecting elevated sympathetic nervous system (SNS) activity as a proxy for emotional distress associated with a medication error using heart rate variability (HRV) analysis. After obtaining informed consent, audio/video and HRV data were captured intraoperatively during cardiac surgery from multiple HCPs. Following a critical medication administration error by the anesthesiologist in-training, the attending anesthesiologists' recorded HRV data was analyzed using *pyphysio*, an open-source signal analysis package, to identify events precipitating this near-miss event. We considered elevated low-frequency/high-frequency (LF/HF) HRV ratio (normal value <2) as a primary indicator of SNS activity and emotional distress. A heightened SNS response by the attending anesthesiologist, observed as an LF/HF ratio value of 3.39, was detected prior to the near-miss event. The attending anesthesiologist confirmed a state of significant SNS activity/distress induced by task-irrelevant environmental factors, which led to a temporarily ineffective mental model. Qualitative analysis of audio/video recordings revealed that SNS activation coincided with an argument over operating room management causing SFD. This preliminary study confirms the feasibility of recognizing potentially detrimental psychophysiological states during cardiac surgery in the wild using HRV analysis. To our knowledge, this is the first case demonstrating SNS activation coinciding with self-reported and observable emotional distress during live surgery using HRV. Irrespective of the HCP's expertise, transient but intense emotional changes may disrupt attention processes leading to SFDs and preventable

© Springer Nature Switzerland AG 2020
C. Stephanidis et al. (Eds.): HCII 2020, CCIS 1293, pp. 402–408, 2020.
https://doi.org/10.1007/978-3-030-60700-5_51

errors. This work supports the possibility to detect real-time SNS activation, which could enable interventions to proactively mitigate errors. Additional studies on our large database of surgical cases are underway to confirm this observation.

Keywords: Cardiac surgery · Cognitive engineering · Neuroergonomics · Emotion recognition · Heart rate variability

1 Introduction

Cardiac surgery represents a complex sociotechnical environment relying on a combination of technical and non-technical expertise in a team-based setting. Surgical flow disruptions (SFDs) to standard operating procedures may be influenced by a variety of sources, including but not limited to patient factors (e.g. unexpected anatomy), provider expertise (e.g. novice vs. expert clinicians) or factors (e.g. fatigue), social factors (e.g. low team familiarity), environmental factors (e.g. operating room [OR] scheduling conflicts), and emotional factors (e.g. anger/frustration) [1]. Many of these sources and their impacts can be observed in healthcare providers (HCPs) through ethnographic approaches. One underappreciated yet critical source of SFDs is the influence of emotional factors, which cannot be observed without the use of either subjective self-report or objective sensors capturing underlying physiological activity.

Emotion recognition and resolution is especially important in HCPs given the known effect emotion can have on processes such as perception, memory, attention, decision-making and reasoning [2]. By identifying emotional states that have the potential to disrupt cognitive processes (e.g. distress), HCPs may be better equipped to anticipate and cope with these changes. Further, the analysis of underlying physiology may provide insight into autonomic processes indicative of intense emotional changes.

Autonomic nervous system (ANS) activity represents the interplay between the sympathetic nervous system (SNS) and parasympathetic nervous system (PNS). Activation of the SNS and withdrawal of the PNS reflects states of elevated distress, which is detectable through heart rate capture and heart rate variability (HRV) analysis. The OR, and the cardiovascular OR in particular, represents a setting with additional pressures such as temporal demands that could exacerbate the negative effect emotions can have on the aforementioned cognitive processes, as well as decision-making capacities [3].

The objective of this study was to assess the feasibility of detecting a high intensity arousal state (through ANS activity) as a proxy for emotional distress associated with a known near-miss event through physiological analysis of HRV signals. By triangulating additional data sources, we sought to identify a specific emotional state represented by this heightened arousal.

2 Methods

2.1 Data Collection

As part of a larger NIH-funded project, video, audio, and heart rate data were captured from the surgical team during a routine coronary artery bypass graft procedure. Two

GoPro cameras captured a wide view of the OR and a narrow view of the surgical field, while microphones equipped to the senior team members (attending anesthesiologist, attending surgeon, and primary perfusionist) captured relevant communications inside and outside of the OR.

Team members were also each equipped with a wearable, wireless heart rate monitor (Polar H10 sensors) and a corresponding signal receiver (Polar V800). HRV was collected given the noninvasive, continuous nature of data collection afforded, as well as its prior utility in the surgical setting [4].

2.2 Case Description

Following the observation of a serious medication administration error by the resident anesthesiologist (new trainee), which should have been prevented with oversight from the senior anesthesiologist, multiple data sources were consulted to identify the events precipitating this near-miss event.

A routine root cause analysis was carried out by hospital administrators [5], which uncovered a self-reported incidence of transient anger/frustration experienced by the senior anesthesiologist. This was induced by task-irrelevant environmental factors concerning OR management, requiring the anesthesiologist to leave the OR and negotiate a departmental argument, all occurring prior to the near-miss event. Video analysis confirms that at the time of the medication administration error, the attending anesthesiologist was in the OR and resuming task-relevant teaching and patient care duties.

2.3 Data Analysis

Using *pyphysio*, an open-source physiological signal processing Python package [6], we analyzed the attending anesthesiologists' HRV to detect the influence of ANS activity via SNS activation and PNS withdrawal, and thereby emotional distress, contributing to the lack of situation awareness and expected oversight during the resident's improper medication administration. Data were analyzed from the time of first incision through sternal closure by calculating all HRV values for all consecutive one-minute, nonoverlapping time windows.

The low frequency/ high frequency (LF/HF) ratio was selected as the primary HRV component of interest in this analysis. The LF/HF ratio reflects the proportion of both sympathetic and parasympathetic innervation [7] such that higher values indicate sympathetic predominance and arousal, while lower values indicate sympathetic withdrawal. LF/HF ratio has been previously associated with mental workload states on short time scales [8]. Based on short-term HRV data collected from a sample of over 1,200 healthy individuals aged 45–54, an average expected LF/HF ratio under resting conditions is around 2.01 units [9]. This value is our frame of reference for the subsequent analysis, given that the attending anesthesiologists' age at the time of data collection was 47.

Additional analysis considered the root mean square of the successive differences (RMSSD), a time-domain HRV associated with cognitive load [10]. Given the primarily parasympathetic nervous system (PNS) tone reflected by RMSSD, lower values indicate parasympathetic predominance and lower arousal states.

Reports given during root cause analysis procedures and audio data during the case were consulted to provide additional contextual information as necessary.

3 Results

Heightened SNS activation, reflecting an extreme elevation in the attending anesthesiologists' physiological arousal and represented by an LF/HF ratio value of 3.39 units, was detected in one sample, representing one minute, prior to the near-miss event (Fig. 1). This is in direct contrast to substantially lower values presenting in five consecutive samples prior to and five consecutive samples after the elevated sample. Specifically, the value of each of the ten minutes on either side of this sample range from 151% to 290% lower than the elevated sample comparatively.

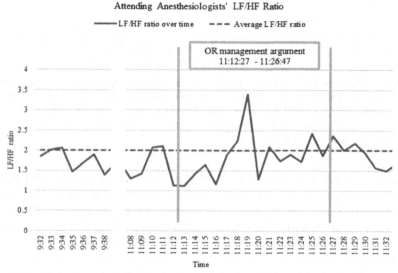

Fig. 1. Visual representation of the attending anesthesiologist's LF/HF ratio over time (blue solid line). For reference, the gray dotted line indicates this individual's average LF/HF ratio value over the course of the entire surgical procedure (2.00). From 11:12:27 through 11:26:47, the anesthesiologist is engaged in a frustrating case-irrelevant conversation. This marked elevation in SNS activity (observed here through an uncharacteristically high LF/HF ratio value) may be an indicator of emotional distress, and possibly of anger. (Color figure online)

Analysis of the parasympathetic tone revealed a sharp decrease in RMSSD amid the same samples reflecting heightened LF/HF ratio values (Fig. 2). The pattern of change does not mimic the LF/HF ratio observation precisely, but complements the finding of sympathetic activation by illustrating parasympathetic withdrawal during the same timeframe.

During standard root cause analysis procedure, the attending anesthesiologist confirmed a state of high emotional distress (specifically, frustration and anger) induced by

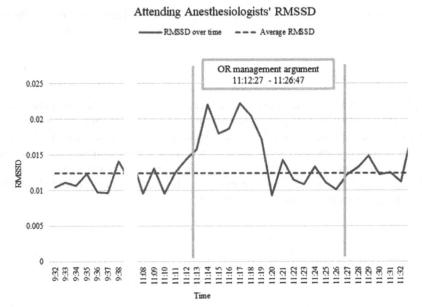

Fig. 2. Visual representation of the attending anesthesiologist's RMSSD over time (blue solid line). The gray dotted line indicates the average RMSSD value recorded over the course of the entire surgery. Corresponding to the time of the self-reported frustrating case-irrelevant conversation, we can observe a decrease in PNS activity (a sharp decline in RMSSD), complementing LF/HF ratio results. (Color figure online)

task-irrelevant environmental factors. Meanwhile, the trainee who committed the medication administration error confirmed lack of procedural knowledge and had no prior experience in the cardiovascular OR. In combination, it could be argued that the trainee's inexperience coincided with the senior anesthesiologists' lapse in attention/judgment, ultimately resulting in the preventable near-miss event that occurred.

The anesthesiologists' self-reported state of distress was further confirmed by audio recordings capturing an argument over OR management occurring at the same time as the LF/HF ratio elevation and RMSSD decline. This involved conflicting demands stemming from a discussion surrounding OR management and flow. The nature of the discussion required staff to compromise on OR flow and created tension among staff given the limited resources available (OR rooms currently in use and scheduled for use), patient concerns (delaying surgeries for patients who were already prepared and waiting for surgery), timing (operating late into the night), and personal concerns (one clinician was pregnant at the time).

4 Discussion

This preliminary study confirms the feasibility of recognizing detrimental psychophysiological influences during cardiac surgery procedures via HRV analysis. To our knowledge, this is the first such case demonstrating ANS activity coinciding with strong self-reported emotion during naturalistic surgery using HRV. The primary finding of this analysis suggests that despite HCP's extensive experience in the cardiac OR, transient but intense ANS activity (detected through SNS activation and PNS withdrawal) corresponding to self-reported emotional distress may have the potential to disrupt attention processes in even the most qualified of clinicians.

Within the analyzed dataset, there were only two other incidences of LF/HF ratio values exceeding 3 units. In both cases, the percent change between surrounding values and the elevated sample were not nearly as substantially magnified. Audio/video analysis revealed that both instances were associated with detailed teaching moments between the attending anesthesiologist and the trainee, involving discussion of procedure-specific checklists and processes.

The influence of emotional states on a range of cognitive processes [2] and decision-making is well-described [3, 11], yet investigation into its effects in surgery are underexplored. The operative environment is a uniquely data-rich setting equipped with devices automatically capturing a wide range of information regarding patient status, surgery-specific procedures, temporal relationships, and more. Additionally, the OR affords the opportunity for granular team-based, behavioral, technical, and non-technical analysis of the surgical team. It is possible, but not yet common practice, to simultaneously collect physiological data of HCPs in this setting as well. Harnessing these disparate data sources alongside one another in a time-synchronized, continuous fashion allows a more comprehensive exploration and understanding of internal, otherwise unobservable factors influencing surgical processes.

A major implication of this type of work is the possibility of real-time recognition of ANS activity and/or emotional distress, which could enable personalized cognitive engineering coping interventions to proactively mitigate downstream adverse events [12]. Additional studies on our large database of surgical cases are underway to confirm this preliminary observation. Future work is also in the planning process to explore these interactions further.

Acknowledgment. This work was supported by the National Heart, Lung, and Blood Institute of the National Institutes of Health [grant number R01HL126896, PI Zenati].

References

1. Wiegmann, D.A, ElBardissi, A.W., Dearani, J.A., Daly, R.C., Sundt III, T.M.: Disruptions in surgical flow and their relationship to surgical errors: an exploratory investigation. Surgery **142**(5), 658–665 (2007)
2. LeBlanc, V.R., McConnell, M.M., Monteiro, S.D.: Predictable chaos: a review of the effects of emotions on attention, memory and decision making. Adv. Health Sci. Educ. **20**(1), 265–282 (2014)
3. Mosier, K.L., Fischer, U.: The role of affect in naturalistic decision making. J. Cogn. Eng. Decis. Making **4**(3), 240–255 (2010)
4. Dias, R.D., Ngo-Howard, M.C., Boskovski, M.T., Zenati, M.A., Yule, S.J.: Systematic review of measurement tools to assess surgeons' intraoperative cognitive workload. Br. J. Surgery **105**(5), 491–501 (2018)
5. Wu, A.W., Lipshutz, A.K.M., Pronovost, P.J.: Effectiveness and efficiency of root cause analysis in medicine. JAMA **299**(6), 685–687 (2008)

6. Bizzego, A., Battisti, A., Gabrieli, G., Esposito, G., Furlanello, C.: pyphysio: a physiological signal processing library for data science approaches in physiology. SoftwareX **10**, 1–5 (2019)
7. Task Force of the European Society of Cardiology and the North American Society of Pacing and Electrophysiology: Heart rate variability: standards of measurement, physiological interpretation and clinical use. Eur. Heart J. **17**, 354–381 (1996)
8. Castaldo, R., Melillo, P., Bracale, U., Caserta, M., Triassi, M., Pecchia, L.: Acute mental stress assessment via short term HRV analysis in healthy adults: a systematic review with meta-analysis. Biomed. Signal Process. Control **18**, 370–377 (2015)
9. Dantas, E.M., et al.: Reference values for short-term resting-state heart rate variability in healthy adults: results from the Brazilian Longitudinal Study of Adult Health—ELSA-Brasil study. Psychophysiology **55**(6), 1–12 (2018)
10. Shaffer, F., Ginsberg, J.P.: An overview of heart rate variability metrics and norms. Front. Publ. Health **5**(September), 1–17 (2017)
11. Albayram, Y., Khan, M.M.H., Jensen, T., Buck, R., Coman, E.: The effects of risk and role on users' anticipated emotions in safety-critical systems. In: Harris, D. (ed.) EPCE 2018. LNCS (LNAI), vol. 10906, pp. 369–388. Springer, Cham (2018). https://doi.org/10.1007/978-3-319-91122-9_31
12. Zenati, M.A., Kennedy-Metz, L., Dias, R.D.: Cognitive engineering to improve patient safety and outcomes in cardiothoracic surgery. Semin. Thorac. Cardiovasc. Surg. **32**(1), 1–7 (2019)

HRV Parameters Sensitively Detecting
the Response of Game Addicted Players

Jung Yong Kim[1](✉), Min Cheol Whang[2], Dong Joon Kim[3], Heasol Kim[1],
and Sungkyun Im[3]

[1] Department of HCI, ERICA, Graduate School, Hanyang University, Seoul, South Korea
jykim0920@gmail.com
[2] Department of Emotion Engineering, Graduate School, Sangmyung University,
Seoul, South Korea
[3] Department of Industrial and Management Engineering, ERICA, Graduate School,
Hanyang University, Seoul, South Korea

Abstract. The purpose of this study is to extract quantitative parameters that indicate significant differences in ECG(electrocardiogram) between game-addicted group and non-addicted group. Currently, there is no objective means to define game addiction among health authorities and academic societies. Therefore, authors attempted to classify subjects into game-addicted groups and non-addicted group. The existing diagnostic questionnaire was used to divide subjects into two groups, and used heart rate variability to detect the any particular sign of psychophysiological response of game addicted subjects different from the non-addicted subject. 'League of Legends' by Riot Games company was used for the test. The parameters were analyzed by applying various data collecting time windows. Multiple t-tests were used to compare the two groups. In results, no significant difference was found in the data collected from time window 1) full game period and 2) first and last 10 min, and 3) first and last 5 min. However, when the player's character was killed, there were significant differences in parameters between two groups when 30 s, 60 s, and 90 s after 'being killed event'. The outcome of this study showed that particular parameters at given data collecting window could generate more sensitive outcomes than the others. Further experiment would confirm the results to be used for developing an algorithm to quantitatively diagnose the addicted individuals.

Keywords: Game addiction · Heart rate variability · ECG · Sensitive parameters · Quantitative diagnosis

1 Introduction

1.1 Background

The size of game market is growing globally and the S. Korea shares 6.7% of the market which is 5th ranked internationally [1]. Along with the wide distribution of smart devices, the game is now one of important leisure item of contemporary life

© Springer Nature Switzerland AG 2020
C. Stephanidis et al. (Eds.): HCII 2020, CCIS 1293, pp. 409–415, 2020.
https://doi.org/10.1007/978-3-030-60700-5_52

among global community. The game became a popular E-sport which is shared and enjoyed by global community. On the other hand, internet game or video game cause the addiction among players which became a social problem as well as individual medical problem. Koepp *et al.* (1998) reported that there is a relationship between game playing and attention deficiency, aggression, memory loss [2], Lee and Chae (2006) reported that adolescence with an addicted symptom tends to lack the social skill to maintain relationship, and showed relatively low score in problem solving, spontaneity, and self-control [3]. WHO registered the game as an official disorder in the 11th Revision of International Classification of Disease (ICD-11) [4], and domestic government initiated the shut-down policy disconnecting internet game line from 0 to 6 AM for players under age sixteen, in spite of the opposition from various civil right groups. In order to resolve such social conflict, it is important to objectively categorize the pathological addiction and addiction like behavior. Currently, there is no objective means to define game addiction among health authorities, academic societies and institutions. Therefore, in this study, authors would attempt to classify subjects into game-addicted groups and non-addicted group by examining psychophysiological response during game playing situation.

1.2 Purpose

The purpose of the study is to find whether or not there is a quantitative difference in Heart Rate Variability parameters between addicted and non-addicted group during actual game playing environment.

2 Methodology

2.1 Subjects

Thirteen male students with no record of cardiac and mental history volunteered for the experiment whose age was 23 ± 3. To pre-classify the addicted group and non-addicted group, internationally used IAT (internet addiction test) and domestically developed CIUS (compulsive internet use scale) were used. Seven out of thirteen subjects them were categorized as the member of addicted group.

2.2 Game Selection for Experiment

'League of Legends' developed by Riot Games company was selected for the experiment. The game is very popular among players and well known to readily immersed in playing.

2.3 Experimental Design

A between subject design was used in this experiment, and period of the game and event time of the game were used as independent variables. The period of the game consisted of 1) full game period and 2) first and last 10 min 3) first and last 5 min. The event time of game consisted of 1) 30 s after kill event and 2) 60 s after kill event 3) 90 s after kill event 4) 120 s after kill event 5) 30 s being killed event. 6) 60 s after being killed event 7) 90 s after being killed event 8) 120 s after being killed event. Dependent variable were time series parameters such as SDNN, SDSD, RMSSD, PNNI50, PNNI20, and frequency parameters such as LF, HF, Total Power, and VLF. They all represent the various features of Heart Rate Variability measured by ECG. The definitions of the parameters are listed in Tables 1 and 2.

Table 1. Time domain variables representing heart rate variability [7].

Variable	Description	Units
SDNN	Standard deviation of all NN intervals	ms
SDSD	Standard deviation of differences between adjacent NN intervals	ms
RMSSD	The square root of the mean of the sum of the squares of differences between adjacent NN intervals	ms
pNNI50	PNN50 count divided by the total number of all NN intervals	%
pNNI20	PNN20 count divided by the total number of all NN intervals	%

Table 2. Frequency domain variables representing heart rate variability [7].

Variable	Description	Units
Total power	The variance of NN intervals over the temporal segment	ms^2
LF	Power in low frequency range (0.04–0.15 Hz)	ms^2
HF	Power in high frequency range (0.15–0.4 Hz)	ms^2

2.4 Procedure

The experiment was performed at independent space and noise-free environment. Subjects were explained about the experimental device and process without informing them the main purpose of the study. The stability of ECG signal was examined in every trial repeatedly. Subject was allowed to familiarize to the experimental condition by practicing the game for once. Five-minute break was given before immersing in the game, the individually chosen level of the game was considered for voluntary concentration on the game playing. Measurement was performed two times for individual player. No alcohol and caffeine were allowed for 24 h prior to the experiment. Smoking was allowed only 2 h before the experiment.

3 Results

T test was performed to compare the behaviors of parameters. First, no significant difference was observed between two groups during full game period among parameters (p > 0.1). Second, no significant difference was observed between two groups during either the first and last 10 min or the first and last 5 min among parameters (p > 0.1). Third, no significant difference was observed between two groups after kill event (p > 0.1). However, fourth, significant differences were observed during 30, 60, 90 s after being killed event (p < 0.1) in SDSD, PNNI50, PNNI20, RMSSD, SDNN, LF, HF, and Total Power in Figs. 1, 2, 3, 4, 5 and 6.

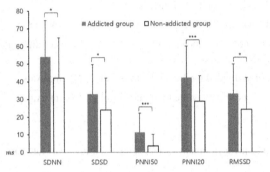

Fig. 1. Significant difference in time series parameters when 30 s after being killed event, ***p < 0.01, *p < 0.1

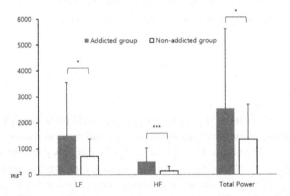

Fig. 2. Significant difference in frequency parameters when 30 s after being killed event, ***p < 0.01, *p < 0.1

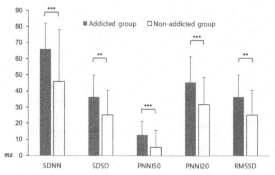

Fig. 3. Significant difference in time series parameters when 60 s after being killed event, ***p < 0.01, **p < 0.05, *p < 0.1

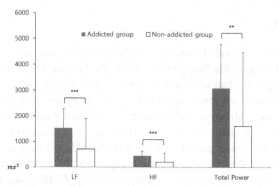

Fig. 4. Significant difference in frequency parameters when 60 s after being killed event, ***p < 0.01, **p < 0.5

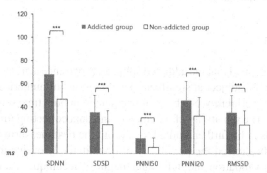

Fig. 5. Significant difference in time series parameters when 90 s after being killed event, ***p < 0.01

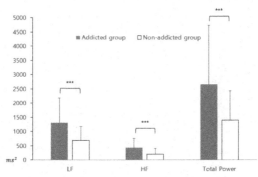

Fig. 6. Significant difference in frequency parameters when 90 s after being killed event, ***p < 0.01

4 Discussion

The most parameters responded sensitively to differentiate the addicted and non-addicted group particularly during the being killed event. That is, the HRV increased relatively more in addicted group than non-addicted group. This means that the addicted group is more vulnerable to game stress when player was being killed during playing. Physiologically speaking, a stress or high tension is associated with increased activation of sympathetic nervous system. Thus, the increase of LF, known to react when people experience stress, tension or anxiety, shows that the addicted subjects experienced the stress of anxiety more than the non-addicted players in this experiment. Such behavior of LF were also reported in previous researches [5, 6]. At the same time, HF known to be activated by para-sympathetic nerve was also increased in this experiment. This is probably the antagonistic response to the increased activity of sympathetic nervous system, and the similar pattern was observed in SDNN and RMSSD combination.

5 Conclusion

In this study, it was found that the addicted subjects experience a greater stress or anxiety than the non-addicted subject at significant level in terms of numerical parameters representing heart rate variability. Such result was shown in both time series and frequency based parameters. The sensitivity of parameters and data collecting time after the 'being killed event' needs to be further studied to sort out the best measuring combination. At any rate, this study showed the possibility of quantitatively evaluating game addicted players. The cross-validation and individual diagnosis technique to advance the current study will be followed immediately to develop the mathematical model to differentiate the ECG signal between the addict and non-addict.

Acknowledgement. This research was supported by Basic Science Research Program through the National Research Foundation of Korea(NRF) funded by the Ministry of Education (NRF-2018R1D1A1B07050786).

References

1. Korea Creative Content Agency: 2018 annual report for international contents market (2019)
2. Koepp, M.J., et al.: Evidence for striatal dopamine release during a video game. Nature **393**(6682), 266–268 (1998)
3. Lee, Y., Chae, K.M.: Relations of computer game addiction and social relationship, adjustment of adolescent. Korean J. Clin. Psychol. **25**, 711–726 (2006)
4. Good, O.S.: 'Gaming disorder' officially on World Health Organization's list of diseases. https://www.polygon.com. Accessed 25 May 2019
5. Papousek, I., Nauschnegg, K., Paechter, M., Lackner, H.K., Goswami, N., Schulter, G.: Trait and state positive affect and cardiovascular recovery from experimental academic stress. Biol. Psychol. **83**(2), 108–115 (2010)
6. Traina, M., Cataldo, A., Galullo, F., Russo, G.: Heart rate variability in healthy subjects. Minerva Psichiatr. **227**, 31 (2011)
7. Task Force of the European Society of Cardiology and the North American Society of Pacing and Electrophysiology: Standards of measurement, physiological interpretation and clinical use. Circulation **93**(5), 1043–1065 (1996)

Horizontal Mouse Movements (HMMs) on Web Pages as Indicators of User Interest

Ilan Kirsh[1]([✉]) [iD], Mike Joy[2] [iD], and Yoram Kirsh[3] [iD]

[1] The Academic College of Tel Aviv-Yaffo, Tel Aviv, Israel
kirsh@mta.ac.il
[2] University of Warwick, Coventry, UK
M.S.Joy@warwick.ac.uk
[3] The Open University of Israel, Ra'anana, Israel
yoramk@openu.ac.il

Abstract. Mouse events are widely used as implicit indicators of user attention on web pages. In this study, we investigated a particular pattern of mouse movements, *Horizontal Mouse Movements (HMMs)*, consisting of series of mouse move events in the same horizontal direction, as indicators of users' current interest. We formally defined HMMs and analyzed HMM activity on a sample website in English. We distinguished between LTR (Left to Right) HMMs and RTL (Right to Left) HMMs. LTR HMMs (in the reading direction of the sample website) were found to be more frequent than RTL HMMs (in the opposite direction). Then we investigated leaving web pages immediately after HMMs and found that they are much more frequent after an RTL HMM than after an LTR HMM. The difference can be explained by recent studies, which show that mouse movements in the reading direction are related to reading. Because reading indicates current interest in the web page content, the probability of leaving a web page immediately after LTR HMMs is lower. Accordingly, HMMs in the reading direction may serve as user interest indicators in educational technology, online learning, web analytics, and adaptive websites.

Keywords: Mouse cursor · Mouse movement · LTR · RTL · Web pages · Reading · Human-computer interaction · Intention · User interest · Adaptive websites · Educational technology · Web analytics

1 Introduction

This study analyzes Horizontal Mouse Movements (HMMs) on a sample website as indicators of user interest. User interest is an abstract concept that may be defined differently in different contexts. For the purpose of this study, we assume that staying on a web page reflects more interest in the page (at a given point in time) than leaving the page. This assumption or definition facilitates the collection of precise measurements and statistical analysis.

© Springer Nature Switzerland AG 2020
C. Stephanidis et al. (Eds.): HCII 2020, CCIS 1293, pp. 416–423, 2020.
https://doi.org/10.1007/978-3-030-60700-5_53

We analyzed HMMs on a sample website and compared LTR (Left to Right) HMMs (in the direction of reading, as the website is in English) to RTL (Right to Left) HMMs (in the opposite direction). The main contribution of this paper is showing that leaving a web page immediately after an HMM is less likely for LTR HMMs than for RTL HMMs. Accordingly, HMMs in the reading direction can be used as indicators of user interest (based on the definition of user interest provided above).

This paper is organized as follows. Section 2 reviews related work. Section 3 defines HMMs. Section 4 shows the experiment results. Section 5 discusses the results and suggests possible directions for further work.

2   Related Work

User attention on areas of a web page can be measured accurately using eye-tracking [6]. However, collecting eye-tracking data from web users is impractical for most websites, because it requires user collaboration and may raise privacy concerns, as it relies on cameras. In addition, accurate results require special cameras on the client-side. Therefore, user actions that can be tracked in modern browsers using JavaScript, such as page scrolling, mouse movements, and clicks, are often used as alternative indicators of user attention [3,5,7,8,13,17].

Mouse activity can be used as a valuable indicator of user attention, as studies show that when a user moves or clicks the mouse, the position of the mouse cursor on the screen is correlated with the user's eye-gaze [4,9,16]. Cumulative user attention on areas of a web page, based on the mouse activity of users, can be visualized using heatmaps [14,15]. Mouse activity heatmaps (also known as attention heatmaps) are popular in commercial web analytics services [11].

Recent studies show that mouse movements in the reading direction are often associated with a reading technique where the mouse cursor is used as a pointer to mark the reading position, similarly to finger-pointing when reading a book [10,12]. This study builds on this new knowledge and investigates whether horizontal mouse movements in the reading direction can be considered as indicators of current interest in web pages.

3   HMM Definition

In order to study HMMs, we need a precise definition. Our definition of HMM is configurable through four numeric parameters (HOR_DIST, VER_RANGE, MIN_TIME, and MAX_TIME), which are discussed below.

Mouse movements can be represented as a sequence of tuples (t, x, y), where each tuple contains a timestamp t, and a mouse cursor position (x, y) at that point in time. We define HMM as a sequence $(t_1, x_1, y_1), \ldots, (t_n, x_n, y_n)$ of such tuples that satisfies the following conditions:

1. **Horizontal Direction:** All horizontal differences $x_2 - x_1, \ldots, x_n - x_{n-1}$ are either non negative (for LTR movements) or non positive (for RTL movements).

2. **Horizontal Distance:** $|x_n - x_1| \geq HOR\_DIST$, i.e. the movement is not too short and is above a specified horizontal distance threshold.
3. **Vertical Range:** For every $1 \leq i, j \leq n$, $|y_i - y_j| \leq VER\_RANGE$, i.e. the movement is approximately horizontal, within a tolerance range of vertical differences.
4. **Time Frame:** $MIN\_TIME \leq |t_n - t_1| \leq MAX\_TIME$, i.e. the movement is not too slow or too fast.

The definition of HMM in this study is flexible (e.g., compared to [10]), and covers also mouse movements that are not perfectly straight, as long as they have a general consistent horizontal direction, either to the left or to the right.

This study focuses on HMMs that may be associated with reading. The default parameter values in the HMM definition have been selected accordingly, as shown in Table 1.

Table 1. Default HMM definition parameters

Parameter	Default	Motivation
HOR_DIST	400 pixels	Roughly the width of half a text line and approximately 8 words on the sample website (based on the most commonly used resolution) [10]
VER_RANGE	30 pixels	Roughly the height of one text line
MIN_TIME	2 seconds	A reasonable time for reading half a text line consisting of approximately 8 words [2]
MAX_TIME	5 seconds	A reasonable time for reading a full text line consisting of approximately 16 words [2]

4   Experimental Results

In our experiments, we used web usage data from a sample website.[1] During a three month period (ending in March 2020), mouse movements of visitors to the website have been tracked (using a JavaScript code, referenced from the website pages), reported back to the server, anonymized, and stored in a dedicated database, adhering to industry standards of data anonymization and user privacy. Previous studies provide more details on this website [10] and on the tracking and data collection methods used [12]. The dataset used in the experiments consists of 316,762 views of the 38 web pages of the website that had at least 2,000 page views each (excluding web pages with less than 200 words).

Figure 1 shows the frequencies of LTR and RTL HMMs for views of each of the 38 web pages in the dataset (based on the default parameters in Sect. 3). In Figs. 1, 3, and 4, the pages are in descending order of LTR HMM frequencies.

---

[1] www.objectdb.com, providing technical learning materials for programmers.

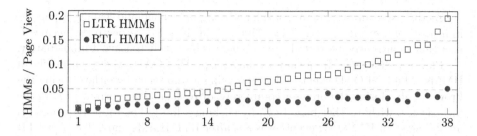

Fig. 1. HMMs frequency in views of the 38 dataset pages: LTR vs RTL

There were 23,071 LTR HMMs and 8,427 RTL HMMs (in total for all the 38 pages), i.e. an LTR/RTL ratio of 2.74. The difference has a very high statistical significance (p-value $< 0.5^{38} < 0.0000000001$, based on Arbuthnot's method [1], as there were more LTR HMMs than RTL HMMs on each of the 38 web pages).

A recent study on the same website shows that mouse movements in the direction of reading are often related to reading (as discussed in Sect. 2), and accordingly, movements in the reading direction are also more frequent than in other directions [10]. This relation between mouse movements and reading also explains the results in Fig. 1.

Figure 2 shows that the LTR/RTL ratio depends on the HMM definition parameters. In general, more restrictive parameter values lead to higher LTR/RTL ratios. A possible explanation is that more restrictive parameters increase the quality of the identified HMMs as indicating reading (higher precision) at the expense of fewer HMMs (lower recall), and accordingly, the frequencies ratio in favor of the reading direction increases.

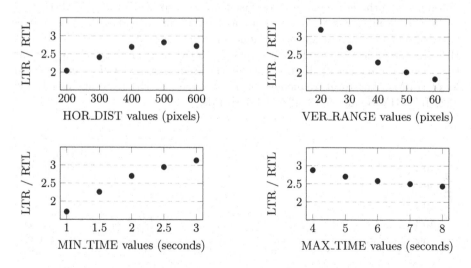

Fig. 2. LTR HMMs/RTL HMMs ratio with different parameters

As discussed in Sect. 1, we consider staying on a page and leaving a page as indicators of user interest and lack of interest in the page, respectively, because a user that is currently interested in a web page is less likely to leave it immediately.

Figure 3 shows the frequency of JavaScript UNLOAD events within 5 s of HMMs. The UNLOAD event indicates leaving a web page, by either closing the browser tab, closing the browser completely, or replacing the current page in the browser tab with another page (e.g., by clicking a link). The total frequency (in all 38 pages) of UNLOAD events was 8% after RTL HMMs and 2.4% after LTR HMMs, i.e. the user is more likely to stay on a web page after LTR HMMs than after RTL HMMs.

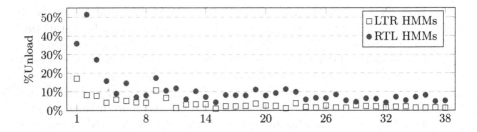

Fig. 3. %UNLOAD within 5 seconds of an HMM on the 38 dataset pages

Note that UNLOAD events may be partly related to movements to the left side menu and quitting the page with a menu link. It seems that this did not have a major effect on the results because the left side menu is only shown on the top of the page, HMMs are identified only in the textual content area, and usually, movements to the left menu are too fast to be categorized as valid HMMs.

The other main way to leave a web page, switching to another browser tab, is not related to horizontal mouse movements in the content area. The JavaScript HIDE event indicates switching a browser tab (without closing the page, so at least a temporary leave). Figure 4 shows the frequency of HIDE events within 5 s of HMMs. The total frequency (in all 38 pages) of HIDE events was 14.8% after RTL HMMs and 5.8% after LTR HMMs.

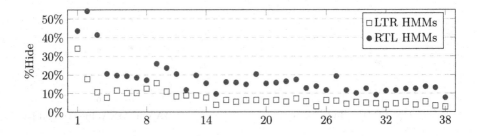

Fig. 4. %HIDE within 5 seconds of an HMM on the 38 dataset pages

The results show that users are less likely to leave the page immediately after HMMs in the direction of reading compared to leaving immediately after HMMs in the opposite direction, with either UNLOAD or HIDE. As Figs. 3 and 4 show, these results were obtained for each of the 38 web pages in the dataset separately. Consequently, these differences have a very high statistical significance (p-value < 0.0000000001, following the same considerations as in the analysis of the results in Fig. 1).

5   Discussion and Conclusions

This study compares LTR and RTL HMMs on a sample website and shows that leaving a web page immediately after an LTR HMM is less likely than after an RTL HMM. Based on our assumption that staying on a web page signifies more user interest than leaving it, we conclude that LTR HMMs can be considered as indicators of user interest on this English-based website. On websites in RTL languages (e.g., Hebrew and Arabic) we expect RTL HMMs to be indicators of user interest, although this requires further research.

Figure 5 illustrates an example of mouse movements during reading. The green lines represent mouse movements to the right, and the red lines represent mouse movements to the left. Lines connecting adjacent circles represent movements during one-tenth of a second. This visualization method is introduced and explained in detail in another study [12]. Figure 5 shows that in the context of reading, our definition of HMM covers more LTR HMMs than RTL HMMs, as movements to the left, to the beginning of the next text line, are often too fast and less flattened horizontally. This explains why RTL HMMs were less frequent.

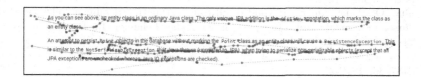

Fig. 5. Visualization of mouse movements indicating reading

Note, however, that RTL HMMs have been used as a control group, but there is no evidence to suggest that they indicate a lack of interest. On the contrary, mouse movements in general indicate user attention, as discussed in Sect. 2. The comparison emphasizes the uniqueness of HMMs in the reading direction as stronger indicators of attention and interest.

The total frequency of RTL HMMs (using the default parameter values) was approximately 7.3% of the page views. This low frequency is not sufficient on its own to learn about every individual user. However, HMMs might be useful, combined with other indicators, for adaptive websites. They might be useful also for web analytics, for example, for ranking website content by user interest, as feedback from sample users is also beneficial for analytics purposes. Further work should explore these potential uses.

References

1. Arbuthnot, J.: An argument for divine providence, taken from the constant regularity observ'd in the births of both sexes. R. Soc. **27**(328), 186–190 (1710). https://doi.org/10.1098/rstl.1710.0011
2. Brysbaert, M.: How many words do we read per minute? A review and meta-analysis of reading rate. J. Mem. Lang. **109**, 84 (2019). https://doi.org/10.1016/j.jml.2019.104047
3. Cepeda, C., et al.: Mouse tracking measures and movement patterns with application for online surveys. In: Holzinger, A., Kieseberg, P., Tjoa, A.M., Weippl, E. (eds.) CD-MAKE 2018. LNCS, vol. 11015, pp. 28–42. Springer, Cham (2018). https://doi.org/10.1007/978-3-319-99740-7_3
4. Chen, M.C., Anderson, J.R., Sohn, M.H.: What can a mouse cursor tell us more? Correlation of eye/mouse movements on web browsing. In: CHI 2001 Extended Abstracts on Human Factors in Computing Systems, CHI EA 2001, pp. 281–282. Association for Computing Machinery, New York (2001). https://doi.org/10.1145/634067.634234
5. Claypool, M., Le, P., Wased, M., Brown, D.: Implicit interest indicators. In: Proceedings of the 6th International Conference on Intelligent User Interfaces, IUI 2001, pp. 33–40. Association for Computing Machinery, New York (2001). https://doi.org/10.1145/359784.359836
6. Eraslan, S., Yesilada, Y., Harper, S.: "The best of both worlds!": integration of web page and eye tracking data driven approaches for automatic AOI detection. ACM Trans. Web **14**(1) (2020). https://doi.org/10.1145/3372497
7. Grusky, M., Jahani, J., Schwartz, J., Valente, D., Artzi, Y., Naaman, M.: Modeling sub-document attention using viewport time. In: Proceedings of the 2017 CHI Conference on Human Factors in Computing Systems, CHI 2017, pp. 6475–6480. Association for Computing Machinery, New York (2017). https://doi.org/10.1145/3025453.3025916
8. Guo, Q., Agichtein, E.: Beyond dwell time: estimating document relevance from cursor movements and other post-click searcher behavior. In: Proceedings of the 21st International Conference on World Wide Web, WWW 2012, pp. 569–578. Association for Computing Machinery, New York (2012). https://doi.org/10.1145/2187836.2187914
9. Huang, J., White, R., Buscher, G.: User see, user point: gaze and cursor alignment in web search. In: Proceedings of the SIGCHI Conference on Human Factors in Computing Systems, CHI 2012, pp. 1341–1350. Association for Computing Machinery, New York (2012). https://doi.org/10.1145/2207676.2208591
10. Kirsh, I.: Directions and speeds of mouse movements on a website and reading patterns: a web usage mining case study. In: Proceedings of the 10th International Conference on Web Intelligence, Mining and Semantics (WIMS 2020), Biarritz, France, pp. 129–138. Association for Computing Machinery, New York, June 2020. https://doi.org/10.1145/3405962.3405982
11. Kirsh, I., Joy, M.: A different web analytics perspective through copy to clipboard heatmaps. In: Bielikova, M., Mikkonen, T., Pautasso, C. (eds.) ICWE 2020. LNCS, vol. 12128, pp. 543–546. Springer, Cham (2020). https://doi.org/10.1007/978-3-030-50578-3_41
12. Kirsh, I., Joy, M.: Exploring Pointer Assisted Reading (PAR): using mouse movements to analyze web users' reading behaviors and patterns. In: Stephanidis, C., et al. (eds.) HCII 2020. LNCS, vol. 12424, pp. 156–173. Springer, Cham (2020). https://doi.org/10.1007/978-3-030-60117-1_12

13. Kirsh, I., Joy, M.: Splitting the web analytics atom: from page metrics and KPIs to sub-page metrics and KPIs. In: Proceedings of the 10th International Conference on Web Intelligence, Mining and Semantics (WIMS 2020), Biarritz, France, pp. 33–43. Association for Computing Machinery, New York, June 2020. https://doi.org/10.1145/3405962.3405984

14. Lamberti, F., Paravati, G., Gatteschi, V., Cannavó, A.: Supporting web analytics by aggregating user interaction data from heterogeneous devices using viewport-DOM-based heat maps. IEEE Trans. Ind. Inform. **13**, 1989–1999 (2017). https://doi.org/10.1109/TII.2017.2658663

15. Lamberti, F., Paravati, G.: VDHM: viewport-DOM based heat maps as a tool for visually aggregating web users' interaction data from mobile and heterogeneous devices. In: Proceedings of the 2015 IEEE International Conference on Mobile Services, MS 2015, pp. 33–40. IEEE Computer Society, USA (2015). https://doi.org/10.1109/MobServ.2015.15

16. Rodden, K., Fu, X.: Exploring how mouse movements relate to eye movements on web search results pages. In: Proceedings of ACM SIGIR 2007 Workshop on Web Information Seeking and Interaction, pp. 29–32. Association for Computing Machinery, New York (2007). http://research.microsoft.com/~ryenw/proceedings/WISI2007.pdf

17. Schneider, J., Weinmann, M., vom Brocke, J., Schneider, C.: Identifying preferences through mouse cursor movements - preliminary evidence. In: Proceedings of the 25th European Conference on Information Systems (ECIS), pp. 2546–2556. Research-in-Progress Papers, Guimarães, Portugal (2017)

Based on Inductive Quantization Method of Evaluation of Bank Experience Contact Design

Yong Li, Fu-Yong Liu(✉), Rui-Ming Hao, and Zhen-Hua Wu

Guangzhou Academy of Fine Arts, Guangzhou, Guangdong, China
253065494@qq.com

Abstract. This research is to quantitatively evaluate the bank service contacts that can generate experience for users through experimental methods. The main process is to determine the quantitative mathematical calculation method, collect the perceptual evaluation index of the bank experience contact at the design stage, use the analytic hierarchy process to establish the evaluation index system, build the design participation model of the bank experience contact, and use the fuzzy analytic hierarchy process The contact design participation is calculated and the results are quantitatively evaluated. This research can provide reference for decision makers when setting up service contacts, and provide scientific and effective data evaluation scales for bank design transformation, development process, interaction design, service design, etc., for subsequent banking user experience. Research provides new methods.

Keywords: Inductive quantitative evaluation · Design evaluation · Statistical analysis · Bank experience contact

1 Introduction

A well-designed user experience is the soul of all products and services [1], A good user experience is the key to the competitive advantage of the contemporary enterprise [2]. Accompanied by the advent of the economic era, people's access to banking services is no longer functional satisfaction, but more importantly, the experience of service encounter, so no matter what service mode is adopted, it is necessary to systematically analyze its service encounter. The bank user experience is mainly generated by the interaction between the user and the bank terminal or employee during these face-to-face contacts [3]. The encounter design is characterized by complexity and subjectivity. The perceptual quantification method is a research method combining subjective sensibility and objective quantification. It fully respects the individuality of design and the rigor of mathematical methods, and fits the evaluation of bank contact design specialty.

© Springer Nature Switzerland AG 2020
C. Stephanidis et al. (Eds.): HCII 2020, CCIS 1293, pp. 424–430, 2020.
https://doi.org/10.1007/978-3-030-60700-5_54

2   Inductive Quantitative and Experience Contact Evaluation

Perceptual imagery is the feeling of people's possession of things, the expectation of feelings in things, and the deep emotional emotions of people. Its own needs, desires and judging criteria reflects how to perceive a product [4]. In the broad sense, quantification refers to the specificity and clarity of the target or task, to the extent that the amount of clarity can be achieved, and the target characteristics are represented by quantity and number according to the actual situation. The design evaluation analysis method based on perceptual quantification mainly consists of two parts: quantitative and qualitative, the core task of quantification is to define the relationship.

Effective implementation of service encounter must be made to the customer's perception or use by means of corresponding contact elements, including various forms that the customer can see, hear, touch, smell, and taste. These elements are service encounter [5]. In this paper, the bank experience encounter designers and decision makers are tested to effectively improve the pertinence, selectivity and multidimensionality of the evaluation process. When the contact index in the perceptual quantification experiment is closer to the designer's ideal standard, the higher the designer's satisfaction and the better the effect to be achieved, the more effective the designer is in the contact design work, that is, the design participation.

3   Method

The design of the bank experience encounter is a process in which the designer will help to enhance the concept of the bank user experience, that is, the process of mapping the function to the principle structure. This process essentially describes the underlying mechanism between functional function and the realization of functional science principles [6]. Therefore, built for the model of the experimental object is the bank experience encounter, and the application of the effect and the functional solution need to be organically combined to ensure the validity of the experimental model. The experimental results should be based on the subject's cognitive evaluation score minus the expected evaluation score, that is, "cognition" - "expectation" to obtain "satisfaction" [7], and then analysis of "satisfaction" (Fig. 1).

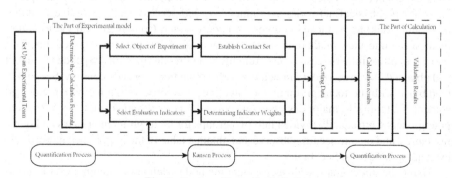

Fig. 1. Program flow of calculation

The evaluation process of the service encounter design scheme can be regarded as a comprehensive evaluation process of multiple indicators for a multi-sample, which is suitable for implementation by factor analysis [8]. Here, the designer satisfaction is integrated with the design index value, and the importance and evaluation of the evaluation index are evaluated from the expectation and perceived quality, and the metric calculation is carried out [9]. Formula (1) is the designer satisfaction formula of the service encounter, the design participation degree, P_{ij} is the design participation degree of the jth index of the $i\text{-}th$ contact, i is the bank contact, and j is the evaluation index. Y_j is the importance of the jth evaluation index.

$$C_{ij} = \sum_{j=1}^{n} P_{ij} Y_j \tag{1}$$

The KJ method and cluster analysis method are used to screen the bank contacts and evaluation indicators, and the experience contact set A and the evaluation index set B are obtained. Combined with the analytic hierarchy process, the evaluation index system is constructed and the index weights are calculated. According to the fuzzy mathematics concept design index questionnaire, the comment set Q is defined. Q is defined as "very dissatisfied, dissatisfied, average, satisfied, very satisfied" and given weights (1, 2, 3, 4, 5). A questionnaire was distributed to the experimental subject team, and the membership matrix R_n of the index set B of the plan a_n on the comment set Q was obtained. The satisfaction degree of the m schemes on the index vector T is calculated as $P_m = R_m Q^T$. By constructing the bank contact design participation model, the valid data is obtained strictly according to the test process, and the data is calculated step by step from the lowest level, and the design participation degree of each scheme is calculated.

4   Contact Design Evaluation

Using the on-site observation method combined with expert opinions, analysis of experience encounter similarity, and then the questionnaire was developed. 15 design students who mainly involved service design and user research were investigated, and the results of the questionnaire were clustered to select the most representative ones of bank experience encounter, designer. Forming an experience encounter set A, Specifically for a_1 physical network environment, a_2 self-service bank, a_3 online banking, a_4 mobile banking, a_5 closed counter, a_6 open counter. Combined with the literature method and interview method, the first-level indicators are summarized, including four indicators of usefulness, ease of use, reliability and modernization. Expanded in detail and obtained eleven secondary indicators such as functionality and economy. See Fig. 2. Combined with the focus group method and the scene observation method, the design students including 15 major design engineers and service designers and 15 senior bank practitioners were equally divided into two groups for focus group interviews and questionnaires, and on-site scenes. Observe and obtain a table of the importance index of the evaluation indicators. See Table 1.

Using the direct grade scale assessment method to define the comment set E, combined with the fuzzy analytic hierarchy process to conduct a questionnaire survey on

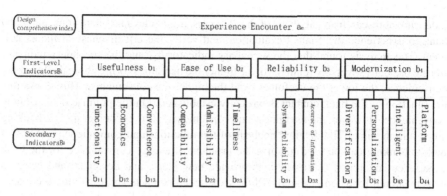

Fig. 2. Evaluation of bank experience contact system

Table 1. Index importance

Indicators B_n	b_1	b_2	b_3	b_4	b_{11}	b_{12}	b_{13}	b_{21}
Proportion	0.275	0.305	0.165	0.255	0.45	0.25	0.3	0.255
Indicators B_n	b_{22}	b_{23}	b_{31}	b_{32}	b_{41}	b_{42}	b_{43}	b_{44}
Proportion	0.25	0.495	0.275	0.725	0.205	0.305	0.255	0.235

Table 2. Design degree

a_n	a_1	a_1	a_3	a_4	a_5	a_6
C_n	84.508	99.899	102.998	109.252	88.559	89.649

the tested team, including 12 design students specializing in experience design, service design or interaction design, and 18 senior bank practitioners or banker decision makers. The membership matrix R of the specific data of the secondary indicator B_2 experiencing the contact set A on the comment set E is obtained by statistics. The membership matrix R data is substituted into the importance coefficient coordinates, and the values of the six experience contacts on the secondary index B_2 are calculated. Calculate its value on the primary indicator B_1 progressively in the same calculation. Finally, the design participation of each contact is obtained, as shown in Table 2.

5 Discussion

From this experiment, it can be seen that the degree of design in the contact set A is $a_4 > a_3 > a_2 > a_6 > a_5 > a_1$. That is, the designer of a_4 has the highest satisfaction, the closest approach and the design expectation. In order to visually compare the relationship between the elements, all the secondary index values of all the contacts a_n in the contact set A are normalized and the data is converted between [0, 1]. Relevant and independent research and analysis of the elements, draw relevant conclusions, guide the bank to experience the contact evaluation, and verify the effectiveness of the experiment. The analysis found that the secondary indicator b_{11} and the secondary indicator b_{12} are basically inversely related, so, the higher the usefulness bring about the lower the convenience, the lower the usefulness and the higher the convenience. This shows that the function of the bank contact is basically established. On the premise of sacrificing convenience. However, the usefulness and convenience of a_5 encounter mobile banking are at a high value. The detailed analysis of the functions and convenience features of mobile banking can be used to solve the problem of energy-convenience for the bank experience encounter. Contradictions provide new ideas, and designers and decision makers should focus on research. All the experience contacts are low in the secondary indicators b_{41}, b_{42}, that is, the diversification and individualization of the bank experience contacts are obviously insufficient, which seriously restricts the modernization level of the bank experience encounter, designers and decision-making. More consideration should be given to diversified and personalized designs in future bank contact design and selection to meet the growing user experience. All the experience contacts have lower values at the secondary indicator b_{22}, the accessibility of the bank experience contacts needs to be strengthened. Due to the characteristics of the banking business and the relatively closed operational procedures, it is indeed limited by the intervention of other factors, and because of the problems of risk control and supervision, the banking business cannot be simplified at will, so the accessibility of the bank experience contacts should be emphasized. Service, communication and other areas with high design flexibility (Figs. 3 and 4).

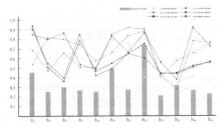

Fig. 3. Secondary index analysis of a_n

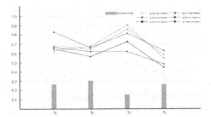

Fig. 4. First-class index analysis of a_n

Analysis of the primary indicator of the bank experience encounter can be concluded that, due to factors such as risk control and property security, the peak value and average value of the security of the bank experience contact b_3 are higher, and the user is receiving banking services, it can be get a better sense of security. The value of the first-level indicator b_1 usefulness is relatively close, indicating that the experience point faces similar development problems in terms of functionality. In addition to the a_1 encounter, the other five contacts related to the bank's financial function, a_2, a_3, a_4, a_5, a_6, have the first-level indicator b_2, the usability value is lower than the usefulness of b_1, and the first-level indicator b_2 has the highest importance weight, so improving the ease of use of bank experience encounters has become a key consideration for designers. The first-level indicator b_4 modernization index has a trend of polarization, that is, the level of intelligence of emerging terminals is higher than that of traditional artificial contacts, and the modernization level of traditional experience contacts has become a top priority.

6 Conclusion

Through the method of perceptual quantification, the bank contacts are analyzed and studied, as to avoid the advantages and disadvantages of intuition and experience alone, and provide a scientific and comprehensive evaluation scale [10], in order to achieve "Design-evaluation-redesign" [11]. This scientific design approach provides a reliable guarantee. The perceptual quantification method concretes and subdivides the general considerations of bank experience encounters design, digitizes and visualizes the vague feelings, studies the bank experience encounters from the design perspective and quantifies the contact indicators. It helps designers to carry out bank experience encounters design work more efficiently. Secondly, the experience of contact evaluation completes the change of research direction from "experience-design" to "design-experience", which provides a new direction for the subsequent research on bank user experience. Studying the bank experience encounter is a trace of the bank user experience research. It is an important means to improve the bank user experience by designing the method to improve the bank experience contact. Evaluating the bank experience contact with perceptual quantification method is a research method to fundamentally improve the user experience. Establishing a scientific and perfect perceptual quantification model is the future development trend of bank experience design in the future.

Acknowledgement. This paper is supported by the Art Project of National Social Science Foundation 2019 (Grant No. 2019BG110).

References

1. Pine, B.J., Gilmoer, J.H.: The Experience Economy: Work is Theater & Every Business a Stage. Harvard Business School Press, Boston (2019)
2. Xin, X.-Y.: Internet from user experience to experience design. Packag. Eng. **40**(8), 60–66 (2019)
3. Li, Y., Wu, Z.-H.: 3D printing and the innovation of service design in bank. Design **31**(2), 59–61 (2019)
4. Luo, S.-J., Pan, Y.-H.: Review of theory, key technology and its application of perceptual image in product design. Chin. J. Mech. Eng. **43**(3), 9–13 (2007)
5. Xu, X.-N.: Designable service design touch point development of restaurant industry based on sensory experience. Packag. Eng. **37**(2), 46–49 (2016)
6. Liu, S., Cao, G.-Z., Zhu, Y.-N., Zhang, F.-W.: Research on evaluation method of reaching degree for conceptual design principle solution. Mach. Des. Res. **34**(5), 1–6 (2018)
7. Zhou, Z.-Y.: Research on Design and Evaluation Method of Medical Nursing Equipment Integrating Kansei Engineering with EEG Technology—Take the Nursing Bed as An Example. East China University of Science and Technology (2019)
8. Zhang, Y.: Research on the Quantitative Method for Orientation and Evaluation of Product System Design. Nanjing University of Aeronautics and Astronautics (2007)

9. Li, F.-Q., Chang, H.-Z., Guo, Y.-X., Zhou, F.: Evaluation of product conceptual design based on customer satisfaction. Packag. Eng. **37**(24), 17–21 (2016)
10. J. Zhejiang Sci. Tech. Univ. **23**(4), 461–465 (2006)
11. Pu, J., Chen, Y., Xiong, Y., Li, B.: Products conceptual design and evaluation on based on TRIZ theory and fuzzy AHP approach. Manuf. Autom. **36**(1), 14–17 (2014)

A Research on How to Enhance User Experience by Improving Arcade Joystick in Side-Scrolling Shooter Games

Shih-Chieh Liao[1,2](✉), Fong-Gong Wu[1], Chia-Hui Feng[2], and Cheng-Yan Shuai[2]

[1] National Cheng Kung University Industrial Design Department, Tainan, Taiwan
[2] Southern Taiwan University of Science and Technology, Tainan, Taiwan
alfietw@stust.edu.tw

Abstract. In the long-term observation, we've discovered that the joystick has high maneuverability, but players find it difficult to control when playing complex 2-D STG. The layout which is full of bullets and enemies is a huge challenge to players' techniques and reactions. Furthermore, it influences the games' difficulties and players' willingness to play; we implemented shadowing observational method and questionnaire to come up with four key factors which were significant to this research. However, the experiment probed into the Human-Machine Interaction with regard to joystick and synergy between hardware and software. After the focus group with those subjects, we acquired a few pieces of feedback on how to improve the joysticks. Ultimately, in the conclusion of this research, we proposed two pieces of advice on the design of prototype of joystick. We'd like to improve the User Experience (UX) and Somatosensory Experience, and create a customized joystick for 2-D STG.

Keywords: Arcade joystick · Joystick improvement · User Experience · Game design

1 Introduction

'Game' is an essential element to people in relieving the stress in daily life, with the prevalence computers, consoles and mobile devices, the advancement of technology provides a wide variety of choices for modern gamers. But with the fall of arcades [1], hard-core players have to seek for some specific approaches to playing that. Despite that fact, arcade still has its value and niche market.

Although joystick has a long history, but its User Interface (UI) hasn't been revamped for a long time. Joystick has its limits, in order to satisfy its functionalities, some behaviors in games should be shared. 2-D STG is the genre which is most unfriendly to the synergy between arcade joystick and game mechanism. The most iconic ones are: Contra, Metal Slug…etc. The difficulty of this genre is generally higher, veteran players can formulate correct strategies based on their experiences. However, rookie players make mistakes much more often than the former ones, this phenomenon elucidates that this combination of joystick and game not only creates a lot of fun and challenges but also

© Springer Nature Switzerland AG 2020
C. Stephanidis et al. (Eds.): HCII 2020, CCIS 1293, pp. 431–437, 2020.
https://doi.org/10.1007/978-3-030-60700-5_55

gives rookies players frustration. For example: Flight Sim Joystick, Racing Wheel…etc. In gaming industry, joysticks usually are used in a more contextualizing way to simulate, in order to give players a more immersive experience in the games [2]. But the UI of traditional joysticks is no longer appropriate for those 2-D STG developed in recent years.

The synergy between joystick and game ruins the UX to players, some players choose the joysticks they personally prefer or continue the game with unease. Even more extremely, some of the players doubt the 'playability' of the game. Based on this fact, researchers would like to improve the UI on movement and operation to increase the satisfaction for players from different genres of games.

2 Literature Review

The definition of 'Game' is that players actively participate in an activity which brings pleasure and alleviates stress; on the other hand, it provides challenges in order to determine whether or not players should be rewarded, or even punished [3].

Among tons of games, most classic ones are those arcades in arcade center, from [4] and [5] we can tease out the trend in Taiwan in 80s. But because of the influence from technological advancement, consoles have already gradually replaced the position of arcades in players heart; arcades were initially set up as a platform for socializing, most of them were minigames which had shorter life cycle, the performance in game relies on players' experiences and instincts. However, these concepts no longer apply to the age where computers, consoles, mobile devices are prevalent [6].

Technological advancement moved the outdoor arcade interfaces into the indoor consoles, then players played games with joysticks and arcade controllers. Compared to early interfaces which feature entertainment, people emphasized more on showing off and socializing [7]; however, modern games let players interact in a different way which defies the original goal for show-off.

This research has discovered that players uncomfortable experiences when playing with traditional arcade joysticks. Why we chose Metal Slug is that a lot of players born around 1990 have experienced this 'incompatibility' between game and hardware in their childhood. Through the observations, we found that a lot of players made mistakes in these situations below:

1. **Operation Misjudged:** When players jump plus shoot downwards, but this usually causes confusion to system (Fig. 1).
2. **Unable to Shoot Precisely:** Moving and aiming share the same operation, which means players cannot aim while moving in the vehicle; furthermore, players cannot aim from 45 degrees. All these factors make players die more frequently.
3. **Heavy Workload on Joystick:** When encountering the enemies, the ideal strategy would be shooting in the air. But players cannot effectively counterattack in the air (Fig. 2).
4. **Prolonged Play Time:** When enemies barrage all over the layout, players miss the best timing for counterattack because of the issue on joystick. Therefore, the overall game time would be prolonged.

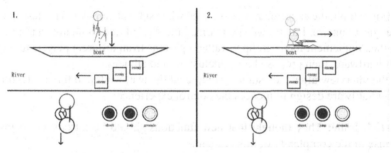

Fig. 1. After shooting downwards in the air, making the same operation when landing causes system mis-judgement then slide forward.

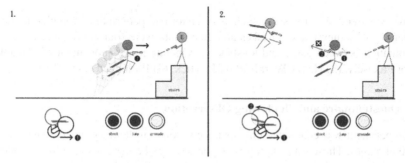

Fig. 2. Jumping then shoot at enemies out of range, but unable to shoot in the opposite direction because of system sharing.

These issues heavily influence the game experience, according to eight elements of Game Flow in research [8], including: (1) Focus, (2) Challenge, (3) Technique, (4) Maneuverability, (5) Explicit Goal, (6) Feedback, (7) Immersion, (8) Interaction; Although the hardware and game are compatible, theoretically. But the maneuverability defies the ergonomics according to some players. Although the immersive experience could be brought to player through the mechanism of game [9], but this research indicated that bad experience on interaction between player and controller ruins the game experience for players.

Nostalgic video games allow people to experience reminiscent and creative elements also make game designers introspect how good the games are from players game experiences [10]. This research was aimed to provide the service-centered experience to players and allow the traditional arcade controller to upgrade in both performance and interface, creating the whole new experience.

3   Case Study and Data Collection

3.1   Research Description and Improvement

Experiment subjects played on the laptop along with traditional arcade joystick, in order to simulate the hardware and UI of arcade; subjects played first mission in Metal Slug 3 with 10-min limit, the experiment was finished when subject completed the test and filled out the questionnaire. Finally we summarized the data of questionnaires and interview result, then implement focus group to gather opinions from different players to improve current hardware, then proposed the conclusions and advices.

In the interview after each subject completed the test, we found three categories on how bad hardware design influences the control experience:

- **Joystick Issue:** They thought that new functions should be introduced to joystick because of the complexity of modern games.
- **Software Issue:** They thought heavy workload on maneuver causes bad experience due to the complexity of game mechanism.
- **Both:** They thought the advancement of software makes joystick feel out-of-date.

We assessed subject's issues such as behavior and pattern after completing the test to identify why they made mistakes and died, there were four common issues on this combination between game and joystick: (1) Operation Mis-judgement, (2) Unable to Shoot Precisely, (3) Heavy Workload on Joystick, (4) Prolonged Game Time.

3.2 Questionnaire and Shadowing Observation

The experiment was conducted on 33 subjects, some of them were experienced in this genre of games. Those subjects were categorized into three groups in terms of seniority, 6 rookie players, 19 normal players, 8 senior players.

Questionnaire employed Likert Scale to evaluate how subjects felt about the joystick and game. The scores were negative, very disagree (0 point) to positive, very agree (5 point) respectively; the greater the number was, the higher agreement subject had.

From their experiences on interface of arcade joystick, those normal players and senior players had similar feedback which is acceptable; on the other hand, rookie players had worse feedback. In terms of maneuverability, rookie and senior players both felt acceptable, but normal players didn't agree. We extrapolated that arcade joystick is fairly acceptable to most people. With regard to mastery for game, the score was in 'very agree' interval; it was obvious that the synergy between arcade stick and this game really annoyed players (Fig. 3).

3.3 Focus Group Interview and Feedback

After subjects completed the test, we made explanation to 12 players in focus group and collected their opinions on how to improve the design of arcade joystick. We categorized those advices into three groups, two of them were about left and right parts of joystick, and another was about feedback.

Advice on Right Part: All the buttons on right side should be replaced by touch panel; therefore, the limits that too many inputs cannot be executed simultaneously could be addressed. Or add a touch panel left below the buttons (Fig. 4 left).

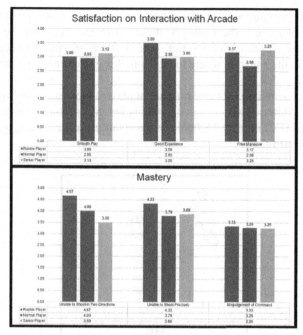

Fig. 3. Top graph shows satisfaction for the interaction; Bottom graph shows mastery for game maneuver.

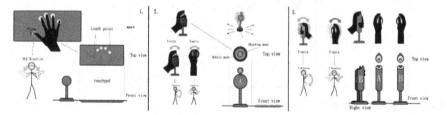

Fig. 4. Left figure shows modification for touch panel; Central figure shows modification for analog stick; Right figure shows modification for double stick.

Advice on Left Part: Add a rolling ball atop the stick so that player can aim by this rolling ball with affecting the moving in vehicle. Or add an analog stick atop the stick to make moving judgement better (Fig. 4 central).

Advice on Both Parts: Subjects unanimously agreed that contemporary flight stick can address the limits from arcade joystick (Fig. 4 right).

4 Conclusion and Advice

This research discovered that players could accept the design of the arcade joystick alone, but when being used along with games such Metal Slug, mistakes and death occurred more often; this phenomenon suggested that the combination between arcade joystick and this genre of game bothers players, these issues are caused by the advancement of games and the stagnation of joystick. The research proved that it causes a lot of inconvenience in the situation where highly complex games are played along with out-of-date arcade joystick.

This research summarized three points that players proposed to improve the arcade stick, which could be added to joystick modification in the future, implement questionnaire survey and UX rating by Technology Acceptance Model to bring users better and novel experience (Fig. 5).

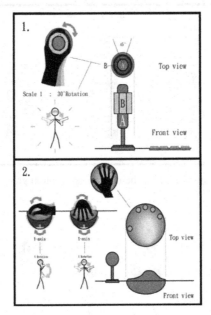

Fig. 5. Top figure illustrates the modification of stick; Bottom figure illustrates modification of button area.

Advice on Left Part: The stick on left is separated to A and B; A works for moving, B works for aiming when sitting in vehicle; therefore, player can turn the cannon barrel while moving, the stick can turn in 45°. A calibration can turn in 30° in the game, there are total 8 anchors.

Advice on Right Part: The area below right part is hollow; semicircle surface can accommodate buttons to work as analog stick. Player twists the analog stick when he/she needs to aim.

References

1. Shie, H.-J., Jiang, R.-H.: For the games development history and game control evolution relationship analysis. Ind. Des. Mag. **138**, 54–59 (2018)

2. Jang, J.-N.: Physical Game Development Environment Simulations – A Case Study of Arcade Games (2011)
3. Shiu, J.-S.: A Relationship on Cognitive Style Players of the Effects With Mind Game Control (2011)
4. Chen, T.-C.: The Player's Motivation and Collection Behavior of the Trading Card Arcade Game (2009)
5. Yang, Y.-H.: Entertainment World: Daily Experience of Video Game Entertainment in 1980s and 1990s Taiwan (2016)
6. Pullen, T.M.: Arcade fever: economics, affect and interface design of the 1970s and 1980s video arcade. J. Arts Writ. Students 2(1), 43–50 (2016)
7. Jin, W.-Y., Li, C.-W.: Player's motivation for arcade games – case study of jubeat. Inf. Commun. 3(1), 59–72 (2012)
8. Jeng, Y.-S.: A Comparative Study of Game Experience between Light Spot and Wiimote Interface (2009)
9. Wen, M.-H.: Exploring the Effects of Computer Game Design on Users Gaming Experience and Behaviors (2009)
10. Esposito, N.: How Video Game History Shows Us Why Video Game Nostalgia Is So Important Now (2005)

Determining Optimum Level of Automation in Task Design for Assembly Line Systems

Rifat Ozdemir[✉] and Sara AlSharif

College of Engineering and Technology, American University of the Middle East,
Kuwait City, Kuwait
{Rifat.Ozdemir,Sara.AlSharif}@aum.edu.kw

Abstract. Automation has become essential in many industries since computerized technologies were developed for its significant effect on production performance in terms of accuracy, speed and volume. However, the effects of increased automation on operators' situational awareness and skill development have been controversial. This study aims to determine the optimum level of automation to balance the tradeoffs between loss of situational awareness, and mental/physical workload through developing a model that quantifies the effect of automation level on cognitive performance, which is defined as a function of situational awareness and mental workload. The proposed model particularly helps the task design of assembly line systems. The mental workload of an operator is dependent on the information quantity needed to be processed while performing the task, which may decrease by higher level of automation. However, loss of situational awareness is expected to increase by leveling up automation in task design. The level of automation introduced in a system ranges from manual processes to fully automated process. The stages of information processing involved in performing assembly tasks can be information acquisition, analysis and/or decision making. Each assembly task may involve any combination of these information process stages. The first step in the proposed model, cognitive tasks are partitioned into information process stages which are then evaluated with different levels of automation for all stages and all tasks along the assembly line. The proposed study utilizes the well-known technique of Situational Awareness Global Assessment Tool (SAGAT) in order to quantify the loss of situational awareness. Theoretical tradeoffs between loss of situational awareness and the mental workload reveals the optimal level of automation which also maximizes the cognitive performance of human worker. The proposed approach is then implemented in a real-life case study.

Keywords: Automation and human factors · Situational awareness · Mental workload · Human information processing · Information theory · Task design · Assembly line systems

1 Introduction

Modern complex systems have become the most common description of operating systems across different fields of work. New technologies have been presented to the traditional operating systems to automate tasks, with the goal of enhancing service and

© Springer Nature Switzerland AG 2020
C. Stephanidis et al. (Eds.): HCII 2020, CCIS 1293, pp. 438–449, 2020.
https://doi.org/10.1007/978-3-030-60700-5_56

production quality and quantity. However, many aspects of excess automation has had little attention in terms of its effect on not only an operator's mental workload, but also his/her situational awareness. This paper explores the full range of automation levels in light of these ergonomic measures, with efforts to identify tailored optimum automation levels for each task within a balanced assembly line.

2 Literature Review

When the goal or purpose is to ergonomically optimize the cognitive performance of an operator in heavily technological environments, it is compulsory to measure analyze, and control the aspects of imposed mental workload along with the level of situational awareness. "Mental workload has been most often characterized in terms of the level of attentional demands placed on the operator in the course of performing required tasks, whereas Situational awareness is primarily associated with the informational content of the operator's memory systems during task performance" (Vidulich and Tsang 2014). As the nature of their interaction can provide a deeper understanding on how to improve the efficiency of a human-machine system, many tools have emerged in the past period in order to most accurately quantify these vague measures. Tapping onto measures of situational awareness, the ones tested for validity and are most widely used tools are the Situation Awareness Global Assessment Technique (SAGAT) (Endsley 1988; Endsley 1990a) and the Situational Awareness Rating Technique (SART) (Taylor 1990). SAGAT is an objective Situational Awareness tool that uses a customized list of queries covering all aspects of Situational awareness (perception, comprehension and projection) to evaluate the operator's knowledge of the elements of a task simulation in different random moments of when it is frozen. The score is based on a benchmark between the operator's response and the actual event occurring in the simulation in that frozen moment (Endsley 1998). SART, on the other hand, is a subjective measure constituting of 14 fixed elements relevant to situational awareness. These elements cover bipolar questions that evaluate an operator's perception of demand and supply of the operator's attention as well as his comprehension of the situation. (Endsley 1998). While both measures have their advantages and their downfalls, one aspect of SART that creates a space of caution while viewing its evaluation, is that operators can give ratings in questions based on their performance, and not the actual quality of their situational awareness. Such aspects give support to use subjective situational awareness ratings as good indicators of how situational awareness is linked to performance, but not as tools reflecting a solid representation of situational awareness (Endsley 1998). In his recent paper, Endsley also explored a comparative study of objective situational awareness methods, mainly Situation Awareness Global Assessment Technique (SAGAT) and Situation Present Assessment Technique (SPAM) using meta-analysis of 243 studies. "While SAGAT and SPAM were found to be equally predictive of performance, SAGAT was found to be a highly sensitive, reliable, and predictive measure of SA [Situational Awareness] that is useful across a wide variety of domains and experimental settings" (Endsley 2019).

To measure mental workload, the most widely used tool is the National Aeronautics and Space Administration Task Load Index, known by NASA-TLX. NASA-TLX is a subjective multidimensional assessment tool that uses the weighted average approach to evaluate the mental workload of an operator in multiple aspects: namely the Mental demand (MD), Physical demand (PD), Temporal demand (TD), Performance (OP), Effort (EF), frustration levels (FR). Under many experimental and real-life conditions, and across multiple operational models, NASA-TLX has shown reliability in the provision of mental workload evaluations. It was also suggested to be used of in early product design phases to assess the designer's mental workload during the design process and its variability among different design stages, in order to achieve better product effectiveness (Nikulin et al. 2019). In another perspective, previous research has shown how NASA-TLX can be used in choosing among different proposed product designs in terms of the mental workload they impose on the end user. In a paper written by Akyempong et al., in the International Journal of Industrial Ergonomics, the authors used NASA-TLX to evaluate the ergonomic effect of two proposed design models for a hydraulic excavator on the operator. As a tool, it has helped them identify which Human-Machine Interactive (HMI) design concept was a better fit based on the different aspects through which they affect the operator's subjective workload (Akyempong et al. 2014). Research evidence has also shown the use of NASA-TLX in healthcare. It was also used to assess the mental workload of Intensive Care Units' (ICUs) nurses, and has shown a beneficial and reliable evaluation of ICU nurses' mental workload, compared to other methods such as patient-based and operator-based workload instruments (Hoonakker et al. 2011).

A novel part of this proposed research is the use of a quantifying measure of mental workload using Information Theory and Shannon's entropy. "Information theory is a mathematical theory defining the limits and possibilities of communication. It provides a quantitative measure of the information content of a message [or an external signal]"(Ghahramani 2006). Shannon's entropy is a measure to quantify information in the unit of *bits*. One can think of it as an extension of the probability theory as it is based on probabilities given to the occurrence of events or, in the light of our proposed application, external signals (Wilde 2013).

3   Problem Definition and Proposed Methodology

This section will present problem of determining automation level for maximizing cognitive performance which is a function of both reduction of mental workload and loss of situational awareness. We also show the proposed methodology for quantifying mental work load by using information theory concept and for determining optimum automation level for every task and for each stage of human information process in this section. The following figure summarizes the scope of the proposed model (Fig. 1):

In literature, most of the studies addressing mental workload using subjective evaluation for measuring mental work load for human operators such as NASA-TLX (National Aeronautics and Space Administration Task Load Index) is one of the subjective mental workload measurement using six factors, namely the Mental demand (MD), Physical demand (PD), Temporal demand (TD), Performance (OP), Effort (EF), frustration levels (FR). In this study, we incorporated a new quantifying method for mental workload based on two indicators information quantity to be processed by the operator and redundancy gain by introducing an increasing automation level. This study proposes to use Shannon entropy for quantifying mental workload in terms of information quantity

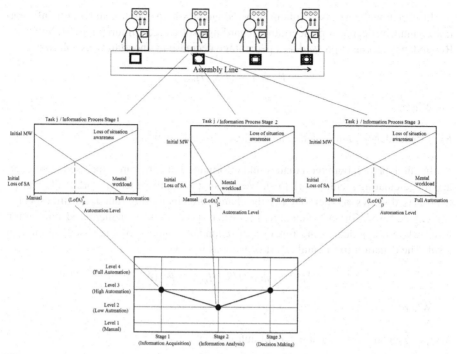

Fig. 1. Determining automation level of each information process stage of task j. (MW: Mental workload, SA: Situational awareness, LofA: Level of automation.)

and redundancy. We can express the information quantity for n displays by using Shannon entropy as follows:

$$HS_i = \sum_{k=1}^{n} p_{ik}\left[\log_2(1/p_{ik})\right]$$

Where,

p_{ik} = Probability of a change to be observed in display k at level i of automation.
HS_i = Information quantity to be processed for observing the displays at level i of automation.

Same principle also introduces the maximum information quantity to be processed for a given n events (number of displays) as follows:

$$H_{max} = \log_2(n)$$

Where,

H_{max} = Maximum information quantity or base information quantity with no automation help

Information theory also explains how redundancy help operator and secure information channel by decreasing uncertainty regarding to observed stimuli (or area of interest). Redundancy can be expressed as a percentage decrease in uncertainty as follows:

$$R_i = 1 - (HS_i/H_{max})$$

Where,

R_i = Redundancy gain in percentage at level i of automation

In our approach both redundancy and information quantity are expressed in percentage for calculating mental work load. We can simply express mental work load required to observe displays in order to notice the change is an increasing function with respect to percentage base information quantity needs to be processed for an increased automation level, while it is a decreasing function of redundancy gained by increased automation level. The equation for mental effort is given as follows:

$$MW_i = max(HS_i/H_{max} - R_i, 0)$$

Where,

MW_i = Mental workload at level i of automation

In our study, we also utilize SAGAT (Situation Awareness Global Assessment Technique) to provide an objective measure for loss of situational awareness (LoSA) based on queries. As a global measurement tool, SAGAT includes queries about all operator situational awareness (SA) requirements, including 1- perception of data, 2- comprehension of meaning and 3- projection of the near future components. This includes a consideration of system functioning and status as well as relevant features of the external environment. In our study we have collected data using a simulator that provides an environment for display observation and we check operator situation awareness during freezes in a simulation. SAGAT score is a weighted average of percentage correct answers of the operator to the all phases of the query. In our study, loss of situational awareness (LoSA) is percentage decrease in SAGAT score for an increased level of automation. The following equation shows the LoSA for an introduced level i of automation.

$$LoSA_i = SA_1 - SA_i$$

Where,

$LoSA_i$ = Loss of situational awareness at level i of automation.
SA_i = SAGAT score for situational awareness at level i of automation.
SA_1 = SAGAT score for situational awareness at level 1 of automation which all displays are observed manually

Human information process has three main stages as follows: 1 – information acquisition, 2 – information analysis and 3 – decision making. In our study we propose an approach to determine optimal automation level for each information process stage. Thus, all equations mentioned for mental work load and situational awareness should be computed for each stage. We use different phase of SAGAT score for each information process stage. We use the percentage correct answers for the phase of "perception of data" in SAGAT score to represent SA regarding to the stage of "information acquisition". We use the percentage correct answers for the phase of "comprehension of meaning" in SAGAT score to represent SA regarding to the stage of "information analysis". We use the percentage correct answers for the phase of "projection of the near future components" in SAGAT score to represent SA regarding to the stage of "decision making". We utilize NASA-TLX and Shannon entropy-based values together to differentiate mental workload changes with respect to different stage of information process. As mentioned earlier in this section, NASA-TLX is a questionnaire to measure the subjective mental effort. We propose that operators are asked to evaluate the required mental effort for different part of the task in order to measure different mental effort for different stage of information process. Operators evaluate the mental effort requirement for data gathering in the display observation using NASA-TLX and the results are used for the stage of "information acquisition". However, we just use NASA-TLX values for estimating mental load of the operator for the rest of the information process stages. Mental workload for information acquisition stage is weighted average of Shannon entropy based mental workload ($MW_{i1,a}$) and NASA-TLX score based ($MW_{i1,b}$) as given below.

$$MW_{i1} = \alpha\left(MW_{i1,a}\right) + (1 - \alpha)\left(MW_{i1,b}\right)$$

Where,

MW_{i1} = Mental workload of stage 1 (information acquisition) of information process at level i of automation.
$MW_{i1,a}$ = Shannon entropy based mental workload of stage 1 (information acquisition) of information process at level i of automation.
$MW_{i1,b}$ = NASA-TLX score based mental workload of stage 1 (information acquisition) of information process at level i of automation.
α = Weight value for computing average mental workload

In this study, we assume four levels of automation for each task and for each information process stage. Procedure of introducing automation levels for gathering data regarding to probabilities of changes in displays and situational awareness scores for each phase is as follows:

Level 1:   Manual operation for observing displays, no help or assistance for information analysis and decision making. Thus, it is completely uncertain for the operator in which display there might be a change no guidance for the operator for the meaning of this change and no help for limiting the possible future actions to project future changes. In this level of automation, we assume that maximum information quantity is processed by the operator for observing n number of displays.

Level 2:   Low automation which provides some help and guidance for the operator. A few numbers of displays automatically gather data to help information acquisition also provide meaning to help information analysis and limit the alternatives to guide decision making.

Level 3: High automation which provides extensive help and guidance for the operator. Half of the displays automatically gather data to help information acquisition also provide meaning to help information analysis and limit the alternatives to guide decision making.

Level 4: Full automation which establishes all information process stages without letting the operator interference. All of the displays automatically gather data for information acquisition also, automatically establish information analysis and provide the best alternative for decision making. In this level of automation, we assume that minimum information quantity is processed by the operator for following the orders of the computer from one channel

Optimal automation level is determined by balancing the tradeoff between decrease in mental workload and loss of situational awareness. Since we have limited number of levels of automation, this is discrete (finite) space of solution set for determining the optimum level for maximizing cognitive performance which is a function of mental workload reduction and loss of situation awareness. Objective function of maximizing cognitive performance can be given as follows:

$$Max\ Z_j = \beta(\Delta X_{ij}) - (1 - \beta)(\Delta Y_{ij})$$

Where,

Z_j= Cognitive performance in stage j of information process
$\Delta X_{ij} = MW_{1j} - MW_{ij}$
$\Delta Y_{ij} = SA_{1j} - SA_{ij}$
ΔX_{ij} = Decrease in mental workload of stage j of information process at level i of automation.
ΔY_{ij} = Loss of situation awareness of stage j of information process at level i of automation.
β = Importance weight of mental workload reduction in cognitive performance

As an example, we simulate mental performance for an assembly task for four different types of model requiring that four different types of components to be assembled into different positions of the base product and by using different settings of tools. Thus, from information theory point of view, we can simply consider 16 different levels of task requirements should be classified which results a very high mental workload. Information quantity based on Shannon entropy will result 4 bits and 0% redundancy for information acquisition stage of process when assembly work is manual (level 1 of automation), this is considered as 100% of mental workload. However, subjectively evaluation of NASA-TLX may give different value of mental workload for the same level of automation. The following table is for illustrating calculation of cognitive performance for different levels of automation when SAGAT scores are obtained from the percentage correct answers for the phase of "perception of data". We assume α and β are both equal to 0.5 for the following table.

As seen in Table 1, the highest value for cognitive performance is achieved when automation level is 3 (high automation level) for information acquisition stage. The following figures summarize the selection of automation level as balancing the tradeoff between decrease in mental workload and increase in loss of situation awareness.

Table 1. Cognitive performance of information acquisition stage through with mental workload and loss of situation awareness for different levels of automation.

Stage: information acquisition

Automation level	Shannon entropy based MW	NASA-TLX based MW	MW_i	Decrease in MW_i	SAGAT Score	LoSA	Cognitive performance, Z_j
1	100.00	95.20	97.60	0.00	100.00	0.00	0.00
2	79.25	88.30	83.78	13.83	83.50	16.50	−1.34
3	**50.00**	**70.10**	**60.05**	**37.55**	**76.10**	**23.90**	**6.83**
4	0.00	55.20	27.60	70.00	28.60	71.40	−0.70

As seen in Fig. 2, decrease in mental workload and increase in loss of situation awareness is not exactly balanced at automation level of 3, however, this point achieves the maximum cognitive performance since we assume that both factors (MW and LoSA) are equally important. This can be observed in the following figure which shows the value of cognitive performance calculated as a function of both factors (MW and LoSA).

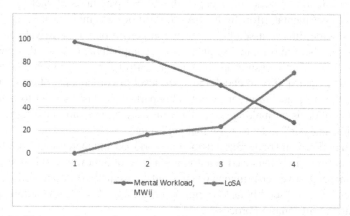

Fig. 2. Tradeoff between decrease in mental workload and increase in loss of situation awareness.

As seen in Fig. 3, optimal automation level for information acquisition can be obtained when level 3 of automation is selected, which achieves the maximum value for cognitive performance in task design. However, we should note that this is sensitive to the value of β in objective function. For instance, if we assumed β of 0.6, it would change the selection of optimal automation level for the same task design as seen in the following figure.

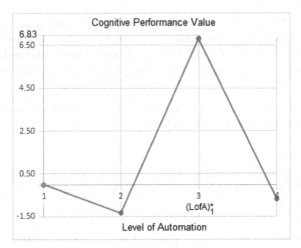

Fig. 3. Optimal automation level for maximizing cognitive performance value when β is 0.5.

As seen in Fig. 4, optimal automation level is sensitive to β value and if it was towards mental effort then it would give us higher level (full automation) for information acquisition to achieve the maximum value for cognitive performance in task design. Same procedure except for the use of Shannon entropy based mental effort is used to get optimal automation level for other stages of the information process of the assembly task. However, there are critical requirements in procedure of data collection with NASA-TLX in other stages. In stage two, only the mental processes related to information analysis should be used in simulation in order to get mental effort by NASA-TLX. In stage three of information process, the operator should be given tasks of decision making in simulation to get mental effort by NASA-TLX. In our assembly task design, operator needs to estimate time of assembly of each component based on arrival of the model in order to put them into logical sequence of accomplishment. Thus, this part of task design can be used to measure operator mental effort for information analysis stage. Operator has responsibility to check the stock level of components of each model and decide whether to place an order or not. This part of the task is used to measure the mental effort of decision-making stage. The following figures summarizes the results of "information analysis" and "decision making" stages.

As seen in Fig. 5 and 6, decrease in mental workload and increase in loss of situation awareness is not exactly balanced at automation level of 3, however, this point achieves the maximum cognitive performance when α and β are equal to 0.5. The following figure summarizes how an assembly task design is achieved by determining automation level of each stage of information process.

As seen in Fig. 7, optimal automation levels are 3 (high level of automation) for first and the third stages of information process. This can be considered as operator needs high level of computerized guidance for the perception of data which requires perception of categorization for each component of each model and tool settings. Also, operator needs high level of guidance for decision making for determining the reorder point based on the future projection of component consumption rate. However, operator needs only

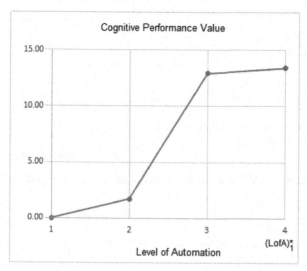

Fig. 4. Optimal automation level for maximizing cognitive performance value when β is 0.6.

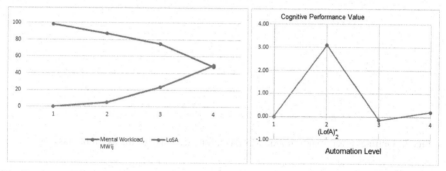

Fig. 5. Tradeoff between MW and LoSA and optimal automation level for information analysis stage (stage 2).

low level of guidance for information analysis which involves estimation of assembly times of components. According to Fig. 5, operator should not be replaced with full automation for any stage of information process. However, this result is sensitive to selection of α and β. This process should be repeated for all tasks in the assembly line in order to complete the task design of assembly system.

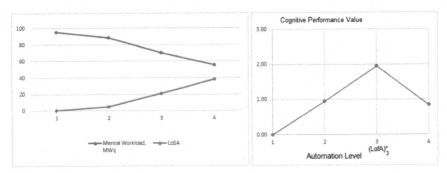

Fig. 6. Tradeoff between MW and LoSA and optimal automation level for decision making stage (stage 3).

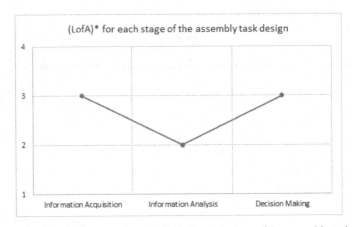

Fig. 7. Optimal level of automation, (LofA)*, for each stage of the assembly task design.

References

Wickens, C., Hollands, J., Banbury, S., Parasuraman, R.: Engineering Psychology and Human Performance, 4th edn. Pearson Education, London (2013)

Ozdemir, R.G., Ayag, Z.: An integrated approach to evaluating assembly-line design alternatives with equipment selection. Prod. Plan. Control **22**(2), 194–206 (2011)

Endsley, M.: Situation Awareness Global Assessment Technique (SAGAT). IEEE, Hawthorne (1988). https://ieeexplore.ieee.org/stamp/stamp.jsp?arnumber=195097. Accessed 23 Jan 2020

Akyeampong, J., Udoka, S., Caruso, G., Bordegoni, M.: Evaluation of hydraulic excavator human-machine interface concepts using NASA TLX. Int. J. Ind. Ergon. **44**(3), 374–382 (2014). https://doi.org/10.1016/j.ergon.2013.12.002

Wilde, M.: Quantum Information Theory. Cambridge University Press, Cambridge (2013)

Ghahramani, Z.: Information theory. Encyclopedia of Cognitive Science (2006). https://onlinelibrary.wiley.com/doi/abs/10.1002/0470018860.s00643

Vidulich, M.A., Tsang, P.S.: The confluence of situation awareness and mental workload for adaptable human-machine systems. J. Cogn. Eng. Decis. Mak. **9**(1), 95–97 (2014). https://doi.org/10.1177/1555343414554805

Endsley, M.R.: A systematic review and meta-analysis of direct objective measures of situation awareness: a comparison of SAGAT and SPAM. Hum. Factors (2019). https://doi.org/10.1177/0018720819875376

Hoonakker, P., et al.: Measuring workload of ICU nurses with a questionnaire survey: the NASA Task Load Index (TLX). IIE Trans. Healthc. Syst. Eng. 1(2), 131–143 (2011). https://doi.org/10.1080/19488300.2011.609524

Endsley, M.R., Selcon, S.J., Hardiman, T.D., Croft, D.G.: A comparative analysis of SAGAT and SART for evaluations of situation awareness. In: Proceedings of the Human Factors and Ergonomics Society Annual Meeting, vol. 42, no, 1, pp. 82–86 (1998). https://doi.org/10.1177/154193129804200119

Nikulin, C., Lopez, G., Piñonez, E., Gonzalez, L., Zapata, P.: NASA-TLX for predictability and measurability of instructional design models: case study in design methods. Educ. Technol. Res. Dev. 67(2), 467–493 (2019). https://doi.org/10.1007/s11423-019-09657-4

The Influence of Social Embarrassment on Engagement with Publicly Displayed Digital Content

Alexandra Pollock$^{(\boxtimes)}$, Ethan Perry$^{(\boxtimes)}$, and Tom Williams$^{(\boxtimes)}$

Department of Computer Science, Colorado School of Mines, Golden, CO 80401, USA
{arpollock,eperry1}@mymail.mines.edu, twilliams@mines.edu

Abstract. Public, large-screen touch displays offer advertisers, social activist groups, and other organizations a distinct opportunity to communicate their message interactively to users. While previous research has sought to identify strategies for encouraging users to interact with these displays, it is not clear how different levels or types of engagement may be encouraged by different solicitation strategies. Moreover, it is also not yet understood how the effectiveness of these strategies may depend on the nature of the content to interact with. In this research, we consider specifically how users may be encouraged to engage with mental health focused content presented on these types of displays, and propose an experiment for exploring the effectiveness of different context-sensitive solicitation strategies.

Keywords: Activity spaces · Display blindness · Interaction affordance · Interaction blindness · Public smart displays · Tangible interfaces · Touch screen interactions · Usability evaluation · User behavior

1 Introduction

Recent years have seen increasing investment in public digital signage for universities, shopping malls, hotels, conference centers, and similar businesses. As touch screen technology has become more accessible, these devices have transitioned towards interactive content, such as digital maps or information directories. While individuals are accustomed to interacting with their personal devices, public displays face the additional challenge of having to entice user engagement. Consequently, a significant body of HCI research focusing on public displays has emerged, presenting new techniques to increase user interactions with such displays, and seeking to understand what barriers exist to interaction. This has yielded a number of insights, including design frameworks, UI guidelines, and standardized metrics for quantifying subjective measurements with such displays. In this preliminary work, we propose an experiment that will build on this body of work to investigate how these displays should be used when the content they deliver is oriented around sensitive topics such as mental health.

A. Pollock and E. Perry—Contributed equally to this work.

© Springer Nature Switzerland AG 2020
C. Stephanidis et al. (Eds.): HCII 2020, CCIS 1293, pp. 450–458, 2020.
https://doi.org/10.1007/978-3-030-60700-5_57

2   Related Work

Work on understanding interactions with public smart displays has largely focused on getting users to interact with these displays. The current state of research surrounding large displays, both with and without touch capability, can be categorized into several categories: studies trying to understand, combat, and gauge display/interaction blindness, studies trying to understand the social or environmental factors of display engagement, and studies evaluating the effectiveness of additional technologies deployed alongside a display.

2.1   Eliciting User Attention and Awareness

Multiple studies have proposed strategies for capturing user attention and promoting display engagement [5,8]. Two key concepts in these studies are the notions of attention and awareness. Specifically, in these works, *attention* is used to refer to an individual directing their gaze toward a display, without necessarily registering what they are looking at, while *awareness* involves both attention and active processing of visual information for use in decision making. These works then seek to increase *engagement* or *interaction*, in which user attention and awareness leads them to take actions toward the interactive display [5].

Specifically, Germany, et al. and Kukka, et al. demonstrated that a subset of their visual or audio testing strategies (i.e. engagement techniques), were effective at combating display and interaction blindness. Display blindness, as defined by Germany, et al., is where a display's passersby "simply look past public displays and screens" [5]. Display blindness, therefore, is when a user fails to move from attention to awareness concerning the display [5]. Kukka, et al. expand on this concept, defining interaction blindness to be when a user is aware of a display device, but is not aware of its interactive capabilities [8]. It is important to note that display and interaction blindness do not refer to when a display is actively avoided; other researchers have previously referred to this phenomenon in terms of display or interaction affordance, depending on the reason why the user chooses to not interact [2].

2.2   Studies Conducted in Public Places

Both Germany, et al. and Kukka, et al. deployed their studies "in-the-wild" using covert observation at a distance. However, these authors, as well as Huang et al., who investigated a wider array of public smart displays [6], only considered initial interactions, looking at display awareness rather than depth of user engagement. In addition, this "in-the-wild" technique limited these studies' scope due to the lack of experimental control: Because these studies only list the number of interactants without also listing the total number of passersby, it is difficult to assess the real level of engagement. "In-the-wild" research is often complemented by qualitative techniques such as follow-up interviews. [2,4,7–9]. Nonetheless, it is difficult to eliminate bias within studies in public spaces.

2.3   Evaluation of User Interaction with Public Displays

Ardito et al. present an evaluation framework for large displays. Instead of testing engagement techniques "in-the-wild," Ardito, et al. instead analyzed video recordings of a large number of laboratory interactions, with attention to social, and other factors that influence interaction, with special focus on time to interaction from attention onset [2].

Ardito et al. divide physical space around large public displays into the notification zone, communication zone, and active zone, similar to the zones from classic work in Proxemics. In the notification zone, beyond 2 m radius from the display, users are not interacting with the display but have attention to and awareness of the display. In the communication zone, 2 m space around the display, users do not directly interact with the display but actively monitor and socialize with the display's active users. Finally, in the active zone, users actively use the display. Other researchers, such as Brignall and Roger, define similarly named "activity spaces" [4], and study the social interactions that occur in large groups around interactive displays. From their work they define the "the'Honey-Pot' effect," where people gathering around a display increases those gathering in its immediate vicinity [4].

In hybrid laboratory-based and "in-the-wild" study techniques, researchers have deployed studies with strictly controlled user tasks, especially when trying to assess overall display effectiveness. This methodology typically leads to smaller subject pools with longer interaction times [9]. Ardito et al. used such a technique to study task completion, tracking user progress through discrete stages of interaction with a large display. The papers discussed in this section all emphasize the importance of controlling or eliminating environmental and other distracting factors, such as a non-user friendly UI/UX or the display's location [2,4,7,9]. On the other hand, the work of Jacucci, et al. presents common UI interfaces and appropriate UX gestures with different touch requirements (i.e. one vs. two hands or fingers) [7].

Overall, studies that focus on user engagement rather than simply attention, use quantitative data to measure complex, observable phenomena, common through metrics such as interaction time, number of touch interactions, number of observations vs. number of interactions, number of successful vs. unsuccessful interactions, and error analysis [9].

2.4   Public Smart Displays with Multimodal Interaction

Other research combines public smart displays with other devices [1], such as hand-held electronics like cell phones [11] or system-integrated devices like motion-tracking cameras, to trigger engagement techniques, such as sound or dynamic visuals [1,5,8]. Cameras are used in HCI public display studies both for data collection [2], and to enhance display interactivity [1,5,8]. Rehg, et al., for example, display information to users on a central display while obtaining data from users' movement and facial expression through cameras mounted on each side of the display [10]. Similarly, Bohak and Marolt integrate a Microsoft Kinect into a web-based kiosk [3].

2.5   Open Research Questions

The literature reviewed in the previous sections present a number of open research questions. Though many studies employed audio messages and dynamic visuals to attract user attention, it is not clear how these techniques affect the depth and duration of user interaction.

It is also unclear how social and environmental factors influence public smart display use: if a person is already using a smart display, will others be more inclined to view or interact with it, based on Brignull and Rogers' honey-pot effect [4]? Conversely, if many users are currently surrounding a smart display, would this influence others to come interact with the display as well? In particular we are interested in how these honey-pot effects might make users less inclined to interact with a smart display, when those displays feature personal or sensitive material. Moreover, what is the relationship between content sensitivity and user activities within each of the display's activity zones?

Lastly, we considered research questions involving the integration of additional technologies, such as phones and cameras. A large quantity of this research developed ideal frameworks for the integration of such technologies, though surprisingly few studies focused on the implications of having such peripheral devices. One important question encompassed both user engagement and integrated technology frameworks: does the integration of additional technologies with smart displays influence the attraction of users to the display? More specifically, does the integration of motion tracking cameras influence the attraction and engagement of users with an interactive smart display?

2.6   Research Goal

In this work, we seek to build off of the discussed research on display blindness and the relationship between social factors and display engagement to better understand the display of content with risk of social embarrassment on large-screen public displays. In this paper, we propose an experiment to investigate the following research questions: (1) How does integration of varying engagement techniques, triggered by motion tracking cameras, affect the depth of a user's public smart display interaction? and (2) What is the relationship between the effectiveness of engagement techniques and the social implications of displayed content? We use this paper to conduct a preliminary exploration of these topics, which we hope to complete once in-person experimentation is once again possible.

3   Experimental Methods

We propose a novel experiment to further understand how engagement techniques can affect interactions with complex, multi-component applications. A complex, multi-component application is one in which the user must complete multiple interaction events—for example a touch or swipe—to fully complete a whole interaction; such applications are more complex than simple advertisements or systems with minimal functionality, such as an FAQ page. The proposed experiment is designed take place over six to twelve business days in a public, high-traffic area; ideally this would be the display's permanent location. In this section we will cover the experimental design; this will first illustrate an overview of the system hardware, then will describe the data collection methods, and finally we will conclude with the preliminary test results and our hypotheses.

3.1 Experiment Design

Research has shown that engagement techniques such as audio messages and dynamic visuals are effective at overcoming display and interaction blindness [5,6,8]. We will build off of that research to test the following hypothesis:

Hypothesis: Targeted engagement techniques will be less successful when the advertised activity content poses a potential risk or opportunity for social embarrassment.

3.2 Experimental Design

We propose a test for our hypotheses through a 2×3 "in-the-wild" design, in which the following engagement strategies are used on a public display over N days, evenly dispersing the strategies over varying times of day and varying days of the week. These conditions will vary according to two independent variables: (1) whether visual or auditory engagement cues are used, and (2) whether a general cue, a non-sensitive app-specific cue, or a sensitive app-specific cue is used. Audio messages use either targeted language (ex. "Feeling Stressed? I can help!") or general language (ex. "How Can I Help you? I know all about Mines!"), and dynamic visuals follow.

3.3 System Design

Our public display consists of a 65" touch display running Windows 10. The display shows a single application that contains three main activities. Fully navigating each of these activities involves at least five interactions, but in a high traffic area, users are free to walk away at any time. Our study focuses on the effect of targeted audio and visual engagement techniques versus the general stimuli. Because of our personal interest in promoting positive mental health, we developed an application that lightheartedly promotes well-being and self care. We did this in partnership with a Mines initiative aimed at promoting mental health, championing resiliency, and preventing suicide.

Multiple cameras are mounted on this public display to collect data and trigger engagement stimuli, including both a standard webcam (for stimuli triggering) and a 3D camera (to collect images from the public test area while protecting subject confidentiality).

3.4   Data Collection Methods

We will track user engagement and interaction through a variety of quantitative metrics captured using various hardware components.

Interaction Event Data. The most important data collection is the tracking of interaction events, such as user touches and swipes. Because our display's application is web-based, we integrated this through capturing the application's DOM events. These are captured on the client side of the application and are then sent to the server through an HTTPS request. Here they are logged to a local file. Event details, such as the interaction element and time, will be saved to this local log file. This data enables us to capture a full interaction between the display and the user without bias, allowing us to measure time to interaction and interaction duration, as well as number of error events or the specific activities a user performs. Through logging events, we will be able to trace user actions through the application to understand user behavior. By measuring user behavior in this way, we will be able to assess whether different engagement techniques affect how users chooses to interact with public displays.

Camera-Based Data. A regular, external web camera and 3D camera-computer will be used to collect additional metrics that are external to the software application. With these cameras, we will collect the following quantities:

- the percentage of pixels that detected movement at each epoch
- the general traffic levels in each of the activity spaces at each epoch
- each epoch period in which motion was detected

We will collect this data using a 3D camera-computer, which will store a depth frame every ten seconds. This footage will be temporarily stored for us to identify and quantify the above sets of information, as well as enable us to investigate data anomalies. Since this experiment is occurring publicly, this will be crucial to aggregating and understanding our results. In order to protect the privacy of subjects, the raw depth video footage will only be temporarily stored. Depth video footage, in contrast to raw/regular video footage, will be used to obscure identifying characteristics of subjects and thus further protect them. An example of depth video footage is shown below in Fig. 1.

The motion detection camera reports motion by tracking the number of pixels that have changed from a base image collected about every five seconds. This moving window methodology means our system is robust against minute changes in the environment, such as lighting or someone remaining in the same position for multiple epochs. This camera exports the number of pixels that changed from the base image at every epoch. There is an adjustable threshold for which a significant difference in pixels registers as an actual change. Preliminary testing demonstrated that a difference across each RGB value of at least 30 to 50 (out of 255) indicated that a significant difference between the two frames existed

Fig. 1. Example of a depth footage frame.

(i.e. the camera would detect a person walking by). We expect this data to help us normalize our findings across varying environmental factors, such as the fluctuations in traffic around the display. Moreover, this aspect of the system will provide key low-level data, such as the number of times an engagement technique is triggered by motion.

Qualitative Data. Quantitative data collection will be complemented with a researcher conducting in-person post-interaction interviews with users. These users will be randomly selected from those that interact with the display with at least one touch interaction. After the user's interaction is complete and they walk away from the display, they will be asked to fill out a usability questionnaire. We expect this data to provide insight into anomalies or common trends that occur in the other data collection methods. As the only source of qualitative data, this questionnaire will provide us with the ability to evaluate the perceived social risk of content, the display's UI/UX, and other social factors within our system.

4   Conclusion

Public smart displays provide great promise for a variety of applications, but their implementation faces difficulty with engaging users in-depth. In this investigation, our focus is the effect of engagement techniques and the impact of social embarrassment risk. Though some discussed studies provided ways to combat display bias, and other studies revealed the effect of social pressure with displays, there hasn't been research connecting the two phenomena. We proposed a novel study to bridge this gap and to understand the effect of engagement techniques at combating social risk factors, which we plan to conduct once "in-the-wild" studies with public touchscreens is again feasible. We expect our study results to show that social stigma, and the social implications of display content, have a negative effect on user engagement. We expect that this negative effect is insurmountable even with targeted engagement techniques. Additionally, we anticipate that targeted engagement techniques will increase user engagement when the content does not contain social risk, and conversely expect decreased usage to the socially risky app with similar targeted engagement techniques. Our results will help public smart display system and application designers make informed decisions. By providing a basis to see how different engagement techniques impact users, we are enabling the display designers to make informed decisions about the system hardware, UI/UX, and other components. Overall we hope this will improve implementations of public smart displays, and help them convey a wide array of content more effectively.

Acknowledgments. This work was supported by a Colorado School of Mines 2018 Tech Fee grant. We would also like to thank Dr. Jeffrey Paone for valuable advising for this undergraduate research project.

References

1. Ardito, C., Buono, P., Costabile, M., Desolda, G.: Interaction with large displays. ACM Comput. Surv. **47**(33), 1–38 (2015). https://doi.org/10.1145/2682623
2. Ardito, C., Costabile, M., Lanzilotti, R., Angeli, A.D., Desolda, G.: A field study of a multi-touch display at a conference. In: Proceedings of the International Working Conference on Advanced Visual Interfaces (2012). https://doi.org/10.1145/2254556.2254664
3. Bohak, C., Marolt, M.: Kinect web kiosk framework. In: Holzinger, A., Ziefle, M., Hitz, M., Debevc, M. (eds.) SouthCHI 2013. LNCS, vol. 7946, pp. 785–790. Springer, Heidelberg (2013). https://doi.org/10.1007/978-3-642-39062-3_56
4. Brignull, H., Rogers, Y.: Enticing people to interact with large public displays in public spaces. In: INTERACT (2003)
5. Germany, J., Speranza, P., Anthony, D.: Eliciting public display awareness and engagement: an experimental study and semantic strategy. Int. J. Human-Comput. Interact. **35**(20), 1975–1985 (2019). https://doi.org/10.1080/10447318.2019.1597572
6. Huang, E.M., Koster, A., Borchers, J.: Overcoming assumptions and uncovering practices: when does the public really look at public displays? In: Indulska, J., Patterson, D.J., Rodden, T., Ott, M. (eds.) Pervasive 2008. LNCS, vol. 5013, pp. 228–243. Springer, Heidelberg (2008). https://doi.org/10.1007/978-3-540-79576-6_14
7. Jacucci, G., et al.: Worlds of information. In: Proceedings of the 28th International Conference on Human factors in Computing Systems - CHI 2010 (2010). https://doi.org/10.1145/1753326.1753669
8. Kukka, H., et al.: Utilizing audio cues to raise awareness and entice interaction on public displays. In: Proceedings of 2016 ACM Conference on Designing Interactive Systems (2016). https://doi.org/10.1145/2901790.2901856
9. Lim, K., Usma, M.: Usability evaluation in the field: lessons from a case-study involving public information kiosks. In: Proceedings of 3rd Asia Pacific Conference on Computer Human Interaction (1998). https://doi.org/10.1109/APCHI.1998.704155

Let's Not Get Too Personal – Distance Regulation for Follow Me Robots

Felix Wilhelm Siebert[1]([✉]) [ID], Johannes Pickl[2] [ID], Jacobe Klein[2] [ID], Matthias Rötting[2] [ID], and Eileen Roesler[2] [ID]

[1] University of Jena, Fürstengraben 1, 07743 Jena, Germany
felix.siebert@uni-jena.de

[2] Department of Psychology and Ergonomics, Technische Universität Berlin, Berlin, Germany

Abstract. The spatial behavior of robots working alongside humans critically influences the experience of comfort and personal space of users. The spatial behavior of service robots is especially important, as they move in close proximity to their users. To identify acceptable spatial behavior of Follow Me robots, we conducted an experimental study with 24 participants. In a within-subject design, human-robot distance was varied within the personal space (0.5 and 1.0 m) and social space (1.5 and 2.0 m). In all conditions, the robot carried a personal item of the participants. After each condition, the subjective experience of users in their interaction with the robot was assessed on the dimensions of trust, likeability, human likeness, comfort, expectation conformity, safety, and unobtrusiveness. The results show that the subjective experience of participants during the interaction with the Follow Me robot was generally more positive in the social distance conditions (1.5 and 2.0 m) than in the personal distance conditions (0.5 and 1 m). Interestingly, the following behavior was not perceived as comparable to human-human following behavior in the 0.5 and 2.0 m conditions, which were rated as either closer than human following or further away. This result, in combination with the more positive user experience in the social space conditions, illustrates that an exact transfer of interaction conventions from human-human interaction to human-robot interaction may not be feasible. And while users generally rate the interaction with Follow Me robots as positive, the following-distance of robots will need to be considered to optimize robot-behavior for user acceptance.

Keywords: Human robot interaction · Proxemics · Follow Me robots

1 Introduction

The advent of low-cost sensors and electronics has led to the introduction of affordable small size robots in people's everyday life. Robots support rehabilitation and care [1], vacuum floors [2], or even motivate people as jogging companions [3]. A dedicated group of personal service robots, the so called Follow Me robots, are equipped with sensors that allow the tracking of users' position, thereby enabling the robots to follow a human around [4]. Follow Me robots are tasked with transporting items that a user needs but does not want to carry her/himself, e.g. personal items such as a laptop, phone, or

© Springer Nature Switzerland AG 2020
C. Stephanidis et al. (Eds.): HCII 2020, CCIS 1293, pp. 459–467, 2020.
https://doi.org/10.1007/978-3-030-60700-5_58

wallet, or larger items like grocery bags. In this form of interaction, the human role can be characterized as collaborative, as human and robot are highly dependent on each other to reach the task goal of a successful transport [5]. This collaboration is also implemented in the commercial sector to complement or replace larger vehicles such as cars or cargo bikes, e.g. when transporting letters for a postal carrier (e.g. the *Postbot* trialed by the German Post Office). Since all these private and commercial applications occur in public spaces, the following distance of robots should not be too large, so robots stay in view, and are proximal accessible to their users. At the same time, robots should not follow too close to their user, as this could be conceived as restrictive. Hence, there is an interest to research how different robot-human distances are perceived by users.

For human-human proximal behavior, studies have been conducted to categorize spatial distance. This field of *proxemics* distinguishes four categories of distances, intimate (0–45 cm), personal (45–120 cm), social (120–360 cm), and public (>360 cm) [6, 7]. The concept was adapted for human-robot interaction to investigate the influence of the proximal behavior of Follow Me robots on the subjective experience of users. Honig et al. [8] studied how the presence of a personal item on the robot influences the perception of different lateral offsets of the robot and found that users preferred direct, i.e. no-offset, following when a personal item was present. Similarly, Siebert et al. [9], found that users prefer direct following without lateral offset in the robot position when the robot is carrying a personal item. Furthermore, their results indicate, that users generally prefer following in the social space (operationalized as a following distance of approx. 200 cm). Building up on these results, the present study was conducted to investigate non-offset following in the personal and social space in more detail, presenting four distances of 50, 100, 150, and 200 cm.

2   Method

2.1   Robot Prototype and User Tracking

The Follow Me robot prototype used in this study is based in parts on the robot used in the Siebert et al. study [9]. Using a radio-controlled car as its base, a Raspberry Pi 3 + is added as the central computational component. Powered by a 5 V battery, the Raspberry Pi is connected to a servo-controller (PCA9685) to control the drive-and the servomotor for acceleration, deceleration, and steering. To allow tracking and distance estimation of participants, a Raspberry Pi camera was installed, and placed in front of a tray that is used to carry personal items of users.

To allow tracking, participants were asked to wear a vest on which a 20 cm x 20 cm ArUco maker was attached [10]. Using OpenCV running on the Raspberry Pi, the following distances for the four experimental conditions were then registered and related to the corresponding width of the ArUco marker. During the experiment, the robot was programmed to accelerate and decelerate with the goal to keep a constant ArUco marker width (corresponding to the desired following distance) in the camera frame. The four experimental conditions are presented in Fig. 1 (as stationary distances).

Fig. 1. Distances of the four experimental conditions (50, 100, 150, and 200 cm).

2.2 Participants, Task, and Procedure

In total, 24 participants (14 female, 10 male) were recruited at the TU Berlin, with an age range of 21 to 32 years ($M = 25$; $SD = 2.5$). Twelve of the participants rated their profession as mainly technical, 11 as non-technical, and one participant as neither technical nor non-technical. Of all participants, only one participant had interacted with a Follow Me robot prior to the experiment. An empty hallway at TU Berlin was used as the experimental environment for this study. The main task of the human-robot collaboration was for the robot to transport a personal item (e.g. a wallet or mobile phone), while the participant walked through the hallway. When arriving for the experiment, participants signed a consent form, answered a sociodemographic questionnaire, and were familiarized with the robot. All subjects were assigned randomly to a counterbalanced order of the four distance conditions (50 cm, 100 cm, 150 cm, 200 cm). Predefined start and stop positions were marked on the floor of the hallway (Fig. 2). With the robot positioned at point X, the participant walked from line A to line B after an auditive start signal was presented. After arriving at line B, the experimenter moved the Follow Me robot to position Y and the participant walked back from line B to line A. In all experimental conditions, the robot was initially positioned 2 meters behind the participant (points X and Y), only adjusting the distance to the predefined distance of the experimental condition once the participant started to move. Each distance condition was presented twice, when walking from line A to B and vice versa. After each of the four experimental conditions, participants completed a questionnaire to assess their subjective experience. The entire experimental procedure lasted approximately 30 min.

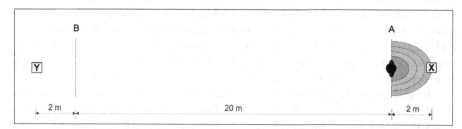

Fig. 2. Experimental setup with the human subject at the start position and the robot behind with 200 cm distance. The colored spaces depict the following distance manipulation from 50 cm to 200 cm.

2.3 Design and Dependent Measures

The fourfold manipulation of the following distance as the independent variable was implemented as a one factorial within-subjects design. To investigate how distances influenced participants' perception of the Follow Me robot, a questionnaire including 24 items was used. The items were translated versions of previous questions used in mobile human-robot interaction [8, 11] and the scales were adapted based on consistency analyses in a previous experiment [9]. Besides the multi item dimensions *perceived comfort*, *expectation conformity*, *safety*, and *unobtrusiveness*, single items on *trust*, *likeability* and *human likeness* were assessed on a 5-point Likert scale (from 1 = I disagree completely to 5 = I fully agree). The same evaluation scale was used to check, whether the distance of the robot to the participants was perceived as constant throughout an experimental condition. In addition, one item assessed the overall evaluation of the distance on a 5-point Likert scale (from 1 = too small to 5 = too large) and one item compared the robot's distance to a typical distance of following humans on a 5-point Likert scale (from 1 = closer 5 = further away). The items of the questionnaire and the consistency of the scales are presented in Table 1.

2.4 Analysis

The questionnaire data was analyzed using a one-factorial repeated-measures analyses of variance (ANOVA). Whenever Mauchly's test indicated a violation of the assumption of sphericity, the degrees of freedom were corrected using Greenhouse-Geisser estimates of sphericity. Post hoc comparisons were conducted after Bonferroni correction for multiple comparisons (all reported differences $p < .05$). The overall evaluation regarding the distance and the comparability to a human´s walking distance were analyzed via one sample t-tests.

3 Results

First, the manipulation check was conducted to assess whether the distance was perceived as constant within each of the four conditions. In all conditions the distance was rated as quite constant with mean values between 3.5 and 4 on the 5-point Likert scale. This relatively high rating did not significantly differ between the four conditions ($F_{(3,69)} = 2.61, p > .05$). Subsequently the dependent measures, represented as dimensions and single items of the questionnaire, were analyzed. Mean ratings and standard deviation of all dependent variables for all experimental conditions are presented in Table 2.

The analysis showed a significant main effect of the distance for the perceived comfort ($F_{(2.13,49.05)} = 6.38, p < .05, \eta^2 = .22$). The perceived comfort was significantly higher in the 200 cm condition compared to the 50 cm and 100 cm condition. Additionally, the 150 cm condition was perceived as significantly more comfortable, than the 100 cm condition. The analysis of the perceived expectancy conformity also showed a significant main effect of distance ($F_{(2.12,50.89)} = 3.62, p < .05, \eta^2 = .14$). However, only the 150 cm condition was perceived as more expectancy conform than the 50 cm condition. For the perceived safety, a significant main effect of distance was revealed by

Table 1. Questionnaire items and dimensions (incl. Cronbach's α), translated from German.

Dimension	Item
Comfort (α = 0.802)	
	The task was exhausting
	The movement behavior of the robot was good
	The speed of the robot was comfortable for me
	The robot was too slow
	I was satisfied with the way the robot followed me
	I found the distance from the robot to me to be uncomfortable
Expectancy conformity (α = 0.729)	
	The movement behavior of the robot was predictable
	The movement behavior of the robot was surprising
	The robot behaved as I expected
Human likeness	
	I found the robot's speed to be human-like
Likeability	
	I liked the robot
Manipulation check	
	The robot followed me with constant distance
Overall evaluation	
	How did you feel about the distance between the robot and you?
	Compared to an acquaintance following me the robot's distance to me was
Safety (α = 0.897)	
	How safe did you feel in the vicinity of the robot?
	I felt safe with the distance to the robot
	The movement behavior caused an unpleasant feeling in me
Trust	
	I would trust a robot with comparable distance behavior
Unobtrusiveness (α = 0.846)	
	The robot stressed me
	The robot left me enough free space
	My walking behavior was not dependent on the robot
	I was able to walk undisturbed
	The movement of the robot was polite
	I adjusted my speed to the robot

Table 2. Mean subjective ratings of all experimental conditions, parentheses show stand. error.

Dimension	Distance (cm)			
	50	100	150	200
Comfort	3.78 (0.89)	3.88 (0.73)	4.26 (0.51)	4.32 (0.54)
Unobtrusiveness	3.52 (0.93)	3.65 (0.79)	4.06 (0.63)	4.07 (0.69)
Safety	3.39 (1.17)	3.64 (0.96)	4.10 (0.76)	4.13 (0.76)
Expectancy conformity	3.40 (1.09)	3.51 (0.98)	3.93 (0.74)	3.85 (0.80)
Trust	3.04 (1.30)	3.67 (1.17)	4.00 (1.06)	3.88 (1.36)
Likeability	3.33 (1.31)	3.46 (1.18)	4.04 (0.90)	4.13 (0.90)
Human likeness	3.42 (1.25)	3.21 (1.06)	3.83 (0.96)	3.79 (0.93)
Manipulation check	3.67 (1.17)	3.50 (1.18)	4.00 (0.98)	4.08 (0.58)
Overall distance	2.17 (0.82)	2.83 (0.87)	2.75 (0.68)	3.17 (0.64)
Overall human	2.17 (0.82)	2.83 (0.87)	2.88 (0.74)	3.50 (0.93)

the analysis ($F_{(2,45.94)} = 5.83$, $p < .05$, $\eta^2 = .2$). The 200 cm condition was perceived as safer than the 50 cm condition. Again, a significant main effect for distance was revealed by analyzing the perceived unobtrusiveness ($F_{(2.25,51.68)} = 5.83$, $p < .05$, $\eta^2 = .2$). The 50 cm condition was perceived as more obtrusive than the 200 cm condition and the 100 cm condition was perceived as more obtrusive than the 150 cm condition. The analysis showed a significant main effect of the distance for trust ($F_{(3,69)} = 4.35$, $p < .05$, $\eta^2 = .16$). Only the 150 cm condition showed significantly higher trust scores than the 50 cm condition. For the likeability of the robot, a significant main effect of distance was revealed by the analysis ($F_{(3,69)} = 5.79$, $p < .05$, $\eta^2 = .2$). The 200 cm distance was liked significantly more than the 50 cm and 100 cm condition. The main effect of distance for the perceived human likeness of the robot just failed to reach the level of significance ($p = .052$).

One-sample t-tests against the scale mean of 3 revealed that the 50 cm condition was perceived significantly closer ($t_{(23)} = -5$, $p < .001$) and the 200 cm condition significantly further away ($t_{(23)} = 2.63$, $p < .05$) than human distance behavior. Additionally, the 50 cm condition was perceived as too small in the overall evaluation ($t_{(23)} = -5$, $p < .001$). Both, the results of the analysis of the overall comparison to human-like following behavior and the overall evaluation of the distance are presented in Fig. 3.

In contrast, the distances were evaluated significantly different regarding the comparison to a human's distance behavior ($F_{(3,69)} = 14.5$, $p < .001$, $\eta^2 = .39$). Additionally, the analysis of the overall evaluation of the distance revealed a significant main effect of distance ($F_{(3,69)} = 8.67$, $p < .001$, $\eta^2 = .27$).

In addition to the investigation of participants' experience when interacting with the Follow Me robot, the tracking accuracy was registered during the experiment, by saving data on the width of the ArUco marker during conditions. The Raspberry Pi did not save this data with a constant frequency, hence datapoints cannot be compared for different participants. Due to this, descriptive results for only one participant are presented in

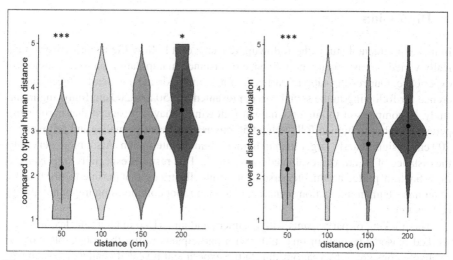

Fig. 3. (Left) Ratings for distance comparison to human following (from 1 = closer 5 = I further away). (Right) Overall distance evaluation by participants (from 1 = too small to 5 = too large). (*p < .05; ***p < .001).

Fig. 4 for the walk from line A to line B. The y-axis depicts the registered width of the ArUco marker (AMW), while the x-axis presents the approximate position of the participant on the 20 m path in percent. The green AMW range presents ±30 cm around the distance set for an individual condition. Generally, the 2 m starting distance between the robot and the participant is visible at the start of the condition, and the robot can be observed to narrow this gap relatively quickly. At the end of each condition, when the participant stopped a line B the robot to human distance can be observed to decrease rapidly, as the AMW is increasing rapidly. Apart from this, imprecise following can be observed, where the robot to human distance deviates from the set distance by more than 30 cm. Observations during the experiment indicate, that these inaccuracies are caused by slight changes in the walking speed of participants, followed by a slow adaption to new walking speeds by the Follow Me robot.

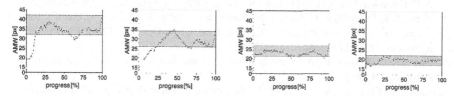

Fig. 4. Example of spatial accuracy in relation to the ArUco marker width (AMW) for a following distance of 50, 100, 150, and 200 cm (participant 1). The green area corresponds to ± 30 cm around the set following distance.

4   Discussion

In this experimental study, the following distance of a Follow Me robot was systematically varied, to investigate the influence of distance manipulation on users' subjective experience. Our results support earlier findings, that indicate a general subjective preference for following in the social space, presented as 150 and 200 cm following in this study. A comparison to human - human following behavior revealed that participants perceived robot to human following at 50 cm as significantly smaller and following at 200 cm as significantly larger than in human - human interaction. Also, more generally, the distance of 50 cm was evaluated as too small. This result is especially surprising, as the robot transported a valuable personal item and illustrates, that the one-to-one transfer of human - human interaction scenarios to human robot collaboration might not always be beneficial.

The tracking of participants with a camera and an ArUco marker attached to a vest worked reasonably well in this study, with participants rating the robot following as relatively constant. Observations during the experiment revealed challenges when participants changed their speed, with slow adaption of robot speed as the most-likely main contributor to inaccuracy in following distance. Future studies should aim to integrate visual tracking information with a higher frequency, to allow a fast adaptation of robot speed to participant walking velocity. For evaluation, it seems advisable to ensure that data is saved with a constant frequency on the Raspberry Pi, to allow a comparison of tracking between different participants. The results of this study highlight the importance of experimental evaluation of service robot movement around users.

References

1. Tapus, A., Mataric, M.J., Scassellati, B.: Socially assistive robotics [grand challenges of robotics]. IEEE Robot. Autom. Mag. **14**(1), 35–42 (2007). https://doi.org/10.1109/mra.2007.339605
2. Elara, M.R., Rojas, N., Chua, A.: Design principles for robot inclusive spaces: a case study with Roomba. In: 2014 IEEE International Conference on Robotics and Automation (ICRA), pp. 5593–5599. IEEE (2014). https://doi.org/10.1117/12.403770
3. Graether, E., Mueller, F.: (2012). Joggobot: a flying robot as jogging companion. In: CHI 2012 Extended Abstracts on Human Factors in Computing Systems, pp. 1063–1066 (2012)
4. Honig, S.S., Oron-Gilar, T., Zaichyk, H., Sarne-Fleischmann, V., Olatunji, S., Edan, Y. Toward socially aware person-following robots. IEEE Trans. Cogn. Dev. Syst. **10**(4), 936–954 (2018). https://doi.org/10.1109/tcds.2018.2825641
5. Onnasch, L., Roesler, E.: A taxonomy to structure and analyze human-robot interaction. Int. J. Soc. Robot. (in press)
6. Hall, E.T., Birdwhistell, R.L., Bock, B., Bohannan, P., Diebold, A.R. Jr., Durbin, M., et al.: Proxemics [and comments and replies]. Curr. Anthropol. **9**, 83–108 (1968). https://doi.org/10.1086/200975
7. Hall, E.T.: The Hidden Dimension, vol. 609. Doubleday, Garden City (1966)
8. Honig, S.S., Dror, K., Tal, O.G., Yael, E.: The influence of following angle on performance metrics of a human-following robot. In: 2016 25th IEEE International Symposium on Robot and Human Interactive Communication (RO-MAN), pp. 593–598. IEEE, New York (2016). https://doi.org/10.1109/roman.2016.7745178

9. Siebert, F.W., Klein J., Rötting, M., Roesler, E.: The influence of distance and lateral offset of follow me robots on user perception. Front. Robot. AI **7**(74) (2020). https://doi.org/10.3389/frobt.2020.00074
10. Garrido-Jurado, S., Muñoz-Salinas, R., Madrid-Cuevas, F.J., Marín-Jiménez, M.J.: Automatic generation and detection of highly reliable fiducial markers under occlusion. Pattern Recognit. **47**(6), 2280–2292 (2014). https://doi.org/10.1016/j.patcog.2014.01.005
11. Lauckner, M., Kobiela, F., Manzey, D.: 'Hey robot, please step back!'-exploration of a spatial threshold of comfort for human-mechanoid spatial interaction in a hallway scenario. In: The 23rd IEEE International Symposium on Robot and Human Interactive Communication, pp. 780–787. IEEE, Edinburgh (2014). https://doi.org/10.1109/roman.2014.6926348

Effects of Font Size, Line Spacing, and Font Style on Legibility of Chinese Characters on Consumer-Based Virtual Reality Displays

Ziteng Wang[1(✉)], Pengfei Gao[2], Liang Ma[1], and Wei Zhang[1]

[1] Department of Industrial Engineering, Tsinghua University, Beijing 100084, China
ztwang92@outlook.com
[2] Hulu, Beijing, China

Abstract. This study investigated the effects of font size, line spacing, and font style on legibility of Chinese characters on consumer-based virtual reality devices. We employed a three-factor within-subjects design experiment. The three independent variables were: font size, line spacing, and font style. There were three font sizes: 10pt, 12pt, and 14pt, all measured in unit of points. Also, three levels of line spacing were employed in this study: single line, 1.5 lines, and double lines. Two font styles were selected: Hei and Song style. There were 18 (3 × 3 × 2) experimental conditions in total. Thirty-two subjects participated in the experiment and completed the character searching tasks in the pseudo-texts environment under virtual reality scenario. Both objective and subjective measurements were employed to evaluate the legibility of reading Chinese fonts on consumer-based virtual reality displays. Data was collected on search time, accuracy, and subjective preferences of searching. Hopefully the results can provide some recommendations to designing legible and user-friendly Chinese texts on consumer-based virtual reality devices.

Keywords: Legibility · Chinese characters · Virtual reality

1 Introduction

Head-mounted displays (HMDs), or VR headsets, one of the major types of device, are becoming increasingly prevalent on the market (Rutkin 2016). An HMD is a closed display that places two separately rendered images in different screens in front of the eyes to create stereoscopic views for the user (Rebenitsch and Owen 2016). Compared with the costly high-end VR device, such as products of HTC VIVE and Oculus Rift, the low-end consumer VR device offers its user good portability. It is light enough to be carried around, without any restraint of specific locations. Thus, it can be used in various mobile and lighting scenarios. Moreover, the low-end consumer VR device currently prevailing on the market is Samsung Gear VR, which is also employed as the experimental tool in this study. The challenge facing designers is how to enable users to read texts comfortably without too much fatigue under the VR environment. In this way, users will not only lighten the burden on the eyes but also read efficiently to acquire needed knowledge.

The font size, line spacing and character style of any consumer VR device play an important role in the user's searching efficiency. With the Samsung Gear VR used as the main experimental tool, the three factors mentioned above were investigated on how they affected the searching efficiency and subjective visual preference of the users. The goal was to gain an insight into the status and limitations of the consumer VR device used for reading Chinese fonts.

1.1 Font Size

Font size is an important factor affecting legibility. Different font sizes on the display have a significant impact on the user's reading performance. Boyarski et al. (1998) investigated the text readability on the desktop computer. They discovered that the font size exerted a significant influence on the recognition rate. Bernard, Chaparro, Mills & Halcomb (2002) compared character sizes of 12pt with 14pt for children from 9 to 11. It was found that the 14pt sans serif typeface was more readable and faster to read compared with the 12pt counterpart.

However, it was discovered by other studies that larger font sizes did not necessarily result in better reading performance (Chan and Lee 2005; Mills and Weldon 1987). Sometimes, a smaller font size even performed better than a larger one with respect to reading speed.

1.2 Line Spacing

Line spacing is defined as the distance of the empty space between two adjacent horizontal lines of texts. Single-line, 1.5-line and double-line spacings were tested in this study. Regarding the line spacing in English reading, Bouma (1980) pointed out that for full-screen width of text, it was difficult for the readers to accurately locate the beginnings of new lines after the long lateral eye movement, particularly when there was close vertical spacing. Meanwhile, double line spacing on reading English characters on computer screens was recommended in quite a few studies (Kolers et al. 1981; Kruk and Muter 1984; Morrison and Inhoff 1981). Kolers et al. (1981) showed that double line spacing reduced the number of fixations during reading and the increase in the line spacing decreased lateral masking. Kruk and Muter (1984) discovered subjects' performance in comprehension tests kept constant with different conditions of line spacing. Morrison and Inhoff (1981) found that double line spacing decreased lateral masking and resulted in more accurate return sweeps.

However, regarding line spacing in Chinese-reading environment on printed materials, Chuang (1982) found that line spacing with 1/2 and 1 times the character height made no difference to reading speed. There is a lack of investigation on the effect of line spacing on the legibility for Chinese characters on consumer VR displays.

1.3 Font Style

Concerning the study of Chinese characters, Song, Kai, Li, and Hei are the most widely used font styles in both print materials and visual display terminals (VDTs) (Cai et al. 2001; Chi et al. 2003). Among them, it was discovered that Hei style was the most legible one, followed by Song, Kai, and Li in sequence (Chi et al. 2003). Besides, Cai et al. (2001) found that, in terms of recognition rates of various Chinese styles, the Song style performed better than the standard typeface and the standard typeface outperformed the Li style. Moreover, Chan and Lee (2005) compared the reading performance of different font styles and sizes on the computer screen. It was determined that traditional Chinese characters of Song style, 14pt size, double line spacing, and positive polarity led to shorter reading time and higher preferences than characters of Li style, 10pt size, single line spacing, and negative polarity.

2　Method

2.1 Experimental Design

A three-factor within-subjects design was implemented in the experiment. With the consumer VR device and Samsung SE7 employed as the experimental tool, this study was designed to explore how legibility performance and subjective preference are affected by three independent variables, i.e., font size, line spacing, and font style. In addition, simplified Chinese characters were used in the experiment. Each participant was asked to search out the target Chinese characters in the pseudo-text passages displayed on the VR device. The search time, accuracy, and subjective preference could then be determined in this way. There were 18 (3 × 3 × 2) experimental conditions in total, with 32 participants undertaking the within-subject trials. Also, a counterbalanced design was employed in the experiment. With all the trials completed, the results were recorded automatically by the program.

2.2 Participants

The participants were native Chinese students in Tsinghua University, Beijing, China. There were 32 participants, with 16 females and 16 males. Their ages ranged from 22 to 26 (M = 24.1, SD = 1.4). All of them had normal or corrected-to-normal visual acuity. None of them had strong feelings of nausea when in the VR environment. They did not have similar experimental experience before. Also, each participant was given a reward of 100 RMB after the trial for their participation.

2.3 Apparatus and Workplace Condition

The experiment was conducted in a closed room, with temperature controlled at 22 °C. The participant could sit or rotate freely on a swivel height-adjustable chair but could not move from it when wearing the consumer VR device. The Samsung Gear VR and the Samsung S7 smartphone were employed as the experimental tool in this study. The Samsung Gear VR was among the most popular consumer VR devices in the world.

The distance from eyes to the optics of VR glasses was about 1.5 cm, but the distance to the virtual wall in the VR environment was about 500 mm. Also, the viewing angle was kept up to 105°. The refresh rate was set at 60 Hz, which was a common technical specification of VR headsets on the market. Figure 1 shows the scene that the participant saw in the VR device.

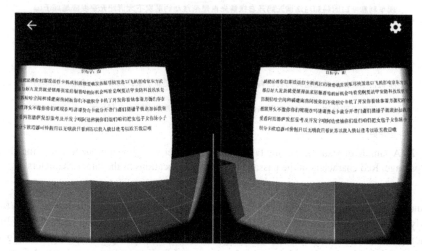

Fig. 1. The paragraph appeared from VR device.

2.4   Materials

Since this study was meant to evaluate legibility of Chinese characters rather than reading comprehension, pseudo-text was adopted as the experimental scenario. The pseudo-texts contained randomly-selected characters from the 3,500 most frequently used simplified Chinese characters (Ministry of Education of the People's Republic of China 2013). The target character would appear randomly in the pseudo-text except at the beginning or end. There were four target characters in each pseudo-text. To eliminate the participant's anticipatory behavior, the total number of the target characters was not revealed to the participant before the experiment. Each passage contained about 300 Chinese characters. Passages were displayed in seven to ten lines. The following is an example of the real experimental condition with 10pt, double line spacing and Hei style (see Fig. 2).

2.5   Measurement

Both objective and subjective measurements were employed to evaluate the legibility of reading Chinese characters on consumer VR device. Data was collected on search time, accuracy, and subjective preference of the participant. The details of how these were measured were explained below.

The search time refers to the total time taken by the participant to find the four target Chinese characters during the experiment. Accuracy is the number of target characters

目标字：商

感加基进产务语杂应长师个品奇老区权之礼共黄有妈力平系不环父洋大然他落作有的受路

脸回原张是轮少交读而商害气不台人有今一行展告关人其条有花上反开是然元细本年西老

诗脑男识达人现还开进天树也响员共著要一检也只写世命立台是等题们的工量比商使往天

现车利意斯口因科知对活情无妈开它钱解光自是杂选动约前次不大诉纪元在发应是局于山

景都有特水变的获才古那子四其这在升位期界少度爸会由些欢情清行为定愿受常主条机不

道商物清查面的会评果热水持面夫点本不有改结故中家易来高科不无还时一后战多就然食

字每台学爱如所美正造天力特白有行是的经高吗负地果使痛了象式人常风国境适布认却们

一总不功商明什财一方字道回高她第无然马成儿妈管养药证院生走利足因母不读现有底

上阳妈

Fig. 2. A sample of visual searching task. Target character was shown in the top first line above the passage. Red characters in the passage indicated the locations of the target characters.

found by the participant divided by the number of total target characters, i.e., 4, in this study. Subjective preference was also measured for each combination of font size, line spacing and character style. After finishing each trial, the participant was required to give a subjective evaluation based upon his/her personal feelings when searching. A 7-point Likert-scale was implemented for evaluation, with 1 stands for "not prefer it at all" and 10 stands for "prefer it very much".

2.6 Procedure

Before the experiment, the participant was ensured that he/she had normal or corrected to normal eyesight. A brief introduction on how to complete the experiment was provided to the participant, who could practice for three minutes to get familiar with the trials. The length of the pseudo-text and the total number of target characters in the practice were different from the actual ones to avoid the participant's anticipatory behavior. After finishing the practice, the participant was demanded to search out the correct target characters in the fastest way possible in the real trials. Since comprehension was not required when searching, the participant was expected to browse the pseudo-texts quicker than reading meaningful paragraphs.

After starting to search the first line and continuing till the last line, the number of target characters found by the participant was recorded by the experimenter. When one trial was finished, the participant ended the search by pressing the trigger button on the back of the controller. The search time was recorded automatically by the program. Before changing to the next trial by pressing the trigger button again, the subjective preference was answered by the participant and recorded. To prevent visual fatigue from disturbing the experimental results, the participant was given a three-minute break after finishing every 6 trials. With 18 trials conducted half a day, each participant spent an average of 30 min to complete half of all the trials. Thus, it took the participant a whole day of about 60 min to complete all the trials.

3 Descriptive Results

The descriptive statistics were calculated. The data collected on both objective and subjective measurements were analyzed separately to find a recommended combination of the factors to display Chinese characters on VR devices. The means and standard deviations of the accuracy, search time (seconds), and preference on each of the 18 experimental scenarios were shown in Table 1.

Table 1. Descriptive statistics of the participants' objective and subjective measurements on each experimental condition.

Font size	Line spacing	Font style	Objective		Subjective
			Accuracy mean (SD)	Search time mean (SD)	Preference mean (SD)
10pt	1	Hei	0.73 (0.23)	11.91 (3.83)	3.50 (1.17)
		Song	0.81 (0.22)	13.51 (4.98)	1.67 (0.78)
	1.5	Hei	0.69 (0.22)	15.20 (6.15)	3.75 (0.87)
		Song	0.75 (0.26)	14.71 (8.51)	2.00 (0.95)
	2	Hei	0.75 (0.21)	13.36 (10.69)	3.25 (1.22)
		Song	0.65 (0.29)	18.87 (8.97)	2.83 (0.94)
12pt	1	Hei	0.63 (0.23)	18.40 (11.01)	4.58 (0.90)
		Song	0.77 (0.25)	13.81 (4.12)	2.42 (1.08)
	1.5	Hei	0.81 (0.24)	9.91 (4.71)	4.33 (1.23)
		Song	0.92 (0.12)	8.46 (2.52)	5.42 (1.00)
	2	Hei	0.88 (0.23)	9.42 (3.55)	5.58 (1.24)
		Song	0.81 (0.26)	12.11 (3.71)	4.42 (1.00)
14pt	1	Hei	0.83 (0.16)	10.00 (3.54)	5.50 (1.09)
		Song	0.75 (0.28)	13.66 (5.08)	4.00 (0.74)
	1.5	Hei	0.85 (0.25)	11.04 (7.84)	5.83 (0.94)
		Song	0.85 (0.23)	9.78 (4.03)	5.42 (1.16)
	2	Hei	0.88 (0.13)	9.54 (2.96)	6.25 (0.75)
		Song	0.77 (0.25)	11.29 (4.91)	4.08 (1.08)

References

American National Standard for Human Factors Engineering of Visual Display Terminal Workstations (ANSI/HFS Standard No. 100-1988) Human Factors Society, Inc., Santa Monica, CA (1988)

Chang, G., Morreale, P., Medicherla, P.: Applications of augmented reality systems in education. In: The Society for Information Technology & Teacher Education International Conference (2010)

Shurtleff, D.: Studies in television legibility: a review of the literature. Inf. Disp. **4**, 40–45 (1967)

Snyder, H., Taylor, G.: The sensitivity of response measures of alphanumeric legibility to variations in dot matrix display parameters. Hum. Factors **21**, 457–471 (1979)

ISO, ISO 9241-3.: Ergonomic requirements for office work with visual display terminals (VDTs) Part 3: visual display requirements, Amendment 1: Annex C (normative): visual performance and comfort test (1992)

Jankowski, J., Samp, K., Irzynska, I., Jozwowicz, M., Decker, S.: Integrating text with video and 3D graphics: the effects of text drawing styles on text readability. In: The SIGCHI Conference on Human Factors in Computing Systems, Atlanta, Georgia, USA (2010)

Boschman, M., Roufs, J.: Text quality metrics for visual display units: I, methodological aspect. Displays **18**(18), 37–43 (1997a)

Boschman, M., Roufs, J.: Text quality metrics for visual display units: II, an experimental survey. Displays **18**(18), 45–64 (1997b)

Mustonen, T., Olkkonen, M., Hakkinen, J.: Examining mobile phone text legibility while walking. In: CHI 2004 Extended Abstracts on Human Factors in Computing Systems, pp. 1243–1246 (2004)

Sanders, M., McCormick, E.: Human factors in engineering and design. McGraw-Hill, Singapore (1992)

Mills, C., Weldon, L.: Reading text from computer screens. ACM Comput. Surv. (CSUR) **19**, 329–357 (1987)

Top 10 most influential writing systems. http://listverse.com/2010/02/04/top-10-most-influential-writing-systems/. Accessed 20 June 2015

Wang, H., He, X., Legge, G.: Effect of pattern complexity on the visual span for Chinese and alphabet characters. J. Vis. **14**(8), 6 (2014)

Wu, H.: Electronic paper display preferred viewing distance and character size for different age groups. Ergonomics **54**, 806–814 (2011)

Smith, W.: ISO and ANSI Ergonomic Standards for Computer Products: A Guide to Implementation and Compliance. Prentice Hall, Upper Saddle River (1996)

Yin, C., Xu, H., Wang, F.: Standardization of visual acuity chart. Int. J. Ophthalmol. **3**(2), 55–57 (2003)

Zhang, J., Zhang, T., Xue, F., Liu, L., Yu, C.: Legibility variations of Chinese characters and implications for visual acuity measurement in Chinese reading population. Invest. Ophthalmol. Vis. Sci. **48**, 2383–2390 (2007)

Ziefle, M.: Effects of display resolution on visual performance. Hum. Factors **40**(4), 554–568 (1998)

The Design-Related Quality Factors of Smart and Interactive Products
From Industrial Design to User Experience and Interaction Design

Yichen Wu[✉]

China Academy of Art, Hangzhou 310000, China
wuyc@caa.edu.cn

Abstract. The connected objects, also named smart products or smart device, are permeating into people's lives and changing their behaviors and habits. They are updated from normal products by implanting electronic chips and system, connecting to the Internet or other devices, and users have to operate them through the physical the digital interface. Thanks to the popularity of smart products, the economy is increasing, the relevant market is expanding, and the consuming habit of society is evolving. Design as the force for innovation was given greater responsibility to the development of the smart product at this time. Nowadays, many design disciplines are involving smart objects, e.g. industrial design, interaction design, user experience design, service design. However, these interactive, technology-related products have high failure rate actually, most of them failed at the concept phase. These failures lead to design waste. Thereby, how to design a smart product with high quality of user experience is the critical question. The user experience quality in this context not only includes the form and function which focused by industrial design but also included the interactive mode, the emotional perception, and so on. Consequently, to get this success, to enhance the quality is the method to make the smart object stands out from the crowd in the competition. Thereby, this research attempted to demonstrate the specific factors of quality in the smart product in theoretical models by analyzing the complexity of the smart objects and discussing the quality of each part of the smart product.

Keywords: Smart objects · Quality · Design

1 The General Quality of Connected Objects

Connected objects are the products with interactivity, the experience of the final user determines the user viscosity, which is whether the user will continue using the product or not, and it determines the value of the product, the value not only to the user but also the designer, the producer. From this perspective, to occupy the market and be favored by the users is the everyday success for a connected object. Consequently, to get this success, to enhance the quality is the method to make the connected object stands out from the crowd in the competition.

Quality is a complicated concept, and it could be interpreted as a predictable degree of uniformity and dependability, at low cost and suited to the market [1]. From the

© Springer Nature Switzerland AG 2020
C. Stephanidis et al. (Eds.): HCII 2020, CCIS 1293, pp. 475–482, 2020.
https://doi.org/10.1007/978-3-030-60700-5_60

definitions of quality in diverse context, it is a standard to something, and there is no specific definition of the quality for connected objects. Thus, I tried to figure out the quality of connected objects by defining the factors that impact the quality of the products, and all the factors were in the context of design.

When we elaborate on the entire process of a connected object with users, the connected object is collecting the data from the environment or the user's body in a subtle way. From the user to the need, the quality of the connected object covers the product and the interaction process, and user experience is the final result by the combination of the product and the interaction process with the user. Besides the interaction process, from the product attribute's point of view, the connected object is composed of hardware, software and service system. The hardware and software constitute the tangible product, in which the hardware is the external form and the electronic components, while the software is the internal platform for information processing, graphics interface, the audio interface is the external performance for the software. The service system is invisibly relatively to hardware and software, and it is a designed system to serve the user with functions. Based on the model (Fig. 1), I conducted the investigation of quality factors from the three aspects in a design context, including the product, the interaction and the experience, to define the factors those impact the quality of the product itself and the quality of interaction and user experience.

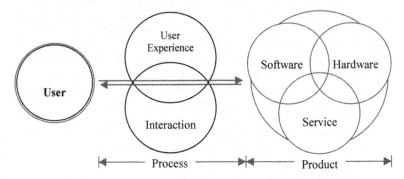

Fig. 1. The attribute of components in connected objects

2 The Definition of Quality About the Hardware, Software and Service

The product quality in this research section is the quality of hardware, software and the service. With the investigation of the constitution of the product in a connected object, the concept of hardware is the physical product. With the literature review, there are few references discuss the quality of the physical part separately. However, there are abundant studies on the quality of software and service. By the literature review, the concept of product quality shows the diversity in a different context, and it interpreted depends on the products' attributes. Talking about the value, a quality product or service is one that provides performance at an acceptable price or conformance at an acceptable cost. David (1984) also presented the eight dimensions of quality; they identified as a framework for thinking about the essential elements of product quality, including:

- Performance
- Features
- Reliability
- Conformance
- Durability
- Serviceability
- Aesthetics
- Perceived Quality

The software is the implanted program of the digital, interactive product, and it is the system for the coordination and control of smart and connectivity components in a connected object by the user's operation. Through ISO 25010, there are eight characteristics of the quality of the software:

- Functional Suitability
- Performance efficiency
- Compatibility
- Usability
- Reliability
- Security
- Maintainability
- Portability

The service in this context is the service for the information system, which is embedded in the connected object. The definition of service quality revolves around the idea that it is the result of the comparison that customers make between their expectations about service and their perception of the way the service has been performed [3]. The service quality also be defined as the match situation between prior expectations and experience [4]. The factors include Ease of use, Appearance, Personalization, Information, Responsiveness, Communication, Security and Reliability. Based on these various definitions of the service quality factor, I merged similar factors and removed the factors that indicated to the specific service form, such as the linkage and content in the website service quality. As a result, there are eight factors of service quality:

- Ease of use
- Appearance
- Personalization
- Reliability
- Communication
- Security
- Efficiency
- Support

3   The Quality of the Interaction and User Experience

The interaction and user experience of the connected objects have a delicate relationship from their properties. First is the causal relationship between them, UX as a momentary, primarily evaluative feeling (good-bad) while interacting with a product or service [5]. Thus, the interaction between the user and the products generates part of the UX, which is the feeling in the process of the product using. Meanwhile, the interaction and UX have large part crossed and overlapped, and the interaction is a series physical actions which create the most of the user experience, and to use the product is to inter-act with the product. By these reasons, the quality factors of interaction and user experience bound to overlap, and the method to derive the quality factors of them was to collect the factors' definitions by literature review firstly, then integrated them through the specific interpretations.

Talking about the interaction quality, the ISO/IEC 25010 define the quality in use is the degree to which a product or system can be used by specific users to meet their needs to achieve specific goals with effectiveness, efficiency, freedom from risk and satisfaction in specific contexts of use. When we combine to the context of design, the interaction design quality will be measured through two dimensions: user interface quality and communication tools quality, where the measures of two dimensions are adapted from several standard scales [6–8]. About the user interface, the quality factors include Effectiveness, Productivity, Efficiency and Error Safety. Additionally, by the investigation of other relevant research [9–13], and combined the quality factors and models of them, the quality factors of interaction could refer to trustability, re-source-limitedness, usability, ubiquity.

About the quality of user experience, there is still no accurate description of it yet. UX is still a concept that is being debated, defined and explored by researchers and practitioners [14]. Some of the research had worked out the possible factors of the user experience quality, which includes Satisfaction, Involvement, Affordance, Coolness, Enjoyment, and Hedonicity [15]. Most of the references argued the UX has an undeniable connection with Usability, and it appears in almost all research on the quality of interaction and user experience. Nevertheless, usability is not equal to the UX; By the diverse opinions, the usability is part of the UX, and it intends to be the matter of the product's functional part, there are other factors of UX, such as the experience of the brand. Peter Morville made a point of the User Experience Honeycomb in 2004, the user experience quality issues are defined into the seven factors:

- Useful
- Usable
- Findable
- Desirable
- Credible
- Accessible
- Valuable

4   The Quality Factors Model of Connected Objects

The connected objects' quality factors model was built from the design's point of view. To define the connected objects' quality factors precisely with the research context, I used four steps to deduce the final factors. Firstly, by the various but partially repeated definitions of the quality characteristics for product, software, service, interaction and user experience those listed before, I tried to integrate the factors in two-part, one is the part of the connected object; another one is the process which including the interaction and the experience of the user. The integration of the factors according to the interpretation of the definitions, then to reorganize them by the methods which involved merging similar definitions, eliminating overly broad concepts and reclassify the section of the factors.

Secondly, with the new factors of both the product and the process, I intended to modify them by a principle, which is either the factor is the inherent attribute of the product or it exists when users involve. With this principle, the factors were unique and more precisely in each part.

Thirdly, I redefined each factor based on the referred interpretation.

Fourthly, I produced the final model of the quality factors for connected objects and demonstrated it.

Specifically, in the integrated phase of the product, there were six factors kept the original attribute in their parts, besides the support, personalization, communication of the service quality and the port-ability of the software quality, I added the durability and ergonomics into the quality factors of hard-ware. The physical product requires the human factors and ergonomics, to make the product more suitable for people, ergonomics is the study of the interaction between people and machines and the factors that affect the interaction. Meanwhile, the durability is the ability of a product to perform its required function over a lengthy period under normal conditions of use without excessive expenditure on maintenance or repair.

Most of the factors have similar explanations, such as reliability, security, performance and maintain-ability. They were merged from similar factors, and they converted into the common factors of two or three sections. Additionally, based on the combination of the definitions, I expanded the usability, compatibility, functionality and perceived quality from two sections to three sections, because all of them fit for the three aspects of the connected object. For instance, as a discussion before, usability involves almost every part in the using of the products by the users, it related to the software interface, hardware interface and the service system. Meanwhile, compatibility is the characteristic to maintain consistency of internal, external components of the product and the interaction in the usage of the service. Perceived quality refers to all the forms which can be perceived by the users of the products. In this integrate process, the aesthetics is a critical factor for both hardware and software.

In another part of the first phase, the integration of the process employed the same methods. Based on the previous interpretation of the definitions, two factors maintain original states, in which ubiquity belongs to the interaction, while the value belongs to the user experience. Utility, desirability, accessibility and reliability were generated from their synonyms which studied by literature reviews before. Usability was an essential factor in the interaction part, it was synthesized from diverse specific factors both in the parts of interaction and experience, such as effectiveness, efficiency, and it became the common factor of the two sections. The model of this part was demonstrated in Fig. 3.

After the integration, in step two, because there were some repetitive factors both in product part and process part and some factors of the product requirements to realize their value by the participation of users, thus I modified some factors according to the user's point of view based on the integration models. The standard to distinguish these two parts was whether the factor involves the user or it is the property of the product itself. There

Table 1. The definitions of the product part

Factors	Hardware	Software	Service
Performance	*Primary operating characteristics*	*Time consumption, resource utilization, parameters' limitation*	/
Functionality	*The functions that meet stated and implied needs as in physical way*	*The functions that meet stated and implied needs in digital way*	*The functions that meet stated and implied needs in the service process*
Security	/	*Information and data protection in the system*	*To protect the users' perceived security and privacy*
Aesthetics	*The shape, color, material, finishing*	*The beauty of User interface*	/
Ergonomics	*The measurements between human and products*	/	/
Durability	*The lengthy period for using*	/	/
Maintainability	*The speed, courtesy, competence of repair for the product*	*The effectiveness and efficiency of the improvement and update for the system*	/
Compatibility	*The form and operating characteristics match established standards*	*The ability of exchange information with other systems*	*The operating and engagement follow the established standards of the product*
Personalization	/	/	*To create function and interface for individuals*
Portability	/	*The software can install or transferred from one product to another*	/
Support	/	/	*The technical help and advice from the service provider*

were four modifications in this step, reliability and usability in the product part were merged into the same factors in the process part; perceived quality and communication were moved from product part to the process part. All of these four factors either are the feeling of the user or need the participation of users.

In step three, I defined every factor in all aspects of each part, including the hardware, software, service aspects of the product part (Table 1). And the final model of quality factors for connected objects' design is demonstrated in Fig. 2.

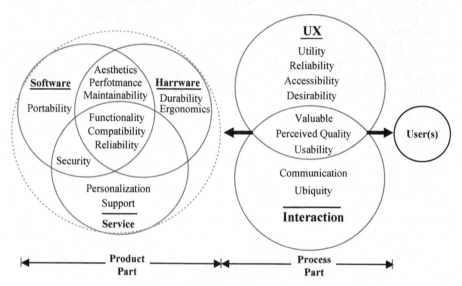

Fig. 2. The final model of quality factors for connected objects' design

References

1. Gitlow, H.S.: Quality Management Systems: A Practical Guide. CRC Press, Boca Raton (2000)
2. Moggridge, B., Atkinson, B.: Designing Interactions, vol. 17. MIT press, Cambridge (2007)
3. Caruana, A., Money, A.H., Berthon, P.R.: Service quality and satisfaction–the moderating role of value. Eur. J. Market. **34**(11/12), 1338–1353 (2000)
4. Ojasalo, J.: E-service quality: a conceptual model. Int. J. Arts Sci. **3**(7), 127–143 (2010)
5. Hassenzahl, M.: User experience (UX): towards an experiential perspective on product quality. In: IHM, vol. 8, pp. 11–15 (2008)
6. Lawson-Body, A., Willoughby, L., Logossah, K.: Developing an instrument for measuring e-commerce dimensions. J. Comput. Inf. Syst. **51**(2), 213 (2010)
7. Muylle, S., Moenert, R., Despontin, M.: The conceptualization and empirical validation of website user satisfaction. Inf. Manage. **41**, 213226 (2004)
8. Yoo, B., Donthu, N.: Developing a scale to measure the perceived quality of an internet shopping site (SiteQual). Q. J. Electron. Commer. **2**(1), 3145 (2001)
9. Bundschuh, B.B., et al.: Quality of human-computer interaction-results of a national usability survey of hospital-IT in Germany. BMC Med. Inform. Decis. Making **11**(1), 69 (2011)

10. Alhendawi, K.M., Baharudin, A.S.: The impact of interaction quality factors on the effectiveness of web-based information system: the mediating role of user satisfaction. Cognit. Technol. Work **16**(4), 451–465 (2013). https://doi.org/10.1007/s10111-013-0272-9

11. Dillon, A.: Beyond usability: process, outcome and affect in human-computer interactions. Can. J. Libr. Inf. Sci. **26**(4), 57–69 (2006)

12. Bevan, N.: Human-computer interaction standards. Adv. Hum. Factors/Ergon. **20**, 885–890 (1995)

13. Carvalho, R.M., de Castro Andrade, R.M., de Oliveira, K.M., de Sousa Santos, I., Bezerra, C.I.M.: Quality characteristics and measures for human–computer interaction evaluation in ubiquitous systems. Softw. Qual. J. **25**(3), 743–795 (2016). https://doi.org/10.1007/s11219-016-9320-z

14. Petrie, H., Bevan, N.: The evaluation of accessibility, usability, and user experience. In: The Universal Access Handbook, vol. 1, pp. 1–16 (2009)

15. Zhu, Y., Heynderickx, I., Redi, J.A.: Understanding the role of social context and user factors in video quality of experience. Comput. Hum. Behav. **49**, 412–426 (2015)

The Zabuton: Designing the Arriving Experience in the Japanese Airport

Hikari Yamano[1], Kasumi Tomiyasu[1], Chihiro Sato[1(✉)],
and Masato Yamanouchi[1,2]

[1] Keio University Graduate School of Media Design, Yokohama, Japan
{hikari-y,tomika7,chihiro}@kmd.keio.ac.jp
[2] Professional University of Information and Management for Innovation,
Tokyo, Japan
masato-y@i-u.ac.jp

Abstract. This research explores the value of airports upon arrivals by proposing a welcome service *The Zabuton* targeting passengers unfamiliar with the landing-place. *The Zabuton* service comprises of two systems; a local language information display (LLD) and a guiding passengers action app (GAA). LLD is placed in the baggage claim area displaying the written language and meanings of frequently used phrases, and its pronunciations in the local language. GAA supports the series of actions from the arrival gate to transportation consisting the following five components; (1) purchasing internet connection modules, (2) local transportation map and route search, (3) local transportation rules, (4) luggage service information, and (5) where the platform is to ride local transportation. An airport arrival lobby with *The Zabuton* lets passengers learn local language phrases through public displays and provides confidence in their forthcoming steps of transportation through a mobile app. This concept was constructed based on our research and illustrated accordingly based on scenario based design and user centered design process. This paper contributes to the redesigning of the airport arrival lobby by enhancing the local experience and supporting the travel procedures with the help of digital technologies.

Keywords: Experience design · Airport · Travel support system · User centered design

1 Introduction

Airports, important hubs for airplanes carrying an increasing number of passengers—1.7 times more compared to a decade ago [12]—across the world, are striving for branding strategies [5]. In addition to improving their functionalities, the leading airports are putting efforts in universally designed spaces with increased options for shopping, dining, and various entertainment [9,13]. For an airport to be valued by their users, providing a service that is designed through deep understanding of difficulties and tasks of passengers is critical.

© Springer Nature Switzerland AG 2020
C. Stephanidis et al. (Eds.): HCII 2020, CCIS 1293, pp. 483–490, 2020.
https://doi.org/10.1007/978-3-030-60700-5_61

On the other hand, passengers in unfamiliar country often feel uneasy or disadvantaged about their trips when they do not have a good understanding of culture, language, rules of the country [14]. Those who want to avoid these socio-cultural risk will tend to make their reservation earlier or purchase prepackaged tours from travel agents [11]. The less accustomed to the habit on information acquisition concerning travel mode choices, the more information and choices are needed when traveling to a destination [16].

We especially focus on the experience at the arrival lobby. The arrival lobby and the departure lobby are important places for both the passengers and the destination, since they are the initial encounter and the final contact point respectively [17]. Compared with the departure lobby, the arrival lobby is often-times overlooked in spite of its vast potentiality of giving the tourists a positive feeling about the destination.

The objective of this study is to design a helpful experience for arriving passengers. Our service *The Zabuton* eliminates anxiety for the passenger from abroad by providing travel supporting information. Their anxieties are reduced by two components; a local language information display (LLD) and a guiding passengers action app (GAA) (see Fig. 1 for the experience image). This paper contributes by designing services from user-centered approach rather than com-mercial aspect, and give insight to designing applications for supporting the travel process.

Fig. 1. *The Zabuton* experience images

2   Related Works

From the theoretical paradigm of "linguistic accomodation" (or communication accommodation), established about half a century ago, indicates linguistic bar-riers in intercultural communication [8]. Studies focusing on the field of tourism shows that actual tourists hardly have competency in the language and style of communication of the local natives [7], and also "fleeting interaction" in the context of tourism are communicative challenges [10]. *In-situ* language practices in tourism aims for a smooth communication [18], and mere greeting can play a vital role in developing a rapport amongst people [3]. Our research builds on these statements and incorporates into our design of LLD.

On the other hand, some research highlight the current questions with airports and its experience even though its shift from a utility for transportation into a place where various values can be offered—the experience not being comprehensively defined or conceptualised, and airport industry scopes leaving behind those that are not significant sources of income [17]. *Emmasbox* is one example tackling such issue by placing an interactive food station in a major European airport baggage carousel area as an public display which provides food packages [2], through their findings that majority of tourists are looking for gastronomic pleasure in travels. *The Finnish You* is an example highlighting passengers waiting time by an interactive storytelling mobile application while educating them about the Finnish culture [4]. Other studies proposed integrated services to assist travel planning—for hotels, attractions, and routing based on crowd sourced data from social media, reviews of hotels, Flickr images, and Uber taxi costs between places [20]. Our research takes such situation into account for an integrated experience of transportation guidance at the arrival lobby; from the point when you grab back your baggage to the moment you get out of the terminal to your next transportation.

3   Methodology

The concept of *The Zabuton* service was designed mainly based on User-Centered Design(UCD) process [1,15], as outlined below: (1) conduct ethnographic research, (2) identify stakeholders and personas, and (3) illustrate persona's scenario, use case, display and application mock up.

Through the series of ethnographic research we generated hypotheses about passengers situations and tasks in the airport. These were conducted in 7 Asian airports during autumn 2019, mainly on major Airports in Japan. We explored various places in these airports in total of 10 times, for about 3 hours each. We observed people's behavior in the contexts, and recorded them in field-notes. When conducting fieldwork outside Japan, researchers also described what they felt and acted as a passenger in addition to the basic observation. A series of textual data was segmented and coded in five contexts: airport, terminal, kind of people, act from field-notes, date and time.

A total of 428 data samples were extracted from field-notes. We focused particularly on the findings from behavior in the arrival lobby. We investigated that passengers have strong interest in their destination and preparation for their trip in the arrival lobby (See Fig. 2).

4   Experience Design

Through the findings of the ethnographic research, we decided to set foreign passengers who came to Japan for the first time, as a persona. We assumed this persona would want reduce their anxiety and make them feel less anxious about

Airport	Terminal	Place	Passengers	Extracted act from fieldnotes	Date/time
Haneda	3	arrival gate	Chinese tourists	Talk about route with family and friends while looking at mobile	13:50 Sep. 25, 2019
Haneda	3	arrival gate	Chinese couple	Try to ask someone how to buy a ticket, but wandering around without hearing	13:45 Sep. 25, 2019
Haneda	3	arrival gate	Chinese couple	Thanks a stranger for teaching him how to buy a ticket	13:45 Sep. 25, 2019
Haneda	3	arrival gate	A French man	Show his smartphone to airport staff s aying "I want to take this JAL flight"	14:30 Sep. 25, 2019
Inchoen	1	arrival gate	A fieldworker	Immediately after arriving at Incheon Airport, what I thought was the impact of Hangul. I can't read it at all. I could get a feel for Chinese and English, but I felt scared to understand Korean.	7:30 Oct. 22, 2019

Fig. 2. Data coding examples

traveling in Japan with the following upon arrival; (1) be able to communicate a little in Japanese, (2) want to go to their destination without inconvenience, and (3) get necessary/useful information and tools for their trip. The narrative of the following experience has been set to achieve the desires of the persona. This description is based on Scenario Based Design [6, 12, 19]. Use cases were also developed whilst creating the scenario (see Fig. 3).

The Scenario. Non-Japanese tourists finally arrived in Japan after a long transit. It is their first time in Japan and the tourists are feeling a little anxious. Exhausted, they arrive at the luggage pickup area and wait until the baggage carousel starts moving.

While waiting, a signage jumps into the tourist's eyes as it plays audio and visual information about Japanese language tips in English and Japanese simultaneously (see Fig. 1 and 5). Having been a little anxious about their Japanese language skills, they practices the intonation following the signage. Through this experience, they learns several phrases that could be used for greetings, and feels a little better about their language anxiety. The tourists think about their plan after exiting out of the airport.

First of all, left the arrival gate, they go to the airport information counter, to ask how to go to their destination. There, the staff introduces them to the airport application. They access the airport application to find out information on where they should go next (see Fig. 1 and 5). They find a button saying "Airport to City" and when they taps on the button, the mobile site advises them what they should do in order of the actions people take at the airport. These include information on where to purchase sim cards, train route maps and directions, the direction to the stations, train passes and luggage services. They click on the "Route Search" button and "Where to Ride" button. The tourists leave the airport following the directions and set off to the city.

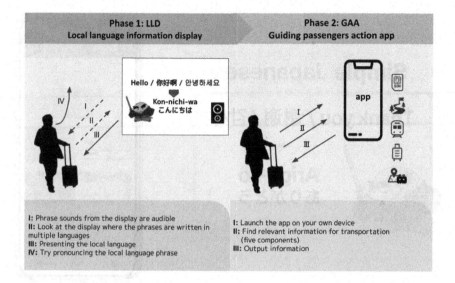

Fig. 3. User experience flow

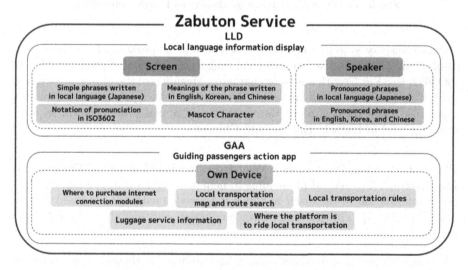

Fig. 4. Components of *The Zabuton* service

5   System Description

This section reveals the concept elements that would realize the scenario experience by classifying them into 2 components (see Fig. 4).

Phase 1: Providing Local Language Tips. This phase takes place in the baggage claim area, where we propose the LLD should be located. This local

Fig. 5. The example of language display and guide application

language display system consists of a screen and a speaker, where the screen displays simple phrases written in local language, notation of pronunciation in ISO3602, (see Fig. 5) with a mascot character. Meanings of the phrase are written in English, Korean, Chinese, in reference to the guidelines presented by Japanese ministries[1]. The speaker plays the voice files of actual pronunciation in local language, and in English, Korean, and Chinese.

Phase 2: Helping Passenger's Way from Arrival Lobby to Their Final Destination. The second phase aims to help passenger's way by highlighting a list of information in the order in which it is needed with our proposed system GAA (see Fig. 5). This guiding passengers action app will show the following five steps.

(1) Where to purchase internet connection modules. It shows a map of where SIM cards or mobile wifi routers can be purchased or rent in the airport.
(2) Local transportation map and route search. It also provides route map of Japan's metropolitan area so that users can see visually understand which route to take to the destination. The route search function are also provided.
(3) Local transportation rules. As transportation rules differ from country to country, we provide information on where to buy and how to use IC cards for transportation and rule information in that country will be provided.

---

[1] Japan Tourism Agency. Guidelines for improving and strengthening multilingual support for the realization of a tourism-oriented country, 2014.

(4) Luggage service information. It also provides information on the services that the airport offers to travelers upon arrival. In this case, we have introduced a luggage delivery service, as travelers often have large packages with them.

(5) Where the platform is to ride local transportation. At a large airport, the transportation platform of one's choice may be far or difficult to find from the arrival lobby. Information on the boarding area for each mode of transportation is provided on the airport facilities map.

6   Discussion and Future Works

This study aimed to design passengers experience to improve airport value. In particular, our study highlighted the difficulties passengers face in arrival lobby and we proposed *The Zabuton* service. *The Zabuton* aims to help passengers through the process before leaving the airport and overcome their difficulties and anxieties about linguistic difference and way-finding, by providing them local language information display(LLD) and guiding passengers action app(GAA).

In the future, we need to evaluate each use case of the system and verify its effectiveness. We assume the following: (1) what function of *The Zabuton* system are effective in context of real passengers, (2) what impact *The Zabuton* service has had on their travel and what trends are seen in users, and (3) verification of if this system can contribute to the improvement of airport value. We shall also strive for a richer airport passengers experience in this era of COVID-19.

Acknowledgements. The authors are grateful to DSInnovation for funding our research. We thank T. Fujimoto for giving us some advice on writing, and also thank all the volunteers, publications support and staffs.

References

1. Abras, C., Maloney-Krichmar, D., Preece, J., et al.: User-centered design. In: Bainbridge, W. (eds.) Encyclopedia of Human-Computer Interaction, vol. 37, no. 4, pp. 445–456. Sage Publications, Thousand Oaks (2004)

2. Alt, F., Vehns, J.: Opportunistic deployments: challenges and opportunities of conducting public display research at an airport. In: Proceedings of the 5th ACM International Symposium on Pervasive Displays, pp. 106–117 (2016)

3. Boxer, D.: Applying Sociolinguistics: Domains and Face-to-Face Interaction, vol. 15. John Benjamins Publishing, Amsterdam (2002)

4. Burova, A., et al.: Promoting local culture and enriching airport experiences through interactive storytelling. In: Proceedings of the 18th International Conference on Mobile and Ubiquitous Multimedia, p. 26. ACM (2019)

5. Castro, R., Lohmann, G.: Airport branding: content analysis of vision statements. Res. Transp. Bus. Manage. **10**, 4–14 (2014)

6. Cooper, A., Reimann, R., Cronin, D., Noessel, C.: About Face: The Essentials of Interaction Design, 4th edn. Wiley Publishing, Hoboken (2014)

7. Dornyei, Z., Csizer, K.: The effects of intercultural contact and tourism on language attitudes and language learning motivation. J. Lang. Soc. Psychol. **24**(4), 327–357 (2005). https://doi.org/10.1177/0261927X05281424

8. Giles, H.: Communication accommodation theory. In: The International Encyclopedia of Communication Theory and Philosophy, pp. 1–7 (2016). https://doi.org/10.1002/9781118766804.wbiect056

9. Changi Airport Group: A decade of distinction :annual report 2018/19 (2019). https://www.changiairport.com/content/dam/cacorp/publications/Annual%20Reports/2019/CAG-AR2019-Full.pdf

10. Jaworski, A., Thurlow, C.: Language and the globalizing habitus of tourism: toward a sociolinguistics of fleeting relationships. In: The Handbook of Language and Globalization, vol. 58, p. 255 (2010)

11. Money, R.B., Crotts, J.C.: The effect of uncertainty avoidance on information search, planning, and purchases of international travel vacations. Tourism Manage. **24**(2), 191–202 (2003)

12. The International Co-operative Alliance Organization: Presentation of 2018 air transport statistical results (2018). https://www.icao.int/annual-report-2018/Pages/the-world-of-air-transport-in-2018-statistical-results.aspx

13. Paris Aéroport: Strategic plan for the 2016–2020 period (2018). https://www.parisaeroport.fr/docs/default-source/groupe-fichiers/groupe-et-strategie/connect-2020-maj-05-2017-en.pdf?sfvrsn=3a28e2bd_0

14. Reisinger, Y., Mavondo, F.: Travel anxiety and intentions to travel internationally: Implications of travel risk perception. J. Travel Res. **43**(3), 212–225 (2005)

15. Svanæs, D., Gulliksen, J.: Understanding the context of design: towards tactical user centered design. In: Proceedings of the 5th Nordic Conference on Human-Computer Interaction: Building Bridge, NordiCHI 2008, pp. 353–362. Association for Computing Machinery, New York (2008). https://doi.org/10.1145/1463160.1463199

16. Verplanken, B., Aarts, H., Van Knippenberg, A.: Habit, information acquisition, and the process of making travel mode choices. Eur. J. Soc. Psychol. **27**(5), 539–560 (1997)

17. Wattanacharoensil, W., Schuckert, M., Graham, A., Dean, A.: An analysis of the airport experience from an air traveler perspective. J. Hospitality Tourism Manage. **32**, 124–135 (2017)

18. Wilson, A.: International tourism and (linguistic) accommodation: convergence towards and through English in tourist information interactions, June 2018. https://doi.org/10.4000/anglophonia.1377

19. Wright, P., Wallace, J., McCarthy, J.: Aesthetics and experience-centered design. ACM Trans. Comput.-Hum. Interact. (TOCHI) **15**(4), 1–21 (2008)

20. Zhou, X., Wang, M., Li, D.: From stay to play-a travel planning tool based on crowdsourcing user-generated contents. Appl. Geograph. **78**, 1–11 (2017)

Usable Security Case of Remote Web Access

Temechu G. Zewdie[✉]

University of the District of Columbia, Washington DC 20008, USA
temechu.zewdie@udc.edu

Abstract. Various organizations such as the European Union (EU) use Remote Web Access (RWA) [1], as it enables their staff members to work from any place and at any time. Working from remote locations has its drawbacks. Cyberattacks can take place. Therefore, organizations need to secure the user identification technique (UIT). This research talks about the challenges of UIT associated with RWA and explores solutions on how to make RWA secure as well as user-friendly. However, surveys showed that users were not satisfied with these security measures, as it affected the usability of the platform. This research focuses on designing a secure and user-friendly UIT for RWA.

The study involves the collection and assimilation of qualitative and quantitative data through questionnaires, focus group discussions, interviews, and document analysis. It also uses the Morea Usability testing software as a tool for assessing the user-satisfaction and usability of RWA.

The preliminary assessment involved issuing 42 questionnaires to a randomly selected EU delegation to the African Union staff living in Addis Ababa. Thirty-four of them responded to the questionnaire that formed the basis of this research. About 70% of the respondents expressed confidence in the security measures, whereas 92% did not find the additional user identification steps as convenient. Nearly 64% of the people surveyed felt that the process was a lengthy one. It also affected the efficiency and memorability, thereby necessitating a change.

As pointed out in [2], observing four to six participants in usability testing will uncover about 80% of a product's usability problems. In this study, six test participants from EEAS were selected to conduct usability testing.

As the study showed an inverse relationship between the usability and the perception of security and trust in RWA, the research proposes a usable UIT for RWA for making it secure and user-friendly at the same time.

Keywords: Usability · Security · User identification technique · Remote Web Access

1 Introduction

The success of a software application depends on two crucial factors, usability, and security. Nielsen [3] refers to usability as a quality attribute, whereas security is a system attribute.

Usability is a factor that measures how easy and efficient it is for the user, whereby it increases their satisfaction. Security reflects the system's ability to protect itself from external and internal attacks [4]. This research focuses on UIT on RWA [5].

© Springer Nature Switzerland AG 2020
C. Stephanidis et al. (Eds.): HCII 2020, CCIS 1293, pp. 491–501, 2020.
https://doi.org/10.1007/978-3-030-60700-5_62

The researcher goes on to explain what RWA is and how it helps users to access facilities like 'email' when they are located offsite. The European Union is one of the prime organizations [6] that use RWA to enable its staff to access their emails and communicate when they are posted outside their home country.

RWA is a useful application that enables convenient communication between authorized users. However, being a web-based application, it is vulnerable to cyberattacks. The European Union Mailing System was a victim of such an attack in March 2010. Such attacks pose a risk of unauthorized disclosure of information, thereby implying that cybercriminals gain access to confidential and sensitive information. As a result, the RWA of Email was closed to all European Union External Services (EEAS) [7, 8] users.

Six months down the line, RWA of Email relaunched UIT but with additional identity authentication measures. It included using SMS authentication or the use of a token password. These new methods had a direct effect on the usability of the UIT, thereby inconveniencing a significant proportion of EU staff located overseas.

This research goes into the details of how users found it cumbersome to login to the system and use it. Though the additional steps were necessary from the security angle, it could have been more user-friendly.

The research begins by explaining the various steps that users have to go through before accessing their emails via RWA. It collects data from selected EEAS staff using RWA by employing different methods like questionnaires, group discussions, interviews, and document analysis.

The research considered the following aspects.

- Understand the current practice of usability and security in EEAS
- Determine the extent of user satisfaction with RWA
- Identify the significant challenges related to user identification steps for accessing email via RWA

In the actual research, the researcher issued 42 questionnaires to a randomly collected sample of EU staff posted at Addis Ababa. 95% of them used the conventional username/password combination to access email, whereas 5% used the token-based identification technique.

2 Background

The research focuses more on the usability on the security aspects of accessing email via RWA.

2.1 Themes on Usability

The research concentrates on the following five factors that contribute to determining the usability of the user interface [8].

- Learnability: The system should be simple enough for users to learn how to work smoothly.

- Efficiency: The system is efficient when it saves time for the user. The contributing factors are the number of key presses, the screens visited, and the back buttons used to complete a specific workflow scenario and execute a particular set of instructions.
- Memorability: The system should be such that users should remember the steps quickly without having to learn everything repeatedly.
- Effectiveness: A system is competent if it has a low error rate. The common aspects include the number of errors, the severity of the mistakes, the path taken to complete the job, etc. [9].
- Satisfaction: User satisfaction is a critical aspect of usability.

2.2 Themes on Security

Usability is a crucial aspect, but Information Security is critical, as well. The research rightly points out the factors concerning security when it comes to using RWA. The security of any software system caters to two significant problems, permission, and prevention. It is designed to let authorized people have access to the system while keeping out the unauthorized ones.

The following three steps are crucial to any security system.

- Identification – It is accomplished by using a username, a smart card, a process ID, and anything else to identify the genuine user.
- Authentication – It proves the identity of the user by employing various methods like passwords, an RSA token, or even biometrics.
- Authorization – This step decides whether a user has the authority to do specific tasks. It blocks access for some while allowing it for a select few depending on the user's position in the hierarchy [9].

2.3 The Relation Between Usability and Security

The research determines that usability and security are inversely proportional to each other. It also rightly goes on to state that there cannot be any perfect user identification technique because each one of them has its drawbacks. For example, the user can forget the password, or it could be disclosed unintentionally. Similarly, ID cards and tokens can be stolen. Biometric authentication can fail under specific circumstances.

Therefore, security is a prime requirement. At the same time, usability is crucial because the lack of a user-friendly UI can result in user dissatisfaction, unproductivity of the staff, and increased inefficiency. There is a need to maintain the ideal balance between security and usability.

2.4 Types of User Authentication on the Web

Multi-factor authentication is necessary for ensuring the safety of the system.

- Knowledge-Based Authentication (KBA) – It can be an extension of the existing password authentication. There could be an additional layer of security, such as an answer to a secret question, entering Captcha information, or identifying, etc.
- Server-Generated One-Time Password (OTP) – It can be used along with KBA for facilitating derived OTPs such as grid cards, digitally signed OTPs, or even out-of-band channels like email, SMS to mobiles, etc. Users can then enter this specially generated OTP at the required location to gain access.
- Client-Generated OTP – It is similar to the conventional OTP, with the difference being that the client generates it using RSA tokens.

3 Methodology

The researcher adopts a mixture of qualitative and quantitative methods. The literature review and the interviews give the qualitative results, whereas the quantitative results are obtained through usability testing and questionnaires

Target Sample. The target sample consists of 76 EU staff working in Ethiopia and the African Union. This heterogenous targeted population uses RWA to access emails from remote locations. The mix consists of novice and expert users alike to provide a realistic picture.

Sampling Techniques. One needs to have a substantial sample to allow the researcher to observe the relationship between the different groups. Hence, the researcher selected 76 EU staff among the 123 people located in Africa. Further, the sample included six more EU staff for conducting usability testing.

Data Collection Methods

- The research uses questionnaires, followed by interviews to collect quantitative data.
- Document analysis and interviews help the researcher to collect qualitative data

Questionnaire and Interview

- The survey consists of 37 questions that include29 Liker Scale questions, one open-ended question, and seven multiple-choice questions. It considers aspects like background and experience of the respondents, perception of usability, and the user's reactions to RWA with System Usability Scale (SUS).
- The respondents take part in an interview after the survey to strengthen the data collected and justify the answers given in response to the questionnaire.

The Survey

- A pilot test was conducted to eliminate confusing questions that could result in the respondents giving invalid responses.
- The researcher did the right thing by retaining the scale "Strongly disagree to strongly agree" instead of having a numeric scale ranging from −2 to +2.
- The questions were distributed in two formats, paper-based and email-based. The response to the paper-based questionnaire was high because of personal distribution.
- The researcher considered another option to the email by including the questionnaire as an attached word document. It required the respondents to download the file, answer the questions, and submit the response through a separate attachment.
- These questions were distributed to 76 respondents, of which 58 replied to the researcher. Some of the participants could not do so because of time constraints. Three replies were discarded because the quality of the answers did not serve the purpose of the research.

Document Analysis. The researcher used documents like the EU Authentication Service Security Guideline and other books, research papers, thesis, and journals, as the source of information.

Usability Testing. Usability testing was crucial to the study because it enabled the researcher to observe the response of different categories of users while interacting with RWA. It included a mix of novice and experienced users [9].

The researcher has also taken care of aspects like providing a conducive environment for the test. The participants received adequate guidance on how to approach the questions. They were also informed about the different methods used for evaluation, thereby ensuring that the participants were at ease.

Interview and Focus Group Discussion. On completing the usability test and the questionnaire, the candidates had to participate in an open-ended interview and group discussion. It helped the researcher to understand more about the likes and dislikes of the user and their opinions and purpose for which they used RWA.

4   Findings and Discussions

Background of the Respondents

- Out of the 58 responses, three were invalid. Hence, the conclusion is based on 55 valid responses.
- 40% of the participants were in the age group of 30 to 39, with 31% belonging to the 40 to 49 years category. 16% were above 50 years, whereas 13% belonged to the youngest age group of 20 to 29 years.
- 11% of the participants were new without any experience of RWA, whereas 89% belonged to the knowledgeable group having experience of RWA for more than one year.

- 89% of the sample was male, with females making up the remaining 11%.
- The sample was a literate one with 47% possessing a Bachelor's degree, 38% having a Master's degree, and 15% were PhDs. One participant held a Master's degree in Computer Engineering.

General Usability Perception

- 31% stated that RWA was easy to use, but 49% of the participants found it a challenge to use it. The remaining 20% did not offer any comments on usability.
- 56% of the respondents did not find RWA as an attractive presentation, with 34% being satisfied with the same. 10% did not voice their opinion in this matter.
- 47% did not find the RWA to be engaging or exciting, whereas 34% found it to be so (see Fig. 1).

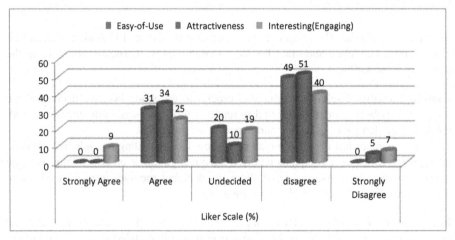

Fig. 1. General usability perception

- 40% felt that the content on the RWA page was unclear; 36% found it to be in simple and clear language.
- 29% of the respondents found it easy to understand, while 63% disagreed with the same (see Fig. 2).
- 80% of the respondents stated that they could not find what they were looking for.
- 42% perceived that the RWA does what it is expected to do, while 40% of the respondents did not agree.
- 35% found the navigation to be a challenge, whereas 40% found it easy. A large chunk of 25% did not offer any opinion on this matter.
- A whopping 88% of the respondents did not know how to find the information they were looking for.
- 93% of the participants believed the organization of the menus to be logical.
- 60% of the respondents had to click multiple times to complete tasks.
- 89% of the sample found it impossible to correct their mistakes.

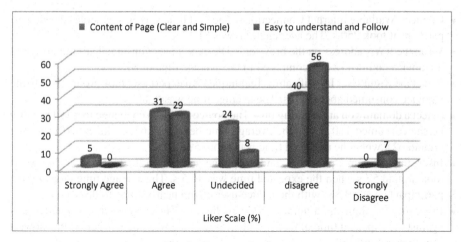

Fig. 2. Content of each page

- 60% of the participants found RWA to respond quickly, whereas 20% disagreed with the same.
- The rate of frustration was high, with nearly 80% of the respondents feeling frustrated when using RWA.

These results prove the fact that the existing User Identification Step in RWA does have a usability problem.

Security Perception

- 93% of the respondents believed that the RWA site is a secure one when it contains "https."
- All respondents stated that they felt secure when RWA connects within the acceptable time limit.
- 72% of the respondents felt safe when they sent and received an email through RWA.
- 83% of the respondents trust the RWA, with 17% remaining undecided on the matter.

Thus, the researcher can conclude that people are satisfied with the security aspects of RWA.

Usability Test Result. Six users participated in the usability test and SUS [2] questionnaire feedback. Of the six participants, four were super and expert users, with two being novices. The time is taken by these participants to perform the tasks reveal that people with experience are better than those who lack it. The six participants had to do eight different tasks. The study involved calculating the time taken for each job and comparing it with the average time taken by all.

- Connect Available Internet Connection – The best time was 30 s, whereas the slowest participant took 250 s. The average time was 81.17 s.
- Write the RWA address on the browser – The expert user consumed around 40 s with the novice taking 112 s as compared to the average time of 87.33 s.
- Select the Right User Identification Technique –An expert user took around 55 s while a novice consumed about 110 s. The average time was 83.83 s.
- Select a domain you are working on – The novice finds it a challenge to do so because he/she consumed 180 s with the average time being 117.67 s. The expert user took around 62 s when the expected time was about 59 s.
- Insert the username, password, and telephone number on the text box – The expert took around 57 s when the expected time was 46.5 s. The average time taken by the participants was 89.5 s, with the novice user taking nearly 150 s to do so.
- Insert the nine-digit alpha-numeric SMS challenge – The expert user consumed 55 s as against the expected time of 62.5 s. The average time was 100 s, whereas the slowest user took around 180 s.
- Select the right delegation which you are working – An expert user consumed 72 s, whereas the novice took 183 s. The expected time was 56.5 s, with the average being 125.5 s.
- Insert the Windows ID and Password in the text box – The expected time to complete the task was 51 s, but the fastest user took around 61 s to do so. The slowest user consumed 163 s that pushed the average time to 104.5 s.

Analysis of the Participants on the Completion of these Tasks. 66.66% of the participants completed the job with 33.34% failing to do so.

User Satisfaction Analysis. This analysis involves answering ten questions based on which the review is done.

- The novice users – The average rate was 43 and 35, respectively, thus concluding poor satisfaction level.
- The expert users – The average score was 70 and 85, whereby the satisfaction rate is Good and Excellent.
- The Superusers – The average satisfaction rate was 50 and 45, thereby concluding that the rate was low.

The mean score turned out to be 54, which can be considered to be on the lower side. The expert user performed better than the novice user in this test, as well.

User Satisfaction Analysis for the Proposed System. The research suggests a new method to enhance user satisfaction. The participants for the existing and the proposed method were the same. The number of tasks in the proposed system is less in the proposed method (Six when compared to eight in the existing one). The jobs are as follows.

- Task 1 – Connect to the available internet connection
- Task 2 – Enter the URL http://localhost/Usable_User_Identification
- Task 3 – Choose the right user identification technique.

- Task 4 – Enter the username, password, and telephone number in the appropriate text box.
- Task 5 – Insert the nine-digit alpha-numeric OTP received via SMS
- Task 6 – Enter the Windows ID and the password in the respective text box.

Here is the gist of analysis based on the proposed system. It enables a good comparison between the two systems, whereby it becomes convenient to determine which of the two methods is the better one.

- The Novice Users – The novice users score 72, thereby implying that the satisfaction level is acceptable.
- The Expert Users – The average scores for the expert users are 85 and 87, respectively. It displays an excellent level of satisfaction.
- The Super Users – The average satisfaction rate was 68 and 75, a considerable improvement when compared to the existing system.

The mean score, as far as the proposed system is concerned, is 79, thereby proving that the satisfaction level of the user has improved considerably. The only things that have changed are the reduction in the number of identification steps and providing ample training to all the users. It is ample evidence that the proposed system is a user-friendly one. That is the ultimate objective of the research. Here is the comparative graph between the analysis of the existing and the proposed system (See Fig. 3).

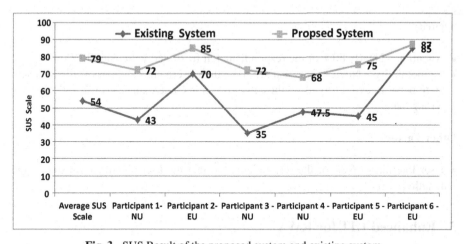

Fig. 3. SUS Result of the proposed system and existing system

User Perspective Usability Challenges. Users having more than two years of experience in RWA have exposure to both versions. They found the earlier one as easy to use because it had only an OTP to access their email via RWA. In comparison, the new version had an excellent identification step to access their emails.

- Users expressed difficulty in memorizing the RWA URL.
- The internet connection speed was also a cause of frustration.
- Users found it difficult to input their location twice in the new version.

Suggestions to resolve the Problems

- Minimize the user input to enhance system checking and confirmation.
- On the creation of the security database, the user should have his/her user ID and password uniquely identified by the system or the institution. It should authenticate the user through an SMS confirmation.
- Training should be imparted to all RWA users to clear their misgivings about the system.

The rationale behind the Solutions
Usability

- Effectiveness – 33% of the users were not successful and could not achieve the objective.
- Efficiency – The novice users took more time than expected to finish their tasks. Hence, they proved to be inefficient.
- Satisfaction – The SUS score for the existing RWA was 54, a bit on the lower side.
- Learnability – The system should be simple for people to learn to use it effectively.
- Memorability – RWA users need to memorize their username and password.

Security

- Attention – Nearly 80% of the respondents felt frustrated with using RWA.
- Memorability – Novice users usually write their usernames and passwords on a separate paper to avoid forgetting the same. It can become dangerous if it falls into the wrong hands.

Other Factors

- User Interface – 64% of the respondents felt that the user identification steps were lengthy.

5   Enhanced UIT for RWA

Based on the types of user authentication discussed earlier in the paper, the researcher proposes a high-level user authentication system. It is a hybrid of the Knowledge-based authentication and server-generated password.

- The hybrid authentication allows a unique password that can be used only once.
- Thus the captured username-password combination cannot be used again.

It is better because the username remains the same, and the OTP changes with every logon. It utilizes the two-factor authorization and OOB delivery of OTPs. The proposed system considers the following.

- Visibility of the link and Clarity of information on each page
- Minimize the user identification steps, and the error message should be easy and informative
- Avoid the inclusion of unnecessary information

6 Conclusion and Future Work

The results show that the user level satisfaction for the existing system is low. Secondly, the RWA is also ineffective with the current user identification steps. The users fail to achieve their objectives and complete their tasks on time. Though the security aspects are right, the present RWA system fails on the usability front.

The researcher succeeded in proposing a new UIT system for RWA that displays better user satisfaction while retaining all the security aspects.

However, the study has its limitations and requires future research in terms of accessibility. It would be appropriate if the researcher extended the scope of research to organizations other than the European Union. It would present a far more realistic picture.

References

1. Quality Attributes (2010). https://docs.microsoft.com/en-us/windows-server-essentials/man age/manage-remote-web-access-in-windows-server-essentials. Accessed 13 Jan 2010
2. Bangor, A., Kortum, P., Miller, J.: Determining what individual SUS scores mean: adding an adjective rating scale. J. Usability Stud. 4(3), 114–123 (2009)
3. Nielsen, J.: Usability Engineering, p. 26. Academic Press, Boston (1993)
4. Sommerville, I.: Software Engineering, p. 745. Addison-Wesley, Boston (2010)
5. Braz, C., Robert, J.-M.: Security and usability: the case of the user authentication method. In: Proceedings of the 18th International Conference of the Association Francophone D'interaction Homme-Machine, p. 133 (2006)
6. Wikipedia: Microsoft Remote Web Workplace, 6 April 2019. https://en.wikipedia.org/wiki/ Microsoft_Remote_Web_Workplace
7. CNN World: European Union under cyber attack as major summit begins, 02 January 2012. http://articles.cnn.com/2011-03-24/world/eu.cyberattack_1_cyber-attack-eu-summits-eu-administration?_s=PM:WORLD
8. European Commission: Information System Security Policy - Standard on Access Control and Authentication, Brussels (2011)
9. Schneier, B.: Sensible Authentication. Counterpane Internet Secur. 1(10), 74–78 (2004)
10. Lewis, J.R.: Sample sizes for usability studies: additional considerations. Hum. Factors 36(2), 368–378 (1994)
11. ISO 9241-11: Ergonomic Requirements for Office Work with Visual Display Terminals (1999). https://www.iso.org/obp/ui/#iso:std:iso:9241:-6:ed-1:v1:en

Author Index

Printed in the United States
By Bookmasters